11e

Public Finance

A Contemporary Application of Theory to Policy

DAVID N. HYMAN
North Carolina State University

CENGAGE
Learning

Australia • Brazil • Mexico • Singapore • United Kingdom • United States

Public Finance: A Contemporary Application of Theory to Policy, Eleventh Edition
David N. Hyman

Senior Vice President, LRS/Acquisitions & Solutions Planning: Jack W. Calhoun

Senior Acquisition Editor: Steven Scoble

Developmental Editor: Ted Knight

Editorial Assistant: Anne Merrill

Senior Brand Manager: Robin Lefevre

Senior Market Development Manager: John Carey

Marketing Coordinator: Chris Walz

Art and Cover Direction, Production Management, and Composition: PreMediaGlobal

Media Editor: Elizabeth Beiting-Lipps

Rights Acquisition Director: Audrey Pettengill

Senior Rights Acquisition Specialist, Text and Image: Deanna Ettinger

Manufacturing Planner: Kevin Kluck

Cover Images: © iStockphoto/Lingbeek, © iStockphoto/Balalaika

Internal Image: © iStockphoto/Balalaika

© 2014, 2011 Cengage Learning

ALL RIGHTS RESERVED. No part of this work covered by the copyright herein may be reproduced, transmitted, stored, or used in any form or by any means graphic, electronic, or mechanical, including but not limited to photocopying, recording, scanning, digitizing, taping, web distribution, information networks, or information storage and retrieval systems, except as permitted under Section 107 or 108 of the 1976 United States Copyright Act, without the prior written permission of the publisher.

For product information and technology assistance, contact us at
Cengage Learning Customer & Sales Support, 1-800-354-9706

For permission to use material from this text or product, submit all requests online at **www.cengage.com/permissions**
Further permissions questions can be emailed to
permissionrequest@cengage.com

Library of Congress Control Number: 2013939864

ISBN-13: 978-1-285-17395-5

ISBN-10: 1-285-17395-3

Cengage Learning
200 First Stamford Place, 4th Floor
Stamford, CT 06902
USA

Cengage Learning is a leading provider of customized learning solutions with office locations around the globe, including Singapore, the United Kingdom, Australia, Mexico, Brazil, and Japan. Locate your local office at **www.cengage.com/global**.

Cengage Learning products are represented in Canada by Nelson Education, Ltd.

To learn more about Cengage Learning Solutions, visit **www.cengage.com**.

Purchase any of our products at your local college store or at our preferred online store **www.cengagebrain.com**.

Printed in the United States of America
4 5 6 7 17 16

About the Author

David N. Hyman, Professor of Economics and Alumni Distinguished Undergraduate Professor at North Carolina State University, has taught both undergraduate and graduate courses in public finance there since 1969. Professor Hyman received his Ph.D. in Economics from Princeton University. He has held Woodrow Wilson, Earhart, and Ford Foundation fellowships and was a Fulbright senior research scholar in Italy in 1980. From 1976 to 1977, he was visiting research professor at the University of Turin in Italy, and in 1997 he was visiting professor of economics at the University of Ferrara in Italy. Professor Hyman is a member of the Academy of Outstanding Teachers at North Carolina State University and received the Alumni Association Outstanding Teacher Award in 1982 and 1996. In 2006, he was a recipient of the North Carolina State University College of Management Teaching Excellence Award. In 2010 and 2012, Professor Hyman was the College of Management recipient of the Board of Governors Award for Excellence in Teaching. He is the author of several widely used textbooks in economics and has published scholarly articles in the *National Tax Journal*, *Public Choice*, *Journal of Economic Education*, and other respected academic journals. In 2005, his *Public Finance* text was translated into Chinese and published by the Peking University Press. Professor Hyman served on the President's Council of Economic Advisers as a consultant and as a senior staff economist from 1988 to 1989. He has also been a guest scholar at the Brookings Institution and has worked as a government budget analyst and as an economist for the Board of Governors of the Federal Reserve System and the U.S. Comptroller of the Currency.

Professor Hyman is also a photographer whose palladium and platinum prints are in the permanent collection of the Corcoran Gallery of Art in Washington, D.C., and the Gregg Museum of Art and Design at North Carolina State University. His photographs have been exhibited by galleries and museums in New York, North Carolina, California, and in China at the Pingyao International Photography Festival and in Beijing, and have been published in art books and on the covers of several novels.

Preface

In view of current pressures to reduce government budget deficits, cut public spending, and reform taxation, the study of public finance is more important than ever. Since the last edition of *Public Finance: A Contemporary Application of Theory to Policy*, the U.S. economy has been rebounding slowly from the severe recession of 2007–2009. Slow economic growth has had an impact on the public sector of the economy as tax collections have lagged and government expenditures for income support, Social Security, and unemployment compensation have grown. Along with growing federal budget deficits and public debt, there have been strong pressures to curtail future government spending and reduce both government budget deficits and the federal debt.

The fastest-growing area of government spending in recent years has been health care. Government spending on health care has been increasing rapidly both on the federal and state levels. The new edition of this text continues to discuss issues related to the provision of health care and the role of government in that sphere with an entire chapter devoted to the subject. In Chapter 9, the provisions of the *Patient Protection and Affordable Care Act of 2010* are discussed along with the impact of these new government regulations on U.S. health insurance markets and taxation in 2014 and beyond.

Fundamental controversies still rage about how to deal with the Social Security system as the population ages. The role of government in supporting education remains an important issue. All these perennial, as well as newer, government issues are covered in this 11th edition. There is a separate chapter on government budget balance and debt (Chapter 12). This unique feature focuses on the implications of government borrowing for the economy and is of major importance in view of the fact that the federal budget deficit and debt has exploded in recent years and must eventually be brought down to avoid future negative consequences for the economy.

The text retains its in-depth coverage of tax theory and policy issues. Sections on taxation have been updated to discuss issues in tax reform and the impact of taxes on incentives and economic growth. The latest data on tax rates and the distribution of tax burden are included. Pressures for reform of the tax code and new revenue are likely to result in a continuing political debate about taxation in the United States at the federal, state, and local levels. The basic theoretical framework developed in this book to analyze taxes on income, consumption, and wealth can provide a basis for evaluating alternative proposals for changes in tax policy.

CHANGES IN THIS EDITION

The 11th edition continues to provide comprehensive coverage of theoretical and applied issues in public finance. The latest data are used to make sure all charts, tables, and analyses are timely and relevant. Environmental protection issues, such as recent changes in "cap and trade" policies to reduce acid rain and greenhouse gases, both in the United States and in the European Union are discussed. Options to reduce future defense spending in the United States are analyzed. Data and analysis relating to poverty and health insurance coverage in the United States have all been updated, and the impact of provisions of the new health care laws and regulations is discussed.

Information on Social Security pensions in the United States has been updated, and a new Global Perspective feature discusses Social Security pensions in the European Union with particular emphasis on the sustainability of pension systems in Euro zone nations at risk for sovereign debt default. There is more discussion of the implications of aging of populations on both pensions systems and health care spending. Data on health care spending in the United States have been updated. Material on the Medicare and Medicaid programs has been updated and new taxes to finance the Medicare program and the costs of extending health insurance under the health care reform to those who have been uninsured are discussed. The section on unemployment insurance has been expanded, and the effects of recent reforms in the United States on replacement rates, number of workers receiving benefits, and the length of the benefit period are discussed.

In the chapters on taxation (Part 4), recent data on the distribution of tax burden and tax rates are included. The provisions of the *American Taxpayer Relief Act of 2012* enacted by Congress are also discussed. The long-term fiscal and economic implications of government budget deficits as well trends in the use of borrowing as a means of public finance receive expanded coverage. A new section on sovereign debt, default risk, and interest rates has been added to the chapter on budget balance and government debt (Chapter 12) with a discussion of the recent situation in several Euro zone nations. Recent proposals for reforming income taxation in the United States are analyzed. Estimates of marginal and average tax rates for income taxation are presented along with estimates of the distribution of the federal tax burden for 2012. Statistics on corporate income taxes, sales taxes, property taxes, and intergovernmental fiscal assistance statistics have been updated. A new Global Perspective on fiscal federalism in the European Union has been added to the last part of the book.

SPECIAL FEATURES OF THIS BOOK

In addition to the boxed features on international issues and public policy, each chapter has pedagogical features such as Learning Objectives and Concept Checks.

To facilitate learning, important concepts are set in colored bold type when first introduced, and every chapter concludes with a summary, a list of important concepts, and a short "Looking Ahead" that explains the relationship between the chapter and those that follow. Also, each chapter includes questions for review. These questions are not problem sets; rather, they are designed to help students review the material covered in the chapter by presenting questions related to its major points or ideas. Several problems follow the review questions. Each chapter also has an annotated bibliography offering suggestions for further reading and in-depth study. The bibliography should prove particularly useful in courses in which term papers are assigned. All chapters have references to Internet sites. Liberal use is made of footnotes throughout the book to provide additional source material and to explain and document material. A glossary at the end of the book lists and defines all important concepts for easy reference.

I have attempted to make this book as self-contained as possible; even students with only a minimal background in economics can use it. Appendixes to several chapters facilitate this process. For example, Chapter 1 includes an appendix that can be used as a convenient reference tool for students unfamiliar with basic microeconomic theory. It features simple, concise explanations of concepts such as indifference curves, income and substitution effects, consumer surplus, producer surplus, cost, and production theory. Although the appendix is not designed as course material, it will help students understand, as well as review, the analyses used throughout the book.

An appendix to Chapter 2 provides a more in-depth analysis of efficiency using Edgeworth box diagrams to derive efficiency loci. The appendix to Chapter 11 derives formulas for the excess burden of taxation and addresses the relevance of compensated demand and supply curves to tax analysis. The appendices to Chapters 2 and 11 cover more advanced material and may be skipped without loss of continuity.

POSSIBLE COURSE OUTLINES

This book contains more material than could possibly be covered in a one-semester (or one-quarter) course in public finance. Instructors of one-semester courses will find enough material to adapt to their own needs and interests. Teachers of the two-semester sequence of the microeconomic aspects of public finance could cover Parts 1 and 2 (the expenditure aspects of public finance) in the first semester, and Parts 3, 4, and 5 (government finance and fiscal federalism) in the second. Instructors of the macroeconomic aspects of public finance could supplement the material in the text with excerpts from one of the many excellent macroeconomic books available.

I suggest four possible course outlines for a one-semester course, each outline having its own emphasis. Instructors may adjust these outlines according to their preferences.

Outline 1: Basic Principles of Public Finance

For intermediate economics courses, with students who have had at least one course in basic microeconomic theory:

1. Chapters 1–5: The economic basis for government activity. Efficiency, market failure, externalities, public goods, public choice, and political equilibrium.
2. Chapters 10–12: Principles of government finance.
3. Chapters 14–17: Application of tax theory to tax policy.
4. Selections from Chapters 6–9 and 18: Topics in public policy or state and local finance, used as time permits and according to the instructor's interests.

Outline 2: The Functions of Government and Government Expenditure

For courses focusing on public policy and government expenditure, with students who have had at least one course in economics:

1. Parts 1 and 2: The economic basis of government activity and application of that theory to selected policy issues.
2. Part 5: State and local government finance.

Outline 3: Tax Theory and Policy

For courses addressing taxation, with students who have had at least one course in economics:

1. Chapters 1 and 2: The functions of government and the concept of efficiency.
2. Chapters 10–17: Government finance, tax theory, and tax policy.

Outline 4: Public Policy

For courses in public affairs or public policy, with students who have had little or no background in economics:

1. Chapters 1 and 2: Efficiency, markets, and the economic basis for government activity.
2. Selections from Chapters 3–5: As appropriate to subject emphasis and student background. Topics could include externalities, public goods, and political equilibrium.
3. Selections from Chapters 6–9: Issues in public policy. The instructor may wish to omit some of the more advanced sections in these chapters.
4. Chapter 10: Introduction to government finance.
5. Selections from Chapters 11–17: Topics in tax policy, chosen according to depth of coverage.
6. Selections from Chapter 18: Topics in fiscal federalism, chosen according to course objectives. More advanced sections could be omitted.

ANCILLARY MATERIALS

Instructor's Manual/Test Bank

The Instructor's Manual includes instructional objectives, changes in this edition, chapter outlines, major points and lecture suggestions, and answers to text problems. The Test Bank for each chapter includes true/false, multiple-choice, and essay questions. This ancillary is available on the Instructor Web site and Instructor's Resource CD.

Lecture Presentation in PowerPoint®

This text features a PowerPoint slide presentation that professors can use to save valuable class preparation time. This supplement covers all the essential topics presented in each chapter of the book, including graphs, tables, and examples. Slides are crisp, clear, and colorful. Instructors may adapt or add slides to customize their lectures. The slides are available on the Instructor Web site and Instructor's Resource CD.

Textbook Support Web Site

Visit the support Web site for this textbook at www.cengagebrain.com to find free Instructor and Student resources. Instructors can find the Instructor's Manual/Test Bank, PowerPoint slides, and an Errata section. Students can find economics applications questions, Internet resources, Flashcards, and an Errata section.

Accessing CengageBrain

1. Use your browser to go to www.CengageBrain.com.

2. The first time you go to the site, you will need to register. It's free. Click on "Sign Up" in the top right corner of the page and fill out the registration information. (After you have signed in once, whenever you return to CengageBrain, you will enter the user name and password you have chosen and you will be taken directly to the companion site for your book.)

3. Once you have registered and logged in for the first time, go to the "Search for Books or Materials" bar and enter the author or ISBN for your textbook. When the title of your text appears, click on it and you will be taken to the companion site. There you can chose among the various folders provided on the Student side of the site. NOTE: If you are currently using more than one Cengage textbook, the same user name and password will give you access to all the companion sites for your Cengage titles. After you have entered the information for each title, all the titles you are using will appear listed in the pull-down menu in the "Search for Books or Materials" bar. Whenever you return to CengageBrain, you can click on the title of the site you wish to visit and go directly there.

Economic Applications

Economic applications include EconNews, EconDebates, and EconData features to deepen understanding of theoretical concepts through hands-on exploration and analysis of the latest economic news stories, policy debates, and data. Organized by topic and continually updated, EconApps are easy to integrate into the classroom.

ACKNOWLEDGMENTS

I am indebted to all of the reviewers of this edition and past editions. Their helpful comments have helped to guide each revision. They include Lori Alden, California State University–Sacramento; Samuel H. Baker, College of William and Mary; Charles L. Ballard, Michigan State University; Kevin Balsam, Hunter College; Donald N. Baum, Dwight Blood, Eric Fredland, Richard McHugh, David Orr, Craig Stubblebine, David Terkla, Temple University; Marcus Berliant, University of Rochester; Katherine Chalmers, Colorado State University; Yuval Cohen and Virginia Wilcox-Gok, Rutgers University; Robert Collinge, University of Texas at San Antonio; Joseph J. Cordes, George Washington University; Eleanor D. Craig, University of Delaware; Steven Cuellar, Sonoma State University; F. Trenery Dolbear, Jr., Brandeis University; William E. Even, Miami University; Lon S. Felker,

East Tennessee State University; Richard Fenner, Utica College; J. Fred Giertz, University of Illinois; Robert J. Gitter, Ohio Wesleyan University; Timothy J. Gronberg, Texas A&M University; Philip Grossman, St. Cloud State University; Mehdi Haririan, Bloomsburg University; Frederic Harris, University of Texas at Arlington; Roberto N. Ifill, Williams College; William Kamps, South Dakota State University; Charles R. Knoeber and Alvin E. Headen, Jr., North Carolina State University; Janet Kohlhase, University of Houston; Wojciech Kopczuk, Columbia University; Charles G. Leathers, University of Alabama; Bill Lee, Saint Mary's College; Jane H. Leuthold, University of Illinois at Urbana-Champaign; Dennis Leyden, University of North Carolina at Greensboro; Stephen E. Lile, Western Kentucky University; Barry Love, Emory and Henry College; Randolph M. Lyon, University of Texas at Austin; James P. Marchand, University of California at Los Angeles; Robert C. McMahon, University of Southern Maine; Amlan Mitra, Purdue University at Calumet; Michael A. Nelson, Illinois State University; Lloyd Orr, Indiana University; Patricia N. Pando, Houston Baptist University; Michael T. Peddle, College of the Holy Cross; Thomas Pogue, University of Iowa; Paul Rothstein, Washington University at St. Louis; Kathleen Segerson and Thomas Miceli, University of Connecticut; James K. Self, Indiana University at Bloomington; Mark Showalter, Brigham Young University; John A. Sondey, South Dakota State University; Michael Spicer, Cleveland State University; Davis Taylor, University of Oregon; Wade L. Thomas and Sherry Wetchler, Ithaca College; John P. Tillman, University of Wisconsin-La Crosse; Gary M. Pecquet, Southwest Texas State University; Michael J. Wasylenko, Syracuse University; James R. White, Hamilton College; Gary Wolfram, Hillsdale College; Michael Wolkoff, University of Rochester; George Zodrow, Rice University; and C. Kurt Zorn, Indiana University.

Thanks also to Joseph Sabatino, Publisher; Steven Scoble, Senior Acquisitions Editor; Jennifer Ziegler, Content Project Manager; Anne Merrill, Editorial Assistant; and Kristina Mose-Libon, Art Director.

David N. Hyman
Raleigh, North Carolina

Brief Contents

Contents

11e

Public Finance

A Contemporary Application of Theory to Policy

PartOne

THE ECONOMIC BASIS FOR GOVERNMENT ACTIVITY

Chapter 1

INDIVIDUALS AND GOVERNMENT

LEARNING OBJECTIVES

After reading this chapter, you should be able to:

- Use a production-possibility curve to explain the trade-off between private goods and services and government goods and services.

- Describe how the provision of government goods and services through political institutions differs from market provision of goods and services and how government affects the circular flow of income and expenditure in a mixed economy.

- Explain the difference between government purchases and transfer payments and discuss the growth of government expenditures in the United States and other nations since 1929.

- Discuss the various categories of federal, state, and local government expenditures in the United States and the way those expenditures are financed.

- Determine some of the issues that must be addressed to evaluate the costs and benefits of government activities.

The role of government in society has been and will always be controversial. Some believe government does too much while others believe it needs to do more. Many look to government to solve problems they believe to be important to them but would rather not have it engage in activities that benefit others. No matter what your view of government, it is clear that its programs and scope have grown significantly from a small share of the economy in the early 1900s to between 30 and 60 percent of the economy in modern industrial nations today. Citizens give up substantial amounts of their income each year to pay the taxes necessary to finance government expenditures.

This book is about the government sector of the economy. A framework for analyzing the role of government will be developed. That framework will be used understand why government has grown and the consequences of future growth. We will study both the economic and political aspects of government. Major government expenditure programs will be analyzed. Alternative mechanisms for financing government activity and their economic effects will be discussed, as will issues relating to the government budget deficits and debt.

Since 2000, government spending in the United States as a share of gross domestic product (GDP) has increased. Federal expenditures for national defense and health care by governments have both gone up as a share of the economy. The recession of 2007–2009 and its aftermath of slow economic growth and high unemployment in the United States resulted in increased federal government spending to stabilize the economy. The recession and anemic economic growth from 2009 through 2011 has adversely affected tax collections for the federal, state, and local governments. Many state and local governments have been forced to curtail spending and raise taxes to balance budgets from 2008 to 2011. The federal government's budget deficit and debt outstanding has been soaring.

Some of the growth in federal spending and the increase in government borrowing is due to the extraordinary circumstances resulting from the financial crisis and recession. The federal government has provided assistance to state and local governments to help them cope with the effect of the recession on their budgets and has also acquired ownership shares in struggling businesses in the banking, financial, and automotive sectors of the economy. Although these shares can be sold in the future, they do pose the risk that economic losses could be borne by taxpayers. The federal government's budget deficit in 2010 was the largest as a share of GDP since the end of the World War II.

As federal deficits have increased, so has the level of federal debt as a share of GDP. Rising levels of government debt both in the United States and nations in Europe using the euro as their currency has been a factor of concern in financial markets. In the United States, political bickering between the president and Congress about the ceiling on federal debt caused one leading credit rating agency to downgrade its rating for U.S. government securities in 2011. And the risk of default on sovereign debt in such euro zone nations as Greece, Italy, Spain, Portugal, Ireland, and even France has caused interest rates to rise on government securities in those nations. Many of these European nations have embarked on "austerity" programs to cut government spending and raise tax revenues that could adversely affect their economic growth rates.

A major factor influencing the growth of government spending in the United States is the expanding role of governments in financing health care. Government expenditures for health care have been rising rapidly in recent years. If current trends continue federal government spending on health care through its two major health insurance programs, Medicare and Medicaid, could account for more than 50 percent of federal government spending by 2080 as the population ages. State government expenditures for health care have also been increasing significantly. Either tax rates will increase in the future to finance growth in government spending or increased federal budget deficits could impact the economy in ways that either slow economic growth or cause inflation. Of course, another alternative would be to attempt to reduce the rate of growth of federal government spending. Given the projected importance of health care spending in the budget, this is unlikely to be possible without some curbs on spending for health care by governments and significant changes in the health care system in the United States. The government's role in health care is likely to remain a divisive issue.

Between 2000 and 2010, total government spending in the United States increased significantly from 30 to 38 percent of GDP. Since 2007 much of that increase resulted from extraordinary expenditure to stabilize the economy while slow growth in GDP also contributed to increased share of government spending in the economy. However, because of rising levels of federal debt and concern about the negative impact of chronic federal budget deficits on the economy, political pressure has now emerged to reduce the share of government in the economies of both the United States and other major industrial nations—particularly those in western Europe.

INDIVIDUALS, SOCIETY, AND GOVERNMENT

What would it be like to live in a nation without government? There would be no system of courts to administer justice. Provision of national defense and homeland security would be difficult or disorganized with no central government to maintain and supply the armed forces. You could forget about such programs as Social Security, unemployment insurance, and welfare that provide income support to the elderly, the unemployed, and the poor or disabled. How would police and fire protection be provided? Driving on roads and over bridges that we take for granted could also be a problem because virtually all the highways, streets, and other public transportation infrastructure we use every day are supplied and maintained by governments or their agencies. There would be no publicly funded elementary and secondary schools. Higher education, which is heavily subsidized by both the federal and state governments, also would be in trouble. Our system of health care depends on government programs to pay the medical bills of many of the poor, the elderly, and veterans. Institutions ranging from medical schools to public clinics and hospitals would have their operations impaired without government support.

Now that you have finished reflecting on what your life would be like without governments, you can better appreciate how much you rely on government services each day. We all benefit from government activities and expenditures. Since 1980, annual government expenditures in the United States averaged one third of GDP.

In economics, we study the ways individuals make choices to use scarce resources to satisfy their desires. If you have taken an introductory economics course, you studied the role of markets as a means of establishing prices that influence individual choices to use resources. In this book, you will study the role governments play in allocating resources and how individual choices influence what governments do. You also will study how government policies affect the incentives of workers, investors, and corporations to engage in productive activities.

If you have completed an introductory economics course, one lesson you have been taught already is that nothing of value can be obtained without some sacrifice. There are costs as well as benefits associated with the activities of governments. The role of government in society is so hotly disputed because we differ in our assessments of the costs and benefits of government programs. Many people think the role of government in the economy needs to be expanded and look to government to help solve their own problems. Others think the role of government in the economy is already excessive and would like to see its scale of influence reduced.

Government expenditures are financed mainly by taxes. U.S. taxpayers give up more of their income each year to support government activities than they do to satisfy their desires for such basic items as food, clothing, and shelter. Taxes collected by governments in the United States are nearly three times the annual expenditures on food, nearly eight times the annual expenditures on clothing, and more than three times the annual expenditures on housing. The average U.S. household devotes nearly four months of annual earnings to meet its total yearly federal, state, and local government tax obligations. Citizens benefit from the many goods and services made available by governments, but they also pay the costs of these services. We differ in our views about what governments should and should not be doing in part because our valuations of the benefits we get from government differ. We also disagree because of variation in the amount of taxes and other costs each of us pay.

GOVERNMENTS AND POLITICAL INSTITUTIONS

Public finance is the field of economics that studies government activities and the alternative means of financing government expenditures. As you study public finance, you will learn about the economic basis for government activities. A crucial objective of the analysis is to understand the impact of government expenditures, regulations, taxes, and borrowing on incentives to work, invest, and spend income. This text develops principles for understanding the role of government in the economy and its impact on resource use and the well-being of citizens.

Governments are organizations formed to exercise authority over the actions of people who live together in a society and to provide and finance essential services. Many citizens and resources are employed in the production of government services. Individuals pay taxes and, in many cases, are recipients of income financed by those taxes. For example, Social Security pensions, unemployment insurance compensation, and subsidies to the poor are financed by taxes.

The extent to which individuals have the right to participate in decisions that determine what governments do varies from society to society. What governments do, how much they spend, and how they obtain the means to finance their functions reflect political interaction of citizens. **Political institutions** constitute the rules and generally accepted procedures that evolve in a community for determining what government does and how government outlays are financed. Through these mediums, individual desires are translated into binding decisions concerning the extent and functions of government.

Such democratic institutions as majority rule and representative government offer citizens an opportunity to express their desires through voting and through attempts to influence the voting of others. Under majority rule, one alternative (such as a political candidate or a referendum to increase spending for education) is chosen over others if it receives more than half the votes cast in an election. Just as economic theory is usefully applied to analysis of market interaction and individual choice, so can it be applied to political interaction and choices. Modern economics bases the study of government activity on a theory of individual behavior.

THE ALLOCATION OF RESOURCES BETWEEN GOVERNMENT AND PRIVATE USE

Government provision of goods and services requires labor, equipment, buildings, and land. The real cost of government goods and services is the value of private goods and services that must be sacrificed when resources are transferred to government use. When citizens pay taxes, their capacity to purchase goods and services for their own exclusive use (such as automobiles, clothing, housing, cameras, and dining out) is reduced. Resources that are thereby diverted from private use are purchased or otherwise obtained by government. Taxes also have indirect costs because they distort choices. Taxes affect prices of goods and services and the incentive to work, save, and allocate expenditures among goods and services. Taxes impair the operation of the economy by inducing individuals to make choices based not only on the benefits and costs of their actions but also on the tax advantages or disadvantages of their decisions. The distortion in resource use and loss in output that results from the effect of taxes on incentives is also part of the cost of government activity.

The resources governments obtain are used to provide citizens with goods and services, such as roads, police and fire protection, and national defense. These government goods and services are shared by all; they cannot be used by any one citizen exclusively. Other goods and services provided by government are limited in availability to certain groups, such as the aged or children, as with Social Security pensions and public primary and secondary schooling.

The trade-off between government and private goods and services can be illustrated with the familiar production-possibility curve. As shown in Figure 1.1, this curve gives the alternative combinations of government goods and services and private goods and services that can be produced in an economy, given its productive resources and technology and assuming that resources are fully employed. **Private goods and services** are those items, such as food and clothing, that are usually made available for sale in markets. **Government goods and services**, such as roads, schooling, and fire protection, usually are not sold in markets. At point A in Figure 1.1, MX_1 units of private goods and services are forgone by individuals so that government can provide $0G_1$ units of goods and services. Resources that would have been employed in producing private goods and services are used by the government to provide services and exercise its functions.

An increase in the amount of government goods and services provided per year from $0G_1$ to $0G_2$ requires a reduction in the amount of private goods available per year. In Figure 1.1, the annual amount of private goods available declines from $0X_1$ to $0X_2$ as the economy moves from point A to point B on the production-possibility curve. For example, suppose that individuals demand more environmental protection services. To make these services available, governments

---

FIGURE 1.1   Production-Possibility Curve

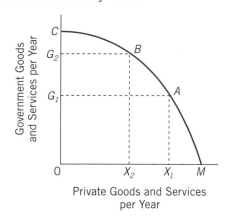

The production-possibility curve shows alternative combinations of government goods and services and private goods and services that can be produced in an economy. The curve assumes that productive resources and technology are given. An increase in government goods from $0G_1$ to $0G_2$ requires a sacrifice of X_1X_2 units of private goods per year.

---

might raise taxes paid by firms that pollute the air or water or they could enact more stringent regulations that prevent pollution. The new regulations or taxes are likely to increase costs of production for business firms, causing the prices of products produced by these firms to increase and the quantities demanded in the marketplace by consumers to decline. The new policies will result in improved environmental quality—a government-supplied good—but will also require that households sacrifice consumption of private goods and services to pay for the cleaner environment.

How Government Goods and Services Are Distributed

Government goods and services are, by and large, distributed to groups of individuals through the use of **nonmarket rationing.** This means that government goods and services are not made available to persons according to their willingness to pay and their use is not rationed by prices. In some cases, the services are available to all, with no direct charge and no eligibility requirements. The provision of national defense services is one strong example of a good that is freely available to all and not rationed by prices. In other cases, criteria such as income, age, family status, residence, or the payment of certain taxes, fees, or charges are used to determine eligibility to receive benefits. For example, to receive Social Security pensions in the United States, individuals must be of a certain age (or be disabled), have worked for a certain period of time (about 10 years) while covered by Social Security, and must have paid their share of Social Security taxes during that time. Similarly, a fare must be paid to use public transportation facilities in cities. If the fares paid do not cover the full cost of operating the system, the deficit is made up by taxes levied by the government. To be eligible for elementary schooling in a given school district, children must reside within the boundaries of that district.

In public finance, we study how the means of rationing the use of government goods and services and financing their resource costs affect incentives, resource use, and production possibilities.

CHECKPOINT

1. What are political institutions?
2. Give four examples of government goods or services and discuss how they are distributed to citizens.
3. Use a production-possibility curve to show the cost of increasing government provision of medical service.

THE MIXED ECONOMY, MARKETS, AND POLITICS

The United States and most other nations today have mixed economies. A **mixed economy** is one in which government supplies a considerable amount of goods and services and regulates private economic activity. In such an economy, government expenditures typically amount to between one quarter and one half of GDP. Taxes absorb at least one quarter of national income in the typical mixed economy, and governments usually regulate private economic activities and use taxes and subsidies to affect incentives to use resources.

In a **pure market economy**, virtually all goods and services would be supplied by private firms for profit and all exchanges of goods and services would take place through markets, with prices determined by free interplay of supply and demand. Individuals would be able to purchase goods and services freely, according to their tastes and economic capacity (their income and wealth), given the market-determined prices. In mixed economies, provision of a significant amount of goods and services takes place through political institutions.

In a market, buyers are not compelled to purchase something they do not want. Political decisions, however, often compel citizens to finance government services and programs, regardless of their personal preferences.

Circular Flow in the Mixed Economy

In a pure market economy, all productive resources are privately owned by individuals who decide how to use these resources. These individuals, together with others living in their households, make decisions about how to use the resources they own. Their decisions are influenced in part by market prices for goods and services. They offer their resources for sale as inputs in the marketplace.

Private business firms are organized to hire resources in input markets to produce goods and services desired by household members. The products, in turn, are sold by businesses to households in output markets.

In a perfectly competitive market economy, no seller can influence prices. Instead, prices are determined by free play of the forces of supply and demand.

FIGURE 1.2 Circular Flow in the Mixed Economy

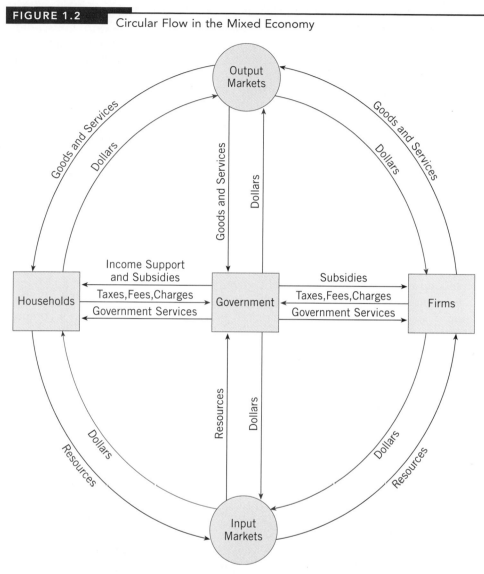

The upper and lower loops represent transactions between households and business firms in markets. Households use the income they earn from the sale of productive services to purchase the outputs of business firms. The inner loop represents transactions between households and government and between business firms and government. Governments purchase productive services from households and outputs of business firms. These purchases are financed with taxes, fees, and charges levied on persons and firms, and the inputs acquired are used to provide government services and transfers.

Given market prices, households decide to sell the resources they own, and firms decide which inputs to buy and what outputs to produce. This process is summarized as a simple circular flow diagram in Figure 1.2. Let's first look at the relationships that would exist in the economy if there were no governments. The lower loop of the diagram represents the input markets, where households sell the resources to firms for market-determined prices. The upper loop is the output market, where an array of outputs is offered for sale to households, which, in turn, pay for them with the dollars earned from the sale of their members' productive resources. The distribution of income depends on the distribution of ownership of productive resources and the prices and other financial returns that resource owners receive from employment of those resources in production. In a pure market economy, all goods and services would be produced by businesses.

In a mixed economy, the government participates in markets as a buyer of goods and services. Figure 1.2 depicts government activities in the central portions of the diagram. Governments purchase inputs from households and acquire ownership rights of such productive resources as land and capital. Governments use these inputs to provide goods and services that are not sold to households and business firms but are made available through nonmarket rationing. However, governments do sometimes own and operate enterprises such as the postal service, railroads, liquor stores, and state lotteries.

Governments also purchase outputs of business firms such as paper, cars, bricks, and guns. To pay for them, the government requires businesses and households to make various payments such as taxes, charges, and fees and might even require resources be made available for use by the government at rates of compensation below actual market prices (as is the case with compulsory military service). Government uses the productive resources it acquires to produce goods and services including national defense, roads, schooling, police and fire protection, and many other essential services.

With reference to Figure 1.2, the question of size of the public sector is one of allocation of total transactions between the upper and lower loops and the central loops. The central loop transactions are made through political institutions, whereas the upper and lower loop transactions are made through market institutions.

GOVERNMENT EXPENDITURES IN THE UNITED STATES

Let's examine government spending in the United States so that we can get a better idea of the kinds of things governments do in mixed economies. Government spending can be divided into two basic categories: purchases and transfers. **Government purchases** are those that require productive resources (land, labor, and capital) to be diverted from private use by individuals and corporations so that such resources can be used by the government. For example, to supply national defense services, the government must acquire steel, labor, and other inputs necessary to support the armed forces and maintain aircraft, tanks, ships, and other capital equipment. A municipal government must acquire trucks and hire labor to administer effectively the collection and disposal of garbage.

The bulk of government purchases are *consumption expenditures* that use resources to satisfy current needs. *Gross investment* by government is expenditure for new capital such as roads, equipment, and structures. In 2010, 9.1 percent of government purchases were for investments while the remainder were consumption.

Government expenditures that redistribute purchasing power among citizens are called **government transfer payments**. These transfer payments constitute a source of income support to recipients who are not required to provide any service in return for the income received. Transfer payments differ from earnings in that they are not payments made in exchange for productive services. You might be surprised to learn that direct transfer payments to individuals constitute more than 50 percent of federal government expenditures in the United States. Included in government transfer payments to individuals are Social Security pension benefits, unemployment insurance benefit payments, and cash payments to low-income families.

Growth of Government Expenditures

Table 1.1 shows government expenditures in the United States from 1929 to 2011. These data reflect outlays each year for federal expenditures, expenditures by state and local governments, and total government expenditures. Ratios of the various categories of government expenditure to GDP in each year provide a rough indication of the relative importance of the government sector's economic activity for each year. Government expenditures are calculated as the sum of government consumption, government transfer payments, and gross government investment as reported in the National Income and Product Accounts (NIPA) for each year since 1929.

The computed ratios provide only a crude index of government activity in the United States. Ideally, an index of the relative importance of government should measure the proportion of total output produced in the public sector. However, measuring government output is virtually impossible because, in most cases, it is not sold or easily measurable in units that can be summed. Actual expenditures are an imperfect proxy for government output.

A further problem with the data is that actual expenditures do not measure the full impact of the government on economic activity. Although the regulatory activities of the public sector increase the costs of producing private goods and services in order to produce collectively enjoyed benefits (such as cleaner air), these increases are not reflected in Table 1.1.

Despite these limitations, the ratios computed in Table 1.1 provide a rough idea of the extent to which government in the United States has grown since 1929. In 1929, government expenditures accounted for only 9.46 percent of GDP. Interestingly, in 1929, the bulk of government expenditures was undertaken by state and local governing bodies. In that year, federal government expenditures accounted for a mere 2.51 percent of GDP, while state and local government expenditures accounted for the remaining 6.95 percent. By 1960, the federal government accounted for 17.8 percent, while state and local government expenditures were only 8.34 percent. The sharp increases in federal expenditures for the years between 1942 and 1945, to over 40 percent of GDP, reflect the influence of World War II on government activity.

Growth of government spending was rapid after 1960, when total government spending as a percentage of GDP rose from about one fourth of GDP to nearly one third of GDP throughout much of the 1970s and 1980s. In the 1980s and 1990s, government expenditures remained at around one third percent of GDP. Total government spending as a share of GDP fell in the late 1990s to a low of 30.36 percent

TABLE 1.1   Government Expenditures in the United States, 2008–2011 (Billions of Dollars)[a]

YEAR	GDP	FEDERAL GOVERNMENT	STATE AND LOCAL GOVERNMENTS[b]	TOTAL GOVERNMENT	PERCENTAGE OF GDP		
					FEDERAL	STATE AND LOCAL	TOTAL
1929	103.6	2.6	7.2	9.8	2.51	6.95	9.46
1930	91.2	2.8	7.9	10.7	3.07	8.66	11.73
1931	76.5	4.1	7.8	11.9	5.36	10.20	15.56
1932	58.7	3.2	6.9	10.1	5.45	11.75	17.21
1933	56.4	3.8	6.4	10.2	6.74	11.35	18.09
1934	66.0	6.2	6.1	12.3	9.39	9.24	18.64
1935	73.3	6.5	6.4	12.9	8.87	8.73	17.60
1936	83.8	8.7	7.0	15.7	10.38	8.35	18.74
1937	91.9	7.3	7.2	14.5	7.94	7.83	15.78
1938	86.1	8.2	7.8	16.0	9.52	9.06	18.58
1939	92.2	9.2	8.2	17.4	9.98	8.89	18.87
1940	101.4	9.7	8.2	17.9	9.57	8.09	17.65
1941	126.7	20.7	7.7	28.4	16.34	6.08	22.42
1942	161.9	56.0	7.4	63.4	34.59	4.57	39.16
1943	198.6	86.1	7.0	93.1	43.35	3.52	46.88
1944	219.8	95.4	7.0	102.4	43.40	3.18	46.59
1945	223.0	85.2	7.5	92.7	38.21	3.36	41.57
1946	222.3	37.2	9.4	46.6	16.73	4.23	20.96
1947	244.2	30.7	11.9	42.6	12.57	4.87	17.44
1948	269.2	33.3	15.9	49.2	12.37	5.91	18.28
1949	267.3	40.7	18.1	58.8	15.23	6.77	22.00
1950	293.8	41.8	19.3	61.1	14.23	6.57	20.80
1951	339.3	58.3	20.3	78.6	17.18	5.98	23.17
1952	358.3	70.8	21.6	92.4	19.76	6.03	25.79
1953	379.4	75.9	23.1	99.0	20.01	6.09	26.09
1954	380.4	69.8	25.8	95.6	18.35	6.78	25.13
1955	414.8	68.2	28.4	96.6	16.44	6.85	23.29
1956	437.5	71.4	30.9	102.3	16.32	7.06	23.38
1957	461.1	79.4	33.7	113.1	17.22	7.31	24.53
1958	467.2	86.7	36.5	123.2	18.56	7.81	26.37
1959	506.6	91.9	38.7	130.6	18.14	7.64	25.78
1960	526.4	93.7	43.9	137.6	17.80	8.34	26.14
1961	544.7	101.7	47.9	149.6	18.67	8.79	27.46
1962	585.6	110.8	50.7	161.5	18.92	8.66	27.58
1963	617.7	114.7	54.4	169.1	18.57	8.81	27.38
1964	663.6	118.8	59.0	177.8	17.90	8.89	26.79
1965	719.1	124.2	64.9	189.1	17.27	9.03	26.30
1966	787.8	144.3	70.4	214.7	18.32	8.94	27.25
1967	832.6	164.1	78.8	242.9	19.71	9.46	29.17
1968	908.8	180.1	88.2	268.3	19.82	9.71	29.52
1969	984.4	189.7	97.0	286.7	19.27	9.85	29.12
1970	1,038.3	205.3	106.9	312.2	19.77	10.30	30.07
1971	1,126.8	221.3	119.4	340.7	19.64	10.60	30.24
1972	1,237.9	245.9	124.8	370.7	19.86	10.08	29.95
1973	1,382.3	262.0	138.7	400.7	18.95	10.03	28.99

TABLE 1.1 Continued

YEAR	GDP	FEDERAL GOVERNMENT	STATE AND LOCAL GOVERNMENTS[b]	TOTAL GOVERNMENT	PERCENTAGE OF GDP		
					FEDERAL	STATE AND LOCAL	TOTAL
1974	1,499.5	295.2	158.6	453.8	19.69	10.58	30.26
1975	1,637.7	357.4	177.8	535.2	21.82	10.86	32.68
1976	1,824.6	386.1	189.5	575.6	21.16	10.39	31.55
1977	2,030.1	421.5	201.1	622.6	20.76	9.91	30.67
1978	2,293.8	466.9	218.3	685.2	20.35	9.52	29.87
1979	2,562.2	517.3	245.8	763.1	20.19	9.59	29.78
1980	2,788.1	608.4	274.7	883.1	21.82	9.85	31.67
1981	3,126.8	695.1	305.4	1,000.5	22.23	9.77	32.00
1982	3,253.2	773.6	337.1	1,110.7	23.78	10.36	34.14
1983	3,534.6	855.9	362.5	1,218.4	24.21	10.26	34.47
1984	3,930.9	915.2	397.0	1,312.2	23.28	10.10	33.38
1985	4,217.5	997.8	441.3	1,439.1	23.66	10.46	34.12
1986	4,460.1	1,056.6	482.0	1,538.6	23.69	10.81	34.50
1987	4,736.4	1,095.2	526.9	1,622.1	23.12	11.12	34.25
1988	5,100.4	1,137.3	562.9	1,700.2	22.30	11.04	33.33
1989	5,482.1	1,211.1	610.2	1,821.3	22.09	11.13	33.22
1990	5,800.5	1,307.4	669.5	1,976.9	22.54	11.54	34.08
1991	5,992.1	1,363.2	713.5	2,076.7	22.75	11.91	34.66
1992	6,342.3	1,487.5	746.5	2,234.0	23.45	11.77	35.22
1993	6,667.4	1,534.8	769.3	2,304.1	23.02	11.54	34.56
1994	7,085.2	1,566.5	807.6	2,374.1	22.11	11.40	33.51
1995	7,414.7	1,631.4	848.7	2,480.1	22.00	11.45	33.45
1996	7,838.5	1,697.8	885.4	2,583.2	21.66	11.30	32.96
1997	8,332.4	1,728.8	929.2	2,658.0	20.75	11.15	31.90
1998	8,793.5	1,761.0	973.2	2,734.2	20.03	11.07	31.09
1999	9,353.5	1,828.7	1,046.1	2,874.8	19.55	11.18	30.74
2000	9,951.5	1,900.6	1,120.9	3,021.5	19.10	11.26	30.36
2001	10,268.2	2,014.1	1,206.7	3,220.8	19.61	11.75	31.37
2002	10,642.3	2,162.6	1,260.3	3,422.9	20.32	11.84	32.16
2003	11,142.2	2,329.3	1,295.3	3,624.6	20.91	11.63	32.53
2004	11,853.2	2,465.2	1,361.8	3,827.0	20.80	11.49	32.29
2005	12,623.0	2,667.4	1,442.5	4,109.9	21.13	11.43	32.56
2006	13,377.2	2,799.4	1,520.4	4,319.8	20.93	11.37	32.29
2007	14,028.7	2,996.2	1,640.7	4,636.9	21.36	11.70	33.05
2008	14,291.5	3,286.7	1,736.2	5,022.9	23.00	12.15	35.15
2009	13,939.0	3,699.4	1,651.1	5,350.5	26.54	11.85	38.39
2010	14,526.5	3,906.9	1,631.9	5,538.8	26.89	11.23	38.13
2011	15,094.4	3,926.6	1,708.4	5,635.0	26.01	11.32	37.33

[a]Calendar years based on National Income and Product Accounts (NIPA) and current dollars for each year. Total government expenditure includes government consumption and government gross investment. For 1929–1959 capital transfer payments and net purchases of nonproduced assets are assumed to be zero.

[b]Excludes federal grants-in-aid. State and local government expenditures are calculated as the difference between total government expenditures and federal government expenditures.

Source: U.S. Department of Commerce, Bureau of Economics Analysis, www.bea.gov interactive NIPA historical tables with latest revisions as of March 2012.

of GDP in 2000. Since 2000 government spending as a share of GDP has resumed its upward march and as of 2010 had risen to 38 percent of GDP. In 2011 government spending fell slightly to 37.33 percent of GDP. The share of GDP accounted for by federal government expenditures has averaged 22 percent of GDP since 1980. The proportion of GDP accounted for by state and local expenditures, exclusive of that portion financed by federal grants, has ranged between 9 and 12 percent of GDP since 1980.

Federal grants-in-aid are contributions made by the federal government to finance services provided by state and local governments. The importance of these grants increased somewhat in the 1970s, when federal grants rose to more than 3 percent of GDP. In the early 1980s, these grants declined, and by 1990 federal grants-in-aid to state and local governments amounted to merely 1 percent of GDP. Since 1990, grants to state and local governments have increased to nearly 3 percent of GDP. In drawing up the table, such grants are viewed as expenditures on the federal level because they are part of a federal program enacted by Congress. But the funds are actually spent by state and local governments, and their omission from such expenditures tends to underestimate state and local government services relative to federal spending.

The general conclusion that can be reached from Table 1.1, given the limitations of its data, is that the importance of the government sector in the United States has grown tremendously since 1929. Since 1929, total government expenditures rose from one tenth to nearly one third of GDP in 1992. From 1992 to 2000, the share of GDP accounted for by government spending declined steadily from 35.22 to 30.36 percent. By 2001, however, government spending started to rise as a share of GDP. Figure 1.3 plots the trend in government spending as a percentage of GDP from 1929 to 2011.

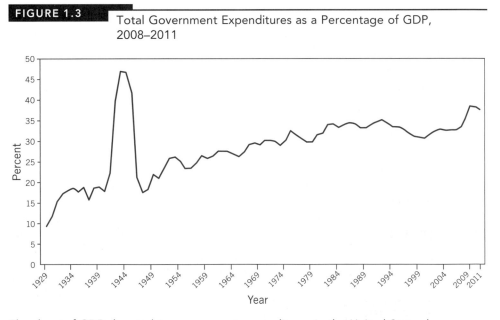

FIGURE 1.3   Total Government Expenditures as a Percentage of GDP, 2008–2011

The share of GDP devoted to government expenditures in the United States has increased dramatically, from about 10 percent to about 38 percent since 1929.

Source: U.S. Department of Commerce, Bureau of Economic Analysis, interactive NIPA historical tables.

The proportion of GDP accounted for by government expenditures in the United States is low compared with that of other industrialized nations. Most European nations all devote more than 40 percent of the value of their GDPs to government expenditures. As of 2011, Denmark, France, Finland, Belgium, Sweden, Austria, the Netherlands, and Slovenia all allocated more than 50 percent of their GDPs to government expenditure.

Current government expenditure in the United States is all the more striking when put in historical perspective. Federal government expenditures from 1870 until the beginning of World War I averaged less than 3 percent of GDP. After the end of World War I, federal government expenditures still remained close to 3 percent of GDP until 1930, when federal government expenditures began to grow at a rapid rate. Federal government expenditures increased less than 1 percent per year until 1940. In contrast, federal government expenditures grew at an average of about 8 percent per year from 1948 to 1980.[1]

Similar trends can be observed in other industrialized nations. The United Kingdom historically has had a large government sector. Surprisingly, the home of Adam Smith, champion of the free market economy, was among the nations with the largest government sectors in the world at the beginning of the 19th century. In 1801, Great Britain devoted 22 percent of its GDP to government expenditures.[2] In 2011, government expenditures in the United Kingdom accounted for 49.8 percent of GDP.

Central government expenditures in Sweden at the beginning of the 20th century amounted to less than 7 percent of GDP.[3] Total government spending in Sweden is now over 50 percent of GDP!

It probably is not an exaggeration to call the 20th century the century of governmental growth throughout the world.

Structure of Federal Government Expenditure

Breaking down government expenditures into a few major components will help us see which kinds of expenditures have been most responsible for the increase in the importance of the government sector in the U.S. economy.

Table 1.2 shows the distribution of federal government expenditure in 2011 among transfer payments, consumption expenditures, and net interest paid on the federal debt. Transfer payments include government social benefits paid to individuals, including Social Security pensions, payments for government-supplied health insurance for the elderly (Medicare) and other social benefits such as cash assistance to the poor and unemployed. Also included in transfer payments are grants-in-aid to state and local governments. Many of these grants also end up financing transfer payments to individuals, including medical insurance for people with incomes low enough to qualify for the Medicaid program and income support for the poor administered by state and local governments.

---

[1]See U.S. Department of Commerce, Bureau of the Census. *Historical Statistics of the U.S., Colonial Times to 1970.* Washington, D.C., 1975 and National Income and Product Accounts.

[2]Based on statistics in Brian R. Mitchell. *Abstract of British Statistics.* Cambridge, England: Cambridge University Press, 1971.

[3]See Brian R. Mitchell. *European Historical Statistics 1750–1970.* New York: Columbia University Press, 1978.

INTERNATIONAL VIEW

How Much Government? The Share of Government Expenditure in Modern Economies

How much government is enough? This is a question that all societies must ask and resolve through their political institutions. In democratic nations, the level of government activity is determined by voting and political interaction in legislatures and through negotiations between leaders. At the extreme, in nondemocratic nations the level of government involvement is determined by dictators or committees that yield political power. For example, for more than 70 years the citizens of the former Soviet Union lived under an economic system that was drastically different from the mixed economies of the Western world. As a centrally planned economy for most of the 20th century, the Soviet Union was dominated by a ponderous government that controlled much of the means of production and regulated most economic activity.

Under central planning, political leaders of the Soviet Union dictated what would be produced through a complex economic plan. Prices set by the planners were not determined by the free interplay of supply and demand in the marketplace; rather, political considerations dominated resource allocation decisions and favored the production of military goods and services and heavy industry. Consumer

goods and services were given low priority by the planners, and consumers often found little merchandise in government-run stores—food shortages were common before the Soviet Union dissolved. The Soviet system was inflexible compared to mixed economies with their large market sectors. Prices in the Soviet economy rarely served as signals that influenced incentives to produce goods.

Modern mixed economies have large government sectors that supply such services as national defense, police and fire protection, roads, and education, and also provide income support and medical insurance for the elderly, the poor, and other groups. The extent of government as a percentage of GDP, the total value of domestic production of a nation, varies considerably among countries. For most modern industrial nations, government expenditures account for between 35 and 60 percent of GDP.

The following table shows estimates of general government outlays for 2011 calculated by the Organization of Economic Cooperation and Development (OECD) for its member states. The outlays include both current and capital expenditures and include

TABLE 1.2   Government Expenditure by Category, 2011 Calendar Year

EXPENDITURE CATEGORY	AMOUNT (BILLIONS OF DOLLARS)	PERCENTAGE OF TOTAL FEDERAL EXPENDITURE
Transfer Payments	2,305.6	58.7
Consumption Expenditures	1,072.6	27.3
Net Interest Paid	312.4	8.0
Other	236.0	6.0
Total	3,926.6	100.0

Source: U.S. Department of Commerce, Bureau of Economic Analysis, National Income and Product Accounts.

Transfer payments accounted for nearly 60 percent of federal government spending in 2011. Net interest paid to holders of federal government securities such as treasury bills, notes, and bonds accounted for nearly 8 percent of federal spending in 2011. Only 27.3 percent of federal government expenditure is accounted for by government purchases for consumption expenditures that provide public services

spending by all levels of government in a nation. In general, spending by governments in European nations is higher than that in the United States when expressed as share of GDP. Most European nations have more extensive Social Security systems that often include government-provided health care and other social programs to support incomes. Government spending in many European nations is over 50 percent of GDP. In Denmark the share of government spending was approaching 60 percent of GDP in 2011. The only OECD nations with government spending below 40 percent of GDP are Australia, Korea, the United States, and Switzerland.

General Government Spending as a Share of GDP, 2011

Australia	35.0
Austria	51.7
Belgium	52.2
Canada	43.2
Czech Republic	43.5
Denmark	59.3
Estonia	38.1
Finland	53.2
France	56.2
Germany	45.5
Greece	49.9
Hungary	48.8
Iceland	46.0
Ireland	45.9
Israel	44.9
Italy	50.1
Japan	42.5
Korea	30.9
Luxembourg	42.5
Netherlands	50.5
New Zealand	49.3
Norway	43.8
Poland	44.7
Portugal	49.4
Slovak Republic	39.4
Slovenia	50.1
Spain	42.7
Sweden	51.8
Switzerland	34.0
Turkey	36.3
United Kingdom	49.8

Source: OECD Economic Outlook, 90, www.oecd.org, December 2011 Projections

such as national defense, homeland security, education, and transportation services.

Figure 1.4 shows how the distribution of federal expenditure has changed since 1960. Transfers have increased from 30 percent of federal spending in 1960 to nearly 60 percent in 2011. While the share of federal spending accounted for by transfers has nearly doubled, government purchases for consumption expenditures have declined from 60 percent to less than 30 percent of spending over the same period. This change is of historical importance and reflects the massive shift to expanded social insurance programs in the 1960s and 1970s, including increases in Social Security pension benefits and indexation of those benefits for inflation, the establishment and growth of the Medicare program that provides health insurance for eligible individuals at age 65, and other programs of income support. In recent years, the growth of the Medicaid program that provides health insurance for the poor has also contributed to the growth of transfer payments.

Interest payments rose from about 8 percent of federal spending in 1960 to a peak of nearly 20 percent of federal spending in 1991, a period of record government deficits and borrowing at high interest rates. Since 2007, despite a soaring federal budget deficit lower interest rates have reduced federal interest payments to 8 percent of total federal spending.

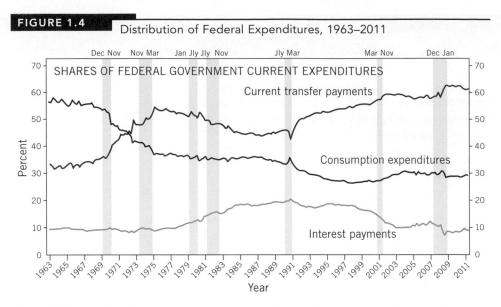

FIGURE 1.4   Distribution of Federal Expenditures, 1963–2011

Since 1963, transfer payments have grown as a share of federal expenditures. (Shaded areas indicate recessions.)

Source: U.S. Department of Commerce, Survey of Current Business, March 2012.

Table 1.3 presents data on the structure of federal government expenditures by major type and function based on NIPA calendar year data. This table is designed to provide information on some of the types of services made available by the federal government.

As of 2011 the biggest and fastest-growing category of federal government expenditure was for health; it accounted for one out of every four dollars of expenditure. The two major federal government health insurance programs, Medicare and Medicaid, constituted the bulk of this spending. Medicare provides health insurance for eligible persons over the age of 65 (and some eligible recipients with disabilities who are below that age), while Medicaid provides medical and long-term care to persons whose incomes and assets are low enough to qualify for benefits under the program.

The second largest category of federal expenditure is national defense, accounting for one fifth of federal spending. Defense spending by the federal government has been rising as a share of total spending since 2001 mainly because of military operations in Iraq and Afghanistan. Social Security and other retirement pensions account for 16.15 percent of federal spending while income security, which provides support for eligible persons with low incomes or to the unemployed accounts for 16.67 percent of spending. Income support payments, particularly unemployment insurance and food assistance, have increased substantially since 2007 as high unemployment rates and slow growth in the U.S. economy have reduced the incomes of many citizens and caused them to apply for benefits under government income support programs.

A very large share of federal spending benefits persons over the age of 65. The sum of spending for Medicare and Social Security pensions to the elderly account for more than 25 percent of federal spending. The top four categories of federal

TABLE 1.3	Federal Government Expenditure by Function	
FEDERAL CURRENT EXPENDITURE 2011*	**AMOUNT (BILLIONS OF DOLLARS)**	**PERCENTAGE OF TOTAL**
Health	939.60	25.01
National Defense	716.60	19.07
Social Security and other Retirement Pensions	606.60	16.15
Income Security	626.40	16.67
Net Interest	325.00	8.65
Education	133.40	3.55
Public Order and Safety	57.90	1.54
Housing and Community Services	63.50	1.69
Transportation	42.50	1.13
All other	245.50	6.53
Total	3.757.00	100.00

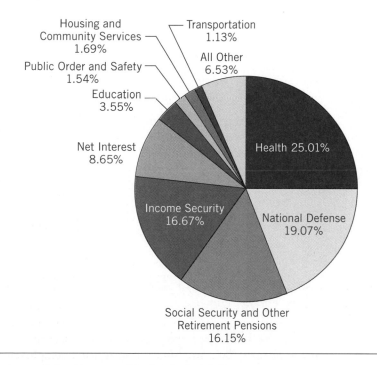

*Based calendar year National Income and Product Account data

Source: National Income and Product Accounts, Interactive Tables, http://bea.gov

spending—health, national defense, Social Security, and income security—account for more than three quarters of total federal spending! Adding interest on the federal debt, which amounts to slightly less than 10 percent of federal outlays to this sum, reveals that only 15 percent of federal spending is accounted for by other types of programs. For example, spending on education by the federal government accounts for only 3.55 percent of its total spending. No other category of federal spending accounts for more than 2 percent of total federal outlays.

THE STRUCTURE OF STATE AND LOCAL GOVERNMENT EXPENDITURE

In contrast to U.S. federal government spending, the 50 state governments in the United States, along with thousands of local governments, spent more than $2 trillion in 2011, of which $492.5 billion was paid for by grants from the federal government.

Education is the most important category of state and local government spending. In 2011, education expenditures accounted for one-third percent of state and local government outlays. Local governments are primarily responsible for providing elementary and secondary education, but state governments assist local governments by providing significant grants-in-aid, and in some cases, financing such expenditures as teacher salaries. States also provide higher education through state colleges, universities, and community colleges.

Health care is the second most important category of spending by state and local governments, accounting for more than 22 percent of spending in 2011. Much of the spending is for Medicaid, which is partially funded by the federal government. In recent years, state governments have been assigned more responsibility for providing health care for the poor. Although much of the health care expenditure is financed by federal grants, these expenses are growing rapidly and putting some strain on state finances.

Public order and safety, which includes police and fire protection, law courts, and prisons accounted for 13 percent of spending by state and local governments in 2011. State and local governments spent nearly 7.5 percent of their budgets on income transfers and 6 percent on transportation. Both income security and transportation are partially funded by grants from the federal government, which has become an important source of finance for state and local governments.

Table 1.4 and its accompanying pie chart show the major categories of state and local government spending in 2011. The pie chart details the distribution of spending.

FINANCING GOVERNMENT EXPENDITURE IN THE UNITED STATES

Taxes, the principal means of financing government expenditures, are compulsory payments that do not necessarily bear any direct relationship to the benefits from government goods and services received. For example, the right to receive the benefits of national defense services or to use public roads is not contingent on payment of taxes. A citizen who pays $10,000 a year in taxes is defended equally and has no more right to use public roads than the individual who pays little or no taxes.

Determining the means of financing government functions is a public choice that is likely to be based on a number of important considerations. Because taxes are compulsory payments required under the powers of authority of government,

TABLE 1.4	State and Local Government current Expenditures by Function, 2011*		
STATE AND LOCAL GOVERNMENT EXPENDITURE 2011	**AMOUNT (BILLIONS OF DOLLARS)**	**PERCENTAGE**
Education	730.1	33.70
Health	480.5	22.18
Public Order and Safety (police, fire protection, law courts, and prisons	285.1	13.16
Income Security	162.9	7.52
Transportation	127.5	5.89
Interest Payments	109.2	5.04
Recreation and Cultural activities	27.2	1.26
Housing and Community Services	7.4	0.34
Other	236.4	10.91
Total	2166.3	100.00

STATE AND LOCAL GOVERNMENT EXPENDITURE

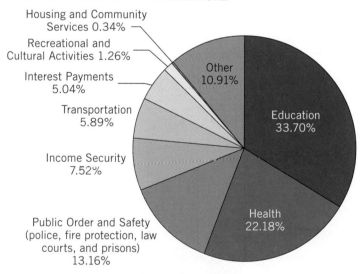

*includes expenditure financed by Federal Grants-in-Aid

Source: U.S. Department of Commerce, Bureau of Economics Analysis, Interactive Tables, http://bea.gov

many citizens believe that taxes should be distributed fairly. However, citizens often differ in their ideas concerning what is a fair distribution of the burden of finance.

Taxes affect economic incentives to produce and consume or to use productive resources in the most gainful way. When part of the gain from a transaction has to be surrendered to the government, the willingness to engage in that activity is naturally reduced. High taxes on interest from savings tend to reduce the incentive to save. Taxes on various consumer goods tend to reduce the amounts of these goods that will be consumed. Taxes on labor earnings can also reduce the incentive to work.

In evaluating alternative means of financing government, desires for fairness in taxation must be balanced with the possible harmful effects of taxes on incentives to produce, consume, and invest. At the extreme, very high taxes on those with high earnings and low taxes on those with low earnings can promote economic equality of income. However, this goal is likely to be achieved at the cost of reduction in incentives for producers to use their resources in activities for which the social returns to production are the highest.

Table 1.5 and its accompanying pie charts provide data on government finances. In 2011, the two major sources of revenue for the federal government

TABLE 1.5 Government Receipts, 2011

FEDERAL GOVERNMENT RECEIPTS 2011		
FEDERAL GOVERNMENT RECEIPTS	AMOUNT (BILLIONS OF DOLLARS)	PERCENTAGE OF TOTAL
Personal Income Taxes	1072	41.80
Payroll Taxes	907.3	35.38
Corporate Profits Taxes	338.2	13.19
Excise Taxes	79.1	3.08
Customs Duties	31.7	1.24
Other	136.5	5.32
Total	2564.6	100.00

FEDERAL REVENUES 2011

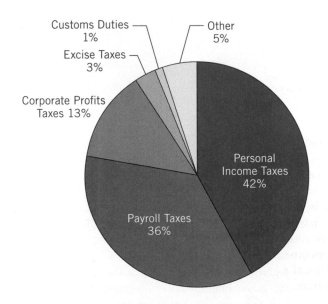

TABLE 1.5   Continued

STATE AND LOCAL GOVERNMENTS, 2011

SATE AND LOCAL GOVERNMENT RECEIPTS	AMOUNT (BILLIONS OF DOLLARS)	PERCENTAGE OF TOTAL
Sales Taxes	458.2	21.98
Federal Grants	492.5	23.63
Income Taxes	293.7	14.09
Payroll Taxes	21.6	1.04
Corporate Profits Taxes	51.5	2.47
Property Taxes	435.3	20.89
Other	331.4	15.90
Total	2084.2	100.00

STATE AND LOCAL GOVERNMENT REVENUES, 2011

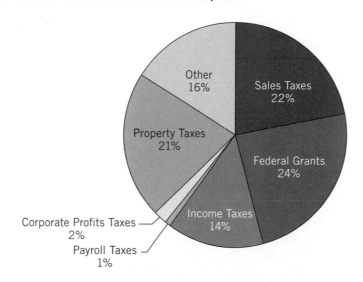

Source: U.S. Department of Commerce, Bureau of Economics Analysis, Interactive Tables, http://bea.gov

were income and payroll taxes, which together accounted for 77.2 percent of government receipts. (Payroll taxes are paid by workers and their employers to finance social insurance programs including Social Security.) Corporate profits taxes accounted for 13.2 percent of federal receipts in 2011. Excise taxes, such as those levied on fuels, telephone service, tires, cigarettes, and alcoholic beverages, accounted for 3.1 percent of federal revenues in 2011. Because of major cuts in federal income tax rates enacted by Congress in 2001 and 2003, the share of revenue coming from income taxes has fallen since 2001.

State and local government receipts were $2,084.2 billion in 2011. Table 1.5 shows the sources of funds for these governments. The most important source of tax revenue for state and local governments is the sales tax, which accounted for 22 percent of receipts in 2011. Personal income taxes accounted for 14 percent, and taxes on property for 21 percent of receipts in 2011. Federal grants accounted for nearly one-quarter percent of state and local receipts in 2011.

CHECKPOINT

1. What is a mixed economy? How does an increase in government taxation and purchases affect the circular flow of income and expenditures in a mixed economy?
2. What is the difference between government purchases and government transfer payments?
3. List the major categories of federal government expenditure and revenue in the United States.

MARKET FAILURE AND THE FUNCTIONS OF GOVERNMENT: HOW MUCH GOVERNMENT IS ENOUGH?

Why do we demand government services? How much government is enough? As citizens, each of us has opinions about what governments should or should not be doing. An economic analysis of government seeks to evaluate the costs and benefits of government activities and also to explain the way government spending, regulations, and finance affect resource use and the distribution of well-being in a society.

One reason we demand government services is that, in many cases, the government can provide us with items that we cannot easily make available for ourselves or purchase from others in markets. For example, governments establish property rights to the use of resources and enforce contracts by providing a system of law enforcement and courts. Government power is exerted through these functions to establish rules that regulate the social interaction among individuals and to settle disputes among citizens. It is almost inconceivable to imagine a society functioning without these rules—and without a government.

Political theorists of the 19th century called the willing submission of individuals to the authority of government the *social compact*. The existence of government gives rise to further demands for its powers to be used to supply various services to its citizens. Governments also use their power to redistribute income and economic opportunity among citizens. For example, the federal government uses tax revenues to provide income support for elderly, unemployed, and poor citizens. Another function is to stabilize economic fluctuations to prevent the waste associated with unemployment of productive resources and the undesirable consequences of inflation. Finally, governments regulate production and consumption to achieve such goals as improved health and the elimination of excessive monopolistic control over prices.

The growth in government spending since 1929 reflects increased demands for government services that markets fail to provide. Demands for social insurance, such as Social Security old-age pensions, unemployment insurance, and government-financed health insurance to the aged and the poor, are responsible for much of the growth of government spending since 1970. National defense is also a service that we cannot purchase for ourselves in markets and has accounted for many billions of dollars in federal government outlays.

But has government grown too much, too rapidly? Do the costs outweigh the benefits of some government functions and services? Could some government services be dispensed with entirely, allowing the resources they absorb to be used elsewhere and allowing a reduction in taxes paid? Should government assets and enterprises, such as the postal service, be sold to private firms to be operated for profit? Have tax-financed Social Security pensions become more generous than initially intended?

How much should governments do, and how much should be left to private enterprise and initiative through market sale of goods and services? This is the core question that occupies much of the first part of this textbook. Once we have established the basis for government activity, we can examine the impact of government finance on private incentives and resource use.

AGING POPULATIONS: IMPLICATIONS FOR PUBLIC FINANCE

The world is getting older. Not just physically—the average age of the population is rising. The aging of populations varies among nations with the effects being most pronounced in the more developed nations, including the European Union, the United States, Japan, and China. In less developed nations, populations are still relatively young, and in the least developed nations, aging is imperceptible.

World population quadrupled in the 20th century. In the 21st century, world population is projected to increase by only 50 percent and is likely to stabilize by the end of the century. Declining population growth is a by-product of economic development. As incomes rise, total fertility rates (measured by births per woman) decline while improved access to health care increases life expectancy at birth.[4] For example, total fertility rates in the United States fell from about 3.5 births per woman in 1950 to about 2 births per woman in 2006. Declines in fertility rates are even more pronounced in China where the rate has fallen from more than 6 in 1950 to about 2 in 2006. These rates are not projected to increase through 2050. Life expectancy at birth in the United States was 69 in 1950 but is projected to be more than 80 by 2050. In China, life expectancy at birth was 40 in 1950 but is projected to be more than 75 by 2050. In short, over the next 50 years we can expect to see more old people around, living longer, and higher percentages of the elderly as a share of total population. Table 1.6 shows observed and forecasted percentages of the population 60 years of age and older

---

[4]For a discussion of the demographics of aging of the population, see Leonid A. Gavrilov and Patrick Heuveline. "Aging of the Population" in *The Encyclopedia of Population*. New York: Macmillan Reference USA, 2003. Also see "Global Population Aging in the 21st Century and Its Economic Implications," A CBO Paper. Washington, D.C.: Congress of the United States, Congressional Budget Office, December 2005.

TABLE 1.6	Population Aging: Percentage of Elderly (aged 60 and older) to Total Population in the World, Selected Regions, and Countries	
REGION OR COUNTRY	2010	2050
World	11.0	21.8
Latin America & Caribbean	10.0	25.0
Africa	5.5	9.8
China	12.3	33.9
India	7.6	19.1
Japan	30.5	41.5
United States	18.4	26.6
Europe	21.8	33.6
Italy	26.5	38.4
Spain	22.3	38.3
Germany	26.0	37.5
Sweden	24.9	30.6

Source: Population Division of the Department of Economic and Social Affairs of the United Nations Secretariat, World Population Prospects: The 2010 Revision. New York: United Nations, 2012.

for the years 2010 and 2050. Notice that Japan, Italy, Spain, and Germany are all expected to have more than one third of their population at age 60 and above by 2050. The aging of the population is less pronounced in the United States, where only 26.6 percent of the population is projected be age 60 or older by 2050. Japan is the nation where aging of the population will be most extreme with 41.5 percent of total population expected to be age 60 or older by 2050. Japan is actually projected to have one sixth of its population aged 80 or more by 2050!

Aging of the population has a profound impact on public finance and government budgets. Most of these effects stem from increased old-age dependency ratios, measured by the percentage of the population 65 years of age and older to the population ages 15 to 64. This is an indicator of the proportion of retired workers to active workers in a nation or region. Because younger people under the age of 65 are likely to be in the labor force and their income generates taxes to pay for government programs (including Social Security pensions), as the old-age dependency ratio rises, a smaller percentage of the population is likely to be productive, taxpaying citizens whose efforts generate taxes to finance government programs. For example, an old-age dependency ratio of 50 percent indicates that on average, there are two people of working age for each retiree (assuming workers on average retire at age 65). The working population must generate enough tax revenue to pay for all government programs including Social Security pensions to avoid government deficits unless some taxes are paid by the elderly. Government expenditure for health care also rises as the population ages because the prevalence of chronic diseases and disability increases with old age. Most European Union

TABLE 1.7	Old Age Dependency Ratios of Population Aged 65 and Older to Population aged 15–64, 1950–2075 (Actual for 1950–2010, Projections for 2010–2075)				
YEAR	UNITED STATES	MORE DEVEL-OPED REGIONS	LESS DEVELOPED REGIONS (EXCLUDES CHINA)	LEAST DEVEL-OPED COUNTRIES	CHINA
1950	13	12	6	6	7
1955	14	13	6	6	7
1960	15	14	6	6	7
1965	16	14	6	6	7
1970	16	15	7	6	7
1975	16	17	7	6	8
1980	17	18	7	6	9
1985	18	17	7	6	9
1990	19	19	7	6	9
1995	19	20	7	6	10
2000	19	21	7	6	10
2005	18	23	8	6	11
2010	20	24	8	6	11
2015	22	26	8	6	13
2020	25	30	9	6	17
2025	29	33	11	7	20
2030	33	36	12	7	24
2035	33	39	14	8	31
2040	35	41	15	9	37
2045	35	43	17	10	39
2050	35	45	19	11	42
2075	40	45	28	18	54

Source: Population Division of the Department of Economic and Social Affairs of the United Nations Secretariat, World Population Prospects: The 2010 Revision. New York: United Nations, 2012.

nations and Japan, for example, are projected to have old-age dependency ratios of 50 percent by 2050. Old-age dependency ratios are projected to be in the range of 35 percent for the United States and 40 percent for China by 2050. Table 1.7 shows dependency ratios based on United Nations data and projections for major world regions.

The impact of aging of the population in the United States will have significant effects on Social Security expenditures and expenditure for health care under the Medicare and Medicaid programs. The Social Security Administration projects, based on current pension formulas, that Social Security outlays will rise from 4.3 percent of GDP in 2004 to 5.8 percent of GDP in 2050 while revenue for

Social Security will amount to only 4.7 percent of GDP at that time. This means that the government will either have to cut pensions at that time, increase tax rates, or borrow to finance the deficit. If current trends continue, spending on Medicare and Medicaid could reach 20 percent of GDP. This implies that government spending on pensions and health care would be more than 25 percent of GDP and could leave little funds available to spend on other government programs such as defense and highways unless taxes are increased or the budget deficit balloons. Such a burden of finance could result in soaring interest rates and declines in private investment that would adversely affect economic growth in the United States.[5]

It is difficult to predict the effects of the aging population on the economy and the federal government's budget. Some forecasts suggest that one third of GDP could be absorbed by health care by the year 2030, mainly as a result of the aging population and consequent demands on the health care system. Other experts suggest that the elderly in the future will be healthier and more productive than their counterparts today. This could lead to higher growth rates for the economy as the elderly retire later. The resulting increase in productivity and tax revenues for the government could offset the demands that retiring baby boomers place on the health care system and government expenditures for pensions. Others suggest that the percentage of the elderly in the future requiring long-term care will actually decline as the health of older people improves.[6]

Tax rates for Social Security pensions are likely to rise as a result of the aging of the population. The extent of the increases depends on the rate of improvement of life expectancy through the year 2070. The current payroll tax rate used to finance Social Security pensions is 12.4 percent. If life expectancy were to remain as currently projected, the tax rate in the year 2070 to finance the pensions would have to increase to 20 percent solely as a result of the aging of the population. If, however, life expectancy were to significantly improve, the tax rate necessary to finance Social Security pensions without incurring any deficit would have to rise to a whopping 32 percent.[7] However, uncertainties about future mortality, fertility, and immigration rates for the nation make it difficult to project exactly the impact of aging on pensions and tax rates required to finance those pensions. This uncertainty combined with problems in forecasting the health and productivity status of the elderly could mean that the situation is not as grave as forecast or it could actually be worse than the most pessimistic projections! Health is crucial because increased spending for government programs that provide health care for the elderly could absorb as much as 10 percent of GDP.

Another factor is the overall rate of growth of the U.S. economy. Programs to aid an aging population could be financed with lower-than-projected tax rates if real GDP grows faster.

The major programs that provide transfers to the elderly, Social Security, and Medicare remain likely to be under fiscal stress in the future. Despite difficulty in making projections, there is a high probability that large federal budget deficits

---

[5]See "The Role of the Economy in the Outlook for Social Security," CBO Testimony, Statement of Douglas Holtz-Eakin, Director, Congressional Budget Office, June 21, 2005; available at www.cbo.gov.

[6]See Ronald Lee and Jonathan Skinner. "Will Aging Baby Boomers Bust the Budget," *Journal of Economic Perspectives*, 13, 1 (Winter 1999): 117–140 for a review of studies on the fiscal impact of aging of the population.

[7]See Lee and Skinner, p. 127.

will result if reforms are not enacted soon. Either tax rates to finance these programs will have to be increased or benefits per recipient will have to decline. One estimate indicates that a 4 percent increase in the payroll tax today might still be insufficient to prevent the Social Security system from spending more per year than it receives in revenues late in the 21st century.[8]

If benefits promised to the elderly are actually paid in the future, it is inevitable that federal government expenditures will grow faster than tax revenues. Excluding interest on the federal debt and expenditures for national defense, more than half of government spending is already allocated to programs that benefit the elderly, and projections indicate that by 2050 these expenditures will account for more than 70 percent of such federal spending. Future deficits will grow after the second half of the 21st century unless tax rates are increased or government expenditures are cut, especially expenditures on programs for the elderly. Reducing the generosity of the programs on average, while maintaining a floor on benefits to those with low incomes, is one alternative. Future deficits could absorb savings, raise interest rates, and cut private investments. The issue in the future may very well be: How much of a share of our GDP should we devote to the elderly?

In 2012 the Congressional Budget Office projected that virtually all the noninterest federal spending growth as a share of GDP in the United States in the next 25 years will result from spending on Social Security, Medicare, and Medicaid and health insurance subsidies under the new Affordable Care Act. Aging of the population results in more beneficiaries under Medicare and Medicaid, and because the elderly have higher health care costs than average, this will cause future health care spending by the government to rise rapidly.

What if nothing is done? The economic implications involving this approach could be devastating because tax rates on a workforce that is a smaller share of the population could soar, and interest rates could increase as government borrowing to cover growing deficits accelerates. The higher tax rates on a shrinking workforce and higher interest rates would likely cause economic growth and real GDP per capita to fall as private investment and work effort are choked off. The situation will be even more dire in other developed nations where old-age dependency ratios will exceed those of the United States. Nations such as Spain, Italy, Germany, Japan, and China will face more severe fiscal pressure because of dependency ratios between 40 and 50 percent and because in some of these nations, it has been traditional for workers to retire between the ages of 55 and 65. Unless some of these nations allow more immigration to permit the workforce to expand or convince the elderly to delay retirement, the fiscal consequences of aging of their populations and the impact on their economies could be catastrophic. Given rising government budget deficits and sovereign debt levels, Denmark, the United Kingdom, and Italy have already passed legislation to increase retirement ages for workers.

There is, therefore, some urgency that something be done within the next few years to halt the scenario of growing expenditures and federal deficits that could cripple the U.S. economy. In later chapters of this text, we will examine options to keep both Social Security pensions and Medicare from growing so rapidly as the U.S. population ages.

---

[8]See Lee and Skinner, p. 135.

SUMMARY

Public finance is the field of economics that studies government activities and alternative means of financing government expenditures. Modern public finance emphasizes the relationships between citizens and governments. Government goods and services are supplied through political institutions, which employ rules and procedures that have evolved in different societies for arriving at collective choices. Increases in government goods and services require decreased private use of resources. Government goods and services are usually made available without charge for their use, and they are financed by compulsory payments (mainly taxes) levied on citizens and their activities. The distribution of the tax burden itself is determined through the political interaction of citizens.

In modern mixed economies, the size of the government sector ranges between one quarter and one half of GDP. A major goal in the study of public finance is to analyze the economic role of government and the costs and benefits of allocating resources to government use as opposed to allowing private enterprise and households to use those resources.

LOOKING AHEAD

The following chapter develops a theoretical basis for understanding and evaluating resource allocation. We introduce the concept of efficiency that appears throughout this textbook. Students who wish to review the basic economic theory that serves as a foundation for much of this textbook will find the appendix at the end of this chapter useful.

KEY CONCEPTS

Government Goods and Services

Government Purchases

Government Transfer Payments

Governments

Mixed Economy

Nonmarket Rationing

Political Institutions

Private Goods and Services

Public Finance

Pure Market Economy

REVIEW QUESTIONS

1. List four government services and the benefits they provide to you and your family. Try to put a monetary value on these benefits by thinking about what you would be willing to give up to receive them if they were not available.
2. Make a rough estimate of how much you and your family pay in taxes each year. Compare this estimate with the value of services received from the government. Do you think government provides you with benefits that are worth what you give up in taxes?
3. How does the mechanism for distributing and rationing most government services differ from that for distributing goods through markets?
4. List some major political institutions and indicate how they translate desires into collective agreements.
5. What is a production-possibility curve? Show how such a curve can be used to explain how private goods and services must be sacrificed to obtain government goods and services.
6. What is the real cost of government expenditures? Think about your estimate of the taxes you pay and what you could have purchased with that money.
7. Discuss the trends in government expenditures and outlays as a percentage of GDP.
8. What are the characteristics of the U.S. economy that make it a "mixed economy" instead of a pure market economy?
9. What is the distinction between government purchases and transfer payments? What is the relative importance of these two types of expenditures in total government expenditures expressed as a percent of GDP? Why are some government purchases necessary to administer transfer payments by government?
10. List the major sources of tax revenue for the federal government. In what ways do the taxes used by state and local governments differ from those used by the federal government? What are other sources of government finance in addition to taxation?

PROBLEMS

1. As productive resources and technological know-how increase, a nation's production-possibility curve shifts outward. Use a production-possibility curve to show how resource growth and improvements in technology can allow a nation to increase its production of government goods and services while also increasing its output of private goods and services.

2. Suppose federal, state, and local governments in the United States were to engage in a massive campaign to deal with AIDS, drug abuse, and other health-related problems. The increase in government medical spending would require a massive tax increase. Assuming that resources and technology are fixed, use a production-possibility curve to show the cost of increased government health services.

3. Suppose governments increase spending for Social Security pensions. Explain why the increased government spending for pensions will not appreciably increase government purchases of productive resources or the products of business firms.

4. Explain why interest payments by the federal government would still be a large share of federal expenditures even if the federal government does not run a deficit again for several years.

5. The proportion of the population over 65 has been increasing and is expected to increase further. How does an aging population affect a *state* government's expenditures? Which state programs are expected to cost more as the population ages? How does an aging population affect a state government's tax revenues? Which types of state taxes are likely to see revenue declines as the population ages?

ADDITIONAL READINGS

Buchanan, James M. *Public Finance in Democratic Process*. Chapel Hill: University of North Carolina Press, 1967. Provides a classic economic analysis of the processes through which individual choices are related to collective actions and government policy with respect to both expenditures and finance.

Kaul, Ingeand and Conceicao Pedro (eds.). *The New Public Finance: Responding to Global Challenges*. New York: Oxford University Press, 2006. A collection of essays on global and international issues in the field of public finance and public policy.

Statistical Abstract of the United States. Washington, D.C.: U.S. Government Printing Office. Published annually. A gold mine of data on U.S. government programs, expenditures, and taxes, as well as facts and figures on just about anything you would care to know about the United States.

Tax Foundation. *Facts & Figures on Government Finances*. Washington, D.C.: The Tax Foundation. Published annually. Provides data and information regarding government spending, revenues, and taxation in the United States.

Wolf, Charles, Jr. *Markets or Governments*. Cambridge, Mass.: The MIT Press, 1993. An analysis of the role of government in a market economy and the failures of government policy. Also discusses the process of transition in formerly socialist countries.

INTERNET RESOURCES

A wealth of current information on government spending and government programs is available on the Internet. In each of the chapters of this book, we supply the addresses of useful Internet sites with data and information on government programs and taxation. Here are several Internet sources of information useful for research along with some hints for surfing these sites.

http://www.whitehouse.gov
The home pages of the president and vice president of the United States provide information about the current administration's policies as well as numerous links to government agencies. You can go to the Web sites of agencies in the Executive Office of the President, including the Council of Economic Advisers and the Office of Management and Budget. Links are provided to Web sites of all the president's cabinet secretaries. This site can serve as an excellent first source when searching for information on government expenditures and finance and current federal government policies.

http://www.usa.gov
At this site you will find a "gateway to government" for citizens. There are interactive services for citizens and businesses at the site. There are also links to help find information about government programs, such as Social Security, laws and regulations, government publications, and federal statistics. There are also links to

state and local government sites. This is a good first stop if you are looking for statistics on government and the economy.

http://www.senate.gov

This is the home page of the U.S. Senate. Click on Committees to obtain information about ongoing work and committee publications on the federal budget. The following committees provide useful information on government spending and taxation: Appropriations, Budget, Finance, The Joint Economic Committee, and The Joint Committee on Taxation.

http://www.house.gov

This is the home page of the U.S. House of Representatives. Click on Committees and a wealth of information on government spending programs can be obtained by accessing the "Green Book" of the Ways and Means Committee. This book can be searched to obtain details on all federal transfer and entitlement programs. Other useful committees to access include Appropriations and Budget.

http://www.state.xx.us

To find information about government spending and taxes in your home state, just replace the *xx* in the address above with your state's postal abbreviation to access your state's home page. Here you can examine your state's budget and its tax system. For example, to access information about North Carolina, simply type: www.state.nc.us.

http://www.oecd.org

The OECD has 34 member nations. You can obtain information about taxation, government spending, and government programs as well as other economic statistics about the member nations (including the United States) at this site. This is a good place to obtain information on international comparisons among industrialized nations.

Appendix 1

TOOLS OF MICROECONOMIC ANALYSIS

This appendix briefly reviews the tools of microeconomic analysis that are used in this textbook. It outlines the uses of these tools and the insights they can provide. The theories are only briefly described. Students who desire a more intensive review and derivation of relationships should consult a textbook on microeconomic theory.

INDIFFERENCE CURVE ANALYSIS

Indifference curve analysis is a useful tool for understanding choices that people make regarding the purchase and use of goods and services. In this text, indifference curve analysis is also applied to understand choices to give up leisure time to obtain income through work, and to give up consumption today for more consumption in the future.

A combination of various goods and services available for consumption over a certain period, say a month, is called a **market basket**. In this book the market baskets discussed are combinations of one particular good and the expenditures on *all* other goods. For example, in discussing a person's monthly purchases of gasoline, the market baskets consist of a certain number of gallons per month and a certain amount of money to spend on all other goods and services.

Assumptions about Preferences

The basic assumptions underlying indifference curve analysis are as follows:

1. People can rank market baskets in terms of most desired and least desired. For any two market baskets, *A* and *B*, the consumer must prefer *A* to *B*, *B* to *A*, or be indifferent between the two.

2. If basket *A* is preferred to basket *B* and basket *B* is preferred to basket *C*, then basket *A* also must be preferred to basket *C*. Similarly, if a person is indifferent between *A* and *B* and also between *B* and *C*, the person also must be indifferent between *A* and *C*. This is called *transitivity*.

3. People always prefer more of a good to less of it, all other things being equal.

4. The amount of money people will give up to obtain additional units of a given good per time period, while being made neither worse nor better off by the exchange, will decrease as more of the good is acquired. This is the *assumption of declining marginal rate of substitution* of a particular good for expenditures on other goods. It is also called the *principle of declining marginal benefit of a good*.

Throughout this book, assume that these assumptions will hold.

Indifference Curves and Indifference Maps

An **indifference curve** is a graph of all combinations of market baskets among which a person is indifferent. All points on an indifference curve give the person the same level of satisfaction, or utility, per month. The preceding assumptions assure that the indifference curves between monthly consumption of a particular good, X (such as gasoline), and monthly expenditures on other goods will be downward sloping and convex to the origin. Figure 1A.1 graphs an indifference curve, labeled U_1, for monthly consumption of gasoline and monthly expenditure on all other goods. The market basket corresponding to point B_1 on the graph has 40 gallons of gasoline per month and $60 expenditures on all other goods per month. Point B_2 must correspond to more gasoline but less expenditure on other goods if it is to be a point on the indifference curve U_1. This has to follow from the assumption that people prefer more to less. If the market basket corresponding to B_2 had more gasoline and more expenditure on other goods than basket B_1, the people would be better off. This means that B_2 would be on an indifference curve, such as U_2, that corresponds to a higher level of satisfaction.

The amount of expenditure on goods other than gasoline that a person will give up to obtain another unit of a good X, such as a gallon of gasoline, while not becoming better or worse off, is called the **marginal rate of substitution** of good X for expenditure on other goods, or the **marginal benefit** of a good. It is equal to the slope of the indifference curve multiplied by –1. The assumption that the marginal benefit of a good declines implies that indifference curves become flatter as good X (in this case, gasoline) is substituted for expenditure on other goods in the person's market basket each month.

FIGURE 1A.1 Indifference Curves

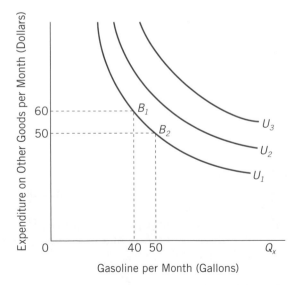

Indifference curves are downward sloping. Curves farther out from the origin correspond to higher levels of satisfaction for a person.

An **indifference map** is a way of describing a person's preferences. It shows a group of indifference curves, as displayed in Figure 1A.1. Because indifference curves farther from the origin include market baskets with more of good X and more expenditures on other goods than those closer to the origin, they correspond to more satisfaction. People prefer points on higher curves to those on lower curves. An indifference map describes a person's preferences by indicating how a person would rank alternative market baskets of goods. Market baskets are ranked according to the level of satisfaction, or utility, that they provide the consumer.

The Budget Constraint

The **budget constraint** indicates the monthly market baskets that the person can afford, given monthly income and the prices of good X and all other goods. Figure 1A.2 shows a person's monthly budget constraint between gasoline and expenditures on other goods. Assume that the price of gasoline is $1 per gallon and that the person's monthly income is $100. A market basket corresponding to 100 gallons of gasoline per month would exhaust the person's monthly income, allowing no expenditures on other goods. This corresponds to point B in Figure 1A.2. Similarly, if the person spent all available monthly income on goods other than gasoline, there would be no gasoline in the monthly market basket. This corresponds to point A on the graph. The budget constraint is a straight line connecting these two points. Market baskets corresponding to points on or below the line are affordable. Those above the line, such as C, cannot be purchased with available monthly income. This equation of the budget line is

$$I = P_xQ_x + \Sigma P_iQ_i \tag{1A.1}$$

FIGURE 1A.2 Budget Constraint Line

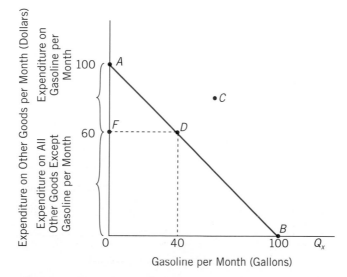

The consumer can afford only those market baskets of gasoline and other goods per month on or below the budget constraint line

where P_x is the price of good X and Q_x is its monthly consumption. The second term represents the sum of expenditure on goods other than gasoline. The market basket that corresponds to point D in Figure 1A.2 is on the budget line. It represents 40 gallons of gasoline per month and $60 expenditures on other goods. The distance OF on the vertical axis is expenditures on other goods corresponding to point D. The distance AF represents the amount of the person's total income given up to buy gasoline that month. This is $40 when the price of gasoline is $1 per gallon.

Consumer Equilibrium

The consumer is assumed to behave so as to obtain the most satisfaction (or utility) possible, given the budget constraint. The consumer substitutes expenditures on goods other than X for purchases of good X, up to the point at which the highest possible satisfaction is obtained. Because indifference curves are convex, this occurs at a point of tangency between the budget line and an indifference curve. In Figure 1A.3, the consumer equilibrium is represented by point E. The corresponding monthly consumption of gasoline is 60 gallons. The person therefore spends $40 on goods other than X each month when the price of gasoline is $1 per gallon.

The **equilibrium condition** is a tangency between the indifference curve and the budget line, implying that the slopes of these two curves are equal. The slope of the budget line is the extra dollars that must be surrendered to obtain each extra gallon of gasoline, which is the price of gasoline multiplied by -1. The slope of the indifference curve is the marginal rate of substitution of gasoline for expenditures on goods other than gasoline per month multiplied by -1. The marginal rate of substitution can be thought of as the marginal benefit of good X.

FIGURE 1A.3 Consumer Equilibrium

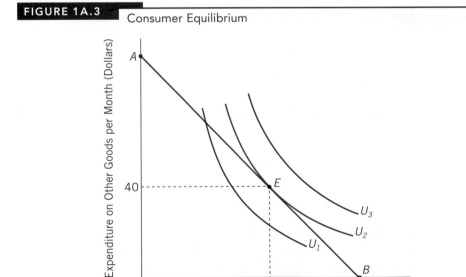

The market basket corresponding to point E is the one that gives the consumer the highest possible level of satisfaction, given the budget constraint.

The equilibrium condition can be written as

$$-P_x = -MB_x$$

or

$$P_x = MB_x \qquad\qquad (1A.2)$$

The consumer purchases a good up to the point at which its price equals its marginal benefit.

Changes in Income and Prices

A change in income shifts the budget constraint line in or out parallel to itself without changing its slope. This is illustrated in Figure 1A.4. An increase in income shifts the budget line outward, expanding the number of affordable market baskets. Similarly, a decrease in income diminishes the number of affordable market baskets.

A change in the price of good X changes the slope of the budget line. As illustrated in Figure 1A.5, a decrease in the price of X swivels the budget line outward to a new intercept, B', on the x-axis. The budget line becomes flatter, reflecting the lower price of X. Similarly, an increase in the price of good X makes the budget line steeper as it rotates to point B''.

Income and Substitution Effects of Price Changes

Useful insights are often obtained by dividing the effect of the price change of a good on the amount purchased per month into two separate effects: income effect and substitution effect. The **income effect** is the change in the monthly (or other period) consumption of a good due to the variation in purchasing power of income

FIGURE 1A.4 Changes in Income

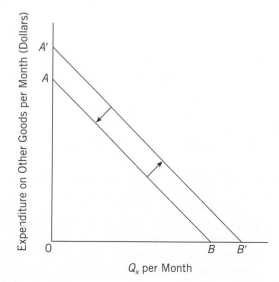

An increase in income shifts the budget constraint line out of parallel to itself. A decrease in income shifts it inward.

FIGURE 1A.5   Changes in the Price of Good X

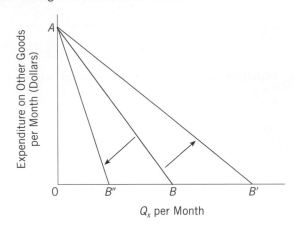

Changes in the price of good rotate the budget constraint line to a new intercept on the
x-axis.

caused by its price change. The **substitution effect** is the change in the monthly (or
other period) consumption of the good due to the change in its price relative to
other goods. This is the change that would be observed if the income effect of the
price change were removed. Income and substitution effects can only rarely be
observed separately. However, it is useful to show how a person's well-being is
affected by each of these effects.

Figure 1A.6 shows how the substitution effect can be isolated from the income
effect. The person whose indifference curves are shown is initially in equilibrium at
E_1. Consuming 60 gallons of gasoline per month and spending \$40 per month on
other goods, this person's monthly income is \$100. If the price of gasoline goes up
to \$2 per gallon as a result of a tax, the budget line would swivel inward. The con-
sumer is now worse off, in a shift from point E_1 to point E_2. At E_2, monthly gasoline consumption falls to 40 gallons per month. The consumer spends \$80 per
month on gasoline at the higher price and uses \$20 of the remaining income to
buy other goods. Suppose the consumer were offered a monthly subsidy (say, by
helpful parents) to help buy gasoline after the price increase. If this monthly
increase in income were sufficient enough to return the consumer to indifference
curve U_2, where the level of satisfaction is the same as before the price increase,
the substitution effect could be isolated.

In Figure 1A.6, a \$50 monthly increase in income returns the consumer to the
level of well-being represented by points on the indifference curve U_2. The consumer's total monthly income would now be \$150. The consumer then would be in
equilibrium at point E', consuming 45 gallons of gasoline per month at a price of
\$2 per gallon (\$90 per month) and spending the remaining \$60 income on other
goods. The 15-gallon monthly decrease in gasoline consumption from the initial
60-gallon monthly consumption level is the substitution effect. The remainder of
the decrease that would be observed in the absence of the monthly compensating
variation in income is an additional 5 gallons per month. This is the income effect.
These two effects are labeled separately in Figure 1A.6.

FIGURE 1A.6 Income and Substitution Effects

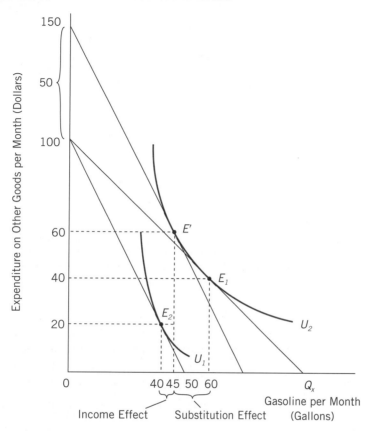

The substitution effect could be observed if the consumer were given an increase in income to offset the decline in satisfaction caused by the price increase of gasoline.

Income and substitution effects are often used in analyzing taxes. For example, taxes that do not affect relative prices but reduce income only have income effects. These taxes are used as benchmarks against which to compare the impact of taxes that have both income effects and substitution effects. The substitution effects stem from the distorting effects that taxes (such as the gasoline tax in this example) have on the relative price of goods and services.

The Law of Demand

For most goods, both the income effects and the substitution effects of price increases tend to decrease the consumption of a good. The opposite is true for price decreases. Goods for which the income effect of a price increase acts to decrease consumption (and for which price decreases have the opposite effect) are called **normal goods**. Throughout this book, the assumption is that all goods and services discussed are normal goods.

The inverse relationship between price and the quantity of a good purchased per time period is the **law of demand**, which holds that demand curves slope

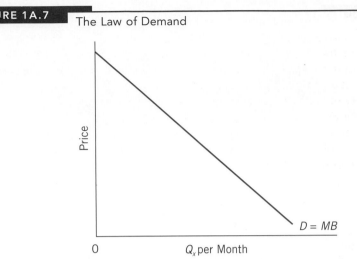

FIGURE 1A.7   The Law of Demand

The demand curve depicts the inverse relationship between price and quantity demanded implied by the law of demand. Points on a demand curve also can be interpreted as the marginal benefit of the various amounts of the good available by month.

© Cengage Learning

downward, other things being equal. Figure 1A.7 shows a demand curve for a good. Movements along that curve in response to price changes are called **changes in quantity demanded**. A shifting in or out of the curve is called a **change in demand**, which can be caused by changes in income, tastes, or the prices of substitutes or complements for the good.

The demand curve also gives information on the maximum price that a consumer will pay for a good. This maximum price represents the marginal benefit of the good to a consumer. Accordingly, the demand curve in Figure 1A.7 is also labeled *MB*. Points on demand curves throughout this book are interpreted as the marginal benefit (*MB*) of the corresponding quantity. Market demand curves are derived from individual demand curves simply by adding the quantities consumed by all purchasers at each possible price.

Price Elasticity of Demand

A useful measure of the responsiveness of quantity demanded to price changes is **price elasticity of demand**, which measures the percentage change in quantity demanded due to a given percentage change in price:

$$E_D = \frac{\%\ \text{Change in Quantity Demanded}}{\%\ \text{Change in Price}} = \frac{\Delta Q_D / Q_D}{\Delta P / P} \tag{1A.3}$$

The price elasticity of demand is negative because an inverse relationship exists between price and quantity demanded. The numerator and denominator of Equation 1A.3 always will be of opposite sign. Demand is elastic with respect to price (relatively responsive) when its value is less than -1. Demand is inelastic (relatively unresponsive) when its value is greater (that is, closer to zero) than -1. Demand is said to be of unitary elasticity when its value is just equal to -1.

Consumer Surplus

Market demand curves can be used to give an approximation of the benefits that consumers obtain from a good. This is found by simply adding up the marginal benefit of each unit consumed to obtain the total benefit of the total consumption per time period. Assuming that the scale of measurement is compact enough along the quantity axis of the market demand curve, this total benefit can be approximated by the area under the market demand curve. In Figure 1A.8, the total benefit of Q_1 units of gasoline consumed per month would be interpreted as the area $0ABQ_1$. This is a dollar approximation of the benefits that consumers obtain from the Q_1 units of monthly consumption.

In most cases, a measure of the *net benefit* that consumers obtain from a good is required. **Consumer surplus** is the total benefit of a given amount of a good less the value of money given up to obtain that monthly quantity. In Figure 1A.8, the amount of money that would have to be given up to purchase Q_1 units of gasoline per month, when its price is P per gallon, is represented by the area $0PBQ_1$. Subtracting this from the total benefit of the gasoline gives the triangular area PAB, which measures the consumer surplus earned on Q_1 gallons per month.

Using Indifference Curves to Explain the Allocation of Time

If leisure is viewed as a good that persons can retain for their own use or supply to others as work, indifference curve analysis can be used to analyze the work–leisure choice. Of the 24 hours available each day, the more leisure hours a person consumes, the fewer hours there are available for paid work. Figure 1A.9 draws a person's indifference curves for leisure hours per day and income per day.

FIGURE 1A.8 Consumer Surplus

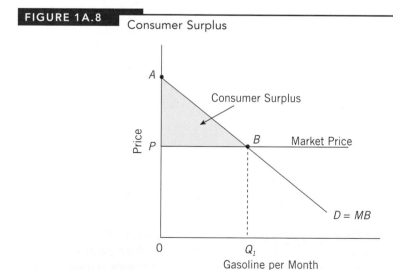

The area *PAB* is a measure of the consumer surplus (net benefit) that consumers receive from consuming gallons of gasoline per month.

FIGURE 1A.9   The Work–Leisure Choice

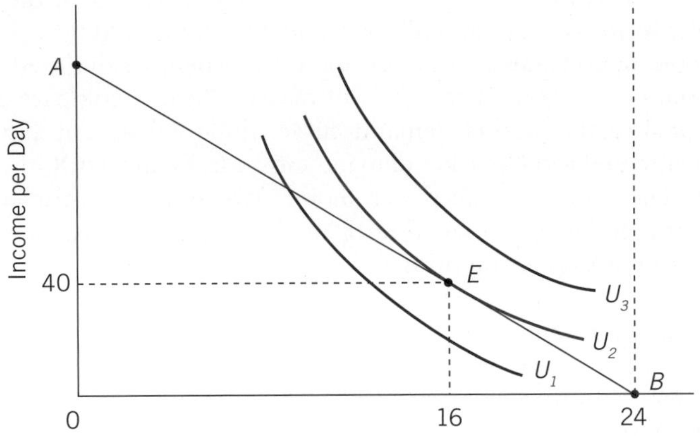

Point *E* represents the combination of leisure and income from work each day that gives the worker the greatest possible level of daily well-being. In equilibrium, the person whose indifference curves are drawn chooses 16 hours of leisure per day. The person therefore works 8 hours per day.

The person's opportunities to earn income by trading leisure hours to employers in a labor market depend on the wage rate. The income–leisure budget constraint shows the opportunities to earn income by trading leisure in the market. If a person can earn w per hour, then the equation of this budget line is

$$I = w(24 - L) \tag{1A.4}$$

where I is daily money income and L is leisure hours per day. *Leisure* is defined simply as using time for any activity other than work for pay. This equation is represented by the line *AB* in Figure 1A.9. For example, if the hourly wage is $5, a person who takes 16 hours per day as leisure will work 8 hours and earn a daily income of $40. This person is in equilibrium at point *E* in Figure 1A.9. The diagram assumes that the only way that the person can earn money income is by giving up leisure. The slope of the indifference curve is the marginal rate of substitution of leisure for income (MRS_{LI}) multiplied by −1. The slope of the budget line in Figure 1A.9 is the wage multiplied by −1. The equilibrium condition at point *E* is

$$MRS_{LI} = w \tag{1A.5}$$

Later in this book, applications of this analysis will show how the equilibrium is affected by taxes and subsidies that affect wages and provide income independent of work.

ANALYSIS OF PRODUCTION AND COST

The amount of goods or services that can be produced depends on the physical resources employed and technical knowledge available. The **production function** is a way of describing the maximum output obtainable from any given combination of inputs, given technology. *Inputs* are the productive services of land, labor, capital (such as equipment, machines, and structures), and materials. Improvements in technology allow more output to be produced with any given combination of inputs.

Production is usually divided into two periods. The **short run** is that period of production when some inputs cannot be varied. The **long run** is the period when *all* inputs are variable.

The **marginal product** of an input is the change in the total output produced by that input when one more unit of the input is employed while all other inputs are held constant. The theory of production presumes that the marginal product of an input will eventually decline in the short run. This implies a limit to the extra output that can be produced in the short run when at least some inputs are fixed.

Isoquant Analysis

Isoquants are curves that show alternative combinations of variable inputs that can be used to produce a given amount of output. Figure 1A.10 shows an isoquant curve for combinations of capital services (measured in machine hours) and labor services (measured in labor hours) that can be used to produce Q_1 units of output per month. The curve is downward sloping. This is because reducing the amount of labor used decreases output unless more capital is used, provided that the marginal product of both inputs is positive. It is usually assumed that producers will never employ inputs in amounts for which the marginal products are negative.

The **marginal rate of technical substitution** of one input, capital, for another, labor ($MRTS_{KL}$), is a measure of the amount of labor services that can be substituted for capital services without increasing or decreasing production. $MRTS_{KL}$ is the slope of the isoquant $\Delta L/\Delta K$ multiplied by -1. The marginal rates of substitution of capital for labor are presumed to decline along a given isoquant, because labor and capital tend to complement one another. Labor can only imperfectly accomplish the tasks of

---

FIGURE 1A.10 Isoquant Analysis

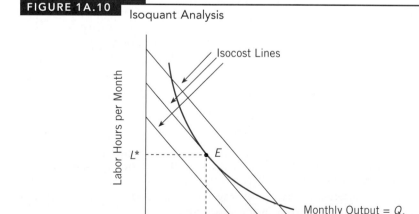

The monthly input combination corresponding to point *E* represents the minimum cost method of producing a monthly output of Q_1 units.

© Cengage Learning

machines and vice versa. As labor is actually substituted for capital, it takes more and more labor hours to make up for each successive reduction in machine hours. The declining $MRTS_{KL}$ gives isoquants their convex shape.

It is assumed that producers seek to produce any given output at minimum cost. **Isocost lines** show combinations of variable input services per month that are of equal cost. Figure 1A.10 also shows a family of isocost lines. The equation of any given isocost line is

$$C = P_L L + P_k K \tag{1A.6}$$

where L is labor hours used per month, K is machine hours used per month, P_L is the price per hour of labor, and P_K is the price per machine hour. C is the cost of the variable inputs, labor, and capital. Isocost lines farther from the origin correspond to higher cost. The slope of any isocost line is $-P_K/P_L$.

Figure 1A.10 shows that the minimum cost combination of labor services and capital services (L^*, K^*) to produce Q_i units of output per month corresponds to point E. At that point, the isoquant is tangent to an isocost line. Because the slope of the isoquant is $-MRTS_{KL}$ and the slope of the isocost line is $-P_K/P_L$, the condition for minimizing the cost of producing any given output can be written as

$$MRTS_{KL} = \frac{P_K}{P_L} \tag{1A.7}$$

Cost

Cost is the monetary value of inputs used to produce goods and services. The opportunity cost of using inputs is their value in their next best use. Assuming that all producers generate any given output at the lowest possible cost, it is possible to derive a cost function from isoquants. A **cost function** gives the minimum cost of producing any given output, given current technology. **Cost curves** describe the way this minimum cost varies with the amount of output produced per year (or any other period). Producers are assumed to use the combination of variable inputs for producing any given output that satisfies Equation 1A.7.

In the short run, the producer can be thought of as being confined to a productive plant or factory of fixed size that cannot easily be altered because of leases and other fixed commitments. In the long run, all inputs can be varied, resulting in more flexibility in production and cost.

Total cost (TC) is the value of all inputs used to produce a given output. In the short run, total cost can be divided into two components: **variable cost** (VC), the cost of variable inputs such as labor, machines, and materials; and **fixed cost** (FC), the cost of inputs that do not vary with output. Monthly rent for a one-year lease on a structure is an example of a fixed cost.

Average cost (AC) is equal to total cost of production divided by the number of units produced. **Average variable cost** (AVC) is variable cost divided by the number of units produced. The difference between average cost and average variable cost is the **average fixed cost** (AFC) of output in the short run.

In the short run, average cost curves are assumed to be U-shaped, because the marginal product of variable inputs tends to decline in the short run. After a point, more and more variable inputs are required to produce more output when some inputs are fixed. This increases average variable cost (and therefore average cost) of production after a point. Given input prices, average cost tends to decline at

FIGURE 1A.11 Short-Run Cost Curves and Profit Maximization under Perfect Competition

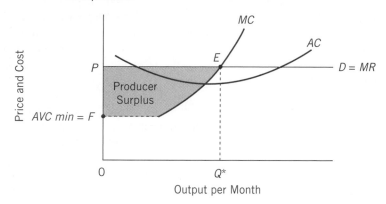

The competitive firm maximizes profits in the short run by adjusting output to Q^*, which corresponds to the point at which $P = MC$. The portion of the marginal cost curve for which MC exceeds minimum possible average variable costs is the short-run supply curve under perfect competition.

© Cengage Learning

first in the short run and then increase. Short-run average cost curves have the characteristic U-shape drawn in Figure 1A.11.

In deciding how much to produce in the short run, the firm's operators need to estimate the marginal cost of production. This is the extra cost associated with producing one more unit of output. Marginal cost tends to rise at low levels of output and continues to rise as output is increased in the plant. The marginal cost curve always intersects the average cost curve at average cost's minimum level. The marginal cost curve, as well as its relation to average costs, is also drawn in Figure 1A.11.

In the long run, firms can build additional plants and expand their capability to produce in various ways not available in the short run. Average costs can vary in three ways, depending on the nature of the production function for a particular good in the long run, assuming that input prices are given. **Increasing returns to scale** exist when long-run average cost declines as output is expanded. **Constant returns to scale** occur when long-run average cost remains constant as the industry expands. **Decreasing returns to scale** mean that long-run average costs rise as the firm expands. The actual cost curve in the long run can reflect all three of these possibilities in sequence. In that case, it will be U-shaped like the short-run average cost curve.

PROFIT MAXIMIZATION, COMPETITION, AND SUPPLY

Perfect Competition

Economists usually assume that a firm seeks to maximize profits. The firm's choice of output depends on the extent to which it can influence the price of its product by its own actions. When the firm is only one of many firms producing a small market share of a standardized product, the quality of which does not differ among firms, **perfect competition** is said to exist. A **competitive firm** is one that sells its output in a perfectly competitive market. The distinguishing feature of perfect competition is that no one firm alone in an industry can influence the selling price of its product in any way. The competitive firm is said to be a **price taker** because it takes the price of its product as given.

The competitive firm will maximize profits by producing that output for which price is equal to marginal cost:

$$P = MC \tag{1A.8}$$

Think of the firm as sequentially increasing output and asking itself whether each increment in output adds or subtracts from profits. It will continue to expand output until the point at which producing another unit will decrease profits. The extra revenue that the firm gets from each extra unit of output is called the marginal revenue (MR). Under perfect competition, the firm cannot influence the price, so it follows that the marginal revenue of an extra unit of output is the price at which that output can be sold. This means that the firm can sell any amount of output at the going market price. From its point of view, the demand curve that it faces is a horizontal line, $D = MR$, as shown in Figure 1A.11.

The firm will add to its profits as long as the price at which it sells one more unit exceeds the marginal cost of producing that unit. When price is exactly equal to marginal cost, the last unit produced will bring in as much revenue as the cost involved in producing it, and the net addition to profits will be zero. If the firm produces beyond that point, profits will decline because the marginal cost of producing that extra unit will exceed the marginal revenue it brings in. It follows that firms maximize profits by producing that output for which price is equal to marginal cost of production.

The Short-Run Supply Curve

The marginal cost curve gives a relation between price and the quantity the firm will produce and supply in the short run. It represents the firm's **short-run supply curve** when price exceeds minimum possible average variable costs (AVC_{min}) of production. When price is below average variable costs, the firm shuts down immediately, because when price (P) is less than minimum possible AVC, the firm will lose more than its fixed costs by continuing to operate in the short run.

The entire market supply curve for a perfectly competitive industry is the sum of the amounts each firm in the industry will produce and offer for sale at all possible output. For any output, points on that supply curve represent the marginal cost to firms of producing that output.

Producer Surplus

Analogous to the concept of consumer surplus is that of **producer surplus**, which is the difference between the market price of an output or input and the minimum price necessary to induce suppliers to make it available for sale on the market. The market supply curve tells how much output or input would be offered for sale at alternative prices. In Figure 1A.11, producer surplus is the area PEF, where F corresponds to minimum possible average variable cost (AVC_{min}). The minimum price at which any producer is willing to supply any given amount of output per month (or year) in a competitive market represents marginal cost. Producer surplus is the difference between price and marginal cost for each quantity.

Long-Run Supply

Perfect competition also requires free entry and exit into the industry. In the long run, firms can enter or leave an industry. The incentives they have to do so depend on the level of profits realizable in an industry. **Normal profits** represent the opportunity costs of resources of owner-supplied (nonpurchased) inputs invested in a firm. Normal profits are, in economic terms, part of a firm's costs. **Economic profits** are those in excess of normal profits. When it is possible to earn economic profits in a competitive industry, new firms will enter. This will increase industry supply and reduce market price. Conversely, when economic profits are negative, firms will leave the industry because they will be unable to cover their opportunity costs (including the normal profit). This will decrease supply and increase the price of the product. The industry is said to be in **long-run competitive equilibrium** when economic profits are zero, so that no incentive exists for firms either to enter or leave.

Under perfect competition, a **long-run industry supply curve** is a relationship between price and quantity supplied for points at which the industry is in equilibrium. Points on such a curve correspond to outputs for which each firm in the industry is maximizing profits. Therefore, price must equal long-run marginal cost ($LRMC$). However, price must also equal long-run average cost ($LRAC$) at the point of equilibrium, because economic profits must be zero in long-run equilibrium. When $P = LRAC$, profit per unit is $P - LRAC = 0$, implying that economic profits, $(P - LRAC)Q$, are zero. The normal profit is included in costs. If $P > LRAC$, new firms would enter the industry until the price fell to make economic profits zero. If $P < LRAC$, firms would incur losses and leave the industry until economic profits were zero.

Figure 1A.12 shows the equilibrium of a typical firm in a perfectly competitive industry when the industry is also in equilibrium. That firm is maximizing profits in the long run because $P = LRMC$. At the maximum profit output, economic profits are zero because $P = LRAC$. Also, at that output, Q^*, $LRAC$ is at its minimum possible level, $LRAC_{min}$. Points on an industry supply curve satisfy the following conditions:

$$P = LRMC = LRAC_{min} \tag{1A.9}$$

Long-run competitive supply curves can be upward sloping, horizontal, or even downward sloping, depending on how the prices of specialized inputs used by an industry change as a result of the industry's expansion or contraction. If the prices of inputs used by the industry do not change as a direct result of expansion or contraction of the industry, then $LRAC_{min}$ for firms in the industry will be independent of the size of the industry. This is the case of a **constant-costs industry**. In other words, other things being equal, any deviation in price from the original $LRAC_{min}$ can be only temporary. Because input prices are independent of the number of firms in the industry, the $LRAC$ curves will not shift up or down as the

FIGURE 1A.12   Long-Run Competitive Equilibrium

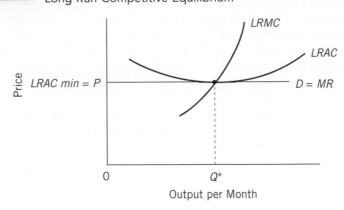

In the long-run competitive equilibrium, $P = LRMC = LRAC$. Points on the long-run supply curve correspond to outputs at which firms in the industry earn zero economic profits.

FIGURE 1A.13   Long-Run Supply: The Case of a Constant-Costs Competitive Industry

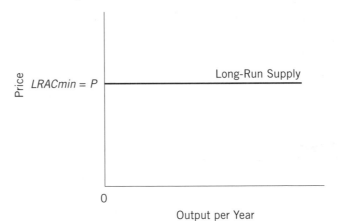

If input prices are independent of the size of an industry, the long-run supply curve is infinitely elastic at a price corresponding to $LRAC_{min}$, which remains constant as the industry increases or decreases in size in the long run.

industry expands or contracts. Price must always return to the original $LRAC_{min}$ in the long run. This implies that the long-run supply curve is a horizontal line, as shown in Figure 1A.13.

In an **increasing-costs industry,** prices of some specialized inputs *increase* as the industry expands and decrease as the industry contracts. This will occur if the firms buy a large portion of the total available supply of these specialized inputs. As the number of firms in the industry increases, the demands for these inputs increase substantially, causing their prices to rise. Consequently, as input prices rise, the *LRAC* curve for all firms in the industry shifts up as the industry expands. This is because the height of the *LRAC* curve for any given output depends on input prices and technology. An increase in input prices drives up the average cost of producing any given output; therefore, an increase in industry output in the long run results in an increase in $LRAC_{min}$. Price must increase in the long run to result in an increase in quantity supplied. If price did not increase, firms could not cover their opportunity costs of production at the higher input prices, and output would not increase.

An increasing-costs industry has an upward-sloping supply curve. For example, if the oil-refining industry purchased a large portion of the total available supply of the services of chemical engineers per year, the wages of the engineers would rise when the industry expanded and fall as it contracted. This would imply that the oil-refining industry is one of increasing costs.

A third possibility is a **decreasing-costs industry**, in which input prices would decline as a direct result of the industry's expansion. This is an extremely rare case. If it were to prevail, *LRACmin* would actually decline as industry output increased in the long run. This would imply that the long-run supply curve was actually downward sloping!

Price Elasticity of Supply

Price elasticity of supply is the percentage change in quantity supplied in response to any given percentage change in price:

$$E_S = \frac{\%\ \text{Change in quantity supplied}}{\%\ \text{Change in price}} = \frac{\Delta Q_S / Q_S}{\Delta P / P} \qquad (1A.10)$$

E_S is elastic when greater than 1 in value and inelastic when less than 1.

FIGURE 1A.14   A Perfectly Inelastic Supply Curve Supply

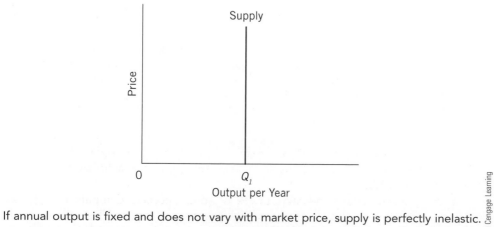

If annual output is fixed and does not vary with market price, supply is perfectly inelastic.

For an industry of constant costs, for which the long-run supply curve is horizontal, the price elasticity of supply is infinite. If the available amount of an input is fixed, as is the case of land, the price elasticity of supply is zero. A perfectly inelastic supply curve is a vertical line at the available quantity. Figure 1A.14 shows the case of a perfectly inelastic supply of a good.

Chapter 2

EFFICIENCY, MARKETS, AND GOVERNMENTS

LEARNING OBJECTIVES

After reading this chapter, you should be able to:

- Discuss the difference between positive and normative economics.

- Define the efficiency criterion and show how the marginal conditions for efficiency can be used to identify the efficient output of a good or service.

- Explain how a system of perfectly competitive markets can achieve efficiency.

- Show how the exercise of monopoly power can prevent markets from achieving efficient levels of output.

- Demonstrate how taxes and subsidies affect incentives and how they can prevent competitive markets from achieving efficient outcomes.

- Use a utility-possibility curve to illustrate the trade-off between efficiency and equity.

Decades of central planning in the former Soviet republics and formerly communist nations of central and eastern Europe resulted in living standards that were, on average, well below those of industrialized nations in which private ownership of productive resources and free markets have prevailed. What is it about free and competitive markets that work to squeeze more out of productive resources than has been possible in centrally planned economies? Can we rely on markets to satisfy all the desires of individuals? When do markets fail to supply useful goods and services, and when does the profit motive, which is necessary to keep a market system going, result in undesirable side effects? To answer such questions, we must first develop some norms for evaluating resource use. We must then examine how well markets achieve results that satisfy the criteria we set up to evaluate resource use. After we evaluate free market performance, we can then discuss possible defects of markets and examine how these defects give rise to demands for government goods and services.

A useful starting point for analyzing government activities is the study of the role of markets in allocating resources. Markets facilitate exchanges of goods and services and inputs. Free exchange between buyers and sellers in unregulated, competitive markets often achieves outcomes that rate high in terms of the standards of economic performance used by many economists. However, markets cannot be relied upon to supply all useful goods and services, and sometimes market transactions have undesirable side effects, such as pollution. In those circumstances, government supply of goods and services through political institutions can result in net gains to citizens' well-being.

In public finance, we study both the virtues and defects of the marketplace. In this chapter, we begin by defining the concept of efficiency. We then discuss conditions under which markets operate efficiently and examine some instances in which they fail to do so. We also show how government subsidies and taxes can distort resource allocation and cause losses in output and efficiency in markets.

In Chapters 3 and 4, we show how government programs can result in improvements in resource use and provide additional benefits to individuals that outweigh any additional costs.

POSITIVE AND NORMATIVE ECONOMICS

Positive economics is a scientific approach to analysis that establishes cause-and-effect relationships among economic variables. Positive theory attempts to be objective, making no presuppositions about what is good or bad or what should be accomplished. It merely formulates hypotheses of the "If ... then" variety that can be checked against facts.[1] For example, a positive analysis of the impact of a proposal to widen a road can be used to predict how the road will benefit users by reducing the time and money costs involved in getting between two locations. A positive analysis of the impact of a food subsidy to low-income persons can be utilized to estimate the effect of the subsidy on the price of food and the quantity available to the recipients. The predictions can then be checked against the facts to determine how well the positive theory has worked.

The normative approach is based on value judgments about what is desirable or what should be done to achieve the desired outcome. Normative theory begins

---

[1]For a classic discussion of the positive approach, see James M. Buchanan, "Positive Economics, Welfare Economics, and Political Economy," *Journal of Law and Economics* 2 (October 1959): 124–138.

with predetermined criteria and is used to prescribe policies that best achieve those criteria. **Normative economics** is designed to formulate recommendations as to what *should* be accomplished. Because it is based on underlying values, this approach, unlike the positive approach, is not objective. It can evaluate alternative policies and actions only on the basis of the underlying value judgments. If you were to disagree with the values on which a normative theory was based, the resulting prescription would be of little use to you. The normative approach used in public finance theory is based on value judgments embodying an individualistic ethic.[2]

Both the positive and the normative approaches are useful. In fact there is a certain dependence between the two approaches. Normative theory cannot make recommendations to achieve certain outcomes without an underlying theory of human behavior. If normative criteria are used to recommend that government authorities undertake a particular policy to increase the incomes of certain individuals, the impact of such actions on incentives to produce and consume must be predicted. Well-intentioned policies can have results opposite to those desired when no account is taken of their effects on economic incentives.

For example, suppose you support government-supplied housing with very heavily subsidized rents for poor families because you believe that such policies will enable them to enjoy better and larger apartments. If positive analysis can show that some persons might actually be induced to move into small, publicly provided housing units from larger apartments, you might reconsider your support of the public-housing program. Similarly, you might favor rent-control legislation to keep rents low enough so that the poor can afford to house their families. If, however, positive analysis predicts that such controls result in housing shortages and reductions in the quality of rental units available on the market, some poor families will be made worse off. If these predictions are borne out by the evidence, you might reconsider your support of rent control as a means of aiding the poor.

Positive theory by itself merely embodies techniques of analysis and so can benefit from the work of normative theorists by using normative guidelines to choose which areas of human interaction to analyze. Therefore, the normative approach is useful to the positive approach in that it defines relevant issues.

NORMATIVE EVALUATION OF RESOURCE USE: THE EFFICIENCY CRITERION

Efficiency is a normative criterion for evaluating the effects of resource use on the well-being of individuals. The **efficiency criterion** is satisfied when resources are used over any given period of time in such a way as to make it impossible to increase the well-being of any one person without reducing the well-being of any other person. Developed by the Italian economist Vilfredo Pareto (1848–1923), it is often referred to as the **criterion of *Pareto optimality***. The criterion represents a precise definition of the concept of efficiency.

The word *efficiency* is part of everyone's vocabulary. To most, efficiency means producing a desired result with a minimum of effort or expense. Synonymous with this is the minimization of wasted effort—that which produces no useful result. The

---

[2]For an advanced discussion of the normative approach, see Richard W. Tresch, *Public Finance: A Normative Theory*, 2nd edition. San Diego, Calif.: Academic Press, 2002, Chapters 1–2.

economist's criterion of efficiency is somewhat more precise than the standard dictionary definition. It does, however, embody the same idea.

Let's begin using the efficiency criterion. First, assume that the well-being of any individual increases with the amount of goods and services that he or she consumes per year. It is easy to show how avoiding waste in production will help achieve efficiency. Given available amounts of productive resources and the existing state of technical knowledge in an economy, elimination of wasted effort will allow more production from available resources. The extra production will make it possible for some persons to consume more without reducing the amounts consumed by others. As a result, it would be possible to make some individuals better off without harming anyone else by avoiding waste in production.

Another important aspect of efficiency is freedom to engage in mutually advantageous exchanges. If you are free to engage in transactions for gain, you can obtain more satisfaction out of your income. For example, suppose you have a collection of heavy-metal-rock compact discs you no longer enjoy. By exchanging those discs for a collection of classic rock-and-roll discs that you value more, you can become more content. If you find a person who really wants your heavy-metal-rock discs and has a set of classic rock-and-roll discs you highly value, then both you and your friend can gain by trading. Freedom to trade is an important aspect of efficiency. Both buyers and sellers can gain in markets when the value a buyer places on an item exceeds the cost the seller incurs by making it available for sale. Constraints that prevent resources being used and traded in such a way as to allow mutual gains will prevent achievement of efficiency. When efficiency is attained, mutual gains from reallocating resources in productive use or through further exchange of goods and services among individuals are no longer possible.

Many citizens argue that not all mutually gainful trades should be allowed. Such individuals demand that the powers of government be used to prevent exchanges they find morally objectionable. They argue that government should exercise paternalistic powers over the choices of its citizens. Thus, it is common to observe laws banning the sale of certain drugs, gambling services, prostitution, and other activities in which some persons might wish to engage but which others find morally objectionable.

The criterion of efficiency is based on an underlying value judgment that individuals should be allowed to pursue their self-interest as they see fit, provided that no one is harmed in the process. Those who wish to intervene to prevent others from pursuing their self-interests disagree with this underlying value judgment. The individualistic ethic underlying the efficiency criterion, therefore, is not acceptable to all persons.

Marginal Conditions for Efficiency

The conditions required for the efficient output of a particular good over a period of time can be derived easily. Analysis of the benefits and costs of making additional amounts of a good available is required to determine whether the existing allocation of resources to its production is efficient. Any given quantity of an economic good available, say per month, will provide a certain amount of satisfaction to those who consume it. This is the **total social benefit** of the monthly quantity. The **marginal social benefit** of a good is the extra benefit obtained by making one more unit of that good available per month (or over any other period). The marginal social benefit can be measured as the maximum amount of money given up by people to obtain the extra unit of the good. For example, if the marginal social benefit of bread is $2 per loaf, some consumers would give up $2 worth of expenditure on other goods to obtain that loaf and be neither worse nor better off by doing so. If these consumers could obtain the bread for less than $2 per loaf, they would be made better off. The marginal social benefit of a good is assumed to decline as more of that good is made available each month.

The **total social cost** of a good is the value of all resources necessary to make a given amount of the good available per month. The **marginal social cost** of a good is the minimum sum of money required to compensate the owners of inputs used in producing the good for making an extra unit of the good available. In computing marginal social costs, it is assumed that output is produced at minimum possible cost, given available technology. If the marginal social cost of bread is $1 per loaf, this is the minimum dollar amount necessary to compensate input owners for the use of their inputs without making them worse off. If they were to receive more than $1 per loaf, they would be made better off. If they were to receive less than $1 per loaf, they would be made worse off by making that extra unit available. The following analysis assumes that the marginal social cost of making more bread available per month does not decrease as the monthly output of bread is increased.

Figure 2.1A graphs the marginal social benefit (MSB) and marginal social cost (MSC) of making various quantities of bread available per month in a nation. Figure 2.1B shows the total social benefit (TSB) and the total social cost (TSC) of producing the bread. The marginal social benefit is $\Delta TSB/\Delta Q$, where ΔTSB is the change in the social benefit of the good and ΔQ is a one-unit increase in the output of bread per month. The marginal social benefit is measured by the slope of the total social benefit curve at any point. Similarly, the marginal social cost, $\Delta TSC/\Delta Q$, is measured by the slope of the total social cost curve at any point.

The efficient output of bread can be determined by comparing its marginal social benefit and marginal social cost at various levels of monthly output. Look at the output corresponding to $Q_1 = 10{,}000$ loaves of bread per month in Figure 2.1A. This monthly output level is inefficient because the marginal social benefit of bread exceeds its marginal social cost. The maximum amount of money consumers would give up to obtain an additional loaf of bread exceeds the minimum amount of money necessary to make input owners, whose resources are used to produce bread, no worse off.

For example, suppose that at Q_1 the $MSB = \$2$ while $MSC = \$1$. The consumer who gives up $2 for the bread is no worse off because the marginal benefit is $2. If the input owners making the bread available were to receive $2 from each buyer, they would be made better off because $2 exceeds the minimum amount they require in compensation for the use of their inputs to produce that bread. This demonstrates that the monthly output of 10,000 loaves is inefficient, because suppliers of bread can be made better off without harming any consumer by making more bread available.

Similarly, the consumer who obtains the loaf of bread for $1 when 10,000 loaves per month are available is better off, because that is less than the maximum amount the consumer would be willing to sacrifice for the bread. If suppliers of bread were to receive $1 for that loaf, they would be no worse off because their marginal costs would be covered. Therefore, at least one buyer can be made better off without making the suppliers of bread worse off when the marginal social benefit exceeds the marginal social cost.

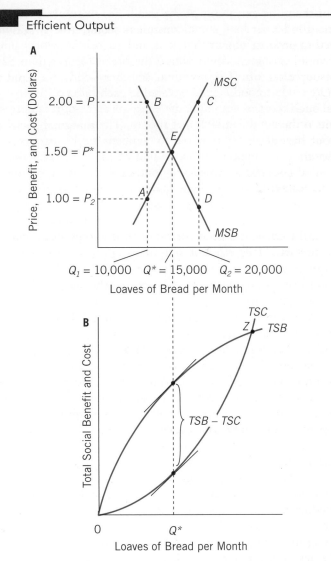

FIGURE 2.1   Efficient Output

A

Price, Benefit, and Cost (Dollars)

$2.00 = P$ ······ B ······ C ······ *MSC*

E

$1.50 = P^*$ ······ E

$1.00 = P_2$ ······ A ······ D

MSB

$Q_1 = 10,000$ $Q^* = 15,000$ $Q_2 = 20,000$

Loaves of Bread per Month

B

Total Social Benefit and Cost

TSC
Z *TSB*

$TSB - TSC$

0 Q^*

Loaves of Bread per Month

The efficient level of output, Q^*, occurs at point E. At that monthly output, $MSB = MSC$. The monthly output Q^* maximizes the difference between *TSB* and *TSC* as shown in B. Extension of monthly output to the level corresponding to equality of *TSB* and *TSC* would involve losses in net benefits. Similarly, output levels Q_1 and Q_2 are inefficient.

© Cengage Learning

The **marginal net benefit** of a good is the difference between its marginal social benefit and its marginal social cost. When marginal net benefits are positive, additional gains from allocating more resources to the production of a good are possible.

Whenever the marginal social benefit of a good exceeds its marginal social cost, it will be possible to make at least one person better off without harming another by producing more of the good. Net gains from allocating resources to additional production of the good continue just up to the point at which the marginal social benefit of the good falls to equal its marginal social cost. If additional resources were allocated to produce more of the good per month beyond that point, marginal social costs would exceed marginal social benefits. The marginal net benefit of such additional resource use would be negative. In other words, if output were increased beyond the $Q^* = 15,000$ loaves of bread per month, consumers would be unwilling to sacrifice enough to compensate input owners for all the costs involved in making the extra units of bread available. The result is that consumers cannot be made better off without harming producers when more than Q^* units of output are produced per month.

The **marginal conditions for efficient resource allocation** require that resources be allocated to the production of each good over each period so that

$$MSB = MSC \qquad\qquad (2.1)$$

In Figure 2.1A, the efficient output corresponds to the point at which the *MSB* and *MSC* curves intersect. This efficient output is $Q^* = 15,000$ loaves of bread per month. If $MSB > MSC$, additional net gains from allocating more resources to monthly production of the good will be possible. The extra net gains possible from increasing output from Q_1 to Q^* are represented by the area *ABE*. When $MSC > MSB$, at least one person can be made better off without harming anyone else by reducing monthly output. The output $Q_2 = 20,000$ loaves per month is inefficient. The additional net gains that would be possible by *reducing* output from Q_2 to Q^* loaves per month is the area of the triangle *CED*.

At the monthly output Q^* at which $MSB = MSC$, the total net satisfaction (benefits less costs) from using resources to produce the item is maximized. As shown in Figure 2.1B, at monthly output Q^*, the slope of the *TSC* curve equals the slope of the *TSB* curve. At the output Q^*, the difference between the two curves in Figure 2.1B is at a maximum. $TSB - TSC$ is the net total monthly benefit of the good. Producing more of the good each month until *TSB* equals *TSC* (at point *Z* in Figure 2.1B) would *decrease* the total *net* monthly satisfaction. This is because the monthly difference between total social benefits and total social costs declines as more than Q^* units per month are produced. At the point where $TSB = TSC$, the total net benefit of the good is actually zero!

Maximizing the total social benefit of a good would require that monthly production and sales be extended indefinitely. This follows from the assumption that more of a good per month always makes persons better off. The efficiency criterion considers *both* the total social cost and the total social benefit of a good. It strikes a balance between the two by recommending maximization of the difference between total social benefit and total social cost.

CHECKPOINT

1. Under what circumstances will a resource allocation be efficient?
2. What are the marginal conditions for efficiency?
3. If the efficient output of mystery books is currently being produced, what is the marginal net benefit of mystery books?

MARKETS, PRICES, AND EFFICIENCY CONDITIONS

Now let's examine the workings of a system of perfectly competitive markets. An efficient economic system allocates resources so as to set the marginal social benefit of each good or service equal to its marginal social cost. Markets are organized for the purpose of allowing mutually gainful trades between buyers and sellers. A system of perfectly competitive markets can result in efficient resource use in an economy. A *perfectly competitive market system* exists if

1. All productive resources are privately owned.
2. All transactions take place in markets, and in each separate market many competing sellers offer a standardized product to many competing buyers.
3. Economic power is dispersed in the sense that no buyers or sellers alone can influence prices.
4. All relevant information is freely available to buyers and sellers.
5. Resources are mobile and may be freely employed in any enterprise.

Assume that both buyers and sellers seek to maximize their gains from trading in such a system. Accordingly, buyers maximize the satisfaction they obtain from exchanging their money for goods and services in markets and sellers maximize the profits they earn from making goods and services available to consumers.

The market prices that emerge reflect the free interplay of supply and demand. Neither businesses nor buyers can control prices; they can only react to them. When deciding how much of a good to purchase, buyers consider their own *marginal private benefit (MPB),* which is the dollar value placed on additional units of the good by individual consumers. When confronted with market prices, consumers trade until they adjust the marginal private benefit received from consuming a good per month to what they must forgo to purchase one more unit of the good per month. What they forgo is measured by the price of one more unit; that is, the amount of money they give up that could have been spent on other items. If the value of the money they give up (the price) exceeds the marginal private benefit of that last unit, they would be made worse off by trading those dollars for the good. Therefore, they maximize their gains from trading by adjusting the amount of any good they consume per month (or any other period of time) until the marginal private benefit, MPB, received is just equal to the price, P:

$$P = MPB = MSB \qquad (2.2)$$

The marginal private benefit received by consumers purchasing the good is also equal to the marginal social benefit of the good, provided that no one except the buyer receives any satisfaction when the good is consumed.

Producers maximize their gains from trading each month when they maximize profits. When it is no longer possible to add any gain by selling one more unit, profits are maximized. The firm will increase profits whenever the revenue obtained from selling an additional unit exceeds the cost of producing and selling that extra unit. The *marginal private cost (MPC)* of output is the cost incurred by sellers to make an additional unit of output available for sale. The extra revenue obtained from selling one more unit is its price, assuming that the firm can sell as much as it likes at the going market price. The firm will maximize profits when it adjusts its output sold per month (or any other time period) to the point at which price is equal to the marginal private cost of output. If marginal private cost exceeds price, the gains from trade (profit) would decline. It follows that producers maximize gains from trade at the point for which

$$P = MPC = MSC \qquad (2.3)$$

The marginal private cost of output incurred by sellers is the marginal social cost, provided that opportunity cost of all resources used in making the product available is included in the sellers' total costs.

Combining Equations 2.2 and 2.3 into one equation gives the following result:

$$P = MPB_i = MPC = MSB = MSC \qquad (2.4)$$

where MPB_i is the marginal private benefit received by any given consumer.

A perfectly competitive market, in which both buyers and sellers maximize their net gains from trade, will result in a level of output for which marginal private benefit equals marginal private cost. If consumers are the only recipients of benefits when a good is sold, and sellers bear all the cost of making that good available, Equation 2.4 implies that $MSB = MSC$ for the good. The market equilibrium will achieve the efficient output. If this condition is met in all markets and all goods are tradable in markets, the overall allocation of resources in the economy will satisfy the efficiency criterion. When the prices of all goods and services equal the marginal social benefits and marginal social costs of these items, the market system achieves an efficient outcome.

Returning to Figure 2.1A, the MSB curve is the market demand curve. It corresponds to the maximum price that would be offered for various quantities of bread available per month. Under perfect competition, the MSC curve is the market supply curve. It represents the minimum price that sellers will accept to make any given monthly quantity of bread available. The market equilibrium is at point E. At that point, the price of a loaf of bread is $P^* = \$1.50$ and the quantity sold is $Q^* = 15,000$ loaves per month. P^* is the efficient price because it reflects *both* the marginal social benefit and the marginal social cost of the good. This equilibrium output, Q^*, is efficient because at monthly output.

$$P^* = \$1.50 = MPB_i = MSB = MSC \qquad (2.5)$$

A system of competitive markets achieves an efficient allocation of resources when Equation 2.4 is satisfied in each market and all goods and services are sold in markets.

When Does Market Interaction Fail to Achieve Efficiency?

It is not surprising that markets operating under conditions of perfect competition produce efficient outcomes. After all, competitive markets are economic institutions that have evolved to allow maximum gains from the exchange of goods and services, and that is what efficiency is all about.

In the study of government, it is more interesting to discuss the conditions under which markets and prices fail to result in the efficient outputs of goods and services. The possibility that political interaction might allow further net benefits to be squeezed from available resources then can be explored. However, political action will not always result in net benefits. Government activity itself can cause inefficiency. For example, the taxes necessary to finance government programs can, as you will soon see, impair the ability of markets to achieve efficiency. The marginal social benefits of a government program must exceed its marginal social costs to result in net benefits.

The basic problem that causes inefficiency in competitive markets is that prices do not always fully reflect the marginal social benefits or marginal social costs of output. This often occurs because of the nature of certain goods, which makes them difficult to package and trade easily in markets. For example, the services of such environmental resources as air and water are often used for disposal of wastes without adequate consideration of the benefits these resources have in alternative uses. This happens because rights to the use of environmental resources are in dispute. Because no one owns these environmental resources, market exchange of the ownership right to use these resources is unlikely. This means that sellers using environmental resources to make goods available do not pay for the right to use those resources. This leads to situations in which the marginal private cost of output incurred falls short of the marginal social cost.

Similarly, for services with collective or shared benefits, it might be difficult to package the benefit flowing from output into units that can be sold to individuals. When packaging into salable units is difficult, so is pricing. A means other than markets must be found to make the social benefits of these goods available. The failure of markets to price and make available certain goods, such as national defense and environmental protection, gives rise to demands for government production and regulation.

Monopolistic Power

Markets will also fail to result in efficient levels of output when monopolistic power is exercised. A firm exercises monopolistic power when it influences the price of the product it sells by reducing output to a level at which the price it sets exceeds marginal cost of production. A monopolist maximizes profits at a level of output per month (or year) at which marginal revenue (MR) equals its marginal private cost. This is illustrated in Figure 2.2.

The demand curve for the monopolist's product reflects the marginal social benefit of possible levels of output. Assume that the monopolist's marginal private costs reflect the value of all inputs used to produce additional output and therefore reflect marginal social costs. The monopoly firm will produce output Q_M per month. This is the monthly output corresponding to point A, at which $MR = MSC$. When that much output is available per month, its price will be P_M. This is the marginal social benefit of that monthly output, MSB_M. Because a monopolist's marginal revenue is less than the price of the product, marginal social cost of production also will be less than the price. Thus, at a monthly output level of Q_M, $P = MSB > MSC$, as shown in Figure 2.2. Efficiency is not attained because $MSB > MSC$ at Q_M.

Efficiency could be attained by forcing the monopolist to increase output until prices fell to a level equal to marginal social cost. The additional net benefits possible from increasing output from Q_M to Q^* units per month are shown by the triangular area ABE in Figure 2.2. This represents the extra social benefits over the extra social costs involved in increasing monthly output up to the point at which $MSB = MSC$. Government intervention in the market to increase output would be prescribed by normative economists seeking to attain efficiency.

FIGURE 2.2 Loss in Net Benefits Due to Monopolistic Power

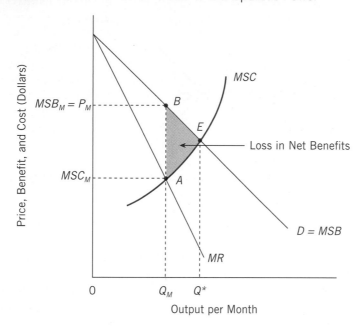

The monopolistic firm maximizes profits by producing Q_M units per month. At that output level, the marginal social benefit of the good exceeds its marginal social cost. Additional net benefits equal to the area *ABE* are possible if output were increased to Q^* units per month.

How Taxes Can Cause Losses in Efficiency in Competitive Markets

In Chapter 1, we discussed how taxes are used to reallocate resources from private to government use. Now that we know the marginal conditions for efficiency, we can begin to show how taxes impair the ability of competitive markets to achieve efficient outcomes.

When a product or a service is taxed, the amount that is traded is influenced by the tax paid per unit, as well as by the marginal social benefit and marginal social cost of the item. The tax *distorts* the decisions of market participants. For example, income taxes influence the decision workers make about the allocation of their time between work and leisure. Workers consider not only the amount of extra income they can get from more work but also the extra taxes they must pay on that income when deciding how many hours per week or year to devote to work. When you work more hours, you receive less than the gross amount of wages paid to you. In deciding whether to work more when you have the opportunity to do so, you weigh the extra income *after taxes* against the value of the leisure time you give up. Taxes influence your decision to work by reducing the net gain from working.

A simple example shows how a tax can prevent a competitive market from achieving the efficient output. Suppose that the market for long-distance telephone service is perfectly competitive. Figure 2.3 shows the demand and supply curves for long-distance telephone service. We assume that points on the demand curve reflect

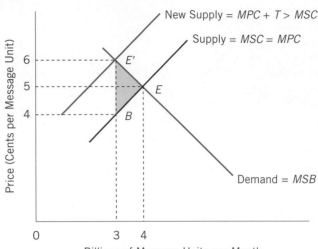

FIGURE 2.3   Taxes and Efficiency

A tax on the sale of a product affects incentives to supply that product. In the graph above, a tax on telephone service decreases the supply of the product. The price of a message unit increases from 5 to 6 cents. There is a loss in net benefits from telephone service because the marginal social cost of the new equilibrium output (corresponding to point E') is less than its marginal social benefit. The loss in net benefits is represented by the triangular area $E'EB$. The tax costs more than the $0.06 billion in revenue collected when the loss in net benefits is added to the amount of revenue collected.

the marginal social benefit of any given number of message units and points on the supply curve reflect the marginal social cost of the service. The equilibrium output in the market, corresponding to point E, is 4 billion message units per month and the equilibrium price is 5 cents per message unit. The market output is efficient because it corresponds to the point at which the marginal social cost of long-distance telephone service is equal to its marginal social benefit.

Now suppose the government levies a 2-cent-per-message unit tax on sellers of long-distance services. Sellers must now consider the fact that each time they supply a message unit, they must not only cover the marginal social cost of that unit but also the 2-cent tax. The effect of the tax is to decrease the supply of the service, as the price required by producers to expand service by one unit must equal the sum of the marginal private cost of the service and the tax per unit of service, T. In Figure 2.3, points on the new supply curve after the tax is imposed correspond to $MPC + T$ for any given quantity.

As a result of the tax-induced decrease in supply, the point of equilibrium now corresponds to E'. At that point, the price of telephone services has increased to 6 cents per message unit and the equilibrium output has fallen to 3 billion units per month.

It is now easy to show how the tax has prevented the market from achieving efficiency and resulted in a loss in net benefits from telephone service. At an output level of 3 billion message units per month, the marginal social benefit of the service is 6 cents per message unit. However, the marginal social cost of that output is only

4 cents! As a result of the change in behavior caused by the tax, the marginal social benefit of telephone service now exceeds its marginal social cost. The loss in net benefits from telephone service is equal to the shaded area $E'EB$ in Figure 2.3. The government will collect a total of \$0.06 billion per month in tax revenue, which is equal to the 2-cent-per-unit tax multiplied by the 3 billion message units sold per month after the tax is imposed. The cost of the tax is not only the \$0.06 billion per month paid by taxpayers. In addition, there is the loss in net benefits, called the *excess burden* of the tax, equal to the area $EE'B$ from telephone service that results from the distortion in the choices after the tax is imposed.

When evaluating the marginal cost of a new government program, we must add any loss in net benefits from distortions in market behavior to the dollar amount of additional tax revenue required to finance the program. Government spending programs can provide net benefits to citizens in the aggregate only when the marginal social benefits of additional spending exceed both the tax revenue collected and the dollar value of the loss in efficiency (the excess burden) in markets that occurs as a result of the distortions in choices caused by the tax.

How Government Subsidies Can Cause Losses in Efficiency

Governments often subsidize private enterprises or operate their own enterprises at a loss, using taxpayer funds to make up the difference. Taxes can impair market efficiency, and so can subsidies. Let's examine the effects of agricultural subsidies and the operation of agricultural markets. Suppose the government guarantees farmers a certain price for their crops. When the market price falls below the "target" price guaranteed by the government, the government will pay eligible farmers a subsidy equal to the difference between the market price of the product and the target price.

Figure 2.4 illustrates how the target price program works and how it results in more than the efficient output of the subsidized grains when the target price is above the market equilibrium price. The graph shows the supply and demand curves for wheat in a competitive market for this product. We assume that the points on the demand curve reflect the marginal social benefit of any given quantity. Similarly, points on the supply curve reflect the marginal social cost of any given quantity. In the absence of any government subsidies, suppose that the equilibrium price of wheat is \$4 per bushel. At that price, farmers produce Q^* bushels of wheat per year because that is the level of output at which price equals their marginal cost. This would be the efficient output level because it corresponds to the point E at which the marginal social benefit of wheat equals its marginal social cost.

Now let's see how the availability of the subsidy will affect farmers' decisions. Farmers know that they will receive a minimum of \$5 per bushel of wheat. In deciding how much to plant, they will base their decision on the target price rather than the market price when they believe that the target price will exceed the market price. In Figure 2.4, they will produce Q_s bushels of wheat per year because that quantity corresponds to point A on the supply curve for wheat, where the marginal cost of wheat is equal to \$5. The output level Q_s is greater than the efficient amount because the marginal social cost of wheat exceeds its marginal social benefit at point A. As a result of the target price program, more than the efficient

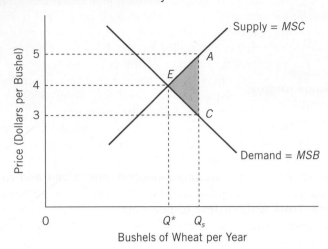

FIGURE 2.4   Subsidies and Efficiency

A target price of $5 per bushel is set by the government. Because this price exceeds the market price of $4 per bushel, the wheat farmers produce Q_s bushels per year instead of Q^*. Q_s is more than the efficient amount of wheat because its marginal social cost is greater than its marginal social benefit. The loss in net benefits from resource use is represented by the area *EAC*. The subsidy the government pays is $2 per bushel multiplied by the Q_s bushels produced annually. After the subsidy, the market price of wheat falls to $3, which is less than the marginal social cost of producing it.

amount of resources are devoted to the production of wheat. Therefore, the loss in net benefits from resource use is equal to the area *EAC* in the graph. In addition to this loss in net benefits that results from the subsidy-induced distortion in resource use, the target price program costs the government $2 per bushel of wheat multiplied by the Q_s bushels of wheat produced per year. The overproduction of wheat relative to the efficient level that results from the program depresses the market price of wheat to $3 per bushel, corresponding to point *C* on the demand curve for wheat. The overproduction of wheat makes it seem cheaper than it would be without any subsidies. In fact, consumers end up paying only $3 per bushel of wheat, while the marginal cost of producing that wheat is $5. The $2 difference between the marginal cost to producers and the price to consumers is paid by the government.

CHECKPOINT

1. Explain how a system of perfectly competitive markets can achieve efficiency.
2. How does the exercise of monopolistic power prevent efficiency from being attained?
3. Describe how taxes can affect incentives and cause losses in net benefits.

MARKET FAILURE: A PREVIEW OF THE BASIS FOR GOVERNMENT ACTIVITY

We cannot rely on markets to provide all goods in efficient amounts. Market failure to make goods and services available in cases for which the marginal social benefits of the goods outweigh the marginal social costs of those goods or services often results in demands for government action. The following forms of market failure to achieve efficient outcomes are commonly used as a basis for recommending government intervention in markets or government provision of services:

1. **Exercise of Monopoly Power in Markets.** When markets are dominated by only a few firms or by a single firm, the potential exists for the exercise of monopoly power. Firms exercising monopoly power can add to their profits by adjusting prices to the point at which marginal revenue equals their marginal private costs without fear of new entrants into the market. To prevent monopoly control over price, governments typically monitor markets to ensure that barriers to entry do not encourage the exercise of monopoly power. Governments also often regulate the pricing policies of monopoly producers of such services as electric power, natural gas, and water.

2. **Effects of Market Transactions on Third Parties Other Than Buyers and Sellers.** When market transactions result in damaging or beneficial effects on third parties who do not participate in the decision, the result will be inefficiency. When the effects are negative, people demand government policies to reduce the damaging effects of market transactions on third parties who do not participate in such decisions. For example, exhaust fumes from cars, trucks, buses, heating systems, factories, and power plants decrease air quality and impair public health. In Chapter 3, the third-party effects resulting from market transactions are discussed, and government policies to deal with these problems are considered. When the effects are beneficial, government policies are often used to encourage production of the item benefiting third parties. This is often the case for education, fire protection, and inoculations for contagious diseases.

3. **Lack of a Market for a Good with a Marginal Social Benefit That Exceeds Its Marginal Social Cost.** In many cases, useful goods and services cannot be provided efficiently through markets because it is impossible or difficult to sell the good by the unit. Benefits of such goods can be shared only. These goods are called "public" goods to distinguish them from private goods, which are consumed by individuals and whose benefits are not shared with others who do not make the purchase. A distinguishing characteristic of public goods is that a given quantity of such goods can be enjoyed by additional consumers at no reduction in benefits to existing consumers. National defense is an example of a public good having this property. Increases in U.S. population occur daily, and the additional population can be defended without any reduction in benefits to the existing population. Another characteristic of public goods is that their benefits cannot be easily withheld from people who choose not to contribute to their finance. Even if you refuse to pay the costs of national defense, you still will be defended. This means that firms selling public goods, like national defense, will have great difficulty collecting revenue necessary to finance costs to produce such goods. Chapter 4 discusses the characteristics of public goods in detail and

explains why it is likely that such goods will be supplied in less than efficient amounts if markets are used to make them available.

Government provision of goods is often justified because of a conviction that the marginal social benefit of the good exceeds the marginal social cost at quantities that would result if the good were supplied through markets. For example, government provision of health insurance, deposit insurance, and flood insurance are common because many persons believe that these are useful services that cannot be provided profitably in efficient amounts by profit-maximizing firms selling in competitive markets. Similarly, direct payments or subsidized loans to students attending institutions of higher education are often justified by arguing that government should encourage education because the marginal social benefits of its consumption exceed the marginal private benefits received by individual students.

4. **Incomplete Information.** We sometimes demand that government intervene in markets because we have incomplete information about the risks of purchasing certain products or working in certain occupations. For example, we rely on government to test new drugs and to prevent hazardous products from being sold. We also rely on government to establish standards for safety in the workplace.

5. **Economic Stabilization.** Market imperfections, such as downwardly rigid wages, give rise to excessive unemployment in response to decreases in aggregate demand. Governments engage in monetary and fiscal policies in an effort to stabilize the economy to correct for these market failures to ensure full employment. Governments also seek to avoid excessive and erratic inflation that can erode purchasing power and can impair the functioning of financial markets. Although the stabilization activities of government do not absorb significant amounts of economic resources, they do represent an important complement to the efficient functioning of markets. Economic stabilization programs are not discussed in this text. Modern public finance concentrates on the microeconomic aspects of government activity and finance rather than the macroeconomic aspects.

EQUITY VERSUS EFFICIENCY

Efficiency is not the only criterion used to evaluate resource allocation. Many citizens argue that outcomes should also be evaluated in terms of **equity**; that is, in terms of the perceived fairness of an outcome. The problem involved with applying criteria of equity is that persons differ in their ideas about fairness.

Economists usually confine their analyses of questions of equity to determinations of the impact of alternative policies on the distribution of well-being among citizens. For example, many people are concerned about the impact of government policies on such groups as the poor, the aged, or children. Positive economic analysis of the outcomes of market and political interaction is useful in providing information about the effects of policies on income distribution. In the field of public finance, analysts usually try to determine the effects of government actions on both resource allocation and the distribution of well-being, thus providing useful information that citizens can use to judge the equity of alternative policies in terms of their own notions of fairness.

The Trade-Off between Efficiency and Equity: A Graphic Analysis

The trade-off between improvements in efficiency and changes in the distribution of welfare can be illustrated with a **utility-possibility curve**.[3] This curve presents the maximum attainable level of well-being (or utility) for any one individual, given the utility level of other individuals in the economy, their tastes, resource availability, and technology. Figure 2.5 gives all the efficient combinations of well-being between two individuals, *A* and *B*, per year.

If, for example, resources are allocated in such a way that the distribution of well-being between *A* and *B* is given at point E_1, then resources are allocated efficiently because, at that point, it is impossible to increase either *A*'s or *B*'s utility without reducing the other's. Similarly, E_2 is also an efficient point. Points E_1 and E_2 differ in the distribution of well-being between *A* and *B* over a given period, such as a year. Both, however, are efficient. Points above the utility frontier, such as *Z*, are unattainable. Given available resources and technology, the economy is simply incapable of producing enough goods and services to achieve the combinations of well-being represented by points outside the frontier. Points within the frontier are inefficient in the sense that it is possible to reallocate resources to improve one person's well-being without decreasing another's.

At point *X*, there would be incentives for either *A* or *B* to increase their individual utility by attempting to change resource allocation so as to arrive at some point

---

FIGURE 2.5   A Utility-Possibility Curve

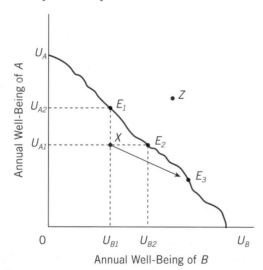

Points on the utility-possibility curve indicate the maximum level of well-being for any one person, *A*, given the level of well-being of any other person, *B*. Points, E_1, E_2, and E_3 are efficient. Point *Z* is unattainable. Point *X* is inefficient. However, a movement from *X* to E_3 will be opposed by *A* because it would make him or her worse off.

© Cengage Learning

---

[3]The utility-possibility frontier is derived in the classic article by Francis M. Bator, "The Simple Analytics of Welfare Maximization," *American Economic Review* 47 (March 1957): 22–59.

PUBLIC POLICY PERSPECTIVE

The Tax System and the Birthrate—An Example of Positive Economic Analysis

What does the tax system have to do with babies? The answer is quite a bit, according to positive economic analysis of the effect of the U.S. system of income taxation on the decision to have children.[1] The U.S. birthrate increased by 3 percent in the early 1990s and it will soon increase more, according to economists Leslie Whittington, James Alm, and H. Elizabeth Peters. These economists have examined how the U.S. tax system has indirectly subsidized the cost of raising children since 1917. They have set up a positive economic model of the choice to have children and then used the model to isolate the effect of the personal exemption of the U.S. income tax on the fertility rate in the United States from 1913 to 1984. The fertility rate measures the number of births per 1,000 women of childbearing age.

The personal exemption is a feature of the federal income tax that, as of 2012, allowed families to exclude $3,800 of income from taxation for each family dependent. For a family subject to a 33 percent tax rate, each additional child reduces the family's annual federal income tax bill by $1,254 = 0.33($3,800). The $1,254 annual tax reduction really amounts to a subsidy that varies with the number of children. Other factors considered equal, the greater the personal exemption, the greater the

subsidy for having children. The value of that subsidy also depends on a family's tax bracket. For example, for a family in the 15 percent tax bracket, the annual reduction in taxes (or subsidy) resulting from a $3,800 personal exemption is merely $570. Finally, a low-income family that does not earn enough income to be subject to income taxation gets little benefit from the personal exemption.

For a middle-income family, the subsidy from the personal exemption ranges from 4 to 9 percent of annual child-rearing costs. For additional children, the subsidy amounts to as much as 14 percent of annual costs.[2] And the subsidy continues until a child reaches age 18, or even longer if that child attends college. By reducing the cost of child rearing, the tax system encourages families to have children. Thus, the positive economic analysis suggests that fertility rates, other factors remaining equal, vary directly with the value of the personal exemption.

Using actual data from 1913 to 1984, the researchers tested their hypothesis by conducting a statistical analysis of the relationship between the fertility rate in the United States, the personal exemption, and a set of other variables that influence the choice to have children. By statistically controlling for all other influences of the fertility

on the section of the frontier E_1E_2. Whichever one makes the attempt, the other will not oppose it because that person would not be made worse off as a result of the change. The only reason a move from X to a point on E_1E_2 might be opposed would be if one individual were ill-informed about the impact of such a move.

Suppose, however, that B wants to move to point E_3. This will be opposed by A because that move would reduce A's well-being. A move from an inefficient resource allocation, such as that represented by point X, to an efficient one, represented by E_3, results in losses to certain groups. The movement from X to E_3 will make B better off at the expense of making A worse off.

Improvements in efficiency represented by the movement from point X to point E_3 are vigorously opposed. Often the losing groups are effectively organized and work tirelessly through political institutions to block the change. It is no surprise that the policy recommendations of many normative economists for elimination of minimum-wage laws and international trade restrictions, on grounds that such elimination would improve efficiency, are continuously defeated in the political arena. These restrictions provide significant benefits to certain groups that prefer to resist losses in income. To understand why inefficient government policies and functions persist, it is necessary to investigate the opportunities that exist for both gainers and losers to protect their interests through political action.

rate, the researchers could isolate the relationship between fertility rates and the real tax reduction value of personal exemptions on average for all taxpayers.

The researchers concluded that an increase in the real tax value of the personal exemption will be associated with an increase in the number of births per 1,000 women. They then used their analysis to estimate the possible effect of recent increases in the personal exemption on fertility rates. The personal exemption increased from $1,080 in 1986 to $3,800 in 2012 and is adjusted each year for inflation. Using the historical relationship between the real tax value of the personal exemption and the birthrate, the researchers conclude that an 11 percent increase in the U.S. birthrate will result from this increase in the personal exemption. Their analysis suggests that middle-income families will get the greatest increase in the subsidy and their fertility rates will increase accordingly. On the other hand, the law actually decreases the incentive of very low- and very high-income families to have children because many low-income families do not now pay any income tax and because the personal exemption was phased out for many families with very high incomes in some tax years during the period of the study.

Some nations directly subsidize children through special family allowances. For example, the Japanese government gives families with more than one preschool child a monthly allowance. Many European nations also have family allowance systems that encourage families to have children. Although the U.S. government does not directly subsidize families with children, the federal tax system provides benefits that vary with family size, and these benefits have been increasing in recent years. The latest innovation is a child tax *credit* for families that will reduce taxes directly with the number of children per family each year. A family that increases the number of dependent children in its household can reduce its tax burden by as much as $1,000 per year for each year the child remains a dependent. A four-child household would pay as much as $4,000 less per year in taxes than a household with the same taxable income but without any dependent children. This is likely to further increase the incentive to have children. It could also create future taxpayers, which will help relieve the per-person tax burden by the middle of the century, when the proportion of retirees in the population will increase dramatically.

---

[1]See Leslie A. Whittington, James Alm, and H. Elizabeth Peters, "Fertility and the Personal Exemption: Implicit Pronatalist Policy in the United States," *American Economic Review* 80, 3 (June 1990): 545–556.
[2]Whittington et al., p. 546.

The Trade-Off between Equity and Efficiency in a System of Competitive Markets

A perfectly competitive market system can be given high marks because it is capable of achieving efficiency. The efficient outcome in a market system is a point on the utility-possibility curve. In a market system, each person's money income will depend on the amount of productive resources owned and the returns obtained from selling productive services to others in markets. The distribution of income will determine the willingness and ability to pay for various goods and services that the economy can produce with available resources and technology.

Many critics of the market system argue that it cannot be given high marks on the basis of equity criteria. They complain that many participants in the system cannot satisfy their most basic needs because low incomes provide them with little capacity to pay for market goods and services. Poverty in the midst of wealth is regarded as inequitable by many people. The market system caters to those with the ability to pay, which depends on earnings. This, in turn, depends on the marginal social benefit of resources that a person owns. The poor lack resources.

Often they are unskilled and undereducated, and, as a result, the quality of their labor service is low. In many cases, the poor are unemployable or employable only at low wages. In addition, they usually own no land or capital, meaning that their nonlabor income is also low.

Critics of the market system also argue that these poor people should receive transfers financed by taxes on more fortunate members of society. The incomes of the poor, and therefore their level of annual well-being, would be kept from falling below minimum standards. This, however, creates a dilemma. Often, as is shown throughout this text, taxes and subsidies used to alter the distribution of income distort incentives to produce in ways that prevent achievement of efficiency. Policy makers are confronted with the inevitable conflict between the quests for both efficiency and equity.

POSITIVE ANALYSIS TRADE-OFF BETWEEN EQUITY AND EFFICIENCY

Positive analysis can be used to evaluate the effectiveness of alternative policies in achieving any given change in the distribution of income. The positive approach attempts to explain why efficient outcomes are, or are not, achieved. It can also be used to predict how government intervention in private affairs affects the likelihood of achieving efficiency while avoiding any direct judgments on the desirability of efficiency as an outcome.

Rather than recommending changes that will result in efficient outcomes, the positive approach attempts to predict whether changes in government policy or spending will be agreed upon through existing political institutions. The analysis is firmly based on models of maximization of personal gains from exchange. For example, it is entirely reasonable to expect individuals to support and vote for inefficient policies if their income shares will be larger under such policies. In effect, these individuals are content with a larger share of a smaller pie. Achievement of efficiency would allow the given amount of resources in the economy to produce more net benefits, but the total shares of this larger pie accruing to groups opposing the change would be less than what they would have with the smaller pie.

Referring to Figure 2.5, person A is better off at point X compared with point E_3, even though point X provides less aggregate net social benefit in the economy. Individuals are not concerned with net *social* benefit. Rather, they maximize their net *personal* benefits. The trick in devising efficient policies is to make maximization of net personal benefits coincide with maximization of net social benefit.

In evaluating public policy, it is important to understand both the efficiency and the distributive consequences of alternatives. Improvements in efficiency are often opposed vigorously by special-interest groups that would suffer losses if the improvements were enacted. These groups are concerned with protecting their income shares at the expense of reduced output and well-being in the economy as a whole. The actual policies and institutions that emerge reflect the conflict between groups of individuals seeking to protect and enlarge their income shares and the benefits of efficient resource use that accrue to individuals comprising the entire community. A further factor affecting the outcome is the effectiveness of economic institutions in allowing those who receive benefits from policy change to bargain with those who bear costs so as to reach a compromise agreement.

One problem in using the efficiency criterion as a normative tool is that the actual number of allocative changes that will satisfy the criterion might be few and quickly exhausted. Most debates concerning resource allocation (for example, how to allocate scarce resources between expenditures on defense and other uses) involve benefits to some groups and losses to others.

In such cases, no one can easily predict whether the change in resource allocation will be made, inasmuch as there will be both gainers and losers. The efficiency criterion, strictly speaking, can only recommend changes when there are gainers only (and no losers) or when the gainers can compensate the losers at transaction costs that do not exceed the gains. Some normative theorists try to overcome this problem by using **compensation criteria**, which attempt to measure the value of the gains to gainers in dollar terms and compare these with the dollar value of the losses to losers. If the value of gains outweighs the value of losses, normative theorists argue that it is efficient to make the change, regardless of whether the losers are compensated for their losses.[4] Such a change, however, still will be opposed by the losers. Although some might argue that the change will improve efficiency, its approval cannot be predicted because it involves losses in income to some individuals. Most public policy issues involve trade-offs between gains in efficiency obtained at the expense of losses by certain groups.

The positive approach can make a genuine contribution by generating information on the gains, losses, and transaction costs associated with particular policy changes and on the distribution of such benefits and costs among citizens. Without such information, it would be impossible for the normative economist to make prescriptions for achieving efficiency in resource allocation and for attaining equity goals. Such information is indispensable to voters themselves when they are deciding how to vote on questions concerning the functions of government and the extent of its powers and expenditures.

SUMMARY

Resources are efficiently allocated when the well-being of any one person cannot be increased without harming another. This condition is attained when all goods are consumed over any period up to the point at which the marginal social benefit of each good equals its marginal social cost.

When prices in competitive markets reflect marginal social costs and benefits, market exchange achieves efficiency. In cases for which interaction between buyers and sellers in competitive markets does not result in an efficient outcome, government intervention can be prescribed to help achieve efficiency.

Changes in policy that move the economy toward efficiency are often opposed because they result in a change in income distribution. Individuals opposing actions that improve efficiency act rationally. They are simply better off with a larger share of a smaller pie. To predict outcomes in any political process, it is necessary to know the benefits of any changes proposed, to whom they accrue, and what changes in the distribution of income result.

LOOKING AHEAD

The appendix to this chapter develops a more rigorous model of efficient resource use. Chapter 3 further explores the implications of market failure to achieve efficiency. The causes, implications, and remedies for the failure of an unregulated system of markets to achieve efficiency are extensively discussed. The framework developed in Chapter 3 is further applied in the discussion of public goods in Chapter 4.

---

[4]This is known as the Kaldor-Hicks criterion. See Nicholas Kaldor's classic discussion of this subject in, "Welfare Propositions of Economics and Interpersonal Comparisons of Utility," *Economic Journal* 49 (September 1939): 549–552.

KEY CONCEPTS

Compensation Criteria	Marginal Social Cost
Efficiency Criterion	Normative Economics
Equity	Positive Economics
Marginal Conditions for Efficient Resource Allocation	Total Social Benefit
Marginal Net Benefit	Total Social Cost
Marginal Social Benefit	Utility-possibility Curve

REVIEW QUESTIONS

1. How are normative statements distinguished from positive statements? Look through a daily newspaper for articles on politics and make a list of statements regarding current issues; indicate which are positive and which are normative.
2. How does trading improve efficiency? Why are trades that apparently provide mutual gains to those involved not undertaken? Show how equating the total social benefit of a good with its total social cost will result in more than the efficient output of the good.
3. Suppose you have more books than you want but would like to have more sporting goods. Explain how your well-being would be affected if a law existed preventing the trading of books for sporting goods. How would such a law affect efficiency in the use of resources? Show how a law banning the sale of books will cause a loss in efficiency. How can these losses be measured?
4. Why might individuals support the status quo over policies that can be shown to improve efficiency? Examine your own views on issues relating to social policy and ask yourself whether you would support such policies as the elimination of tariffs and other barriers to international trade, which might improve efficiency in the use of productive resources. How would quotas on imports of Japanese cars affect you personally? If you owned stock in General Motors or worked in an automobile factory, would that affect your support for the quotas?

5. Relate the concept of efficiency to points on a utility-possibility curve.
6. Suppose a politician asks consultants to calculate the total social cost and the social benefit of the activities in a government agency. The politician discovers that total social benefits exceed total social costs. Does this imply that the activities of the agency should be increased to achieve efficiency?
7. Suppose the marginal social cost of fighter aircraft each year exceeds their marginal social benefit. Are fighter aircraft being produced at an efficient level?
8. The marginal social benefit of college enrollments currently exceeds its marginal social cost. Use a graph to demonstrate the gain in efficiency that would result from an increase in college enrollment.
9. The price of automobiles currently equals both the marginal social benefit and the marginal social cost at existing annual output. A tax is levied on the sale of cars. Assuming that the tax increases the marginal private cost of sellers, show how it will cause a loss in efficiency in the automobile market.
10. Efficiency can correspond to more than one distribution of well-being. Can the efficiency criterion be used to rank one distribution over another?

PROBLEMS

1. The following table shows how the total social benefit and total social cost of summer outdoor concerts in Central City vary with the number of performances.

NUMBER OF CONCERTS	TOTAL SOCIAL BENEFIT ($)	TOTAL SOCIAL COST ($)
1	10,000	5,000
2	15,000	11,000
3	18,000	18,000
4	20,000	26,000
5	21,000	36,000

What is the efficient number of concerts?

2. a. Suppose the marginal social cost of television sets is $100. This is constant and equal to the average cost of television sets. The annual demand for television sets is given by the following equation: $Q = 200,000 - 500P$, where Q is the quantity sold per year and P is the price of television sets. If television sets are sold in a perfectly competitive market, calculate the annual number sold. Under what circumstances will the market equilibrium be efficient?
   b. Show the losses in well-being each year that would result from a law limiting sales of television sets to 100,000 per year. Show the effect on

the price, marginal social benefit, and marginal social cost of television sets. Show the net loss in well-being that will result from a complete ban on the sales of television sets.

3. A prominent senator has calculated the total social benefit of the current amount of space exploration at $3 billion per year. The total social cost of space exploration is currently only $2 billion. The senator argues that a net gain to society would result by increasing the amount of space exploration until total costs rise enough to equal total benefits. Is the senator's logic correct?

4. The market equilibrium price for rice in Japan would be $3 per pound in the absence of government subsidies to rice production. However, the government sets the price of rice at $5 per pound and agrees to buy all the rice produced by farmers at that price. Assume that points on the demand curve for rice equal the marginal social benefit of alternative quantities, while points on an upward-sloping supply curve equal the marginal social cost of various quantities. Show how the subsidy program will result in losses in efficiency.

5. Suppose perfect competition prevails in the market for hotel rooms. The current market equilibrium price of a standard hotel room is $100 per night. Show that the current market equilibrium is efficient, assuming that both the marginal cost incurred by sellers and the marginal benefit perceived by buyers reflect all costs and benefits associated with production and use of hotel rooms. Suppose a $10 per night tax is levied on hotel occupancy. Show how this tax will prevent the market from achieving efficient output. Show the loss in net benefits from hotel use resulting from the tax.

ADDITIONAL READINGS

Bator, Francis M. "The Simple Analytics of Welfare Maximization." *American Economic Review* 47 (March 1957): 22–59. This classic article provides a clear and crisp exposition of the Paretian model of welfare economics.

Just, Richard E., Darrell L. Hueth, and Andrew Schmitz. *The Welfare Economics of Public Policy*, Northhampton, Mass.: Edward Elgar Publishing, 2005. An advanced overview of the field of welfare economics with practical applications to public policy and project evaluation.

Tresch, Richard. *Public Finance: A Normative Theory*, 2nd edition. San Diego, Calif.: Academic Press, 2002. A comprehensive advanced text on the normative theory public economics. The text provides a framework for analyzing public policy and is a good reference book for those wanting to do research in public finance.

INTERNET RESOURCES

http://www.cbo.gov
This is the home page of the Congressional Budget Office—the "think tank" of Congress. You can access studies analyzing issues of public policy as well as other information about government programs at this site.

http://www.cato.org
http://www.brookings.org
http://www.urban.org
These three private think tanks, the CATO Institute, the Brookings Institution, and the Urban Institute, study economic policy and the public sector. Access these sites to find studies on various public policy issues and on allocation of resources between the government and the private sectors of the economy.

www.taxfoundation.org
The Tax Foundation provides information and analysis of the nation's tax system. You can find current data on federal, state, and local taxation at this site along with analysis of the effects of taxes on resource use and income distribution.

Appendix 2

WELFARE ECONOMICS

Welfare economics is the normative analysis of economic interaction that seeks to determine the conditions for efficient resource use. This appendix develops a basic model to investigate how people's economic well-being is related to economic variables. Extensive use is made of graphic analysis. Efficiency conditions are derived from the analysis. A good background in microeconomics is necessary for understanding the material in this appendix. For those who skip the appendix, the basic notions of efficiency and the efficiency conditions derived in Chapter 2 are sufficient for understanding the analysis to follow in the rest of this book.

A MODEL OF EFFICIENT RESOURCE USE

Suppose two individuals annually produce and consume two goods produced with two inputs, given technology.[5] The consumption or production of each good is at costs that reflect the full social value of all resources used. The two inputs are labor and capital. These are used to produce food and clothing. The problem is to allocate inputs to the alternative outputs and to allocate outputs among individuals (*A* and *B*) that satisfy the efficiency conditions.

Production and Technology

Consider first the technological relationships within this economy. The two production functions are one for food and another for clothing. Such functions, by definition, give the maximum attainable output from any input combination. Call the annual output of food F and the annual output of clothing C. If L_F is the amount of labor used in the production of food and K_F is the amount of capital used in the production of food each year, then

$$F = F(L_F, K_F) \qquad (2A.1)$$

is the production function for food.

Similarly, if C is the annual output of clothing, L_C the amount of labor used in the production of clothing, and K_C is the amount of capital used in the production of clothing each year, then

$$C = C(L_C, K_C) \qquad (2A.2)$$

is the production function for clothing.

The output of food depends only on the inputs used in producing food and not on those used in producing clothing. Similarly, the output of clothing depends only on the amounts of labor and capital used in the process of producing clothing.

---

[5]The model can easily be expanded to include many goods, inputs, and persons. A multidimensional model requires the use of calculus to derive the efficiency conditions.

In addition, all available labor and capital will be fully employed in the production of food and clothing. If L is the total annual available labor services and K is the annual available capital services, then this condition can be written as

$$L = L_F + L_C \qquad\qquad\qquad (2A.3)$$

$$K = K_F + K_C \qquad\qquad\qquad (2A.4)$$

L_F, L_C, K_F, and K_C are variables with values to be solved in the model. L and K are assumed to be fixed in supply.

PRODUCTIVE EFFICIENCY

Productive efficiency exists if it is not possible to reallocate inputs to alternative uses in such a manner as to increase the output of any one good without reducing the output of some alternative good. For a two-good world, this criterion will be met when, for any specified output level of one good, the maximum possible amount of the alternative good is being produced, given the community's endowment of inputs and technology.

The next step is to determine the condition that will lead to productive efficiency in the use of inputs. This may be accomplished by employing an *Edgeworth box*. The length of the horizontal side of the rectangle illustrated in Figure 2A.1 equals the total available labor services per year, L. The length of the vertical side of the box represents the total available capital services per year, K. Measure the amount of capital used in the production of food upward along the vertical side of the box, $0K$, and measure the amount of labor used in production of food along the horizontal side of the box, $0L$. If productive resources are presumed to be always fully employed, then it must follow that any labor or capital not used in the

---

FIGURE 2A.1   Productive Efficiency

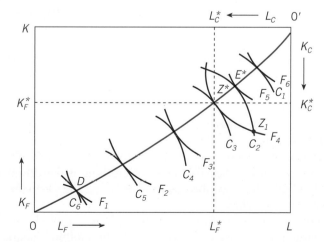

All input allocations corresponding to tangencies of the food and clothing isoquants satisfy the conditions for productive efficiency.

production of food must be used in the production of clothing. This can be seen by simply rearranging terms in Equations 2A.3 and 2A.4 as follows:

$$L_C = L - L_F \qquad (2A.5)$$

$$K_C = K - K_F \qquad (2A.6)$$

The diagram accounts for Equations 2A.5 and 2A.6 by measuring the amounts of labor and capital used in the production of clothing from the origin $0'$. Any point within the Edgeworth box will correspond to certain values of the four variables L_F, K_F, L_C, and K_C. For example, at point Z^*, the four values are

$$L_C = 0L_F^*, \ L_C = 0'L_C^*$$

$$K_F = 0K_F^*, \ K_C = 0'K_C^*$$

It is a simple matter to plot the isoquants corresponding to the production functions for food and clothing within the box. Use 0 as the origin for plotting the food isoquants labeled F_1 to F_6. The marginal rate of technical substitution of labor for capital diminishes as more labor is substituted for capital in the production of food. Through any point within the box will be, of course, an isoquant corresponding to some level of production of food. Isoquants farther away from the origin 0 represent higher production levels for food.

In the same fashion, isoquants corresponding to different levels of production for clothing can be plotted. Now, however, $0'$ is used as the origin. The isoquants for clothing, labeled C_1 to C_6, are convex to $0'$, and those farther from $0'$ correspond to higher levels of production of clothing. It easily can be seen that each point within the box corresponds to values for six variables. Referring again to point Z^*, it has already been shown that it corresponds to values of L_F, K_F, L_C, and K_C. As soon as the input mix is specified, so are the production levels of the two outputs (see Equations 2A.1 and 2A.2). Therefore, at point Z^*, the use of L_F^* labor and K_F^* capital in the production of food implies an annual output level of F_4 of food, where F_4 is the level of production of the good corresponding to the isoquant through Z^*. The annual output of clothing at Z^* is C_3.

At point Z_1 in Figure 2A.1, the input combination used results in an annual output F_4 of food and C_2 of clothing. The input mix at Z_1 is not efficient. Why? Because it is possible to increase the production of clothing to C_3, which represents a higher level of production for clothing, without decreasing the production of food. This is accomplished by moving along the isoquant F_4 until the highest clothing isoquant is reached. (Remember that even though they have not been drawn in Figure 2A.1, there is a clothing isoquant through every point on F_4.) The highest that can be reached is clearly C_3, where C_3 is tangent to F_4. To move from Z_1 to Z^*, simply reallocate labor away from the production of food while replacing it with capital. Once point Z^* is reached, it is no longer possible to increase the production of clothing while the production of food is held at F_4.

Similarly, it can be shown easily that, at Z_1, the production of food could be increased without decreasing the production of clothing if the production of clothing is held at C_2. This is accomplished by moving along the isoquant corresponding to C_2 until point E^* is reached.

Similar exercises can be performed for any point within the box. Only those points corresponding to tangencies between food and clothing isoquants will fulfill the requirements of productive efficiency. The line $00'$ has been drawn to connect all the points of tangency. Along $00'$, it is impossible to increase the production of any one good without decreasing the production of the other. Accordingly, $00'$ defines all values for F, C, L_F, L_C, K_F, and K_C that satisfy the requirement of productive efficiency. All the points of 00′ correspond to tangencies between some food isoquant and some clothing isoquant.

The slope of the food isoquant is its marginal rate of technical substitution of labor for capital multiplied by −1 in the production of food. Writing this slope as $MRTS_{LK}^{F}$, it follows that all points on the efficiency locus 00' are defined by

$$MRTS_{LK}^{F} = MRTS_{LK}^{C} \qquad\qquad (2A.7)$$

where $MRTS_{LK}^{C}$ is the slope of any clothing isoquant multiplied by −1.

The Production-Possibility Curve

The economic information displayed in the efficiency locus may be summarized in an alternative fashion. To do this, consider what the efficiency locus implies. Given the economy's resources (L and K), any point on 00′ gives the maximum amount of food that can be produced for any given level of production of clothing each year and the maximum amount of clothing that can be produced given any level of production for food each year. This is precisely the definition of an economy's production-possibility curve. Plotting the annual quantity of food on the vertical axis of Figure 2A.2, and the annual quantity of clothing on the horizontal axis, the curve TT' gives the economy's potential for producing combinations of food and clothing efficiently, given its endowment of resources (L and K). The production-possibility curve has the usual shape. It is concave to the origin, implying an increasing marginal rate of transformation of food into clothing as more resources are devoted to clothing production in a year.

Each point on TT' gives a different annual output allocation for the economy; that is, a different combination of F and C. This serves to emphasize that an infinity of output allocations satisfies the criterion of productive efficiency. However, no basis exists to decide whether a move from a point which is not efficient (a point within $T0T'$) to a point which is efficient (one on TT') is desirable in all cases. Referring to Figure 2A.2, a movement from point A to any point on arc E_1E_2 can be said to be *desirable* because it increases the output of both food and clothing. However, no basis exists for saying that a movement from point A to a point off

FIGURE 2A.2   Production-Possibility Curve

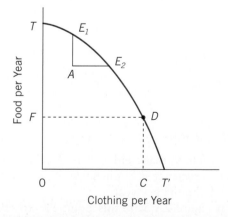

The curve TT' gives all the efficient combinations of food and clothing per year that can be produced in the economy, given the resource constraints and technology.

the arc E_1E_2, like D, is desirable. A movement from A to D increases the output of one good while reducing the output of the other. The same will hold for any movement from A to a point on TT' off the arc E_1E_2. Only movements to points on E_1E_2 from A will be costless in terms of efficiency.

PARETO EFFICIENCY

Tastes and Utility

The welfare and tastes of individuals A and B are described by the following two utility functions:

$$U_A = U(F_A, C_A) \tag{2A.8}$$

$$U_B = U(F_B, C_B) \tag{2A.9}$$

where U_A is A's utility level taken as a function of the amount of food and clothing that A alone consumes each year. Similarly, U_B is B's utility level that is taken to depend on the food and clothing that B alone consumes each year. To derive the conditions for Pareto efficiency, it is again necessary to construct an Edgeworth box similar to that used for the case of production. However, a number of differences exist between the box to be drawn now and Figure 2A.2. The first difference concerns what goes inside the box. Instead of production functions for food and clothing, utility functions are plotted. Second, whereas the sides of the production box were taken to be fixed, the sides of the consumption box are variable; that is, the assumption was a fixed annual amount of labor and capital available to produce food and clothing. The side of the Edgeworth box for consumption represents the total amount of food and clothing available for consumption each year. It is clear that these are variables. One such box corresponding to the output of F and C, represented by point D in Figure 2A.2, is drawn as Figure 2A.3. An infinite number of boxes can be drawn—one for each point on TT'. A's utility is measured from the origin 0; B's utility is measured from the origin D. Moving northeast from 0, A is successively better off as he moves to higher indifference curves. Similarly, B is placed on higher utility curves as she moves from D to 0. Any point within the box corresponds to values for the allocation of the total available supplies of food and clothing between A and B—F_A, F_B, C_A, C_B—such that the total available supply of food and clothing produced are consumed; that is,

$$C = C_A + C_B \tag{2A.10}$$

$$F = F_A + F_B \tag{2A.11}$$

In addition, each such point within the box implies some level of utility for both A and B (this follows from Equations 2A.8 and 2A.9). It is not necessary to compare the utility levels of A and B; it is required only that A and B know when they are better or worse off.

Attainment of Efficiency

When it is no longer possible to make either A or B better off without making one of them worse off, Pareto efficiency is attained. Assume that the output of food and clothing is fixed at F and C units per year.

Look at point E in Figure 2A.3. Is this point Pareto efficient? The answer is clearly no. Why? Because it is possible to make B better off without harming A by

FIGURE 2A.3 Efficient Allocation of a Given Amount of Food and Clothing per Year for Two Consumers

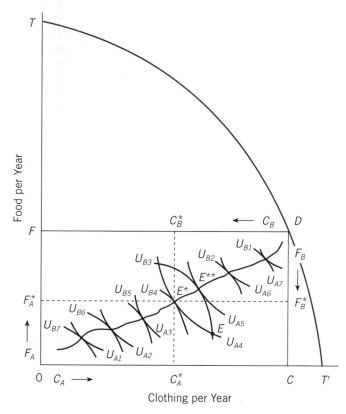

An efficient allocation of the two goods requires that the marginal rate of substitution of food for clothing be the same for both consumers.

moving along the indifference curve labeled U_{A4} to point E^*. Moving from E to E^*, A receives more food at the expense of giving up some clothing each year while B gains clothing and loses food each year. At E^*, where the indifference curve corresponding to U_{A4} is tangent to that corresponding to U_{B4}, it is no longer possible to reallocate clothing and food between A and B so as to make one better off without making the other worse off. At point E^*, A consumes $0C_A^*$ of clothing and $0F_A^*$ of food while B consumes DC_B^* of clothing and DF_B^* of food. Point E^{**} is also a Pareto-efficient allocation of the fixed amount of food and clothing between A and B.

Points E^* and E^{**} are not the only positions of Pareto efficiency. There are many such points—one for each possible tangency between the two sets of indifference curves. Each tangency represents a different annual distribution of goods and well-being between A and B.

Multiplying the slope of any indifference curve in the box by -1 gives the marginal rate of substitution of clothing for food. MRS_{CF}^A measures A's willingness to exchange food for a unit of clothing. MRS_{CF}^B measures B's willingness to exchange food for a unit of clothing. All points of efficiency within the box must satisfy the following criterion:

$$MRS_{CF}^A = MRS_{CF}^B \tag{2A.12}$$

Equation 2A.12 merely states that, for an allocation of the fixed amount of goods to be efficient, the two relevant indifference curves must be tangent, implying that their slopes are equal.

Suppose that the annual outputs of food and clothing can be varied. It is now necessary to determine the efficient production levels of the two outputs, as well as the efficient allocation of goods among A and B. It is possible to "transform" food into clothing according to the terms implied by the slope of the transformation curve of Figure 2A.3 (the marginal rate of transformation of food into clothing). Not all the points on the locus of tangencies between the two sets of indifference curves in Figure 2A.3 are really efficient when the annual production of the two goods is variable. To understand this, suppose that at point E^* in Figure 2A.3, the marginal rate of substitution of clothing for food is 1 for both A and B. Thus,

$$MRS_{CF}^A = MRS_{CF}^B = 1 \tag{2A.13}$$

Call the marginal rate of transformation of food into clothing MRT_{CF}, and suppose its value is 2 at point D in Figure 2A.3. This implies that, at that particular point on the transformation curve, two units of food can be produced by diverting into food production the labor and capital used to produce one unit of clothing. But, by assumption, only one unit of food is necessary to replace one unit of clothing to keep A and B at the same level of utility at point E^* in Figure 2A.3.

Therefore, if one unit of food is taken from A and replaced with one unit of clothing, he will not be made any worse off by this exchange. A unit of clothing taken from A has no effect on B's utility. Now, the resources that were previously employed to produce this unit of clothing for A can be diverted to food production, and, by assumption, two units of food can be produced. One of these must be given to A to compensate for the loss of a unit of clothing. But, this leaves one extra unit of food. The extra food can be given to either A or B or divided between them. In any event, either both of them will be better off than they were previously or one can be made better off without making the other worse off. It follows that no allocation of resources can be efficient until all gains from an exchange of this kind have been exhausted. This will occur only for those points where the rates at which A and B are willing to substitute food and clothing while retaining the same level of utility are precisely equal to the rate at which clothing may be transformed into food at the margin by diverting resources (labor and capital) from the production of one commodity to the other. That is, the following must hold:

$$MRS_{CF}^A = MRS_{CF}^B = MRT_{CF} \tag{2A.14}$$

An Interpretation of Efficiency Conditions

A more intuitive interpretation of the efficiency conditions is made possible by allowing one of the two goods to be "money." Efficient substitution of money for clothing in Equation 2A.14 requires that A's willingness to substitute clothing for money be equal to B's willingness to substitute clothing for money, which, in turn, must equal the capability of the economy to transform money into clothing. The willingness to substitute clothing for money for both A and B is a measure of the marginal benefits they obtain from clothing. Assume as well that the marginal benefits obtained by each consumer reflect the marginal social benefit of the good. The capability to transform money into clothing is a measure of the value of alternative goods that must be forgone to produce another unit of clothing. This is the marginal social cost of clothing. Rewriting Equation 2A.14,

$$MSB = MB_C^A = MB_C^B = MSC_C \qquad (2A.15)$$

At least one output combination will satisfy the efficiency condition. The actual number of efficient output solutions depends on the differences in tastes among households. If A and B have different tastes, then any change in income distribution would alter relative demands and cause a change in the efficient output mix (that is, lead the economy to a new efficient point on the production-possibility curve).

Therefore, many allocations are likely to satisfy the efficiency criteria when tastes differ among households. Each one still differs in terms of the distribution of welfare. Insofar as A and B have different tastes, changes in income distribution alter the efficient resource-use pattern. Thus, for any income distribution, the model specifies from the utility functions (Equations 2A.8 and 2A.9) the output demands of A and B. Given the income distribution, some efficient output mix (F, C) exists where $F = F_A + F_B$ and $C = C_A + C_B$, allowing both A and B to maximize their welfare within their income. The production functions (Equations 2A.1 and 2A.2) give the efficient allocation of inputs L_F, L_C, K_F, and K_C that are necessary to produce that mix. Thus, for any income distribution, the model produces a solution for the variables F, C, L_F, L_C, K_F, K_C, U_A, U_B, F_A, F_B, C_A, and C_B. All points satisfying the efficiency criterion of Equation 2A.14 are represented by the utility-possibility frontier (Figure 2A.5).

Ranking Efficient Outcomes: Social-Welfare Functions

Some normative economists attempt to do more than simply specify the efficient outcomes. They try to develop criteria to rank alternative income distributions. No objective way exists to do this. Positive economists have been extremely critical of attempts to rank alternative income distributions.[6]

The technique used by the normative economists is to postulate the existence of a social-welfare function. Social welfare, W, is taken as a function of individual welfare. Social welfare depends on the utility levels of A and B:

$$W = W(U_A, U_B) \qquad (2A.16)$$

This function embodies ethical evaluation of the importance of A's and B's relative welfare in determining social welfare. The actual form of the function depends on the weights, or coefficients, applied to individual utilities. The function then can be used to choose among alternative efficient welfare distributions. Thus, the welfare distribution that maximizes social welfare is chosen as "best." Once the social-welfare maximizing values of U_A and U_B are known, the values of the other variables are determined easily from the utility and production functions.

---

[6]James Buchanan has argued, quite convincingly, that resorting to the social-welfare function is inconsistent with the basic value judgments of Paretian welfare economics precisely because it is based on a nonindividualistic ethic. See his classic discussion of this topic in *Demand and Supply of Public Goods* (Chicago: Rand McNally, 1968), 193–197.

EFFICIENCY AND ECONOMIC INSTITUTIONS

Pure Market Economy and Productive Efficiency

The efficiency criterion can be used to evaluate resource allocation in a pure market economy operating under conditions of perfect competition in all markets. Assume that productive resources are privately owned and that no individual market participant has any power whatsoever to affect prices of the commodities or inputs that are bought or sold. The price of any given commodity must be assumed to be identical for all buyers and sellers of that particular commodity. This implies no distortions in the marketplace, such as taxes, cause the price received by sellers to differ from the price paid by buyers.

In a perfectly competitive market, producers take the prices of labor and capital as fixed. Under these constraints, firms minimize the cost of producing any output. If the price of labor is P_L and the price of capital is P_K, then the total cost of producing any given annual output is

$$C = P_K K + P_L L \qquad (2A.17)$$

As more labor and capital are used, the cost of production becomes greater. If cost is held constant at C, Equation 2A.17 can be plotted on a set of axes, with capital measured on the vertical axis and labor on the horizontal axis. The resultant relationship is an isocost line, defining all those combinations of labor and capital that cost C dollars. This is illustrated in Figure 2A.4. There will be one isocost line through every point within the set of axes. Each isocost line corresponds to a different value of C. Lines farther from the origin imply greater purchases of both L and K and therefore greater total cost.

Now, consider the combinations of labor and capital that might be used to produce a particular amount of food, say $F = F_1$. The slope of the isoquant is the marginal rate of technical substitution of labor for capital in the production of food, say $F = F_1$. This information is summarized in the isoquant corresponding to $F = F_1$ and is illustrated in Figure 2A.4. To produce this particular output of food at minimum cost, the input combination corresponding to the tangency of the isoquant with some isocost

---

FIGURE 2A.4   Cost Minimization and Productive Efficiency

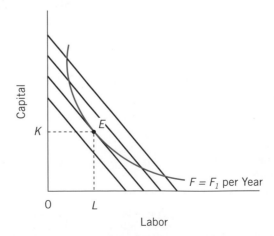

Competitive firms maximizing profits choose the efficient input allocation.

line is chosen. At that point, the slope of the isocost line equals the slope of the iso-quant corresponding to $F = F_1$. The slope of the isoquant is the marginal rate of technical substitution of labor for capital in the production of food multiplied by -1, while the slope of the isocost line is the ratio of the price of labor to the price of capital multiplied by -1. The cost of producing any output of food will be minimized when the isoquant corresponding to that level of production is tangent to an isocost line. Thus, the condition for minimizing the cost of production of any output of food is

$$MRTS_{LK}^F = \frac{P_L}{P_K} \tag{2A.18}$$

A similar argument can be advanced for the production of clothing. The only necessary alteration is to draw the isoquant corresponding to a particular level of clothing production in Figure 2A.4. The conclusion is similar. To minimize costs of production for any output level, the clothing producer must set the marginal rate of technical substitution of labor for capital in the production of clothing equal to the ratio of the price of labor to the price of capital:

$$MRTS_{LK}^C = \frac{P_L}{P_K} \tag{2A.19}$$

Now, assuming no distortions in the market, such as taxes, ratio of the price of labor with respect to capital (P_L/P_K) will be the same for producers of food and clothing. Because both producers adjust to equate their marginal rates of technical substitution to the same ratio of prices, it follows that they also adjust to set these rates of substitution equal to one another. Therefore, combining Equations 2A.18 and 2A.19 yields

$$MRTS_{LK}^F = MRTS_{LK}^C = \frac{P_L}{P_K} \tag{2A.20}$$

Equation 2A.20 is the condition for efficiency in production. It follows that perfect competition in the markets for labor and capital implies that the criterion of productive efficiency will be satisfied. That is, the economy automatically will be led to a point on, as opposed to within, its production-possibility frontier.

A Pure Market Economy and Pareto Efficiency

Next, consider the decisions concerning the level of production for food and clothing. If P_F is the price of food and P_C is the price of clothing, the producers can maximize profits by selecting that level of output for which the price of each commodity is equal to the marginal cost of producing that output. Accordingly, profits are maximum for both food and clothing producers when they have adjusted their output to satisfy the following conditions:

$$P_F = MC_F \tag{2A.21}$$

$$P_C = MC_C \tag{2A.22}$$

where MC_F and MC_C are the marginal costs of food and clothing, respectively. The information represented in these two equations may be combined into one equation by dividing Equation 2A.22 by Equation 2A.21:

$$\frac{P_C}{P_F} = \frac{MC_C}{MC_F} \tag{2A.23}$$

It easily can be shown that the ratio of marginal costs in Equation 2A.23 represents the marginal rate of transformation of food into clothing.

The slope of the production-possibility curve can be interpreted as the amount of one commodity that must be forgone in order to produce one more unit of the other commodity. The value of the extra resources necessary to produce this one more unit is the marginal cost of producing that unit, as measured by the forgone alternative commodity output that could have been produced by them. In symbolic form, if ΔF is a change in food output and ΔC is a change in clothing output, then

$$MC_F = \Delta C \tag{2A.24}$$

$$MC_C = \Delta F \tag{2A.25}$$

Dividing Equation 2A.25 by Equation 2A.24 gives

$$\frac{\Delta F}{\Delta C} = \frac{MC_C}{MC_F} = MRT_{CF} = \frac{P_C}{P_F} \tag{2A.26}$$

The bowed-out shape of the curve shows that marginal costs of production increase as the production of any good increases. To see the shape, move along the production-possibility curve from T to T' in Figure 2A.2, thereby increasing the output of clothing at the expense of decreasing the output of food. When this is done, the marginal cost of food will decrease because less is produced. The ratio of the marginal cost of clothing to food therefore increases, causing the slope of TT' to increase as point T' is approached.

Prices of food and clothing are given to persons A and B. Both A and B have a certain income level dependent both on the amount of labor and capital they own and on prices. This income level, together with the prices of food and clothing, determines their budget constraint. The tangency between their budget constraint line and an indifference curve in their indifference map defines the market basket of goods they choose in order to maximize their utility. This is illustrated in Figure 2A.5.

Given the budget line and indifference curves for A, point E represents A's equilibrium position, implying that he consumes F_A units of food and C_A units of clothing in order to maximize his utility. At E, the slope of an indifference curve is equal to the slope of the budget line. It follows that

$$\frac{P_C}{P_F} = MRS_{CF}^A \tag{2A.27}$$

Similarly, for B at equilibrium, given B's indifference curve and budget constraint,

$$\frac{P_C}{P_F} = MRS_{CF}^B \tag{2A.28}$$

If both producers and consumers react to the same price ratio, they will behave in a manner that will satisfy the condition for efficiency. To understand this, refer to Equations 2A.26, 2A.27, and 2A.28; the relevant slopes are equal to the same price ratio. It follows that these slopes must be equal to each other; that is,

$$MRS_{CF}^A = MRS_{CF}^B = MRT_{CF} = \frac{P_C}{P_F} \tag{2A.29}$$

which is the condition for efficiency. From a normative point of view, therefore, a perfectly competitive economy is desirable because it leads to efficiency.

Income Distribution

But many possible efficient resource allocations are likely if tastes differ between A and B. Which one will the market economy achieve? This depends on the initial income distribution between A and B, which, in turn, depends in part on the

FIGURE 2A.5 Consumer Choice

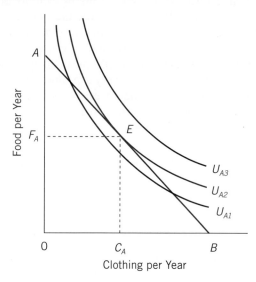

In equilibrium, each consumer purchases food and clothing in markets to satisfy the following condition:

$$MRS_{CF} = \frac{P_C}{P_F}$$

amount of productive resources owned by each individual. Their annual income is the sum of payments received by them in return for the services of the productive resources they own. Call the amount of labor and capital that A owns L_A and K_A, respectively. B's labor supply is L_B while K_B is B's capital. All the available capital and labor is distributed between A and B, so that

$$L = L_A + L_B \tag{2A.30}$$

and

$$K = K_A + K_B \tag{2A.31}$$

Given the prices of labor and capital services, A's and B's annual income levels are I_A and I_B, respectively, and can be expressed as

$$I_A = P_L L_A + P_K K_A \tag{2A.32}$$

and

$$I_B = P_L L_B + P_K K_B \tag{2A.33}$$

If A and B have differing preferences, any change in the distribution of annual income will shift the relative demand for food and clothing, thereby resulting in a change to a new efficient annual output mix.

Under certain circumstances, A and B might agree to an alteration in the distribution of income. For example, A's welfare might be interdependent with that of

B's. In this case, A might be able to improve his own welfare by making B better off. It would be in his interest to give some of his income to B without asking for any service to be given in return. While such mutually beneficial transfers are easy to administer in a two-person world, they might require a more sophisticated administrative mechanism when many individuals are involved, each with different ideas about what constitutes a desirable distribution. Under these circumstances, a government might emerge from the community's political institutions to act as an agent for redistributing income according to an agreed plan that allows mutual gains (due to interdependent utility functions) to be realized through income redistribution. This implies that some households will pay taxes while others will receive transfer payments.

The kind of taxes that the government uses must be of a special type, and the government must be careful not to destroy the identity of relative prices, as seen by producers and consumers. That is, the taxes must not be reflected in any of the relative prices of outputs or inputs so as to distort them in such a way as to make the attainment of efficiency impossible.

Alternative Economic Institutions and Efficiency

Alternative economic institutions could conceivably satisfy the efficiency criteria. Productive resources might be owned by the state and could be allocated according to a central plan devised by a managerial agency. In such a socialist economy, resource allocation would be efficient if the planners succeeded in setting prices of resources and commodities to equal their marginal social benefits and marginal social costs. Given the prices, households and plant managers would then proceed to maximize their returns from trade. In the same way as described in the market economy, this would lead to an efficient outcome and would satisfy Equation 2A.14. The actual efficient resource allocation that would emerge under such a set of institutions would depend again on the income distribution. Because resources are not privately owned, the planners would have to determine the income distribution, and stipends would have to be paid to all citizens to achieve both that distribution and its implied resource allocation.

However, it's reasonable to believe that such a planned socialist economy would not attain efficiency in a dynamic or rapidly changing environment. In such a world, knowledge about productive relations and consumption possibilities is likely to be a scarce good. Prices represent an avenue for communication of such knowledge. If a natural disaster occurs that destroys half of the world's oil supply, information on the economic consequences gets to the citizen through an increase in the price of oil products. The market economy, with its allowance for rapid price changes, provides a mechanism for economizing on such scarce knowledge.[7] The complex interrelationships between and among markets, however, permit rapid communication of occurrences in other markets.

In a planned economy, the managerial committee would require knowledge of changes in all markets simultaneously to achieve the same result and likewise the ability to change prices rapidly. If knowledge is costly to acquire, then it can be difficult for planners both to acquire it and to use it to adjust prices in a way that would accommodate shifts in supply and demand. Thus, when knowledge is a

---

[7]For a classic discussion of the knowledge problem and alternative economic institutions, see Friedrich A. Hayek, "The Use of Knowledge in Society," *American Economic Review* 35 (September 1945): 519–530.

scarce "good," a market economy then, in fact, might be preferable to a planned one, on the basis of the efficiency criteria.

MARKET IMPERFECTIONS

A number of conclusions can be reached concerning the desirable market structure in terms of the efficiency criteria. When producers possess a degree of monopoly power, they might influence the price of their output by manipulating their production. Prices can no longer be taken as given for these producers. To maximize their profits, producers no longer set prices equal to marginal costs. Instead, they produce that amount of output that corresponds to a point where marginal cost of output is less than price.

Because the demand curve slopes downward, the marginal revenue is always less than the price of the product. To reach the output level that maximizes profits, the monopolist must restrict the amount of production per time period to a level below that which would prevail if the monopoly were organized as a perfectly competitive industry. When the monopolist firm equates marginal revenues with marginal costs, it finds that marginal revenues are less than prices because the demand curve is not infinitely elastic (as is the case for firms operating under conditions of perfect competition).

If the producer of, say, food has a monopoly, it produces that output corresponding to

$$MR_F = MC_F \tag{2A.34}$$

where MR_F is the marginal revenue of food $(P_F > MR_F)$ and MC_F is the marginal cost of producing food. If perfect competition remains in the production of clothing, the following will be true for the profit-maximizing output of clothing:

$$P_C = MC_C \tag{2A.35}$$

Dividing Equation 2A.35 by Equation 2A.34 gives

$$\frac{P_C}{MR_F} = \frac{MC_C}{MC_F} = MRT_{CF} \tag{2A.36}$$

Because consumers set their MRS_{CF} equal to the ratio of prices P_C/P_F, it follows that, for any consumer,

$$MRS_{CF} > MRT_{CF} \tag{2A.37}$$

that is, the independent maximizing behavior of producers and consumers no longer acts to achieve efficiency automatically. For this reason, monopoly is considered undesirable by normative economists. To maximize profits, a monopolist produces less than a perfectly competitive industry producing the same good would produce. In doing so, the monopolist prevents the market from attaining an efficient resource allocation.

Similarly, monopolistic power in input markets results in less of the input, say labor, being offered for sale, so that sellers of the input might maximize their return. Monopolistic power in input markets prevents the attainment of efficiency in production. The normative economist therefore often recommends governmental regulation of competition insofar as this is necessary to attain an efficient resource allocation.

Chapter 3

EXTERNALITIES AND GOVERNMENT POLICY

LEARNING OBJECTIVES

After reading this chapter, you should be able to:

- Define an externality, and explain how positive and negative externalities can prevent efficiency from being achieved even when markets are perfectly competitive.

- Describe how corrective taxes and subsidies can be used to internalize externalities.

- Explain the Coase theorem and its significance.

- Prove how a system of tradable pollution rights for emissions can work to reduce pollution at lower cost than emissions standards.

- Discuss command and control methods of environmental protection, and compare the economic effects of these with such market-based alternatives as corrective taxes and marketable pollution rights.

The federal and state governments have been in the business of environmental protection now for many years. As a result of government regulations and other programs, emissions of sulfur dioxide, smoke, and other particulates have declined substantially. There also has been considerable progress in the United States and in other nations in cleansing rivers, lakes, and streams of pollutants. However, environmental pollution remains a serious health and social problem.

Many citizens believe they have the right to a clean environment, and they naturally look to government to protect that right. Cleaner air will result in many benefits, including a reduction in diseases from pollution and a decrease in the medical costs to treat those diseases. A decline in smog and acid rain will preserve the beauty of natural resources that provide recreational benefits to millions of Americans.

Some of you undoubtedly have very strong feelings about environmental protection, and many of you regard it as a moral rather than an economic issue. However, environmental protection is an issue that has an important economic dimension because it boils down to a question of resource use and the legal rights to use the air, water, and land for disposal of wastes. Because it is technologically impossible to recycle all wastes (such as residues and gases that result from the burning of fuels), a complete ban on the emissions of wastes in the environment could grind modern industrial societies to a screeching halt.

Business firms in the United States spend billions of dollars on pollution abatement and control. Some state governments are adopting even more stringent emissions control legislation than the federal rules. The increased costs of pollution control ultimately will result in higher prices for many products.

But is it possible to improve the quality of the environment to the same degree at lower cost? To find out, we need to examine how competing uses for resources result in pollution and the issues involved when governments limit the rights to emit wastes. We begin by demonstrating how the rights of some resource users are sometimes ignored as buyers and sellers go about their business in the marketplace.

EXTERNALITIES: A CLASSIFICATION AND SOME EXAMPLES

Let's examine some of the reasons why buyers and sellers in markets sometimes fail to consider effects on third parties. Externalities are costs or benefits of market transactions not reflected in prices. When an externality prevails, a third party (other than the buyers or sellers of an item) is affected by its production or consumption. The benefits or costs of the third party (either a household or a business) are not considered by either buyers or sellers of an item whose production or use results in an externality.

The third parties are people like you who bear the costs of polluted air and water. These third parties often organize politically through groups such as the Sierra Club to lobby legislators and public officials to protect their rights to a clean environment. In the United States and other industrial nations, environmentalists have emerged as an effective, potent political force to induce governments to pass laws that limit the rights of producers and consumers to emit wastes that pollute the air, water, and land.

Market prices do not accurately reflect either all the marginal social benefit or all the marginal social cost of traded items when an externality is involved.

Negative externalities, also called *external costs*, are costs to third parties other than the buyers or the sellers of an item not reflected in the market price. An example of a negative externality is the damage done by industrial pollution to people and their property. The harmful effects of pollution are impairments to good health and reductions in the value of business and personal property and resources. Another example of a negative externality is the dissatisfaction caused by the noise of low-flying aircraft as experienced by residents who are located near an airport. Those bearing pollution damages are third parties to market exchanges between the buyers and the sellers of goods or services. Their interests are not considered by the buyers and sellers of goods and services when an externality is present.

Positive externalities are benefits to third parties other than the buyers or the sellers of a good or service not reflected in prices. Buyers and sellers of goods that, when sold, result in positive externalities, do not consider the fact that each unit produced provides benefits to others. For example, a positive externality is likely to exist for fire prevention, because the purchase of smoke alarms and fireproofing materials benefits those other than the buyers and sellers by reducing the risk of the spread of fire. Buyers and sellers of these goods do not consider the fact that such protection decreases the probability of damage to the property of third parties. Fewer resources are devoted to fire prevention than would be the case if it were possible to charge third parties for the external benefits that they receive.

Effects of market exchanges on third parties are not externalities when those effects are included in prices. For example, if a person's hobby is photography, increases in the demand for photographic equipment by others could make that person worse off by increasing the price of the equipment. These higher prices, however, merely reflect the fact that such goods have become scarcer relative to the demands placed on them. The higher price serves to transfer income from buyers to sellers and to increase incentive to produce these goods, while existing production is rationed through higher prices. Some economists refer to these as *pecuniary externalities,* that is, the effects of increases (or decreases) in the price of a good on existing consumers as a result of changes in the demand or supply of a good. Pecuniary externalities merely result in changes in real income of buyers or sellers. *Real externalities* are unpriced costs or benefits. They are the effects of market exchanges external to prices.

Externalities and Efficiency

Why do externalities pose problems for resource allocation in a market system? Unregulated competitive markets result in prices that equal the marginal costs and marginal benefits that sellers incur and buyers enjoy. When an externality exists, the marginal costs or marginal benefits that market participants base their decisions on diverge from the actual marginal *social* costs or benefits. For example, with a negative externality, business firms producing a product for sale in the marketplace neither pay for nor consider the damage the production or consumption of that product can do to the environment. Similarly, with a positive externality, buyers and sellers of a product in the marketplace do not consider the fact that their production or consumption of the item benefits third parties.

We can now apply the framework developed in Chapter 2 to understand why externalities prevent competitive markets from achieving efficient outcomes. Once this is understood, we can look at alternative government policies to correct resource allocation problems that result from externalities.

Negative Externalities

When a negative externality exists, the price of a good or service does not reflect the full marginal social cost of resources allocated to its production. Suppose, for example, that in the production of paper, each unit of output results in cost to parties other than the buyers or the sellers of the product. Neither the buyers nor the sellers of the good consider these costs to third parties. The **marginal external cost (MEC)** is the extra cost to third parties resulting from production of another unit of a good or service. MEC is part of the marginal social cost of making a good available. However, it is not reflected in the price of the good.

A negative externality might be associated with paper production because of damages done by pollutants emitted into streams and rivers. Pollutants decrease the benefit obtained by other users of streams, rivers, or lakes. For example, industrial pollution from paper production could decrease the catch of commercial fishers. It also could reduce the benefit that recreational users of lakes and streams can receive from swimming, boating, and other activities.

Assume that the paper industry operates under perfect competition, implying that market power is diffused and that no one seller or buyer can influence price. The market equilibrium price and quantity in the competitive market corresponds to point A in Figure 3.1. The current price of paper is $100 per ton, and the industry produces 5 million tons per year at that price. The demand curve, D, is based on the marginal benefit that buyers receive from each ton of paper, also assumed to be

FIGURE 3.1   Market Equilibrium, Negative Externality, and Efficiency

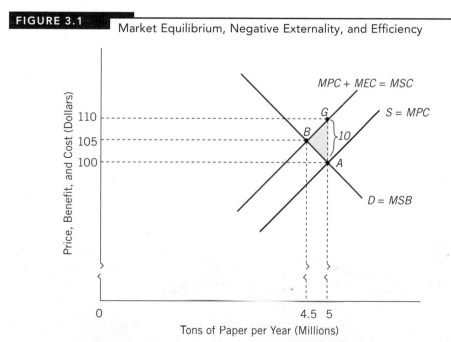

The market equilibrium output of 5 million tons per year is inefficient because MSC > MSB at that output. The efficient output corresponds to point B, where the annual output of paper is 4.5 million tons per year. The price of paper would have to rise to $105 per ton to move to the efficient output. This will reduce the marginal social cost of paper from $110 to $105 per ton and result in net gains equal to the area BGA.

© Cengage Learning

the marginal social benefit of paper. The supply curve is based on the marginal cost actually incurred to produce additional units, such as additional wages and material cost, as firms in the industry produce more. But the marginal cost curve, as seen by producers, does not include all the cost incurred in producing extra units of paper. Suppose that a marginal external cost of $10 is associated with each ton of paper produced. In reality, the marginal external cost could increase with output either because emissions per ton increase as more output is produced or because the damages done by the fixed amount of emissions per ton of output are greater when more is emitted per year. When the marginal external cost of production increases with output, the pollution damages per ton of paper are a more serious social problem at higher levels of paper output than at lower levels of output. For simplicity in this example, we assume that the marginal external cost associated with each ton of paper is constant.

The marginal external cost of $10 per ton is not considered in the producers' choice of output. But external cost is as much a part of the opportunity cost of making paper available as are wages and materials cost. If the stream had no other use, then dumping wastes into it would cause no problem inasmuch as the usefulness of the stream to others would not be impaired. The negative externality in this case stems from the fact that dumping industrial wastes in the stream decreases its usefulness to other users.

The marginal cost that producers base their decisions on is the **marginal private cost (MPC)** of producing paper. To obtain the marginal social cost, the marginal external cost of output, MEC, must be added to the marginal private costs, MPC:

$$MPC + MEC = MSC \qquad (3.1)$$

When a negative externality exists, the marginal private cost of a good falls short of its marginal social cost of output. To obtain the marginal social cost of paper in Figure 3.1, MEC must be added to MPC for each possible output. Because $MEC = \$10$ at all output levels, the MSC curve is above the MPC curve. The distance between the MPC curve and MSC curve in Figure 3.1 is $10, independent of annual output. If, instead, MEC were to increase with annual output, the distance between the MPC curve and the MSC curve would increase as annual output increased.

The competitive market equilibrium corresponds to point A, at which

$$MPC = MSB \qquad (3.2)$$

Efficiency requires that the full marginal social cost of a good be considered in the productive decision. As shown in Figure 3.1, the efficient equilibrium will be at point B rather than at point A. At point B, the following condition is satisfied:

$$MSC = MPC + MEC = MSB \qquad (3.3)$$

The marginal social cost of the good, including the marginal external cost, must be equal to its marginal social benefit to attain efficiency.

The market equilibrium output of 5 million tons of paper per year is inefficient because its marginal social cost equals $110 per ton at point G, while its marginal social benefit is only $100 per ton at point A. Because the marginal social cost of paper production exceeds its marginal social benefit, too much is being sold in the competitive market relative to the efficient amount. A gain in net social benefit equal to the triangular area BGA is possible by reducing annual output from 5 million tons to 4.5 million tons. The price of paper would have to increase to $105 per ton to induce consumers to cut back consumption from 5 million tons to 4.5 million tons per year. *When a negative externality exists, too much output is produced and sold in a competitive market relative to the efficient amount.*

Positive Externalities

When a positive externality is present, prices do not fully equal the marginal social benefit of a good or service. For example, suppose inoculation against a disease results in a positive externality. Those who are vaccinated benefit themselves, of course, by reducing the probability that they will contract a contagious disease. But they also provide benefits to those who do not receive inoculations by reducing the number of persons who will become hosts for the disease. This, in turn, reduces the probability of outbreaks of the disease for the entire population, including those who are not vaccinated. Eventually, if the disease is eradicated in this way, the entire world population will benefit. The external benefit of inoculations is the reduction in the probability that those other than the persons purchasing vaccinations will contract the disease.

Figure 3.2 illustrates how the sale of inoculation services in a competitive market will result in less than the efficient annual number if a positive externality exists. The market equilibrium occurs at point U. At that point, 10 million inoculations are sold per year at a price of $25 per inoculation. Suppose that the **marginal external benefit** (**MEB**), the benefit of additional output accruing to parties other than buyers or

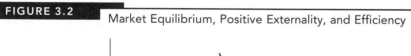

FIGURE 3.2   Market Equilibrium, Positive Externality, and Efficiency

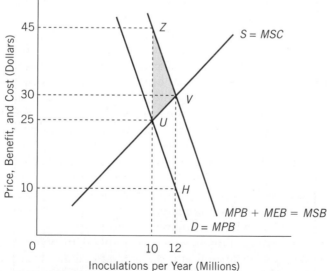

The market equilibrium corresponds to point U, at which $MPB_i = MSC$. The resulting output of 10 million inoculations per year is inefficient because $MSB > MSC$ at that point. The efficient annual output corresponds to point V, at which 12 million inoculations would be consumed per year. The price to consumers would have to fall from $25 to $10 per inoculation to move to that point. Moving to the efficient point allows net gains equal to the area UZV.

© Cengage Learning

sellers of the good, is $20 for each inoculation. The marginal benefit that consumers base their decisions on is the **marginal private benefit** (*MPB*). In Figure 3.2, market equilibrium corresponds to the equality of each person's marginal private benefit, MPB_i, of an inoculation with the marginal social cost of providing it. Assume that the marginal private cost of an inoculation to sellers accurately reflects its marginal social cost. At the market equilibrium, point *U*, the actual marginal social benefit of an inoculation exceeds the $25 price each consumer uses in deciding whether to be inoculated. The actual marginal social benefit of an inoculation, when 10 million are purchased per year, is $45. This equals the sum of the marginal private benefit received by consumers and the marginal external benefit to others of $20.

$$MPB_i + MEB = MSB \qquad (3.4)$$

In general, when a positive externality exists, marginal private benefit will fall short of marginal social benefit at each level of annual output.

Less than the efficient output results from market interaction because the marginal social benefit at the market equilibrium exceeds the marginal social cost. The efficient output of inoculations corresponds to point *V* in Figure 3.2. At that point, the marginal social benefit of inoculations equals the marginal social cost incurred to produce them. The marginal conditions for efficiency are met at that point because

$$MPB_i + MEB = MSB = MSC \qquad (3.5)$$

At *V*, the marginal social cost of an inoculation would be $30. To get to that point, the price of inoculations to consumers would have to *decrease* to $10, which corresponds to point *H* on the market demand curve for inoculations. At that point, the quantity of inoculations demanded by consumers per year would be the efficient number of 12 million. The marginal social benefit of inoculations, $MPB_i + MEB$, equals their marginal social cost of production at the efficient output. The increase in net benefits that would be possible by movement to point *V* is represented by the shaded triangular area *UZV* in Figure 3.2.

In actuality, the marginal external benefit per inoculation is likely to fall as more of the population is inoculated because fewer people will be susceptible to the disease. If this were the case, the marginal external benefit would eventually fall to zero when enough people were inoculated. Suppose that *MEB* gradually declined, eventually becoming zero at 16 million inoculations per year. In Figure 3.3, *MSB* exceeds MPB_i only if annual output is less than 16 million inoculations per year. The *MSB* curve gives the sum of the marginal private benefit and the marginal external benefit at each level of output. The distance between the *MSB* and the MPB_i curves decreases because *MEB* declines with output, as shown on the graph.

The implications of this type of externality for market failure are quite important. For example, suppose that the marginal social cost curve was *S*. This would also be the supply curve under conditions of perfect competition. Under these circumstances, the market equilibrium would correspond to point *A*, at which the price would be $25 per inoculation and the annual quantity consumed would be 10 million per year. This would be inefficient because the marginal social benefit of an inoculation exceeds its marginal social cost at that annual output. The efficient output would correspond to point *B*, at which $MSC = MSB = MPB_i + MEB$ and annual output is 12 million inoculations. Thus, a market failure exists.

If, instead, the supply were $S' = MSC'$, the market equilibrium would correspond to point *C*. At that point, the price per inoculation would be $20, and the quantity consumed per year would be 20 million. Is the market equilibrium

FIGURE 3.3 A Positive Externality for which Declines with Annual Output

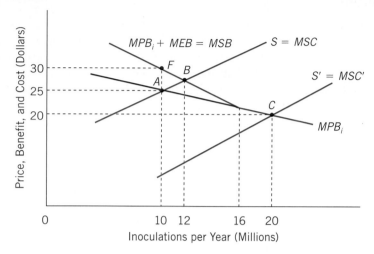

In this case, *MEB* declines as more persons are inoculated per year. If market price is $25 per inoculation, a loss in efficiency occurs because *MEB* > 0 at the corresponding output of 10 million inoculations per year. However, when the market price is $20, the market equilibrium is efficient because *MEB* = 0 at the corresponding output of 20 million inoculations per year.

inefficient in this case? The answer is no! This is because *MEB* = 0 at an annual output of 20 million. Therefore, no divergence exists between marginal social cost and marginal social benefit. For positive externalities such as these, with a marginal value that declines with output, competitive markets fail to perform efficiently only at low levels of output.

INTERNALIZATION OF EXTERNALITIES

Internalization of an externality occurs when the marginal private benefit or cost of goods and services are adjusted so that the users consider the actual marginal social benefit or cost of their decisions. In the case of a negative externality, the marginal external cost is added to marginal private cost for internalization. For a positive externality, the marginal external benefit is added to marginal private benefit to internalize the externality. Internalizing an externality results in changes in prices to reflect full marginal social cost or benefit of a good.

Internalization of externalities requires *identification* of the individuals involved and *measurement* of the monetary value of the marginal external benefit or cost. The data required for such identification and measurement are often difficult to obtain. Economic policy toward externalities is sometimes controversial because of strong differences of opinion concerning the actual value of the external cost or external benefit. For example, how can all the sources of air pollution be identified? How are damages done to property and personal well-being evaluated? This is a formidable scientific, engineering, and economic detective problem. Because strong disagreement exists among physical and biological scientists as to the costs of pollution, the necessary information required for internalizing the externality can be elusive.

Corrective Taxes: A Method of Internalizing Negative Externalities

A **corrective tax** is designed to adjust the marginal private cost of a good or service in such a way as to internalize the externality. The tax must equal the marginal external cost per unit of output to achieve this objective. In effect, a corrective tax is exactly like a charge for emitting wastes. It is designed to internalize a negative externality by making sellers of the product pay a fee equal to the marginal external costs per unit of output sold.

Suppose a corrective tax were levied on producers of paper to internalize the negative externality resulting from their output. Figure 3.4 shows the impact of such a tax. The marginal external cost per unit of output is assumed to be $MEC = $10. The corrective tax, T, is

$$T = MEC \tag{3.6}$$

In this case, the tax would be set at $10 per ton of paper, the marginal external cost of paper per year. This tax is levied on each unit produced and will be treated by producers as an increase in the marginal private cost of production. Consequently, the supply curve shifts up from S to S', where S' reflects the full marginal social cost of producing paper. The increase in cost caused by the tax changes the point corresponding to the market equilibrium from A to B. The market price of paper increases to $105 per ton, and the equilibrium quantity of paper consumed

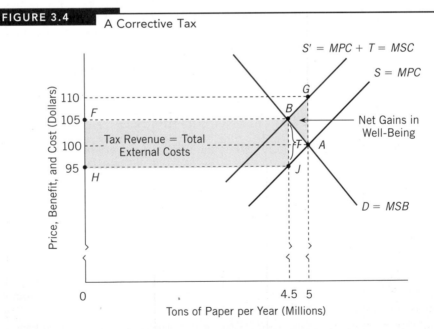

FIGURE 3.4   A Corrective Tax

A corrective tax of $T = $10 per unit output increases marginal private cost by an amount equal to the marginal external cost and results in the efficient annual output of paper. The tax revenue collected is represented by the area $FBJH$. This revenue equals the total external costs at the efficient output, provided that MEC does not vary with output. The tax allows net gains in well-being equal to the area BGA.

declines from 5 million tons to 4.5 million tons per year. This is exactly equal to the efficient annual output.

The tax of $10 per ton will collect $45 million of revenue per year at the equilibrium output of 4.5 million tons. This is represented by the area *FBJH* in Figure 3.4. After the tax is imposed, the annual value of pollution costs to alternative users of the stream declines. Initially, these costs were $50 million per year, equal to the $10 per ton cost of pollution multiplied by the annual output of 5 million tons. Because annual output declines to 4.5 million tons after the tax, the annual cost of pollution from paper produced declines to $45 million.

The corrective tax does *not* reduce the pollutants in the streams to zero. It merely raises the cost of using the stream to reflect the marginal damage done to alternative users of the stream. Paper producers that use the stream now compare this extra cost ($10 per unit output) with other alternatives of waste disposal and then decide how much of the stream's services to use at that cost. It is unlikely, though possible, that all producers will completely stop dumping in the stream. But, given the costs of alternatives, including the recycling of any wastes, purifying the wastes before disposal, reducing output, or going out of business, most certainly fewer wastes will be emitted. The actual amount of that reduction will depend on the availability and cost of alternative disposal methods relative to the corrective tax and on the impact of the tax on the profitability of producing paper. The tax is designed to force the producer to compare the marginal benefit (in terms of profits) of dumping wastes in the stream with the marginal external cost of emitting untreated wastes. It does so by adding the marginal external cost to producers' marginal private cost.

The tax revenue collected can be used for a variety of purposes. If the competing users of the stream are easily identifiable, the tax revenue collected, $45 million, could be used to compensate other users of the stream for $45 million in damages that remain after the externality is internalized by the corrective tax.[1] Alternatively, paper producers might argue that they should receive compensation for their losses in the form of a once-and-for-all payment to each producer. This payment would compensate them for the loss of their free right to dump. Finally, the revenue collected could go toward a reduction in other taxes or an increment in government services.

In summary, the corrective tax causes the following results:

1. An increase in the price of paper and a reduction in the quantity demanded, to the efficient level, where the marginal social cost equals the marginal social benefit of paper.

2. A consequent transfer of income away from paper producers and consumers in favor of individuals who use the recreational services of streams and of others who might have their taxes reduced or enjoy the benefit of increased government services if the revenue collected is used for those purposes.

3. A reduction in, but not the elimination of, use of the stream for disposal purposes and a consequent reduction in damage to alternative users of the stream.

---

[1]Compensation for damages in this way is likely to cause allocation problems if the number of alternative users of the stream is not fixed. New users would be able to enter without considering the effect of their presence on the paper producers' cost. For this reason, many economists argue against the use of tax funds for compensation.

In view of these results, the following predictions can be made concerning political support for enactment of such a corrective tax:

1. Paper producers, employees, and consumers will likely vote against it to the extent to which they are not involved in alternative uses of the stream and will not be compensated for their losses.

2. Recreational and commercial users of the stream, as well as taxpayers in general, will vote in favor of the corrective tax to the extent to which they have few interests in paper production or consumption.

To internalize the externality through the use of a corrective tax will result in some groups receiving benefits at the expense of other groups bearing the costs. In other words, the internalization of the externality also will result in income redistributive effects, which, in turn, will influence the willingness of the individuals involved to support the scheme.[2]

The gain in efficiency resulting from the corrective tax is represented by the triangular area *BGA* in Figure 3.4. This area measures the increase in net social benefits when annual paper output is reduced to the point at which its marginal social benefit equals its marginal social cost.

How a Corrective Tax Could Be Used to Reduce Global Warming

A corrective tax on the emission of carbon wastes is one possible way to reduce the economic costs associated with global warming. Global warming results from the "greenhouse effect" of carbon dioxide and other gases that trap energy in the atmosphere. Carbon dioxide is a waste from the burning of fossil fuels, such as coal, oil, and gasoline. The costs and extent of global warming are issues of enough concern to world leaders that delegates to a United Nations Conference on Development and the Environment in 1992 agreed to recommend a goal of reducing carbon dioxide emissions. Some scientific forecasts suggest that the amount of carbon dioxide in the atmosphere could double in the future, causing average temperatures to increase by as much as 9 degrees. The resulting global warming could then have high costs, including reduced agricultural productivity, increased flooding from rising sea levels, and other damage to the natural environment. In 1990, 1.5 trillion tons of carbon were emitted in the United States alone!

A corrective tax on carbon emissions could hold U.S. emissions of carbon to the 1990 level.[3] The tax could initially be set at $2 per ton of carbon waste. The tax will have to grow with the demand for fuel to encourage conservation in later years. Because coal has the highest carbon content of all fuels, its tax would have to be highest, amounting to $11.46 per ton in 2020. In the same year, the tax on oil would be $2.41 per barrel and the tax on natural gas would be 29 cents per thousand cubic feet. The higher taxes on coal are likely to raise its price by about 40 percent and, based on the elasticity of demand assumed by the researchers, the

---

[2]Refer to the utility frontier in Chapter 2. Unless paper producers are compensated for the loss of their unlimited right to dump, they will oppose the corrective tax and attempt to block benefits to those groups that use the stream for alternative purposes. Lack of compensation would imply a move such as the one from *X* to E_3 in Figure 2.5.

[3]See Timothy Tregarthen, "Economists Propose Taxes to Avert Global Warming," *The Margin* 8 (Spring 1993): 32–33. The tax levels are based on research by Dale W. Jorgenson of Harvard University, Daniel T. Slesnick, and Peter J. Wilcoxen, both of the University of Texas at Austin.

quantity demanded would decline by 25 percent. Higher coal prices would raise the price of electricity and induce power–generating firms and users of electricity to conserve energy. The corrective tax on carbon also would raise the prices of gasoline, heating oil, and natural gas.

The tax on carbon could double current U.S. pollution control costs. To decide whether these additional costs are worthwhile requires a comparison of the marginal benefit of preventing global warming. Unfortunately, scientists themselves disagree on the possible effects of global warming, making calculation of such benefits difficult.

Internalizing Negative Externalities Associated with Goods Sold in Imperfectly Competitive Markets

Such economic problems as externalities are typically looked at one at a time. In many cases, however, two or more factors contributing to losses in efficiency might exist in a single market. Suppose that a negative externality is associated with output sold by a monopoly. Also assume that the transactions costs (through political or other action) involved in attempting to break it up are too high to make this a feasible alternative.

In this case, two distortions prevent the attainment of the efficient output. The firm's monopolistic power results in less than the efficient output. On the other hand, because the monopoly causes negative externalities, other things being equal, it produces more than the efficient output. A "first best" solution would be to break up the monopoly, thereby increasing output as competition among firms in the industry lowers price to a level that equals marginal social cost. The output of the competitive industry then could be taxed to internalize the negative externality. This would increase price in the industry and decrease output.

However, an alternative way exists to achieve the same efficient outcome. The monopoly initially is producing an annual output level lower than the one corresponding to the equality between price and marginal social cost. This is equivalent to saying that it is behaving as a perfectly competitive industry for which marginal cost has been increased to account, say, for a negative externality. In effect, the monopolistic distortion can offset part or all of the distortion resulting from the negative externality.

Figure 3.5 shows a monopoly producing output Q_M per year, corresponding to point C, at which its marginal private cost equals its marginal revenue. This output level is inefficient when the marginal private cost is also the marginal social cost. The efficient output would be Q^*, which corresponds to point B. The exercise of monopolistic power would result in a loss of net benefits corresponding to the area ABC.

If, however, a negative externality is also associated with the monopolist's output, marginal social costs would be $MPC + MEC$ at any output and therefore would exceed marginal private costs. The output Q^* would not be efficient because its marginal social cost would exceed its marginal social benefit. The efficient output, as shown in Figure 3.5, would be Q_M, corresponding to point A, at which $MSC = MSB$. As the graph is drawn, the monopolistic output *is* the efficient output!

In actuality, the efficient output could be greater or less than the monopolist's output. To emphasize the point being made, the graph assumes that the monopolist's output is, in fact, the efficient one when the externality is present. The monopolist's power thereby allows net gains in well-being equal to the triangular area AFB. This would not be possible in a competitive market. These gains offset the social losses from monopolistic power. A "second best" alternative to achieve efficiency is to allow the monopoly to continue operating. Efficiency could

FIGURE 3.5   A Second Best Efficient Solution

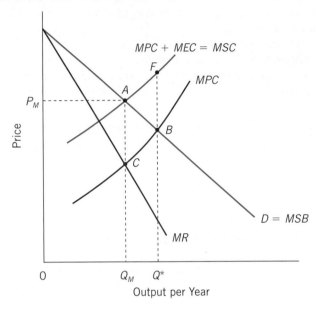

The monopolist produces less than the efficient output under normal circumstances. Here, however, the monopolist also generates external costs. The loss in well-being due to monopoly power is the area *ABC*. This is offset by a gain in well-being equal to the area *AFB* that would be lost if a competitive industry produced this output.

be attainable without even taxing the monopolist's output if the output reduction due to monopolistic power exactly offsets the external cost. In general, a corrective tax on the monopolist's output must be *less* than the corrective tax that would be necessary to achieve efficiency if the good were produced by a competitive industry.

This example illustrates an application of the **general theory of second best.**[4] Essentially, the theory states that when two opposing factors contribute to efficiency losses, they can offset one another's distortions. If it is costly to eliminate a market distortion associated with some given economic activity, then, to achieve efficiency, an offsetting distortion in another economic activity departing from the standard efficiency conditions in that activity is required. In evaluating resource allocations, the economist has to treat each problem on an ad hoc basis to determine if there are any "second best" problems present.

Corrective Subsidies: A Means of Internalizing Positive Externalities

A corrective subsidy is similar in concept to a corrective tax. Figure 3.6 shows how a corrective subsidy for inoculations can result in the efficient output of this good. The competitive market equilibrium output would be 10 million inoculations per

---

[4]For a classic discussion of this topic, see Richard G. Lipsey and Kelvin Lancaster. "The General Theory of Second Best," *Review of Economic Studies* 24 (1956): 11–32.

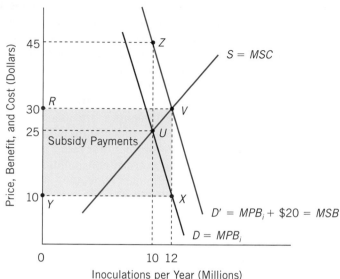

FIGURE 3.6 A Corrective Subsidy

A corrective subsidy to consumers increases the demand for inoculations and achieves the efficient output. After subsidy payments are received by consumers, the net price of an inoculation falls to $10, inducing them to purchase the efficient amount of 12 million per year. The area $RVXY$ represents the total subsidy payments at the efficient output.

year at the competitive market price of $25 per inoculation. This is inefficient because the marginal social benefit $(MPB_i + MEB)$ at that level of consumption exceeds the marginal social cost.

A **corrective subsidy** is a payment made by government to either buyers or sellers of a good so that the price paid by consumers is reduced. The payment must equal the marginal external benefit of the good or service. In this case, $20 is the marginal external benefit associated with each person inoculated. Suppose the government announces that it will pay each person inoculated a subsidy of $20. This subsidy adds $20 to the marginal private benefit of each inoculation. The demand curve for inoculations shifts upward from $D = MPB_i$ to $D' = MPB_i + 20. As the demand for inoculations increases, the market equilibrium moves from point U to point V in Figure 3.6. At that point, the market price of an inoculation *increases* to $30 to cover increased marginal costs of production. However, the *net price after receiving the subsidy declines for consumers.* The net price is now $30 − $20 = $10 per inoculation. This reduction in the net price to consumers increases the quantity demanded to 12 million per year, the efficient output.

The effect of the subsidy is to increase the benefit of inoculations accruing to those other than the buyers or the sellers of inoculations from $200 million per year to $240 million per year ($20 per person inoculated multiplied by 12 million inoculations per year). The government accomplishes this by making a total of $240 million in subsidy payments to the 12 million people inoculated each year. This is represented by the area $RVXY$ in Figure 3.6. The subsidy is paid from tax revenues.

Examples of corrective subsidies include the provision of certain government services at levels below the marginal cost of such services. For example, many municipal governments make special pickups of trash and such large waste items as discarded furniture at prices well below marginal cost. The difference between the actual price and the marginal cost of the pickup can be regarded as a corrective subsidy designed to avoid accumulation of trash and unauthorized dumping. Some city governments also subsidize property owners who plant trees by the curbs of their property. They might, for example, pay half the price of those trees. This is designed to internalize the positive externality associated with property beautification.

Many citizens believe that positive externalities are associated with college enrollments. Some states provide subsidies to students attending both public and private colleges. Governments often provide services that result in positive externalities free of charge and establish minimum levels of consumption, as is commonly the case for elementary and secondary schooling. However, not all subsidies are designed to internalize positive externalities. Many subsidies are based on other goals, such as alleviating poverty.

CHECKPOINT

1. What are externalities? Use a supply-and-demand analysis to show how a negative or positive externality prevents a perfectly competitive market from achieving efficiency.
2. What does it mean to internalize an externality?
3. Explain how corrective taxes and subsidies can be used to internalize an `externality.

PROPERTY RIGHTS TO RESOURCE USE AND INTERNALIZATION OF EXTERNALITIES: THE COASE THEOREM

Let's look more closely into the causes of externalities. Externalities arise because the property rights of some resource users are not considered in the marketplace by buyers or sellers of products. The willingness of people to engage in market transactions involving property or goods and services depends on both the gains expected from the transactions and the costs involved in acquiring those gains. **Transactions costs** include the time, effort, and cash outlays involved in locating someone to trade with, negotiating terms of trade, drawing contracts, and assuming risks associated with the contracts. Transactions costs depend, in part, on property rights to use resources. Government has the power to change property rights. By doing so, transactions costs will be affected, as will the potential net gains realizable through market exchanges. If a government lowers transactions costs, efficiency will be improved in cases for which new gains from trading outweigh the costs involved in establishing or modifying preexisting property rights.

Governments can and have modified the right of business firms to emit wastes in the air and water and can lower transactions costs involved in trading existing rights to dispose of wastes in the environment. For example, users of a lake or stream could be granted the right to unpolluted water. Suppose an industrial firm can purchase the right to pollute from those who have been granted the right to a pollution-free lake. If the firm's owners can still be better off after purchasing the right to pollute, and users better or at least no worse off than they would otherwise have been, a gain in net benefits is possible. Provided that transactions costs of the exchange do not outweigh the net benefits possible to the parties, exchange of these property rights will help achieve efficiency. By establishing property rights and seeking to lower transactions costs associated with their exchange, governmental authority can increase net benefits to citizens.

The **Coase theorem** states that governments, by merely establishing the rights to use resources, can internalize externalities when transactions costs of bargaining are zero.[5] Once these property rights to resource use are established, the Coase theorem holds that free exchange of established rights for cash payments among the affected parties will achieve efficiency. This result holds irrespective of which of the involved parties is granted the right.

For example, suppose only two competing uses exist for a stream: a convenient place to dump wastes from paper production and a site for recreation. Suppose the transactions costs of trading established rights to use the stream between the paper factory and the recreational users of the stream are zero. Under these circumstances, the Coase theorem maintains that it makes no difference whether the factory is granted the right to pollute the stream or the recreational users are given the right to a pollution-free stream. In either case, an efficient mix of industrial and recreational uses of the stream will emerge from private bargaining between the factory and the recreational users. Corrective taxes or any other charges are not needed, because competition for use of the stream by the interested parties will internalize the externality.

If the factory is granted the right, it will be in its interest to reduce pollution if the recreational users will offer a payment that more than offsets the reduction in profits resulting from reduced polluting. If, instead, the recreational users have the right to a pollution-free stream, they would give up part of this right if the factory can offer them a payment in excess of the losses they incur from increased pollution. By creating the right, the government gives the user who receives it a valuable asset that can be exchanged for a cash payment from the other user. The exchange of those rights will lead to efficient resource use, provided that no third parties are affected by the exchange of the government-created rights.

The transactions costs of bargaining to exchange rights include the costs of locating a trading partner and agreeing on the value of the traded right. In general, these transactions costs tend to be close to zero when the parties involved in trading the right are few in number. Under such circumstances, those who are granted a right are likely to know who (if anyone) is willing to purchase it, and a price can easily be agreed upon to internalize any externality. Those who purchase the rights of others to pollute, for example, know that no other polluters will continue to cause damages after the deal is completed. The kinds of externalities for which the Coase theorem is relevant are called **small-number externalities**. In dealing with externalities of this type, or any externality for that matter, it is useful to divide the parties involved into two groups: emitters and receptors. The distinction is, however, somewhat arbitrary because, as is shown in the following section, the emitter could as well be designated the receptor and the receptor could be

[5]Ronald Coase, "The Problem of Social Cost," *Journal of Law and Economics* 3 (October 1960): 1–44. The examples used in this section are similar to those used by Coase.

considered the emitter. The essential social problem that exists for any externality is the disputed use of a productive resource.

Exchange of Property Rights to Internalize a Negative Externality: An Example Illustrating the Coase Theorem

Suppose a cattle rancher and a wheat farmer operate on two adjoining plots of land. Currently, the border between the two plots is unfenced. Both producers sell their outputs in perfectly competitive markets; therefore, they have no control over the prices they receive for their goods. The cattle occasionally stray into the wheat fields, damaging the crop. As the size of the cattle producer's herd increases, it is inevitable that more steers will stray into the wheat fields and more wheat will be damaged. Thus, an increase in the output of beef is obtainable only with a corresponding decrease in the output of wheat. Only the wheat farmer is harmed by the damage done by the cattle.

Assume the governing authorities grant the wheat producer the right to cattle-free land, requiring that the cattle producer pay the wheat farmer for damages incurred by the cattle. This forces the cattle producer to take into account the external cost, measured in wheat damage, caused by the herd. In effect, the law acts to internalize the externality in such a way as to increase the cattle producer's marginal private cost to the point where it is equal to marginal social cost (the direct cost incurred by the cattle producer plus the value of the damage to the wheat crop).

Figure 3.7A shows how the cattle producer behaves, assuming that his goal is to maximize profits. The current price per pound of beef, P_B, is established in a competitive market. The rancher can sell all the beef produced at that price. The profit-maximizing output of beef is Q_{B1} pounds of beef per year when the rancher is *not* liable for damages to the farmer. This is the output corresponding to the point at which the marginal private cost of beef equals the price per pound: $P_B = MPC$. At that output, the marginal social cost of beef produced on this ranch would exceed the price of beef by the marginal external cost to the wheat producer. For any given level of beef output, the marginal external cost to the wheat farmer is the loss in wheat output, Q_W, multiplied by the market price of wheat, P_W:

$$MEC = P_W Q_W \tag{3.7}$$

Therefore, the cost of any given amount of physical damage to the wheat crop will become higher as the price of wheat goes higher.

In Figure 3.7A, the marginal social cost of beef is $MPC_B + MEC$. When liable for damage, the rancher must consider MEC as part of his marginal costs. He produces the output Q_B^* per year, corresponding to the point where $P_B = MSC$, when the wheat farmer has the right to cattle-free land. The annual output Q_B^* is the efficient output because P_B also equals the marginal social benefit of beef in a competitive market.

If the maximum revenues that the rancher can earn when producing the efficient output, Q_B^*, per year fall short of the opportunity costs of production, the rancher will go out of business. The land adjacent to the wheat farm then will be converted to some other use. If the rancher can increase profits by building a fence to eliminate the straying, the fence will go up. Building the fence increases average costs of production but does not affect marginal costs, because the amount of fencing does not vary with the size of the herd. After building the fence, the rancher will produce output, Q_{B1}, per year because MEC will be zero at any level of output after the fence is constructed.

FIGURE 3.7   The Coase Theorem

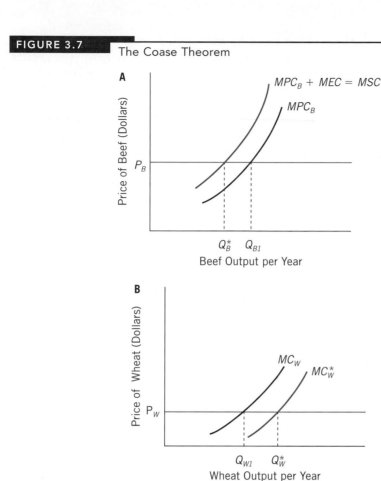

The graph A in shows the marginal cost of producing beef and the price of beef, while that in B indicates marginal cost and price for a neighboring wheat farmer. The Coase theorem holds that the efficient output of beef, Q_B^*, and the efficient output of wheat, Q_W^*, will be produced on the adjacent lands, irrespective of who is liable for damages the cattle cause to the wheat crop each year.

Finally, the rancher looks at the option of purchasing the wheat farmer's land. If the annual payment necessary to buy the land allows greater annual profits than available by producing output, Q_B^*, and paying damages or building a fence, the rancher will choose that option. Buying the land eliminates the liability for damage and, in effect, results in the purchase of the right to cattle-free land from the farmer. Once again, this has no effect on marginal cost of beef and allows the rancher to produce output Q_{B1} without payment of damages. The rancher chooses the alternative that allows the greatest profit.

An Alternative Property Right Assignment

Suppose the cattle rancher is *not* liable for damages. This means that the right to use unfenced land for grazing is granted to the rancher. How much will the wheat farmer be willing to pay to buy back any portion of the rancher's right of unlimited grazing? Such payments will act to reduce the size of the rancher's herd.

Figure 3.7B shows the problem faced by the wheat farmer. The marginal cost of producing wheat depends on the size of the neighboring cattle herd. The greater the size of the herd, the greater the marginal cost of producing any given quantity of wheat on the adjoining wheat farm. When the rancher produces Q_{B1} pounds of beef to maximize profits, the marginal costs of beef production are MC_W, as shown in Figure 3.7B. Under those circumstances, the farmer produces the output Q_{W1}, corresponding to the point at which the price of wheat, P_W, equals MC_W. A decrease in the output of the rancher to the efficient annual output, Q_B^*, will *reduce* the marginal costs of wheat, because it will take less seed, labor, and other variable inputs to harvest a given amount of wheat. If the rancher could be induced to cut back output to the efficient level, the marginal cost curve of producing wheat would shift downward to MC_W^*.

The rancher will accept a payment to reduce annual output of beef if it allows an increase in profits. The farmer is no worse off by making an annual payment up to the marginal external cost that would be caused by a given amount of annual beef output.

The maximum amount of money the farmer would pay for each unit reduction in beef output by the rancher is equal to the marginal external cost of beef. Making such a payment will increase wheat revenues per year by an amount exactly equal to *MEC*. In effect, this internalizes the externality. The payment that the farmer would be willing to make to prevent each increase in beef output becomes, in effect, part of the rancher's marginal costs. This is because the rancher forgoes receipt of this payment each time output is increased. The wheat damage is part of the opportunity cost of beef! The rancher now maximizes profits by setting $MPC_B + MEC = P_B$, where *MEC* is now the maximum payment per pound of beef received from the farmer. The rancher reduces the size of his herd to the efficient amount Q_B^*. This is the same annual output that would prevail if the rancher were liable for damages! When the rancher produces the efficient annual output of beef, the farmer's marginal costs are lower. The farmer will produce Q_B^*, corresponding to the point at which $MC_W^* = P_W$.

The mix of output produced on the adjoining lands will be exactly the same, independent of which party is liable for the damages. In this case, the farmer must make annual payments to the rancher, independent of the amount of wheat produced, to compensate the rancher for the reduction in the size of the herd. Therefore, the farmer's profits will be lower and the rancher's profits will be higher than was the case when the farmer had the right to claim damages from the rancher.

As was the case when the rancher was liable for damages incurred by his cattle, the wheat farmer can be expected to choose the option that will give maximum possible profits. The farmer will compare the alternative of annual payments to the rancher to reduce output or to build a fence with that of buying the rancher's land outright. The farmer will also consider the option of going out of business and then will choose the option that maximizes profits.

Significance of the Coase Theorem

The remarkable conclusion of the Coase theorem is that the efficient mix of output will result simply as a consequence of the establishment of exchangeable property rights. It makes no difference which party is assigned the right to use a resource. Provided the transactions costs of exchanging the right are zero, the efficient mix of outputs among competing uses of the resource (in this case, land) will emerge.

However, governments assigning property rights provide a valuable resource to those who get the rights. Although it makes no difference for resource allocation who gets the rights, it makes a big difference to the parties involved in terms of their incomes! Clearly, a corporation is better off if it is granted the right to pollute. Under those circumstances, those who want cleaner air will have lower incomes because they will have to pay to get the corporation to reduce pollution. On the other hand, the corporation would be worse off if environmentalists and citizens at large were granted the right to pollution-free air. Under those circumstances, the corporation would have to pay for the right to pollute and its annual income would be lower. *The users who are initially granted the right are better off, because then they own a valuable property right that can either be used or be exchanged. Therefore, the assignment of the property right by the government affects the distribution of income between the two parties using the resource.*

The Coase theorem also points out that negative externalities are really disputes concerning the rights to use certain resources. The parties involved have conflicting claims on the use of certain resources for their own benefit. However, the use of the disputed resource for one purpose diminishes its usefulness for the other purpose. This emphasizes that the externality is a reciprocal relationship between the parties involved, with no need to label good guys or bad guys. The efficient solution, involving a trade-off between the social value of competing resource uses, strikes a balance between the net social value of both uses.

To make this point still stronger, consider the plight of the American farmer. In recent years, significant concern has arisen about the problem of agricultural runoff. Increased use of chemicals by farmers, as well as new methods of raising livestock in confined spaces, have resulted in external costs, because these chemical and organic wastes washed away by rains can cause offensive odors and illness stemming from contamination of drinking water. Fifty years ago, most farms were located in low-density, rural areas. Damages done by runoff would be borne by the farmers themselves. These costs would have automatically been considered in agricultural decisions, and no externality could be said to have existed. As urbanization increased, more homes were built on the periphery of urban areas, and, in many cases, land use in previously all-rural and all-agricultural areas became mixed with such nonagricultural uses as housing. Agricultural runoff now had the effect of decreasing the usefulness of the area for housing purposes because of the potential contamination of wells and the discomfort caused by offensive odors.

The introduction of a competing use of land in an all-agricultural area had the effect of externalizing an internal cost. As the number of homes built in the zone increases, the number of inhabitants with no direct interest in agriculture, as well as the external cost of any given amount of agricultural runoff, also increases. Establishing the rights of the parties involved in this case is no easy matter. The farmers might argue that they have disposed of waste through runoff for years and that the individuals who purchased homes in the area should have considered these costs before deciding to locate their residences in the vicinity of their farms. The homeowners, on the other hand, could argue that they have a right to safe drinking water and sweet-smelling country air and that the farmers cannot infringe upon those rights.

If the liability for damages were assigned exclusively to farmers, and if they were required to compensate homeowners for damages, little incentive would remain for developers to refrain from constructing homes in the area. New residents could expect to bear some costs of agricultural runoff if they chose to locate in the area, but they would receive full compensation for these costs. Damages paid by farmers would rise continually with increases in nonagricultural population, and if population continually increased, farmers eventually would be induced to sell their farms for nonagricultural use. This result is contingent on full payment of compensation to homeowners. If, however, the homeowners were forced to bear some or all of the costs of cleaning up the agricultural runoff, the process would be much slower. The issue of compensation for damages remains controversial in view of its influence on the dynamics of social change. This example illustrates again how competing for the right to use certain resources (in this case, land) for alternative uses (in this case, runoff versus housing) results in an externality.[6]

There are difficulties involved in applying the principles of the Coase theorem in practice. For example, consider the problem of urban flooding in the United States. A chief cause of flooding is inadequate consideration of the costs of land development. As an urban area grows, more land is built up and covered with concrete for homes, roads, and businesses. This diminishes the capacity of the land to naturally absorb rainfall and increases runoff of rainfall into streams and estuaries. During heavy rainfall streams and rivers swell and often overflow their banks, causing flooding in low-lying areas. Existing residents and business owners in an area often complain about unlimited land development and demand that "impact" fees be charged to developers to both discourage further building in the area and to help finance flood control projects (including dams and levies). They also seek to limit development in flood prone, low-lying areas.

Here the resource in question is land and its alternative uses. Existing residents want the right to a flood-free environment, while developers and residents who would like to move to the area want the right to build their homes and businesses where land is available. If existing residents are given the right to halt further development of land in the area, they can prevent further economic growth and limit new building unless they are fully compensated for the increased risks of flood damage. To efficiently enforce a Coasian scheme the link between flooding and land development would first have to be established. Scientific studies would have to be done to determine how much increased risk of flooding and damages from flood was associated with each additional acre of land development in the community and how much was due to natural processes unrelated to land development. Further, if many existing residents are subject to this risk they would have to be organized and bargain collectively as a single unit to determine the total compensation that would be acceptable for each additional acre of land development. If this was not the case and individual residents bargained separately with developers, then any one resident could hold out for high payments after additional residents agreed to accept compensation. This could prevent any additional land development or result in less than the efficient amount of land development.

Similarly, if many developers were involved and the developers had unlimited rights to develop land, then each developer would forgo a payment not to develop additional land. Some residents might avoid making payments to prevent land development if they felt that enough of their neighbors would make those payments. If sufficient numbers of existing residents tried to get a "free ride" on the payments of their neighbors or refused to pay at all to stop development, then

---

[6]The type of externality described here is often referred to as "undepletable." An undepletable externality is one for which the external costs borne by existing receptors are not affected by the number of receptors. In this case, no matter how many houses are built, the costs borne by each homeowner are not decreased as more homes are built. Depletable externalities are those that additional receptors decrease the costs borne by the existing receptors.

there likely would be more than the efficient amount of land development in the region given the risk of flooding associated with that development.

Finally, the transactions costs of negotiating an agreement could be quite high when there are many existing residents and developers involved. The parties involved might also play strategies to minimize the costs of achieving their desired outcomes. Given the uncertainties of the costs involved and actual risks associated with development of each acre of land, there would be ample opportunity for bargaining and threats that could make achievement of agreement on pricing the right to develop each acre of land (or the right to prevent each acre of land from being developed) difficult. This often leads to political action to establish government-imposed impact fees or regulations that limit development.

Many issues such as these discussed earlier will affect redevelopment issues for New Orleans in its recovery from the catastrophic floods of 2005 resulting from Hurricane Katrina. Given the fact that much of New Orleans is below sea level and the difficulty in protecting the city through rebuilding destroyed or compromised levies, limits on redevelopment of land in low-lying areas may be the efficient way of reducing the risks of future flooding. Low-lying areas would be converted to marshland that would serve as a natural sink to absorb rainwater and prevent flooding. It is unlikely that private bargaining in a Coase-like environment will help resolve the issues regarding the trade-off between land development and the return of displaced residents and future protection against the risk of flooding.

Applying the Coase Theorem: Pollution Rights

One possible market-based solution to the problem of controlling pollution is the establishment of transferable permits to pollute.[7] **Pollution rights** are transferable permits to emit a certain amount of particular wastes into the atmosphere or water per year. Regulatory authorities would issue a certain amount of these rights and monitor firms to make sure that only those with permits emitted the wastes. The permits would be offered for sale in a market. Firms that purchased the pollution rights then would be free to sell them to other firms if they wished. An advantage of permits over emissions charges or corrective taxes is that the regulatory authorities could strictly control the amount of emissions by issuing a fixed number of permits.

Suppose, for example, in the absence of any regulations or charges, the current amount of annual emissions of a certain type of air pollutant is estimated to be 100,000 tons. As illustrated in Figure 3.8, this is the amount that firms emit at zero price for emissions. The demand curve, D, represents the marginal social benefit of emitting wastes to business firms. The current level of emissions corresponds to the point at which the demand curve intersects the horizontal axis.

If regulatory authorities wish to reduce emissions to 75,000 tons per year, they would issue 75,000 pollution rights, requiring that one right be purchased for the privilege of emitting 1 ton of waste per year. This might or might not be the efficient level of emissions. To determine the actual efficient level, authorities would have to estimate the marginal social costs of emissions and compare them with the marginal social benefits.

A pollution control board would auction off the rights to those firms that desire to emit wastes. The market price would correspond to the intersection of the fixed

---

[7]This scheme was first proposed by J. H. Dales. See John H. Dales, *Pollution, Property, and Prices.* Toronto: University of Toronto Press, 1970.

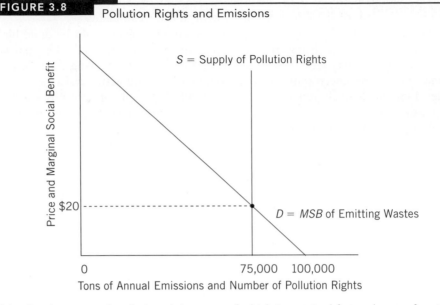

FIGURE 3.8   Pollution Rights and Emissions

If the fixed amount of pollution rights, one of which is required for each ton of emissions, is issued, the price of rights will be determined by the demand, which reflects the marginal social benefit of emitting wastes. In this case, competition for the 75,000 pollution rights issued results in a price of $20 per right.

supply curve, S, and the demand curve, D, in Figure 3.8. Assuming that the scheme could be easily enforced, each polluter would have to buy one right per ton of waste emitted per year. As shown in Figure 3.8, the resulting price is $20 per pollution right. At that price, some firms find it cheaper to change their production methods, reduce output, or go out of business rather than purchase the rights. The result is an immediate reduction in emissions from 100,000 tons per year to 75,000 tons per year.

Changes in market conditions would change the price of pollution rights. For example, if the marginal social benefit of emissions were to increase, the demand for pollution rights would also increase. Provided that the supply of permits remained fixed, their price would increase. The regulatory authority could periodically increase the number of permits available. It could also purchase some of the permits of existing firms and remove them from circulation. This would affect the supply and thereby change the price. By controlling the number of rights in circulation, the authorities can strictly regulate the amount of pollution. Firms have the choice of paying the price to pollute or taking measures to reduce emissions. Pollution rights are used today in the United States to control sulfur dioxide emissions.

Efficient Pollution Abatement Levels

How much pollution control is enough? Figure 3.9 illustrates the marginal social benefit and marginal social cost of pollution abatement. The marginal social cost of pollution abatement is likely to increase with increased abatement. Each successive 1 percent reduction in wastes emitted per year is likely to be more costly to

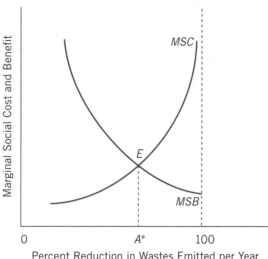

FIGURE 3.9 The Efficient Amount of Pollution Abatement

The efficient amount of abatement corresponds to the point at which the marginal social cost of additional reduction in wastes emitted just equals the marginal social benefit of that reduction. This corresponds A^* to percent of abatement per year.

achieve than the previously abated 1 percent. At the extreme, once abatement levels of more than 95 percent are achieved, additional levels of improved environmental quality might be difficult, if not impossible, to achieve with given technology for recycling, cleaning, or collecting waste products before they are disposed of in the environment.

Similarly, the marginal social benefit of increased pollution abatement is likely to decline as more pollution is abated. The efficient level of pollution abatement will occur at point E. This is the point at which the marginal social cost of pollution abatement equals its marginal social benefit. The efficient amount of abatement is an A^* percent reduction in wastes emitted per year.

An ideal pollution abatement policy therefore is one that balances the forgone output that results from increased cost of pollution abatement with the added benefit of improved environmental quality. Failure to consider the opportunity cost of a cleaner environment can result in a cure more painful than the disease.

CHECKPOINT

1. What is the Coase theorem? How is it significant to the understanding of social conflicts caused by externalities?
2. How can the sale of pollution rights reduce emissions by polluters and make them pay for the use of environmental resources?
3. Explain why the efficient level of pollution abatement is unlikely to be 100 percent.

ENVIRONMENTAL PROTECTION POLICIES IN THE UNITED STATES

In practice, the primary method of treating the problem of pollution in the United States is government regulation. Market-based corrective taxes or other pollution rights schemes that charge firms for the damages done by their emissions are the exception rather than the rule in U.S. environmental protection policies. However, in recent years more market-based policies that allow trading of pollution rights have been initiated. Let's look at how government actually intervenes in the marketplace to deal with environmental pollution in the United States and compare the effects of regulation with those we might expect if emissions were reduced by corrective taxes or the issuance of a limited number of tradable pollution rights.

Emissions Standards versus Corrective Taxes

The typical method used to control the external costs of pollution is the establishment of standards that limit the amount of pollutants that can be emitted into the air or water. For example, the 1970 Amendments to the Clean Air Act established stringent limits on automobile emissions per vehicle. Maximum levels of emissions of hydrocarbons, nitrogen oxides, and carbon monoxide per vehicle were specified. These limits led to the adoption of catalytic converters on vehicles, serving to increase the price of automobiles in this country. The emissions standards specify the maximum amount of grams per mile that can be emitted while driving.

Emissions standards differ from corrective taxes in that they *do not charge for emissions damages if the amounts emitted are less than legally established standards.* In effect, those who emit pollutants in amounts less than the standards can do so for free! Emissions levels that exceed the standards are strictly outlawed. When the marginal social benefit or cost of emissions varies among firms or locations, rigid emissions standards do not achieve an efficient outcome.

Figure 3.10 shows the marginal social benefit and marginal social cost of emission of a certain pollutant into the air by two firms, A and B. The marginal social benefit of the emissions reflects the maximum amount that a firm will pay for the right to emit those wastes. If no emissions charges currently exist at all, firms emit wastes up to the point at which the marginal social benefit is zero. Thus, firm A emits Q_{A1} tons of waste per year, while firm B emits Q_{B1} tons of waste per year.

This would be efficient only if the marginal external cost associated with emissions were zero.

In Figure 3.10, we assume that the marginal external cost associated with each ton of emissions per year is $10 for each firm. This is also the marginal social cost of emissions. The efficient level of annual emissions is Q_A^* for firm A and Q_B^* for firm B. This is the amount of emissions that would be observed per year if each firm were charged a fee of $10 per ton of emissions for the right to emit wastes. Notice that $Q_A^* > Q_B^*$ because the marginal social benefit of emissions is greater for any given quantity for firm A than it is for firm B. The marginal social benefit of emissions can vary from firm to firm or from region to region because of differences in the cost of reducing emissions or differences in the prices of output produced with inputs that pollute.

Now suppose that government emissions standards allow each firm to emit up to Q_R tons per year at no charge. Emission of more than Q_R tons per year is then

FIGURE 3.10   Regulating Emissions: Losses in Efficiency from Differences in the Marginal Social Benefit of Emissions

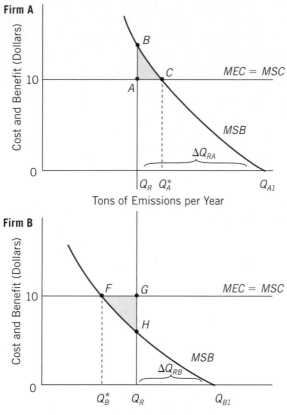

When the marginal social benefits of emissions differ among firms, uniform emissions regulations at Q_R result in less than the efficient level of emissions for firms such as A and more than the efficient amount of emissions for firms such as B.

© Cengage Learning

strictly prohibited. Accordingly, firm A is forced to cut back wastes from Q_{A1} to Q_R tons per year. Similarly, the regulations force firm B to cut back emissions from Q_{B1} tons to Q_R tons per year.

These standards do not achieve efficiency. They result in *less* than the efficient level of annual emissions for firm A. At Q_R, the marginal social benefit of emissions exceeds their marginal social cost for A. If, instead, this firm were charged $10, the marginal social cost of the damages per ton of emissions, it would choose to emit $Q_A^* > Q_R$ tons of waste per year. The extra net gain in well-being made possible by using an emissions charge is represented by the triangular area ABC in Figure 3.10.

Standards set at Q_R result in more than the efficient amount of emissions from firm B. The efficient amount of emissions corresponds to $Q_B^* > Q_R$. This is the amount that firm B would choose to emit per year if it were charged according to the marginal external cost of $10. The extra net gain possible by using the $10 emissions charge is represented by the area FGH.

From another perspective, uniform standards result in a greater *reduction* in emissions than is efficient for firm A. **Pollution abatement** is the reduction in pollution that results from reduced emissions. As shown in Figure 3.10, under uniform standards of emissions, firm A reduces emissions by ΔQ_{RA} tons per year. This results in *more* than the efficient amount of pollution abatement. Similarly, reduction in emissions of ΔQ_{RB} by firm B is *less* than the efficient amount of abatement by this firm.

Similarly, uniform regulations would not achieve efficiency if the marginal external cost of emissions varied by region in a nation. Suppose the marginal external cost per ton of emissions were $20 in urban areas but only $5 in rural areas. These represent the marginal social costs of emitting wastes in the two regions. Assume as well that the marginal social benefit of any given quantity of a certain type of pollutant that is emitted is the same for all firms, irrespective of their location. Figure 3.11 shows that the efficient amount of emissions for firm C, located in

---

FIGURE 3.11   Losses in Efficiency from Emissions Standards When MEC Differs among Regions

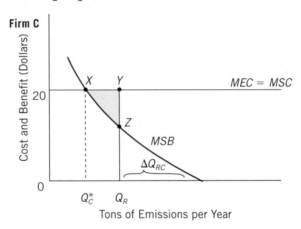

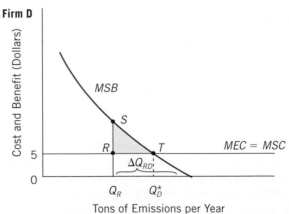

The marginal social cost of a ton of emissions is greater for firm C, located in an urban area, than for firm D, located in a rural area. A uniform standard of emissions of tons per year results in more than the efficient amount of emissions from firm C and less than the efficient amount from firm D.

an urban area, is Q_C^*. This is the amount for which *MSB* of emissions = $20. The efficient amount of emissions for firm D, located in a rural area, is Q_D^*. This is the level at which *MSB* of emissions = $5. If all firms, irrespective of their location, are subject to the same emissions standard of Q_R tons, the efficient level of emissions will not be achieved. The standard would allow all firms to emit Q_R tons of emissions per year at zero cost and prohibit more than this amount. This results in *more* than the efficient amount of emissions by the firm in the urban area because $Q_R > Q_C^*$. On the other hand, *less* than the efficient amount of emissions is allowed in the urban area because $Q_R > Q_D^*$.

The efficient amount of emissions could be attained by an emissions charge of $20 per ton in the urban area and $5 per ton in the rural area. The loss in net benefits when uniform emissions standards, and not charges, are used is the sum of the areas *XYZ* for firm C, and *RST* for firm D. The amount of pollution abatement for the urban firm is ΔQ_{RC}. This is *less* than the efficient amount of abatement for that firm. On the other hand, *more* than the efficient amount of abatement occurs under uniform emissions standards for firms in the rural area, where ΔQ_{RD} tons of emissions are abated.

Uniform standards for controlling emissions that result in negative externalities therefore are unlikely to achieve efficiency. Use of a standards approach to controlling negative externalities, such as pollution, will have to be flexible to achieve an efficient outcome. This can be accomplished by adjusting for differences in the marginal social benefit and marginal external cost of pollution among firms and regions.

Command-and-Control Policies and Environmental Quality

The standards approach has given the federal government both the power and the responsibility of regulating the emissions of every polluter in the nation. Such direct controls often result in the Environmental Protection Agency (EPA) specifying rigid standards and techniques for coping with emissions, without duly considering the special conditions and difficulties encountered by certain industries in meeting those standards. **Command-and-control regulation** is a system of rules established by government authorities that requires all emitters to meet strict emissions standards for sources of pollution and requires the use of specific pollution control devices. In other words, under this system, the government not only tells emitters how much they can emit, but it also tells them which technology they must employ to reduce emissions.

Rigid command-and-control regulation discourages private innovation in pollution control and entails an administrative burden that cannot possibly be carried out effectively, given the enormous amount of information required to specify the "best" way of treating the variety of environmental pollutants already in existence. Standards imposed by the EPA have experienced considerable delays in implementation due to court challenges by private business interests. The costs of complying with the new regulations and standards often run into the hundreds of billions of dollars, and it is not surprising that various political forces have developed to oppose the standards, both through the courts and through standard political channels.

It is also naive to assume that regulations, merely because they exist, can be enforced. It is costly to police emissions standards, and the standards are often exceeded by businesses that know that the EPA cannot monitor emissions of all polluters in the nation. When a business is caught exceeding the standards, it often denies any wrongdoing and, more often than not, it is difficult to prove in court that the standards were violated. In many cases, even when a polluter is found guilty in court, the fines paid are low.

MARKETS FOR POLLUTION RIGHTS IN PRACTICE: SULFUR DIOXIDE ALLOWANCES, AND CAPPING AND TRADING THE RIGHT TO EMIT

In July 1991, the nation's largest commodity market, the Chicago Board of Trade, voted to create a market for the rights to emit sulfur dioxide. This historic decision was made possible by provisions of the Clean Air Act of 1990, empowering the EPA to issue marketable rights to emit sulfur dioxides to electric power–generating companies. The pollution rights provide these firms with a new way of complying with emissions reductions of this compound, which is a major cause of acid rain.

By a stroke of the pen, Congress established the property rights necessary to create a market. The tradable emissions permits under the program to control pollution from sulfur dioxide are called "allowances" and are part of a long-term environmental program to clean up the air in the United States. Begun in 1995, the program's goal was to reduce acid rain by cutting sulfur dioxide emissions from electric power–generating plants to half the level that prevailed in 1980—a 10-million ton reduction. Owners of power–generating plants were given a fixed number of allowances each year based on historic patterns of emissions and fuel use. The allowance is a tradable emissions right that entitles its holder to emit one ton of sulfur dioxide per year. Each year the EPA auctions off a small number of additional allowances and the revenues from these sales are rebated to existing permit holders in proportion to their initial allowance allocations.

New power–generating plants must buy allowances to emit pollutants from existing owners of the permits or from the annual EPA auctions. Power–generating plants that do not have sufficient allowances to cover each year's emissions are subject to severe financial penalties ($2,000 per ton of emissions). The EPA continually monitors emissions from all plants. If a plant emits more than its allowances, it must pay the fine per ton and also must reduce emissions the following year by the amount exceeded in the current year. Plant owners can choose to continue to emit as allowed by the allowances they hold or reduce emissions and sell their allowances to others. They can also hold onto unused allowances for future use or sale. Emissions can be reduced by switching to cleaner burning fuels with less sulfur or by scrubbing techniques that reduce the sulfur dioxide levels from burning of high sulfur fuels (mainly coal). To install a scrubbing technology, the typical power plant would incur capital costs in the range of $125 million.

The program has been effective in reducing emissions. Emissions dropped sharply in 1995 from more than 8 million tons to 5.3 million tons. This amount was below the amount allowed under the new program and many power–generating companies "banked" their allowances for future use or sale. The reason for the sharp drop was that in anticipation of the program in 1992, after allowance allocations were announced and based on early estimates of the expected price of the permits, many companies chose to install scrubbers or shift to other fuels. This shift decreased demand for the allowances after they were required in 1995 and their market price turned out to be lower than initially anticipated. The market price of the sulfur dioxide allowances in 1995 ended up at $100 per ton—less than anticipated and much less than the amount incurred by the companies per ton to install scrubbers. Emissions abatement through installation of scrubbers cost the power companies an average of about $210 per ton of sulfur dioxide abatement per year—more than the 1995 market price of allowances but less than the $300 to $400 per ton that the power companies expected the allowances to cost.[8] Anticipation of the program resulted in more pollution abatement than expected! Once a scrubber is built, its marginal cost is only $65 per ton of sulfur dioxide abated, and since this was less than the $100 per ton cost of the permits, the plants continued to use their scrubbers even though the price of the allowances were lower than anticipated.

Power–generating firms will now be under pressure by their stockholders to compare the cost of continuing to emit sulfur dioxide with the price they can get for their pollution rights. The higher the market price of the pollution rights, the greater the incentive to reduce emissions. In this way, the cost of polluting becomes a factor in the profit calculation of the power companies.

The trading of the pollution rights is likely to allow electric power companies to meet the new emissions reductions requirements at lower costs than would otherwise be possible. For example, suppose the market price of a pollution right to emit a ton of sulfur dioxide is $150. If a firm can recycle or remove that ton of wastes from its smokestack for only $75, it can add $75 to its annual profits by reducing the emissions and selling one pollution right for $150 on the market. Power companies can also reduce their emissions by shifting to low-sulfur coal. The only plants that would want pollution rights would be those for which the cost of cleaning up one ton of emissions would be greater than the $150 market price of the right. Naturally, the price of the pollution right will vary with the value of emitting wastes. As new technologies for reducing emissions develop, the price of the pollution rights could fall. Increases in the demand for electricity would be likely to increase the price of the pollution rights.

The new scheme also encourages electric power companies to develop new technology for reducing emissions. By doing so, they can add to their profits by selling their pollution rights! This new market-based approach to emissions reduction is a great improvement over the old command-and-control approach that required all firms to reduce their emissions by the same percentage and often dictated the technology they must use to achieve that result.

In 1996 the cost of abatement under the program was estimated at $1 billion less than the amount that would have prevailed to achieve the same emission reductions under older command-and-control programs.[9] Because emissions reductions have been greater than anticipated, electric power companies banked (for future use) allowances for 6 million tons of annual emissions. More than 4 million allowances were traded in 1996, and trading volume has continually increased as power companies seek to maximize profits while reducing emissions and considering the market value of their allowances both today and tomorrow (providing incentives to save allowances for future use). The program therefore is successful in putting a

---

[8]See Richard Schmalensee, Paul L. Joskow, A. Denny Ellerman, Juan Pablo Montero, and Elizabeth M. Bailey, "Interim Evaluation of Sulfur Dioxide Emissions Trading," *Journal of Economic Perspectives*, 12, 3 (Summer 1998): 53–68.

[9]See Robert N. Stavins, "What Can We Learn from the Grand Policy Experiment? Lessons for SO2 Allowance Trading," *Journal of Economic Perspectives*, 12, 3 (Summer 1998): 69–88.

cap on emissions that cause acid rain while giving participants incentives to achieve their reductions in an economically efficient way. For example, rather than requiring all power companies to use the same technology to reduce emissions, as would have been the case under command-and-control, Midwestern companies took advantage of low rail rates to reduce their emissions by buying low-sulfur coal from Wyoming and Montana rather than installing scrubbers.

The success of the allowance trading program shows how economic theory can be put to practical use by solving pollution problems (acid rain in this case) while economizing on resources. The program, in effect, puts a cap on emissions at a certain level per year and allows holders of the rights to emit to trade those rights in a market. In general, government approaches to control emissions in ways that provide economic incentives to trade rights so as to lower the costs of reducing emissions are referred to as "cap-and-trade" policies. A cap-and-trade program is also used in the United States to control nitrogen oxide emissions. In the European Union (EU), cap-and-trade programs are used to control greenhouse gasses. Recently, proposals have been made to use this method of emissions control to put a cap on carbon emissions in the United States by issuing tradable rights to emit various carbon compounds.

In effect, cap-and-trade programs can have effects on incentives similar to those of corrective taxes. Whereas a corrective tax is used to internalize externalities by "pricing" marginal external costs, cap-and-trade policies "cap" the quantity of emissions below existing levels and then issue the rights to emit. As competition among emitters for the rights to emit occurs in the market for the emission rights, a price for the emission rights is established. That price helps internalize the externality at minimum cost by forcing emitters to compare the price of the right to emit with the cost of various alternatives for reducing emissions. Compared to command-and control-emissions reduction programs cap-and-trade programs allow a given reduction emissions to be achieved at lower opportunity cost by providing incentives for emitters to trade rights and choose minimum cost alternatives for meeting the cap.

Figure 3.12 shows variation in the price of sulfur dioxide allowances from March 1994 through March 2008. Notice how the price of allowances was fairly stable in a range of $200 per allowance between 1994 and 2004. During the same period, there was considerable variability in the volume of rights transferred in the market for the sulfur dioxide allowances. From 2004 to 2006, the price of allowances soared from $200 to nearly $1,600. The reason for the spike in prices is explained in part by a sharp increase in the price of low sulfur coal over the same period. Use of low sulfur coal by power plants was a major method used to reduce emissions and therefore the need to hold or buy emissions allowances. As the price of low sulfur coal increased, many power companies found it more economical to shift to high sulfur coal and the pay for the right to emit. As this increased the demand for allowances, their prices increased. Another factor causing the price of allowances to increase had to do with the fact that the cap on emissions was lowered beginning in the year 2000 and many power companies who in the past had been "banking" allowances for future use now had to buy new allowances as they started using the ones that they had been holding in reserve. Also the demand for allowances increased as companies started to try to buy more in anticipation of possible future decreases in the cap on emissions. After the price increased trading volume stabilized within a narrow range of about 1 million transfers per year. At a price of $1,600 per allowance, many companies were considering installing scrubbers.

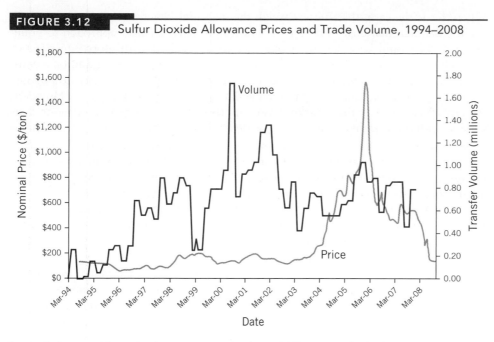

FIGURE 3.12   Sulfur Dioxide Allowance Prices and Trade Volume, 1994–2008

Source: Environmental Protection Agency, www.epa.gov/captrade/allowance-trading.html

Also notice how the price of plummeted after 2006 back to a level of $200. Some of this decline in price was due to plans to install scrubbers. However, a dramatic event in 2008 called the cap-and-trade programs administered by the EPA into question. A court ruling based on challenges to the legality of the EPA's "Clean Air Interstate Rule" resulted in suspension of the program. The price of allowances promptly fell dramatically to a level below $100. However, later in 2008 an appeals court reinstated to Clean Air Interstate Rule and once again allowed the cap-and-trade acid rain program to function until the legal issue could be resolved in a way that would allow the program to achieve its goals of reduction in harmful emissions by further reducing the cap applied.

Because of the legal challenges to expansion of the cap-and-trade program, the EPA imposed tougher limits on the emissions of sulfur dioxide in 2010 and decided to rely less on allowances to limit such emissions. As a result, the price of allowances in the acid rain program plunged to nearly zero in that year.

However, in September of 2011 the EPA established a replacement program for sulfur dioxide and nitrogen dioxide allowance trading. The first brokered trade was executed at that time with vintage 2012 sulfur dioxide allowance selling at $2,600 a ton.

More on Market-Based Approaches to Pollution Control: How Trading Pollution Rights Can Reduce the Cost of Environmental Protection

We have discussed two market-based approaches to dealing with negative externalities: corrective taxes and pollution rights. Both of these approaches are similar in that they offer firms an opportunity to pay for the damages done by their emissions.

When this is the case, the emitters weigh the marginal benefit of continuing to emit against the marginal cost of doing so, which in a market-based approach to pollution control would be either the corrective tax associated with more emissions or the pollution rights (or emissions permits) they must buy to pay for additional emissions. Many environmentalists oppose the idea of giving firms a "license to pollute" by offering them the option to pay for the damage their emissions cause. However, the remarkable fact is that market-based approaches like corrective taxes or marketable pollution rights can lower the cost of a given amount of emissions reduction.

Both tradable pollution rights and corrective taxes provide incentives to reduce pollution at the minimum possible cost. However, corrective taxes generate revenue for the government that can be used for other purposes or to compensate victims of the efficient level of pollution. Tradable pollution rights result in the creation of a valuable asset for those who can clean up pollution at a cost per unit less than the price of a pollution right. Tradable pollution rights provide incentives to clean up pollution by adding to the profits of some firms.

Rigid standards, such as those established by the EPA for ambient air quality, could constrain economic growth substantially for certain regions. Suppose a city exceeds the standard for a certain pollutant. A new firm that emits even small amounts of such pollutants into the air wants to locate in the city. Under rigid standards, the firm would not be allowed to do so. As a result, employment opportunities and economic growth in the city would be curtailed.

Concerns about the difficulties of meeting standards, and the social costs of doing so, have led to innovations in EPA policies, which have moved in the direction of the pollution rights scheme. The EPA now uses an "emissions offset policy" in most regions of the United States. Under this policy, new firms can enter an area in which standards are already met or exceeded, provided that they pay other firms to reduce their pollutants in an amount equal to or greater than that to be generated by the new firms. For example, suppose a new factory will discharge 500 pounds of sulfur dioxide per day in an area that already exceeds EPA ambient air standards. Without an offset, the firm would be unable to obtain a permit for operation from state authorities. If, however, the owners of the factory persuaded or paid other polluters to reduce pollution by 500 pounds of sulfur dioxide per day, they would obtain the necessary offset for approval of the permit. For example, the EPA allowed construction of a new General Motors plant in Oklahoma City after the local chamber of commerce arranged for a reduction in hydrocarbon emissions from oil companies in the area. The offset policy is similar to the pollution right policy in that it allows firms to "purchase" the right to emit wastes by paying other firms to reduce emissions.

Another scheme used by the EPA is the "bubble." Under this approach, an imaginary bubble is placed over the firm. Subject to an overall emissions limit, the firm is allowed to exceed emissions standards for one type of pollutant if it compensates for this by reducing emissions by more than the required standard for another pollutant. This is another approach designed to add flexibility to rigid standards and to decrease the costs of attaining a given level of environmental quality.

Finally, the EPA has allowed "banking" of emissions reductions in excess of current standards. Firms that exceed current standards are given credits that will allow them to fall short of the standards at some point in the future. The firm is even allowed to sell these credits to other firms that wish to exceed current standards. This is another move in the direction of a system of transferable pollution permits.

Let's examine how a trading approach can make it cheaper to obtain a given amount of emissions reduction. Suppose a new regulation requires all firms in your city to cut emissions of particulates, such as smoke, by one ton a day. An electric power–generating plant in the region finds that the marginal cost of meeting the new standards will be $1,000 per day. A steel manufacturer in the region finds that it can meet the new standard at a daily cost of only $100. Under the command-and-control regulation, the marginal social cost of the two tons of particulate emissions reduction will be $1,100 per day. If, instead, the same two-ton daily reduction emissions were obtained by allowing the power plant to continue to emit wastes while requiring the steel manufacturer to reduce emissions by two tons, the marginal social cost of obtaining the given reduction in emissions would be only $200 per day—a daily savings of $900!

It would, however, be wishful thinking to expect regulators to be able to assign the cleanup to the least-cost sources—it would require more information than a central agency could expect to have. No one knows the costs of reducing emissions better than the emitters themselves, and they cannot be expected to volunteer that information to the government if they know they are going to be ordered to increase the amount of their emissions reductions as a consequence! A better approach is to let the firms trade rights to pollute among themselves. For example, by allowing trading of the right to pollute, the steel manufacturer can make a profit by offering to reduce emissions by an extra ton per day so that the power plant manager can avoid the $1,000 daily cost of cleaning up an extra ton of particulates. As long as the steel manufacturer gets more than $100 marginal cost of reducing emissions from the electric power plant to clean up an extra ton, it would be more advantageous to offer to reduce its emissions still further. Similarly, the power plant manager will agree to pay to have its ton of emissions reduced by the steel manufacturer as long as the amount paid for that ton is less than the $1,000 marginal cost incurred by reducing emissions itself. If the two firms can strike a mutually agreeable bargain to trade, the two tons of emissions can be obtained for a cost of less than $1,100. For example, if the power plant pays the steel manufacturer $200 to reduce emissions by one additional ton per day, the marginal cost of two tons of emissions reduction would only be $300.

Benefits and Costs of Environmental Protection Policy

The costs of environmental policy in the United States have been considerable. In 1990 the EPA estimated annual compliance costs to be $152 billion and estimates for 2000 indicate that current costs could be in the range of $225 billion per year.[10]

Although these are just rough estimates of annual costs, we can try to determine whether the benefits from current policies exceed these costs and whether, on the whole, there have been net gains from government policies to improve environmental quality.

The motivating force behind environmental protection policy in the United States has been the protection of human health. Standards have been set to provide benefits, and there was no mandate to explicitly consider costs in setting standards. There is no doubt that the EPA reduced emissions of such harmful gasses as nitrogen oxides and of particulates. Millions of additional tons of many pollutants

---

[10]See A. Myrick Freeman III, "Environmental Policy Since Earth Day I: What Have We Gained?" *Journal of Economic Perspectives* 16, 1 (Winter 2002): 125–146.

G L O B A L   P E R S P E C T I V E

Global Pollution: Externalities That Cross Borders

Are you worried about depletion of the earth's ozone layer? Will continued reduction of stratospheric ozone increase your risks of getting skin cancer? Will global warming result from continued use of fossil fuels and from deforestation of the Amazon in Brazil? Do we need more intergovernmental cooperation on the international level to save the planet?

Let's first look at the issue of ozone depletion. Chlorofluorocarbons (CFCs) and other chemicals used in the production of solvents and insulation materials disperse into the atmosphere no matter where they are used. The use of these chemicals increases the concentrations of chlorine and bromine in the atmosphere, creating chemical reactions that deplete the ozone. Ozone depletion means that more ultraviolet radiation will reach earth, increasing the risk of skin cancer and cataracts. Depletion of the ozone layer also will reduce agricultural yields and have unfavorable effects on fishing and industrial materials.

It is clear that externalities do not stop at the borders of a nation. Even if the United States develops policies to reduce the emissions of CFCs, which are used in refrigeration, aerosol propellants, and fire extinguishers, continued use of these and other chemicals in other nations will threaten the ozone layer. It is going to take action by more than one government to internalize the externalities associated with the use of CFCs. Some progress has already been made through international agreements that resulted in a sharp reduction in CFC production in 1998.

Global warming is another international problem that is aggravated by the fact that users of fossil fuels and timber do not consider the full social cost of their use of these products. The greenhouse effect results when concentrations of carbon dioxide and other gases increase in the atmosphere and absorb heat that then radiates down toward earth. The concentrations of these gases do not depend only on the amounts emitted, but they also depend on the vegetation cover of the earth because vegetation naturally absorbs carbon dioxide. Much of the world vegetation cover is forest. In recent years, deforestation in Africa and Brazil has contributed to fears that the greenhouse effect would become worse. However, harvesting of timber is a key source of income and well-being to citizens in low-income regions of the world. Governments of these nations naturally resist concerns for them to restrain from clearing and harvesting their forest resources. This has led to calls for international cooperation to compensate Brazil and nations in Africa in return for their promises to reduce harvesting forest resources.

Of course, another way to reduce the risk of global warming is to discourage the use of fossil fuels, which spew forth the gases that create the greenhouse effect. This could be accomplished through very high corrective taxes on the use of these fuels. The high taxes could slow world economic growth unless alternative fuels that are cleaner burning can be developed.

Externalities have a very important international dimension that cannot be ignored in social policy. Effectively dealing with the problems of protecting our environment will ultimately require coordinated actions by all governments of the world. A United Nations–sponsored Conference on Environment and Development in Rio de Janeiro in 1992 made some progress in such coordination. The conference resulted in 160 nations signing an agreement that commits richer nations to assist poorer nations to develop while minimizing environmental damage. In exchange for international aid and technology transfer, poorer nations will pursue policies that reduce high birth rates.

In 1997, an international conference on climate change in Kyoto, Japan, established the "Kyoto Protocol," which set targets for nations to reduce greenhouse gases thought to be responsible for global warming. These gases include carbon dioxide, methane, nitrous oxide, and other gases. The protocol set specific targets for each country to reduce emissions from 2008 through 2012. The targets are designed to cut emissions of greenhouse gases believed to be responsible for global warming by 5.2 percent of the 1990 level. To be effective, since global warming is a worldwide phenomenon, the targets must be international. However, the actual distribution among nations must be worked out through negotiation and agreed upon by all nations to be effective in reducing global levels of greenhouse gases. The protocol would require the United States to cut its emissions of greenhouse gases by 7 percent of the 1990 level. This would mean that the level of emissions of these gases in the United States would have to be 30 percent less than expected with no action between 2008 and 2012.

Greenhouse gases result from carbon emissions mainly from combustion of fossil fuels: petroleum, coal, and natural gas. Because combustion of coal emits much more carbon waste than petroleum or natural gas (which emits the lowest levels), one way to achieve the reduction is through a shift away from coal and petroleum to natural gas or such other forms of energy production as hydroelectric or nuclear power generation.

As of January 2013, the Kyoto Protocol had been ratified by 191 nations and the European Economic Community. The United States has not ratified the protocol. One estimate is that if permits to emit carbon were priced at $100 to $200 per ton, annual costs to businesses in the United States would run from $27 to $54 billion per year. Corrective taxes on oil necessary to meet the reductions in greenhouse gases in the United States under the Kyoto Protocol could more than triple the price of a barrel of oil and cause the price of a ton of coal to go up by more than 1,000 percent. These costs would be even higher for European nations. The high cost of abating carbon emissions permits in industrial nations virtually assures failure of the international treaty.[1]

Benefits of reducing carbon emissions are very difficult to quantify and assess. Uncertainties regarding the impact of pollution on climate stem from scientific problems in assessing the extent of global warming and its effects. There is no doubt that carbon dioxide and other greenhouse gases are transparent to ultraviolet light. As ultraviolet light passes through these gasses, they warm objects on the ground, which, in turn, release infrared energy. This energy would normally escape into space but is trapped by the greenhouse gases, thereby warming the earth's atmosphere. And emission of greenhouse gasses has been increasing with industrial development. However, it is unclear whether atmospheric temperatures have, in fact, been increasing, and it is also unclear

whether ocean temperatures will rise even if the atmosphere is warming. The consequences of global warming, if it were to take effect, include higher sea levels, more heat waves and droughts, more intense storms—but the magnitude of the effects is also difficult to assess.

It is unlikely that an international agreement on reductions of carbon and other greenhouse gas emissions will be reached any time soon. More pragmatic solutions to the problem are needed.[2]

The EU has made a unilateral commitment to reduce emissions of greenhouse gases by at least 20 percent of 1990 levels by 2020. To accomplish this goal, new regulations to improve energy efficiency of equipment and appliances have been issued for EU member nations. Other regulations mandate increased use of renewable energy sources including wind, solar, and biofuels. The EU has also embarked on a new cap-and-trade system for greenhouse gases requiring industries to have allowances for carbon emissions. Under the EU emissions trading scheme, emitters of large volumes of carbon dioxide are required to monitor and report amounts emitted each year and have to give up allocated allowances according to the amount they emit annually. The allowances were initially allocated freely to industries based on historical emissions levels. The price of the allowances were determined by free market trading. In 2012 the EU also began assessing a carbon tax on airlines flying in EU airspace by requiring them to purchase allowances at market prices for emissions of greenhouse gasses. The requirement that aviation firms purchase allowances for emissions was expected to increase the demand for allowances by as much as 12 million tons in 2012 putting upward pressure on prices. The extension of the program to aviation has been challenged by the United States, China, and other countries flying in European airspace.

---

[1]See Warwick J. McKibbin and Peter J. Wilcoxen, "The Role of Economics in Climate Change Policy," *Journal of Economic Perspectives* 16, 2 (Spring 2002): 107–129.
[2]See McKibbin and Wilcoxen, pp. 116–122 for discussion of a hybrid permit-tax plan designed to lower the costs of achieving reductions in emissions.

would have been dumped in the environment in the absence of EPA policies. The EPA has argued that the benefits of environmental protection programs far outweigh the costs. In 1990, the EPA estimated that the benefits of the Clean Air Act were nearly 50 times the costs.[11] This would imply that, in the aggregate, programs designed to clean up the air have resulted in net gains and thereby have improved efficiency.

However, the EPA's calculations have been criticized. A. Myrick Freeman argues that by disaggregating the programs a better picture of the effect of specific air quality control programs on efficiency of resource use can be obtained. The researcher estimates that 82 percent of the benefits claimed by EPA for the Clean Air Act come from programs that have reduced mortality and disease associated with fine particles (particulates) suspended in the air. Fine particles mainly come from stationary sources, such as power plants and factories. Removing lead from gasoline accounts for an additional 8 percent of benefits. Thus, according to Freeman, programs targeting leaded gasoline power plants and factories account for 90 percent of the benefits and also outweigh the total costs of compliance for all programs as reported by the EPA.[12] Other programs involved in control of mobile sources of pollution account for less than 10 percent of total benefits reported by the EPA and Freeman calculates that their costs exceed the benefits. Freeman argues that better information would be provided if benefits and costs for specific EPA policies were broken down to examine which programs actually do provide net gains in welfare.

The Clean Water Act of 1972 established national goals for water quality and sought to eliminate discharge of pollutants from industrial sources and municipal sewage treatment plants into navigable rivers. The policy for water pollution control was classic command-and-control. Maximum emission standards were established based on current technologies. No attempts were made to estimate the ability of water bodies to assimilate pollutants, and the same standards were applied to all dischargers of a given type. Water quality effects of emissions were not considered—all emissions were to be controlled.

The effects of the Clean Water Act have apparently only been modest. Although some rivers have shown remarkable improvements in water quality, overall the number of river miles meeting the standards since 1972 has increased by less than 10 percent.[13] The poor result is because the impact of the Clean Water Act has primarily been on point sources of pollution, such as industrial plants and sewage treatment facilities, while such sources as runoff of pollutants from both urban and industrial areas has received little attention. Freeman believes that, in the aggregate, the costs of meeting water quality standards exceed the benefits. The EPA estimated the costs at about $60 billion in 1990. Additional analysis by Hahn for some specific rules under the Clean Water Act indicates that the benefits of these directives were equal to about 5 percent of costs.[14]

---

[11]U.S. Environmental Protection Agency. *The Benefits and Cost of the Clean Air Act: 1970–1990.* Washington, D.C.: Office of Policy Analysis, 1997.

[12]See Freeman, pp. 130–132.

[13]See Freeman, p. 137.

[14]Robert W. Hahn, *Reviving Regulatory Reform: A Global Perspective.* Washington, D.C.: AEI-Brookings Joint Center for Regulatory Studies, 2000.

1. What are the major differences between emissions standards and market-based approaches, such as corrective taxes and marketable pollution rights, to pollution abatement?
2. What is command-and-control regulation?
3. How can market-based approaches to pollution control work to obtain a given amount of emissions reduction at the minimum possible social cost?

SUMMARY

Externalities are costs or benefits of market transactions not reflected in prices. They are a dominant form of market failure to achieve efficiency in industrial economies. When externalities are present, market prices fail to equal the marginal social cost or benefit of goods. Exchange of goods and services in an unregulated system of competitive markets fails to achieve efficiency when externalities prevail. When the marginal external cost or benefit is priced so that buyers and sellers consider it in their decisions, an externality is internalized.

Externalities can be negative or positive. Negative externalities result in costs, while positive externalities result in benefits to third parties of market exchanges. To internalize an externality, the parties involved must

be identified and the marginal external cost or benefit must be measured.

In some cases, particularly that of few individual emitters and receptors, private action through informal bargaining can be expected to internalize the externality without recourse to collective action through political institutions. The Coase theorem shows that, in such cases, government assignment of rights to resource use, along with facilitation of free exchange of those rights, achieves efficiency, independent of which party is granted the right. When larger numbers of individuals are involved, a solution will require collective action to internalize the externality. Among the techniques used for this are corrective taxes and subsidies, regulations, and the establishment of standards.

LOOKING AHEAD

Chapter 4 discusses the nature of public goods and shows that their market provision results in positive externalities. The difficulties involved in efficiently

supplying public goods through markets make government a logical candidate for their production and distribution.

KEY CONCEPTS

Coase Theorem

Command-and-Control Regulation

Corrective Subsidy

Corrective Tax

Externalities

General Theory of Second Best

Internalization of an Externality

Marginal External Benefit (*MEB*)

Marginal External Cost (*MEC*)

Marginal Private Benefit (*MPB*)

Marginal Private Cost (*MPC*)

Negative Externalities

Pollution Abatement

Pollution Rights

Positive Externalities

Small-Number Externalities

Transactions Costs

REVIEW QUESTIONS

1. Explain why externalities prevent the attainment of efficiency when goods are traded in competitive markets.
2. Do you agree with the following statement? "Efficiency cannot be achieved when externalities exist." Explain your view.
3. Why do prices fail to represent the opportunity costs of resources when externalities exist?
4. How can a corrective tax adjust costs to reflect externalities? What effects will a corrective tax have on prices, output, and pollution?
5. Suppose a positive externality is associated with college enrollment. Assume that college instruction is sold in a competitive market and that the marginal social cost of providing it increases with enrollment. Show how a corrective subsidy to college students will increase the market price of instruction. Show the net gain in well-being possible from the subsidy and the amount of tax revenue required to finance its costs on your graph.
6. What kinds of information must be gathered to internalize an externality?
7. Why do limits on pollution emissions fail to internalize the externality that generates the pollution?
8. Under what conditions are externalities likely to be internalized without the necessity of government intervention?
9. Why might it be argued that the distinction between emitters and receptors of an externality involves an arbitrary judgment?
10. What criteria can be used to determine if a small-number externality exists? Why is it undesirable to compensate receptors of external damage in cases where there are few emitters and many receptors?

PROBLEMS

1. The supply of paper is described by the following equation:

$$Q_s = 5,000P$$

where Q_s is tons supplied per year and P is the price per ton. The demand is described by

$$Q_D = 400,000 - 1,000P$$

where Q_D is tons demanded per year. Because of the pollution associated with paper production, marginal external costs of $20 are associated with each ton of paper. Assuming that paper is sold in a competitive market, what is the market price? How many tons of paper will be produced per year at that price? What is the efficient annual output of paper? How can a corrective tax achieve efficiency?

2. The following data show how the marginal external benefit and marginal private benefit associated with a soil treatment agent to control Japanese beetles vary with the gallons of the control agent sold per year: Draw the demand curve for the control agent and show how the marginal private benefit differs from the marginal social benefit. Suppose the supply of the agent is infinitely elastic at the current price of $25 per gallon. Will the market equilibrium be efficient? How would your answer differ if the market supply were infinitely elastic at a price of $15 per gallon? What policies could you suggest to achieve efficiency?

3. The EPA wants to reduce emissions of sulfur dioxides from electric power–generating plants by 20 percent during the next year. To achieve this goal, the EPA will require each power–generating plant in the nation to reduce emissions by 100 tons per year. Suppose five power plants emit sulfur dioxides and serve a given metropolitan area. The following table shows the cost per ton of reducing emissions for each of the five plants:

GALLONS PER YEAR (IN MILLIONS)	MPB ($)	MEB ($)
20	30	10
30	25	6
40	20	2
50	15	0

COST PER TON OF PLANT	EMISSIONS REDUCTION ($)
1	600
2	500
3	500
4	400
5	200

Assuming that the cost per ton of emissions reduction is constant and that the improvement in the air for the metropolitan area is the same no matter which plant reduces emissions, calculate the following:

    a. Cost of meeting EPA regulations.

    b. Least-cost method of achieving the EPA goal of reducing emissions of sulfur dioxides from power plants in the metropolitan area.

4. Instead of using regulations to achieve the 20 percent reduction in emissions discussed in the preceding problem, suppose the EPA requires each of the five emitters to pay a fee of $450 for each ton of sulfur dioxide it dumps in the air during the year.

Use the data from the table for problem 3 to predict which companies will purchase pollution rights, total cost of achieving the reduction in sulfur dioxide emissions, and revenue generated from the sale of pollution rights in the area.

5. Economists argue that there is an efficient amount of pollution abatement. Explain why the efficient amount of abatement is unlikely to be either 0 or 100 percent. List all the information that would be required to determine the efficient amount of pollution abatement. Why is it difficult in practice to determine the efficient amount of pollution abatement?

ADDITIONAL READINGS

Barthold, Thomas A. "Issues in the Design of Environmental Excise Taxes." *Journal of Economic Perspectives* 8, 1 (Winter 1994): 133–151. An analysis of some of the practical problems involved in the implementation of corrective taxes to deal with pollution control.

Baumol, William J. and Wallace E. Oates. *The Theory of Environmental Policy.* Englewood Cliffs, N.J.: Prentice-Hall, 1975. A technical application of the theory of externalities to environmental problems.

Coase, Ronald. "The Problem of Social Cost." *Journal of Law and Economics* 3 (October 1960): 1–44. A modern classic on the nature of externalities and the nexus between economics and the law.

Cropper, Maureen L. and Wallace E. Oates. "Environmental Economics: A Survey." *Journal of Economic Literature* 30, 2 (June 1992): 675–740. A survey of the state of knowledge in environmental economics along with analysis of recent economic policy to deal with environmental problems in the United States and other nations.

Dahlman, Carl J. "The Problem of Externality." *Journal of Law and Economics* 22 (April 1979): 141–168. A discussion of transactions costs, efficiency, and externalities.

Economic Report of the President, 2002. Washington, D. C.: U.S. Government Printing Office, February 2002. Chapter 6 provides a review of environmental protection programs in use in both the United States and foreign nations. Regulatory programs are discussed along with market-based systems including tradable quotas.

Freeman, A. Myrick, III. "Environmental Policy Since Earth Day I: What Have We Gained?" *Journal of Economic Perspectives* 16, 1 (Winter 2002): 125–146. A discussion of the costs and benefits of environmental protection programs in the United States and a critical evaluation of the impact of these policies on the achievement of more efficient use of resources.

Hahn, Robert W. "Economic Prescriptions for Environmental Problems: How the Patient Followed the Doctor's Orders." *Journal of Economic Perspectives* 3, 2 (Spring 1989): 95–114. In this article, Hahn discusses how market-based pollution control policies have actually been implemented in several nations.

Poterba, James M. "Global Warming Policy: A Public Finance Perspective." *Journal of Economic Perspectives* 7, 4 (Fall 1993): 47–63. An analysis of the use of corrective taxes and other policies to deal with the problem of global warming.

Schmalensee, Richard, Paul L. Joskow, A. Denny Ellerman, Juan Pablo Montero, and Elizabeth M. Bailey. "Interim Evaluation of Sulfur Dioxide Emissions Trading." *Journal of Economic Perspectives* 12, 3 (Summer 1998): 53–68. A survey of the history and effects of a major environmental policy innovation in the United States that established marketable emissions permits in the power–generating industry and substantially reduced the cost of pollution abatement.

INTERNET RESOURCES

http://www.epa.gov

At the EPA Web site, you can obtain data and information about government programs concerning environmental protection and environmental quality. Click on "Acid Rain" under "Popular Topics" to find details on sulfur dioxide trading and other emissions trading programs.

http://yosemite.epa.gov/ee/epa/eed.nsf/pages/homepage

At the home page of the National Center of Environmental Economics, you can access information on analytical methods and economic research on environmental issues.

http://www.aere.org

This is the home page of the Association of Environmental and Resource Economists. Here you can access research on environmental issues through newsletters and economic journals.

Chapter 4

PUBLIC GOODS

LEARNING OBJECTIVES

After reading this chapter, you should be able to:

- Define public goods and discuss their characteristics.

- Explain the difference between pure public goods and pure private goods.

- Derive the demand curve for a pure public good and explain how it differs from the demand curve for a pure private good.

- Determine the conditions for efficient output

of a pure public good and explain why positive externalities associated with the production of pure public goods imply that market provision of the good is likely to be inefficient.

- Discuss cooperative methods of supplying pure public goods and the characteristics of the Lindahl equilibrium.

- Analyze the free-rider problem.

Defense spending in the United States increased rapidly in 2003 in response to global threats and the war on terrorism. Wars in Afghanistan and Iraq started in 2002 and 2003 have contributed to increased defense spending and Congress allocated more funds for defense and homeland security. Defense-related spending in the United States rose from 3 percent of GDP in 2001 to 5.5 percent of GDP in 2011. When the federal government provides national defense, it must employ labor and procure capital in the form of weapons systems, aircraft, naval vessels, and land to use as military bases and airfields. The production aspect of national defense is very similar to that of any business operation. Labor must be hired; work rules must be established; research and development contracts must be negotiated for new capital equipment and new products, such as weapons that can penetrate deep bunkers, stealth fighter planes, and remote-controlled aircraft. However, the similarity with business ends on the output side of the picture. The output of the federal government agencies that supply national defense is not sold in the market to buyers like cars, cookies, or clothing. In fact, it is inconceivable to imagine defense services being packaged into neat bundles that can be sold over the counter to eager buyers. Although the production of national defense is similar to that of any other good, its *consumption* is fundamentally different. Products such as national defense are *collectively consumed*. As soon as we defend any one person, we defend all.

Because defense is not sold by the unit in markets and cannot be parceled out to individuals to enjoy in greater or smaller amounts according to their tastes, we all consume the total amount produced. We all pay taxes to finance the production of national defense, and we must consume the amount made available, even though we might prefer to have more or less than the government provides. An issue that concerns us all is how much of our resources we allocate to services such as national defense.

This chapter explores the characteristics of goods that are collectively consumed. We evaluate alternative methods of supplying public goods and show why it is efficient for people to *share* the costs of producing goods with shared benefits.

CHARACTERISTICS OF PUBLIC GOODS

Chapter 3 showed how markets tend to fail to produce efficient amounts of goods that result in externalities when exchanged. Many of the goods and services actually provided by governments, such as national defense, would result in positive externalities were they made available for sale to individual buyers in markets. An entire class of goods, including environmental protection, roads, and public safety, has benefits that must be shared by large groups of individuals. The production of these goods for sale in the marketplace would be accompanied by positive externalities because any such items purchased for individual use would provide external benefits to a large number of third parties as well. Market provision of goods with benefits shared by people other than those who purchase them for their own use is unlikely to result in an efficiently large amount of output.

Goods with benefits that cannot be withheld from those who do not pay and are shared by large groups of consumers are **public goods**. Public goods are usually made available politically through the ballot box as people vote to decide how much to supply rather than through the marketplace, where those who care to pay the price can buy as much as they like for their own exclusive use. In most cases, government provision of public goods implies that the goods are freely available to all rather than being sold in markets. The costs of making the goods available are usually financed by taxes.

Let's begin our analysis of public goods by examining their characteristics more closely. Public goods are **nonrival in consumption**, meaning that a given quantity of a public good can be enjoyed by more than one consumer without decreasing the amounts enjoyed by rival consumers. For example, television and radio transmissions are nonrival in consumption. A given amount of programming per day can be enjoyed by a large number of consumers. When an additional viewer switches on a television set, the quantity of programming enjoyed by other viewers is not reduced. Similarly, the benefits of national defense services are nonrival. When the population of a nation increases, no citizen suffers a reduction in the quantity of national defense because more people are being defended at any time.

Goods that are rival in consumption are called **private goods**. A given quantity of fish available on a dock is said to be rival in consumption. As the number of fish made available to any one consumer increases, the quantity available for rival consumers who desire the fish decreases. Except when externalities are present, prices can efficiently allocate goods that are rival in consumption. The price serves the purpose of making any one person who desires a unit of the good consider the decrease in benefits to rivals who wish to consume that unit.

Pricing a good that is nonrival in consumption serves no useful purpose. After all, an additional consumer of a nonrival good does not reduce the benefit to others who wish to consume it. In other words, the marginal cost of allowing additional people to consume a given amount of a good with nonrival benefits is zero. It is therefore inefficient to price goods that are nonrival in consumption.

In most cases, it is also unfeasible to price units of a public good. This characteristic of public goods, called **nonexclusion**, implies that it is too costly to develop a means of excluding those who refuse to pay from enjoying the benefits of a given quantity of a public good. For example, it is unfeasible to exclude those who refuse to pay for cleaner air from enjoying the benefits of a given amount of air quality improvement, once it has been supplied for the benefit of other people. Air quality improvement has the property of nonexclusion.

From a practical point of view, goods that are nonrival in consumption need not necessarily be subject to nonexclusion. Television broadcasting services, as was pointed out earlier, are nonrival. However, it is feasible to exclude those who refuse to pay from the benefits of transmissions through cable provision of the broadcasts or use of signal coding for satellite transmission. Similarly, the benefits of roads are often nonrival. However, it is feasible to use tolls to exclude those who refuse to pay. The characteristics of nonrival consumption and nonexclusion vary in degree from good to good. Much, however, can be learned from further investigation of the problems involved in making available efficient amounts of a good that is *both* nonrival in consumption and the benefits of which are nonexclusive.

Pure Public Goods and Pure Private Goods

A **pure public good** is nonrival in consumption for an entire population of consumers, and its benefits have the characteristic of nonexclusion. A given quantity of a pure public good is consumed by all members of a community as soon as it is produced for, or by, any one member. In contrast, a **pure private good** is one that, after

PUBLIC POLICY PERSPECTIVE

National Defense Spending in the United States

Trends in Defense Spending

National defense is a classic example of a public good. Spending on national defense in the United States amounted to nearly 10 percent of GDP in 1968 during the Vietnam conflict. Between 1968 and 1978 defense spending as a share of GDP steadily declined to less than 5 percent. In the 1980s there was another increase in defense spending in the United States as government purchases for new military hardware and weapons systems increased. By 1986 defense spending absorbed 6.2 percent of GDP. With the demise of the former Soviet Union and the communist regimes of Eastern Europe, defense spending began to decline significantly. Military bases were closed and military procurement was sharply reduced. By 1999 defense spending in the United States amounted to only 3 percent of GDP. However, terrorism attacks in 2001 on the United States and subsequent military operations in Afghanistan and Iraq reversed the downward trend in military spending. By 2008 defense spending in the United States was 5.2 percent of GDP. With the end of military operations in Iraq in 2011, defense spending declined slightly from a peak of 5.6 percent of GDP in 2009 and 2010 to 5.5 percent of GDP in 2011. The following chart shows the trend in defense spending as a share of GDP in the United States since 1962.

The military operations in Iraq and Afghanistan have been costly with total appropriations by Congress running at about $1.4 trillion (including an estimated $127 billion for fiscal year 2012). Of the total appropriations, about $1.25 trillion has gone to the Department of Defense. An additional $150 billion was allocated for training indigenous security forces and for foreign aid for Iraq and Afghanistan. These costs only include government outlays and do not measure other costs such as loss of lives and other human casualties. Because these military operations are a component of national defense (a public good) that all must consume, the mounting costs of the war have given rise to controversy and political conflict as many citizens come to different conclusions about the benefits of the military

operations. It is clear that costs have exceeded estimates when the operations were initiated. Also, some of the initial benefits upon which the decision to engage in the operations were made were evaluated on the basis of faulty intelligence about weapons of mass destruction and terrorism links in Iraq.

The economic aspect of the debate on military operations ultimately relates to disagreements about the marginal social benefits and marginal social costs of continuing to spend scarce resources in Iraq. Critics of the military operations argue that the marginal social costs are too high relative to the marginal social benefits and that military and other resources could be spent more efficiently in other ways to protect against terrorism and military aggression by national governments. Others argue that national defense efforts need to be better coordinated within government by allowing more cooperation between the military and those charged with providing homeland security.

Cutting Military Spending

In future years the Department of Defense is planning for a leaner and more focused military. As part of an overall plan to cut the federal government's budget deficit, the U.S. armed forces are likely to be reduced in number and revamped to use new technology for an effective defense against future threats to national security. It is difficult to forecast how much the budget of the U.S. Department of Defense will actually be cut in the future because of political uncertainty within the nation and uncertainty about the actual threats that will be faced in the future. However, the fiscal reality is that defense spending is likely to be subject to substantial reductions in future years. The hope is that by using more effective technology to achieve limited goals defense output could be provided for citizens at a reasonable level with lower costs. Of course, the actual, if any, reductions in defense spending until hinge on political considerations. As of 2012, some politicians were arguing that defense spending in future years should remain fixed in real terms—with appropriations growing with the rate of inflation.

Defense Expenditures as a Share of GDP, 1962–2011

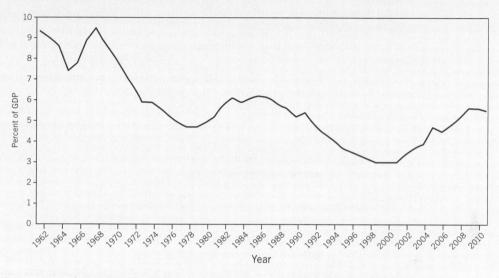

Source: U.S. Department of Commerce, National Income and Product Accounts Tables, March, 2012.

A number of possible areas for cuts were being considered as of 2012. The Obama administration proposed cuts in military spending by $450 billion over a ten-year period. However, some have been calling for even more substantial cuts of $1 trillion over the same period, which would amount to a 17 percent cut in the Department of Defense base budget. The issue that remains is how much of a cut in spending can allow an effective level of national security.

Some cuts in spending, such as those for military health insurance and retiree benefits, would not directly affect the level of output of national defense. Other areas for cuts such as reduction in military personnel, closing of bases, and reduction in the number of air wings decrease the inputs used in providing national defense and, unless offset by increased efficiency, can also reduce output of defense services. Cuts were also being considered in new weapons purchases and the nuclear arsenal of the nation. Technological improvement including cyber warfare, more use of sophisticated drones, and special operations can allow more focused objectives that protect against threats from terrorists with a minimum of labor input. Substitution of capital and technology for labor can maintain levels of national security at lower costs. Labor costs currently account for one third of total national defense spending. As of 2012 total labor costs were $181 billion per year, and $50 billion of that amount was allocated to health care while another $24 billion was for retired personnel pensions.

Health care costs are a significant problem for the military as it is for the nation as a whole. The Department of Defense is actually the nation's largest employer and in recent years the share of its budget going to health care for its workers, including active military and retired military personnel has been increasing as a share of total costs. Changes in the military retirement system can also cut costs. The health insurance plan for the military, called Tricare, currently has only minimal co-pays and deductibles. Changing the system for retired personnel allowing higher out-of-pocket fees for service could reduce military spending.

producers receive compensation for the full opportunity costs of production, provides benefits *only* to the person who acquires the good, and not to anyone else. A pure private good is rival in consumption, and its benefits are easily excluded from those who choose not to pay its market price.

Market exchange for pure private goods results in neither positive nor negative externalities. A pure public good, on the other hand, results in widely consumed external benefits to all people, even if made available for only one person. These two extremes can be considered as poles on a continuum, where goods are ranked according to their degree of publicness or privateness in terms of the range and extent to which their production or consumption generates externalities.

Pure public "bads" can also exist. These activities result in external costs affecting a wide range of the population. The quantities of public bads are of concern to all individuals. Air pollution, for example, is a pure public bad if pollutants diffuse in the atmosphere, thereby affecting all individuals, independent of the location of their residence. At the other extreme, national defense can be considered a pure public good. It is impossible to protect any one individual against harm from a foreign invasion or attack without protecting all other individuals in the nation at the same time.

The marginal cost of distributing a pure public good to an additional consumer is zero for a given amount of the public good. This follows from the nonrival characteristic of pure public goods. Figure 4.1A shows that the marginal cost of allowing additional people to consume certain amounts of a pure public good falls to zero after the good has been made available for any one person. Be careful not to confuse *distribution* cost with *production* cost. The marginal costs of accommodating an additional consumer will be zero for a *given quantity* of a pure public good. However, the marginal cost of producing *additional units* of the public good will be positive, as is the case for all economic goods, because increasing the quantity of a pure public good requires additional resources. This is illustrated in Figure 4.1B, where we assume that the average cost of a pure public good is constant. Two units of the public good cost twice as much as one unit. In this case, if the average cost of the public good is $200 per unit, the marginal cost will also be $200.

We can emphasize the distinction between pure public goods and pure private goods in still another way.[1] A pure public good is not divisible into units that can be apportioned among consumers. A given quantity of a pure public good can only be shared rather than enjoyed individually. Its benefits are collectively consumed by the entire population. A unit of a pure private good, on the other hand, can be enjoyed only by a single consumer. The more units of a given amount available to be consumed by one person, the less is available to rival consumers.

An Example: Bread versus Heat

A simple example will help to clarify the distinction between pure public goods and pure private goods. Suppose a community of a certain number of people is confined to a room. Decisions made in that room affect only those in the room and no one else. Each day, residents of the room receive a fixed quantity of bread and a certain amount of fuel to heat the room. The bread is a pure private good in the sense that

---

[1]This point is emphasized by Samuelson in his classic papers on pure public goods: Paul Samuelson, "The Pure Theory of Public Expenditure," Review of *Economics and Statistics* 36 (November 1954): 387–389 and "Diagrammatic Exposition of the Theory of Public Expenditure," *Review of Economics and Statistics* 37 (November 1955): 350–356.

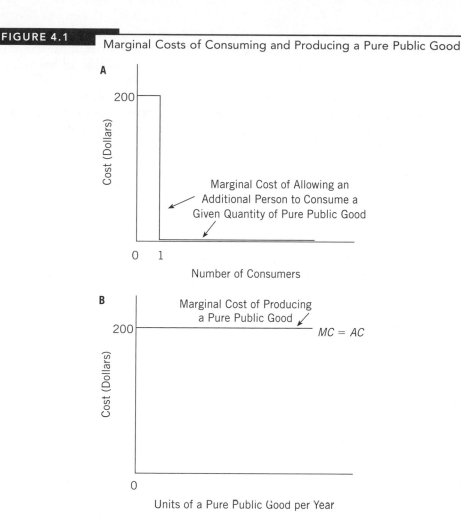

FIGURE 4.1 Marginal Costs of Consuming and Producing a Pure Public Good

The diagram in **A** shows that the marginal cost of allowing an additional person to consume a given quantity of a pure public good falls to zero after it is made available to any one person. The graph in **B** shows that the marginal cost of producing the good is always positive. In this case, the marginal cost of each extra unit of the good is $200.

© Cengage Learning

it is possible to slice it and divide it among the individuals. The total amount of bread available each day equals the sum of the amounts consumed by the people in the room. If more bread is allocated to any one person, less will remain available per day for the others. Bread could be easily sold in a market where the price would be established each day by the interaction of demand and supply. Given the daily price of bread, the people in the room could adjust their consumption of bread according to their preferences and economic circumstances.

On the other hand, it is impossible to divide the room's heat among the people. All individuals in the room at any point in time experience the same temperature level. Assume that the room is large enough so that the effect of the heat emitted by additional bodies on the amount of fuel needed is negligible. Therefore, additional people can be accommodated in the room at a given temperature without using more or less fuel. It is impossible for one person to consume more heat in such a way as to reduce the amount made available to others. Finally, it is impossible for different people in the room to consume different quantities of heat; that is, the level of heat produced for any one individual is the level that all individuals must consume. Individual consumers of heat will lack the ability to adjust the amount of heat they consume in accordance with their own tastes and economic circumstances. It is impossible for two individuals simultaneously to occupy a room in which the temperature is both 65 degrees and 78 degrees Fahrenheit. The level of heat in the room will have all the characteristics of a pure public good for those who occupy the room.

An important consideration in discussing public goods is the range of their benefits. Some public goods, such as world peace, might conceivably provide collectively consumed benefits to every single individual, no matter where they are on the face of the earth. Some goods are collectively consumed within the confines of given nations, although others might produce collectively consumed benefits that are locally consumed. The geographic range of shared benefits influences the desirability of having public goods supplied by various levels of government (for example, federal, state, or local). This problem is extensively investigated in Part 5 of this book.

CHECKPOINT

1. What are the characteristics of public goods?
2. How do pure public goods differ from pure private goods?
3. Why is the marginal cost of allowing another consumer to enjoy the benefits of a pure public good always zero even though the marginal cost of producing the good is positive?

PROVISION OF PRIVATE GOODS AND PUBLIC GOODS: MARKETS AND GOVERNMENT

The supply of goods and services and the mechanisms of distributing them among individuals reflect collectively agreed-upon institutional arrangements that have emerged in a community. It is difficult to make generalizations about the most appropriate means for making goods and services available. Private goods that are individually consumed are sometimes supplied through markets by government, as is the case for certain transportation services, electricity, and other public utility services. On the other hand, many goods that are nonrival in consumption and which have characteristics of public goods, are privately produced and supplied through markets. This is the case for certain recreational services sold through private clubs, television and other communication services, and private police protection. In many cases, goods and services are supplied both through markets under private production and by governments through political institutions. For example, both private and public schools are available. Recreational services and facilities, such as parks, tennis courts, and golf courses, are supplied by both the government and the private sector.

It is possible to imagine, at the extreme, pure private goods being supplied through government and financed through taxation. For example, citizens could agree collectively to supply clothing through government and allow every person one identical suit of clothes per year at no direct charge, financing the production and distribution of the clothing through taxation. Similarly, it is possible to envision goods that have the characteristics of public goods being produced privately and sold through markets when the costs of exclusion are not very high. This is the case for cable television services in which programming that is nonrival in consumption is produced by profit-maximizing firms that sell monthly subscriptions to their programming services. The fee serves as an exclusion device, making the service available only to those who sign a contract and agree to pay.

In practice, it is not possible to draw a neat line between pure private goods and pure public goods. Many intermediate cases exist in which external benefits or costs accrue only to some people, and the transaction costs associated with trading goods with collectively consumed benefits are not prohibitive. In those cases, both private supply and government supply are feasible, and it is often difficult to determine which supply method is appropriate.

Congestible Public Goods and Private Goods with Externalities

Government supply through political institutions and private supply through markets are alternative means of making any good available. These two alternatives can be evaluated according to the extent to which externalities are associated with either the production or consumption of the good and the extent to which it is possible to develop a means of selling rights to use the good or service.

Congestible public goods are those for which crowding or congestion reduces the benefits to existing consumers when more consumers are accommodated. The marginal cost of accommodating an additional consumer is not zero after the point of congestion is reached. For example, an additional user of a congested road decreases the benefits to existing users by slowing down traffic and increasing the risk of an accident. This is illustrated in Figure 4.2. After N^* users of a road have been accommodated per hour, the marginal cost of allowing another user on that road becomes positive.

Price-excludable public goods are those with benefits that can be priced. Private clubs are often set up to share facilities, such as tennis courts, swimming pools, and dining areas for small groups. Membership rights, which are sold in the market, are sometimes negotiable and can be sold by their holders to others. By joining clubs and paying dues, members share in the cost of facilities and services that they otherwise would be unable to afford. Dues and limits on the number of members are determined by collective agreement of existing members.[2] The dues ration the facilities of the club to avoid the effects of congestion. Other price-excludable public goods include such public facilities as schools and hospitals. These goods can be priced, but their provision results in positive externalities.

Table 4.1 summarizes alternative means for producing, distributing, and financing goods and services. Goods and services have been divided into four categories:

1. Pure private goods
2. Price-excludable public goods
3. Congestible public goods
4. Pure public goods

---

[2]See Todd Sandler and John T. Tschirhart, "The Economic Theory of Clubs: An Evaluative Survey," *Journal of Economic Literature* 18 (December 1980): 1481–1521.

FIGURE 4.2   Congestible Public Good

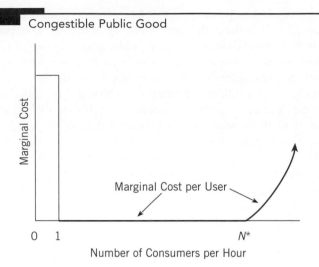

Number of Consumers per Hour

The marginal cost of allowing additional users to consume the congestible public good falls to zero after the good is made available to any one user but then rises above zero after N^* users are accommodated per hour.

The first category represents goods that approximate the ideal of a pure private good that is individually consumed and subject to low-cost exclusion from benefits for those who do not pay for the right to receive such benefits. The production of these goods usually does not generate an externality, but some individuals believe that external benefits are associated with others who consume these goods. Such private goods might be sold in markets either by private firms or by government. When sold in markets, their costs of production are financed by the revenue obtained from sales to individual buyers. Alternatively, they may be produced or purchased by government from private firms, distributed free of direct charge to eligible recipients, and financed by taxes. Such is the case for public welfare programs that give medical services, food, housing, and other services to low-income citizens who meet certain eligibility tests. These services also could be sold at subsidized prices, with losses made up from tax-financed subsidies.

Second, some goods can be individually consumed and are subject to exclusion, but their production or consumption is likely to generate externalities. These are price-excludable public goods. Again, such goods can be distributed through markets when produced either by private firms or by government. The production or consumption of these goods can be subsidized to account for the positive externality associated with their sale. The good would be financed by both the revenue from sales and the taxes used to finance the subsidy. Such is the case for private and public hospitals, mass transit facilities, and schooling. These goods also can be produced by government and distributed with no direct charge. In such cases, however, the quantity and quality of the service would be determined collectively through political institutions, and costs would be financed through taxation. This is the case for public schooling, public sanitation service, and government-supplied inoculations that are available at public health facilities.

Congestible public goods are nonrival in consumption only up to a certain point. After the number of consumers exceeds a certain amount, the goods become

TABLE 4.1 Alternative Means of Producing, Distributing, and Financing Goods and Services

CHARACTERISTICS OF THE GOOD OR SERVICE	MEANS OF PRODUCTION	METHODS OF DISTRIBUTION	METHODS OF FINANCE	EXAMPLES	
				PRIVATE	PUBLIC
Pure Private Goods No externality; low-cost exclusion	1. Private firms; government	Markets; direct unit charge	Revenue from sales	Food; clothing; cars	Government liquor stores; government tobacco monopoly
	2. Government; private firms under contract with government	No direct unit charge; eligibility to consume various amounts determined politically	Taxes		Government distribution of medical services and food to low-income citizens
Price-Excludable Public Goods External benefits when produced or consumed; low-cost exclusion	1. Private firms; government	Markets; direct unit charge (may be subsidized)	Revenue from sales; taxes	Schools; hospitals; transportation	Transit facilities; public hospitals
	2. Government; private firms under contract with government	No direct unit charge; consumption available or required only at collectively chosen quantity and quality	Taxes		Public schools; public sanitation; inoculations
Congestible Public Goods Collectively consumed benefits subject to crowding; possibility of exclusion	1. Private firms; government	Fees for the right to use the facility sold in markets	Revenue from sales	Clubs; theaters; amusement parks sporting events	Public golf courses; roads
Pure Public Goods Collectively consumed benefits not subject to crowding; high-cost exclusion	1. Private firms; government	No direct unit charge; quantity dependent on amount collected	Fees; contributions	Private charity	Public television and radio
	2. Government; private firms under contract with government	No direct unit charge; quantity and quality of service collectively chosen	Taxes		National defense; environmental protection

at least partially rival in consumption. An increase in the use of the good by one consumer decreases the benefits from a given amount of the good that can be enjoyed by others. Exclusion from benefits of these goods is often possible through application of certain fees. Congestible public goods, in some cases, are also price-excludable public goods. These goods are often in the form of services flowing from shared facilities that can be distributed in markets either by government or by firms through the sale of admissions, memberships, or other use-related fees; these might receive public subsidies. Privately supplied examples include clubs for sharing recreational or other facilities, amusement parks, theaters, and sporting events. Government-supplied goods of this type might be partially or fully financed by taxes. Public parks are an example, as are other forms of public recreation, civic centers, auditoriums, roads, bridges, and similar public facilities.

Pure public goods result in collectively consumed benefits that are not subject to crowding and are subject to high-cost exclusion. It is difficult to sell use rights to the benefits of these goods, and markets are unlikely to provide a convenient mechanism for distributing them. Conceivably, they could be produced privately through voluntary contributions, with the quantity and quality of service provided being contingent on the amount of revenue collected. Private charity is often provided and financed in this manner. However, goods resembling pure public goods are most likely to be distributed free of direct charge by governments, with the quantity and quality of the service determined through political institutions and financed by taxes. Such is the case for national defense, environmental protection, and other goods resembling pure public goods.

Semipublic goods exist in a continuum ranging from pure private goods to pure public goods. Figure 4.3 shows how goods could be categorized according to the degree of rivalry in consumption and the degree of excludability. The horizontal

FIGURE 4.3   Classifying Goods According to the Degree of Rivalry and Excludability of Benefits from Their Use

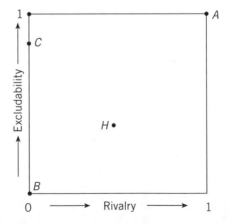

A pure public good corresponds to point *B*, where there is no rivalry for benefits and excludability from benefits is impossible. A pure private good corresponds to point *A* on the graph. A nonrival good, such as TV transmissions, for which exclusion is possible, corresponds to a point like *C*. A congestible public good for which it is possible to charge for use, such as a limited access highway, corresponds to a point like *H*.

axis of the graph plots the extent to which the benefits of the good are rival on a scale of zero to one. A pure private good with benefits that are fully rival in consumption would rate a value of one on the horizontal axis, while a pure public good with benefits that are completely nonrival in consumption would rate a zero on the horizontal axis. A congestible public good with benefits that are only partially nonrival would be assigned a number between zero and one on the horizontal axis depending on the degree of its congestibility.

The vertical axis measures the excludability of the good on a scale of zero to one. A pure private good, which is perfectly excludable because its benefits can be fully withheld from someone who does not pay, would be assigned a one on the vertical axis. Similarly, a pure public good that is not price excludable would be assigned a zero. Goods, such as highways for which tolls can be charged and other price-excludable goods, would be assigned a number between zero and one depending on the ease with which the benefits of the product can be priced.

According to this classification scheme, a pure private good would correspond to point A on the graph. At that point, there is full excludability and full rivalry for the benefits of the good. Similarly, a pure public good would correspond to point B at which the benefits are fully nonrival and price excludability is impossible. Some goods, such as cable TV transmissions, would correspond to a point on the vertical axis like C. For such a product, the benefits are nonrival, but price exclusion is relatively easy because signals can be scrambled and those who decline to pay for a hookup can be denied the benefits. A highway subject to congestion would correspond to a point like H, where there is a degree of rivalry, and price exclusion is possible through tolls.

Education as a Public Good

Education is a service that has some characteristics of a public good while at the same time having characteristics of a private good. Education is commonly believed to result in widely ranging external benefits when it is provided at least at some minimal level to all children in a society. However, at the same time, the exclusion principle can easily be applied to educational services so that it can be withheld from those who do not pay for it. Education is a clear example of a partially public good. Decisions must be made, therefore, about how to supply it. Education can be made available through the marketplace like any private good. Education can also be supplied by governments and given out free of charge in equal amounts to all children in a society.

In the United States, as well as in most other nations, a mix of both private and public schools has emerged both through the marketplace and political interaction as a means of supplying education. However, in the United States and in most other nations as well, on the primary and secondary level, education is mainly a government-supplied service. For example, in the United States approximately 90 percent of children attend public elementary and secondary schools. For higher education there are, of course, many public colleges and universities. But few public institutions of higher learning fully finance their activities with tax revenues. Students at colleges and universities pay a portion of the cost of their education through tuition and fees, and these prices have been increasing in recent years. Furthermore, about 40 percent of students at institutions of higher learning in the United States attend private schools.

It is clearly feasible to price educational services. And because the marginal cost of educating a student is certainly not zero, a zero price for the service is not an efficient alternative. Nonetheless, it is commonly agreed that education is such an important generator of positive externalities that it should be universally subsidized by government tax revenues. In the case of elementary and secondary education, the subsidization is complete and the price to families of children attending public schools is set at zero. In the United States, the costs of providing educational services is financed with a combination of local, state, and federal tax revenue, with the bulk of the revenues (more than 90 percent) coming from state and local tax coffers. State governments, through direct appropriations to colleges and universities, also heavily subsidize higher education. Federal subsidies to individuals and institutions and tax credits to individuals also help finance higher education. Education at the elementary and secondary level is almost universally compulsory up to a certain age. Thus, governments intervene in the supply of education to make sure every citizen consumes at least a minimal amount of this service.

What are the externalities associated with the production and consumption of education that result in such universal support of government supply and subsidization? Many believe that wide-ranging externalities exist when we live in a society where we can be sure everyone has a minimal level of education so that they can be productive citizens. We want to be sure everyone can read, have minimal computational skills so that they can manage their finances, and have adequate appreciation of public institutions and the duties of citizens to each other. This minimal level of education helps us all live in a reasonably civil society and therefore has a component that can be viewed as a public good that is equally consumed by all. Education has a "socializing" function. It provides students with the ability to function effectively in a society by following rules, obeying orders, and working together with colleagues. It also provides students with such basic skills as punctuality, ability to follow directions, and other skills that increase their productivity as workers.[3] Universal education also screens students by helping them to identify their abilities and to choose appropriate occupations as adults. In this way another public good aspect of education is its function of providing a better match of workers to jobs, thereby increasing productivity levels for a nation.

Many believe that some citizens would purchase less than the efficient amount of education for their children if it were provided in a competitive market. If this were the case, many brilliant minds could be deprived of sufficient education, and we would all be deprived of their possible future contributions to society. Further, some parents might not value education as much as others, and this could deprive their children of an adequate education. Whether or not underconsumption of education would actually result, it is clear that this idea is behind the principle of free and compulsory public education. Public education helps integrate all children into society. Education is especially useful for helping immigrant groups to understand the basics of an adopted culture and political system and to learn a new language.

However, the fact remains that education has characteristics of a private good. No government can guarantee that all children in a society receive an equal amount of education. Wide disparities exist in the quantity and quality of education provided among school districts in the United States. Production of a given output of education might take varying amounts of inputs depending on the students being taught. In areas where schools have a disproportionate number of disadvantaged students, higher expenditures per pupil are necessary to achieve the same level of output as

---

[3]See Andrew Weiss, "Human Capital versus Signaling Explanations of Wages," *Journal of Economic Perspectives* 9, 4 (Fall 1995): 133–154.

those areas where students have better home environments. Most studies show that the level of support parents can give students at home increases with household incomes, and home support is an important factor in learning for children.

Even if it were possible to equalize the quality and quantity of education provided in public schools, there is no way to prevent parents who want more than this standardized quantity and quality of education for their children from buying it in the marketplace. And since upper-income parents have more ability to pay for educational services, their children are more likely to obtain supplementary instruction or attend private schools where the quality and quantity of instruction could be higher.

CHECKPOINT

1. How do congestible public goods differ from pure public goods?
2. How do price-excludable public goods differ from pure public goods?
3. Give some examples of "semipublic goods" that are provided through the marketplace by profit-motivated businesses. Discuss the characteristics of these goods in terms of the excludability of their benefits and the rivalry among consumers for the benefits of given amounts of the goods.

THE DEMAND FOR A PURE PUBLIC GOOD

The demand for a pure public good must be interpreted differently from the demand for a pure private good. The market demand curve for a pure private good gives the sum of the quantities demanded by all consumers at each possible price per unit of the good. The market demand curve for a pure private good, such as bread, is illustrated in Figure 4.4. For any given price, a point on the market

FIGURE 4.4 Demand for a Private Good

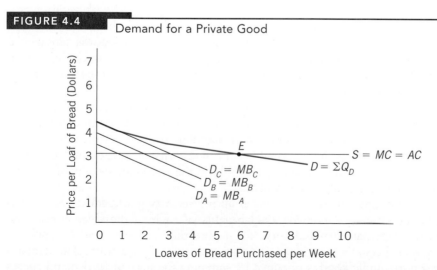

The demand for a private good is obtained by adding the quantities demanded by each consumer at each possible price. The efficient output is six units per week, which corresponds to point E. At a price of $3 per loaf, $MB_A = MB_B = MB_C = MC$.

demand curve for a pure private good is found by simply adding the quantity that each individual would purchase at that price. The individual demand curves are added laterally over the horizontal axis to obtain the market demand curve.

In Figure 4.4, there are only three consumers of the private good. At a price of $3 per loaf, the person whose demand curve is D_A purchases one loaf per week. That is the quantity for which the price equals his or her marginal benefit per week ($MB_A = \$3$). The person whose demand curve is represented by D_B purchases two loaves per week at a price of $3 per loaf. At that amount of weekly purchase of bread, $MB_B = \$3$. Finally, the person with demand curve D_C purchases three loaves per week at a price of $3 per loaf because $MB_C = \$3$ at that amount of weekly consumption. The total market quantity demanded by these three consumers is six loaves per week at a price of $3 per loaf. This is represented by point E on the market demand curve. Until the price falls below $4 per loaf, the only individual purchasing the good will be the one whose demand curve is represented by D_C. At lower prices, the other individuals whose demands are represented by D_B and D_A progressively enter the market, and the quantities that they demand as prices are lowered are added to that of the consumer whose demand is D_C. The market demand curve for the private good is labeled $D = \Sigma Q_D$.

For a pure public good, *all consumers must consume the same quantity of the good*. Purchasers of a pure public good would not be able to adjust their consumption so that one person had one unit per week, while another person enjoyed two units per week, and still another had three units per week. If consumer A had three units per week, all other people would consume three units per week. For a pure public good, consumers cannot adjust the amounts purchased until the price of the good equals their marginal benefit from the good per week. In fact, a pure public good cannot be priced because of its nonexclusion property.

How then can a demand curve for a pure public good be derived? The variables on the vertical axes are not market prices. Instead, they are the maximum amounts that people would pay per unit of the pure public good as a function of the amount of the good actually available. For example, suppose the three consumers live together in a small community and desire to provide themselves with security protection. The quantity of security protection can be measured by the number of security guards hired per week to patrol their community. Security guards represent a pure public good for these three consumers. No way exists for any one person in this community of three to hire a security guard for his or her own benefit without benefiting his or her neighbors.

Figure 4.5 shows each person's demand curve for security guards. A point on any of the individual demand curves represents the maximum amount that the consumer would pay to get *each unit* of the corresponding quantity of the public good. This maximum amount is the marginal benefit of security protection at each quantity. Each individual's demand curve shows how the marginal benefit of security guards declines as more are made available.

The total amount that would be given up per security guard hired per week is the sum of the annual weekly marginal benefits of each of the three consumers. Points on the aggregate demand curve for a pure public good could be obtained by adding each person's marginal benefit at each possible quantity. The demand curve for a pure public good is obtained by summing the individual demand curves vertically. The marginal benefit, or demand price, that each person would pay per unit of the public good is summed at each quantity of the good, because all people must consume the same quantity.

Demand for a Pure Public Good

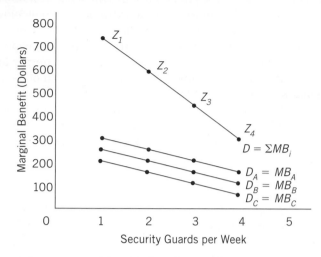

The demand curve for a pure public good is obtained by summing the individual marginal benefits at each quantity.

For example, the person with the demand curve D_A would pay a maximum of $300 per security guard if only one guard were provided per week. Similarly, the maximum amounts the people with demand curves D_B and D_C would give up per security guard if only one were provided per week would be $250 and $200, respectively. A point on the market demand curve therefore is obtained by adding these maximum amounts. Because the maximum amounts reflect the marginal benefit of security protection, the point on the market demand curve represented by point Z_1 corresponds to the sum of the marginal benefits of all three consumers. This equals $750 per year when only one security guard is provided.

The marginal benefit of additional units of a pure public good declines in the same fashion as do those of pure private goods. The amount per security guard that could be collected if two guards were made available per week is less than that which could be collected per guard when only one is provided per week. This too is shown in Figure 4.5. The maximum amount per guard that each of the three consumers would give up when two guards are made available per week is $250 for A, $200 for B, and $150 for C. Therefore, the sum of the marginal benefits when two security guards per week are provided is $600, as represented by point Z_2 in Figure 4.5. Adding the marginal benefit received by each consumer from any number of security guards in this way gives points on the demand curve for the pure public good. This curve is labeled $D = \Sigma MB_i$.

EFFICIENT OUTPUT OF A PURE PUBLIC GOOD

Efficiency requires that all economic activities be undertaken up to the point that their marginal social benefit is equated with their marginal social cost. This principle holds for pure public goods as well.

Suppose a person were to attempt to produce or purchase a pure public good for his or her own use. By making a unit of the public good available in the community, this person will generate benefits not only for himself or herself but also for every other member of the community in which she resides. The marginal social benefit of this good will be more than the extra benefit to its purchaser. Additional benefits will accrue to each and every other person who will simultaneously enjoy each unit made available. Summing up these benefits to all people in the community gives the marginal social benefit for each extra unit of output produced. The marginal social benefit of any given amount of a pure public good is the *sum of the individual marginal benefits received by all consumers.*

The efficient quantity per time period of a pure public good corresponds to the point at which output is increased so that the sum of the marginal benefits of consumers equals the marginal social cost of the good. The efficiency conditions for a pure public good are

$$MSB = \sum MB = MSC. \tag{4.1}$$

Market sale of a pure public good for individual purchase would generate wide-ranging positive externalities, because a purchaser of the good would consider only *his* or *her* marginal benefit in deciding how much to buy. The marginal external benefit would be the sum of the marginal benefits to all other consumers. When individual buyers do not take the marginal external benefit into account, sale of the good to individuals in a market is likely to result in less than the efficient annual quantity. A pure private good has no external benefits of additional production. In evaluating the benefit of extra production, it is necessary to count only the benefit received by the individual who actually purchases and consumes the extra output.

The efficiency conditions for a pure public good can also be written as

$$MSB = MB_i + \sum_{j=1}^{n-1} MB_j \tag{4.2}$$

Equation 4.2 states the marginal social benefit of a unit of a pure public good as the sum of the benefits accruing to any one person acquiring it (MB_i) and of the extra benefits that accrue to the remaining ($n - 1$) members of the community (ΣMB_j). The marginal social benefit is the sum of an individual benefit and an external benefit accruing to all other members of the community. The summation term

$$\sum_{j=1}^{n-1} MB_j$$

represents the marginal external benefit of a unit of a pure public good made available to any one person. The production of a pure public good generates external benefits that are positively valued by all members of a community.

A Numerical Example

Table 4.2 provides data on the marginal benefits of three consumers who desire security protection in a community. These data summarize the numbers used to derive the demand curve for security protection in Figure 4.5. In the table, the marginal benefits of as many as four security guards per week are shown for each consumer.

Suppose the weekly cost per security guard is $450. If as many guards as desired can be hired at that rate, the average cost of security protection would be constant at $450 per unit. In this case, a unit of security protection per week is presumed to be perfectly correlated with the services of one security guard per week.

TABLE 4.2   Hypothetical Marginal Benefits of Security Protection
for a Community of Three People

| | NUMBER OF SECURITY GUARDS PER WEEK | | | |
	1	2	3	4
MB_A	$300	$250	$200	$150
MB_B	250	200	150	100
MB_C	200	150	100	50
ΣMB_i	$750	$600	$450	$300

© Cengage Learning

Because average cost is constant, it is also equal to the marginal cost. Assuming no negative externalities associated with security protection, the marginal social cost of security protection also will be constant and equal to $450.

Table 4.2 also shows the sum of the marginal benefits, ΣMB_i, of security guards for the three consumers at each weekly quantity. Figure 4.6 plots the marginal benefit curve of each of the three consumers on the same set of axes as the marginal social cost curve. This latter curve is a straight line drawn at $450. Also plotted on the axes is the sum of the marginal benefits for the three consumers at each level of output. This latter curve gives the marginal social benefit of alternative weekly amounts of security protection.

FIGURE 4.6   Efficient Output of a Pure Public Good

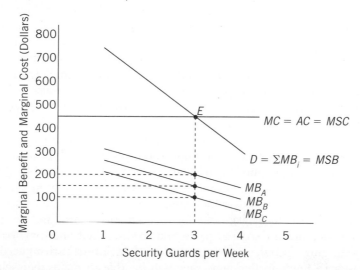

The efficient output occurs at point *E*, which corresponds to three security guards per week. At that point, $\Sigma MB_i = MSC$. The Lindahl equilibrium is also at point *E*. At that point, voluntary contributions of the three people would cover the cost of the public good. Each person would demand three security guards per week at a price per unit equal to the marginal benefit received from three guards per week.

© Cengage Learning

The efficient number of security guards for the three members of the community is three per week. At that level of supply, corresponding to point E, the sum of the marginal benefits equals the marginal social cost. At that level of weekly supply, the marginal social benefit equals the marginal social cost for members of the community.

Figure 4.6 can quickly show why market provision of security protection would not result in the efficient output. If the services of security guards were available to individuals only through market purchases, the quantity supplied to this community would be zero! This is because it costs $450 per week to hire each security guard. No single resident alone values the services of the first security guard that highly. The most any one person would pay for a security guard is $300 per week. The marginal benefit of the first security guard for any one buyer falls short of the market price per unit necessary to cover the marginal costs of sellers.

However, an output of zero is inefficient. The market equilibrium would be inefficient because, as is shown in Figure 4.6, the sum of the marginal benefits of the three consumers when one security guard per week is provided exceeds the marginal social cost of making that guard available. The marginal social benefit of the first guard is $750, while the marginal social cost is only $450. Therefore, it is certainly inefficient not to hire *at least* one security guard per week. The efficient output is actually three security guards per week, corresponding to point E in Figure 4.6. At that point, the sum of the individual marginal benefits equals the marginal social cost of security protection.

A Cooperative Method of Efficiently Supplying Pure Public Goods: Voluntary Contributions and Cost Sharing

To achieve the efficient output of three guards per week, members of the community will have to cooperate to share the costs per unit of security protection. By sharing the costs, members can pool their resources to enjoy public goods that they could not afford if they had to purchase them on their own in a market. In small communities, pure public goods conceivably could be made available in efficient amounts and financed by voluntary contributions. Understanding why this is unlikely to occur in larger communities is the key to understanding the reasons that citizens resort to governments to provide many public goods. It also helps provide insights into the reasons governments finance most of their activities with compulsory taxes instead of voluntary contributions.[4]

Suppose the three people previously discussed try to cooperate to satisfy and finance their desires for security protection. These people are confronted with the problem of financing a pure public good that is collectively consumed by them alone. All three must consume the identical quantity of security protection per week and must voluntarily contribute to cover the annual costs of making the protection available. Remember, it costs $450 per week for each security guard, and no member of the community will purchase security protection service if he has to pay for it alone.

Suppose the three people pool their resources to hire security guards. If they can obtain enough funds in this way, they will be able to make themselves better off by acquiring benefits none of them can individually afford. They will continue

---

[4]A classic model of a cooperative mechanism for supplying public goods was developed by Erik Lindahl in the early 1900s. See Erik Lindahl, "Just Taxation: A Positive Solution," in *Classics in the Theory of Public Finance*, eds. Richard A. Musgrave and Alan T. Peacock (New York: Cromwell-Collier, 1958): 168–177. Also see Cecil Bohanan, "McCaleb on Lindahl, Comment," *Public Finance* 38 (1983): 326–331.

to cooperate in this way by hiring guards up to the point at which their pooled contributions can no longer finance additional guards.

Suppose they try to hire one guard per week. How much would they collect in contributions? Figure 4.6 shows that A would contribute $300 for the first guard, B would contribute $250, and C would contribute $200. These amounts represent the marginal benefits for these people when only one guard per week is hired. Because the sum of the voluntary contributions exceeds the marginal cost of the first guard, the members conclude that it might be worthwhile to try to finance two guards per week instead. Hiring only one guard per week leaves a budget surplus for security protection. The budget surplus indicates that the marginal social benefit of the first security guard in the community exceeds the marginal social cost of providing the protection.

The sum of the marginal benefits of two security guards per week is $600. The members of the community would contribute $600 per guard if two would be hired per week. This also exceeds the marginal cost of making two guards per week available. The members of the community would collect more than enough funds to finance two units of security protection per week. The community security budget still has a surplus as long as each member faithfully contributes an amount equal to the marginal benefit per guard. The total cost of two guards per week would be $900. Because each person contributes an amount equal to the marginal benefit per guard, the total amounts collected to finance two security guards would be $500 from A, $400 from B, and $300 from C. The total revenue would be $1,200. The surplus is $300 per week.

The marginal benefits when three guards per week are available are $MB_A = \$200$, $MB_B = \$150$, and $MB_C = \$100$. The sum of the marginal benefits exactly equals the marginal cost of the third guard, $450. The community can finance still another unit of security protection. The total cost of three security guards per week is $1,350. Person A contributes $200 per guard or $600 per week for three guards. Person B contributes $150 per guard and pays $450 per week for three guards. Finally, C contributes $100 per guard, making a total weekly contribution equal to $300 for three guards. The total contributions exactly equal the total cost of $1,350 per week for three guards. This occurs at point E in Figure 4.6, where the ΣMB_i curve for the public good intersects the marginal cost curve for the good. At point E, $MSB = \Sigma MB_i = MC = MSC$ for the three consumers.

Any output greater than three could not be financed with voluntary contributions, because the sum of the marginal benefits of security protection in excess of three guards per week would fall short of the marginal cost of that level of security. Voluntary contributions would fail to collect enough to finance more than three security guards per week.

The equilibrium achieved through voluntary contributions results in the support of three security guards per week, which is efficient. This is because $MSB = MSC$ at the equilibrium number of guards per week. Thus, voluntary contributions in small groups can achieve the efficient output of a pure public good.

The Lindahl Equilibrium

Point E in Figure 4.6 is called a **Lindahl equilibrium**, after the Swedish economist Erik Lindahl.[5] The voluntary contribution per unit of the public good of each member of the community equals his or her marginal benefit of the public good at the

---

[5]Erik Lindahl, "Just Taxation."

efficient level of output. These equilibrium contributions per unit of the public good are sometimes called **Lindahl prices**. If the good were made available at these prices per unit for each of the consumers, the quantity demanded by *each* consumer would be the efficient amount of three security guards per week.

In effect, the Lindahl equilibrium also could be achieved by assigning each participant a Lindahl price per unit of the public good. Each person would have to be assigned a price that equals his or her marginal benefit at the efficient output of the good. In equilibrium, all three individuals would unanimously agree on the efficient quantity of the good to be made available, given their assigned Lindahl prices. In the preceding example, the Lindahl prices for each security guard would have to equal each community member's marginal benefit at the efficient output of three guards per week. If disagreement about the quantity of the good arose, the Lindahl prices per unit of the good would have to be adjusted until all individuals demand the quantity for which $MSB = MSC$. If disagreement ensued about the Lindahl prices, the quantity of the good would have to be adjusted until all individuals accepted their share and no surplus or deficit in the budget existed at the efficient output.

The solution to the model is similar to a market equilibrium, because it results in a set of price shares per unit of the good that are unanimously accepted to finance the cost of production of a simultaneously agreed-upon quantity. No one is forced or coerced to enter into the agreement. Given the distribution of income and other factors that affect the demands (or willingness to pay) of the three individuals for security protection, the outcome is a determinate quantity of the public good and an associated cost-sharing scheme. The voluntary cooperation model presented is one in which contributions are accepted for alternative quantities of the public good which, in turn, are compared with the marginal cost of additional production. Other similar models have auctioneer-announcing schemes for the division of the cost per unit of a public good in terms of the percentages to be borne by each individual, independent of the number of units produced. This ensures that the budget will always be in balance. Such tax-sharing schemes continually are called out until the quantity demanded of the public good is the same for all individuals.[6] The result in both cases is identical: The public good is produced at the level where the sum of the marginal benefits is equal to the marginal social cost, and each individual's Lindahl price in equilibrium reflects that person's marginal benefit at the equilibrium level of production.

Generalizing the Results

The Lindahl equilibrium consists of an agreement on the division of the costs of producing the equilibrium quantity of a pure public good. Conditions for equilibrium can now be generalized. Call t_i the amount contributed by each person per unit for any quantity of a pure public good made available and Q^* the equilibrium annual quantity of the pure public good. The equilibrium under the model of voluntary cooperation meets the following conditions:

1. The amount contributed per unit of the public good by each person, t_i, must be adjusted so that each individual desires the identical amount of the public good. This requirement stems from the nature of public goods. It is impossible for any one member of a community to consume, for example, more security protection than another, assuming that protection is truly a public good.

---

[6]This is the approach used by Lindahl in his classic model.

GLOBAL PERSPECTIVE

The Marginal Cost of the Persian Gulf War to the United States and How International Cost Sharing Financed It

World security is an international public good. Conflicts that affect the supplies of essential resources, such as crude oil from the Middle East, can play havoc with the economies of most industrial nations. When Iraq invaded Kuwait in August 1990, and stood poised to invade Saudi Arabia, the industrial nations of the world and many Arab nations who saw their security at risk were quick to unite against Iraqi aggression. With the Soviet Union and other old U.S. adversaries no longer opposed to U.S. intervention, the stage was set for a massive military buildup in the region to counter the Iraqi threat to other nations.

Although the bulk of the military effort came from the United States, millions around the world saw not only unprecedented cooperation among the many nations in the conflict but also commitments of cash and material from industrial nations that did not send troops to the region. The voluntary contributions to finance the U.S. cost of Operations Desert Shield and Desert Storm is a classic case of cooperation in the supply of a public good.

Let's take a look at the numbers to see how the U.S. cost of the war was shared by the group of nations threatened by the Iraqi aggression. The U.S. Office of Management and Budget has calculated the "incremental" costs of the war. These costs reflect the additional resources that were used to transport and supply troops during Operations Desert Shield and Desert Storm. These incremental costs are an indication of the marginal social cost of the war. Additional wages for military personnel and military operations are included in the estimate of the marginal social cost. Other costs include the transport of personnel and equipment by sea and by air to the Persian Gulf, support operations once there, fuel for military vehicles, and military construction.

According to the Office of Management and Budget, weapons and other nonpersonnel costs amounted to 70 percent of the total costs of the war. About one third of the costs were for personnel, including the difference between reserve pay and active duty pay for reservists called to active duty, combat pay, and long-term costs, such as increased veterans' benefits for soldiers who served in the conflict.

The official estimate of the incremental costs of Operations Desert Shield and Desert Storm was a total of $61 billion. However, much of these costs have been offset by contributions of foreign nations that voluntarily pledged to contribute to expenses incurred by the United States. Here is an example of the Lindahl model at work on an international scale: Total pledges by allies of the United States amounted to $54 billion! Of this total, $48 billion were monetary contributions and the remainder were contributions of fuel and other materials to the war effort. These contributions have been allocated to the U.S. Defense Department to offset war-related expenses. The net cost of the war to the U.S. taxpayers was expected to amount to only $7 billion.

The following table shows the pledges of the major allies.

Voluntary Contributions to Finance the Marginal Social Cost of Operations Desert Shield and Desert Storm (Billions of Dollars, Rounded to the Nearest Whole Number)

NATION	CONTRIBUTION
Saudi Arabia	$17
Kuwait	16
Japan	11
Germany	7
United Arab Emirates	4
Total Pledged	54
U.S. Share	7
Total	61

Source: Office of Management and Budget and Congressional Budget Office.

When the United States went to war in Iraq again in 2003, such cooperation failed to materialize. The costs of the 2003 war and the occupation of Iraq were borne almost entirely by U.S. taxpayers with some help from a small coalition of allied nations and the United Kingdom.

2. The sum of the amounts contributed by each member of the community per unit must equal the marginal social cost of producing the public good. When marginal social cost equals the average cost of the good, this implies that the voluntary contributions will constitute amounts sufficient to finance the good without any surplus or deficit.[7] The revenue collected can be expressed as the sum of the cost shares per unit of the public good, Σt_i, multiplied by the number of units produced in equilibrium, Q^*. The total cost of production is average cost, AC, multiplied by the quantity produced, Q^*. It follows that

$$\sum t_i Q^* = MC(Q^*) = AC(Q^*) \qquad (4.3)$$

or

$$\sum t_i = MC = AC.$$

3. All individuals must agree voluntarily, with no coercion whatsoever, on the cost-sharing arrangement and the quantity of the good. The equilibrium must occur under unanimous consent. This ensures an efficient outcome, because any individual made worse off by any arrangement can block its approval.

THE FREE-RIDER PROBLEM

A system of voluntary contributions for reaching agreement on the financing and quantity of a pure public good could work well when a community comprises only a few individuals. In fact, a great deal of similarity exists between voluntary agreements on the supply of pure public goods and the Coasian small-number externalities discussed in Chapter 3. When the number of people involved in reaching the voluntary agreement is small, the transaction costs are likely to be low. In small groups, individuals know each other well and have a good idea of each other's benefits from the availability of a public good. People in the community are well aware of the common benefit of the shared good. Any attempts by individuals to conceal their actual marginal benefits from the good can be easily detected.

For example, people living in a condominium often meet to determine the extent of maintenance on roads jointly owned by the owners of individual apartments. They might also meet to pool their resources to provide security protection. Members of the association are likely to be sufficiently aware of the tastes and incomes of their neighbors to have a good notion of their true marginal benefits of additional maintenance services. Under such circumstances, individual members have little incentive to conceal their preferences in the bidding process. Similarly, in small communities, moral obligations of members might act as strong constraints in preventing inaccurate preference revelation. For this reason, churches and many civic clubs successfully finance projects of common benefit to their members through donations.

However, as the number of people involved in the decision increases, and information about neighbors' tastes and economic circumstances becomes scarcer, the likelihood that individuals will inaccurately reveal their preferences becomes higher.

---

[7]When marginal costs of producing the pure public good are increasing, $MC > AC$ at any given quantity. This implies that $\Sigma MB_i > AC$ at the efficient output for which $\Sigma MB_i = MC$. In this case, the sum of voluntary contributions per unit exceeds the average cost of production in equilibrium. The equilibrium budget will have a surplus, which could be returned as a lump-sum payment to members of the community after the cost of the public good is financed.

This is because no one person in a large group is likely to have accurate information on the actual marginal benefits of others.

If people know that they are required to pay a share of the unit cost of the public good dependent on their marginal benefits, they have an incentive to understate their true marginal benefits. To do this is in their interest because it conserves their incomes. At the same time, they do not have to forgo all the benefits of public goods because these benefits are nonexclusive. A person might, in fact, choose to contribute nothing toward the financing of government activity in the hope of enjoying benefits made possible by other people's contributions. Clearly, if all citizens behave in this way, no source of finance for the budget exists, and therefore no benefits. But the individual who behaves in this manner assumes others will continue to contribute.[8]

A good example of this problem is public television and radio programming. Listener- and viewer-financed stations fund a good portion of their operations from voluntary contributions. Many viewers and listeners who receive benefits from the station give nothing or contribute amounts below their marginal benefits from existing programming. A likely result is less than the efficient amount of programming.

A **free-rider** is a person who seeks to enjoy the benefits of a public good without contributing anything to the cost of financing the amount made available. The free-rider problem stems from the incentive people have to enjoy the external benefits financed by others, with no cost to themselves. Free-riding can be a reasonable strategy for any one individual, provided that no penalty exists and that only a few individuals choose the strategy. If all members of the community choose the free-rider strategy, no vehicle is available to hitch a ride on because no production of the public good would be forthcoming. Everyone would be worse off under this strategy, because the benefits of the public good will be forgone completely.

Under a system of voluntary contributions when large numbers of people are involved, attempts by individuals to play the free-rider strategy almost guarantee that the equilibrium amount of pure public good will be less than the efficient amount. Therefore, voluntary cost sharing of pure public goods will result in insufficient amounts of the public good being produced relative to the efficient amounts.

Individual members of the community can be made better off by engaging in free-rider strategies. Suppose person C, whose marginal benefit curve is drawn in Figure 4.6, tries to be a free-rider. To see how he can gain, calculate his net benefits from security protection at the efficient output of three guards per week. His total benefit, $450, is the sum of his marginal benefit from each of the three guards. If he truthfully reveals his marginal benefit for three guards per week, his cost share per guard will be $100. His total cost for the three guards will be $300, and he will enjoy net benefits of $150 at the efficient output.

If he were to be a free-rider, he would contribute zero per guard. The cost of a third guard could not be covered even if the other two members truthfully contributed their marginal benefits. This is because $MB_A + MB_B = \$350$ at three guards per week. However, two guards per week could be financed because $MB_A + MB_B = \$450$ at two guards, barely covering the marginal cost of the second guard. At that level of weekly output, person C would enjoy net benefits of $350 (the sum of $200 for the first guard and $150 for the second guard) without contributing a cent. Because his net benefit while pursuing the free-rider strategy exceeds his net benefit from truthfully

[8]This problem can be avoided if a collectively agreed-upon mechanism can be established to provide artificial incentives for individuals to reveal their true preferences. For a review of this literature, see Martin Loeb, "Alternative Versions of the Demand Revealing Process," *Public Choice* 29 (Spring 1977): 15–26. Also see O. Kim and M. Walker, "The Free-Rider Problem: Experimental Evidence," *Public Choice* 43 (1984): 3–24.

contributing, he is better off. Other members of the community also could gain by pursuing a free-rider strategy. However, if more than one person were to attempt to be a free-rider, not enough would be contributed to finance even one security guard per week! Each one of the three people would be worse off under those circumstances because they would forgo the security protection completely.

The free-rider problem tends to become more acute as the size of the group benefiting from a pure public good becomes larger. This is because each individual member of a small group reasons that if he or she withholds his or her contribution, the result could be a significant reduction in the quantity of the good that is supplied in equilibrium. In the three-member group example, the individuals know that if more than one of them is a free-rider, no security protection is possible. This provides a strong incentive for them to cooperate. If, on the other hand, 10,000 members are in the community, C's attempt to be a free-rider might reduce the equilibrium amount of security only slightly if enough of the others still contribute. In large groups, the incentive for any one person to be a free-rider is greater because each person might reason that the vast multitude of other beneficiaries will contribute enough to finance the good. Therefore, the probability of the free-rider problem reducing the actual contributions to zero is all the greater in a community with a large number of members.

Compulsory Finance

In view of the free-rider problem, communities commonly require compulsory payments to help finance the costs of public goods made available to large groups. This leads to government supply of public goods and financing of the cost by taxation. Of course, not all goods supplied by governments are pure public goods. Some government services, such as schooling, roads, and postal services, can be priced and, in fact, could be sold in markets to individuals. However, it is common for government services that involve some degree of collective consumption to be financed through a compulsory tax scheme to avoid the possibility of free-riding.

An important lesson remains from the model of voluntary cost sharing of public goods. Under compulsory taxation, a voter is told, not asked, to contribute. In democratic nations, because political outcomes are determined by voting, the willingness of any voter to vote in favor of a proposal depends on his or her tax share per unit of the good. As demonstrated in Chapter 5, a person decides how to vote in an election by comparing the tax share per unit of a public good with the marginal benefit of the proposed output.

CHECKPOINT

1. How does the demand for a pure public good differ from that of a pure private good? How can the demand curve for a pure public good be derived?
2. Under what conditions is the output level of a pure public good efficient?
3. What are the characteristics of the Lindahl equilibrium for cooperative supply of a pure public good? How does the free-rider problem affect the effectiveness of voluntary cooperative methods in achieving efficient levels of output for pure public goods?

SUMMARY

A pure public good is one that is consumed by all members of a community as soon as it is produced for any one member. Its benefits are nonrival and nonexcludable to consumers. The market supply of such a good would result in positive externalities to all members of the community. Therefore, its benefits are collectively consumed, and the exclusion of any one member from those benefits is costly. A pure private good is one that generates no externalities, neither when produced nor when consumed.

Efficiency requires that the production of pure public goods be undertaken to the point where the sum of the marginal private benefits is exactly equal to the marginal social cost of production. Market supply of public goods for individual purchase is likely to be inefficient. This results from the positive externalities associated with market provision of such goods. People often attempt to consume the benefits of others' purchases of pure public goods while bearing no costs themselves. These people try to become free-riders.

Ideally, an efficient output of a pure public good could be achieved if each person contributed an amount equal to the marginal benefits received per unit of a public good. This is known as the Lindahl equilibrium. However, problems in inducing households to reveal their true preferences for public goods resulting from free-rider effects make this solution difficult to implement.

In actuality, many goods and services fall between the extremes of pure public goods and pure private goods. In evaluating the alternatives of government and market supply for intermediate cases, the external benefits of the good and the efficiency of alternative methods of exclusion have to be considered.

LOOKING AHEAD

Public goods supplied through political institutions require collective agreement on the quantity to produce and the means of finance. Chapter 5 examines public choices and the political process.

KEY CONCEPTS

Congestible Public Goods

Free-rider

Lindahl Equilibrium

Lindahl Prices

Nonexclusion

Nonrival in Consumption

Price-Excludable Public Goods

Private Goods

Public Goods

Pure Private Good

Pure Public Good

REVIEW QUESTIONS

1. What are the essential differences between pure public goods and pure private goods?
2. Although the marginal cost of producing a pure public good is always positive, some consumers can enjoy the benefits of pure public goods at zero marginal costs. Explain the apparent paradox, if there is one!
3. Why does the definition of a pure public good imply that its benefits are not subject to congestion?
4. How does the condition for efficiency differ between pure public goods and pure private goods?
5. What problems are likely to arise if people try to supply public goods for themselves without cooperating and sharing costs?
6. In what sense does the demand curve for a pure public good differ from that of a pure private good?
7. How will shares in the finance of public goods vary among contributors in a model of voluntary cooperative supply of such goods?
8. Give some examples of goods sold by governments in markets. Also, think of examples of partially public goods produced and distributed by private firms for profit.
9. Suppose the price of hiring a security guard increases from $450 to $600 per week. Using the data in Table 4.2, show how this will affect the Lindahl equilibrium.
10. Use the data in Table 4.2 to show how a decrease in the demand for security protection by any one voter will affect the Lindahl equilibrium.

PROBLEMS

1. The following table shows how the marginal benefit of a service varies for four consumers:

Marginal Benefit (in Dollars)

	CONSUMERS			
QUANTITY	ALICE	BEN	CAROLYN	DON
1	1000	800	600	400
2	800	600	400	200
3	600	400	200	100
4	400	200	100	50

a. Suppose the service is a pure private good and is sold in a competitive market with the only buyers being the four people whose marginal benefits are shown in the table. If the market price of the product is $400, what is the quantity demanded?

b. Suppose the service is a pure public good with the only consumers being the four people whose marginal benefits are shown in the table. What is the marginal social benefit of two units of the service?

c. If the marginal social cost of the good is $2,000, what is the efficient output assuming that it is a pure private good?

d. If the marginal social cost of the good is $2,000, what is the efficient output assuming it is a pure public good?

2. Suppose the marginal cost of a pure public good increases as more is purchased by a community. Prove that the Lindahl equilibrium will result in a budget surplus at the efficient annual output of the pure public good.

3. Suppose the services of a road are subject to congestion after 50,000 vehicles per hour enter the road. Assume that it is feasible to price road services on an hourly basis. Use a graph like that drawn in Figure 4.2 to show how the services of the road should be priced per hour when fewer than and more than 50,000 vehicles per hour are expected so as to achieve efficiency.

4. The following table shows how the marginal benefit enjoyed by John, Mary, Loren, and all other consumers of outdoor rock concerts varies with the number made available by a city government per summer.

Marginal Benefit of Number of Rock Concerts per Consumer (in Dollars)

	NUMBER OF CONCERTS			
CONSUMERS	1	2	3	4
John	150	125	100	75
Mary	125	100	75	50
Loren	100	75	50	25
All Others	600	400	200	100

a. Derive the demand curve for rock concerts assuming that it is a pure public good.

b. If the marginal cost of producing rock concerts is $1,000 no matter how many are produced, then what is the efficient number of concerts to have each summer? What would be the efficient number of concerts to produce if the marginal cost of production were $425 instead of $1,000?

5. Suppose the marginal cost of producing rock concerts is only $250 per concert no matter how many are produced. Use the data from the previous question to calculate the efficient number of concerts. If a Lindahl scheme is used to finance the concerts, what prices of admission should be charged to John, Loren, and Mary?

ADDITIONAL READINGS

Bank, Stevan A., Stark, Kirk J., and Thorndike, Joseph J., *War and Taxes*, Baltimore, Md.: The Urban Institute Press, 2008. An analysis of the way national defense spending is financed within the context of American history from the revolutionary war to 9/11 and the war in Iraq.

Buchanan, James M. *The Demand and Supply of Public Goods*. Chicago, Ill.: Rand McNally, 1968. A pioneering work applying principles of exchange to the public sector and attempting to formulate a theory of supply as well as demand for public goods.

Collender, Stanley E. *The Guide to the Federal Budget*. Washington, D.C.: Urban Institute Press, published annually. Analysis of what is in the federal budget.

Ferroni, Marco, and Ashoka, Mody, editors, *International Public Goods: Incentives, Measurement, and Financing*. Boston, Mass.: Kluwer Academic Publishers, 2002. A collection of studies on international public goods including security concerns, control of epidemics, and other aspects of issues relating to global stability. An extension of the theory of public goods to international concerns and cooperation.

Mueller, Dennis C., *Public Choice III*, 3rd ed. Cambridge, England: Cambridge University Press, 2003. An excellent integration of the theory of public goods with the notion of collective choice.

Touffut, Jean-Philippe, *Advancing Public Goods*, Northampton, Mass.: Edward Elgar Publishing, 2006. A selection of papers on issues in the theory of public goods with application to issues regarding the supply of public services in mixed economies.

INTERNET RESOURCES

http://www.whitehouse.gov
Information on the federal budget and agencies of the federal government can be accessed through the White House home page. Click on "Our Government" to access all major departments of the federal government.

http://www.defense.gov/.
This is the home page for the Department of Defense. If you are interested in military spending and programs for national defense, information can be obtained from this site. Find the defense budget to examine various military programs, including personnel, weapons systems, and items requested by the military in its current budget.

Chapter 5

PUBLIC CHOICE AND THE POLITICAL PROCESS

LEARNING OBJECTIVES

After reading this chapter, you should be able to:

- Define a public choice and the concept of political equilibrium.

- Explain how voting decisions are influenced by tax shares.

- Discuss incentives to vote.

- Discuss the characteristics of political equilibrium for a single public good under majority rule, the importance of the median voter, and how cycling of outcomes can result when all voters do not have single-peaked preferences.

- Describe the role of political parties and special-interest groups in the political process.

- Show how logrolling can influence political equilibrium.

- Analyze how bureaucrats behave and how they can influence political outcomes.

Have you ever thought about how many decisions affecting your daily life are made through the political process? Everything from the quality of your local public educational system and road network to the commitment of U.S. military forces to war is determined through political decisions. Politics also influences the amount of taxes you pay and how the burden of financing government programs is distributed among citizens. The process is also used to compete for the favors of government. Politics determines who gets income support from the government and which businesses are the fortunate recipients of government subsidies.

The political process is based on rules embodied in a nation's constitution. In democratic nations, citizens have the opportunity to vote on issues or for candidates who take positions on those issues. The outcome of the process depends on voting and the behavior of a host of characters, including politicians, elected officials, special-interest groups, and bureaucrats.

The political process involves more than merely counting votes and deciding on the rules for reaching agreement. Agendas for political action are drawn up by political parties, and alternative proposals are placed before Congress and legislatures. A variety of groups then seek to provide voters with information on the costs and benefits of alternatives so they can decide how to vote.

The theory of *public choice* studies how decisions to allocate resources and redistribute income are made through a nation's political system. The political process is, of course, influenced by factors other than economics, such as ideology. However, from an economic point of view, the purpose of politics is to provide citizens with useful goods and services. The theory of public choice examines how the political process is used to determine the quantity of goods and services supplied by governments.

THE SUPPLY OF PUBLIC GOODS THROUGH POLITICAL INSTITUTIONS: THE CONCEPT OF POLITICAL EQUILIBRIUM

A **public choice** is one made through political interaction of many people according to established rules. The supply of a public good through political institutions requires agreements on the quantity of the public good and the means of finance. Political institutions rarely require unanimous agreement on both the quantity of the public good to produce and the cost-sharing scheme. In fact, a variety of public choice rules are used to make decisions in communities, the most familiar of which is majority rule.

The model of voluntary cooperation for supplying public goods, discussed in Chapter 4, is useful in gaining insights into the factors that influence the actual political choices. Under government supply of goods and services, taxes rather than voluntary contributions are usually used to finance the goods and services provided. Citizens who vote against an outcome that is enacted must abide by the results. This differs from the voluntary cost-sharing model for supplying public goods in which individual citizens can veto proposed outcomes if they are dissatisfied with their share of the costs.

Political Equilibrium

A **political equilibrium** is an agreement on the level of production of one or more public goods, given the specified rule for making the collective choice and the distribution of tax shares among individuals. **Tax shares**, sometimes called *tax prices*, are preannounced levies assigned to citizens and are equal to a portion of the unit cost of a good proposed to be provided by government. To a voter, these tax shares represent price per unit of a government-supplied good. The sum of the tax shares must equal the average cost of the public good to avoid budget surpluses or deficits. If t_i is the share of the cost per unit of a pure public good for voter i, then Σt_i for all the voters must equal the average cost of the good.

The cost of producing a public good influences the amount of taxes that citizens must pay to finance the production of each unit of the good. Given the distribution of tax shares per unit of a public good among individuals, an increase in the average cost of producing the public good will increase the individual's tax bill per unit of the public good. Unless such increases in cost are accompanied by increases in benefits, the increased taxes likely will serve to diminish support for increases in the output of the public good.

In reality, information on costs of producing the good is difficult to obtain. Debates preceding an election may influence the willingness of voters to support various levels of output of the public good. Political campaigns provide information on both the costs and the benefits of the alternative programs being offered to voters for their consideration. Control over information concerning the costs and benefits of public goods is an important factor influencing collective choices and their efficiency.

The actual outcome depends, in part, on the particular public choice rule used to make the decision. Proposals that cannot gain approval under unanimous consent might very well be approved under majority rule. In general, the smaller the proportion of the community required to approve any given issue, the greater the probability the issue will be approved. The analysis in this chapter concentrates on choices made through **simple majority rule**, under which a proposal is approved if it receives more than half the votes cast in an election.

Elections and Voting

Public choices are made formally through elections in which each individual is usually allowed one vote. The economic analysis of the political process assumes that people evaluate the desirability of goods supplied by government in the same way they consider market goods and services. They are presumed to vote in favor of a proposal only if they will be made better off by its passage.

A rational person's **most-preferred political outcome** is the quantity of the government-supplied good corresponding to the point at which the person's tax share is exactly equal to the marginal benefit of the good. This level of output of the good provides the maximum possible satisfaction to that person. Increasing the quantity of the government-supplied good a fraction of a unit over this amount would make the person worse off.

The most-preferred political outcome for the person whose marginal benefit curve and tax share are illustrated in Figure 5.1 is Q^* units of the good per year. This is the output corresponding to point Z, at which $MB_i = t_i$, where t_i is the voter's tax per unit of the public good. Increments in the output of the good up to Q^* per year make this voter better off because the extra benefit of those units exceeds the extra taxes the voter must pay to make those units available. If, however, the output were to increase above Q^* units per year, the extra taxes would exceed the extra benefit, and the voter would be made worse off. In effect, the voter acts as though the public good could be bought at price t_i in a market.

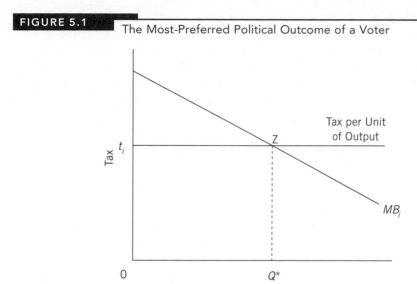

FIGURE 5.1 The Most-Preferred Political Outcome of a Voter

The voter achieves maximum net satisfaction at point Z. This is the point at which $MB_i = t_i$. The voter's most-preferred political outcome corresponding to this point is Q^* units of the public good per year.

A voter will vote in favor of any quantity of a public good as long as the marginal benefit of that quantity is not less than the marginal tax he or she must pay to finance that amount.

For a given public choice rule, the outcome of an election will depend, in part, on the distribution of tax shares among individuals. Proposals to increase the output of public goods that cannot gain approval under a certain distribution of tax shares might be approved under a different distribution of tax shares, because a change in tax shares will change the most-preferred outcomes of voters. Similarly, the political equilibrium will depend on the distribution of benefits among individuals. A change in the distribution of benefits for a given public project alters its chances of approval, because it changes the most-preferred outcomes of voters. The distribution of benefits of such programs as military installations in the United States is often a crucial factor influencing congressional approval of increases or decreases in spending. Politicians, by manipulating the distribution of benefits of certain programs, can alter the chances of those programs being enacted.

To Vote or Not to Vote

A person's decision to vote depends on the benefits and costs of doing so, as well as on the probability that voting will help to achieve the anticipated benefits. The individual also might receive benefits from voting that do not necessarily depend on whether the desired alternative is approved. One such benefit is the pleasure received from exercising the duties of being a citizen.

One of the costs involved in voting is the time and effort it takes to go to the polls. Other costs include those of gathering the information necessary to make a choice. This involves reading newspapers and going to meetings to understand the issues and positions of the candidates. This can be a time-consuming process.

Many citizens quite rationally believe that their votes will not make any difference in the outcome of an election. Indeed, any given citizen's choosing not to bother to vote very likely does not affect the outcome of any given election. Voters reason that the probability of their votes influencing the election will be close to zero when the number of voters is large. Because the costs of voting are positive while the expected benefits, in terms of influencing the outcome, are close to zero for an individual voter, it is rational not to vote. In effect, nonvoters try to become free riders on the time and effort put in by those who do vote.

If all voters were to reason this way, a democratic nation would not be able to function as such because no one would vote! In fact, some democratic nations make voting a legal requirement for citizens in order to avoid free riding by nonvoters. However, even in nations where voting is not legally required, voters turn out to the polls in surprisingly large numbers. This indicates that other forces, such as the pleasure of exercising the duties of being a citizen or social pressures, motivate citizens to vote. Nevertheless, voter turnout in the United States has decreased in recent years. Fifty-one percent of eligible voters actually voted in the 2000 presidential election! Voter turnout in presidential elections has been declining in the United States since 1960, when 62.8 percent of the electorate voted. In the 2002 elections, an estimated 39.9 percent of the electorate voted.[1] In the 2004 presidential elections, there was an increase in voter turnout when 55.3 percent of the voting age population went to the polls. In the 2006 Congressional elections voter turnout was a mere 37.1 percent of the voting age population. The 2008 presidential election between John McCain and Barack Obama resulted in a turnout of 57.1 percent of the voting age population while the 2012 election between Obama and Mitt Romney had a turnout rate of 57.5 percent.

In general, the closer the alternatives are, the less the benefit obtained from choosing one alternative over another. In these cases, the net benefit of voting is likely to be very low, even if the probability of influencing the result of the election is significantly greater than zero. Therefore, some might argue that voters are less likely to vote when they see little or no differences between the alternatives considered in the election.

In other cases, a given voter's most-preferred position might be so far from the alternatives being offered that the probability of receiving any net benefits as a result of casting a vote is very low. The voter will choose to stay away from the polls under these circumstances. The decision to vote therefore depends on the cost and the expected benefit of that action, as is the case for any economic activity.

Some voters who do vote do so on the basis of scanty information, and their votes might be different if they knew more about the issues. When an individual casts a vote based on poor information, it is doubtful that the social benefit obtained is any greater than if the voter had stayed away from the polls. To vote intelligently, voters must have information on the marginal costs, including extra taxes, which they will bear if the issue under consideration passes. They also must know the marginal benefits they will receive if the issue passes. A voter cannot vote

[1]Estimate by Michael P. McDonald. For a discussion of the methodology used, see Michael P. McDonald, "The Turnout Rate among Eligible Voters for U.S. States, 1998–2000," *State Politics and Policy Quarterly* 2, 2 (June 2002): 199–212.

rationally in an election to increase the quantity of a public good, such as more roads, without accurate information on the extra taxes and marginal benefits that will result if the issue wins. Unfortunately, because information on taxes paid and the benefits of many public programs is hard to obtain, many voters do not take the time to become fully informed. **Rational ignorance** is the lack of information about public issues that results because the marginal cost of obtaining the information exceeds the apparent marginal benefits of doing so. When voting for congressional representatives, few people take the time to find out where candidates stand on all the issues and what taxes the candidates support. As a result, many voters who do vote may be making decisions that are not in their own interests. For example, voters who do not research their decisions might actually vote in favor of extensions of public services, such as roads, beyond the point at which marginal benefits to them fall to equal the marginal costs they must bear as a result of the public choice.

Determinants of Political Equilibrium

In summary, all of the following factors influence whether a public choice will result in approval or disapproval of any proposal regarding the level of production of a public good (or any other issue of collective interest):

- The public choice rules itself, that is, the proportion of yes votes in relation to the number of votes required for approval of the issue.

- The average and marginal costs of the public good.

- The information available to voters on the cost and benefit associated with the issue.

- The distribution of tax shares among voters and the way in which extra taxes vary with extra output of the good provided. In the models developed here, the marginal tax per unit of output is assumed to be constant.

- The distribution of benefits among voters.

If any one of these factors is changed, the equilibrium itself will respond accordingly.

In any election, each of these determinants of political equilibrium affects the outcome. All candidates seek to formulate policies that will give them a majority of the votes cast. In some elections, the issue of tax increases or decreases and the distribution of the tax burden is important. Walter Mondale's pledge to raise taxes might very well have been a major fact contributing to his defeat in the 1984 presidential election. In the 1988 election, George Bush pledged not to raise taxes and emphasized that a great deal of uncertainty surrounded the costs and benefits of programs proposed by Michael Dukakis, who argued that proposals for tax changes by Bush would alter the distribution of tax shares to favor the rich. Dukakis argued that his programs for spending and taxation would provide more benefit to middle-income groups. Both candidates argued that they would cut federal spending to reduce the deficit but remained vague about which programs would be cut for fear of suggesting that they would alter the distribution of benefits of spending in a way that would harm their chances of being elected. In the 1992 presidential election, Bill Clinton promised to raise taxes on upper-income groups to help reduce the budget deficit. This combined with an economy barely recovering from a recession helped Clinton win the election over George Bush, who once again promised not to raise taxes (a pledge he did not keep in his term in office after the 1988 election). And in the 1996 presidential election, both Bill Clinton and Bob Dole vowed to reduce taxes *and* cut the deficit. In the 2000 election, both George W. Bush and Al Gore sought to reduce taxes and to appeal to middle-income voters. The result was a virtual tie that had to be settled in the courts! During the 2004 presidential campaign, George W. Bush once again promised not to increase taxes despite a growing federal budget deficit and increasing military expenditures for wars in Iraq and Afghanistan. Bush defeated John Kerry in that election, obtaining 50.7 percent of the popular vote. However, by 2008 the median voter appeared to be growing less conservative on issues relating to military activities, taxation, and the economy, and the result was a major victory by the Democratic candidate, Barack Obama, over the more conservative Republican candidate, John McCain. In that election, Obama received 53 percent of the popular vote, a margin of victory significantly greater than Bush's in the 2004 presidential election. In 2012 President Obama promised to raise income tax rates for upper income taxpayers to help reduce the federal budget deficit and he won the election defeating the more conservative Mitt Romney.

CHECKPOINT

1. What are public choices?
2. Under what circumstances does a rational voter choose to vote in favor of a proposal to increase the output of a public good? Why do some voters choose not to vote?
3. What are the major determinants of a political equilibrium?

A MODEL OF POLITICAL EQUILIBRIUM UNDER MAJORITY RULE

To illustrate political equilibrium under simple majority rule, assume that citizens must decide on the quantity of a pure public good to produce. Given the average cost of producing the good, a tax-sharing scheme is announced whereby each individual will pay the same tax per unit of the good. If the good can be produced under conditions of constant costs and there are n individuals in the community, each individual will pay a tax equal to AC/n per unit of the public good. Assuming seven voters, Figure 5.2 shows the marginal benefit curves of the voters, the marginal (and average) cost line for the public good, and the tax share per unit of the public good of each of the voters.[2]

Suppose that the seven voters, whose marginal benefit curves are subscripted A, B, C, M, F, G, and H, respectively, constitute a community of people trying to provide themselves with security protection. Assume that the quantity of protection

---

[2]This analysis follows the classic model of political equilibrium developed by Howard R. Bowen in "The Interpretation of Voting in the Allocation of Economic Resources," *Quarterly Journal of Economics* 58 (February 1943): 27–48; reprinted in *Readings in Welfare Economics*, Kenneth Arrow and Tibor Scitovsky, eds. (Homewood, Ill.: Irwin, 1969): 115–132.

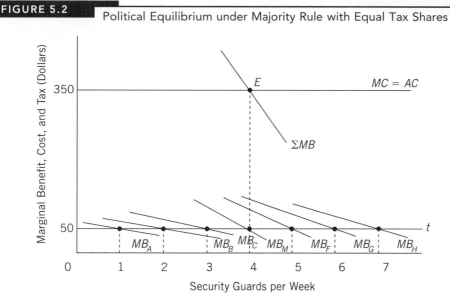

FIGURE 5.2 Political Equilibrium under Majority Rule with Equal Tax Shares

The political equilibrium occurs at the median most-preferred outcome of four security guards per week under simple majority rule. Each voter pays a tax share of $50 per guard per week. In equilibrium, the weekly tax bill of each voter is $200.

© Cengage Learning

provided varies with the number of security guards hired per week to patrol their neighborhood. Security protection services have all the characteristics of a pure public good for the seven members of the community. Given their tax shares per guard, each of the seven individuals has his or her own most-preferred output level, corresponding to the point where each marginal benefit curve crosses the tax share line, t, in Figure 5.2. Suppose the cost of each security guard is $350 per week. This represents both the average and the marginal cost of security protection. The weekly tax share of each voter per security guard will be $50 if the tax shares are to be equal for each voter. This is because $AC/n = \$350/7 = \$50$.

If security protection were a private good available at price t per unit, each person would be able to consume the most-preferred amount of the good, which ranges from one to seven security guards per week. However, because it is a pure public good, all must consume the same quantity. That quantity is the number of security guards per week that can gain approval under majority rule.

Election Results under Majority Rule

Elections now will be held to approve or disapprove successive increases in the output of the public good. Proposals to increase production from zero to any positive amount will be successively voted on. As long as a proposal to increase the amount of guards per week by one more unit achieves more than half the seven votes, it will pass. Therefore, at least four votes are required for a proposal to pass. Assume that all members of the community vote.

Table 5.1 shows the vote tallies for each election and the results, as referenda to increase output from zero to seven are successively held. The election held to increase output from zero to one unit of security protection passes unanimously,

TABLE 5.1		Voting to Provide Security Protection and Election Results under Simple Majority Rule						
		INCREASE SECURITY GUARDS PER WEEK TO						
		1	2	3	4	5	6	7
Voters	A	Yes	No	No	No	No	No	No
	B	Yes	Yes	No	No	No	No	No
	C	Yes	Yes	Yes	No	No	No	No
	M	Yes	Yes	Yes	Yes	No	No	No
	F	Yes	Yes	Yes	Yes	Yes	No	No
	G	Yes	Yes	Yes	Yes	Yes	Yes	No
	H	Yes	Yes	Yes	Yes	Yes	Yes	Yes
Results		Pass	Pass	Pass	Pass	Fail	Fail	Fail

© Cengage Learning

because the marginal benefit of the first unit is not less than the tax cost of that unit for any of the voters. As shown in the tally sheet, all vote yes.

A proposal then is made to increase weekly security protection by increasing the number of guards from one to two per week. This proposal also passes under majority rule. Only voter A votes against this proposal. He or she does so because the marginal benefit of the second security guard falls short of the extra taxes he or she will have to pay per week to finance that extra protection ($MB_A < \$50$). Under majority rule, the proposal to increase output to two guards per week passes six to one even though an individual is made worse off by the move. Similarly, expansion in the output of the public good to three and four units per week obtains the majority necessary for passage. This is because at least half the members of the community will be made better off when the number of security guards increases up to four per week.

Increases in the output of the public good beyond four security guards per week, however, will not receive a majority of votes. The election to expand output to five guards per week, for example, will receive only three yes votes. The other four voters will have reached levels of consumption at which marginal benefits are less than their tax shares and therefore vote no.

The political equilibrium under majority rule and equal tax shares, given the marginal benefit curves shown in Figure 5.2, will be four security guards per week. If voters were asked to choose between this number of guards and any alternative number, four would win. This is because four guards per week is closer to the most-preferred outcome of a majority of voters. As long as the alternative of four guards per week is put on the ballot, it will emerge as the political equilibrium under simple majority rule.

The Median Voter

The **median voter** is the one whose most-preferred outcome is the median of the most-preferred outcomes of all those voting. In Figure 5.2, the voter with the marginal benefit curve MB_M is the median voter. The most-preferred outcomes of all voters range from one to seven security guards per week. Voter *M*'s most-preferred outcome is the median of four guards per week. Three voters have a most-preferred outcome of less than four guards per week, and three voters have a most-preferred alternative of more than four guards per week.

The median voter ends up consuming the same amount of the public good that he or she would choose to consume if it were sold in a market at a price $t = \$50$. In equilibrium, under majority rule, voters *A*, *B*, and *C* consume more than their most-preferred levels of security protection, given the tax shares. Similarly, voters *F*, *G*, and *H* end up consuming less than their most-preferred levels, under the majority rule equilibrium.

If the marginal benefit of a public good declines for all voters, the median most-preferred quantity of the good always is the political equilibrium under majority rule. As shown in the following section, this holds even if each voter does not pay the same tax share. Voters whose most-preferred outcomes deviate from the median must consume either more or less of the public good than they would choose independently, given their tax shares.

The greater the dispersion of most-preferred outcomes from the median, the more likely there will be dissatisfaction with public choices under majority rule. At one extreme, all voters could have the *same* most-preferred outcome. If this were the case, *all* voters would agree unanimously on the quantity of the good to supply. Any one voter could be regarded as the median voter in this case. The other extreme is the one shown in Figure 5.2 for which each voter has a different most-preferred outcome. The more voters whose most-preferred outcomes are clustered toward the median voter's most-preferred outcome, the greater will be the satisfaction with the political equilibrium under majority rule. This emphasizes an important point about majority rule: When more than two outcomes are possible, majority rule does not necessarily ensure that 51 percent of the voters will receive their most-preferred outcomes. *Only the median voter obtains his or her most-preferred outcome.* Differences in the most-preferred outcomes of voters can be explained either by differences in the marginal benefits they receive from alternative quantities of the public good or differences in their assigned tax shares.

Political externalities are losses in well-being that occur when voters do not obtain their most-preferred outcomes, given their tax shares. Political externalities would be zero if the tax shares of all voters of government goods and services were adjusted until they equaled the marginal benefits received from government output. When political externalities prevail, additional gains to voters are possible either through changes in the output of government goods or through changes in voters' tax shares.

Do not confuse political externalities with market externalities. Market externalities, as defined in Chapter 3, are costs or benefits of market exchanges not reflected in prices. Political externalities are costs borne by those who would like to have either more or less of a government good or service, given their tax shares, than the amounts agreed upon through political interaction. If all decisions were made under unanimous agreement, political externalities would not exist. This is because any single voter could veto a proposal if he or she did not attain his or her most-preferred political outcome.

If political externalities were the only costs of political interaction, unanimous agreement would minimize the costs of the political process. In fact, some proponents of democracy argue that more inclusive majorities (for example, two-thirds majority) required for approving government programs would more adequately protect minorities. However, other costs also are involved in actually reaching an agreement. **Political transactions costs** measure the value of time, effort, and other resources expended to reach and enforce a collective agreement. These are additional costs of the political process that must be considered in evaluating the efficiency of government supply compared with market supply. Political institutions that require high percentages of agreement in the population before increments in government activity can be undertaken are likely to result in a minimal amount of political externalities. On the other hand, rules that require close to unanimous agreement are likely to take a great deal of time and effort before an agreement can be achieved. In choosing political institutions, citizens must weigh the political externalities associated with these rules against the political transactions costs of the rules.

The prevalence of representative government in all democratic nations is best explained by an effort to economize on political transactions costs. In a large nation, decisions never would be made (or would be made too late) if the entire nation had to vote before action could be undertaken. Other costs of political interaction are those resulting from bureaucratic inefficiency. If bureaucrats do not produce their output at minimum possible cost, or if they succeed in getting more than the efficient amount approved, losses in net benefits to citizens will occur.

CHECKPOINT

1. Who is the median voter?
2. What are political externalities?
3. What are political transaction costs?

UNIQUENESS AND CYCLING OF OUTCOMES UNDER MAJORITY RULE

Under certain circumstances, a unique political equilibrium cannot emerge under majority rule. When this is the case, for any output of the public good that can achieve a majority of the votes, another output level will exist that also can achieve a majority.

When no equilibrium exists, the outcome of elections decided under simple majority rule can depend on factors other than the benefits of the proposed changes in output and the costs to voters. These other factors could include the order in which alternatives are presented to voters or the addition or subtraction of an alternative to the ballot. This possibility is particularly disturbing because it suggests that the outcome under majority rule could depend on factors other than the merits of the proposed changes. For example, it implies that skillful politicians might be able to manipulate the results of elections by controlling the order in which proposals are considered by the electorate.

Single-Peaked and Multiple-Peaked Preferences

To illustrate the problems associated with simple majority rule, consider the following hypothetical election. A community of three citizens must vote to decide on the number of fireworks displays to have per year. Each display costs $200. Voter A must pay a tax, t_A, of $100 per display. Voter B's tax share per display is $t_B = \$75$, and voter C pays a tax share of $t_C = \$25$ per display. The voters agree to consider three alternatives: one display per year, two displays per year, or three displays per year. The results of an election between any pair of alternatives will be determined by simple majority rule. Table 5.2 shows how each of the voters ranks the three alternatives. Given their tax shares, the three individuals are presumed to rank these alternatives in terms of highest to lowest levels of net benefits received. In other words, the rankings are obtained for each voter by subtracting the taxes paid from the benefit gained from availability of each alternative. The net benefit of each output for a voter is the difference, as evaluated by the voter, between the total benefit of the output and the total costs of the output measured by taxes.

In Figure 5.3, the information contained in Table 5.2 is used to plot the net benefits of the three voters, A, B, and C, for each of the three alternatives. A's preferences are apparently such that, for the three alternatives available, her net benefit increases with the number of displays per year. B obtains the greatest net benefit when only one display is provided per year. However, his second-ranked alternative is three displays per year, the greatest number of displays being considered by the voters. The moderate alternative of two displays per year apparently gives him the least net benefit. B is an individual who prefers the extremes to the moderate alternatives. Finally, C's preferences are such that she gets the greatest net benefit from two displays per year and lower net benefits when either one or three displays are provided per year.

Single-peaked preferences imply that individuals behave as if a unique optimal outcome exists for them. The further away from their optima, either in the positive or in the negative direction, the worse things are. **Multiple-peaked preferences** imply that people who move away from their most-preferred alternative become worse off at first *but eventually become better off as the movement continues in the same direction.* Of the three voters whose rankings are shown earlier, B is the only one with multiple-peaked preferences. As shown in Figure 5.3, B becomes worse off as fireworks displays are increased from one to two per year. However, this voter becomes *better off as* output is increased from two to three displays per year. Voters A and C both have single-peaked preferences. If output is reduced below three displays per year, A is made continually worse off. If displays per year deviate in any direction from C's most-preferred outcome of two, she is made worse off.

Pair-Wise Elections: The Phenomenon of Cycling

Pair-wise elections are those held between any two alternatives when three or more alternatives are possible. Begin with one display per year against the alternative of two displays per year. The tally sheet for that election is given in Table 5.3. Each voter is presumed to vote for the alternative that gives the highest net benefit. Because the alternative of two displays per year receives two votes versus only one vote for one display per year, it receives the simple majority and is declared the winner.

Now, suppose the next pair-wise election were held between the losing alternative of one display per year and the remaining alternative of three displays per year.

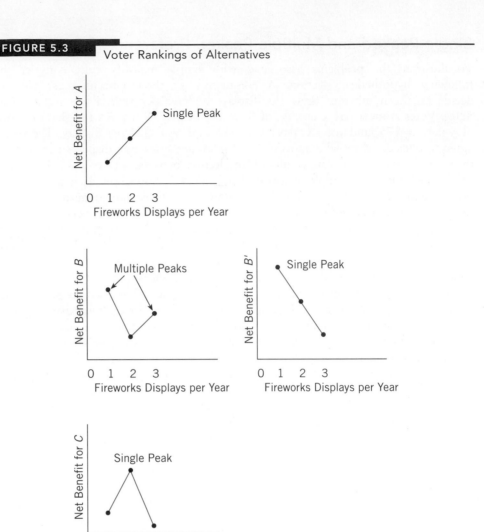

FIGURE 5.3   Voter Rankings of Alternatives

All voters have single-peaked preferences except for voter *B*, who becomes worse off as he moves from his most-preferred outcome of one display per year but then better off as he moves to three displays per year.

TABLE 5.2   Voter Rankings for Fireworks Displays per Year

	FIRST CHOICE	SECOND CHOICE	THIRD CHOICE
Voters			
A	3	2	1
B	1	3	2
C	2	1	3

TABLE 5.3		Electoral Tally Sheets for Pair-Wise Elections (Based on Rankings in Table 5.2)

ELECTION 1	1 DISPLAY PER YEAR	2 DISPLAYS PER YEAR
Voters		
A		X
B	X	
C		X
Total	1 Vote	2 Votes

Result: 2 displays per year wins.

ELECTION 2	3 DISPLAYS PER YEAR	1 DISPLAY PER YEAR
Voters		
A	X	
B		X
C		X
Total	1 Vote	2 Votes

Result: 1 display per year wins.

ELECTION 3	2 DISPLAYS PER YEAR	3 DISPLAYS PER YEAR
Voters		
A		X
B		X
C	X	
Total	1 Vote	2 Votes

Result: 3 displays per year wins.

© Cengage Learning

As shown in the tally sheet for election 2, the alternative of one display per year would win. Finally, suppose an election were held between the alternative of three displays per year and two displays per year. The result, under simple majority rule, would be three displays per year.

The result of pair-wise voting in this fashion among the three alternatives is a never-ending cycle. In the three elections held, two displays per year defeats the alternative of one display per year; then one display per year emerges as the winner when paired against three displays per year; and finally three displays per year wins when paired against two displays per year. Each loser can become a winner when paired with another alternative. The outcome of the election between pairs of alternatives is arbitrary. Depending on the order in which the elections are held, any of the three alternatives can emerge as the winner under simple majority rule. This phenomenon is called *cycling*. In pair-wise elections, no political equilibrium exists. No one alternative can defeat all others *whenever* it appears on the ballot.

Elections could be held for any pair of alternatives. The winner of that election then could be paired against the remaining alternative. In a series of such elections, any of the three alternatives can win the runoff elections, depending on the order in which the alternatives are presented to the voters.

The phenomenon of cycling is very disturbing to our confidence in the democratic institutions of voting and majority rule to reach public choices because it suggests that perhaps no rhyme or reason explains the choices that emerge. Cycling implies that public choices can be influenced by such factors as the order in which issues are placed on the agenda for consideration by voters and legislatures. It also suggests that with three or more alternatives on the agenda, elimination of one of the alternatives can change the way the remaining two are ranked in a public choice.

Arrow's impossibility theorem generalizes the results discussed here for majority rule by stating that it is impossible to devise a voting rule that meets a set of conditions that can guarantee a unique political equilibrium for a public choice. To prove his theorem, Kenneth Arrow, who received a Nobel Prize for his groundbreaking work on the properties of political equilibrium, sets up a number of conditions for "collective rationality." These conditions require that public choices meet the same criteria we expect for rational individual choices. Arrow's work is expressed in terms of mathematics. The analysis here simplifies the theorem. Arrow's conditions can be roughly summarized to include the following:[3]

1. All voters must have free choices among alternatives in elections, and the public choices cannot be made by any one individual who would act as a dictator.

2. A unique political equilibrium must be attained no matter what the preferences of individuals comprising the electorate. We cannot rule out the possibility that some voters have multiple-peaked preferences.

3. If all voters change their rankings of a particular alternative (either moving it up or down), the public choice that emerges must not move in the opposite direction. For example, if all voters now prefer less national defense, we would not expect a public choice to emerge in which more national defense is chosen.

4. Public choices and political equilibrium must not be influenced by the order in which alternatives are presented to voters.

5. Public choices must not be affected by the elimination or addition of an alternative to the ballot. If voters choose A over B in an election when A and B are the only alternatives, then they must not choose B over A when a third alternative, C, enters the race.

6. Public choices should be transitive: If A is chosen over B and B is chosen over C, then A should be chosen over C.

Arrow's conditions imply that no "paradox of voting" should exist such that a third-party candidate can act as a "spoiler" in an election. For example, suppose a Republican candidate for president runs against a Democrat and that the Republican would win if the Democrat and the Republican were on the ballot alone. However, a third-party Conservative candidate who enters the race takes votes away from the Republican and the Democrat wins. This means that the ranking between Republicans and Democrats changes when the third-party candidate enters.

Arrow's theorem is disturbing because it implies that any alternative could emerge as a political equilibrium. It also implies that strategies such as controlling the agenda for political debate or manipulating the order in which issues are discussed in a legislature can influence political outcomes. However, Arrow's theorem does not imply that public choices are always inconsistent. It merely points out that

---

[3]See Kenneth Arrow, *Social Choice and Individual Values*, 2nd ed. (New York: Wiley, 1963).

no voting rule, such as majority rule, can always be relied on to reach a unique political equilibrium. However, a given voting rule can produce unique public choices when voters themselves have preferences that meet certain properties. To find out the conditions under which public choices *are* consistent under simple majority rule, we need to examine the causes of the cycling phenomenon.

The Cause of Cycling

Cycling and the lack of a political equilibrium under pair-wise voting in majority rule are caused by multiple-peaked preferences. When all voters have single-peaked preferences, simple majority rule is capable of achieving a political equilibrium for a single-issue election at the median peak for all voters.[4]

This theorem can be illustrated with the preceding example. Simply replace voter *B*, who has multiple-peaked preferences, with voter *B′*, whose preferences are single-peaked at the fewest number of fireworks displays per year. Assume that voter *B′* pays the same tax share per display as did voter *B*. The net benefit from fireworks displays for voter *B′* declines as more are provided. This is shown in Table 5.4. The net benefit functions of the three voters, *A*, *B′*, and *C*, are plotted together in Figure 5.4, which now shows three single peaks (or maxima) for each of the three voters. Voter *A* would enjoy maximum net benefit at three displays per year. Voter *B′* would enjoy maximum net benefits if one display per year were provided. Finally, voter *C* would have maximum net benefit if two displays per year would emerge as the political equilibrium. For each voter, now, movement away from his or her most-preferred outcome in any direction results in decreased net benefit over the range of the possible outcomes. All voters have single-peaked preferences. The median peak is at two displays per year. Because voter *C* is the one whose first choice corresponds to the median peak, this voter is the median voter.

Now hold elections between pairs of alternatives as before but base the votes on the preferences in Table 5.4. The electoral tally sheets for these elections are given in Table 5.5. In this case, the alternative of two displays per year emerges as the political equilibrium. In elections 1 and 3, in which two displays per year is paired directly with the alternatives of one display per year and three displays per year, two

TABLE 5.4	Voter Rankings for Fireworks Displays per Year: All Voters with Single-Peaked Preferences		
	FIRST CHOICE	**SECOND CHOICE**	**THIRD CHOICE**
Voters			
A	3	2	1
B′	1	2	3
C	2	1	3

© Cengage Learning

[4]This is sometimes called the Black theorem, after Duncan Black, who first developed it. Black's pioneering efforts are described in his book, *The Theory of Committees and Elections* (Cambridge, Eng.: Cambridge University Press, 1958). Also see his work, "On the Rationale of Group Decision Making," *Journal of Political Economy* 56 (February 1948): 23–24 and "The Decisions of a Committee Using a Special Majority," *Econometrica* 16 (July 1948): 245–261.

FIGURE 5.4 The Median Peak as the Political Equilibrium under Majority Rule

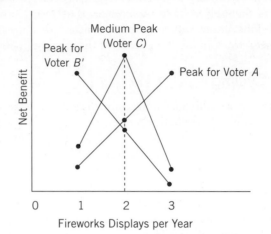

The median voter is C, whose most-preferred outcome of two fireworks displays per year is the political equilibrium under majority rule.

TABLE 5.5 Electoral Tally Sheets for Pair-Wise Elections (Based on Rankings in Table 5.4)

ELECTION 1	1 DISPLAY PER YEAR	2 DISPLAYS PER YEAR
Voters		
A		X
B'	X	
C		X
Total	1 Vote	2 Votes

Result: 2 displays per year wins.

ELECTION 2	3 DISPLAYS PER YEAR	1 DISPLAY PER YEAR
Voters		
A	X	
B'		X
C		X
Total	1 Vote	2 Votes

Result: 1 display per year wins.

ELECTION 3	2 DISPLAYS PER YEAR	3 DISPLAYS PER YEAR
Voters		
A		X
B'	X	
C	X	
Total	2 Votes	1 Vote

Result: 2 displays per year wins.

displays per year receives a simple majority in both cases. In election 2, between the alternatives of one and three displays per year, one display per year is victorious. But this alternative will lose when paired with the most-preferred outcome of the median voter: two displays per year.

The median peak of two displays per year is the political equilibrium. When all preferences are single peaked, neither cycling of outcomes nor arbitrariness is involved in the collective choice. One and only one outcome of the three emerges as victorious: the one corresponding to the median peak. This is the median most-preferred outcome of all voters and is sometimes called the **median voter rule**. The rule holds for any tax-sharing arrangement as long as voter preferences are single peaked.

Existence of Multiple-Peaked Preferences

Economists typically assume that the marginal benefit of any good tends to decline as more of the good is made available. It easily can be demonstrated that multiple-peaked preferences are inconsistent with declining marginal benefit of public goods. Figure 5.5A plots the net benefits received by a voter whose tax share and marginal benefit curve for a pure public good are shown in Figure 5.5B. When the voter's marginal benefit exceeds his or her tax per unit of the good, his or her net benefit increases. The net benefit is at a maximum when Q^* units of output per year are provided. If more than Q^* per year are made available, the marginal benefit would be less than taxes per unit, and net benefit would decline. It follows that the net benefit curve for any voter with declining marginal benefit for the good will have an inverted U-shape, as shown in Figure 5.5A. This is a single-peaked net benefit function, with the peak at the output corresponding to $MB = t$.

Unfortunately, the possibility of multiple-peaked preferences cannot be ruled out. For example, individuals voting in a school budget election can have multiple-peaked preferences. Suppose the voters have the alternative to send children to private schools. In part, the incentive depends on the quality of public schools, which presumably is correlated with the size of the public school budget.

The voter's first choice might be to send his or her children to private schools. If he or she does this, it is in his or her interest to keep the size of the public school budget as small as possible, because he or she will receive no direct benefit from public schooling for his or her taxes. The voter's first choice will be a budget that allows minimum-quality public schooling. If it is assumed that the taxes necessary to finance a school budget that allows only moderate-quality schooling will make it difficult for the voter to afford private schooling, his or her second choice may very well be the budget that allows the highest-quality public schooling. Under such circumstances, he or she might view the quality of public schools adequate enough to forgo sending his or her children to private schools. The voter's least-favored alternative will be a school budget that allows only moderate-quality public schooling. The taxes required to finance moderate-quality public schooling will not leave him or her enough income after taxes to afford private schooling. Thus, given the alternative of private schooling, multiple-peaked preferences might be quite reasonable for a voter who seeks to maximize the quality of schooling for his or her children.

During the 1960s and the early 1970s, multiple-peaked preferences by U.S. citizens were prevalent on the issue of the Vietnam War. Many citizens argued that wars, if fought, should be fought to win. They preferred the alternative of all-out war (including the use of nuclear weapons) or no war at all to the alternative of a limited war that did not use the full military capability of the armed forces for the purposes of

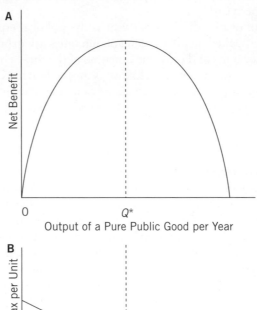

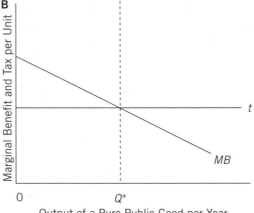

FIGURE 5.5   Declining Marginal Benefit of a Pure Public Good Meaning That Performances Are Single Peaked

If the marginal benefit of a pure public good declines with annual output for a voter, total net benefits received per year will first increase, and then decrease. This implies that preferences are single peaked, with the peak occurring at the point at which $t = MB$.

winning territory and subduing the enemy. Again, these individuals were expressing preferences for extreme solutions over a moderate, solution. Multiple-peaked preferences might be common therefore on a wide variety of issues. This leaves open the specter of absence of political equilibrium under majority rule as a possibility.

CHECKPOINT

1. What are single-peaked preferences?
2. What can cause cycling of outcomes under majority rule?
3. What is the median voter rule?

THE POLITICAL PROCESS

A prerequisite to the study of the political process is an analysis of how political institutions themselves are established. In almost all nations, the rules for making choices on issues of common interest comprise a constitution. In effect, a constitution pairs choices regarding specific activities with a specific decision rule. Those activities for which the constitution specifies no rule are usually left as private or market decisions. The advantages and disadvantages of various collective choice rules require study to determine which rules are most likely to be paired with which economic activities.

Constitutions

Constitutions are the generally accepted set of rules by which decisions are made in a society. Constitutions may be written or unwritten. They evolve over time, and they are generally accepted by individuals comprising a society. The process by which the rules for making choices regarding how goods are produced and distributed is itself an interesting philosophical problem. In some cases, the rules allow individuals to choose what to do, and how to do it, by themselves—with no approval required by their peers. For example, the kind of clothes one wears and the kind and amounts of food one eats are most often private decisions. The decision to go to war with another nation, however, is always a collective decision—made according to specified rules. The evolution of constitutions has received only scant attention by economists. It is clear, however, that if constitutions are to be viable, the "social contracts" inherent in their rules must receive broad support by members of the society.

Analysis of the philosophical basis for the establishment of "social contracts" by John Rawls argues that individuals are likely to establish such contracts by unanimous agreement when each individual is uncertain of his or her skills and future opportunities relative to other individuals or "players." Rawls argues that incentives to "get on with the game," combined with the "veil of ignorance" regarding future opportunities, will provide strong incentives for individuals to approve a "just" and "fair" social contract under unanimous agreement.[5]

Assuming then that members of the community can unanimously agree on the rules of the game embodied in a constitution, one can go on to analyze the advantages and disadvantages of particular rules and their pairing with particular issues. Given the pros and cons of each rule, the possibility of its acceptance for particular issues by individual voters may be assessed.

A Classification of Collective Choice Rules

Alternative decision rules may be classified on a spectrum according to the percentage of the community required to reach the decisions. On this basis, rules run the gamut from 0 percent to 100 percent of the voters. If a community has N voting citizens, then the proportion of voters required to reach a decision under simple majority rule will be $(N/2 + 1)/N$. If unanimous consent is required, the proportion will be N/N or 1. If a minority rule is chosen, then the required proportion of voters

---

[5]John Rawls, *A Theory of Justice*. (Cambridge: Harvard University Press, Belknap Press, 1971).

necessary to make the choice will be less than one-half. If a two-thirds majority is required, it will be necessary to have (2/3) N of the voters agreeing, and so on.

Minority Rule

Consider minority rule first. If the community agrees to such a decision-making rule, it runs the risk of making decisions that do not satisfy a majority of the community. In such cases, those who disagree with the decision bear political externalities imposed on them by a minority of citizens. When decisions are always made by a *specific* minority group, the result is called *oligarchy*.

The extreme form of minority rule is that in which decisions are made by only one member of the community. In other words, only one vote will pass an issue. In the case where the decisions are always made by one specific individual, the result is monarchy (or dictatorship). It is even possible to conceive of a voting rule where decisions are made by 0 percent of the population! In such a case, the community would be ruled by some external power, such as a colonial power or a set of traditions. In these limiting cases, there is no collective decision making at all because the decisions are the result of the whims of one individual or some external force that commands the obedience of the community.

Majority Rule

Simple majority rule, which we have already analyzed, merely requires agreement among approximately 51 percent of the community. This is a rule commonly used to elect representatives in the United States and other countries. However, the constitutional structure of the federal government is such that other rules (such as two-thirds majority rule) are used as well. For example, confirmation of certain presidential appointees by the Senate requires a two-thirds majority.

For simple majority rule, it is quite possible that slightly less than one-half of the community will be dissatisfied with the resultant decision. For the case of the two-thirds majority rule, the maximum possible amount of dissatisfied voters declines to about 33 percent of the voting population.

Choice of the Collective Decision-Making Rule

An analysis of the factors influencing the choice of collective decision-making rules has been offered by James Buchanan and Gordon Tullock.[6] Their technique is to concentrate on the factors from the point of view of the individual voting members of the community. Each individual weighs the costs and benefits of alternative decision rules in relation to his or her own particular interests. Political externalities decline as higher proportions of the community are required for collective agreement. Conversely, decision rules requiring agreement among a very high proportion of the population also are likely to be very costly in terms of transactions costs because they imply that a great deal of time might be necessary to work out a compromise agreeable to all factions within the community.

Most nations actually employ a multitude of decision-making rules. Indeed, it is the essence of a constitution to embody a set of diverse decision rules. That is to say, there is a generally agreed-upon procedure through which decisions are made.

---

[6]See James Buchanan and Gordon Tullock's study of collective decision-making rules, *The Calculus of Consent*. (Ann Arbor: University of Michigan Press, 1962), for a path-breaking analysis of collective decision-making rules.

Citizens in the United States elect a president once every four years. Between presidential elections, the chief executive has a considerable amount of power to make decisions within the framework of the Constitution, subject to the constraints of legislative action and judicial review. It is possible that presidential decision-making power in the interval between elections might impose high costs on a significant portion of the population who finds the president's policies repugnant.

Costs and Benefits of Collective Action

The benefits of collective action may be measured by the efficiency gains obtained from the internalization of any external effects of private action. The costs of collective action are the sum of newly generated political externalities and the transactions costs of collective choices. The political process can be expected to generate political externalities for all decision-making rules aside from unanimity. The actions of the citizens' positive voting on any issue passed according to some decision rule result in political externalities being imposed on those citizens who voted negatively on the issue and are therefore dissatisfied with the resulting decision. For example, the individual who is forced by majority rule to bear an increase in taxes to finance increased public services from which he or she receives no benefits is bearing political externalities of the political process. For any single individual, the political externalities associated with any one particular activity may be defined as the costs he or she expects to bear as a result of the actions of others through the political process.

For any given individual and any given issue, the probability that one will bear political externalities tends to decline as the percentage of the community required for a collective agreement rises. This is simply because the probability that one will be in the losing coalition of voters declines as the percentage of the population required to pass an issue increases. At the extreme, if unanimous agreement were required before collective action by governing authorities could be undertaken, no one would be forced to bear political externalities, because every single voter would have veto power over any action. It is therefore reasonable to expect that the costs associated with political externalities will tend to decline as the percentage of the population required for agreement increases.

If political externalities were the only costs associated with the political process, all decisions would be made under unanimous agreement, because this is the rule that minimizes those costs. Unfortunately, there are political transactions costs that are likely to make unanimous agreement an unattractive alternative for many citizens. These transactions costs tend to rise as higher percentages of the population are required to vote yes before collective action can be undertaken.

If unanimous consent is required for action, decision-making costs may be extremely high, not only because of the time required to reach agreement, but also because the knowledge by any one individual that he or she can prevent action by being obstinate leads to the possibility of strategic behavior by individuals. They may withhold their consent until they succeed in extorting "bribes" from those individuals who strongly desire action on the issue. Once again, the costs are likely to differ among voters and between issues.

When asked which decision rule he or she prefers on each possible issue, the rational individual will choose the one that minimizes the sum of the expected political externalities and transactions costs he or she must incur in the collective choice process.

It must be emphasized that the cost function associated with each possible decision rule depends both on the nature of the issue being decided and the preferences of particular individuals. In general, it may be argued that for a given issue, individuals with preferences that may be considered extreme in one way or another will generally prefer more inclusive majorities in order to minimize the probability of being in the losing minority. Similarly, other things being equal, individuals with high opportunity costs of time may be expected to prefer less inclusive majorities for a given issue.

Unanimous Consent

The rule of unanimity has the advantage of allowing only Pareto-efficient changes to be approved. As long as any particular issue must receive the approval of all voters before being enacted, it remains impossible for any one individual to be made worse off while others are made better off. This advantage led early scholars in the field of public choice, such as Knut Wicksell, the famous 19th-century Swedish economist, to favor unanimity rule strongly as a mechanism for reaching collective choices on issues of common interest.[7] However, it must be emphasized that Wicksell and others favoring unanimous consent as the optimal decision rule presumed that, prior to approval of the unanimous consent rule, the community had previously agreed on and implemented the "just" distribution of income. The necessity of such a prerequisite is obvious. Unanimous consent as a collective choice rule is capable of approving only those measures that result in net gains at zero cost to others.

If the initial distribution of income or property rights to wealth is not considered ideal by all voters, the possibility of changing that distribution under unanimous consent is nil unless those who will lose as a result of the change are fully compensated by the gainers. In other words, unanimous consent will block all those changes that involve any redistribution of either property rights, to ownership or wealth, or income.

The advantages of unanimous consent in terms of its potential for achieving only Pareto-efficient outcomes must be balanced against its potential costs. The most obvious disadvantages are the high transactions costs already discussed. Reaching a decision under unanimous consent may take too long. Inaction on an issue can be costly. Failure to pass an issue with substantial collective benefits may occur under unanimity rule.

Further, unanimous consent may tend to encourage strategic behavior on the part of voters. If each voter knows that he or she has the power to block action on particular issues of interest to other voters, he or she may act in such a way as to minimize his or her tax burden by attempting to force other voters to pay their maximum tax bid for any given amount of output of the public good. However, such strategic behavior always entails a certain amount of risk to the individual. If the individual over-guesses the maximum bids of others, or if others "call his bluff" or play counter-strategies, the outcome may once again be blockage of any action at all—with the resulting loss in welfare due to inability of the collective choice process to approve efficient outcomes.

On the other hand, if all individuals truthfully reveal their preferences and refrain from strategic behavior, the unanimous consent rule is not only capable of achieving that political equilibrium corresponding to the efficient level of output of the public good, but will likewise do so at the distribution of tax shares corresponding to the marginal benefits. Given the distribution of income, it is possible to imagine a process of "trades" developing among voters that will modify any initial set of tax shares in such a way as to make them reflect the marginal benefits associated with additional units of public output. Under such arrangements, individuals who strongly favor

---

[7]For a classic discussion of unanimous consent, see Knut Wicksell, "A New Principle of Just Taxation," reprinted in Richard A. Musgrave and Alan T. Peacock, eds., *Classics in the Theory of Public Finance* (London: Macmillan, 1958): 72–118.

action on particular issues will attempt to "buy" the votes of others for whom the initial tax share exceeds marginal benefits. On a given issue, the bribes can take the form of explicit pecuniary compensation. The end result will be a distribution of tax shares reflecting marginal benefits and a level of output of the public good where the sum of the marginal benefits will be equal to marginal costs.

Relative Unanimity and the Rights of Minorities

Concern for the rights of minorities led Wicksell to favor a rule of "relative unanimity." Under such a rule, referendums on the extension of government activity, combined with specific tax-sharing plans, must pass by margins close to unanimity, such as seven-eighths of the voters, for positive action. The rule still has the drawbacks of unanimous consent in the sense that it is likely to involve excessive transactions costs as the "price" paid for protecting the rights of minority groups. An advantage of relative unanimity is that the resulting distribution of tax shares is contingent on the induced "bribes." It is likely that those who most strongly prefer the particular action will finance the bulk of it after bribes are paid. If preferences are truthfully revealed, this approximates the Lindahl solution in the sense that equilibrium tax shares are close to individual marginal benefits of government activity.

Plurality Rule

Plurality rule is a commonly used collective decision-making rule when at least three alternatives are on the ballot. An obvious disadvantage of simple majority rule in such cases is that when more than two alternatives are on the agenda, no single one may receive a simple majority. This may lead to high transactions costs and runoff elections. It may in fact be impossible for any one of the alternatives to emerge as a unique political equilibrium if multiple-peaked preferences exist. Under plurality rule, the alternative that receives the highest percentage of total votes cast is declared the winner.

Such a voting rule often allows a minority to decide. For example, if there are three issues on the ballot and the vote is split 32, 32, and 36 percent, the alternative receiving the 36 percent will be declared the winner—despite the fact that 64 percent of the electorate voted against it.

Plurality rule can result in cycling similar to that which occurs under majority rule. Further, it may result in extremely unstable political equilibrium inasmuch as incentives exist always to reformulate the agenda in such a way as to change the winning plurality. Thus, both a given issue *and* its converse may pass under plurality rule. Voters may vote to increase expenditures by 10 percent and then vote again to reduce them by 10 percent.

Point-Count Voting

Point-count voting allows a refined expression of intensity of feeling. Under this system, each voter is assigned a number of "points" (for example, 100) that he or she is free to allocate in any manner he or she wishes among the possible alternatives. As an example, if there are three alternatives and the voter is given 100 points, he or she may assign 50 points to one alternative and 25 points each to the other two. If he or she has a very strong preference for one alternative versus the other two, he or she may choose to put all 100 points on that alternative and allocate zero points to each of the other two. The outcome is determined by adding the points assigned by all voters to each alternative. The alternative that earns the greatest number of points is declared the winner.

Point-count voting affords the opportunity for a greater revelation of preferences. As such, it may serve to protect the rights of minorities with strong feelings on particular issues. It also greatly increases the possibility of strategic behavior on the part of the voters and the possibility of high decision-making costs. It is conceivable that a "market" for points will develop as individual voters make trades on different issues. It is also possible that some voters may attempt to guess how other voters will allocate their points and base their own behavior in part on such guesses.

Instant Runoff Voting

When more than three alternatives are put before the electorate, it is possible that no one alternative can receive a simple majority. In many cases, the alternative that gets only a plurality of votes is declared a winner. Depending on the rules, some states declare a new, and costly, runoff election between the two alternatives that get the highest number of votes, guaranteeing that only the alternative that achieves a simple majority can win.

A new technique that keeps the costs of elections down and prevents a third alternative from acting as a spoiler is now used in Hawaii for state elections and in San Francisco for mayoral elections. Instant runoff voting is a scheme that makes it more likely that a winning candidate receives a simple majority rather than a plurality. In most cases in the United States when more than two candidates are running for a single office, it is possible that a candidate with less than a simple majority of the votes can be elected.

Under instant runoff voting, voters rank candidates according to their first, second, third choices, and so on, if there are more than two alternatives. If no candidate receives a simple majority based on first-choice votes in the election, the candidate with the fewest first place votes is eliminated automatically. A recount is then taken for the remaining candidates. The ballots are then retabulated with votes registered based on rankings for the remaining candidates. For example, if your first choice is eliminated for the second election, then you will have a vote registered for whomever your second choice might have been. The process of elimination of candidates continues until a winner achieves a simple majority. All this can be accomplished very quickly with the use of a computer program.

Proponents of this new method of voting argue that it guarantees that only a candidate preferred by the majority of voters is likely to win. It can also save substantial sums of money and time by avoiding special runoff elections. It gives voters a greater range of choices to express their preferences and could increase voter turnout. It could also induce candidates to concentrate more on issues as they seek to be not only the first but also the second and even third choice of voters.

CHECKPOINT

1. What are constitutions?
2. Describe and compare various collection choice rules.
3. How can a rule of "relative unanimity" protect the rights of minorities?

PUBLIC POLICY PERSPECTIVE

Public Choice in U.S. Cities: Do Political Institutions Matter?

In the United States, municipal government takes two basic forms. One form relies heavily on a professional city manager who, along with a staff, makes the day-to-day decisions about how to run the city and plays an important role in advising elected public officials on expansion of public facilities. The city-manager form of government typically involves nonpartisan elections for mayor and city council members. In the second form, a mayor, deputy mayor, and other public officials are elected directly, usually in partisan elections (in which candidates are members of a political party). In this form of government, the mayor and city council members wield considerably more power than they do under the city-manager form of government.

Does the form of city government affect the public choices made in municipalities? Some scholars have argued that politicians under partisan governments respond to different incentives than city managers. For example, one researcher has argued that city managers act as technicians who view city capital and labor simply as inputs for the production of city services. However, partisan mayors view these inputs partly as political assets that can affect their power base and ability to be reelected.[1]

To test the hypothesis that the form of city government makes a difference for public choices, Kevin Duffy-Deno and Douglas R. Dalenberg collected data from 26 large U.S. cities chosen at random. Half were city-manager governments and half were run by elected mayors.[2] Using estimates of the capital stock for each city, researchers sought to explain differences in city capital per person and capital-labor ratios between cities. City capital included police and fire facilities, parks, recreation centers, highways, water and sewer systems, and health and welfare facilities. Among the variables used to explain these differences were the number of facilities located in the metropolitan area of each city of the sample, municipal population density, number of manufacturing firms in the city, per capita personal income, percentage of owner-occupied homes, median age of city residents, the city's region, population change in the preceding five years, percentage of homes built in or before 1950, and number of services offered by the city.

After accounting for the influence of all variables, the researchers found that the per capita stock of capital was 12.5 percent greater in those cities managed by elected mayors than those with the city-manager form of government. The capital-labor ratio was also higher in the cities run by elected mayors rather than city managers. Although the form of government did not seem to influence total municipal expenditures, it did seem to influence the means by which services are produced. Public choices in cities managed by elected mayors appear to result in more capital-intensive production methods and larger stocks of capital relative to population. Therefore, public choice rules do seem to matter when it comes to choices of input mixes of U.S. cities!

---

[1]See J. S. Zax, "Economics Effects of Municipal Government Institutions," Working Paper No. 1657, National Bureau of Economic Research, 1985.
[2]See Kevin T. Duffy-Deno and Douglas R. Dalenberg, "Do Institutions Matter? An Empirical Note," *National Tax Journal*, 43, 2 (June 1990): 207–215.

POLITICAL PARTIES AND POLITICAL EQUILIBRIUM

Individuals with similar ideas on the role of government and other issues often group together to form **political parties**. Politicians seek elective office for a variety of reasons: power, prestige, desire to serve others, and personal financial returns after leaving office. They are influential in formulating the alternatives that are presented to voters and in dispersing information on the relative merits of alternative measures and candidates on the agenda for approval. When information is scarce, the behavior of politicians can be influential in determining the actual political equilibrium that emerges. Competition among political parties, particularly under a system of majority rule, has been analyzed by economists in an attempt to gain a better understanding of the political process.[8]

Thus far, little has been said about the role of political parties in the formulation of the alternatives presented to the electorate. Clearly, political parties play an important part in defining issues and in attempting to influence the results of elections. For the individual voter, the marginal benefit of any particular budget proposal will depend not only on the level of expenditures but also on the mix of types of expenditures within the budget. The willingness of any citizen to vote favorably on any given budget also will depend on the particular tax-sharing plan proposed to finance the expenditures. In some ways, political parties act as brokers to encourage vote trading among voters. Political platforms often include proposals for programs that benefit only a minority of voters. However, by including these benefits and spreading the costs over the majority, the party can gain votes.

Economists characterize political parties as vote maximizers, because they tend to put together political programs and tax-sharing arrangements designed to maximize the votes that they receive. Under majority rule, the party most successful at maximizing votes wins the election. Therefore, vote maximization is a prerequisite to successfully obtaining political power in a democracy.

The Median Voter, Political Parties, and Political Equilibrium under Majority Rule

Suppose the positions of political parties can be ranked according to a scale that measures the quantity of government activity per year. For example, conservatives who argue that government activity should be reduced or curtailed would rank low according to this scale. Liberal candidates who propose more government activity would rank high on the scale.

Political candidates tend to take a position that represents the median on the scale. Political parties and candidates who take extreme positions are likely to lose elections. The candidate who most accurately approximates the median most-preferred outcome will emerge as the victor.

This is illustrated in Figure 5.6. The graph plots the net benefit (after paying taxes) that each voter receives from each possible political platform on government activity. Assume that the greater the quantity of government goods and services per year, the more liberal is the platform.

The graph assumes that the most-preferred outcome of voters varies considerably. Some conservative voters' most-preferred outcome occurs at zero government goods and services per year. The most-preferred outcome of more liberal voters corresponds to higher amounts of government goods and services per year. In Figure 5.6, the net benefit curves of nine voters are drawn. The median most-preferred outcome is Q^*, which corresponds to the peak of the net benefit function of the median voter. Assuming that each voter has a single-peaked net benefit function, Q^* will emerge as the political equilibrium. This is because the net benefits of more than half of the voters will be higher under Q^* than for any alternative quantity of government goods and services, given tax shares.

Figure 5.7 shows that if the most-preferred outcomes of voters are normally distributed, a political party can maximize the number of votes by taking a center

---

[8]Political parties and their influence on the political process are described in the classic study by Anthony Downs, *An Economic Theory of Democracy*. (New York: Harper & Row, 1957).

FIGURE 5.6 The Median Voter and Political Reforms

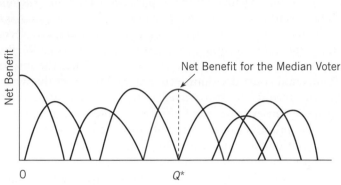

Given tax shares, the political party proposing Q^* units of government goods and services per year will win an election over any other party proposing an alternative quantity. This is because Q^* is closer to the most-preferred outcome of a simple majority of the voters.

© Cengage Learning

FIGURE 5.7 Number of Voters and Government Output

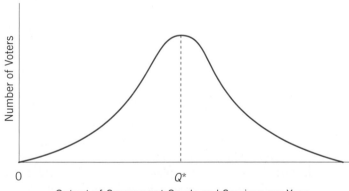

The annual output, Q^*, is the political equilibrium under majority rule because it can obtain more votes than any other alternative.

© Cengage Learning

position corresponding to Q^*. The implication of this analysis is that political parties or candidates who take extreme positions on issues are doomed to lose elections. Political parties that seek to maximize votes will always have an incentive to straddle the median position.

Ample evidence exists to prove that when political candidates in the United States take extreme positions they do in fact lose. For example, in the 1964 presidential election, Barry Goldwater, a presidential candidate, proposed a platform that was apparently far more conservative than the one preferred by the median voter of that time. The result was a landslide victory by his Democratic opponent,

Lyndon Johnson. Similarly, in 1972, the Democrats chose George McGovern as their candidate, but his position was apparently far to the left of the median peak. The result was a landslide victory by the Republican candidate, Richard Nixon. In 1976, in the Jimmy Carter versus Gerald Ford race, both candidates proposed platforms close to the median most-preferred position. As a result, the election was very close. Similarly, in the 2000 election as both Al Gore and George W. Bush straddled the median on issues, the result was an election so close that the results were hotly disputed. Recounts and court decisions were required to select the winner.

Over time, the median most-preferred outcome can change. For example, a movement to a more conservative point of view by voters can provide opportunities for candidates who propose conservative platforms to win elections. Perhaps the landslide victory of Ronald Reagan in 1984 can be interpreted as the result of a movement to a more conservative median most-preferred outcome. In 1992, the victory of the more liberal Bill Clinton over a conservative George Bush reflected a movement to a more liberal median most-preferred outcome. The election of Barack Obama over the more conservative John McCain in 2008 can also be interpreted as a result of a movement to a less-conservative median most-preferred outcome than the previous eight years of the George W. Bush presidency. In any event, political issues are seldom single dimensional. In presidential elections in particular, many issues are bundled together in the platforms of the political parties. Often, ranking of candidates along a single dimension is impossible. For example, a candidate might be regarded as conservative on domestic policy but liberal on foreign policy.

The Effect of Nonvoting on Political Equilibrium

Politicians seek to offer a political platform in line with the median most-preferred outcome of all *voters*. If all citizens do not vote, this outcome can differ from the median most-preferred outcomes of all *citizens*.

Voters might abstain from voting because they are indifferent to the platforms of two competing political parties. Barry Goldwater's campaign slogan in 1964 was "A choice, not an echo!" Perhaps he hoped that a significant number of conservative citizens who had not turned out in the past because they were indifferent to the positions of the candidates might turn out in hordes to support his position even though it was to the right of that espoused by the median voter. Apparently, he was mistaken.

When voters do not vote because the platforms of the candidates appear to be similar, the impact on political equilibrium depends on the number of voters on each end of the political spectrum who do not vote. Assume that candidates can be ranked on a single-dimensional scale, such as the liberalness of their positions. The median most-preferred outcome of citizens still will be the political equilibrium, provided that as many conservative citizens as liberal citizens do not vote because of indifference. Only in the case in which nonvoters are predominantly conservative or liberal will the median most-preferred outcome of all citizens diverge from the median most-preferred outcome of all actual voters.

Another reason for abstaining from voting is alienation. Citizens might find the positions of the candidates too far from their own most-preferred positions to bother to vote at all. The effects of alienation on the outcome of elections are complex. Assume once again that the positions of voters can be ranked according to a single scale of liberalness. When voters choose not to vote because they are alienated, the tendency for political parties is to move toward the mode rather than the median of the most-preferred outcome of citizens. If the distribution of the most-preferred outcome of voters is symmetric (as is the case for the familiar bell-shaped normal distribution shown in Figure 5.7), then the median and the mode will coincide. Under these circumstances, the median most-preferred outcome of all citizens still will dominate, provided that the distribution is unimodal. When the distribution of most-preferred outcomes is either asymmetric or multimodal (one that has two peaks), alienation can result in political equilibriums that differ from the median most-preferred outcome of all citizens.[9]

VOTING ON MORE THAN ONE ISSUE AT A TIME: LOGROLLING

When more than one issue is voted on simultaneously as a package—as is commonly the case—voters are sometimes confronted with political packages that include both favorable and unfavorable items. If the voter feels more strongly about some issues compared with others, or if he or she is better informed on some issues than on others, then his or her vote may be a function of the extent to which the package supports those issues he or she strongly favors. When intensities of preference differ on issues, there are incentives for groups to trade votes for those issues of great interest to them. Such a vote-trading process is called **logrolling**.

Suppose, for example, the ballot contains two issues, neither of which can pass separately because each issue provides benefits to only a minority of voters. One of the issues significantly benefits oil producers, and the other greatly benefits shoe manufacturers. Suppose that oil producers can gain considerably when their issue passes, and these gains outweigh any losses they might incur by voting for the issue favored by the shoe manufacturers. They then will have incentives to offer to vote for the issue of interest to shoe manufacturers in exchange for the shoe manufacturers' positive vote on the issue of interest to the oil producers. The shoe producers will agree to such a trade, provided that simultaneous passage of both issues will provide them with net benefits.

Incentives to trade votes exist when an asymmetry of gains on the issues is involved. If the oil producers' gains resulting from passage of their issue were exactly offset by losses from passage of the legislation of interest to shoe manufacturers, the incentive to trade votes disappears.

Trading votes might not be successful in accumulating enough votes to pass an issue. However, opportunities for logrolling clearly result in passage of some issues that otherwise could not command a simple majority.

Incentives to engage in logrolling depend on the relative intensities of voters' preferences on issues. If voters felt the same about all issues, the gains from passage of any one issue would be exactly offset by the losses expected as a result of passage of any other paired issue. Again, no incentive to trade votes exists under those circumstances.[10]

Implicit Logrolling

Implicit logrolling occurs when political interests succeed in pairing two (or more) issues of strong interest to divergent groups on the same ballot or the same bill. This is a common practice in legislatures, where riders are often attached to bills.

---

[9]Otto A. Davis, Melvin J. Hinich, and Peter C. Ordeshook, "An Expository Development of a Mathematical Model of the Electoral Process," *American Political Science Review* 64 (June 1970): 426–448.

[10]For an analysis of logrolling, see James S. Coleman, "The Possibility of a Social Welfare Function," *American Economic Review* 57 (December 1967): 1311–1317.

PUBLIC POLICY PERSPECTIVE

State Government Spending: Does the Size of the Legislature Matter?

State legislatures have grown in size during the 20th century. Only a minority of U.S. state governments (about 20 percent) have the same number of seats in their legislatures that they did in 1902. In more than half the states, the size of the upper house has increased since the beginning of the 1900s, while 23 states have expanded their lower house as well. For state programs, a larger number of districts represented in the legislature suggests that the tax costs per district for state public goods and services if distributed equally among districts will be lower. If constituents of each legislator's district pay one nth of the cost of a statewide program, where n is the number of districts, the cost in each district falls when the number of districts goes up. The theory of logrolling suggests that as more districts are available to distribute the costs of public spending, there will be more incentives for individual legislators to engage in vote trading to expand state government spending.

To test this theory, Thomas Gilligan and John Matsusaka collected data on spending by the 48 contiguous states from 1902 to 1942.[1] According to their research, the number of seats in state legislatures had a significantly positive impact on state and local government expenditure in the first half of the 20th century. However, it is the number of seats in the upper house (the Senate) that accounts for the upward effect of government spending. The impact on the number of seats in the lower house did not have a statistically significant impact on state and local government spending during this period.

Gilligan and Matsusaka also examined the impact of political parties on spending. They could not find any significant effects from control of the legislature of the governor's office by varying political parties on spending over the period. The increment in spending attributable to increased legislature size was most concentrated in government spending on highways and education. Since these are two aspects of government spending that tend to result in geographically restricted benefits, this suggests that increased legislature size does contribute to more logrolling. The researchers also conclude that much of this increased spending was by local governments that often benefit from state aid.

As with most economic studies of this type, the researchers used statistical methods to account for other possible influences on state and local government spending including population, income, federal aid, population growth, percent of population in rural areas, and other demographic and political characteristics. The results indicate that after controlling for these influences, growth in legislature size in states during the period studied, in fact, contributed to higher government spending.

---

[1]See Thomas W. Gilligan and John G. Matsusaka, "Fiscal Policy, Legislature Size, and Political Parties: Evidence from State and Local Government in the First Half of the 20th Century," *National Tax Journal* LIV, 1 (March 2001): 57–82.

For example, two unrelated issues, such as import quotas for textiles and the funding of a new bomber, might be included on the same ballot. By doing so, legislators will have to vote for each of the issues together even if they would gain from the passage of only one issue. Each issue, if voted on separately, would be defeated because each alone provides benefits only to a minority of voters. However, the combined package might succeed in passing by a simple majority if each minority special-interest group votes for it to get its favored program. In effect, each special-interest group is induced to support the program of another special-interest group in order to receive benefits from its most-favored program.

Again, the willingness of each special-interest group to vote for the combined package is a function of the relative intensity of preference on the two issues. If the gains on the most-favored issue are balanced equally by the losses resulting from passage of the issue most favored by the other group, no incentive exists to muster support for the combined package. Citizens will have incentives to engage in implicit logrolling only to the extent to which it provides them with positive net benefits.

Many argue that logrolling is a positive safety valve in a democratic society because it allows citizens an opportunity to express their intensity of preference for particular outcomes in terms of their willingness to trade votes. A problem often overlooked in democratic societies is that allowing one vote per voter on each issue provides no direct basis for individuals to express their intensity of preference on issues. A vote is a vote. It says nothing about the extent to which a citizen is made better or worse off by a given political change. Under simple majority rule, a coalition of individuals can succeed in defeating issues about which certain minority groups have extremely strong feelings. If the minorities have no outlet for venting these intense preferences, the result might very well be social instability and eventually a revolution to change political institutions. Thus, logrolling can be thought of as a safety valve.

Although logrolling has the potential to account for intensity of preference, the danger remains that it will be used by skillful politicians as a means of gaining approval for programs with purely redistributive benefits. In fact, the common judgment is unfavorable toward logrolling because of its reputation as a mechanism for members of Congress to use the political system to gain benefits that accrue only to their constituents. Those who argue against logrolling believe that it extends the size of the public sector over and above what would be the case in its absence. Many believe that this extension is primarily in programs that redistribute income to certain groups, rather than providing positive net benefit.

Logrolling and Efficiency

Suppose citizens in a community vote whether to support both security protection and community entertainment. Both these goods are pure public goods for the citizens. Security protection is measured by the number of security guards hired per week. Entertainment is measured by the number of fireworks displays per week. Assume three voters agree to share equally in the unit costs of these two goods. Assume each fireworks display costs $300 per week and the cost of a security guard is also $300 per week. The marginal and average cost of each of these public goods is $300. At first, these issues are voted on separately, and no logrolling agreements are made. Each voter is assigned a tax share of $100 for each unit of the good. The collective decisions are made according to majority rule.

In Figure 5.8, the marginal benefit, tax per unit, and marginal cost of each of the goods are shown. Figure 5.8A assumes that the marginal benefit received by voters A and B is zero at one fireworks display per week. The MB_A and MB_B curves intersect the horizontal axis at one display per year. However, voter C receives a marginal benefit of $250 from the first fireworks display. C is the only person whose tax does not exceed the marginal benefit of the first display. She will cast the only favorable vote. Under majority rule, no fireworks displays will be provided because A and B vote against the first unit, given their $100 tax per display.

Figure 5.8B shows the marginal benefit, marginal cost, and tax per unit of security guards. In this case, voter A is the only one whose marginal benefit does not fall short of the $100 tax per guard. The marginal benefit that A receives from the first security guard is $250. Voters B and C are presumed to have zero marginal benefit at a weekly level of protection corresponding to one security guard per week. It follows that, given their $100 tax shares, they vote no. No security protection will be provided under majority rule. Given the assumptions, neither security

FIGURE 5.8   Logrolling

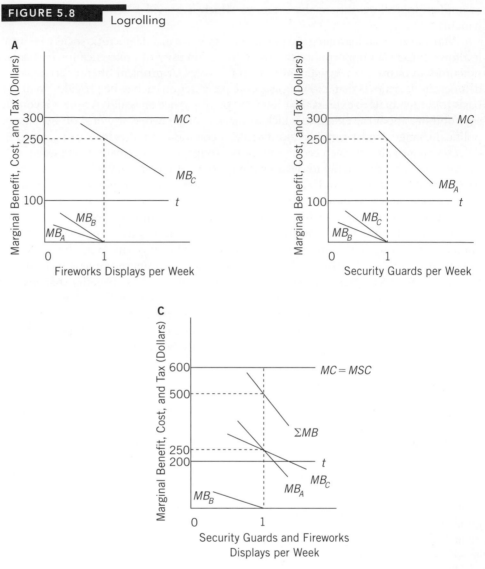

Logrolling can result in the passage of two issues together that could not pass if voted on separately.

© Cengage Learning

protection nor fireworks displays will be provided under majority rule. The median most-preferred outcome of the three voters is zero in both cases.

Now suppose that *A* and *C* collude to get fireworks displays and security guards paired together as an issue. The election now consists of approval of a budget that includes one fireworks display per week for each security guard hired per week. In Figure 5.8C, the total output of security and fireworks is plotted against the marginal cost, benefit, and tax shares. A budget of $600 is proposed. All voters understand that this budget consists of one fireworks display and one security guard per week. The tax share for each voter is $200 for each combined security guard and fireworks display per week. Voter *B*, who evaluates the marginal benefit of both of these goods as zero, votes against the proposed budget. However, both voters *A* and *C* will vote in favor of this budget because the sum of the marginal benefits of fireworks and security protection exceeds their taxes. For voter A, the marginal benefit of the budget is $250, which consists entirely of the benefit received from security protection. For voter C, the marginal benefit of the budget is also $250 and consists entirely of the marginal benefit received from fireworks displays. When they agree to pair the issues, both A and C are better off than they otherwise would have been if the issues had been voted on separately. Thus, pairing of the issues results in passage of both, while neither would pass if voted on alone on its own merits.

The same result would emerge if voters A and C agree to trade votes if each of the issues were voted on separately. That is, C would agree to vote in favor of security protection, even though that would make her worse off, provided that A agreed to vote in favor of fireworks displays. The net weekly gain to A from agreeing to vote for security protection would be $50. This is the difference between the weekly marginal benefit of $250 from one security guard and the weekly tax bill of $200 that would finance *both* fireworks and security. Similarly, voter C also would get a net weekly gain of $50 by agreeing to trade votes. The big loser in this process is voter B, who ends up paying $200 per week in taxes to pay for both a security guard and a fireworks display, neither of which provides positive marginal benefit to him!

Notice how the result depends on the intensity of preferences of voters A and C. Suppose that the marginal benefit of the first fireworks display was only $125 for voter C. She would still vote in favor of it if it were proposed on its own merits, because her marginal benefit would exceed her $100 tax share. However, under these circumstances, she would have no incentive to engage in logrolling, because the sum of her marginal benefits for the first fireworks display and the first security guard would be only $125, assuming again that she receives zero marginal benefit from one security guard. Because this falls short of the $200 tax share necessary to support both programs together, she would vote against the combined budget of one fireworks display and one security guard per week.

Logrolling also can cause losses in efficiency. At the political equilibrium budget of $600 per week, the marginal benefit received by A and C from both security protection and fireworks is $500. Because the marginal benefit from both of these public goods is zero for voter B, the sum of the marginal benefits for all three is only $500 in equilibrium. This is less than the marginal cost of $600 necessary to provide both goods. Because the marginal social cost of the budget exceeds its marginal social benefit by $100, approval of the budget means that more than the efficient amount of public spending occurs.

However, logrolling does not always cause losses in efficiency. For example, if B and A were each to get $25 in positive benefits from fireworks displays, then it would be efficient to have one display per year. But one display per year would not pass when voted on alone because both B and A still would vote against the program that would cost each of them $100 per week in taxes for $25 per week in benefits. However, the sum of the marginal benefits in this case would equal the $300 marginal cost. Similarly, if both B and C were to get $25 per week in marginal benefits from security guards, it would be efficient to have one guard per week because the sum of the marginal benefit of the guards would be $300, which equals the marginal cost. Pairing the two issues as before still would result in B voting against the two goods, because his $200 tax share would fall short of the $50 benefit he got from the two goods. However, A and C would each get $275 in benefits from passage and would both vote in favor of it, given a $200 tax share for each. The sum of the marginal benefits of the combined programs would be $275 + $275 + $50 = $600, which equals the marginal cost of $600.

It is not possible to reach an unequivocal conclusion about the impact of logrolling on the efficient use of resources. In some cases, logrolling can allow improved efficiency by contributing to passage of programs with a marginal social benefit that equals or exceeds their marginal social costs. In other cases, logrolling results in an overallocation of resources to government use by allowing passage of government programs with marginal social costs that exceed their marginal social benefits.

SPECIAL-INTEREST GROUPS AND THEIR IMPACT ON POLITICAL EQUILIBRIUM

Special-interest groups are organizations that seek to increase government expenditures that benefit their constituents. They differ from political parties in that their leaders do not actually run for political office. They do, however, seek to put pressure on political candidates, bureaucrats, and ultimately on voters to support issues that benefit the members of their groups. Special-interest groups can apply pressure to politicians by threatening to tell their constituents to vote against them. They also can make campaign contributions to politicians who support their positions and finance advertisements against candidates who do not support their interests.

Special-interest groups exist to promote policies favorable to workers, particular industries, regions, racial minorities, ethnic groups, environmental preservation, and taxpayers in general. The Sierra Club, for example, often acts as a special-interest group in trying to persuade environmental protection agencies to preserve wilderness areas. In recent years, such groups as the Sierra Club and AARP, which is a special-interest group representing retirees, have become potent political forces. Many of these special-interest groups have used their power to influence the votes of those who are not members or direct beneficiaries of their efforts. In effect, special-interest groups in modern democracies often campaign with as much zeal and actual expenditure of money and resources as do the political candidates themselves. The technical efficiency of the group in influencing the votes of nonmembers can make small groups, such as those representing farmers, or environmentalists, formidable and powerful influences on voters and therefore on the political equilibrium. Research on the effectiveness of several special-interest groups in Switzerland in achieving their objectives measures their influence and suggests that they have influenced the political equilibrium in that nation.[11]

Gary Becker has analyzed how special-interest groups affect political equilibrium.[12] Successful pressure groups succeed in manipulating taxes, government subsidies, and government regulations to raise the well-being of their members. Becker points out that pressure groups that succeed in obtaining increased benefits from government must make the members of competing pressure groups worse off. This is because an increase in government spending for one group increases taxes, or imposes other costs, on other groups. Increased influence of any one particular

[11]F. Schneider and J. Naumann, "Interest Groups in Democracies—How Influential Are They? An Empirical Examination for Switzerland," *Public Choice* 38 (1982): 281–303.

[12]Gary S. Becker, "A Theory of Competition among Pressure Groups for Political Influence," *Quarterly Journal of Economics* 98 (August 1983): 371–400.

group is also assumed to decrease the influence of competing groups. The pressure groups themselves compete for political influence by spending time, effort, and some of their income on the production of political pressure. The number of members in a group and the resources spent per member in supporting the group's pressure activities determine the amount of political pressure that a group can deliver. To the extent to which those who benefit from the special-interest group's efforts try to be free riders, the effectiveness in producing pressure declines. By spending money to reduce free riding, the leaders of the groups can increase pressure on political agents.

Becker's model can be used to gain some insights into the success or failure of competing special-interest groups. *Successful special-interest groups are likely to be small relative to the portion of the population that pays taxes to support their subsidies.* This result might seem surprising, but it is really very logical. After all, the greater the number of citizens who pay taxes to support even a rather large subsidy to a group with only a few members, the lower is the tax per citizen relative to the subsidy per beneficiary. Becker points out that this result is consistent with empirical observations. For example, agriculture tends to be heavily subsidized in nations where it is a small sector, as is the case in the United States and in Japan. Agriculture tends to be heavily taxed in nations where it is a large sector, as in Poland and in many African nations.

People are often members of more than one special-interest group. For example, a person could be a member of an occupational pressure group and of a group that supports regional growth. This person could spend money and effort as a member of his or her occupational pressure group in ways that result in increases in the costs of obtaining the benefits desired for his or her special interest in regional growth. In effect, the activities of various special-interest groups often result in both taxes and subsidies for their constituents. Many people could be equally as well off if both their taxes and subsidies from each pressure group were reduced in equal amounts. If the effect of these taxes and subsidies is to cancel each other, members of the various special-interest groups will not be harmed. But, because taxes and subsidies to particular activities result in efficiency losses, the result will be net gains from reducing taxes and subsidies.

BUREAUCRACY AND THE SUPPLY OF PUBLIC OUTPUT

The establishment of a government also implies the development of a **bureaucracy** that is in charge of implementing public choices made through political institutions. The bureaucracy itself influences the actual delivery of services and the efficiency with which such services can be produced.[13] Insofar as bureaucrats influence the cost of producing public goods, their behavior is an important determinant of the actual terms on which such goods can be produced and offered to citizens. In other words, bureaucrats influence the terms of supply of public goods and thus influence the resulting political equilibrium.

A basic problem exists in measuring the efficiency of production by bureaucrats. In most cases, the output produced is neither easily quantifiable into units nor easily sold for profit in markets. Therefore, it is difficult to determine whether government bureaus produce their output at minimum possible cost. For a private firm competing with other firms producing a similar output, such information is rapidly made available to owners through the firm's profit and loss statement. A business firm with costs of production that are higher than those of competing

---

[13]See Thomas E. Borcherding, ed., *Budgets and Bureaucrats.* (Durham, N.C.: Duke University Press, 1977).

firms will quickly discover that it will be difficult to make a profit unless costs are lowered. Bureaucrats do not directly own the inputs they use for production. Funding comes from an external source (such as Congress), and any net financial gains to bureaucrats who produce efficiently are rare.

Bureaucratic Behavior

Among the most significant contributions by economists who have analyzed bureaucracy is the work of William Niskanen.[14] He has argued that bureaucrats seek to maximize the power associated with holding public office. Such power is likely to be correlated with the resources that the bureaucrat has under command. This, in turn, is related to the size of the bureau's budget. Niskanen therefore assumes that the bureaucrat seeks to maximize the size of the bureau's budget. The implication of Niskanen's analysis is that attempts by bureaucrats to maximize their budgets lead to a general overextension of the government sector in excess of the efficient level of output.

Figure 5.9 shows the bureaucratic incentive to supply more than the efficient amount of output. The marginal social benefit and marginal social cost of the bureau's output per year are shown in Figure 5.9A. The output could be the number of new missiles deployed per year for a military bureau such as the air force. For a civilian agency, such as a bureau of public roads, the output could be measured as the miles of new road supplied per year. The efficient output, Q^* units per year, corresponds to point E, where the marginal social benefit of output just equals its marginal social cost. Bureaucrats, however, seek to maximize the size of their budgets. They seek to obtain as much funding as possible for their output. If they reason that they can obtain additional funds as long as the total social benefit (TSB) of the output exceeds its total social cost (TSC), they will try to increase output beyond the efficient level of Q^* units per year. This is illustrated in Figure 5.9B, where the TSB and TSC of the bureau's output are plotted. The efficient output corresponds to the point where the slope of the TSC curve equals the slope of the TSB curve. At that output, $MSB = MSC$ in Figure 5.9A. The output that the bureau will try to get approved is Q_B, which corresponds to the point where $TSC = TSB$. The bureau's desired level of output therefore exceeds the efficient amount.

Figure 5.9A shows the loss in well-being that results if the bureaucrats succeed in getting their desired level of output approved. The loss in net benefits is the triangular area EAB.

An additional problem with managing bureaucracies to achieve efficiency is that bureaucrats often have monopolistic power. Single agencies provide such services as environmental protection, defense, and social insurance. In many cases, the bureaucrats themselves have specialized information not available elsewhere. The bureaucrats could seek to attain the budget-maximizing output by trying to make politicians believe that the social benefit of their output is greater than it is in fact. This would shift the TSB curve up to the TSB' curve in the eyes of funding agencies, as shown in Figure 5.9B. The maximum output that the agency could fund would increase to Q'_B.

A funding agent often has difficulty monitoring the activities of its bureaus because of high transactions costs. Budgeting and managerial improvements that

---

[14]For more details on William A. Niskanen, Jr.'s pioneering views on bureaucratic behavior, see his works, *Bureaucracy and Representative Government.* (Chicago: Aldine-Atherton, 1971) and "Bureaucrats and Politicians," *Journal of Law and Economics* 18 (December 1975): 617–643.

FIGURE 5.9   Bureaucracy and Efficiency

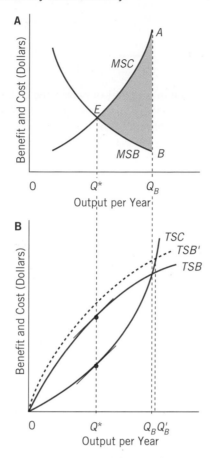

The efficient output is Q^* per year. A budget-maximizing bureau tries to get its sponsor to approve Q_B units per year. This amount would result in a decrease in well-being equal to the area EAB. A bureau could try to get Q'_B approved if it convinced its sponsor that its benefits at any given output level were given by the curve TSB' instead of TSB.

lower these transactions costs would contribute to better monitoring of bureaucrat behavior and would help achieve efficient output levels.

Bureaucrats can increase the size of their budgets in two ways. They can seek to convince governing authorities that their output needs to be increased, as in the preceding analysis. Alternatively, they can increase the amounts of input necessary to produce any given amount of output by using inefficient production techniques. In this latter case, the loss in efficiency results from misuse of input rather than excessive production of the bureau's service. Bureaucrats do not achieve efficiency because they maximize a utility function that depends not only on net benefit to their "sponsors" (funding authorities) but also on the growth of their budget, fringe benefits, job security, and reduced workload.

The behavior of bureaucrats depends on the constraints that they face. Most of the models of bureaucracy presume that sponsors are at the mercy of the bureaucrats. In fact, however, adequate budgeting procedures can establish a set of constraints that could govern the tendencies of bureaucrats to overexpand or produce inefficiently.

CHECKPOINT

1. What is logrolling?

2. How can logrolling result in approval of extensions of public services that could not be approved under majority rule when they are voted on as single issues?

3. How does bureaucratic behavior influence public spending? How can bureaucrats influence information in ways that increase government spending beyond the efficient levels?

SUMMARY

A political equilibrium is an agreement on the level of production of one or more public goods, given a specified rule for making the public choice and the distribution of tax shares among individuals. The political equilibrium is also influenced by the cost of production of the public good or goods and information available to voters on both costs and benefits. Individuals base their votes on a comparison of their marginal benefits and tax shares for proposed increases in output. A voter's most-preferred outcome corresponds to the point at which the marginal benefit of a given quantity of a public good is equal to the extra taxes that must be paid for that quantity.

Collective, or public, choices are agreements resulting in political equilibrium on issues of common concern. The most commonly used public choice rule is simple majority rule. Under certain circumstances, when two or more alternatives are to be decided upon, majority rule might be incapable of achieving a unique political equilibrium. However, when all voters have single-peaked preferences, majority rule will produce a unique political equilibrium at the median most-preferred outcome. Single-peaked preferences exist when a unique optimal outcome exists for each individual, such that movement away from the optimum always makes that individual worse off.

Political equilibriums are influenced by politicians and bureaucrats. Models of political behavior presume that political parties attempt to maximize votes. When all voters have single-peaked preferences, parties will tend to move to the median position to win elections.

When all voters do not vote, the median most-preferred outcome of all citizens could differ from the median most-preferred outcome of all voters. Voters might choose not to vote because they believe that their votes will have no effect on the outcome of an election. The costs of voting might outweigh the expected benefits of doing so.

Political parties have incentives to propose less than the efficient amount of government services when voters are better informed on costs than on benefits of those services. However, vote-maximizing behavior also provides incentive for politicians to engage in logrolling.

Logrolling is the explicit trading of votes on issues of great interest to voters. When two or more issues are voted on simultaneously, implicit logrolling can occur. Under these circumstances, two issues that could not be approved if voted on separately could pass. Logrolling offers an outlet to express intensity of feeling on an issue in a one-person, one-vote democracy. However, logrolling also can cause losses in efficiency.

Models of bureaucratic behavior presume that bureaucrats attempt to maximize the size of their budgets. If they face no competition and no restraints from budgeting procedures, this leads to a tendency of oversupply of government output or inefficient production techniques. Special-interest groups also influence political outcomes by seeking to increase government subsidies to their constituents that are financed by taxes on others.

LOOKING AHEAD

Chapter 6 examines some practical techniques for evaluating the costs and benefits of government programs. We show how the budgeting process can be used to help achieve the least-cost means of providing public goods and how government projects to increase the output of government goods and services can be evaluated with cost-benefit analysis.

KEY CONCEPTS

Arrow's Impossibility Theorem

Bureaucracy

Constitutions

Implicit Logrolling

Logrolling

Median Voter

Median Voter Rule

Most-Preferred Political Outcome

Multiple-Peaked Preferences

Political Equilibrium

Political Externalities

Political Parties

Political Transactions Costs

Public Choice

Rational Ignorance

Simple Majority Rule

Single-Peaked Preferences

Special-Interest Groups

Tax Shares

REVIEW QUESTIONS

1. What factors influence the costs of supplying such public goods as police protection and national defense? What might cause these costs to go up or down, and how would such change affect your taxes?

2. How does a person decide to vote on any issue that proposes to change the amount of public goods supplied by the government?

3. What factors influence the political equilibrium?

4. Using the data in Table 5.1, show that the median most-preferred outcome will defeat any other alternative in elections decided by majority rule.

5. Given tax shares, explain why only the median voter consumes his or her most-preferred quantity of a public good under majority rule. Show how other voters are prevented from obtaining maximum satisfaction from the public good. Show the losses in well-being that can be prevented if the tax paid by *each* voter equaled that voter's marginal benefit.

6. Use Figure 5.2 to show how an increase in weekly wages of security guards to $420 will affect the most-preferred outcome of each voter and the political equilibrium under majority rule.

7. When does majority rule lead to the possibility of public choices that result in the outcome of an election being contingent on the order in which alternatives are presented to the electorate? Under what conditions will a unique collective choice result from simple majority rule?

8. Under what conditions will the median peak correspond to an extreme outcome, such as no output of a good?

9. What is logrolling? Under what conditions is logrolling likely to emerge? How can logrolling prevent the attainment of efficiency?

10. Show how an increase in the average cost of supplying a pure public good will reduce the output resulting from simple majority rule. Is the median voter always the same person? Show how a change in tax shares could change the identity of the median voter.

PROBLEMS

1. The average cost of landscaping services for members of a condominium community is $350 per week. Assume that the quantity of landscaping services is perfectly correlated with the number of gardeners per week. Suppose the community consists of seven residents, each with the identical marginal benefit curve for landscaping services. The marginal benefit of the first gardener is $100 per resident.

   a. How many gardeners would be hired if their services were sold in a market to individual buyers at a price of $350 per week? Explain why the market arrangement is inefficient.

   b. Assume that the efficient number of gardeners is three per week. What is the political equilibrium under majority rule if each voter is assigned a tax share of $50 per gardener per week? Does the political equilibrium under majority rule differ from the Lindahl equilibrium?

2. Instead of all residents having identical marginal benefit schedules, the marginal benefit per gardener

varies for five residents according to the following table:

Marginal Benefit for Each Gardener (Dollars)

VOTER	1	2	3	4
Mike	325	275	225	175
Jan	225	150	75	0
Franklin	75	50	25	0
Susan	75	50	25	0
Megan	50	25	0	0

If each voter is assigned a tax share of $50, what is the political equilibrium under majority rule? Show that this equilibrium does not result in the efficient output of gardening services. Show how the Lindahl equilibrium will differ from the political equilibrium under majority rule.[15]

3. The example of logrolling used in the text assumes that the transactions costs of vote trading are zero. Suppose instead that voters A and C have to incur expenditures equal to $60 per week to reach agreement on the vote-trading scheme. Show how this would prevent successful logrolling. Also show how logrolling would be impossible if the marginal benefit of the first security guard were only $150 to voter A and transactions costs were zero.

4. Suppose the positions of political candidates on all issues can be ranked on a scale of conservative to liberal. The more conservative a candidate, the less the quantity of public goods he or she will supply. Suppose as well that all voters favoring liberal candidates will vote while only 50 percent of those favoring conservative candidates will vote. Use a graph like the one drawn in Figure 5.6 to show how the political equilibrium will differ from an election in which all citizens vote.

5. Suppose the military bureaucracy consistently misinforms Congress on the total costs of producing military hardware. Assume that it underestimates the actual costs and that the political representatives believe these estimates. Show how this is likely to cause a loss in efficiency. Show the efficient output of military hardware, the output desired by the military bureaucracy, and how the output chosen will differ from the efficient output even if Congress attempts to achieve efficiency. In your answer, assume that the military seeks to maximize the size of its budget.

ADDITIONAL READINGS

Arrow, Kenneth. *Social Choice and Individual Values*, 2nd edition. New York: Wiley, 1963. A treatise on collective choice that led to a Nobel Prize in economics for the author. Requires a strong background in mathematics.

Becker, Gary S. "A Theory of Competition among Pressure Groups for Political Influence." *Quarterly Journal of Economics* 9 (August 1983): 371–400. A path-breaking technical application of economic theory to political interaction. It analyzes the behavior and impact of special-interest groups on political equilibrium.

Black, Duncan. *The Theory of Committees and Elections*. Cambridge, Eng.: Cambridge University Press, 1958. A classic in the theory of collective choice.

Breton, Albert. *The Economic Theory of Representative Government*. Chicago: Aldine, 1974. An analysis of the demand and supply of government output and policy.

Buchanan, James, and Gordon Tullock. *The Calculus of Consent*. Ann Arbor: University of Michigan Press, 1962. An application of economic theory to political interaction in constitutional democracy.

Downs, Anthony. *An Economic Theory of Democracy*. New York: Harper & Row, 1957. A pioneering application of techniques of economic analysis to political interaction. Very readable.

McLean, Iain, and Arnold B. Urken, eds. *Classics of Social Choice*. Ann Arbor: The University of Michigan Press, 1993. A collection of classic articles on public choice issues.

Mueller, Dennis C. *Public Choice III*, 3rd ed. Cambridge, Eng.: Cambridge University Press, 2003. A summary of the literature on public choice.

Niskanen, William A., Jr. *Bureaucracy and Representative Government*. Chicago: Aldine-Atherton, 1971. A modern classic that analyzes bureaucratic incentives and the influence of bureaucracy on public policy.

---

[15]I am indebted to Michael Wentz of Salisbury University for this problem and for providing clarification on the first problem in this chapter.

INTERNET RESOURCES

http://www.house.gov
This is the home page of the U.S. House of Representatives. Click on Leadership to obtain information on the political agendas of both Democratic and Republican party leaders.

http://www.senate.gov
This is the home page of the U.S. Senate. Information on legislation proposed by both Republicans and Democrats can be obtained from this site.

http://www.fairvote.org
The Center for Voting and Democracy maintains this site to help inform the public about how voting systems affect political participation, representation, and government in a democracy. An online library is provided to access information and studies on proportional representation, instant runoff voting, redistricting, voter rights, voter turnout, and many other issues relating to voting systems in a democratic nation.

http://www.whitehouse.gov
The political agenda of the president, including his recent speeches, are available at this site.

PartTwo

GOVERNMENT EXPENDITURES AND POLICY IN THE UNITED STATES: SELECTED ISSUES

Chapter 6

COST-BENEFIT ANALYSIS AND GOVERNMENT INVESTMENTS

LEARNING OBJECTIVES

After reading this chapter, you should be able to:

- Discuss cost-effectiveness analysis and explain how it can be used to help government select the least-cost means of achieving given objectives.

- Describe how cost-benefit analysis can be used to help government choose among alternative investment projects.

- Explain how benefits and costs of government investment projects can be measured and list some of the difficulties involved in doing so.

- Define the social rate of discount, the difficulties involved in estimating it, and how it is used to obtain the present value of future net benefits of government investments.

- Put all the steps of cost-benefit analysis together and show how a typical cost-benefit tableau can be set up.

- Analyze the role of cost-benefit analysis in government investment budgeting and in the political process.

How many times have you heard political candidates claim that the problem with government is that it is not run like a business? The average citizen believes, perhaps for good reason, that considerable waste and mismanagement exists in government that would not be tolerated in a profit-maximizing business. You have all heard about outrageous prices for screwdrivers and other components in defense contracting, and many believe that federal and state bureaucracies are inflated with workers whose productivity is low.

It would be nice if government could be run like a business, but some fundamental differences between the nature of government and the nature of business make this impossible. First, governments do not sell their products for a profit. Because they do not earn profits, they do not receive very good signals about how well they are doing in satisfying the demands of the citizens they serve. Second, governments do not usually face competition. Even if they are doing a poor job because they are supplying a product or service that has little value or because their costs are excessively high, no competing producer can quickly enter to produce a better service or one that costs less. Finally, government projects and programs are often chosen through the political process because of their effects on the incomes of special-interest groups rather than their contribution to the efficient allocation of resources.

Many government programs involve investment in roads, water and sewer facilities, air and sea ports, education, and other projects that provide social capital that enhances the productivity of inputs employed by both government and the private sector. For example, roads provided by governments in the United States are used as inputs into trucking services and provide transportation benefits to many segments of the U.S. population. The air traffic control system run by the federal government makes it possible for both businesses and households to enjoy the benefits of safe air travel. Government investments usually take several years to develop and construct, but once completed yield a stream of benefits to citizens for many years to come. However, because the government projects do not usually result in output sold in the marketplace, it is difficult to compute the return earned on the government funds invested. We need a way of estimating net return to government investments to determine whether they provide net benefits to society. This chapter discusses some practical techniques that can be used to help government economize the use of resources and rank alternative investment projects according to their net benefits.

THE BUDGET PROCESS

The budgeting process for the federal government in the United States follows an established procedure to authorize federal expenditures and the means of financing those expenditures for each fiscal year that begins on October 1. The process usually begins on the first Monday in February when the president of the United States presents his budget request to the Congress. The president's budget is compiled by the president's Office of Management and Budget and represents the administration's plan for spending and funding that expenditure based on its political priorities. The budget request indicates total spending in various areas such as national defense, health, and education. The actual document transmitted to Congress is huge and contains very specific requests for funding of a broad array of individual federal programs, estimates for total spending, tax revenues, and any budget deficit or surplus that results when expenditures do not exactly equal revenues. There is also considerable analysis of spending and revenues over the next five years based on the president's priorities.

The president's budget indicates any changes in spending or tax policy proposals the administration wants the Congress to approve. However, nearly 70 percent of the federal budget is based on existing legislation, including the spending for major entitlement programs (Social Security, Medicare, and Medicaid) and net interest on the federal debt. Spending for entitlements and net interest are automatically funded with no action by Congress required, and the bulk of revenue can be raised by the existing tax code unless Congress chooses to approve changes in tax policy.

Discretionary programs are those that Congress must renew funding for each year. Included in discretionary spending are programs for national defense, education, health, housing, highways, and many others. Discretionary spending accounts for about 30 percent of federal spending and is under the jurisdiction of the House and Senate Appropriations Committees. The president's budget request includes recommendations for funding of all discretionary programs. The Congress must appropriate funds for discretionary spending each year. *Entitlement programs* include spending for such transfers as Social Security, Medicare, Medicaid, military retirement, and veterans' benefits that are determined by the number of individuals eligible for payments under existing rules and are automatically funded. However, the president and Congress can change the rules for the programs or propose new programs. The president can also propose changes in the tax system, and Congress can approve or reject (or modify) the president's proposals.

After the president's budget request is received, the House and Senate Budget Committees hold hearings and draft a budget resolution to be discussed and possibly amended by the House of Representatives and the Senate. After differences are ironed out, a *budget resolution* is passed by Congress (usually by April 15) that indicates funding levels for 19 broad federal spending categories for the next five years. There is a spending ceiling and a revenue floor in the resolution, and the difference between the two is the anticipated federal budget deficit or surplus for each of the five years.

The budget resolution specifies *budget authority* that the Congress will allow federal government agencies to spend in each of the 19 spending categories for broad budget functions. Budget authority does not always equal budget outlays in a given year because agencies might not actually spend all the funds that have been authorized in a given fiscal year, and these funds could be spent in a subsequent fiscal year. The budget authority does, however, represent a limit on agency spending over the five-year period with the budget deficit or surplus in any given year dependent on how much of budget authority actually ends up as outlays in that fiscal year.

Finally, Congress can enact a *budget reconciliation bill* that contains specific provisions for federal spending and tax policy or changes in entitlement spending. This bill can be voted on by both the House and Senate and then goes to the president to be signed into law or vetoed. Final enactment of the budget legislation and its approval by the president provides the budget authority for federal government spending in the coming fiscal year.

ECONOMIC ANALYSIS FOR THE BUDGET PROCESS: ACHIEVING THE LEAST-COST MEANS OF ACCOMPLISHING AN AUTHORIZED OBJECTIVE

In this section, we discuss some budgeting techniques that can be used to help government choose the best mix of programs to accomplish various objectives, such as providing children with a certain amount and quality of schooling. We then discuss techniques to help government choose among alternative investment projects.

Governments are like enormous multiproduct firms. To choose among alternative products, we must evaluate both the marginal social benefits and marginal social costs of additional investments and rank projects according to their marginal social net gain.

Program Budgeting

A **program** is a combination of government activities producing a distinguishable output. **Program budgeting** is a system of managing government expenditures by attempting to compare the program proposals of all government agencies authorized to achieve similar objectives. The **mission** of a government agency is comparable to a business firm's product. Program budgeting seeks to measure the outputs of agencies in quantitative terms. Then the goal is to choose the combination of programs that achieves the mission at minimum cost. The minimum-cost combination of programs is sometimes called the cost-effective program mix.

An advantage of program budgeting is that it has the potential to allow budget managers to see trade-offs that are not immediately obvious when agency or department budgets are viewed in isolation. For example, suppose all agencies with the basic function of improving health and safety are required to submit their proposed programs to a central budget office. The programs of many agencies in such diverse departments as Health and Human Services and Transportation are designed to accomplish similar objectives. For example, highway safety, cancer research, antipollution controls, and medical subsidies all ultimately serve the purpose of prolonging human lives. Under program budgeting, each agency would estimate the years of human life that their programs will produce over time. The budget managers then would seek to achieve a given number of years of life prolongation by choosing the cost-effective mix of programs.

Trade-offs between the programs of agencies with similar missions in the two departments would not be as easily discovered under a *line budgeting system*, which compares the budget proposals of agencies in a given department with each other, even though those agencies have very different missions. Consistent use of program budgeting techniques, and skillful grouping of alternative programs according to the actual outputs produced, can result in considerable tax savings by allowing choice of least-cost mixes of programs achieving given objectives.

Cost-Effectiveness Analysis

Cost-effectiveness analysis is a technique for determining the minimum-cost combination of government programs to achieve a given objective. The first step in implementing a cost-effectiveness analysis would be to choose an objective that alternative government programs can achieve. For example, suppose we want to achieve the objective of reducing deaths from disease or accidents by 5,000 per year on average over the next 10 years. We can choose from many programs, all of which help reduce deaths. We can use tax funds to provide more information about the risks of smoking, drinking alcohol, or having a diet high in fat. We also could require that all buildings be equipped with smoke detectors and provide them for free in low-income neighborhoods where the quality of housing is so poor that the incidence of deaths as a result of residential fires is high. We could provide subsidies to improve the cardiac-care facilities of hospitals in the nation. Finally, we could invest funds in improving the safety of our highways so as to reduce accidental traffic deaths or improve air traffic control techniques to reduce aircraft accidents.

Let's look at two programs: government provision of free smoke detectors to urban neighborhoods and government provision of free inoculations against the flu to the same neighborhoods. The objective of both programs is to save an extra 5,000 lives per year. The problem is to choose the mix of the two programs that achieves this objective at minimum possible cost.

The first step to solve the problem is to find all the combinations of the two programs in appropriate amounts that can be used to save 5,000 lives per year. In this way, we can derive an isoquant for the two programs. Such an isoquant is illustrated in Figure 6.1. Each point on the isoquant shows a specific combination of the two programs that will save 5,000 lives per year. For example, point A corresponds to 20,000 smoke detectors and 10,000 free inoculations per year. Point B corresponds to 10,000 smoke detectors and 20,000 free inoculations. Because both points are on the isoquant, they are both equally effective in achieving the objective of saving 5,000 lives per year. To actually construct the isoquant, budget analysis requires estimates of the marginal product of each of the two programs in terms of lives saved and information on how the marginal products will vary with the level of the program, which in this case is easily measured by the number of smoke detectors and inoculations provided.

With information on the marginal products, we also can calculate the slope of the isoquant at each point. The slope provides information on the marginal rate of technical substitution of one program for the other. It tells us, for example, how many more inoculations we will have to provide to keep the number of lives saved

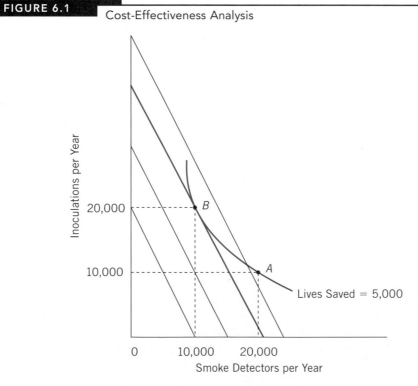

FIGURE 6.1   Cost-Effectiveness Analysis

The minimum-cost combination of programs corresponds to point B.

at 5,000 when we reduce the number of smoke detectors by any given amount. The marginal rate of technical substitution (*MRTS*) is the slope of the isoquant multiplied by −1 and equals the ratio of the marginal product of smoke detectors (*SD*) to the marginal product of inoculations (*I*):

$$MRTS = Marginal\ Product\ of\ SD/Marginal\ Product\ of\ I. \qquad (6.1)$$

To determine the cost-effective mix of the two programs, we must then get information on the prices of the two alternatives. If the price of a smoke detector is P_{SD} while the price of an inoculation is P_I, then the cost of any combination of smoke detector and inoculation can be calculated as follows:

$$C = (SD)P_{SD} + (I)P_I. \qquad (6.2)$$

This equation defines a family of isocost lines. The slope of each isocost line is the price of smoke detectors divided by the price of inoculation multiplied by −1. (See the appendixes of Chapters 1 and 2 for a review of isoquant analysis.) Suppose each smoke detector installed costs \$30 and each inoculation costs \$15. The equation of the family of isocost lines would be

$$C = 30(SD) + 15(I). \qquad (6.3)$$

Figure 6.1 plots a hypothetical isoquant for the two programs, giving all the combinations of smoke detectors and inoculations per year that can be used to save 5,000 additional lives per year. Also plotted on the same set of axes is the family of isocost lines.

The cost-effective mix of the two programs occurs at point *B*, where 20,000 free inoculations are provided and 10,000 free smoke detectors are installed. At that point, the isoquant becomes tangent to an isocost line. No other combination of programs other than that at point *B* can save lives at lower annual cost. At the point of tangency, the slope of the isoquant is equal to the slope of the isocost lines, and the following condition is satisfied:

$$MRTS = P_{SD}/P_I. \qquad (6.4)$$

Remember, the *MRTS* depends on the marginal productivities of both programs. The analysis shows that the cost-effective mix of the two programs depends both on their productivity in terms of lives saved and the prices of units of services provided by the programs themselves.

Cost-effectiveness analysis allows policy makers to see trade-offs between programs by budgeting together for all agencies with similar missions. In this way, governments can lower the costs of achieving certain goals, such as improving health or reducing delays from congestion in travel. By encouraging government agencies to compete for scarce budget funds through the development of more effective programs, this system can also reduce taxpayer expense further by encouraging innovation that reduces the cost of government programs or increases their productivity. The trick in making the government more cost effective is to group all agencies having similar goals together for budgeting purposes. For example, programs in the Department of Transportation and the Department of Health and Human Services and even the Department of Housing and Urban Development could all serve similar purposes. By budgeting together for these agencies, we can help reduce the costs of achieving such objectives as reducing deaths each year or improving health.

Performance Measures and Government Budgeting in Practice

Program budgeting has had only limited use in the United States. At the federal level, variants of program budgeting and cost-effectiveness analysis were used in the 1960s and 1970s. In the 1960s, the variant used by the Johnson administration was called the "planning-programming-budgeting system" (PPBS). In the 1970s, under the Carter administration, a system called "zero-based budgeting" (ZBB) was used. ZBB required each agency to justify its programs each year or risk a funding cut to zero (eliminating the program entirely). ZBB required a major effort to generate numbers and information to justify spending and absorbed considerable resources that could otherwise have gone into providing government services instead of evaluating those services. After a few years of use, it was generally agreed that the extra resources required under ZBB were not resulting in any improvement in government efficiency, and the extra costs of the process itself exceeded any extra benefits. Both systems failed to change the process by which resources were allocated to federal programs largely because the information they generated was ignored by Congress. The federal bureaucracy also had considerable difficulty in generating the information necessary to effectively implement these program budgeting schemes. Currently, no system of program budgeting is being used by the federal government. Systems of program budgeting are still used by some state and local governments in combination with other budgeting techniques.

In an assessment of the value of such systems, the Congressional Budget Office (CBO) has argued that they have only limited ability to improve resource allocation but that they do improve management and finance reporting.[1] The study also indicated that federal agencies do attempt to measure results of their programs in various ways to determine their effectiveness. However, none of the agencies surveyed by the CBO used cost-effectiveness analysis to make decisions about how to allocate resources among programs.

Incremental Budgeting

Given the politics of the budget process and the time constraints in enacting annual budgets, the approach that many governments actually use views budgeting as an "incremental process." Instead of making bold changes each year, the previous year's budget is viewed as embodying previous collective choices and a political equilibrium for levels of spending for existing government programs. The current fiscal year budget becomes the base for making small changes in the next fiscal year budget under this approach. *Incremental budgeting* bases the current budget on the previous year's budget with only minor changes in funding levels for various programs included in the budget. Incremental budgeting is a pragmatic approach that seeks to minimize the resources that go into the budgetary process each year and make it easier for governments to enact budgets. Under this approach, programs are rarely terminated, although poorly performing programs could endure incremental cuts for several years that would ultimately result in elimination of spending for the program. Proponents of incremental budgeting argue that it

---

[1]See Congress of the United States, Congressional Budget Office, "Using Performance Measures in the Federal Budget Process" (July 1993).

minimizes political conflict, reduces the cost of the budget process, and avoids disruptive changes in government spending policy in any given year.[2]

CHECKPOINT

1. What is program budgeting?
2. What information and procedures are required to implement a cost-effectiveness analysis of government programs?
3. How can cost-effectiveness analysis help keep government spending down?

COST-BENEFIT ANALYSIS

Cost-benefit analysis represents a practical technique for determining the relative merits of alternative government projects over time. Use of cost-benefit analysis can contribute to efficiency by making sure that new projects for which marginal social cost exceeds marginal social benefit are not considered for approval. Cost-benefit analysis, if done well, provides essential information to be used by government authorities and citizens in making choices among alternative government projects.

Cost-benefit analysis is not a new tool. It has been used in the United States since 1900 by the Army Corps of Engineers to evaluate the desirability of alternative water resource projects. In commonsense terms, cost-benefit analysis is nothing more than a statement of the pros and cons of a particular activity over a period of time. It is a very systematic way of gathering information.

Since 1981, all new regulations proposed by the federal government must be subjected to a cost-benefit analysis. This practice was instituted by the Reagan administration to control the growth of new social regulations in the 1980s. Cost-benefit analysis is applied to new social regulations dealing with products, job safety, and environmental protection.

Essentially, the three steps involved in a cost-benefit analysis are:

1. Enumerate all costs and benefits of the proposed project.

2. Evaluate all costs and benefits in dollar terms.

3. Discount future net benefits. This allows future benefits and costs to be reduced to their present values so that they can be compared with the dollar amount of budget authority necessary to finance the project.

Although the steps may seem simple, an adequate analysis demands a great deal of ingenuity. It might require the combined talents of economists, engineers, and scientists to correctly enumerate and evaluate costs and benefits. Benefits must include all indirect effects (externalities) generated by the project. Costs must be defined correctly as alternative benefits forgone if the project is adopted

[2]For a discussion of budgeting from various perspectives, see Albert C. Hyde (ed.), *Government Budgeting: Theory, Process, Politics*, 3rd edition, Wadsworth, 2002, and Janet Kelly, "A Century of Public Budgeting Reform," *Administration and Society*, 37, pp. 89–109 (March 2005).

(the opportunity cost). An appropriate discount rate must be chosen to compare present and future returns from alternative projects.

Enumerating Benefits and Costs

The preliminary step is to define both the project under consideration and its output. Once this is done, the analysts can proceed to enumerate the costs incurred and the benefits generated over the life of the project.

Benefits can be divided into two categories: direct and indirect. Direct benefits are those increases in output or productivity attributable to the purpose of the project. For example, in an irrigation project, the purpose is to increase the fertility of a particular tract of land. The direct benefits in this case will be the net increase over time in agricultural output on the tract of land being irrigated. Indirect, or spillover, benefits are those accruing to individuals not directly associated with the purpose of the project. In an irrigation project, spillover benefits might include the improved fertility of adjoining land that is not actually irrigated by the scheme that results from changes in the height of the water table in the area.

In enumerating benefits, only real increases in output and welfare are considered. Care must be exercised not to double-count benefits of a particular project. For example, agricultural land values are likely to increase as a result of an irrigation project. However, such appreciation merely reflects the increased output potential of the land. Counting the increase in land value along with the value of the increase in agricultural output results in double-counting the benefits of the project. Unfortunately, this is not always understood by those undertaking cost-benefit analyses, and double-counting does occur on occasion.[3]

Another problem is the definition of indirect, or spillover, effects of a project. In some cases, analysts include as a benefit the extra profits of third parties not directly affected by a project. For example, retailers will sell more goods in a region where incomes rise as a result of a government project. In a full-employment economy, these extra retail sales and profits merely reflect changes in the distribution of income as a result of the project. That is, they reflect increases in income to owners of resources, attracted from alternative uses rather than from increases in output. The increase in retail sales in the area that benefits from the project is balanced by a *reduction* in retail sales elsewhere, because the taxes to finance the project reduce incomes elsewhere. The practice of counting extra profits of third parties has been common in some cost-benefit analyses of irrigation projects.[4] In these cases, the profits of businesses that process the increased agricultural outputs, as well as the profits of firms that supply goods to farmers, have been included in the enumeration of benefits.

For some projects, enumeration of benefits is difficult. How are the benefits of an education program or a health program defined? Again, the answer must yield a quantifiable result that avoids double-counting. In a particular vocational education program, benefits might include the increased output as reflected in the higher earnings of those who attain new skills as a result of the program. In an accident prevention project, benefits might include the increased output that results from reduced injuries and fatalities.

---

[3]Examples of double-counting are offered by Alan R. Prest and Ralph Turvey, " Cost-Benefit Analysis: A Survey," in *Surveys of Economic Theory*, 3 Vols. (New York: St. Martin's, 1966) 3: 155–207.

[4]*Ibid.*, 181.

In enumerating costs of a project, listing direct resource costs gives only a partial account of real costs when external costs also will occur. Any costs not reflected in the prices of inputs must be included. Suppose, for example, that a new project in a given area will have the effect of reducing water resources available to nearby agricultural land. The corresponding reduction in agricultural output must be included as a cost of the project.

Evaluating Benefits and Costs

After all costs and benefits have been satisfactorily enumerated, the next step is to evaluate these costs and benefits in dollar terms. Valuing output requires an estimate of the demand for increased production and calculation of consumer surplus.[5] When the outputs of particular programs are not sold in markets, the problem of valuation is difficult. Surrogate measures of the willingness of beneficiaries to pay for outputs that are not sold must be obtained. For example, although the benefits of many public health programs are consumed collectively, the value of these benefits might be reflected in increased earnings of those whose health is improved by the project. An estimate of such increased earnings over time can be a good reflection of the value of the benefits for the project. Similarly, the benefits of an education program might be measured by an estimate of the increased earnings accruing over time to former students.

An additional problem occurs with outputs and inputs that are marketable but have prices that do not reflect their true social value. This results when any output attributable to a project is sold in monopolistic markets, when external effects are generated by production of the output, or when distortions due to subsidies or taxes are present. Under such conditions, prices must be adjusted to reflect the actual marginal social cost or benefit. For example, if the prices of increased agricultural outputs of an irrigation project reflect the price supports of U.S. agricultural policy, then the prices must be adjusted downward to reflect the actual marginal social benefit of the output to consumers. If the prices of inputs used are distorted upward from actual marginal social cost by the monopolistic power of sellers, then a downward adjustment must be made in the input prices. The elimination of such price distortions might require some arbitrary estimating decisions by the analysts.

Discounting Future Net Benefits

The next step after enumerating and evaluating costs and benefits is to discount all future net benefits. The choice of an appropriate discount rate is of crucial importance here. The need to discount stems from the existence of positive interest rates in the economy. Positive interest rates imply that a dollar of benefits in the future will be worth less than an equivalent dollar of present benefits, because it takes less than today to produce a dollar of resources tomorrow (say, one year from today), when interest rates are positive.

For example, if the interest rate is 5 percent per year, then only $95.24 needs to be invested today to obtain $100 one year from today. That is to say, $100 received one year from today is worth only $95.24 today. The $95.24 is called the *present value* (*PV*) of $100 to be received in one year. At the end of the year, $95.24 will be equal to $95.24 + (0.05)($95.24) = $100.

---

[5]For an excellent discussion of calculating consumer surplus for cost-benefit analysis, see Edward J. Mishan, *Cost-Benefit Analysis* (New York: Praeger, 1976), Chapter 7.

In general, the present value of X dollars to be received n years from now at simple interest rate r is obtained by solving the equation $X = PV(1 + r)^n$.

$$PV = \frac{X}{(1+r)^n} \tag{6.5}$$

The higher the interest rate used to discount a certain amount of future income X, the lower the present value of X. The interest r, called the **social rate of discount**, is used to compute the present value of X. If a particular project yields benefits over a number of years, the net benefits, X_i, per year must be discounted in each year as follows:

$$PV = \sum_{i=1}^{n} \frac{X}{(1+r)^i}. \tag{6.6}$$

For example, if a project yields X_1 dollars in net benefits after the first year and X_2 dollars after the second year, its present value is

$$PV = \frac{X_1}{(1+r)^1} + \frac{X_2}{(1+r)^2}. \tag{6.7}$$

How the Discount Rate Affects the Present Value of Projects

Why is the choice of an appropriate discount rate important? First, it is no more important than the proper enumeration and evaluation of costs and benefits. An analysis that uses the correct discount rate but seriously miscalculates costs and benefits will produce results as misleading as a study that uses a zero discount rate. All phases of cost-benefit analysis are equally important if such studies are to yield useful information. However, the choice of the discount rate affects the ranking of alternative projects and the number of projects that can be approved. A low discount rate tends to favor projects that yield net benefits further into the future relative to projects that yield current net benefits.

An arithmetical example illustrates this effect. Consider two alternative projects. Project 1 yields $90 in net benefits immediately. Project 2 yields $100 two years after it is undertaken but nothing at present or after one year. The present values of net benefits from these two projects can be calculated with a variety of discount rates and then ranked according to their present values. Consider three alternative discount rates: 0 percent, 5 percent, and 10 percent. The present value of project 1 is always $90 because it yields only present net benefits. The present value of project 2 will vary with the discount rate. Table 6.1 gives the present values of net benefits for project 2 under the alternative discount rates.

TABLE 6.1	Discount Rate and Project Rankings	
DISCOUNT RATE	**PRESENT VALUE OF PROJECT 1**	**PRESENT VALUE OF PROJECT 2**
0%	$90	$\dfrac{\$100}{(1+0)^2} = \$100$
5	$90	$\dfrac{\$100}{(1+0.05)^2} = \$90.7$
10	$90	$\dfrac{\$100}{(1+0.01)^2} = \$82.6$

As shown in Table 6.1, the present value of project 2 is greater than that of project 1 under a discount rate of 0 percent and 5 percent. But if a discount rate of 10 percent is chosen, the result is such that project 1 is ranked above project 2. In general, the higher the discount rate, the less is the weight given to the value of future net benefits.

Furthermore, higher discount rates result in fewer government projects that can be approved. Insofar as the discount rate reflects the return to private consumption and investment, a higher rate implies that the opportunity cost of government expenditure in terms of private satisfaction forgone is greater. This, in turn, implies that efficiency requires a relatively smaller amount of government expenditure as a percentage of gross domestic product (GDP). Some projects that yield a positive value for the present value of net benefits under low discount rates will have negative net present benefits at higher discount rates.

Choosing the Social Rate of Discount

The social rate of discount should reflect the return that can be earned on resources employed in alternative private use.[6] This is the opportunity cost of funds invested by the government in a project. To avoid losses in well-being, resources should not be transferred from the private sector to government use if those resources can earn a higher social return in the private sector.

Setting the discount rate equal to the **social opportunity cost of funds** ensures that misallocations do not occur. The social opportunity cost depends on the rate at which savers and investors are willing to give up either consumption or investment to finance the government project. For example, if the rate of interest in the economy is 10 percent, a government project must yield at least that much to justify the transfer of funds from private to government use.

Because of the existence of distortions (the corporate income tax, for example), the net return that savers can earn often is different from that earned by investors. For example, with a 50 percent tax on corporate profits, the return to investments in the corporate sector of the economy is only one-half of the actual gross percentage rate of return. If investors must pay 10 percent interest to borrow funds, they will require a return in excess of 20 percent to undertake any project. A gross return greater than 20 percent is necessary to earn a positive net return after paying 10 percent interest. The existence of such taxes causes investors and savers to adjust to different interest rates.

This is illustrated in Figure 6.2. The curve D represents the demand for funds for investment in the absence of any taxes. Points on this curve give the gross return to investors for any quantity of funds invested per year. S is the supply curve of investible funds. It gives the rate that would have to be paid to savers to induce them to supply any given amount of funds per year. In the absence of any taxes, the market equilibrium would be at point E. The gross return to investors, r_G, would equal the interest rate paid to savers. Suppose this rate is 16 percent.

Now suppose that investors are subject to a 50 percent tax on the return to investment but that the interest earned by savers is not subject to taxation. The tax causes the *net return* to investors to fall short of the gross return by a factor of 50 percent. In Figure 6.2, this is represented by a downward shift of the

---

[6]For a comprehensive discussion of the discount rate, see Raymond F. Mikesell, *The Rate of Discount for Evaluating Public Projects* (Washington, D.C.: American Enterprise Institute, 1977).

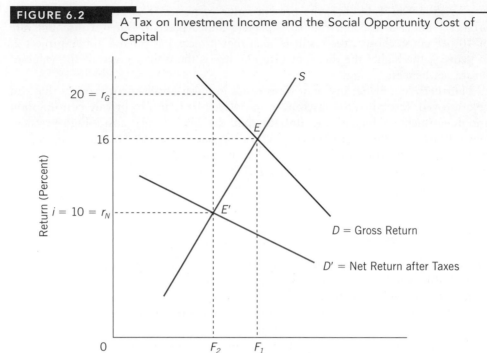

FIGURE 6.2   A Tax on Investment Income and the Social Opportunity Cost of Capital

A tax-on-investment income causes the gross return to investment to exceed the market rate of interest earned by savers, i. The social opportunity cost of government investment is 20 percent if private investment funds are displaced. However, the social opportunity cost of government funds will be only 10 percent if taxes displace private saving.

investment demand curve from D to D'. Investors now make their decisions according to points on D', which give the net return to investment after the 50 percent is paid. The new market equilibrium corresponds to point E'. As the amount of funds invested declines from F_1 dollars to F_2 dollars per year, the gross return rises to $r_G = 20$ percent. However, the net return after payment of the tax is only $r_N = 10$ percent. The net rate of return is also the market rate of interest necessary to induce savers to supply F_2 dollars per year for investors to use. If the funds used to finance the project displace investment, the appropriate discount rate is 20 percent. If, however, they displace consumption, the opportunity cost is only the 10 percent that those funds could have earned had they been saved.

An ideal technique for determining the social rate of discount is to ascertain the kind of private expenditures that are displaced by a government activity and to use an average of the return on displaced expenditures.[7] However, such an estimate of the distribution of expenditure displaced may be difficult to obtain.

From a pragmatic point of view, it is often convenient to estimate the social rate of discount by considering a variety of factors. These factors include the riskiness of

---

[7]For an analysis that yields such an estimate, see Arnold C. Harberger, "On Measuring the Social Opportunity Cost of Public Funds," *Project Evaluation* (Chicago: Markham, 1972): 94–122.

displaced investment and taxes.[8] For example, if risk and other complications are ignored, assume that the market rate of interest would be 10 percent. With a 50 percent tax on business profits, the gross actual return on business investment must be 20 percent before taxes, as shown in Figure 6.2. This results in a *net return* after taxes of 10 percent. The opportunity cost of displaced business investment, therefore, will be 20 percent. Similarly, risk and inflation often result in higher returns on private investment. If higher returns are required on private investment in equilibrium to compensate investors for risk and expected inflation, then these must be added into the opportunity cost of government use of those displaced funds.[9]

Weighting and Disaggregating Net Benefits

Cost-benefit analysis is a tool designed primarily to aid in choosing government projects that are efficient. However, some practitioners attempt to modify its techniques to build in equity as well as efficiency criteria in ranking projects. The effects of a given project on the distribution of income can be built in by weighting the costs or benefits according to whom or where they accrue.[10] This technique would disaggregate both benefits and costs according to income of recipients and also would weight those benefits and costs borne by low-income groups relatively.

A variant of the weighting of benefits according to income of recipients is to weight net benefits according to their regional location. Many argue that a legitimate function of government is to base decisions on which public expenditures to undertake according to the region in which benefits and costs would flow and that the higher weight should be placed on benefits and costs in depressed or declining regions.

Attempts to formalize distributional considerations through weighting of benefits and costs might not be in accord with the distributional goals of all citizens. For this reason, formal weighting of benefits and costs might serve only to confound the distribution and efficiency aspects of projects by confusing net increases in welfare with their distribution. Separate consideration of efficiency and distributive consequences allows the trade-offs between net benefits and their distribution to be more clearly seen.

Another proposal that would allow cost-benefit analysis to take into account distributional considerations is to disaggregate benefits according to demographic, income, and other social characteristics of the citizens who will receive benefits and bear the costs. This avoids the problem of how to weight benefits and provides direct information on the distribution of costs and benefits among citizens. Insofar as this provides information on the distribution of marginal benefits of increased government expenditure and on the manner in which costs are distributed among citizens, it allows both citizens and their political representatives to vote on a more informed basis.

---

[8]For an analysis using the opportunity cost approach, see William J. Baumol, "On the Social Rate of Discount," *American Economic Review* 58 (September 1968): 788–802.

[9]Some controversy exists as to whether a risk premium should be added to the social rate of discount. For a discussion of the desirability of using a riskless versus a risk-adjusted discount rate, see Mikesell, *The Rate of Discount*, 28–32.

[10]See Arnold C. Harberger, "On the Use of Distributional Weights in Social Cost-Benefit Analysis," *Journal of Political Economy* 86 (April 1978): S87–S120. No unique set of weights to apply exists; the weights would reflect either the opinions of those who do the analysis or some consensus on the relative "deservingness" of individuals according to their income. Universal agreement on a set of norms to do this remains difficult and requires interpersonal comparisons of utility.

Treatment of Inflation

Inflation creates a problem in cost-benefit analysis by making the measuring rod of money a poor standard for comparing benefits over time. There are two alternative ways of dealing with the problem of inflation. First, both benefits and costs could be measured through time in nominal values by estimating the rate of inflation over time and inflating both future benefits and costs accordingly. If this is done, the analyst must take care to use the nominal interest rate as well in discounting future net benefits. The **nominal interest rate** is the sum of the real interest rate and the rate of inflation. If inflated values of net benefits are used, they must, in turn, be deflated by the nominal interest rate to account for the inflation.

Similarly, if benefits and costs are measured over time in real terms, meaning that future benefits and costs are deflated, then one also must use the real interest rate (the nominal interest rate less the rate of inflation) to discount future benefits and costs.[11]

Ranking Projects

Projects are usually ranked according to the present value of their discounted net benefits $(B - C)$ or according to the ratio of the present value of benefits to the present value of costs. All projects with positive net benefits are considered for approval. Similarly, all projects with benefit-cost ratios in excess of a value of 1 are considered for approval. These two criteria are shown in Equations 6.8 and 6.9.

$$\text{Net Benefit Criterion: } B - C = \sum_{i=1}^{n} (B_i - C_i)/(1 + r)^i, \tag{6.8}$$

$$\text{Benefit} - \text{Cost Ratio: } \frac{B}{C} = \frac{\sum_{i=1}^{n} B_i/(1 + r)^i}{\sum_{i=1}^{n} C_i/(1 + r)^i} \tag{6.9}$$

where B_i are benefits in year i, C_i are costs in year i, n is the life of a project, and r is the discount rate.

Use of these rules can ensure that inefficient projects will not be considered for approval. In any given year for any agency, a certain level of service has already been provided. It is difficult to determine whether this level of service is the efficient amount. For example, in a given year, a certain amount of interstate highways exists. Proposed projects for new highway construction represent additional units of this transportation service. The new highway construction will improve efficiency only if its marginal social benefit exceeds its marginal social cost. Projects are ranked according to the net social gain they provide.

Figure 6.3 shows the marginal social benefit and marginal social cost of highways, measured in miles available each year. Suppose the amount of highway mileage currently existing is Q_1 miles of four-lane, limited-access roads. A new project is proposed that will increase road mileage to Q_2. The project will add an additional ΔQ_1 miles of road to available highways. Suppose that a cost-benefit analysis of the project finds that the ΔQ_1 miles have a positive net benefit (or a benefit-cost ratio greater than 1). This would imply that the area $Q_1 A B Q_2$, representing the marginal social benefit of the project, would exceed the area $Q_1 C D Q_2$, which represents the marginal social cost of the extra highway miles. Approval of the project moves output closer to the efficient level Q^*, at which $MSB = MSC$.

---

[11]For proof of this, see Edward M. Gramlich, *A Guide to Benefit-Cost Analysis*, 2nd edition. (Englewood Cliffs, N.J.: Prentice-Hall, 1990).

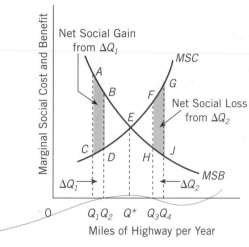

FIGURE 6.3 Cost-Benefit Analysis and Efficiency

If ΔQ_1 miles of new roads are made available, a net gain results. However, the increment ΔQ_2 involves a net loss.

© Cengage Learning

Suppose instead that Q_3 miles of highways already exist. If proposals to increase miles available to Q_4 are made, the increment in roads supplied, ΔQ_2, will be inefficient, because the marginal social cost of ΔQ_2 miles of road, Q_3FGQ_4, exceeds the marginal social benefit of Q_3HJQ_4. This is because at an output of Q_3, more than the efficient amount of roads, Q^*, exists. A correctly executed cost-benefit analysis of the project resulting in ΔQ_2 units of road should reveal a negative net benefit or a benefit-cost ratio less than 1.

CHECKPOINT

1. What are the steps necessary to implement a cost-benefit analysis of a government program?
2. Why must future net benefits be discounted in a cost-benefit analysis?
3. What are some of the difficulties in choosing an appropriate social rate of discount? How does the discount rate affect the net benefits and the ranking of projects?

ANALYSIS OF GOVERNMENT INVESTMENTS: COST-BENEFIT ANALYSIS IN PRACTICE

Governments supply a considerable amount of capital used in production. A nation's **physical infrastructure** is its transportation and environmental capital, including its schools, power and communication networks, and health care system. Much of the capital that constitutes a nation's physical infrastructure is supplied by governments.

In the United States, both the private sector and governments provide infrastructure. Most of the communication and power supply networks are provided for profit by business firms, and the output is sold through the marketplace. Local governments are active in supplying educational and health care facilities, although some of these facilities also are provided by business firms motivated by profit. The federal government is active in providing and helping to fund highways, bridges, mass transit facilities, railways, airports and airways, and water resources, including fresh water supply. Government-provided infrastructure accounts for a significant portion (about one-fifth) of U.S. nonresidential capital stock. Governments also invest in *human* capital through programs designed to improve the skills and education of its citizens.

Government-provided infrastructure complements private capital and improves its productivity. Better roads and bridges reduce travel time and make private cars and trucks more productive. Government-provided airports and air traffic control systems improve both the performance and the safety of private air carriers. Similarly, the Intracoastal Waterway as well as public ports, locks, and dams make shipping more productive. Government facilities for wastewater treatment lower the costs of production for business and help improve the environment.

In the United States, roads and bridges are aging. The nation's physical infrastructure is in need of repair. Federal spending for roads, mass transit, railways, airports and airways, water resources, and water treatment has grown little after adjustment for inflation since 1980. In 1990, the federal government spent $26.2 billion on the nation's infrastructure and more than half of that amount was allocated to highways, particularly the interstate highway system. Real spending on infrastructure grew rapidly between 1956 and 1966, and then stagnated throughout much of the 1970s during a massive reallocation of federal spending to transfer programs including Social Security. Some growth in federal spending for infrastructure occurred in the late 1970s, but on average, spending during the 1980s did not increase at all. In 2008, federal government spending on gross investment amounted to $148.2 billion, which was less than 5 percent of total federal spending.

Investment in infrastructure in the United States amounts to a mere 2 percent of GDP compared to 5 percent in Europe and 9 percent in China. The Bureau of Transportation Statistics estimated that in 2008 about 21 percent of urban interstate highways and 35 percent of other urban roads were in need of repairs and in 2009 nearly 10 percent of the bridges in the United States were structurally deficient. Traffic congestion was also a problem resulting in excessive fuel use and travel delays in many urban areas.

During periods of recession when there is significant unemployment of construction workers and capital, the opportunity cost of using resources for infrastructure is reduced. Recent stimulus programs from 2007 to 2009 have allocated resources toward infrastructure improvement in the United States. For example, nearly $50 billion was allocated toward transportation infrastructure investment in 2009.

Is it economically desirable to spend more than we are currently spending on government investment projects for transportation and water resources? Is the return to additional government investment higher than the return to private investment that will be forgone if more funds are allocated to government investment? Unfortunately, the answers to these questions are not easy, but cost-benefit analysis is useful in providing a framework to help guide economic policy decisions on the mix of investment spending.

Additional investments in infrastructure or government education and research programs result in net benefits to society if the return on these investments exceeds the opportunity cost of the private funds that must be diverted to government use to finance government projects. Cost-benefit analysis is a useful tool to analyze the net benefits and social return provided through government investments that yield a stream of net benefits through time. Cost-benefit analysis can be used to help calculate the net benefits of government investments in infrastructure and human capital and provides information on the social return to government investment relative to the private investment that must be sacrificed when funds are diverted from private to government use.

In practice, cost-benefit analysis is more of an art than a science. Many simplifying assumptions must be made to obtain measures of benefits of both marketable and nonmarketable goods resulting from projects. In addition, when projects involve negative externalities, considerable differences of opinion often exist among experts about how they should be valued. Economists can develop principles to use as guidelines in enumerating and evaluating costs and benefits. In practice, actual enumeration and valuation require a cooperative effort of scientists, engineers, and other experts. Differences of opinion are common. A few examples can illustrate these problems.

Water Resource Development: An Irrigation Project

Irrigation increases the supply of water for agricultural and other purposes. The direct benefits of the project include the increase in water available to farmers. Estimates must be made of the value of the increased annual flow of water from the project over the life of the facility. Ideally, the water should be valued on the basis of the price that farmers would be willing to pay for extra units. However, in the absence of a market for water or water rights, such evaluation is difficult.[12] Instead, with the help of agronomists and other scientists, it is possible to approximate the amount that farmers would be willing to pay by estimating the increase in agricultural yields attributable to the increased water supply. This represents an estimate of the marginal productivity due to the increased water supply. Multiplying this estimate of increased agricultural output over the life of the project by the appropriate price will give an estimate of the value of the marginal product of the increased water supply, which, in turn, can be used as a proxy for the price that farmers would pay for the extra water.

For example, a proposed project for Nebraska by the Bureau of Reclamation would have irrigated 44,000 acres of dry farming lands. In 1967, the Bureau used data based on cropping patterns, input costs, farm yields, and other information to estimate that benefits from the project totaled nearly $2.5 million. This was 43 percent of the total benefit from the land reclamation project for the area. However, the prices that the Bureau used to calculate the agricultural benefit included the effect of agricultural support programs. These programs caused prices to be higher than they would have been otherwise. Therefore, part of the price of the output included a subsidy to farmers that represents a transfer to them from taxpayers rather than a benefit of the project. In addition, some of the inputs used to produce the goods were also subsidized. In particular, farmers in the area were eligible for subsidized loans for their crops. Finally, those doing the cost-benefit analysis underestimated the value of labor of owner-operators relative to the opportunity cost of that labor. Adjusting for these effects, a critical analysis found that the value of

---

[12]For a method of actually evaluating the water, see Harberger, *Project Evaluation*, Chapter 11.

increased agricultural output falls from $2.5 million to only slightly more than $1 million. This illustrates the pitfalls in doing cost-benefit analysis incorrectly, even in cases in which marketable output exists.[13]

Suppose an artificial lake is created as part of the irrigation system. The lake will have the potential for recreational use. If it is feasible to exploit the lake for recreational purposes, the resulting recreational benefits should be included as part of the project. As is always the case, the test for benefits on the national level involves answering the question of whether the proposed benefits represent a net increase in potential well-being not offset by reductions in well-being elsewhere. If new recreational facilities result from the project, they qualify as a real benefit. Such benefits might include fishing, picnicking, boating, swimming, and so forth. If the lake is available for use free of charge, the evaluation of benefits becomes difficult. Usually, rough estimates are made concerning potential use of the recreational resource and the willingness of users to pay for a day of recreation, on average, at the new facility.[14]

The cost of the project would include all labor costs necessary to construct and maintain the irrigation facility and the lake; all capital that would need to be acquired, such as pipes, or rented, such as backhoes and derricks, in the process of construction and maintenance; and all land acquisition costs, right-of-way costs, and rental payments that would be required for construction of the facilities. These are the direct costs of the project.

One issue of dispute concerns the proper valuation of labor costs when the economy suffers from unemployment. Some economists argue that in periods of unemployment, the social costs of using labor should be set at zero because the project provides work that would not otherwise be available. This argument is faulty for two reasons. First, unless deficit finance is used, with no effect on the price level, the revenues necessary to finance the project withdraw effective demand from the private sector, thereby further decreasing the ability of the economy to provide jobs. Increased employment on the irrigation project therefore is offset by at least some decrease in employment opportunities elsewhere in the economy. Second, the labor skills required to construct the irrigation facilities might not be those possessed by workers currently unemployed. This being the case, the irrigation workers would have to be attracted from other employment, with no net increase in employment to workers currently out of work. For both these reasons, it is good practice to value labor resources positively, even in periods of unemployment, when computing project costs.

Indirect costs include lost agricultural output on land that has to be flooded as a result of the project, provided that these costs were not already included in the price paid by the government to acquire that land. Similarly, if the project diverts water, it can reduce the water table in locations not served by the irrigation system, with the consequent effect of a reduction in agricultural output not otherwise reflected in land acquisition costs. If wilderness areas are harmed as a result of the project, with a consequent loss in the recreational services provided by the wilderness (hunting and fishing, for example), estimates must be made of these costs and included as a cost of the project.

[13]See Steve H. Hanke and Richard A. Walker, "Benefit-Cost Analysis Reconsidered: An Evaluation of the Mid-state Project," in *Public Expenditure and Policy Analysis*, 3rd edition, Robert H. Haveman and Julius Margolis, eds. (Boston: Houghton Mifflin, 1983).

[14]On valuing recreation, see Marion Clawson and Jack Knetsch, *Economics of Outdoor Recreation* (Baltimore: Resources for the Future, 1966).

Cost-Benefit Tableau

When all costs and benefits have been enumerated and evaluated, a tableau that lists all such costs and benefits over the life of the project can be drawn up. Assume that in this case the expected life of the irrigation system is 50 years. In a capital-intensive project, such as the construction of an irrigation system, costs in early years are likely to be high relative to benefits (for example, no benefits at all until the system is completed, which might take a considerable number of years). In later years, benefits might be high relative to costs as construction costs fall to zero and only maintenance costs are required.

The tableau for the irrigation project is shown in Table 6.2. The costs and benefits for this hypothetical example are shown symbolically rather than as actual dollar amounts. Costs are likely to be very high in the first five years of the project as construction is carried out. These costs then are likely to decline rapidly in the sixth year, when construction will have been completed, so that only maintenance costs and indirect losses (agricultural output having declined on lands suffering from the effects of declines in the water table and reduced benefits from wilderness destroyed) will be incurred. In Table 6.2, construction costs, F, falls to zero in the

TABLE 6.2   Cost-Benefit Analysis of a Hypothetical Irrigation Project

| | YEAR | | | | | | | |
COSTS[a]	1	2	3	4	5	6	...	N
Engineering and Planning Studies	E	—	—	—	—	—		—
Building and Construction								
Labor								
Pipes								
Heavy Equipment	F_1	F_2	F_3	F_4	F_5	—		—
Land Acquisition								
Easements (Right-of-Way)								
Maintenance	—	—	—	—	—	M_6		M_N
Loss in Agricultural Output on Other Lands	A_1	A_2	A_3	A_4	A_5	A_6		A_N
Loss in Recreation Due to Destruction of								
Wilderness	R_1	R_2	R_3	R_4	R_5	R_6		R_N
Total Costs	C_1	C_2	C_3	C_4	C_5	C_6		C_N
BENEFITS[a]	**1**	**2**	**3**	**4**	**5**	**6**	**...**	**N**
Increased Agricultural Output	—	—	—	—	—	A_6		A_N
Increased Recreation	—	—	—	—	—	R_6		R_N
Total Benefits	—	—	—	—	—	B_6		B_N

[a]A dash indicates either zero benefit or zero cost in that year.

© Cengage Learning

sixth year. On the other hand, no direct benefits occur until the project is completed. Thus, in the first five years, the total benefits in the tableau are zero, as indicated by a dash. Only in the sixth year will benefits accrue. To account for inflation, all projections would have to be done in constant dollars.

Finally, because the decision to approve the project must be made today, the stream of benefits and the stream of costs over the life of the project must be collapsed down to their present values by discounting with an appropriate discount rate, as discussed previously. Typically, cost-benefit analysis done by the federal government computes a benefit-cost ratio, B/C, and considers those projects for which B/C exceeds 1. Projects then are ranked according to the magnitude of their benefit-cost ratios.

The tableau does not include any secondary benefits, such as increased purchases of farm equipment and consumer goods by farmers whose incomes are increased as a result of the project. As discussed, these are transfers rather than real benefits produced by the irrigation project. Nothing in the project increases the capability of the economy to produce tractors or consumer goods. Hence, any increased purchases of these items by farmers merely represent a transfer of resources from elsewhere to the area of the project.

Transportation: Widening an Existing Highway

To evaluate the benefits of adding two more lanes to a highway, an estimate must be made of the demand for travel between the points involved as a function of the average cost per trip. The average cost per trip includes fuel, depreciation, vehicle maintenance, and, most important, the value of time involved. Improvement of the facility makes trips between two points faster. This will result in cost savings to existing users and will encourage new users to take trips on the road. The major benefit of the improved facility will be the cost saving on existing trips plus the net benefits on new trips along the improved route.

Assuming enough information is available, these benefits can be estimated from the demand for travel between the points involved. This is illustrated in Figure 6.4. D_T is the demand for travel. The current average cost of travel per trip for points served by the existing road is C, and the current number of trips per year is measured as T. Widening the facility is estimated to lower the average cost of a trip to C' and increase the number of trips per year to T'. The annual cost saving on existing trips is CC' multiplied by T, or the area $CBAC'$. The net increase in trips is TT'. The cost of making these new trips is, on average, C'. The net benefits on new trips are additional consumer surplus over and above the cost of making the new trips.[15] This is the area ABD. The net benefits from widening the road are the sum of the two areas $CBAC'$ and ABD.

Cost of the project would include all labor, capital, and land costs to construct the new facility, as well as maintenance costs over the life of the facility after construction is completed. Additional costs would include damage and injuries, including possible fatalities caused by hazards during the construction period. Losses from slowdowns in traffic and congestion during construction are also part of the costs of the project. Any external costs, such as destruction of wilderness or increased pollution due to the increased traffic generated on the road (less any pollution reduction elsewhere if some of the new traffic previously used alternative routes), would have to be included as a real cost of the project.

[15]For a discussion of valuation of travel time, see Gramlich, *Benefit-Cost Analysis*, 72–74.

FIGURE 6.4 The Benefits of Widening a Highway

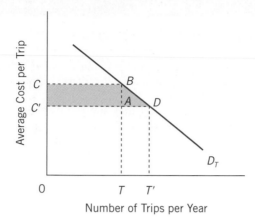

The total benefit is the reduction in the cost of *T* trips per year to existing users plus the benefits of additional trips by new users. This is the sum of the areas *CBAC'* and *ABD*.

© Cengage Learning

After all such costs are estimated over time, a tableau similar to that done for the irrigation project would be constructed, giving the flow of both costs and benefits over the life of the project. Both benefits and costs could then be discounted, and the present value of net benefits, or a benefit-cost ratio, could be calculated to evaluate the project.[16]

Health: How Is Human Life Valued?

Among the most difficult projects to evaluate with cost-benefit analysis are those involving human resources. The problem is particularly difficult for health programs of various kinds that involve benefits in the form of a decrease in mortality rates and reduced loss of human welfare due to injury or illness. Many programs seek to prolong life by avoiding accidental death. For example, suppose a proposed project seeks to reduce accidents by redesigning dangerous superhighway access points. The benefit-cost ratio for this project should be compared with other projects that are more traditionally thought of as health programs; that is, those with major goals of reducing mortality, injury, or disabling illness. These would include inoculation programs, research, and various preventive medicine programs.

The primary benefit of redesigning a highway access will be a reduction in accidents. Fairly good data might exist on the current accident rate for various fatalities, and estimation of the decrease in accidents could be fairly easy. In all cases, such estimates would have to adjust for the possibility that improved access might increase traffic on the road, which, in turn, will offset some of the benefits by contributing to increased accidents, unless a corresponding decrease occurs in accidents on alternative routes.

The basic problem encountered in such a cost-benefit analysis, after the accident reduction is estimated, is to place a value on the lives saved and the reduction in injuries. A number of techniques have been used to estimate the value of human

---

[16]For a more complete and detailed analysis, see Harberger, *Project Evaluation*, Chapter 10.

P U B L I C   P O L I C Y   P E R S P E C T I V E

Cost-Benefit Analysis of the Job Corps Program

Cost-benefit analysis is valuable to evaluate the success or failure of programs that have been in operation for a while. Data for existing programs are usually easier to obtain and more accurate than data for programs under proposal. One such study was done for a controversial federal program designed to increase the future earnings of disadvantaged teenagers: the Job Corps.

The Job Corps provides education and training in a residential setting to disadvantaged teenagers and young adults between the ages of 16 and 24. The goal of the program is to provide participants with skills that increase their potential to earn income while improving their education and literacy to make them more productive and law-abiding citizens. While enrolled in the program participants receive food, clothing, and modest pay from the government. Each year about 60,000 new participants enter the program and receive such services as basic education, vocational skills training, health care, and counseling. There are 120 centers throughout the United States and the annual budget for the program was in the range of $1.5 billion in 2006. Current annual cost per participant is therefore $25,000, making the Job Corps a very expensive program on a per participant basis. Is the program worth its costs? To find out, the U.S. Department of Labor commissioned a cost-benefit analysis of the program by Mathematica Policy Research, Inc.

Let's look at the benefits and costs of the program. Because the costs for the sample of participants were incurred in 1995, all benefits are also valued in 1995 dollars. Earnings after 1995 are discounted and the effect of inflation is removed. The initial study tracked the earnings of the two groups for a four-year period after 1995 and assumed that any positive differential in the earnings of participants over non-participants would continue over their entire working lives. The most recent study tracked earnings for a seven-year period after 1995.

The benefits of the Job Corp program include:

1. Increased output from increased productivity of Job Corps participants after they enter the labor market, measured by the impact of the program on their compensation in the labor market (including fringe benefits from work) less the costs of child care associated with working.

2. Reduced outlays for other programs that would otherwise provide the participants with assistance, such as other education and training programs, welfare programs, and health care programs.

3. Reduced costs of crime committed by participants and against the participants.

The costs of the Job Corp program include:

1. Outlays for operating costs of the Job Corp Program. However, the student pay, as well as food and clothing received by participants, is treated as a transfer and not included in these costs (this is a cost to taxpayers but it is offset by a direct benefit in the year of the outlay to Job Corp enrollees).

life saved. A common method is to value lives saved according to the discounted present value of future earnings. This requires estimates of the number of lives that would be saved and the ages of individuals whose lives are likely to be saved (for two individuals of equal earning capacity, an older life will be worth less than a young life). One problem with such an approach is that it places a zero value on the leisure time of the potential lives saved and a higher value on lives of persons with high earnings relative to those with low earnings.

An alternative approach to valuing life argues that it is not really necessary to value or identify the lives saved to get meaningful data on the benefits of various health-related programs. This approach argues that public programs that save lives really produce a public good, which, in turn, reduces the probability that any given

2. Donated goods and services for the program.

3. Economic costs of capital (real estate, furniture, and equipment) used by the program.

The Mathematica National Job Corps Study is based on a national random sample of eligible applicants for the Job Corp in 1994 and 1995. With both a program group in the sample that actually enrolled in the Job Corps and a control group that did not the study was able to use statistical methods to compare the earning gains and other gains of program participants over and above the earnings of non-participants. The study was conducted over a number of years and initial results published in 2001 indicated that the benefits of the Job Corp program exceeded its costs per participant by nearly $17,000. However, a revised study released in 2003, based on improved methodology and a longer term perspective, reached the opposite conclusion: On average, the benefits of the Job Corps program per participant fall short of the costs.

The increments in earnings of participants in the program, on average, do not persist after a four-year period. Because increased labor compensation is a major benefit of the program, the new research concludes that the decay of the earnings differential attributable to the program after four years results in benefits falling short of costs. The net benefit per participant is estimated at −$10,150.

The following table shows the estimated benefits and costs per participant in the Job Corp program.

However, by disaggregating the data, the researchers were able to reach some other interesting conclusions. Although the impact of the program on earnings for the entire sample after the fourth year were close to zero, the impact on participants between the ages of 20 and 24 remained positive. This age group accounts for about one-quarter of all Job Corps participants.

Benefits and Costs of the Job Corps (1995 Dollars per Participant over Working Lifetime)[a]

BENEFIT	VALUE
Increased output	269
Reduced use of other Programs	2,186
Reduced crime	1,240
Total benefit	3,695
COSTS	
Operating costs net of transfers	12,285
Misc. other costs	543
Capital costs	1,016
Total costs	13,844
NET BENEFIT	**−10,150**

[a]Based on Sochet, Peter Z., McConnell, Sheena, and Burghardt, John. "National Job Corps Study: Findings Using Administrative Earnings Records Data," Final Report, October 2003. Submitted to the U.S. Department of Labor by Mathematica Policy Research, Inc. Numbers might not add due to rounding.

This suggests that the program could result in benefits that exceed costs if it concentrates its efforts on an older group of participants. The program still remains a good deal for participants because the transfers they enjoy while participating typically offset the earnings they forego by enrolling in the program.

individual will die or suffer harm as a result of a particular hazard—in this case, accidents upon entering a highway. The benefits of such programs should be measured in terms of the willingness of individuals affected by the programs to pay for such reduction in hazards or risks to which they are exposed. Such information, however, might be difficult to obtain because of the familiar free-rider problems associated with public goods. Some attempts have been made to get estimates of the willingness of individuals to pay for reduction in the risk of death and injury by sending questionnaires to a random sampling of the population.

The questionnaires specify the odds of a person being exposed to the hazard in question (an accident upon entering a highway) and surviving the accident. The person then is presented with an estimate of the impact of the proposed project on those odds and asked how much he or she would be willing to pay in taxes for improvements in the odds. The average dollar response then is calculated and used as a crude index of the willingness to pay, or, in other words, the benefits per taxpayer of the project in terms of saved lives.[17]

Whichever method is used, the outcome will be a dollar value of benefits for the project in terms of reduced mortality and disability, which will be estimated over time, adjusting for any changes in traffic flow as a result of the project.[18] The costs will be any capital, labor, and right-of-way acquired to improve the facility and any subsequent maintenance. As before, a tableau can be constructed, and both benefits and costs can be discounted to calculate a benefit-cost ratio.

Cost-Benefit Analysis of Government Regulations

Cost-benefit analysis has been used for many years to analyze the impact of new government regulations on economic well-being. Regulations impose costs on businesses or individuals but also provide such benefits as environmental protection, improved health, and better safety that reduce the probability of injury or death from accidents.

In 2007, a new regulation by the U.S. Department of Transportation required all new passenger vehicles weighing less than 10,000 pounds to be equipped with electronic stability control (ESC) beginning in 2012.[19] The ESC system improves safety on roads by electronically controlling breaking systems during emergency situations to reduce the risk of loss of control of the vehicle by a driver and therefore reduce the probability of accidents.

Prior to the new regulation, many consumers purchasing new vehicles chose not to equip them with ESC when it was offered as an option. It can be argued that there are external benefits involved with ESC systems because when given a choice to equip a car with the device, buyers consider only their personal benefits and neglect the possible benefits to other drivers from crash avoidance. To decide whether mandating that all new passenger vehicles be equipped with ESC would result in net benefits, the Department of Transportation conducted a cost-benefit analysis of the regulation.

In doing the analysis it was first estimated that by 2011 approximately 70 percent of vehicles that would be subject to the regulation would already have ESC as standard equipment and therefore would not be affected by the new regulation. The analysis therefore looked at the benefits and costs of raising the number of vehicles equipped with the device from about 70 percent to 100 percent beginning in 2012. To analyze the benefits of the new regulation the first step would be to forecast the number of crashes that could be avoided as a result of the increase in the number of vehicles equipped with ESC. Once this was done, estimates had to be made of the reduction in death, injury, property damage, and traffic jams that would be avoided as a result of the new regulation. A dollar value would then be placed on these benefits. Based on traffic accident data it was estimated that about 1,500 lives per year

---

[17]For a thought-provoking discussion of this topic, see Steven E. Rhoads, "How Much Should We Spend to Save a Life," *The Public Interest* 51 (Spring, 1978): 74–92.

[18]An additional method is the use of wage differentials in risky occupations as an indicator of the amount of payment necessary to induce individuals to bear the risk of loss of life. However, a number of difficulties are involved in using such data to calculate willingness to pay. See Gramlich, *A Guide to Benefit-Cost Analysis*, 67–71.

[19]See *Economic Report of the President*, 2012, Washington, D.C.: U.S. Government Printing Office (February 2012), Chapter 8, pp. 236–237.

TABLE 6.3	Annual Benefits at Costs of the ESC Mandate (Billions of 2005 Dollars)	
	AT 3% DISCOUNT RATE	**AT 7% DISCOUNT RATE**
BENEFITS		
Reduction in Deaths and Injuries	7.965	6.360
Reduction in Damage and Delays	0.309	0.247
Total Benefits	8.274	6.607
COSTS		
Increase in Vehicle Cost	0.985	0.985
Increase in Fuel Use	0.027	0.022
Total Costs	1.012	1.007
NET BENEFITS	*7.262*	*5.600*

© Cengage Learning

would be saved as a result of the new regulation while about 47,000 injuries would be avoided. Future benefits were then projected using constant 2005 dollars and discounted accordingly. The benefits from reduced property damage and traffic delays were also estimated. Costs included the increased cost of production per vehicle as a result of the mandate and because the device added weight to the vehicles, the reduction in gas mileage and the cost of increased fuel to operate the vehicles was also estimated over the life of the vehicles. In the study, both a 3 percent and a 7 percent discount rate was used to see how the results would be sensitive to changing financial conditions in credit markets. Vehicle costs were not discounted because they occur in the year of purchase. Future benefits and increased fuel over the life of the vehicles were discounted.

The cost-benefit analysis resulted in positive estimated net benefits each year using either the 3 percent discount rate or a 7 percent discount rate with the net benefit lower, of course, at the higher rate of discount. Table 6.3 shows the benefits and costs estimated by the National Highway Safety Administration in 2007. Net benefits were $7.262 billion per year at a 3 percent discount rate and $5.6 billion per year at a 7 percent discount rate. Given the historically low interest rates prevailing in 2012, the larger number is a more accurate estimate of the impact of the regulation over time. It was concluded that the new mandate to require all passenger vehicles to have ESC would improve efficiency of resource use and the mandate was put into effect.

Sports Stadiums: Cost-Benefit Analysis of State and Local Government Subsidies

Cost-benefit analysis is often used by state and local governments to justify subsidies to such projects as sports stadiums and civic centers. When we analyze projects from the perspective of a particular state or local region, benefits must be examined in terms of the way they affect individuals and taxpayers living in that area. For example, suppose there are 20 teams in a professional football league. Many citizens in your city would like to have one of the teams in the league relocate to the local area. Many are willing to help the team by paying increased city or state taxes to subsidize the building of a new stadium. If the team is successfully wooed to your city, it will relocate its business headquarters to the new stadium. The city that the team previously regarded as home will now lose the team and its stadium will be worthless unless a new team can be found to adopt it as its new home.

From a national perspective, the benefits of building the new stadium will be nil. If your city attracts the team, its gain will be another city's loss. However, from the local view there is a gain. New sports services are now available that were not present before, and local fans now have the pleasure of a home team to root for and games to attend locally. Although it is legitimate to view this as a local benefit, it is amazing how cost-benefit analysis is used on this level to overestimate the benefits and even count costs of the project as benefits to the locality!

The federal government indirectly subsidizes the construction of sports facilities by allowing state and local governments to issue tax-exempt bonds to finance capital costs of the facility. Tax exemption means that the federal government does not tax the interest earned by holders of the bonds and this, in turn, allows money to be borrowed at lower interest rates than would otherwise be the case. The loss in tax revenues amounts to millions of dollars per year. Such facilities as the Superdome in New Orleans and Giants Stadium in New Jersey were financed this way, and the annual tax loss for each of these stadiums amounted to $1 million per year. Local residents provide even more subsidies by directly financing some of the costs of new stadiums. These subsidies average in excess of $10 million per year per stadium. Oriole Park, for example, costs Maryland residents $14 million per year in tax revenue allocated to the stadium.[20] In many cases, however, government bonds issued to finance the stadium are paid off, in part, from revenues by sale of tickets, luxury seating sales, and other revenues from the stadium's use. However, competition for professional sports teams has led many cities to allocate substantial tax revenues to either attract new teams or keep the teams they have from leaving.

The local political debate that precedes approval of public funds for stadiums usually concentrates on jobs. Often it is argued that construction jobs (a cost of the project) are really a benefit for the community. This reasoning could have some validity on the local level if it actually permanently attracts construction firms to locate and employ workers who would not have otherwise been in the area. However, more likely than not, the workers are merely diverted from other jobs in the area or are temporarily brought in while construction is underway. This is clearly a misuse of cost-benefit analysis because it erroneously translates a cost into benefit!

Local supporters of public subsidies to stadiums also argue that fans attending games will spend more in the local area and that tourists who would otherwise not spend their dollars in the local area will be attracted and generate jobs as they spend on hotels, meals, and souvenirs. These so-called benefits are then multiplied several times over as the spending is re-spent by those who are paid to provide services to tourists. This is clearly a secondary benefit of the project that

---

[20]For detailed analysis, see Roger G. Noll and Andrew Zimbalist, *Sports, Jobs, and Taxes* (Washington, D.C.: The Brookings Institution, 1997).

should not be included even in its nonmultiplied initial stage because the project does not provide new resources to the area to produce more tourist services. By inflating the benefits, supporters of the stadium say that the combined benefits of the community will more than offset the costs. They often argue that the local benefits will be so huge that enough state and local tax revenue will be generated from additional spending so that taxpayers will not have to pay any extra taxes for subsidizing the stadium!

Unfortunately, the logic used by supporters of sports stadiums is seriously flawed, and they usually substantially overestimate benefits while underestimating costs. According to Roger Noll and Andrew Zimbalist,[21] sports facilities in reality have very little, and in some cases a negative, impact on local production and employment. The facilities do not generate enough revenue on their own to pay a return that would allow a private developer to profit, which explains why they require subsidies. The facilities scarcely generate enough tax revenue to pay for the heavy subsidies by local taxpayers.

Sports facilities generate spending primarily by local residents. Only a small percentage of fans attending a game are typically from other cities. Insofar as the stadium or new team's presence in the city does not generate spending or production from elsewhere, it will not increase output. Unfortunately for many citizens, the athletes themselves often reside elsewhere and so their salaries do not always add to local spending despite the high salaries they earn. Even when they reside locally, they tend to have a high savings rate because they know they can work only a limited number of years in professional sports.

Spectator sports are, in reality, a form of entertainment, so when a stadium opens, the spending it generates is usually a substitute for other forms of entertainment. Spending on other forms of entertainment and dining in other locations decline. As tax revenues generated from ticket sales, spending on food and souvenirs, and other spending in the stadium increase, spending elsewhere falls. The main beneficiaries of the subsidies end up being the sports team owners who enjoy revenues generated by the new stadium. Some of those revenues also accrue to the league with which the sports team is associated.

One intangible benefit to the local community that is real but difficult to value is the public benefit to fans of having their own local team. These fans are voters and their support for the public subsidy of the stadium and willingness to pay higher taxes to induce a team to locate in their area often is enough to provide the political support for a program whose benefits otherwise fall short of costs.

CHECKPOINT

1. What are some of the difficulties involved in actually implementing a cost-benefit analysis?
2. How would you estimate the benefits and costs of an irrigation project?
3. How would you estimate the benefits and costs of a project to widen the beltway that surrounds a city?

---

[21]*Ibid.*

The Role of Cost-Benefit Analysis in Budgeting

Cost-benefit analysis is a valuable tool for evaluating the net benefits of proposed government projects. It can be used to organize information in a way that aids citizens, politicians, and bureaucrats. However, it remains difficult to measure the benefit of government goods and services accurately. Difficulties also arise in accurately measuring social costs. Differences of opinion exist regarding what benefits and costs to include and how to value the output of various projects.

It is also difficult to reduce the problem of selecting government goods and services to a few simple, objective criteria. Political interaction is influenced by many factors. As has been pointed out many times in this text, not all citizens benefit when efficient outcomes are chosen. Some are often better off when the less efficient mix of government goods and services is produced. Very few politicians or citizens will abandon their favorite proposed government projects because those projects have benefit-cost ratios that are lower than competing projects.

SUMMARY

Program budgeting and cost-benefit analysis can be used to improve efficiency by lowering the cost of government activities and ensuring that only programs for which marginal social benefits exceed marginal social costs are considered for approval. Cost effectiveness is achieved when governments achieve their missions by choosing a combination of programs with the minimum cost. Cost-benefit analysis is a technique for determining net increases in well-being that result from alternative government projects. Cost-benefit analysis is particularly useful in evaluating government investment projects that will yield a stream of benefits through time. A cost-benefit analysis lists and evaluates all benefits and costs of a project and discounts all future net benefits. The discount rate should reflect the opportunity costs of funds used to finance the project. Projects are ranked according to the discounted present values of net benefits or the ratio of discounted benefits to costs.

LOOKING AHEAD

Modern governments allocate a considerable amount of the funds they raise to the transfer of income among citizens. Chapters 7 and 8 evaluate two major types of transfer programs: transfers to the poor and transfers to the elderly. Chapter 7 looks at the problem of poverty in the United States and how government-subsidized programs designed to alleviate poverty affect resource use.

KEY CONCEPTS

Cost-Benefit Analysis

Cost-Effectiveness Analysis

Mission (of a government agency)

Nominal Interest Rate

Physical Infrastructure

Program

Program Budgeting

Social Opportunity Cost of Funds

Social Rate of Discount

REVIEW QUESTIONS

1. What are the steps necessary to implement a program budgeting system? How does program budgeting differ from line budgeting?

2. What information is required to find out whether a given combination of programs designed to achieve the same objective is cost effective?

3. Explain how program budgeting systems seek to improve efficiency within government. How are decisions made under program budgeting similar to those made by profit-maximizing business firms?

4. Explain how the cost-effective mix of government programs to provide national security can be determined. How does approval of programs that are not cost effective prevent the attainment of efficiency?

5. Why would counting retail sales that result from increased farmer income resulting from an irrigation project overstate the benefits of the project? When should increases in land values that result from government projects be included as a benefit of the project?

6. Suppose investment income is taxed at a higher rate than the interest that consumers earn on their savings. Explain why the social opportunity cost of funds used for government projects will depend on whether investment or consumption will be displaced as a result of the project.

7. How does the social rate of discount used affect the number of projects that can be approved and their ranking in cost-benefit analysis?

8. Suppose more than the efficient number of hydroelectric power projects have already been approved. Show why a properly executed cost-benefit analysis would result in a benefit-cost ratio that is less than 1.

9. Suppose a new project to expand air traffic control facilities will allow reductions in the cost of air travel and increases in the volume of travel. How would you measure the benefits of the new facilities?

10. What are some of the problems involved in measuring the value of human life? Explain why saying that each life is priceless is likely to result in more than the efficient amount of investment in life-saving programs.

PROBLEMS

1. Two alternative programs to save 50 more lives per year entail providing more cardiac intensive care facilities and redesigning dangerous highway interchanges. The price of a new cardiac intensive care unit is $500,000, and the price of redesigning and renovating a highway interchange is $1 million. One combination of the two programs that can save 500 lives is five cardiac units and three highway exit renovations. If five cardiac units are built, the marginal product of this program will be 10 lives saved per year. If three highway interchanges are redesigned, the marginal product of this program also will be 10 lives saved per year. Is the mix involving five cardiac units and three highway exit renovations cost effective? Assuming that the marginal products of both programs decline, what needs to be done to achieve the cost-effective mix of programs?

2. Suppose a proposed new road to be constructed in North Carolina between Raleigh and Morehead City will lower the average cost per trip by car from $5 to $4. Currently, 500,000 trips are made between the two cities per year. An estimate indicates that, all other things being equal, the new road will increase the number of trips per year to 600,000. Calculate the annual benefits to motorists of the new road as based on their willingness to pay.

3. A new tax is levied on airline profits to finance improvements in the nation's airports. The current market rate of interest is 8 percent. However, airline profits are subject to a 50 percent tax. A cost-benefit analysis calculates the percent return to the investment in new air facilities to be 12 percent. Will net benefits from resource use increase as a result of construction of new air travel facilities?

4. A cost-benefit analysis of a new irrigation project indicates that the net benefits $(B - C)$ of the project in each of the first four years will be $2 million. Thereafter, the project will yield positive net benefits of $750,000 for the next 20 years. Calculate the present value of benefits minus costs when the social rate of discount is 10 percent. You can use spreadsheet software to do this calculation. Does the program merit approval? How would the present value of the net benefits change if the social rate of discount were 15 percent?

5. A workshop designed to retrain workers 55 years of age and older who have lost their jobs is proposed. Suppose the workshop will increase the income of each participant by $1,000 per year for a period of 10 years.
   a. Calculate the present value of the increased income per participant with each of the following discount rates: 0 percent, 1 percent, 3 percent, 5 percent, and 10 percent.
   b. If the cost per participant is $8,000 and all those costs are incurred in the first year, at what discount rates will the benefit-cost ratio of the project exceed 1?

ADDITIONAL READINGS

Adler, Matthew D., and Eric A. Posner, eds. *Cost-Benefit Analysis: Legal, Economic, and Philosophical Perspectives*. Chicago: University of Chicago Press, 2001. A collection of essays providing critical discussion of cost-benefit analysis, its application, and its limitations.

Anderson, Lee G., and Russell F. Settle. *Benefit-Cost Analysis: A Practical Guide*. Lexington, Ky.: D. C. Heath, 1977. A practical "how-to-do-it" approach to cost-benefit analysis.

Boardman, Anthony E., David H. Greenberg, Aidan R. Vining, and David L. Weimer, eds. *Cost-Benefit Analysis: Concept and Practice*, 2nd edition. Englewood Cliffs, N.J.: Prentice Hall, 2000. A text developing the theory of cost-benefit analysis along with exposition of techniques for applying it in practice.

Gramlich, Edward M. *A Guide to Benefit-Cost Analysis*, 2nd edition. Englewood Cliffs, N.J.: Prentice-Hall, 1990. A comprehensive treatment and guide to all aspects of cost-benefit analysis.

Lynch, Thomas D. *Public Budgeting in America*, 4th edition. Englewood Cliffs, N.J.: Prentice-Hall, 1994. A descriptive account of budgeting procedures for both the federal and nonfederal governments in the United States.

Mishan, Edward J. *Cost-Benefit Analysis*. New York: Praeger, 1976. A complete discussion of theoretical and practical aspects of cost-benefit analysis. Contains many examples.

U.S. Congress, Congressional Budget Office. *How Federal Spending for Infrastructures and Other Public Investments Affects the Economy*. Washington, D.C.: U.S. Government Printing Office, July 1991. An analysis of federal investment spending in the United States.

Zerbe, Richard O. Jr., and Allen S. Belas, *A Primer for Benefit-Cost Analysis*. Northampton, Mass.: Edward Elgar Publishing, 2006. A discussion of the underlying economic theory and foundations of cost-benefit analysis, along with practical methods for applying the tool to evaluate government projects and policies.

INTERNET RESOURCES

http://www.cbo.gov
The home page of the Congressional Budget Office (CBO) can be used to access CBO studies on specific government programs and on the budgeting process.

http://www.cbpp.org
This is the home page of the Center on Budget and Policy Priorities. The Center analyzes major federal budget and tax proposals from the standpoint of fiscal responsibility, examining their effects on the economy and the federal budget, especially over the long term. There is material on the budget process at the site along with studies that explore the potential impact of budgetary proposals on households in different income groups.

Chapter 7

GOVERNMENT SUBSIDIES AND INCOME SUPPORT FOR THE POOR

LEARNING OBJECTIVES

After reading this chapter, you should be able to:

- Discuss the extent of poverty in the United States.

- Understand the basis for government assistance to the poor and the major government programs that benefit the poor in the United States.

- Explain the difference between cash assistance, price-distorting subsidies, and in-kind allotments of benefits, and

discuss their effects on incentives and resource allocation.

- Analyze the impact of transfer payments to the poor on work incentives.

- Examine the negative income tax, wage rate subsidies, and the Earned Income Tax Credit as alternative programs to aid the poor.

In 2011, 46.2 million people in the United States were classified as poor—a number corresponding to 15 percent of the population. Despite the vast wealth of the United States, poverty remains a serious social problem, the signs of which are visible to us daily in large cities and rural areas. Many live in dilapidated substandard housing. Many of the poor lack access to adequate health care and education.

Poverty breeds crime and social unrest. Many citizens believe that it is their moral responsibility to help the poor through charitable contributions. Philanthropic organizations and religious institutions have traditionally acted as intermediaries to channel such contributions to the poor. However, charitable contributions are unreliable and are unstable as a means of providing income support for the poor. Many citizens do not contribute in the belief that others will take up the slack. During recessions, when the ranks of the poor swell, charitable contributions typically decline because the incomes of the nonpoor decline.

Support for the poor has evolved into a government function in the United States and most other industrialized nations. In 2011, 15 percent of federal government expenditures in the United States were allocated to programs that support the poor. The *Personal Responsibility and Work Opportunity Act of 1996* enacted by Congress has fundamentally overhauled the nation's system of welfare support to the poor. The concept of income support for the poor as an "entitlement" program was scrapped. In its place, the law created two types of grants to state governments and directed state governments to develop systems of welfare support that allow families with children to provide the means to care for themselves while they make efforts to find work and avoid births outside of marriage. The law strictly limits eligibility for welfare payments to five years for most families and withholds benefits from most noncitizens. Additional grants to states provide funds to subsidize child care for families on welfare and other families to assist them in working.

The U.S system of support for the poor is designed to encourage work and to eliminate the so-called welfare trap that made the prospect of remaining on welfare more desirable than finding work for many of the nation's poor. Under the old law, a family receiving cash assistance from the government often found that its disposable income actually declined as welfare benefits were reduced once a family member began earning income from a job. This situation reduced work incentive and encouraged dependency on government welfare support. All programs of support to the poor and proposals to reform these programs must come to grips with the trade-off between providing a minimum living standard to those who are poor—a group that is alarmingly composed of a growing number of children—while at the same time trying to minimize the work disincentive for those who are eligible for support.

The major recession that began in the United States in late 2007 is straining the system of support for the poor. As unemployment rates soared to the range of 10 percent in 2009, more and more people have had their incomes reduced and have been seeking public assistance. A new emergency fund of $5 billion was created as part of the federal *American Recovery and Reinvestment Act of 2009* to assist state governments in providing relief to families that have fallen into poverty in 2009 and 2010. However, the patchwork of federal and state government programs to help them has been criticized by many as not doing enough to provide assistance to eligible applicants and failing to provide benefits to large portions of the population entitled to receive them. Much of the responsibility to provide increased support to those in need during a recession falls on state governments, most of which are facing extreme budget limits as their tax revenues decline in response to reduced economic activity.

In this chapter, we examine the major government programs that assist the poor in the United States. We also develop a general framework for analyzing the impact of subsidies and transfers to individuals on the allocation of resources. Government assistance to the poor requires redistribution of income from the nonpoor to the poor. The generosity of the programs affects the tax burdens on those who must finance their costs. Of course, social costs of programs designed to redistribute income are inevitable. Transfer programs that subsidize the consumption of particular goods, such as food or medical services, are likely to affect the choices of recipients in ways that cause losses in efficiency. The availability of transfers also can affect the incentives of eligible recipients to work. The social losses from distortions in work and spending decisions of transfer recipients are matters of concern to those who finance the programs.

Economic analysis of transfer and subsidy programs provides insight into their effects that are not immediately obvious. Much of this chapter is devoted to an in-depth analysis of the impact of the major transfer programs on incentives of those eligible, or potentially eligible, for the benefits.

POVERTY IN THE UNITED STATES

Federal statistics classify as poor those people who live in households having annual income below the established poverty level. According to a definition developed by the Social Security Administration, people are poor if their income is less than three times the cost of a "nutritionally adequate diet." This method of measuring poverty assumes that a poor family does not have enough income to purchase a low-cost diet and twice that amount to spend on other goods and services. The official poverty-level income varies with the size of the family and whether the family has a head of household older than 65. A two-person household headed by a person older than 65 is classified as poor at a lower level of income than a two-person household not headed by an elderly person. Larger households are classified as poor at higher levels of income than smaller households.

The **poverty threshold** is the level of money income below which a household is classified as poor in the United States. The poverty threshold is adjusted each year by multiplying the previous year's threshold by the change in the Consumer Price Index and adding the increase to the previous year's threshold. This threshold varies by family size, age of householder, and the number of related children under age 18 in the household. In 2011, the poverty threshold for a U.S. family of four consisting of two adults and two related children under the age of 18 was $22,811 per year. For a family consisting of a single parent and two related children under the age of 18, the threshold was $18,123. By contrast, for a single person under the age of 65, the threshold was $11,702.

The definition of poverty is arbitrary, and many would argue that it is either too low or too high. Be that as it may, this definition has become the poverty standard for statistical purposes. Families with children have a greater likelihood of living in poverty in the United States than those with no children. More than 30 percent of the people classified as poor are children. More than 30 percent of the poor live in families headed by a female with no husband. The female-headed family accounts for more than half the families classified as poor. The elderly have lower poverty rates than other demographic groups. In 2011 only 8.7 percent of the elderly (those over 65 years of age) in the United States were poor.

PUBLIC POLICY PERSPECTIVE

Changing the Poverty Threshold: When Are People Really Poor?

Measuring poverty is an art rather than a science. Definitions of poverty are in many ways arbitrary and loaded with subjective value judgments. A person who is classified as poor in the United States has a standard of living that would be considered quite satisfactory or even luxurious in such third world countries as Bangladesh. The Census Bureau has been considering a change in the definition of poverty in the United States that would result in millions of people being added to the official poverty rolls.

The new definition would have raised the average poverty threshold for a family of four in 1998 from $16,660 to $19,500. Such a change in 1998 would have added enough people to the poverty rolls to increase the percentage of the population living in poverty from 12.7 to 17 percent. Some critics argue that the old guidelines set in 1965 for the poverty threshold based only on the cost of a minimal diet does not represent current eating habits or spending. For example, the threshold does not include an adequate amount for such basics as transportation, car expenses, and car repair. In the modern United States, a car, which would be a luxury in a third world nation, is a necessity to get people to work in suburban areas without adequate public transportation. The fact is that poverty is a relative concept that varies from society to society depending on the average living standard for the nation as a whole. So a more generous poverty standard for the United States is reasonable to many. Some argue that for a family of four in the United States, a reasonable poverty threshold would be an amount equivalent to 60 percent of the median family income in the United States. This amount would include minimal sums necessary to provide the poor with socially acceptable housing, health insurance, and a few luxuries that could be viewed as acceptable to the poor in a nation as rich as the modern United States. Median household income in 2011 was $50,054. Using a 60 percent standard for defining poverty would give a poverty threshold of $30,032 in 2011, which is considerably above the $23,021 poverty threshold used on average for a family of four in that year.

There is a lot of politics involved in setting poverty thresholds because many government means-tested programs are tied to the definition of poverty. For example, government spending for the Supplemental Nutrition Assistance Program (formerly called the food stamp program) and the Head Start program would increase if the poverty threshold were raised. The politicians, rather than the statisticians, could therefore decide the extent of poverty in the United States in the future.

In 2011 the Census Bureau began using a new "Supplemental Poverty Measure." The new experimental measure adds the monetary value of in-kind assistance received by the poor, including nutritional assistance and subsidized housing to the income of the poor and also adds the Earned Income Tax Credit (EITC) to their income. It also subtracts from income expenses such as taxes, childcare and other work-related expenses, and out-of-pocket medical expenses from income. According to the new supplemental measure, 16 percent of the U.S. population would have been classified as poor in 2010 compared with 15.1 percent of the population according to the current official measure of poverty. The new measure also reveals the EITC has a large anti-poverty effect and when incorporated in the new supplemental measure. As a result of the impact of the EITC, 6.1 million fewer people would be classified as poor in 2010 of which half this number would be children. Children in poor families also disproportionately benefit from Supplemental Nutritional Assistance Program. So the new supplemental measure would show that fewer children are classified as poor compared to the number considered poor under the official measure of poverty. On the other hand because the elderly tend to have high out of pocket medical costs, more people over the age of 65 would be classified as poor according to the new supplemental measure of poverty.

Table 7.1 and the accompanying chart show the extent of poverty in the United States from 1959 to 2011. The official rate of poverty in the United States declined from 22.4 percent of the population in 1959 to 11.1 percent in 1973. From 1973 to 1983, the official poverty rate increased to more than 15 percent of the population,

TABLE 7.1   Number of Poor and Poverty Rate: 1959–2011

YEAR	NUMBER	PERCENTAGE OF POPULATION	YEAR	NUMBER	PERCENTAGE OF POPULATION
1959	39,490,000	22.4	1986	32,370,000	13.6
1960	39,851,000	22.2	1987	32,341,000	13.4
1961	39,628,000	21.9	1988	31,745,000	13.0
1962	38,625,000	21.0	1989	31,534,000	12.8
1963	36,436,000	19.5	1990	33,534,000	13.5
1964	36,055,000	19.0	1991	35,000,000	14.2
1965	33,185,000	17.3	1992	38,000,000	14.8
1966	28,510,000	14.7	1993	39,300,000	15.1
1967	27,769,000	14.2	1994	38,100,000	14.5
1968	25,389,000	12.8	1995	36,400,000	13.8
1969	24,147,000	12.1	1996	36,500,000	13.7
1970	25,420,000	12.6	1997	35,600,000	13.3
1971	25,559,000	12.5	1998	34,500,000	12.7
1972	24,460,000	11.9	1999	32,300,000	11.8
1973	22,973,000	11.1	2000	31,581,000	11.3
1974	23,370,000	11.2	2001	32,907,000	11.7
1975	25,877,000	12.3	2002	34,570,000	12.1
1976	24,975,000	11.8	2003	35,861,000	12.5
1977	24,720,000	11.6	2004	36,957,000	12.7
1978	24,497,000	11.4	2005	37,040,000	12.6
1979	26,072,000	11.7	2006	36,460,000	12.3
1980	29,272,000	13.0	2007	37,276,000	12.5
1981	31,822,000	14.0	2008	39,824,000	13.2
1982	34,398,000	15.0	2009	43,569,000	14.3
1983	35,266,000	15.2	2010	46,180,000	15.1
1984	33,700,000	14.4	2011	46,247,000	15.0
1985	33,064,000	14.0			

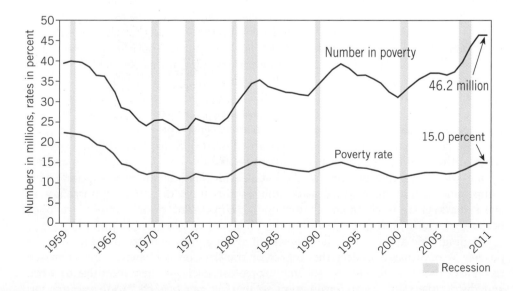

Note: The data points are placed at the midpoints of the respective years.

Source: U.S. Census Bureau, Current Populations Survey, 1960 to 2011 Annual Social and Economic Supplements.

then fell by 1989 to 12.8 percent. The chart accompanying Table 7.1 shows that the poverty rate in the United States fell significantly in the 1960s but rose sharply between 1977 and 1983, and then fell again after 1983. However, partly as a result of a recession, the poverty rate increased again from 1990 to 1993. Then the poverty rate fell steadily until 2001, when the effects of recession increased poverty rates. Between 2001 and 2004 the poverty rate increased each year. However, between 2004 and 2007, the poverty rate declined slightly to 12.5 percent. The effects of the recession in 2008 threw more people below the poverty line and the poverty rate in that year increased to 13.2 percent of the population. Slow recovery from the recession in 2010 resulted in the poverty rate climbing to 15.1 percent in that year. In 2011 the poverty rate declined only slightly to 15 percent.

One problem with the official poverty statistics is that they measure only cash income. They do not include government transfers of goods and services received by the poor. This is significant because, as shown in the following discussion, transfers of goods and services rather than cash are the dominant means of aiding the poor in the United States. However, these figures can be adjusted to account for such transfers.

For example, by adding the market value of noncash assistance in food, housing, medical care, and other forms of noncash income in 2001, the overall rate of poverty would have been reduced from 11.7 to 7.8 percent of the population.

GOVERNMENT PROGRAMS TO AID THE POOR: THE BASIS AND THE TRADE-OFFS

Needs versus Earnings and the Equity-Efficiency Trade-Off

Government programs to aid the poor establish minimum standards of living for those eligible for assistance. A common justification for establishing minimum standards of well-being through transfers is that market outcomes can result in households earning less than the minimum level required for survival. The result is low-income families who cannot earn enough to support their children and otherwise meet their needs. Such outcomes are viewed as unacceptable by many citizens and provide a basis of support for a program of "safety-net" measures to prevent citizens' incomes from falling below minimally acceptable levels. This approach justifies programs and policies that provide the poor with the transfers discussed in this chapter.

Disagreement on what is minimally required for survival would have to be resolved to implement such policies. At the extreme, if it were agreed that needs do not differ among individuals, policies that distribute income according to need would call for an equal distribution of income. This notion, however, conflicts with the belief that people should be rewarded according to their abilities and the value of their work. A compromise solution would allow people to obtain earnings in line with the value of their work, but provide minimal income support. This compromise could be coupled with policies that provide equal opportunity in labor markets and schooling. A substantial number of poor families are poor because of insufficient earnings rather than inability to work.

A pragmatic approach to the problem of altering income distribution to alleviate poverty is one that considers the impact of transfers on efficiency. This approach recognizes that transfers to low-income people can decrease their incentive to work and distort the pattern of consumption so that the net benefits from resource use are less than would be possible if resources were efficiently utilized. In effect, this approach recognizes that the way the "pie" is divided can ultimately affect its size. Under such circumstances, losses in efficiency decrease the economy's potential for producing goods and services and jobs. Insofar as transfers cause such losses, these losses must be weighed against the gains of improved equity. At the extreme, many argue that the best way to improve the lot of the poor is to pursue efficient policies because efficiency maximizes job opportunities. However, many of the poor are not employable because of age or health, so programs that create jobs do little to help them. In fact, as shown in this chapter, many of the transfer policies in the United States are designed to help people incapable of working or to benefit poor children.

Collective Benefits Resulting from Aid to the Poor: Social Stability and Safety Nets

Changes in the distribution of income that reduce the incidence of poverty can result in benefits that are collectively enjoyed. From this perspective, income redistribution to the poor can be viewed as a public good. Many people who support government efforts to redistribute income do so because they believe that they, and other nonpoor citizens, will benefit when poverty is reduced. They might also believe that government programs that establish a safety net to prevent personal income from falling below certain levels provide the nonpoor with insurance; that is, if individuals should suffer a financial or health-related catastrophe, government policies would prevent them from becoming destitute.

In addition, many people have genuine compassion for those who are unfortunate enough to be unable to provide for their own needs and indeed experience satisfaction when the government provides subsidies to the poor. Income redistribution also can provide collective benefits through social stability. Many people reason that a society in which poverty is prevalent breeds discontent and revolution, with the potential for chaos and violence. Upper-income groups tend to support income transfers to the poor to secure the benefits of social stability, thereby reducing the probability of revolutionary upheaval.

But why do we rely on government rather than on private charity to provide assistance to the poor? The answer lies in the public-good nature of charity. Voluntary donations to the poor are likely to result in an undersupply of income redistribution to low-income groups relative to the efficient amount because of the free-rider problem discussed in Chapter 4. Government action to redistribute income can establish uniform standards of eligibility for aid. Such standards might not be ideal from the point of view of all citizens, but these government standards reflect the political compromise necessary to obtain a public program of ensured tax-financed income redistribution.

GOVERNMENT PROGRAMS OF ASSISTANCE TO THE POOR IN THE UNITED STATES

Eligibility

One of the crucial concerns in the development of programs to aid the poor in the United States has been the effect of transfers on the work incentive of the recipients. As a result, the major welfare programs for the poor in the United States have mainly assisted those who, for one reason or other, cannot work. These groups include the disabled, the aged, and families of needy children headed mainly by women. Those falling into these demographic categories satisfy the **status test** for public assistance. The status test ensures that they belong to one of the particular groups that is eligible for poverty relief. Because people in these groups are not usually in the labor force, transfers to them are believed to have minimal effects on work incentive. In effect, this policy "tags" certain groups of limited work capacity and makes them eligible for government assistance.

Under the reformed system of income support for the poor in the United States, the status test for eligibility has been revised. Depending on individual state policy, most recipients of welfare are required to work or seek work training and are eligible for income support only for a limited time. Thereafter, their status will be irrelevant because they will no longer be eligible for assistance. Except for a limited number of poor who are disabled, the new program has greatly increased the incentive to work for all people with low incomes.

To be eligible for cash and other forms of assistance in the United States, recipients also must pass a **means test,** which establishes that those passing the status test also have incomes and asset levels that are below the minimally required amounts to be eligible for aid. Those meeting both the means test and the status test are *automatically entitled to the transfers*. For this reason, these transfer programs, often called **entitlement programs,** require payments to all those people meeting eligibility requirements established by law. However, under the reformed system in the United States, even those families meeting the means test could be denied income support after a certain period of entitlement.

Government programs to aid the poor consist of direct cash transfers, direct provision of such basic goods and services as medical care, subsidies to assist the poor in obtaining housing and food, and various programs designed to aid children and provide incentives to the poor to become self-sufficient. The bulk of the aid, however, is in direct provision of goods and services or subsidies to assist the poor in obtaining goods and services.

Cash Assistance to the Poor in the United States: Temporary Assistance to Needy Families and Supplemental Security Income

Two major programs provide welfare assistance in the form of cash transfers to the poor in the United States: **Temporary Assistance to Needy Families** (TANF) and **Supplemental Security Income** (SSI). TANF provides family support payments on a temporary and limited basis through grants to state governments, which in turn determine eligibility by income and conditions for receiving welfare payments. All states began implementing the new federal welfare system on July 1, 1997.

TANF is a federal block grant that provides funding to states to support the poor. TANF replaces three programs of support to the poor that existed prior to 1996: Aid to Families with Dependent Children (AFDC), which provided income support to families with children deprived of parental support; JOBS, an employment and training program for AFDC recipients; and Emergency Assistance (EA), which provided short-term emergency services and benefits to needy families.

The old AFDC program was widely criticized for discouraging work effort by recipients. Single females headed most AFDC families. If the head of the family began to work, her AFDC cash payments were reduced. Most states allowed welfare recipients to earn a standard allowance of $120 per month before cutting welfare benefits after the first year of work. Allowances were also made for child-care costs equal to 20 percent of earnings up to a maximum amount per year. After the maximum allowances were reached, AFDC payments began to decline by 67 cents per dollar earned during the first four months of employment. When the welfare recipient had been employed for four consecutive months, AFDC benefits were reduced by $1 for each $1 of earnings after the standard allowances of $120 and those for child care expenses. By working, welfare recipients also incurred expenses for commuting, nonreimbursed child care costs, clothing, taxes, and other costs. And as income rose, families found that eventually they became ineligible for other government programs that subsidized food, medical care, or housing. After getting off welfare, household heads, most of whom had skills that could command only low wages in the labor market, found that their family's income ended up lower than it was under welfare!

The old system severely dampened the incentive to work by reducing the net gains from accepting employment. Welfare under AFDC became a bitter trap for many families. They knew that if they were to enter the labor market given their skill set, they would not be able to earn more than they could have under welfare. The incentive for many was to remain a welfare recipient under AFDC. In effect, many families could not improve their living standard by going off welfare, so they found ways to remain eligible for AFDC. Some families remained on welfare for more than one generation. Despite attempts to fix the system in the late 1980s by providing more training and education for recipients, by the mid-1990s the political forces had moved toward a more radical reform. The result was the *Personal Responsibility and Work Opportunity Act of 1996* that established TANF. The new system is often called "workfare" because it does not give recipients of temporary cash assistance the option of not working. All recipients must accept work training and are expected to eventually find a job unless the recipient is disabled. Cash assistance to the poor is limited to a maximum of five years over a recipient's lifetime. In short, the emphasis of the current system of welfare in the United States is to make sure people are only allowed temporary government assistance and to help them eventually become self-sufficient.

The system of assistance to needy families under TANF is fundamentally different from that under previous programs. Under AFDC and EA, funding was open-ended as entitlement programs that required payment of benefits to all who met status and means tests. The amount spent supporting the poor was therefore not directly under the control of the federal and state governments and could vary year by year, depending on the number of people entitled to receive benefits. TANF caps federal spending each year and allocates funds to states on the basis of historical spending for AFDC, EA, and JOBS.

TANF is fully administered by state governments. Each state determines criteria for eligibility to receive benefits, and monthly payments under the program vary widely from state to state. To assist the states and the poor in finding jobs, the workfare law also provides funds to states to help subsidize child care for families in need so that they can seek employment. It also limits welfare payments to noncitizens and provides funding to develop new policies that will reduce the rate of nonmarital births and make sure that child support payments by absent spouses are collected. State governments are required by the federal government to spend some of their own funds on programs to assist needy families or be subject to penalties. The amount a state government must spend is set at 80 percent of their 1994 contribution to AFDC-related programs. In recent years, states have been spending approximately $12 billion of their own funds annually to assist the poor. The federal funding for TANF has been capped at $17 billion annually, but during periods of recession Congress has authorized additional emergency fund assistance to state governments.

Legislation in 1996 did not fundamentally change the SSI program. However, it did change the criteria by which some children are classified as disabled. The new law resulted in a reduction in the number of children eligible for aid under this program.

SSI is a federally funded and operated program that provides cash transfers to the aged, the blind, and the disabled who pass a means test. Most states supplement the basic SSI payments made to individuals by the federal government. Because of the state supplements, SSI benefits vary considerably; payments received by the individuals also vary with their income from other sources.

In addition, state governments have programs of *general assistance* to the poor, which provide financial aid to couples without children and unrelated individuals who pass a means test but are ineligible for benefits under SSI or TANF. The federal government provides additional assistance to the poor through the **Earned Income Tax Credit (EITC)**, a program for those who work that provides assistance in the form of supplements to earnings that are transfers paid out when eligible recipients file appropriate federal income tax forms. The maximum credit per family was $5,751 in 2011. The EITC has emerged as a major means of support to the poor in the United States. The features of the EITC are discussed at the end of this chapter.

In-Kind Aid to the Poor: Supplemental Nutrition Assistance, Medicaid, Housing Assistance, and Other Programs

The federal and state governments also assist the poor through **in-kind benefits**, which are noncash benefits that increase the quantities of certain goods and services that will be consumed by the recipients. In-kind benefits are those received in some form other than money that improve the well-being of recipients. These benefits consist of medical services, food, housing, and other services provided either directly to recipients or at subsidized prices to eligible families and individuals. In dollar terms, in-kind subsidies are much more important than cash transfers to the poor. Some poor people also receive subsidies that lower the prices they pay for services such as housing they purchase in the marketplace.

Medicaid was enacted by Congress in 1965 to provide, at government expense, medical care services for the poor. The program is jointly financed by the federal and state governments but administered by state governments. It provides benefits for most of those eligible for TANF and SSI cash subsidies and others who pass a means test. Under Medicaid, all states (except Arizona) provide basic health services to eligible recipients. Each state determines eligibility requirements under Medicaid and can provide benefits above the minimum established by federal law. Each state establishes its own reimbursement policies to medical providers who supply services to Medicaid patients. Service provider fees are billed directly to the various state governments. State governments are required to provide Medicaid coverage for all children age 19 or younger in families with income at or below the poverty threshold. Some states also provide Medicaid to dependent children over the age of 19 in families that are above the poverty line. In most states adults are provided with Medicaid coverage only if their family income is below the poverty threshold.

Medicaid has become the most expensive of all programs of public assistance to the poor. Federal government expenditures for the Medicaid program in 2011 amounted to $275 billion, or 7.6 percent of total federal spending. An additional $9 million of outlay was incurred for the Child Health Insurance Program (CHIP) that provides health insurance to some children in households with incomes as much as 200 percent of the official poverty level. Medicaid costs have been rising rapidly and are expected to continue to do so at an even more rapid rate. State governments have been struggling with rapidly rising Medicaid costs and their spending has been approaching $200 billion per year amounting to about 20 percent of their budgets. The Medicaid program benefits more than 40 million recipients. Beneficiaries under the program receive a card that they can use in lieu of cash to pay for medical services from physicians and hospitals. The Congressional Budget Office projects that unless reforms are enacted to change the Medicaid system, it will absorb 2.5 percent of GDP in the United States by 2030.

The **Supplemental Nutrition Assistance Program** (formerly called the food stamp program) is a federally financed subsidy program that began in 1971. Under this program administered by state governments, recipients receive electronic benefits transfer (EBT) cards that can be redeemed for food and related items at stores. An eligible recipient must pass a means test. The actual amount of stamps received per month varies with a person's earned income, less allowable deductions. The benefits received by recipients decline as earned income increases. Total federal government outlays for the Supplemental Nutrition Assistance Program in 2011 were $77 billion. Since 2008 outlays under this program have nearly doubled and in 2011 outlays for food assistance amounted to slightly more than 2 percent of federal government expenditure.

Finally, various other programs, including those for social services (such as foster care, child nutrition, and state children's health insurance) are available through state and local governments for those who meet both means and status tests.

Federal Expenditures for Assistance to the Poor in the United States

Table 7.2 shows federal government expenditures under the major programs of government aid to the poor in the United States in fiscal year 2011. Total expenditures under the major transfer programs to low-income people in the United States absorbed 15 percent of total federal government expenditures in 2011. The numbers in Table 7.2 include only federal spending. State and local governments also provide cash assistance to the poor and spend over $2 billion per year out of their own budgets doing so.

Cash transfers to the poor accounted for only about one third of total federal spending to aid the poor in 2011. The remaining two-thirds is accounted for by in-kind benefits. Cash transfers consist of TANF and SSI benefits paid to individuals and families and assistance to the working poor through the Earned Income Tax Credit. Federal cash transfers to the poor accounted for only 4.36 percent of total federal government spending in 2011. Federal grants under TANF go to state governments and do not necessarily end up as support to the poor.

In-Kind versus Cash Transfers

As the data in Table 7.2 demonstrate, the welfare system of aid to the poor in the United States is heavily weighted toward the provision of goods and services. The reasons for this are complex. Political realities make it more likely that a given

TABLE 7.2   Major Federal Government Expenditures to Aid the Poor, 2011

PROGRAM	AMOUNT (BILLIONS OF DOLLARS)	PERCENTAGE OF FEDERAL SPENDING
SSI	53	1.47
Family Support*	26	0.72
Earned Income Tax Credit and Child Tax Credits	78	2.17
Subtotal: All Cash Transfers	**157**	**4.36**
Medicaid and CHIP	284	7.88
Supplemental Nutrition Assistance	77	2.14
Child Nutrition, Health, Foster Care and Social Service	25	0.69
Subtotal: All In-Kind Transfers	**386**	**10.71**
Total	**543**	**15.07**

*Includes Temporary Assistance for Needy Families (TANF), programs for child support enforcement, other family and childcare programs, and research to benefit children.

Source: Congressional Budget Office. Percentages calculated on the basis of $3,603 billion total federal government expenditure in 2011.

dollar amount of in-kind assistance can gain approval, whereas equivalent amounts of cash assistance cannot. Apparently, assistance to the poor is more likely to obtain votes when a particular issue is clarified. For example, programs of food assistance to the poor were expanded after an investigation of the extent of hunger in the United States in the 1960s. It also appears that programs of in-kind assistance to the poor are more easily approved during periods of high unemployment.

The rationale for many in-kind benefits to the poor is that they allow some control over the spending patterns of recipients. Many people who support such programs as Supplemental Nutritional Assistance, public housing, and government-supplied training and schooling argue that these programs ensure that the recipients will spend their grants on necessities rather than luxuries. However, in-kind benefits free up cash that would have been spent on the subsidized items. This cash then can be spent on nonsubsidized items. In other words, in-kind subsidies, like cash subsidies, allow increased purchases of all goods.

CHECKPOINT

1. How is poverty officially defined in the United States? Based on the official definition of poverty, has any progress been made in reducing its incidence in the United States since 1960?
2. How is eligibility determined for government programs designed to assist the poor in the United States?
3. What are the major types of government programs that provide support for the poor in the United States?

SUBSIDIES AND TRANSFERS TO INDIVIDUALS: ECONOMIC ANALYSIS OF THEIR EFFECTS

A major concern about all transfer programs is their effect on resource allocation. In-kind programs of assistance can distort the behavior of the recipients in ways that cause losses in efficiency. The programs can result in consumption of goods or services by recipients beyond the point at which the marginal benefit of the item to the consumer falls to equal its marginal social cost. In addition, the availability of the programs themselves could result in changes in the behavior of those who would take advantage of eligibility requirements. Finally, those who are already receiving government assistance might lose their incentive to work if earning income results in a loss of cash and in-kind benefits. The effects of government assistance programs to the poor on resource allocation highlight the realities of the equity-efficiency trade-off.

All forms of assistance to the poor in the United States can be regarded as subsidies. In effect, subsidies are the opposite of taxes. They are payments to individuals, usually from governing authorities, subject to certain terms and conditions. Economic analysis of in-kind and cash subsidies helps to isolate their impact on efficiency.

Price-Distorting Subsidies

Let's begin our analysis with a discussion of subsidies that decrease the price of consuming a good or service to the recipient. For example, poor people often are eligible for housing subsidies that allow them to rent apartments at monthly rents below the market equilibrium rent for similar housing. The government then pays the difference between the actual rent and the amount that the tenant pays. The difference between the market rent paid to the landlord and the tenant's rent is the subsidy. Some government programs subsidize payments on mortgage loans to enable low-income individuals to buy their own homes. Similarly, some poor people also receive subsidies that reduce the price of energy and other services.

Subsidies that reduce prices to consumers below the market price are called **price-distorting subsidies**, which (other things being equal) are likely to result in losses in efficiency as individuals act to substitute the subsidized good for other goods in their annual budgets. Figure 7.1 illustrates the impact of a price-distorting subsidy for housing services. Suppose, for example, the government agrees to pay a certain fraction (such as 40 percent) of monthly rents of low-income citizens. Initially, before the subsidy is available, the person (whose indifference curves are drawn in Figure 7.1) is in equilibrium at point E_1. At that point, she purchases H_1 units of housing services (measured in terms of, say, square feet or number of rooms rented per month) and spends N_1 on other goods each month. Total expenditure on housing per month is represented by the distance N_1I.

The government subsidy reduces the price of housing services to the recipient and therefore swivels the budget line outward from IA to IB. The consumer now is in equilibrium at point E_2, at which she consumes H_2 units of housing per month. Her total monthly expenditure on housing services now is represented by the distance IS. However, only a portion of this comes out of her income. Of the total annual expenditures on housing after receipt of the subsidy, IN_2 is paid by the recipient and N_2S is paid by the government. The total amount of the subsidy received by the individual is therefore N_2S per year. After receipt of the subsidy, then, she enjoys H_2 units of housing services each month and spends N_2 on other goods each year.

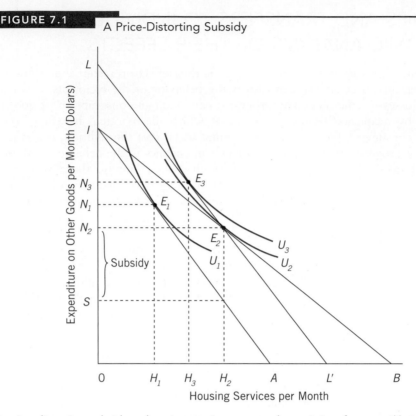

FIGURE 7.1   A Price-Distorting Subsidy

A price-distorting subsidy to housing services moves the recipient from equilibrium at point E_1 to equilibrium at E_2, as the price that must be paid for such services declines. If instead the recipient were given N_2S per year as a cash subsidy, she would be in equilibrium at point E_3. The person is better off at E_3 than at E_2 because she achieves utility level $U_3 > U_2$.

Suppose instead this consumer were given a monthly cash subsidy exactly equal to the amount that would be received under the price-distorting housing subsidy. The amount of the monthly cash subsidy would be N_2S. The budget line would now be LL'. This budget line goes through point E_2, with the result that the consumer could still buy the combination of housing services and other goods that would be affordable under the price-distorting subsidy. However, the increase in cash income now enables the consumer to purchase more of all goods, not only housing services. The equilibrium under the cash subsidy is at point E_3, where the consumer chooses to purchase H_3 units of housing services per month and to spend N_3 on other goods each month. This result will hold as long as the marginal rate of substitution of housing services for expenditure on other goods, which is the marginal benefit of housing services to the person, declines. Because the slope of the budget line LL' is steeper to the left of point E_2, the equilibrium must be at a point on an indifference curve that is also steeper. The consumer must substitute expenditure on other goods for housing to increase the marginal benefit of housing, thereby moving to a steeper point on the indifference curve at point E_3. The price-distorting subsidy induces the consumer to purchase a larger amount of housing services than would be the case if she received an equivalent cash grant.

A cash grant to an individual equal to the amount received under the price-distorting subsidy would therefore allow the person to enjoy a higher level of utility. After all, the consumer could always use the cash grant to purchase the combination of housing and other goods at point E_2. The cash subsidy gives the recipient greater freedom of choice, thereby allowing the achievement of a higher level of satisfaction. The difference between the utility level U_3 and the utility level U_2 is a loss in utility to the recipient from the N_2S dollars of subsidy compared to the unrestricted cash grant. This **deadweight loss** of price-distorting subsidy is the extra benefit a recipient can enjoy from the dollar amount of the price-distorting subsidy if instead the grant was received in a lump sum. Here the deadweight loss of the subsidy is the difference in well-being of the individual at point E_2 compared to what she can enjoy at point E_3 for the same dollar amount of subsidy. A net gain would result if each individual receiving a price-distorting subsidy were able to get the same sum in the form of a lump-sum unrestricted cash transfer. Naturally, with the cash transfer, the individuals would choose to consume less of the subsidized good.

The Excess Burden of a Price-Distorting Subsidy: Market Effects

Now let's examine the effect of a price-distorting subsidy on the market for a product like housing services. To make the analysis simple, assume that the housing industry operates under conditions of constant costs so that the long-run supply curve of housing is perfectly elastic. Figure 7.2 shows the long-run market supply curve for a standard one-bedroom apartment along with the demand curves for these apartments by low-income tenants. Because the supply curve is perfectly

FIGURE 7.2   Excess Burden of a Subsidy

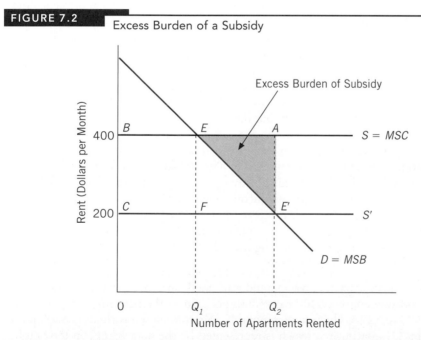

The cost of a subsidy to low-income tenants to taxpayers is represented by the rectangular area *BAE'C*. The net benefits to recipients of the subsidy are represented by the area *BEE'FC*. The excess burden of the subsidy is the difference between its costs to taxpayers and the benefits to recipients, represented by the triangular area *EAE'*. The subsidy causes more than the efficient amount of resources to be devoted to housing because the marginal social cost of housing after the subsidy exceeds the marginal social benefit received by tenants.

elastic, the rent for the apartments is independent of the demand by low-income tenants. The marginal social cost of making one-bedroom apartments available to tenants is assumed to be $400 per month. Assuming no externalities in the production or consumption of housing, and perfect competition in the housing market, the supply curve of housing gives the marginal social cost of any given number of apartments, which is constant at $400 per month.

The demand curve shows that the marginal benefit of one-bedroom apartments to low-income tenants varies with the number rented. In the absence of any subsidy, the market equilibrium rent would be $400 per month for the apartment and the number of apartments rented would be Q_1. This would be efficient because at point E the marginal benefit of the apartments equals their marginal social cost to low-income tenants. Assuming no positive externalities are associated with housing consumption to low-income tenants, the marginal benefit they receive from renting a one-bedroom apartment is also the marginal social benefit of making that apartment available to them.

Now suppose that the government agrees to pay one-half the rent for low-income tenants. As a result of the subsidy, the price to low-income tenants falls to $200 and the quantity demanded by these tenants increases to Q_2, corresponding to point E'. At that point, tenants pay only $200 per month rent but landlords receive $400. The $200 difference between the market rent and the rent paid by tenants is the price-distorting subsidy per tenant represented by the distance AE'. Naturally, this housing subsidy distorts prices and this induces low-income tenants to increase their consumption of housing services. Families who would normally live in small one-room apartments or with relatives now move into one-bedroom apartments and are made better off as they consume more housing. Because of the price-distorting subsidy, more resources are devoted to making one-bedroom apartments available to low-income tenants. When Q_2 units are supplied each month to these tenants, the $400 marginal social cost of the apartments exceeds the marginal social benefit to tenants of only $200. Too many apartments are being supplied to low-income tenants relative to the efficient number. In effect, the subsidy program induces a reallocation of resources toward housing, but the value of the resources used exceeds the benefits they provide to the tenants. The result is a loss in net benefits from resource use because the subsidy induces tenants to consume housing beyond the point at which its marginal benefit to them equals the marginal social cost of the service.

Now let's look at the cost of the subsidy to taxpayers and compare those costs with the net increment in benefits low-income tenants enjoy as a result of the subsidy. The monthly cost of the subsidy to taxpayers is the $200 subsidy per apartment multiplied by the Q_2 apartments rented by the recipients of the subsidy. This is represented by the area $BAE'C$ in Figure 7.2. The total value of the subsidy to recipients can be calculated as follows:

1. Those low-income tenants who would rent one-bedroom apartments even without the subsidy enjoy a $200 per month net gain as the net rent they pay is cut from $400 to $200. The total net monthly gain to these individuals is $200 multiplied by Q_1 apartments, which is represented by the area $BEFC$ on the graph.

2. As a result of the subsidy, the number of apartments rented to low-income tenants increases. The monthly net gain to each of these tenants is the difference between the monthly marginal benefit they place on housing and the monthly $200 rent. The total monthly net gain for these tenants is represented in the graph as the triangular area $EE'F$.

The total increase in net benefits to recipients of the subsidy is therefore the sum of the rectangular area *BEFC* and the triangular area *EE'F*. The sum of the two areas is the area *BEE'FC*.

The area *BEE'FC* is *less* than the area *BAE'C*, representing taxes paid to finance the subsidy to tenants. The subsidy costs more to taxpayers than it is worth to those who receive it. This difference between the cost of the program to taxpayers and the gain in net benefits to the tenants is called the **excess burden of the subsidy**, represented by the triangular area *EAE'*. The excess burden measures the additional cost over and above the taxes paid for the subsidy. This additional cost is the loss in efficiency in housing markets from overconsumption of housing beyond the point at which its marginal social benefit equals its marginal social cost.

Price-distorting subsidies result in an excess burden because they encourage recipients of the subsidy to consume the subsidized good beyond the point at which its marginal social benefit falls to equal its marginal social cost. A smaller lump-sum cash subsidy (in this case equal to the area *BEE'FC*) can be substituted for the dollar value of the price-distorting subsidy that would make recipients equally as well-off and cost taxpayers less in taxes. If we wish to preserve efficiency in the marketplace, then lump-sum transfers to the poor are preferable to price-distorting subsidies.

A Price-Distorting Subsidy That Lowers the Price to Zero

The analysis of the effects of subsidies on resource use is pertinent to the economic effects of Medicaid, which is the largest program of assistance to the poor in the United States. Although its actual provisions are quite complex, the program, up until recently, effectively reduced to zero the money price of medical services to most eligible low-income persons.

Figure 7.3 analyzes the effect of such a medical subsidy program as Medicaid on consumption of medical services by the poor. Assume that the annual quantity of

FIGURE 7.3 Full Subsidization of Medical Services

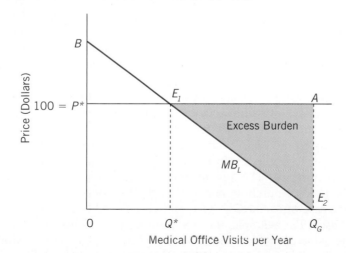

A full subsidy reduces the price of the subsidized good to zero for consumers, who continue consuming the good until its marginal benefit is zero.

medical services consumed can be measured by office or hospital visits to medical practitioners. Medical services are presumed to be supplied by a perfectly competitive industry. In Figure 7.3, the marginal social costs of supplying medical services do not increase as more are made available to the poor. In the absence of any subsidies, the poor would have to pay the market equilibrium price of an office visit. This price would equal the marginal social cost of medical service of $P^* = \$100$. Given the demand for medical services by low-income people, the quantity that they would consume at the market price would be Q^*. The demand curve for medical services by the poor reflects their willingness to pay, given their low incomes. This is their marginal benefit for medical services. The equilibrium at P^* would be efficient because $P^* = MC = MB_L$ of medical services.

Assume that when low-income people are eligible for Medicaid, the price of medical services becomes zero. At zero price, the quantity demanded by Medicaid recipients is Q_G. At this level of annual consumption, recipients of Medicaid are consuming medical services beyond the point at which their marginal benefits equal the marginal cost of the service. At point E_2, the marginal social cost of providing medical service to low-income people exceeds the marginal benefit that they obtain. This is because, at zero price, recipients of the subsidy consume medical services up to the point at which their marginal benefit (MB_L) is zero.

The total annual cost of the Medicaid program to taxpayers is represented by the area P^*AE_20. However, the dollar value of the gain in well-being for recipients of Medicaid is *less* than the cost of the program to taxpayers. In the absence of a subsidy, low-income people would consume Q^* units of medical services (a certain number of office visits per year). The difference between the maximum amount that they would pay for that amount of medical services and the market price of $100 per office visit is represented by the triangular area P^*BE_1. This is the consumer surplus that they earn on Q^* office visits per year. The gain in consumer surplus to recipients of the Medicaid program is the area $P^*E_1E_20$. This represents the net gain in well-being to recipients of Medicaid (see the appendix to Chapter 1 for a discussion of consumer surplus).

Part of the increase in consumer surplus is the extra net benefit on the Q^* units of medical service that would have been purchased anyway. This is represented by the rectangular area $0P^*E_1Q^*$. The remainder is the area $Q^*E_1E_2$. This is the consumer surplus on the extra medical services consumed after the price falls to zero.

The excess burden of the Medicaid subsidy is represented by the triangular area E_1AE_2. This is a measure of the loss in efficiency due to the in-kind subsidy as the recipients consume medical services beyond the point at which their marginal benefit falls to equal the marginal social cost of the services. The recipients of Medicaid could be made as well-off with a cash subsidy, which would be less than the amount the government would have to pay to finance the program!

A cash subsidy to the poor would increase their ability, and therefore willingness, to pay for medical services. In Figure 7.3, this would shift the demand curve for such services outward. The advantage of the cash subsidy to the recipients is that it could be used to purchase not only medical services but also other services or goods. In the case of Medicaid, the subsidy is enjoyed only if more medical services are purchased. For example, the U.S. Bureau of the Census estimated that the average market value of medical services received by a single parent with two children under Medicaid was $2,166 in 1987. However, based on ability and willingness to pay, the bureau estimated that these benefits were worth on average only $652 in 1987 for such a family if its income were $10,000 per year. Instead of receiving Medicaid, the recipient could be given an unrestricted lump-sum grant of $652 and be as well off as with Medicaid, while taxpayers would save $1,514! The prices of medical services have more than doubled in the United States since 1987 and more services are available. Roughly adjusting the 1987 estimates for inflation would indicate that in 2011 dollars, a cash grant of about $1,500 would make the family just as well off as Medicaid insurance costing approximately $5,000 in 2011. The savings to taxpayers in 2011 dollars would roughly be about $3,500 per Medicaid family.

Additional Effects of Subsidies: The Case of Increasing Costs

Suppose the long-run supply curve of medical services is upward sloping. This would imply that the prices of inputs, such as the services of physicians and hospitals, would increase as a result of increased annual production of medical services. Figure 7.4 shows that in this case the market for medical services would be affected by the Medicaid program.

The market demand for medical services, again measured as office visits per year, is D_M in Figure 7.4. This demand curve is the lateral summation of the demand curve for medical services for low-income people, D_L, and everyone else, D_O. The market price, $100 per office visit, corresponds to the point at which D_M intersects the upward-sloping supply curve at point E_1. At that price, low-income people consume Q_L visits per year and others consume Q_O visits per year, for a total of Q_1.

The Medicaid program reduces the price of an office visit to zero only for low-income people. As a result, their quantity demanded increases to Q_G. The total market demand curve is now the sum of the quantity demanded by all others at any given price and Q_G, where Q_G is independent of price because $P = 0$ to Medicaid

FIGURE 7.4   Impact of the Medicaid Program on Price: The Case of Increasing Cost

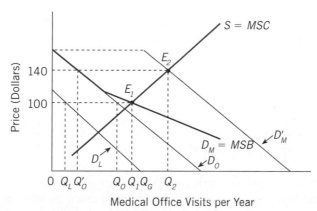

The initial market equilibrium corresponds to point E_1, at which the market demand curve D_M intersects the market supply curve S. If low-income people are eligible for Medicaid, their quantity demanded increases to Q_G. The market demand curve D'_M is obtained by adding Q_G to the demand curve D_O. Given the new increased demand by the poor for medical services, the price of an office visit increases from $100 to $140.

recipients. The new market demand curve, D'_M, intersects the market supply curve at point E_2. The market price *increases* to \$140 per office visit. At that higher price, those who are not receiving Medicaid decrease the quantity of medical services demanded per year to Q'_O. Total quantity demanded is $Q_2 = Q'_O + Q_G$.

It follows that when the supply of medical services is upward sloping, the government subsidy program will cause the price of medical services to increase. This means that those paying the taxes to finance the program *also* will pay more for their own medical services but that owners of specialized inputs necessary to provide medical services, such as physicians and hospitals, will enjoy increases in income. Consumers of medical services who are ineligible for the subsidies therefore suffer a reduction in real income, whereas medical practitioners are likely to enjoy an increase in real income. This points out how price-distorting subsidies, in addition to causing losses in efficiency, also can cause changes in the distribution of income through changes in the market price of the subsidized goods or services.

Concern about the impact of Medicaid and other government subsidy programs for medical care, such as those enjoyed by the elderly and veterans, on the prices of medical services has led to recent cutbacks in coverage. These cutbacks have reduced the subsidy received by the poor by limiting the kinds of medical services that are provided free. Cost-containment measures that limit reimbursement to hospitals and physicians decrease incentives to offer such services to Medicaid patients.

We discuss the economics of health care and the role of government in providing medical services in greater detail in Chapter 9.

CHECKPOINT

1. What is a price-distorting subsidy? Why do price-distorting subsidies result in a deadweight loss?
2. What is the excess burden of a subsidy?
3. Explain why the Medicaid program contributes to an overallocation of resources to health care in the United States relative to the efficient amount. Under what circumstance does subsidized medical care contribute to increases in the price of medical services?

MEDICAID AND STATE GOVERNMENT BUDGETS: SKYROCKETING COSTS

As of 2011 Medicaid absorbed nearly one-quarter percent of state government budgets in the United States, making it the single biggest category of state government expense having surpassed elementary and secondary education spending. Medicaid spending has risen from 17.8 percent of state government spending in 1992.

Under federal guidelines, each state establishes its own eligibility standards, determines the type of services to be provided, sets payment rates to providers, and in general administers the program. There is considerable variability in policies regarding Medicaid coverage and payment among the states. A person who is eligible for Medicaid benefits in one state may not qualify for those benefits in another state.

The federal government pays a share, called the *Federal Medical Assistance Percentage (FMAP)*, of each state's Medicaid costs. FMAP is determined each year using a formula that considers per capita income in each state relative to the national average per capita income. States with lower than average per capita income are reimbursed with a higher share of their Medicaid outlays than states with per capita income that is higher than average. In 2011, FMAP ranged from 50 percent in the highest income states to 74.8 percent in Mississippi. Combined federal and state government spending for Medicaid in 2011 was approaching $400 billion annually.

In general, federal guidelines require states to provide Medicaid coverage for most individuals receiving federally assisted income support (these include all those who meet criteria for public assistance under income-support programs that were in effect in mid-1996). The *Children's Health Insurance Program (CHIP)* is also jointly funded by the state and the federal governments. As of 2012 eligibility for CHIP benefits is a family income of 200 percent of the poverty level or greater in 47 states and the District of Columbia. CHIP has contributed to a reduction in the percent of children without health insurance coverage. For the CHIP program and other health programs affecting children FMAP is higher than for regular Medicaid, meaning that the federal government pays a higher percentage of the costs of these programs. Medicaid is similar to most private health insurance plans in that it provides inpatient and outpatient hospital benefits, physician services, and diagnostic services. Most states also provide prescription drug coverage, clinic, transportation services, and other services. Long-term nursing care, a benefit not available under most private health insurance plans, is part of the benefits available under Medicaid.

States pay most health care providers directly on a fee-for-service basis. As discussed earlier in this chapter, the Medicaid recipient is not billed and in most cases the price to the recipient is zero (although cost pressures could change this policy in many states). Some states also use managed-care facilities (health maintenance organizations) under prepayment contractual arrangements. States can set rates of payment to providers with the federal requirement that rates must be high enough to generate a supply of services comparable to that available to the general population in the area. Providers participating in Medicaid must accept the state payment rates under the program as payment in full. States also make special payments to hospitals that serve a disproportionate number of Medicaid recipients or uninsured patients. This disproportionate share hospital (DSH) payment was used heavily and, in many cases, inappropriately between 1988 and 1991 and has since become severely restricted.

State governments do have the power to require some Medicaid recipients to pay a share of some of the cost of medical services they receive. Those who receive long-term care in nursing facilities are usually expected to contribute some of their income to their care. Average Medicaid payments per enrollee was $5,337 as of 2008. However, costs for aged Medicaid recipients, who comprise about 9 percent of all Medicaid enrollees, averaged more than $13,800 per person in 2008. This is a cause of concern to the Medicaid program because as the population ages, the percentage of total Medicaid recipients who are elderly will rise. In the past, Medicaid has paid 45 percent of the cost of long-term institutional care for the elderly, and these costs will rise sharply in the future. Another concern under Medicaid is the growth of spending for prescription drugs.

SUBSIDIES TO HOUSING AND FOOD

Public Housing

Let's return to the issue of housing subsidies. Some housing subsidies for the poor in the United States reduce the price of housing only if the poor agree to move into specially constructed government-supplied housing reserved for low-income families. This housing is usually rented to eligible citizens at rates considerably below those prevailing in the market. Public-housing programs are expected to increase the recipient's consumption of housing. Unfortunately, the availability of these programs could actually *reduce* the consumption of housing by restricting the freedom of choice of the consumer.

Suppose, for example, a government program makes available a standard three-room apartment at a rental rate of $30 per room per month. The total rent paid by those eligible for the government housing is $90 per month. Assume the housing can be measured in standardized rooms per unit. This, of course, is a simplification because housing can vary greatly in quality and other characteristics (such as the neighborhood in which it is located). Assume that the market rent for a standardized room (the same size and quality as that provided in public housing) is $100 per month. The three-room public-housing apartment would cost $300 per month if rented on the free market. The cash equivalent of the public-housing subsidy to eligible tenants is $210 per month, which is the difference between the market rent and the subsidized rent.

Figure 7.5 shows that a person who is eligible for public housing could be induced to move from a larger privately rented apartment to a smaller government-subsidized

FIGURE 7.5   Eligibility for Public Housing and the Effect on Housing Consumption

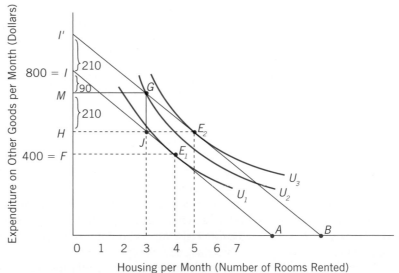

A person eligible for a standardized three-room apartment at a subsidized rent, whose indifference curves are shown in the graph, reduces consumption of housing from four to three rooms per month. If the person were given the monthly cash value of the in-kind subsidy, $210, he or she would increase housing consumption.

unit. This person *would reduce* monthly consumption of housing as a result of the availability of the subsidy. Those taking advantage of the subsidy have no choice in the size or quality of their apartments. They must accept the standardized three-room units offered in the public-housing projects or forgo the subsidy.

The person whose indifference curves are illustrated in Figure 7.5 is currently in equilibrium at point E_1. He currently rents a four-room apartment at the going market rent of \$400 per month. After paying rent, he has $0F$ remaining to spend on other goods. For example, if his monthly income were \$800, he would spend \$400 on housing and have \$400 left over each month to spend on other goods.

Now suppose the person becomes eligible for a new public-housing program. He can move into a standardized three-room public-housing apartment at the subsidized rent of \$90 per month if he chooses. Point G on the graph represents this alternative. At that point, the tenant would be consuming a three-room apartment, which normally would cost \$300. He spends only $IM = \$90$ a month for this apartment. The remainder is paid by government as a subsidy represented on the graph by the distance $MH = \$210$. If the eligible recipient chooses to move to public housing, he will spend \$90 per month on housing, and assuming an \$800 monthly income, have \$710, represented by the distance $M0$, left over to spend on other goods.

The analysis shows that the eligible tenant in fact will choose to move out of the nonsubsidized four-room apartment and into the subsidized three-room apartment, because he is better off at point G compared with his initial equilibrium at point E_1. If he were to remain in the four-room apartment, he would achieve utility level U_1 at point E_1. By moving into the subsidized three-room apartment, he can increase his utility level to U_2 at point G. Therefore, given the choice, he accepts the subsidized apartment and *reduces* the amount of housing consumed per month.

The analysis also shows that if the person were to receive the cash value of the housing subsidy, he *would increase* his consumption of housing. The subsidy of \$210 per month is represented by the distance $GJ = MH$ on the graph. If this amount were given in cash each month to the person, the budget line would become $I'B$. With the monthly cash grant, he would be in equilibrium at point E_2. He would move from his four-room apartment into a five-room apartment. He would spend \$500 per month on housing. His total income would be \$800 (monthly earnings) plus \$210 (monthly grant), for a total of \$1,010. He would spend \$510 on other goods. This person would consume more housing and be better off (because $U_3 > U_2$) at point E_2 than at point G.

Thus, for some people, a public-housing program could have results opposite to those intended. Some people would not want to reduce the quantity of housing if they were eligible for public housing. For example, a person currently in equilibrium consuming the services of a three-room apartment per month would clearly be made better off by the subsidy. She would gladly move into the government-supplied three-room apartment, provided it was of the same quality as her current residence. This is because the subsidy would enable her to have more of other goods while consuming the same amount of housing per month. For this person, the housing subsidy would be equivalent to a cash grant.

Figure 7.6 shows the case of a person who will turn down the opportunity to enter a government housing project even with no differences in the quality of government- and market-supplied housing. This person's indifference curves are steeper than those drawn in Figure 7.5. The person is originally in equilibrium at point E_1 in a four-room apartment. If he were to move to point G, the

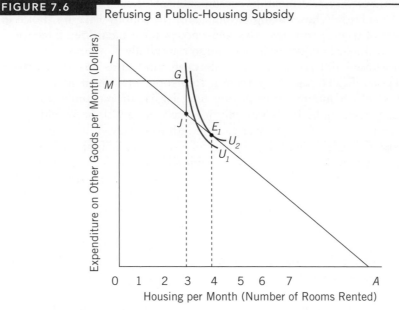

© Cengage Learning

FIGURE 7.6   Refusing a Public-Housing Subsidy

The person whose indifference curves are drawn is better off remaining in his or her four-room apartment than moving into the three-room public housing at point *G*. This person does not accept the offer of subsidized public housing.

government-supplied three-room housing, he would be made worse off, achieving utility level $U_1 < U_2$. He therefore remains at point E_1 by refusing subsidized housing.

In fact, many argue that in some cases government housing is of lower quality than market housing, because the housing projects have been concentrated in low-income neighborhoods. The concentration of poverty-level households in deteriorating neighborhoods results in crime and other social problems that plague tenants. Public housing is also an expensive subsidy. One estimate is that new construction of public housing in 1984 required a federal subsidy of $5,000 per unit per year![1] Given the magnitude of that subsidy, few new public-housing projects have been built in recent years. An equivalent cash grant of that amount would clearly contribute greatly to pull many low-income people out of poverty.

The Housing and Community Development Act of 1987 authorized a new voucher program that gives low-income households funds that can only be used to rent housing. These vouchers provide subsidies to rent privately owned housing units instead of limiting the subsidy to public housing.

Supplemental Nutrition Assistance: A Fixed Allotment Subsidy

Some subsidy programs do not distort prices. **Fixed allotment subsidies** give eligible recipients the right to consume a certain amount of a good or service each month either through direct allotment of the item or through the issuance of vouchers that can be used only to buy a specific item. An example of a fixed allotment subsidy is the Supplemental Nutrition Assistance Program (SNAP) in the United States.

[1]See Sar A. Levitan, *Programs in Aid of the Poor*, 5th ed. (Baltimore: John Hopkins University Press, 1985): 72.

The Supplemental Nutrition Assistance Program, formerly called the food stamp program, grants low-income people the right to purchase a certain amount of food per month through using a special electronic benefit transfer (EBT) card that is similar to a bank debit card. For most recipients of the allotment of benefits in the form of food in the United States, the stamps received are equivalent to a cash transfer. This is illustrated in Figure 7.7.

FIGURE 7.7 The Impact of an In-Kind Transfer: Food Stamps

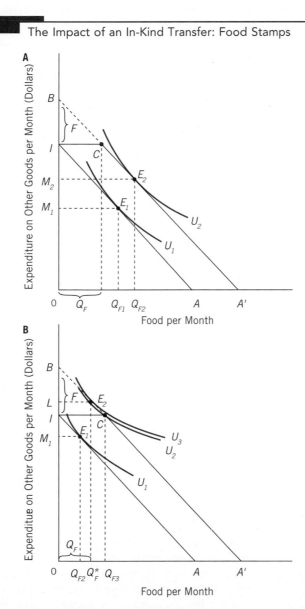

In **A**, a food grant in the form of an electronic benefit transfer that allows the purchase of Q_F units of food per month have the same effect as a cash grant of F. In **B**, food stamps result in more consumption of food than would be the case if the recipient received an equivalent cash grant of F.

© Cengage Learning

The person whose indifference curves are illustrated in Figure 7.7A has a current monthly income equal to $0I$. Given the price of food, the person is initially in equilibrium at point E_1, where she purchases Q_{F1} units of food per month and spends M_1 per month on other goods. Suppose that this person now becomes eligible for a monthly grant of food that will allow her to purchase Q_F units of food each month.

The cash value of the fixed allotment of food benefits, given the current price of food, is F. This represents the amount of cash necessary to purchase Q_F units of food per month. For example, the average value of nutritional assistance benefits per person in 2011 was \$134 per month in the United States and its territories. A monthly cash grant of F would allow the recipient to increase her purchase of other goods by IB. However, because the grant can be used only to purchase food (and related items), the budget constraint, after the monthly food grant, becomes ICA'. If instead a monthly cash grant of F were given to the recipient, the budget line would be BA'. Under the food grant, the market baskets of goods represented by the section BC on the budget line BA' cannot be purchased. This is because food benefits can be used to buy only food, whereas cash can buy anything. With an equivalent cash grant of \$134 per month, the person could purchase *all* the market baskets along the budget line BA'.

Suppose the person is in equilibrium at point E_2 after receiving the monthly grant of food. At that point, she consumes Q_{F2} units of food each month and spends $0M_2$ on other goods. The effect of the grant in this case is to increase *both* the quantity of food consumed per month and monthly expenditure on other goods. In effect, the recipient spends the equivalent of F in food benefits received per month on food, along with some of her own money. However, because the grant frees some of her own monthly income that would have been spent on food, she is able to increase her consumption of other goods as well. The equilibrium at E_2 in Figure 7.7A is exactly the same as that which would occur if the recipient were given a cash grant of F per month instead of the food grant. The effects of the cash grant and the food grant on consumption are identical in this case.

Figure 7.7B illustrates the case of a person who, under a cash grant, would be in equilibrium along the line segment BC. This person is initially in equilibrium at point E_1. A cash grant of F would move him to point E_2, which in Figure 7.7B falls on BC, and he would consume Q_F^* units of food per month. If instead he were given a monthly amount of food grants valued at F per month, he would be forced to point C. At that point, his maximum possible monthly utility is U_2, which is less than U_3, obtained with the equivalent cash grant. This is because he cannot use the food grant to purchase combinations of food and other goods on the line segment BC. At C, he consumes Q_{F3} units of food per month, which is greater than Q_F^* units that he would choose to consume each month if he were given a cash grant. For this person, the food grant does increase food consumption above the monthly level he would choose with an equivalent cash grant. He is also forced to spend F per month on food. He would spend only BL on food (and $0L$ on other goods) with the cash grant. However, this person is worse off with a fixed allotment food grant than he would be with an equivalent monthly cash grant. It is commonly believed that the cash value of the fixed allotment food grant under the Supplemental Food Nutrition Program in the United States is so low (only about \$134 per month per recipient in 2011) that recipients would be likely to spend at least that much on food even if they were given cash. Given that most recipients are likely to spend more than this amount per person per meal, food grants can be regarded as equivalent to a cash grant. Contrary to common belief, this program is unlikely to increase the consumption of food over the levels that would prevail if recipients were given the cash value of the food grant.

Does the Supplemental Nutrition Assistance Program contribute to an increase in the price of food? Keep in mind that although the program provided $77 billion for food expenditures in 2011, it does not increase actual expenditures by that amount because recipients normally would spend some of their own cash on food even in the absence of the program. Part of the food grants increases expenditures on other goods. Total expenditures on food in the United States exceed $500 billion per year. It is therefore unlikely that the injection of only a portion of the $77 billion from the Supplemental Nutrition Assistance Program into the food market is likely to have a major effect on the price of food.

Between 1994 and 2000 food stamp caseloads fell by 37.5 percent. Apparently many of those still eligible for food grant program benefits simply did not apply for them after they stopped receiving public assistance under TANF in the late 1990s. However, between 2000 and 2005, the number of people receiving benefits in the United States has grown from 17.2 million to nearly 26 million according to the U.S. Department of Agriculture. Even though the number of people participating in the food grant program has increased significantly since 2000, estimates indicate that only 60 percent of those eligible for food benefits are actually enrolled in the program. However, the severe recession that began in 2007 in the United States has resulted in a sharp increase in the number of recipients of Supplemental Nutrition Assistance. By 2011 the number of SNAP recipients had increased to 45 million, a 40 percent increase over the number of recipients in 2005!

CHECKPOINT

1. How do public-housing programs affect the choices of those eligible for apartments in public-housing projects?
2. How does the Supplemental Nutrition Assistance Program operate in the United States?
3. Explain why the consumption of food by most SNAP recipients would be unchanged if, instead of food benefits, they received the cash value of those benefits.

THE IMPACT OF GOVERNMENT ASSISTANCE PROGRAMS FOR THE POOR ON THE WORK INCENTIVE OF RECIPIENTS

Welfare benefits in cash or in kind assure the recipient of a minimum level of real income independent of work. The more generous the grant, the greater is the disincentive to work. In other words, a transfer results in an income effect that is unfavorable to work. This is illustrated in Figure 7.8. The indifference curves drawn illustrate a person's preference for leisure or income. Leisure per day is plotted on the horizontal axis. The maximum hours of leisure that a person can enjoy per day is 24. Leisure is defined as engaging in any activity other than work for pay.

FIGURE 7.8   The Income Effect of a Transfer

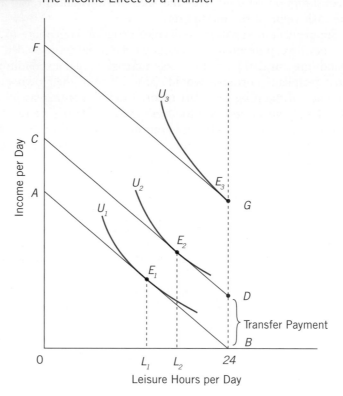

If leisure is a normal good, an increase in income caused by a transfer increases leisure hours per day. The income effect of the transfer therefore is unfavorable to work. A transfer of *BG* dollars per day will reduce hours worked per day to zero for the person whose indifference curves are illustrated.

The line *AB* shows a person's opportunity for giving up leisure for income by working, assuming that the only way the person can obtain income (or goods and services) is by working for an employer. In other words, the line *AB* assumes that nonwage income is zero. If the person can work at a wage of per hour, the equation of the budget line is

$$I = w(24 - L), \tag{7.1}$$

where *I* is income per day and *L* is leisure hours per day. If $L = 24$, along *AB*, the person's income will be zero.

The slope of the budget line is $-w$. The person whose indifference curves are illustrated is in equilibrium at point E_1, where he enjoys L_1 hours of leisure per day. He therefore works $(24 - L_1)$ hours each day.

If the person were to receive a transfer payment of $BD = AC$ per day, his income per day would increase by that amount. Even if he took 24 hours per day in leisure, he would enjoy positive income. The increase in income leads to an increase in the consumption of all normal goods. If leisure is a normal good, the person will increase the amount consumed. In Figure 7.8, the transfer payment to the person shifts the budget line upward to *CD* and results in a new equilibrium at E_2, where the individual increases hours of leisure per day by L_1L_2. He decreases hours worked per day. If the person were eligible for a transfer of ($BG = AF$) per day, he would be in equilibrium at point E_3, where he would consume 24 hours per day in leisure, therefore not working at all. Eligibility for a subsidy of that amount would cause the person to drop out of the labor force!

Another work disincentive effect results from the way in which benefits are reduced as the recipient earns more income. This is illustrated in Figure 7.9. Given the wage rate that a person can earn, the amount of the transfer for which the person is eligible varies with hours worked per day (or any other time period). In Figure 7.9, the maximum subsidy per day a person is eligible for is BD. This is granted if the person does not work at all. As the person works, the subsidy steadily declines. At point C, where the person works ($24 - L^*$) hours per day, the daily transfer would be zero.

This subsidy program shifts the person's budget line up to CD and *decreases its slope* at points corresponding to more than L^* hours of leisure per day. This means that the net effect of the program is to *reduce* the person's real wage rate if he works less than ($24 - L^*$) hours per day. In Figure 7.9, the person is in equilibrium at point E_2 after the subsidy. The subsidy program reduces hours worked per day from ($24 - L_1$) to ($24 - L_2$). This type of subsidy has a *substitution effect* in addition to an income effect for people who work less than ($24 - L^*$) hours per day. It decreases work incentive by causing the wage a recipient can earn to decline,

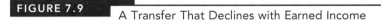

FIGURE 7.9 A Transfer That Declines with Earned Income

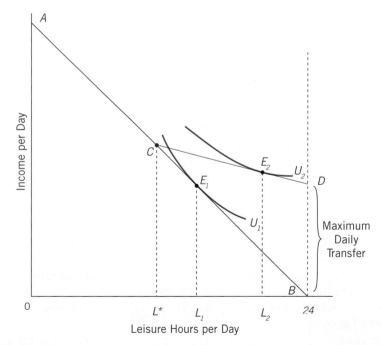

Transfer income per day declines as the recipient's earned income per day increases. At point C, the subsidy per day would be zero. The subsidy reduces the net wage if the person takes more than L^* hours of leisure per day. This transfer reduces the incentive to work because it generates both income and substitution effects unfavorable to work.

© Cengage Learning

because working increases earned income but *decreases* transfer income. As a result, the recipient has an incentive to substitute leisure for work. In effect, the subsidy decreases the opportunity cost of an hour of leisure by reducing the wage when more than L^* hours per day are enjoyed. In this case, both the income and the substitution effects of the transfer act to decrease hours worked per day.

When a transfer recipient starts working, the transfer usually gets phased out. For example, suppose a recipient is eligible for a $300 per month transfer if she has no earnings at all. Suppose her transfer is reduced by 70 cents for each dollar of earnings. At any level of earned income, I_E, her monthly transfer, T, can be calculated from the following formula:

$$T = 300 - .7I_E. \tag{7.2}$$

For example, if she earns $300 per month, her transfer would be reduced from $300 to $90 per month. The transfer eventually would be terminated if she earns sufficient income. To calculate this level of income, set T equal to zero in the preceding equation and solve for I_E. In this case, I_E is equal to $428.57 per month. This would correspond to the level of earned income at point C in Figure 7.9.

If recipients of welfare are out of the labor force, these unfavorable effects on work incentive will be minimal. The cash benefits of many programs are often at values low enough to minimize their income effects. Most states, for example, have paid benefits that are insufficient to raise a recipient's income above the poverty level, even at the maximum monthly amounts. Evidence does indicate that recipients have been more likely to work in states where welfare benefits are minimal than in states where benefits are more generous.[2] TANF deals with work disincentives by limiting the period of eligibility for assistance and requiring recipients to work.

Work and Welfare: Empirical Evidence

Numerous empirical studies and even some experiments have attempted to measure the impact of welfare programs on the work incentive of recipients. One research study has concluded that in the absence of income support, women whose families received these benefits would have worked between 10 and 15 hours per week more than they actually did in the early 1980s.[3] However, because most welfare recipients are unskilled and earn very low wages, this extra work would have increased their disposable income by a mere $1,500 per year—hardly enough to bring them out of poverty and certainly not enough to take the place of the welfare stipends. Most of the experimental evidence also suggests that means-tested transfers have an effect on work effort but that the effect on low-income men and women with dependent children is small.[4] A 10 percent increase in cash transfers will reduce hours worked by less than 2 percent, according to estimates based on these experiments. These findings suggest that even if welfare benefits were to be reduced substantially, or if the rate at which they are phased out with earnings is reduced, work would increase but the increase would not be sufficient to bring the workers out of poverty.

---

[2]Frederick Doolittle, Frank Levy, and Michael Wiseman, "The Mirage of Welfare Reform," *The Public Interest* 47 (Spring 1977): 62–87.

[3]Robert A. Moffitt, "Incentive Effects of the U.S. Welfare System: A Review," *Journal of Economic Literature* 30, 1 (March 1992): 1–61.

[4]*Ibid.*

PROGRAMS WITH NO STATUS TESTS: THE NEGATIVE INCOME TAX AND SUBSIDIES TO THE WORKING POOR

Critics of the U.S. system of assistance to the poor argue that the status tests are demeaning to the recipients. They also argue that the "patchwork quilt" overlap of programs lacks consistent goals. Some have proposed scrapping the system in favor of a **negative income tax (NIT)**[5] cash assistance program that would provide a minimum income guarantee for all Americans. All those with income below the floor would receive cash subsidies from the government, whereas those above the floor would pay taxes. An NIT plan would integrate the system of government assistance with the federal income tax.

How an NIT Would Work

The first step in developing an NIT plan is to decide on the income guarantee. This represents a floor on family income. A person with zero earnings would be guaranteed the standard of living represented by the floor. Suppose the floor is set at $I_G = \$5,000$ per year for a family of four. The floor, of course, would vary with household size.

The second step in the plan is to determine the rate, t_N, at which the transfer received by those with zero income would be phased out as recipients' annual earnings increase. Assuming $t_N = 50$ percent, for every $2 earned the transfer to eligible recipients from the government will be reduced by $1.

The annual transfer, T, received by any eligible family can be expressed as

$$T = I_G - t_N I_E, \tag{7.3}$$

where I_E is earned income per year. For example, if I_E is zero, the family will receive a transfer of $I_G = \$5,000$. As the family's annual earnings increase, the annual transfer will be reduced accordingly. Table 7.3 shows how the transfer will decline with income.

If the family earns enough, the transfer will fall to zero, and the family will begin to pay taxes instead of receiving transfers (which are negative taxes) from the government. The level of income at which this occurs is called the *break-even income* and can be determined from Equation 7.3 by setting $T = 0$ and solving for I_E. This gives the annual earned income, designated as I_B, at which $T = 0$:

$$0 = I_G - t_N I_B \tag{7.4}$$

$$I_B = I_G / t_N. \tag{7.5}$$

I_B is the annual income at which the taxpayer is neither paying taxes nor receiving transfers. As shown in Table 7.3, when $I_G = \$5,000$ and $t_N = 50$ percent, $I_B = \$10,000$.

The disposable income, I_D, of a family receiving a transfer is obtained by adding earned income and the transfer, as shown in Table 7.3. For example, the disposable income of a family of four with $2,000 earned income is $2,000 + [\$5,000 - 0.5(\$2,000)] = \$6,000$. A family of four with income *greater than* the break-even level of $10,000 per year would pay positive taxes. Its disposable income would be earned income *minus* taxes paid.

---

[5]The economist Milton Friedman proposed the original idea for an NIT in the late 1960s. Friedman suggested replacing all income support programs for the poor with a minimal income guarantee for all Americans. See Milton Friedman, "The Case for the Negative Income Tax," in *Republican Papers*, Melvin R. Laird, ed. (New York: Praeger, 1968).

TABLE 7.3	NIT: Disposable Income of Recipients in Relation to Earned Income	
EARNED INCOME (I_E)	**TRANSFER FROM GOVERNMENT** $(T = I_G - T_N I_E)$	**DISPOSABLE INCOME** $(I_D = I_E + T)$
$ 0	$5,000	$ 5,000
1,000	5,000 − [0.5 (1,000)] = 4,500	5,500
2,000	5,000 − [0.5 (2,000)] = 4,000	6,000
3,000	5,000 − [0.5 (3,000)] = 3,500	6,500
4,000	5,000 − [0.5 (4,000)] = 3,000	7,000
5,000	5,000 − [0.5 (5,000)] = 2,500	7,500
6,000	5,000 − [0.5 (6,000)] = 2,000	8,000
7,000	5,000 − [0.5 (7,000)] = 1,500	8,500
8,000	5,000 − [0.5 (8,000)] = 1,000	9,000
9,000	5,000 − [0.5 (9,000)] = 500	9,500
10,000	5,000 − [0.5 (10,000)] = 0	10,000[a]

[a]Break-even income.

© Cengage Learning

FIGURE 7.10	A NIT Plan

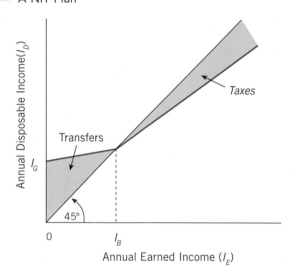

All people with less than the break-even level of income, I_B, would receive transfers. The annual disposable income of these people therefore would exceed their annual earned income. All people with annual earned income greater than I_B would pay taxes. Disposable income for these people therefore would fall short of earned income.

© Cengage Learning

A crucial step in implementing an NIT comes after a family reaches the break-even level of annual income. If income is taxed at a flat rate of, say, 20 percent, after the break-even point, the effective tax rate paid by taxpayers would actually be lower than that paid by transfer recipients whose income declines by 50 percent with earnings! Figure 7.10 shows that disposable income would vary with earned income assuming that t_N is 50 percent and that income above the break-even level is taxed at 20 percent.

A problem with a national income guarantee plan such as NIT is that it can end up being very expensive if the income guarantee is set at any reasonable level, because the plan requires no status test. For example, suppose the income guarantee is set at the level of about $20,000 for a family of four and at correspondingly lower levels for smaller families and higher levels for larger families. With t_N equal to 50 percent, all families of four with income of less than $40,000 per year would be transfer recipients. This could be a substantial portion of the population. The taxes on the remaining portion of the population would have to be quite high to finance the transfers and other government services. If a lower t_N is used to encourage work effort, it would be even worse. If $t_N = 0.2$, and $I_G = \$20,000$, the break-even income level would be $I_B = \$100,000$. Therefore, all families of four with income of less than $100,000 per year would receive transfers! Only families of four with incomes above $100,000 per year would be paying taxes to finance these benefits and all other public services. The higher the break-even level of income, the fewer the number of families paying taxes.

Wage Rate Subsidies

Concern about the work disincentive effects of existing transfer programs for the poor has led to proposals for **wage rate subsidies (WRS)** as a means of both supporting the incomes of the working poor and providing them with incentives to work. Under a WRS plan, minimum-wage legislation would be repealed and workers would be induced to search for jobs at the market-determined wage. Those working at the lowest wages would receive subsidies from the government to raise their incomes to some minimum level. The subsidy would vary with hours worked and would be phased out as a worker's hourly wage rate increased.

For example, if a worker earned $2.00 per hour, the government might subsidize the hourly wage at the rate of $1.50, bringing up actual take-home wages per hour to $3.50 for the worker. Employers would still pay $2.00 per hour. The lower wages made possible by the plan would provide more employment opportunities but maintain the worker's income and incentive to work. Table 7.4 shows how the WRS might vary with hourly wages. For a worker earning wages of, say, $3.00 per hour, the subsidy might be reduced to only $1.00 per hour, giving the

TABLE 7.4	Wage Rate Subsidies	
WAGE PAID	**SUBSIDY (PER HOUR)**	**TOTAL WAGE RECEIVED**
$2.00	$1.50	$3.50
2.50	1.25	3.75
3.00	1.00	4.00
3.50	0.75	4.25
4.00	0.50	4.50
4.50	0.25	4.75
5.00	0.00	5.00

© Cengage Learning

worker a net wage of $4.00 per hour. The subsidy might decrease with an increase in wages until it fell to zero at, say, wages of $5.00 per hour.

The subsidization schedule would have to be designed to provide incentive for workers to move on to higher paying jobs. The subsidy also would have to be phased out at some reasonable level of wages to keep the costs of the plan down.

An obvious advantage of WRS is that it directly increases wages and encourages low-income people to seek and find work. It also encourages employers to hire low-income workers, assuming that wages under the plan would be below those that would prevail under minimum-wage laws.

The Earned Income Tax Credit

The Earned Income Tax Credit (EITC) has emerged in the United States as a form of wage subsidy that is a major means of income support for the working poor. The EITC has only minimal status tests. The EITC is available *only* to those who work.

The EITC is actually part of the Federal Income Tax code. It was first introduced in 1975 as a modest program to stimulate consumption when the United States was in recession. The program provides a *negative tax payment* (actually a transfer of income) to low-income earners. Notice that this is not a tax refund—it is a payment from the federal government to workers who file income tax returns. People eligible for the EITC file a regular income tax return but instead of paying taxes or receiving a full or partial refund on taxes already paid, they actually get a payment from the federal government! The EITC works to reduce some of the work disincentive effects of the tax system on welfare recipients who take a job, and it also reduces the burden of Social Security taxes that all workers must pay when they have earnings.

The EITC was expanded as an income support program for the working poor in 1979 and 1986. Legislation enacted in 1990 raised the maximum credit to $1,998 per year in 1994 and simplified eligibility for the EITC. The amount a household can receive under the EITC is dependent on its income, the number of children in the household, payments the family makes for health insurance, whether a new child was born during the year, and whether the family receives other tax benefits. The benefits under the program are phased out as a family's income rises over a certain threshold amount, like the NIT plan discussed in the preceding sections. Several states, including New York, Maryland, Massachusetts, and Wisconsin, have their own EITC programs that supplement the federal EITC.

The EITC was greatly expanded as a result of legislation enacted in 1993.[6] In 2011, for a family with two children, the maximum credit was $5,112. This amount is indexed for inflation to keep the real amount constant in future years. In 2011, the maximum payment was paid to a single-parent family with two children beginning at $12,750 annual earned income until income reached $16,650 annually. After income increases greater than $16,650 per year, the tax credit is reduced for each extra dollar of income (see Table 7.5). The break-even level of income under the EITC for a single-parent family with two children was $41,000 in 2011.

The EITC was estimated to benefit more than 26 million families in 2011. It typically can increase the money income of a family with one earner working full time at the minimum wage to a level above the poverty threshold. Prior to 1993, only workers with children were eligible for credits. Now single workers are also

---

[6]For analysis of the changes, see Alicia H. Munnell, "The Coming of Age of the Earned Income Tax Credit," National Tax Association, *NTA Forum* (Winter 1994).

TABLE 7.5	The EITC: Single-Parent, Two-Child Family in 2011
TOTAL EARNED INCOME	**EITC**
$ 0	$ 0
2,000	810
4,000	1,610
6,000	2,410
8,000	3,210
11,000	4,410
15,000	5,112
20,000	4,410
30,000	2,304
41,000	0

Source: Internal Revenue Service.

eligible for the EITC. However, payments to single workers are limited to a portion of the workers' Social Security tax up to a maximum of $464 in 2011.

The changes in the EITC represent an increase in the cash support for the poor and an increased federal commitment to support the working poor. Payments under the EITC are entirely the responsibility of the federal government, although as pointed out above, several states have their own programs.

EITC versus NIT

A common criticism against the NIT was that it would discourage work effort. The EITC is more favorable to work effort than the NIT because it is available only to those who work. In that sense, it is more like a wage rate subsidy than an NIT. In effect, the EITC turns an $8 per hour wage into an $11.20 hourly wage (a 40 percent increase) for workers eligible for the full credit. The EITC can also be viewed as a substitute for an increase in the minimum wage. Also, because the credits are a percentage of income earned, tax rates at low levels of income are actually negative, which encourages recipients to work more. For the program, the tax rate is as much as *minus* 40 percent of earnings for a two-child family.

The EITC differs from the NIT plans already discussed in that the basic income guarantee is a percent of earnings and increases as earnings increase until it reaches the maximum amount allowed. Also, the negative tax rate for phasing out benefits is only slightly more than 20 percent. This low tax rate is much more conducive to encouraging work than is the case for a system with a 50 percent negative tax rate. However, the break-even level of income is much higher, which adds to the cost of the plan. Under existing legislation, all two-child families with income less than $41,000 or $46,000 (2011 dollars—these amounts are adjusted each year for inflation), depending on marital status, per year receive EITC *payments* from the federal government rather than paying federal personal income taxes! Families still pay the payroll tax and any applicable state income tax. Also, recipients with incomes greater than $20,000 per year are subject to both payroll and income taxes that increase the effective taxes they pay on additional earnings to as much as 50 percent.

When combined with other programs, such as SNAP and Medicaid, which in effect provide an income guarantee for those with zero income who are eligible for these programs, the EITC represents a way of increasing support for the poor in the United States while increasing their incentive to work.

Of course, the EITC does not exempt the working poor from all taxes. Working poor still must pay the employee share of the payroll tax that supports Social Security and Medicare in the United States and could be subject to state income taxes. However, for low-income childless workers, the EITC amounts to a refund of much of the employee share of the federal payroll tax. The EITC for low-income workers with children, in most cases, more than offsets their share of the federal payroll tax.

Figure 7.11 shows how the EITC varied with taxpayer (or adjusted gross income) for childless families, families with one child, and families with two or more children in 2011.

CHECKPOINT

1. What is the income effect of a transfer on incentives to work?
2. How does the TANF program diminish the work disincentive of cash transfers in the United States?
3. How would an NIT program with no status test differ from the current U.S. system of public assistance to the poor? What is the advantage of a WRS plan to assist the poor? How does the EITC benefit low-income workers?

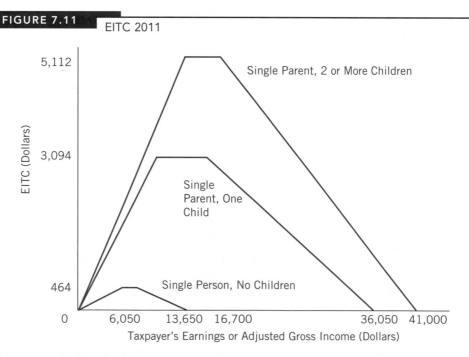

FIGURE 7.11   EITC 2011

Source: Internal Revenue Service.

TANF, WORK, AND PUBLIC ASSISTANCE: WELFARE REFORM IN THE UNITED STATES

The *Personal Responsibility and Work Opportunity Act of 1996* was a fundamental change in the system of income support to the poor in the United States that *requires* most welfare recipients to work. Under the TANF, cash assistance can only be a temporary source of income to most low-income recipients who meet status and means tests. Further, each state government is now required to set up plans to assist recipients who receive funds under the TANF program in developing work skills and finding work. The law also provides federal funds in the form of a grant to state governments to subsidize child care expenses for families on welfare, families leaving welfare, and low-income families. The function of welfare as a safety net for families experiencing temporary financial problems is preserved while reducing long-term dependency on means-tested government transfer programs. Here are the provisions of TANF designed to achieve these objectives:

1. Means-tested cash transfers are limited to five years to any family over their lifetime. However, states may exempt up to 20 percent of their caseload for families in which work is difficult or impossible because of disabilities and other problems. *All able-bodied recipients of welfare payments who have been on welfare for two years must participate in some activity designed to help them become self-supporting.* Federal standards now require states to have one-half of their welfare recipients in work programs for 30 hours per week. States can set up even stricter programs and will be penalized by the federal government if they do not get a set percentage of their welfare recipients to work.

2. To enable heads of families with dependent children to work, each state receives a grant to subsidize child care services to the poor.

3. To reduce future caseloads and the number of welfare recipients, TANF includes policies to reduce the number of nonmarital births. Teen mothers are required to live at home with a responsible adult and attend school. Those unmarried mothers who do not help establish paternity for their children have their cash benefits reduced by 25 percent. Funds are also provided to help states enforce child support laws.

4. A parent with a child over the age of five who refuses an offer of work approved by social service caseworkers will lose benefits. Some states may put children of nonworking parents in foster homes. Only adults with children under one year old—about 15 percent of recipients—are exempt from the work requirement. Legal immigrants who arrived in the United States after August 1996 are denied access to TANF for a period of five years.

Each state has the responsibility of implementing these laws. In general, states have developed programs to provide training, child care, health care, transportation, and wage rate subsidies, and are putting some of their block grant funds into contingency funds to provide additional support for the poor during periods of economic downturns.

TANF has increased the supply of unskilled labor in the marketplace. In growing areas where jobs are plentiful, the increased supply is likely to be easily accommodated. However, in areas experiencing declines in growth, unemployment among those who have exhausted their five-year supply of benefits could be a problem. These individuals and their families would have no source of income unless they received private charity or the state developed some contingency plans to support them during recessions. Lower wages could result in more payments through the EITC program.

Because of the way TANF benefits are structured only about 30 percent (based on fiscal year 2007 data) of each dollar spent goes to cash assistance. Except for 8 percent administrative cost the bulk of each dollar spent (more than 60 percent) provides services to recipients in the form of child care, work support, training, transportation, and other services designed to help recipients support themselves financially.

The Impact of Welfare Reform in the United States: TANF, Declining Caseloads, and Increased Labor Force Participation of the Poor

Since the introduction of TANF, welfare caseloads in the United States have declined. The labor force participation among less-skilled single mothers has increased more than expected.[7] State programs have focused on providing job preparation skills (interviewing skills, getting along on the job, getting child care, and assistance with searching for a job) to those enrolled in TANF. Relatively small amounts are actually spent on training for specific jobs. State governments have greatly increased their spending for work support including child care subsidies and transportation subsidies. States also assist those enrolled in TANF with job search expenses and, in some cases, subsidize wages.

Prior to 1996, it was typical for state governments to spend 70 percent of their welfare budgets on cash assistance to the poor. By 2000, a study of six states showed that 38 percent of state assistance of the poor was going to child care subsidies, whereas direct cash assistance had fallen to less than one-third of state assistance to the poor.[8] There has been a substantial and rapid decline in welfare caseloads throughout the United States since 1996. Former recipients are being weaned off public assistance and are staying off. Labor force participation rates of single mothers with children increased by 10 percentage points between 1994 and 1999. The increased labor force participation rates have not only increased earnings but have also increased labor force experience, which over time leads to increased worker productivity and higher wages.

Poverty rates through 2001, particularly for families headed by single mothers, declined more quickly than poverty rates on average. Most research on the impact of TANF indicates that the new program explains a significant portion of the decline in caseloads although other factors, including the strong growth in jobs in the booming U.S. economy from 1996 through 2000, also were important factors in explaining declining caseloads. In addition, there is general agreement that the EITC, which is basically a WRS to low-income workers, also helped increase labor force participation and decrease caseloads particularly for single parents. One estimate is that welfare reform increased labor supply among less-skilled women in the

---

[7]For a thorough review of the impact of welfare reform in the United States, see Rebecca M. Blank, "Evaluating Welfare Reform in the United States," *Journal of Economic Literature* XL, 4 (December 2002): 1105–1166.

[8]See *Economic Report of the President*, 2002. (Washington, D.C.: U.S. Government Printing Office, 2002): 202–206.

United States by more than 1 million workers between 1996 and 2002. Although this labor supply effect put downward pressure on market wages, it was offset by increased demand for labor over the same period and, as a result, there was no significant decline in market equilibrium wages paid to less-skilled workers.[9]

The increased expenditures on work support for the poor, particularly child care, have made a substantial impact on labor supply and work among single parents. The increase in labor supply by single parents has been substantial since 1996 and exceeded increases in labor supply among married women and less-skilled men in the labor force. TANF has also apparently been successful in reducing poverty rates among less-skilled and disadvantaged women.[10]

The reforms in the United States have influenced other nations. Some communities in Germany are now imposing time limits on public assistance. Canada has given local governments greater control over social assistance programs and has experimented with programs designed to move women from dependence on welfare to work in the labor market. In the United Kingdom, a program similar to the U.S. EITC is now in place.

The impact of the new welfare system on work is actually part of a long-term trend. There has been a steady shift away from means-tested and status-tested grants to the poor toward support for the working poor. This has diminished the income and substitution effects unfavorable to work inherent in grant programs with phase-outs that subject the poor to high effective tax rates that discourage work. The new programs have provided strong incentives to work, particularly in single-parent families.[11] The decline in families on welfare began in 1993 and by 1998 the number of families receiving welfare payments through either AFDC or TANF had declined by 50 percent. There is good reason to believe that the declines in welfare rolls are due primarily to changes in incentives for the poor to work. The expansion of the EITC for families encourages work. New rules introduced in the 1990s also prohibit states from removing children from the Medicaid rolls if they are in families with income below the poverty level. This means that a poor single mother does not risk losing health insurance for her children if she works.

Although it is difficult to accurately assess the reasons for the decline in welfare cases, one expert has estimated that 50 percent of the decline is a result of the new welfare law. Another 30 percent of the decline can be attributed to the EITC and other programs that support workers. Finally, 20 percent was due to a strong economy.[12]

Overall, the new system has been effective in reducing poverty rates. The shift from means-tested cash transfers to work support has reduced poverty rates of single-parent families from 51 percent to 44 percent.[13] From 1997 to 2000 welfare rolls have been lower than anticipated and most states received more under TANF from the federal government than they would have under the old entitlement programs. In many states, including Connecticut, Texas, and Minnesota, federal grant money has been used to replace state funds for existing antipoverty programs, thus

---

[9]See Timothy J. Bartik, "Displacement and Wage Effects of Welfare Reform," in *Finding Jobs: Work and Welfare Reform*, eds. David Card and Rebecca M. Blank (New York: Russell Sage, 2000): 119–158.

[10]See Blank, op. cit., p. 1144.

[11]See David T. Ellwood, "Anti-Poverty Policy for Families in the Next Century: From Welfare to Work and Worries," *Journal of Economic Perspectives* 14, 1 (Winter 2000): 187–198.

[12]See Ellwood, p. 192.

[13]*Ibid.*, p. 195.

freeing up money in the state budgets for either tax cuts or funding of other pro-grams. The shift away from means-tested cash support for the poor leaves many unprotected by a safety net if unemployment rates soar and job opportunities for the unskilled dry up. Although unemployment insurance could provide some sup-port to the poor in a recession, the current system replaces only a small fraction of wages and is unlikely to keep the unemployed poor from being mired in poverty if their jobs evaporate.

The program's attempt to reduce out-of-wedlock births has not been especially successful. Only 12 states showed miniscule reductions since 1996. As of 2012 about 40 percent of the births in the United States are to unwed mothers.

Recessions and TANF

TANF was introduced during a period of almost unprecedented prosperity in the United States. A booming job market and tight labor markets in many large cities made it relatively easy to find jobs for those on the new temporary assistance pro-gram. A major concern with the reformed welfare program was how well it would hold up under the pressure of the rising unemployment rates that accompany a recession. When the first recession of the new millennium began in March 2001, the reformed welfare program met its first test.

Despite the recession, the number of people enrolled in welfare programs in many large cities actually fell in 2002. For example, in New York City, which has the most enrolled in welfare programs of all cities in the United States, the number of people receiving aid under public assistance actually decreased by 10 percent during the first nine months of 2002. Some have argued that many of the poor have merely fallen through the safety net and are looking for other sorts of aid from private charity. However, it is more likely that many of the single mothers who have found jobs under TANF are in occupations that were relatively un-affected by the recession. Single mothers have found jobs in such industries as edu-cation, health care, and social services. These service occupations expanded, rather than contracted, during the downturn of 2001 and the slow recovery in 2002. And jobs in these areas are increasing. In other cities, many single mothers who found work under TANF were employed in travel-related industries such as hotels and restaurants. These industries were hard hit during the recession, and welfare rolls in states such as California have increased.[14]

There were, however, some concerns that the situation could change unless the sluggish recovery from the recession picked up. By mid-2002 there was an increase in monthly applications for public assistance in New York City.

Between 2002 and 2004 federal welfare rolls continued to decline. In general, it appears as though more people actively seek work under the TANF system rather than applying for welfare assistance. The pool of previous welfare recipients have now learned job skills and are a more stable portion of the labor force. This group appears to have acquired the ability to maintain employment. Between 2001 and 2004 federal welfare rolls declined by about 45 percent. However, over the same period the number of households receiving food stamps increased by about 35 percent. Given the choice of work or applying for public assistance through TANF, it is clear that more people now find work to be the more attractive alternative.

---

[14]See Leslie Kaufman, "Economy Dips While Welfare Drop in Cities," *The New York Times*, August 31, 2002.

The major recession that began in late 2007 provided new challenges to TANF and other programs that provide a safety net of assistance to needy families. A report by the U.S. Department of Health and Human Services expresses some concern about the effectiveness of TANF in actually getting support to the poor. In 2005 only 40 percent of those who can meet the means test for benefits actually received assistance. Many of those who are not receiving benefits they or their families qualify for are children. Following the pattern from 2002 to 2004, TANF caseloads continued to decline during the period 2005 to 2008 despite the onset of a major recession. During the first six months of 2008 these caseloads declined in all states except California, Delaware, Florida, New Mexico, South Carolina, Washington, and West Virginia. During the same period caseloads under the Supplemental Nutrition Assistance Program increased significantly.

From mid-2008 to the end of 2010 cash assistance under TANF increased by about 16 percent. However, the number of families receiving such cash assistance by late 2010 was only 1.9 million compared to 5.1 million in March of 1994. In the aftermath of the recession of 2007–2009, TANF was playing a much smaller role in lifting families out of poverty than the pre-1996 welfare system in the United States. During this last recession and the slow recovery that followed, a greater share of income support was coming from Unemployment Insurance, SNAP, and Medicaid than has been the case for past recessions and their aftermaths.

PROGRAMS TO AID THE POOR AND THE DISTRIBUTION OF MONEY INCOME IN THE UNITED STATES

How effective have U.S. transfers to the poor been in changing the distribution of income in the United States? Table 7.6 shows the distribution of annual money income before taxes for selected years from 1947 to 2010. The money income of each one-fifth of households includes cash transfers. The table provides some indication of the degree of inequality in the distribution of money income among these households. If the distribution of income were perfectly equal, each one-fifth of households would receive one-fifth, or 20 percent, of total aggregate annual money income. The data in the table indicate significant inequality of income in the United States.

The 1970s were marked by a sharp increase in the importance of transfers and aid to the poor, as associated with President Johnson's "war on poverty." The data, however, seem to indicate that during the 1970s, these programs had little impact on the actual distribution of money income. These data do not include the impact of the many income in-kind transfers for which the poor are eligible. Adjustment can be made for in-kind transfers. If assumed that each dollar's worth of in-kind benefits is worth a dollar to the recipient, inclusion of in-kind transfers would increase the share of income of the lowest group. This indicates that in-kind transfers have reduced income inequality. Despite the sharp increases in spending to aid the poor, their income shares have fallen since 1967, whereas income shares of the rich (the highest fifth) have increased. One explanation for this could be that the growth in transfers has been accompanied by an increase in the number of poor people.

TABLE 7.6		Percent Share of Aggregate Money Income of Each One-Fifth of Households, Including Cash Transfers, Selected Years, 1947–2010			
YEAR	LOWEST FIFTH	SECOND FIFTH	THIRD FIFTH	FOURTH FIFTH	HIGHEST FIFTH
1947	5.0	11.9	17.0	23.1	43.0
1967	4.0	11.1	17.6	24.6	42.7
1969	4.1	11.0	17.5	24.5	42.8
1971	4.1	10.7	17.3	24.5	43.4
1973	4.3	10.6	17.2	24.4	43.5
1974	4.4	10.6	17.0	24.5	43.5
1976	4.3	10.4	17.0	24.7	43.6
1978	4.3	10.3	16.9	24.8	43.7
1983	4.1	10.0	16.5	24.7	44.7
1987	3.8	9.6	16.1	23.3	46.7
1989	3.8	9.5	15.8	24.0	46.8
1991	3.8	9.6	15.9	24.2	46.5
1995	3.7	9.1	15.2	23.3	48.7
1996	3.7	9.0	15.1	23.3	49.0
1997	3.6	8.9	15.0	22.2	49.4
1998	3.6	9.0	15.0	23.2	49.2
2001	3.5	8.7	14.6	23.0	50.1
2005	3.4	8.6	14.6	23.0	50.4
2007	3.4	8.7	14.8	23.4	49.7
2010	3.3	8.5	14.6	23.4	50.2

Source: U.S. Department of Commerce, Bureau of the Census, Money Income of Households in the United States, Current Population Reports, Series P-60, various years.

Interpreting Data on Income Inequality: Some Pitfalls

It is quite difficult to interpret the data on income distribution in Table 7.6. Part of the problem of interpretation stems from the fact that the income data are for households rather than for individuals. For example, over time in the United States the number of households with two earners has increased. If there is a greater tendency for upper-income households to have more than one earner, then any increased share of income going to them overstates their individual gains relative to lower-income households.

For example, between 1979 and 1993, the average real family income of the richest fifth of families increased by 18 percent, whereas the poorest fifth of families suffered a 15 percent decline in income. Much of the decline in income in the lowest fifth could be accounted for by an increase in the proportion of female-headed families. Female-headed families typically earn less than male-headed families. If *all* families experienced increased income in the lowest fifth but the proportion of families headed by females increased, then the share going to this fifth could decline even if all families in the lowest fifth had higher incomes.

Similarly, it is possible that the income shares going to the upper fifth can increase even if individual incomes do not grow within this fifth if more upper-income people marry other upper-income people. For example, suppose two mid-level managers each earn $50,000 per year and would normally fall in the fourth fifth of families if they were single. If they marry each other, then their household income doubles to $100,000 even though their individual earnings have not increased. Therefore, they will be in the highest fifth of families, thereby increasing the share going to that group.

There are other problems involved in interpreting the raw income distribution data in Table 7.6. Besides not including the value of in-kind transfers to the poor in their income, the numbers are based on before-tax incomes. If the rich tend to pay higher percentages of their income in taxes than the poor, the degree of inequality shown in the table is likely to be less if it were based on after-tax income instead. In particular, the Earned Income Tax Credit, which can add more than $4,000 per year to the income of qualifying families, is not included in the cash income of the lowest income groups when calculating their income shares.

Differences in income shares can be the result of differences in work effort. This is particularly true for middle- and upper-income households in which both spouses work. If those in the middle- and upper-income groups simply choose to work more, this will increase their income shares while some people in the lower income quintiles might be there because they choose to work fewer hours (possibly to spend time at home taking care of children). For single-parent households the option of a two-person income does not exist unless older children have earnings.

Also, lower income groups are more likely to consume more than their income by borrowing or receiving support from other family members not in their households. If data for grouping households into quintiles were based on consumption instead of income, it is likely that it would show less inequality. For example, suppose two medical students married to each other show up as a low-income family in the first or second quintile based on their incomes. If, however, they have borrowed heavily to finance their education and are receiving financial aid from their parents, then their consumption might be much higher than their income and their living standard higher than would be suggested by their reported income. There is some evidence that low-income households on average somehow manage to consume dollar amounts of goods and services nearly twice their income as a result of borrowing, public or family assistance. However, upper-income households tend to save and this means that their consumption is less than their income.

Finally, it is not always the same people in each quintile. There is considerable mobility from year to year. Someone who is poor one year might enjoy income increases in later years thereby moving up into a higher income quintile. Some studies have shown that this mobility is significant with as much as two-thirds of the people in the lowest quintile moving up to a higher quintile within 15 years. Also, sometime upper income people fall into hard times and move from a higher to a lower quintile.[15]

---

[15]For a review of studies on income distribution data, see Edgar K. Browning, *Stealing from Each Other*, Westport Connecticut: Praeger, 2008. Chapter 2 provides a comprehensive analysis of possible flaws in data on income distribution in the United States.

To better understand what is happening to income distribution, it would be more useful to look at how earnings and other sources of income vary among people of similar characteristics (for example, 18- to 24-year-old males with only a high school education) and other distinct groups (such as retirees) and how the proportion of people with differing characteristics changes over time.

Further, remember that incentives to earn income are part of the engine that drives economic growth. We can't necessarily conclude that a higher share of income going to the rich is bad if the alternative is to tax it away and reduce the incentive to work and invest, which decreases economic growth and opportunities for all, including the lower-income groups of society.

SUMMARY

Many government subsidies benefit low-income people. Eligibility for these subsidies is determined by a status test and a means test. The status test determines whether a person belongs to one of the demographic groups eligible for government assistance. The means test determines whether the person's income and wealth are low enough to be eligible for government assistance.

In the United States, both in-kind and cash subsidies are used to assist the poor. In-kind subsidies include transfers in the form of food, medical services, and housing to the poor. They account for about two-thirds of federal assistance to the poor in the United States. In-kind subsidies can result in an excess burden that results from inefficient resource use. In most cases, in-kind subsidies free enough cash for other uses by recipients that they can be regarded as equivalent to cash transfers.

Most transfers reduce the incentive to work. In evaluating transfer programs, voters must weigh the desire to obtain changes in the distribution of income against the decreases in efficiency and work incentive resulting from the subsidy programs.

LOOKING AHEAD

Chapter 8 looks at social insurance programs. These programs transfer income to people who need not pass a means test. The major social insurance program in the United States is the Social Security pension system, and its functions are closely analyzed.

KEY CONCEPTS

Deadweight Loss

Earned Income Tax Credit (EITC)

Entitlement Programs

Excess Burden of the Subsidy

Fixed Allotment Subsidies

In-kind Benefits

Means Test

Medicaid

Negative Income Tax (NIT)

Poverty Threshold

Price-Distorting Subsidies

Status Test

Supplemental Nutrition Assistance Program

Supplemental Security Income (SSI)

Temporary Assistance to Needy Families (TANF)

Wage Rate Subsidies (WRS)

REVIEW QUESTIONS

1. List the major programs of government assistance to the poor in the United States. What percentage of the population is poor? Do all the poor qualify for government assistance programs?

2. What is a means test? How does it differ from a status test? What are entitlement programs, and how are the expenditures under these programs related to means tests and status tests?

3. Suppose the government gave away heating oil free to eligible low-income citizens. Use a graphic analysis to show the excess burden in the market for this good. Under what circumstances will the subsidy cause the market price of fuel oil to increase?

4. What are the possible collective benefits of government assistance to the poor? Why are in-kind benefits to the poor more prevalent than cash benefits?

5. Explain why in many cases in-kind transfers to the poor are likely to be equivalent to cash transfers in their effects.

6. Suppose a person receives a grant from the government that allows the purchase of $300 worth of clothes per year. This grant cannot be used to buy any other items. Show how this grant affects the person's budget line. Show the various market baskets of goods that could be purchased with a $300 cash grant and that *cannot* be purchased with the grant.

7. Explain how cash and in-kind transfer programs can reduce the incentive to work by recipients.

8. Suppose a person will receive $50 per day as a transfer if he does not work at all. This transfer is reduced by 60 cents for each $1 of earned income. How much daily earned income will reduce the transfer to zero?

9. Has poverty in the United States been eliminated as a result of transfers to the poor? What are some of the problems involved in measuring poverty?

10. Explain why the negative income tax plan is likely to be more expensive than the current system of assistance to the poor. What are the advantages of wage rate subsidies?

PROBLEMS

1. Suppose bread is subsidized in a small Caribbean nation with a high percentage of citizens who live in poverty. The subsidy is paid to suppliers of bread by the government in the amount of 50 pesos per loaf. In the absence of the subsidy, the price of bread would be 100 pesos per loaf. Assuming that the supply of bread is perfectly elastic at the 100 peso price, show the effect of the subsidy on the market equilibrium price of bread. Assuming no externalities, show that the subsidy will result in more than the efficient amount of bread being produced. Show the excess burden of the subsidy on your graph. Explain why the subsidy will provide benefits to the nonpoor as well as the poor.

2. Suppose low-income people are given vouchers worth $200 per month that they can use only to pay rent on housing. Use indifference curve analysis to show how the person could be made as well off with a $200 cash transfer. Would the consumer's choice of the amount of housing to rent be any different if he receives cash instead of housing vouchers? Use indifference curve analysis to show under what circumstance the $200 per month housing vouchers would cause the recipient to increase the amount of housing rented (measured in square feet) compared to what would be rented if the recipient received $200 in cash each month in lieu of the housing vouchers. Would this recipient be as well off under the housing voucher scheme as he would be with a cash transfer of equal value?

3. A needy family consisting of a mother and three children currently receives cash benefits that average $12 per day. The mother of this family is allowed to earn an average of $4 per day before her benefits begin to decline. After that, for each dollar earned, cash benefits decline by 67 cents. Plot the recipient's money income–leisure tradeoff (budget) line under these circumstances. Assume that she can find work at $4 per hour. How many hours will she have to work per day before her benefits are eliminated? Assuming that her indifference curves for work and leisure are convex, show her equilibrium allocation of time between work and leisure per day. Show that it is possible to have *more* than one most-preferred outcome.

4. A proposal for a negative income tax is designed to provide an income guarantee for each person, irrespective of his or her age or status, of $3,000 per year. Thus, a family of four would have an income guarantee of $12,000 per year. The transfers under the program will be phased out at a rate of 25 percent as earned income increases. Calculate the break-even level of income for a family of four. If all families above the break-even level of income pay a flat-rate 25 percent tax on their earnings, plot disposable income as a function of earned income. Comment on the costs of this plan.

5. Get the directions for the Federal Income Tax or go to http://www.irs.gov to obtain the tables for the EITC for the current year. Explain how the program increases earnings for low-income workers and affects their incentives. Draw a curve for single workers, married workers filing jointly, and single parents showing how the EITC will vary with earnings. Why does the EITC encourage low-income workers to work? Use indifference curve analysis

to show the income and substitution effects resulting from the EITC up to the point at which the maximum credit level of earnings is reached. How does the EITC phaseout affect tax rates paid for workers after they go past the level of earnings that pays the maximum credit under the EITC?

ADDITIONAL READINGS

Blank, Rebecca M. "Distinguished Lecture on Economics in Government—Fighting Poverty: Lessons from Recent U.S. History." *Journal of Economic Perspectives* 14, 2, (Spring 2000): 3–19. A useful review of antipoverty policy and its effects in the United States.

Blank, Rebecca M. "Evaluating Welfare Reform in the United States." *Journal of Economic Literature XL*, 4 (December 2002): 1105–1166. A comprehensive review of research on the impact of welfare reform in the United States.

Browning, Edgar K. *Stealing from Each Other*, Westport, Conn.: Praeger, 2008. A critique of programs that redistribute income in the United States along with analysis of data on income distribution, the methodology of measuring income distribution, and the impact of transfer programs on incentives.

Burtless, Gary. "The Economist's Lament: Public Assistance in America." *Journal of Economic Perspectives* 4, 1 (Winter 1990). An excellent review of how cash transfer programs to aid the poor have worked in the United States and an analysis of their economic effects.

Ellwood, David T. "Anti-Poverty Policy for Families in the Next Century: From Welfare to Work and Worries." *Journal of Economic Perspectives* 14, 1 (Winter 2000): 187–198. A discussion and analysis of the major shift in U.S. welfare policy away from means-tested grants toward work subsidies.

Moffitt, Robert A. "Incentive Effects of the U.S. Welfare System: A Review." *Journal of Economic Literature* 30, 1 (March 1992): 1–61. A review of economic analysis of the effects of the U.S. system of support to the poor on their incentives to work and engage in other economic activities.

Weil, Alan and Finegold, Kenneth, eds. *Welfare Reform: The Next Act*. Washington, D.C.: Urban Institute Press, 2002. A comprehensive examination of the changes in the system of support for the poor resulting from the welfare reform legislation of 1996. The effects of the new system on family structure, children, work incentive, and immigrants are analyzed.

INTERNET RESOURCES

http://www.house.gov

This is the home page of the U.S. House of Representatives. Click on Committees. A wealth of information on government spending programs can be obtained by accessing the Overview of Entitlement Programs also known as the "Green Book" of the Ways and Means Committee. This book can be searched to obtain details on all federal transfer and entitlement programs. Other useful committees to access include Appropriations and Budget.

http://www.census.gov

The Census Bureau's home page includes a search engine that allows you to access information on the population of the United States and its characteristics, including income levels and income distribution, poverty rates, and other information.

http://www.dhhs.gov

The home page of the U.S. Department of Health and Human Services has information on welfare programs and on the Medicaid program.

http://www.irp.wisc.edu

This is the home page for the Institute for Research on Poverty of the University of Wisconsin. You can use it to browse for issues related to welfare reform and the status of the poor in the United States.

Chapter 8

SOCIAL SECURITY AND SOCIAL INSURANCE

LEARNING OBJECTIVES

After reading this chapter, you should be able to:

- Discuss the Social Security system and how it is financed by payroll taxes in the United States.

- Explain how the Social Security retirement system differs from private pension systems and how Social Security retirement benefits are computed.

- Describe the concepts of gross and net replacement rates for retirees and how these rates vary for Social Security pensions with preretirement earnings and other factors.

- Examine the intergenerational aspects of the Social Security system and how changing demographic factors, Social Security tax rates, and changes in gross replacement rates influence the effective return on taxes paid into the system by retirees.

- Analyze the impact of the Social Security system on work incentives and labor force participation of the elderly.

- Estimate the possible impact of the Social Security system on savings rates in the United States.

- Discuss the Medicare system of health insurance for the elderly and unemployment insurance in the United States.

As of January 2012, there were 53 million beneficiaries receiving Social Security pensions. Of this total 37 million were retired workers. The 16 million who were not retired workers received such benefits either because they were disabled workers or they were dependents or survivors of eligible pension recipients. Nearly 70 percent of Social Security pension recipients are therefore retired workers. The amount spent for such pensions will grow rapidly as the fraction of the population eligible for pensions increases. The elderly (65 and older) accounted for 11 percent of the U.S. population in 1980, and are forecasted to account for about 21 percent of the U.S. population by 2050. As the number of retirees increases relative to the total population, the Social Security system will have greater demands placed on it to support a larger number of elderly persons who, thanks in part to improved health care, will live longer. The social insurance system of the United States and other economically developed nations will be challenged by the aging populations. As the proportion of the population over the age of 65 increases, and the ratio of tax-paying workers to retirees declines, either tax rates will have to increase or benefits to recipients will have to decline to avoid ruinous government budget deficits later in the 21st century. We will look at these challenges to social insurance and Social Security in this chapter and consider some alternatives for reforming existing systems.

Social Security pensions accounted for about 16 percent of expenditures by the federal government in the United States in 2011. Social Security pensions absorbed 4.5 percent of gross domestic product (GDP) in 2008 and are expected to absorb more than 6.2 percent of GDP by 2035. The Social Security Act of 1935 remains one of the most significant and enduring mandates for government activity in the United States. Originally proposed by President Franklin D. Roosevelt as part of his New Deal, the act provided, for the first time in the United States, a system of compulsory taxation to finance pensions to the aged and the disabled and their survivors, and unemployment benefits to workers (in most occupations) who, laid off from their jobs, are temporarily out of work. The system is designed to ensure adequate income security to individuals during periods of unemployment, in the event of disability, and in old age. The pension system is financed through a tax on payrolls, up to a certain limit for each worker's annual wages. The tax is split between the workers and the employers. The proceeds of the payroll tax are earmarked to finance pensions for the aged. An additional payroll tax finances health insurance for people older than 65, and a tax paid only by employers finances unemployment insurance benefits.

Social insurance and Social Security programs provide income and health benefits financed by taxes to eligible individuals. Compared to major European countries, the United States was relatively tardy in passing social insurance legislation. The first Social Security legislation was enacted in Germany in 1889. Similar plans were established in the United Kingdom in 1908, France in 1910, Sweden in 1913, and Italy in 1919. Social insurance in the United States is still not as comprehensive as it is in some other countries. More than 170 countries have some form of social security system today, many of them providing sickness and maternity benefits (national health insurance) and family allowances (subsidies for child expenses, most often payable to families with two or more children). The first national health insurance system was established in 1912 by the United Kingdom.

Social Security pensions have had a profound effect on the well-being of the elderly in the United States. The average age at which Americans retire from working has fallen sharply since 1965. The average real income of the elderly increased relative to the rest of the population. On average, the elderly are less likely to be poor than the rest of the population. Research on the economic status of the elderly in the United States suggests that they are at least as well-off as the nonelderly and their living standards might, in fact, be much better than the nonelderly. Social Security, which accounts for an average of nearly 40 percent of the income of the elderly in the United States, has vastly improved the economic status of the aged.

This chapter shows how social insurance programs, particularly those that aid the elderly, operate in the United States. The economic effects of the benefit programs on incentives to work and save are highlighted.

SOCIAL SECURITY IN THE UNITED STATES

Social Security in the United States is a rubric that includes many programs benefiting diverse groups of citizens. In general, **social security and insurance programs** include government-provided pensions, disability payments, unemployment compensation, and health benefits. As pointed out in Chapter 7, many of the government assistance programs for the poor in this country are administered by the Social Security Administration. This chapter confines the discussion exclusively to social insurance and pension programs administered under the Social Security Act. This category of expense includes a multitude of other programs, such as railroad retirement, public employee retirement, disability insurance, and worker's compensation. However, the most important programs from the point of view of public policy are (1) old-age, survivors, and disability insurance (OASDI)—the system of government-supplied pensions; (2) Medicare (HI)—the system of health insurance for the elderly; and (3) unemployment insurance (UI). This chapter emphasizes government pension programs. Social Security pays pensions to retired workers, their spouses and dependent children, and to disabled workers. About 14 percent of pension recipients are disabled workers.

Eligibility for benefits payable under the Social Security system and other social insurance programs is usually contingent on paying a tax or having that tax paid on one's behalf by virtue of employment in a job for which coverage is required. In the United States today, self-employed individuals are required by law to pay Social Security taxes for the pension program (OASDI) and for Medicare (HI) and thereby are covered by the Social Security system. The taxes paid are in accordance with the provisions of the Federal Insurance Contribution Act (FICA), established to finance Social Security pensions, and are usually deducted from employee wages and salaries. In addition, employers pay the tax based on their payrolls. In 2012, the tax rate was 7.65 percent for workers and 7.65 percent for employers. The combined OASDI-HI rate was 15.3 percent and was levied on wages up to $110,100 per year per worker for OASDI. The maximum amount of wages per worker subject to the Social Security payroll taxes is adjusted for inflation each year. The HI tax (2.9 percent total) has no maximum earning limit.

To be eligible for benefits, a worker must have worked and paid the tax on a certain minimum amount of earnings. Forty quarters of coverage (10 years of covered work) qualifies a worker for Social Security retirement benefits. The monetary amount of the pension that a worker receives depends on previous earnings history, marital status, dependents, and the amount of time that Social Security taxes have been paid by the worker.

Unemployment insurance benefits are financed by a special tax on payrolls levied on employers alone. They are administered by state governments, and some variation in eligibility and benefits paid exists among the states. On average, however, the unemployment benefits equal about one third of the wages previously earned, up to a certain limit. Benefits are usually paid for a maximum period of 26 weeks; however, they can be extended automatically during a period of high unemployment. In periods of deep recession and other extraordinary circumstances, Congress can enact legislation that extends benefits for even longer periods. Benefits are available to all workers who, through no fault of their own, involuntarily lose their jobs and whose previous employers paid unemployment insurance taxes on the workers' behalf. No means test is required to be eligible for benefits.

Social insurance and Social Security pensions are transfer programs open to all workers regardless of their income. However, the way in which benefits are paid can affect the income distribution somewhat, because they are distributed according to the worker's wages. Low-income workers receive benefits that are higher proportions of their preretirement earnings than higher-income workers or workers for whom nonwage sources of income are relatively important. All workers in jobs covered by the Social Security system must pay the Social Security tax, as must their employers, regardless of their own personal circumstances or evaluation of the program's future benefits.

THE SOCIAL SECURITY RETIREMENT SYSTEM

Pay-as-You-Go versus Fully Funded Pension Systems

Government-supplied retirement benefits under Social Security are financed in a radically different manner than are the benefits under most private retirement systems. A **fully funded pension system** is one in which benefits are paid out of a fund built up from contributions by, or on behalf of, members in the retirement system. The dollar value of the fund must equal at least the discounted present value of pensions promised to members of the system in the future.

A member of a fully funded private pension system contributes monthly to the pension plan (or the employer contributes along with or instead of the employee). When the workers retire, they receive a pension based on the amount of contributions (a form of saving) plus the return earned (net of administration costs) on those contributions over the period of time the money was held (and invested) by the retirement system. This is called a defined-contribution pension plan, under which the worker (or the employer) contributes a certain amount per year and receives a pension based on the contributions, earnings of the pension fund, and the fund's payout experience. Defined-benefit plans promise the employee a certain pension. To be fully funded, these plans must collect contributions to finance a fund that will amass adequate earnings to pay the promised pensions. Administrators of fully funded retirement systems invest the funds of the pension system in various financial obligations, seeking to obtain reasonable rates of return on the fund while balancing the return earned with any risks associated with their investments.

The Social Security retirement system uses revenues collected from the payroll tax to provide pensions for the aged, the disabled, and their survivors eligible for benefits.[1] The **Old-Age, Survivors, and Disability Insurance (OASDI)** program is a

---

[1] Taxes collected from any portions of Social Security pensions subject to the federal income tax are also used to finance Social Security retirement benefits.

tax-financed pension system; retirement benefits are financed through taxes levied on the working population.

A **pay-as-you-go pension system** is one that finances pensions for retired workers in a given year entirely by contributions or taxes paid by currently employed workers. Because the bulk of payroll taxes collected to finance Social Security pensions in recent years has been used to pay pensions of currently retired workers, the Social Security system has been characterized as a pay-as-you-go retirement system. A special trust fund invests revenue in federal government securities. However, in the 1970s and early 1980s, the amount in this fund equaled less than two months of annual pension benefits. In recent years, the Social Security retirement system has been one that is financed by directly transferring taxes collected from those working to those who are retired. The Social Security pension system represents an implicit contract between workers and retirees. It is this "contract" that keeps the system functioning.

The Social Security trust fund is now growing because of increases in the payroll tax collections and other changes in the Social Security system made in 1977 and 1983. Without these changes, the Social Security system would have been unable to pay promised pensions benefits from payroll taxes. As the trust fund builds, some current workers will be contributing not only to finance the pensions of currently retired workers but also to fund their own future retirement benefits.

The Social Security trust fund is projected to increase until sometime in the first quarter of the 21st century. Thereafter, as the proportion of retirees in the population increases, revenues taken into the fund are projected to fall below outlays from the fund, and the trust fund will begin to decline. From now until the time the trust fund is depleted, the U.S. Social Security system will not be strictly on a pay-as-you-go basis. If it were to return to such a basis, payroll tax rates could be reduced from their scheduled levels until about the first quarter of the 21st century. However, these rates would be much higher later on in the 21st century if the system were to remain pay-as-you-go.

Currently, workers who are paying the payroll tax expect that future generations of workers also will be taxed in a similar way so that when they retire, they too will receive a pension under Social Security. In simple terms, the Social Security system pays benefits today only because of the government's ability to tax and because of the willingness of individuals to agree collectively to such taxes in exchange for the promise of future retirement benefits.[2]

How Retirement Benefits Are Computed under Social Security

In the year 2000, the age at which workers became eligible for full Social Security retirement benefits was increased from 65. The *full retirement age* (also called normal retirement age) is the age at which a worker is entitled to full (as opposed to reduced) Social Security retirement benefits. For workers retiring in 2009, the full retirement age was 66. The full retirement age will then remain at 66 for workers born between 1943 and 1954. Beginning with workers born in 1955 the full retirement age will start to increase by two months every year until it reaches 67 for workers born in 1960. If you were born in 1960 or later your full retirement age is therefore 67 under current law.

---

[2]To the extent to which a private pension system is not fully funded, it too might be forced to use pay-as-you-go means of finance or forgo paying full promised benefits to retirees. For a general discussion of private pensions and their problems, see Bruno Stein, *Social Security and Pensions in Transition* (The Free Press: New York 1980). Also see Dan M. McGill, Kyle N. Brown, John J. Haley, and Sylvester J. Schieber, *Fundamentals of Private Pensions*, 8th edition. (Oxford University Press: USA, 2005).

Workers can still retire at age 62—the increase in the full retirement age has not reduced the minimum retirement age. Workers can still choose to retire at any time between age 62 and their full retirement age. However, the benefit reduction at age 62 (or any age below full retirement age) will depend on the worker's full retirement age. For workers with a full retirement age of 66, the benefit reduction was 20 percent. Workers with a full retirement age of 67 will suffer a benefit reduction of 30 percent if they retire at age 62. Workers who choose to retire after their full retirement age get an increment in their Social Security pensions of 8 percent per year (up to age 70) over what they would receive if they retired and started collecting benefits at their full retirement age.

The initial monthly pension benefits that a particular worker receives upon retirement depend on a benefit formula used by the Social Security Administration. Such personal information as a person's earnings history and age is considered. The formula calculates an employee's **average indexed monthly earnings (AIME)**, which are based on the worker's average monthly earnings (on which payroll taxes are paid). The 35 years of highest actual earnings prior to retirement, adjusted for changes in average wage levels each year, are used in the formula. In effect, AIME is a measure of a worker's real average taxable monthly earnings, up to a certain maximum, over a lifetime in jobs covered by Social Security benefits. In calculating AIME, the worker's nominal earnings in each year are indexed to convert actual dollar earnings in the year to approximately current levels. The indexing factor for each year prior to age 60 is obtained by dividing the average wage index for the year the person attains age 60 by the average wage index for that year. For example, if a worker earned $5,000 in 1966, and the ratio of average wage index when he attained age 60 in 2004 was seven times the average wage index for earnings in 1966, his nominal earnings will be multiplied by 7 to give indexed earnings of $35,000. A similar calculation will be done for up to 35 years of highest actual earnings prior to retirement to adjust previous earnings prior to age 60 for changes in average wage levels. Then the highest 35 years of indexed earnings are averaged and the result is divided by 12 to obtain average indexed monthly earnings.

After AIME has been calculated, it is used in another formula to determine a worker's primary insurance amount (PIA). This represents the basic monthly pension for which a worker who is retiring at full retirement age is eligible. The formula for PIA changes from year to year and also depends on the year the worker reaches age 62. PIA gives the retirement benefit a worker would receive if he or she retires at full retirement age. PIA is adjusted downward if a worker retires before reaching full retirement age and adjusted upward if a worker retires after reaching full retirement age. A certain amount of AIME, called the first "bend point" is multiplied by 0.9; then as AIME rises above the first bend point, a second bend point is reached and the amount (if any) between the first and second bend point is multiplied by 0.32. If AIME exceeds the amount specified by the second bend point, then any excess over that amount is multiplied by 0.15. For example, suppose a worker reached age 60 in 2009 and his AIME was calculated to be $5,000. For 2009 the first bend point was $744 and the second bend point was $4,483. His PIA will be $0.9(744) + 0.32(4,483 − 744) + 0.15($5,000 − $4,483) = $1,943.60$. This will be his actual monthly pension if he were to retire at his full retirement age. The bend points change each year. Also once PIA is calculated, it is adjusted each year for changes in the cost of living. PIA is also adjusted if the retiree has a dependent spouse or other dependents.

The Social Security pension for which a person qualifies is considered an earned right. This means that it is paid regardless of the worker's wealth and nonlabor income. However, retired workers between 62 and full retirement age are subject to an **earnings test,** which reduces Social Security benefits by $1 for each $2 of earnings over a certain maximum amount of earnings that is adjusted each year when they retire before the year they reach their full retirement age. For example, the maximum earnings for these retirees amounted to $14,640 per year in 2012. This implies that if a worker earns enough wages in a given year, the Social Security pension benefit will become zero. Workers who retire during the year they reach their full retirement age were allowed to earn $38,880 in 2012 (this amount is adjusted for inflation each year) and their benefits are reduced by only $1 for every $3 earned over that amount if they retire before the month in which they reach their full retirement age. However, once a retiree reaches full retirement age, the earnings test is no longer applied and retirees do not have their pensions reduced no matter how much they earn.

Social Security benefits are also paid to a worker's family under certain circumstances. Dependent spouses who reach full retirement age are entitled to one-half a worker's basic monthly benefit. In addition, in most cases, widows and widowers receive the amount to which their spouse would have been entitled. Benefits are also paid to dependent children of retirees.

Workers who have 20 quarters of their past 40 quarters of earnings in a job covered by the Social Security system are eligible for disability pensions if they become severely disabled. These pensions are also available for disabled workers younger than 31 if they have worked a certain number of quarters after turning 21. These pensions require proof of disability and are paid after a five-month waiting period.

CHECKPOINT

1. How are Social Security pensions financed in the United States? Is Social Security a fully funded pension system?
2. How is eligibility for Social Security pensions determined?
3. What factors will influence a retiree's Social Security pension?

SOCIAL SECURITY REPLACEMENT RATES

Gross Replacement Rate

A useful measure of the standard of living allowable under Social Security retirement benefits compared with that enjoyed prior to retirement is the extent to which these benefits replace preretirement earnings. The **gross replacement rate (GRR)** is the worker's monthly retirement benefit divided by monthly earnings *in the year prior to retirement*:

$$\text{GRR} = \frac{\text{Monthly Retirement Benefit}}{\text{Monthly Labor Earnings in the Year Prior to Retirement}} \tag{8.1}$$

Table 8.1 shows 2012 gross replacement rates for four typical workers who retired at age 66 in January 2012 (the worker's full retirement age.

The average earner has had average earnings in relation to all retiring workers covered by Social Security pensions in the year of retirement. The high earner had

TABLE 8.1	Gross Replacement Rates under Social Security (Percentage for Workers Retiring at Full Retirement Age in January 2012)
WORKER STATUS	**GROSS REPLACEMENT RATE (GRR)**
Low Earner[a]	57.3
Average Earner	42.5
High Earner[b]	35.7
Maximum Earner[c]	28.6

[a]Earnings equal 45 percent of average earner.
[b]Earnings equal 160 percent of the average earner.
[c]Earnings equal the maximum taxable wages under OASDI each year.

Source: Social Security Administration, 2011 OASDI Trustees Report.

earnings equal to 160 percent of the average earner in the year prior to retirement. The low earner had earnings equal to 45 percent of the average earner in the year prior to retirement. The maximum earner had earnings equal to the maximum taxable earnings. In 2012 the average earner retiring at age 66 received a Social Security pension of $18,204 per year.

Average earnings in the year prior to retirement were $42,333 in 2011 dollars, which gives the average worker a 42.5 percent gross replacement rate. Notice how the GRR declines with earnings. This is not an accident. The formulas for determining Social Security pensions have a built-in income redistribution component that is designed to provide more generous gross replacement rates to low-earners and the generosity of the pension relative to earnings declines with preretirement earnings.

Two-earner households receive benefits based on the earnings histories of both spouses (with a floor on the benefits available to the one spouse with lower earnings equal to 50 percent of the benefits due to the spouse with higher earnings). For example, a two-earner household with each worker retiring in 2012, both at full retirement age, and receiving the maximum possible Social Security benefit of approximately $28,879 in 2011 dollars would have a total household Social Security pension of 57,758 in 2011 dollars.

Social Security pensions are based on "need" as well as earnings histories. Adjustments for family size reflect the underlying belief that married couples and households with dependents will require greater retirement income than single-person households. Therefore, two workers with identical earnings histories may well receive pensions of different amounts based on their marital status and the number of dependents they support.

Figure 8.1 shows how GRRs decline with annual preretirement earnings for workers with various annual incomes. For a worker with a $200,000 annual earning, the GRR for the Social Security retirement pension is only 13 percent.

Net Replacement Rate: A Better Measure of the Generosity of Social Security Pension Benefits

The GRR underestimates the extent to which Social Security pension benefits replace a retiree's actual disposable earnings. Disposable income is gross income minus taxes paid on those earnings. Social Security pension benefits are nontaxable

FIGURE 8.1 Gross Replacement Rates (Percentage) for Social Security Retirement Pensions for Workers Retiring at Full Retirement Age

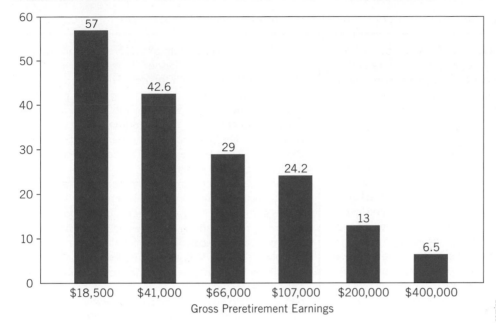

GRRs decline with monthly preretirement earnings. In 2010, the average earner's GRR was 42.6.

for about two-thirds of retirees.[3] For most workers, the entire Social Security pension is disposable income.

A better measure of the generosity of the pension benefits is the **net replacement rate (NRR):**

$$NRR = \frac{\text{Monthly Social Security Pension Benefits}}{\text{Monthly Labor Earnings After Payment of Taxes in the Year Prior to Retirement}} \quad (8.2)$$

NRRs are higher than gross replacement rates (GRRs). To see this, consider the case of the average earner. This worker is likely to have paid a total of 20 percent of labor earnings in federal and state (and possibly local) income taxes and Social Security payroll taxes in 2010. Assume this worker's preretirement earnings in 2009 were $41,300. Taxes on these earnings at a 20 percent rate would be $8,260 per year.

Assume that this is the average earner and he receives a Social Security pension of $17,600 not subject to taxation, which gives a gross replacement rate of 42.6 percent. The NRR would therefore be

$$NRR = \frac{\$17,600}{\$41,300 - \$8,260} = \frac{\$17,600}{\$33,040} = 53.27\% \quad (8.3)$$

which exceeds the 42.6 percent GRR.

[3]Workers whose income (including private pension and annuity income, investment earnings and earnings from work) plus one-half of their Social Security pensions exceeds $25,000 ($32,000 for married couples who file joint returns) do pay income tax on a portion of their Social Security pensions. Income taxes collected on Social Security pensions are used to finance Social Security benefits. As of 2012, as much as 85 percent of pensions for these workers were subject to income tax. Many state governments also tax Social Security benefits.

G L O B A L   P E R S P E C T I V E

Social Security throughout the World: Trends toward Privatization

Social security is a general term for a number of programs established by governments to insure individuals against interruption or loss of earning power and to meet costs resulting from marriage, maternity, children, sickness or injury, unemployment, or death.

Social Security Payments

The most common form of social security protection is the replacement of a portion of income resulting from retirement. Most nations have social security old-age pension systems similar to those in the United States. However, some countries pay retirees a fixed pension that is not related to prior average earnings as are Social Security pensions in the United States. Other nations do not provide pensions but instead give a large lump-sum payment to workers on retirement, which is equal to a refund of the employees' and employers' contributions to a fund plus the accumulated interest on those contributions.[1]

Unemployment insurance is not as common as social security old-age pensions. In less-developed nations, the family, and in some cases the tribe or community, has informal mechanisms for providing support to the unemployed. However, in many of these less-developed nations, labor markets are not developed, and much of the work is carried on within the household through subsistence farming.

Other programs that are common to social security programs throughout the world, but not available as part of the U.S. Social Security system, are universal health insurance and systems of allowances to families to assist them with the expenses of rearing children. The U.S. government does provide the elderly and the poor with health insurance. However, in many nations, including Great Britain and Canada, health insurance is provided universally to all citizens as part of the system of social security. Many nations also supplement their health insurance programs to pay medical costs with sickness and maternity benefits. These programs offer cash benefits to replace earnings lost as a result of short-term illness or maternity leaves.

Some nations offer citizens a lump-sum "demogrant" payment, a flat cash payment to citizens irrespective of their income, employment, or wealth. These payments are basic, no-strings-attached

subsidies designed to help all citizens, but they generally account for a higher percentage of the incomes of the poor than the rich. The United States does not have a similar program, but it does provide cash assistance to the poor through various means-tested programs such as Temporary Assistance to Needy Families (TANF) and Supplemental Security Income (SSI). (See Chapter 7 for detailed descriptions of these programs.)

Family allowances are regular cash payments for families with children. In some nations, this form of social security protection includes grants for birth expenses, for schooling, for prenatal, maternal, and for child care services. The family allowance system originated in several European nations in the 1920s and 1930s. More than 60 countries have family allowance systems that subsidize the cost of having and nurturing children. The programs typically consist of monthly payments to families with children irrespective of the family's income and wealth. Some systems, such as that of Italy, pay allowances for an unemployed dependent spouse, but most begin payment only with the arrival of the first child. Payments commonly terminate when the child reaches a certain age—usually between 14 and 18 years (although in some nations the payments terminate as early as age 5). In nations desiring to increase their population, no limit is placed on the number of children that can be covered with the allowances. Some nations, however, reduce the payment per child as the family size increases. Although the United States does not have a family allowance program, in 1997 Congress enacted a tax credit program for middle-income families with children under the age of 16. As of 2012 this program provided benefits of up to $1,000 per child for families below certain income levels.

Aging of Populations

Many of the social security systems around the world are under stress because of demographic change. Government-financed pensions represent a vast public enterprise in most nations. In almost all cases, the pay-as-you-go social security pensions systems require higher tax rates to pay benefits at promised levels when the ratio of the working-age population to retirees declines. In the United States, this support ratio has declined from 7.1 workers for each retiree in 1950 to only 4.7 workers per retiree in 1990. By 2020, projections indicate that there will only be 3.3 workers per retiree in the United States. In other nations, particularly those with very low birth rates like Japan, projections indicate that there will be only two workers paying taxes to support each retired worker by the year 2030!

The aging of the population will become more severe in Japan and in Western Europe by the middle of the 21st century. In 2000 for most industrialized nations the number of people age 65 and older averaged between 20 and 25 percent of the number age 15 to 64. For most nations, the ratio of older people to that of working age will stabilize at around 40 to 45 percent by 2030. However, France, Germany, Italy, and Japan will have ratios of nearly 50 percent and higher if current trends do not change.

Both Italy and Japan are projected to have old-age dependency ratios in the range of 70 percent by 2050! By contrast, the projected ratio of those over 65 to the potential working population of age 15 to 64 in the United States is projected to be only 33 percent by 2050. If all those over 65 in Italy and Japan in 2050 were retired, only about 30 percent of the population would be working to support the remaining 70 percent. The situation could even be worse in Italy because since 1950, workers in that country have typically retired well before they reached age 65! The consequences of aging for tax rates and budget deficits would be catastrophic for nations such as Italy and Japan, and it is likely that their pension systems will be reformed before they reach such a situation.

The following table shows ratios of people age 65 and older to those age 15 to 64 for seven leading industrial nations in the world.

COUNTRY	2000	2010	2030	2050
Canada	18	20	38	44
France	25	26	42	47
Germany	24	31	45	50
Italy	27	32	49	69
Japan	25	35	52	71
U.K.	24	25	35	38
U.S.	19	19	31	33

Source: United Nations, World Population Prospects, 2004 Revision Population Database.

Privatization

Declining death rates combined with low birth rates spell trouble for many social security pensions systems throughout the world. As the populace ages, the cost of financing pension benefits at any given per capita level implies higher taxes imposed on relatively fewer workers. This problem has led some nations to seek alternatives to the traditional pay-as-you-go government pensions plans. For example, Chile in the 1970s forecasted that a whopping 65 percent tax rate would be required on earnings of workers to finance social security benefits at promised replacement rates to workers in the future. To avoid the incentive problems that would result from such high tax rates, Chile took the radical step of privatizing its social security pension system. It accomplished this by mandating retirement contributions into special accounts and then allowing private pension plans to compete for the right to manage these accounts. Older workers in Chile were given the option to remain in the old system and receive pensions at the promised replacement rates or to receive a bond equal in value to their past contributions to be invested in the new privatized system. Most workers opted out of the old system. The new system has been quite successful in that it has resulted in an annual real return on retirement contributions of 10 percent! This is much better than the 2 percent average return that U.S. workers can expect on their retirement contributions.

Other countries have also begun to partially or totally privatize their social security retirement systems. Argentina and Peru have followed Chile in moving to a privatized system of saving for social security retirement pensions. Mexico and Sweden have schemes to partially privatize their social security systems. Australia, while maintaining its basic social security system, is mandating employer-provided retirement savings accounts for workers in the same way that governments mandate health insurance for workers.

One problem with privatization schemes has been the high cost of administering the plans. Other problems involve transition to the new system from the old system. Administrative costs for government-run, pay-as-you-go pension systems have been quite low. In the United States these costs have run less than 1 percent of taxes collected, not counting costs borne by employers. The privatized scheme in Chile has administrative costs that have been running 19 percent of contributions. Shifting from a government-run plan to a privatized plan could result in significant reductions in replacement rates to retirees as much of the funds previously allocated to pensions are absorbed in administration. These administrative expenses include the costs of managing both investments and annuities by decentralized private firms and include the costs of sales agents competing for retirement savings of workers.

Plans similar to Chile's have been adopted by several other Latin American nations. Similar plans exist in Hungary and Poland. In the United Kingdom a hybrid system has been developed to assure that all workers are covered by a basic social security plan. There is basic traditional coverage that provides a modest pension for all workers. Either an employer-sponsored plan, a state-sponsored supplemental plan, or a personal pension in which persons open individual retirement accounts at financial institutions also covers higher-income workers. This system amounts to government-mandated saving for retirement for some workers and is similar to what has evolved in the United States through a system of tax-preferred accounts voluntarily set up by individuals or employers.

In Sweden, a new system collects a contribution of 2.5 percent of earnings from workers to be deposited in a government-managed, interest-bearing account. Workers are allowed to move funds from the government retirement accounts into individual private mutual funds each year. The mutual funds make investments and are regulated by the government. The system seeks to economize on administrative costs by creating a special government organization that serves as the sole intermediary between workers and the mutual fund, thus eliminating the need for agents that deal directly with workers in such countries as Chile.

Any privatization scheme that does not raise total taxes or contributions allocated to social security reduces the funds available to existing retirees. In a pay-as-you-go system, this could mean that higher taxes or additional taxes will be needed to finance the pensions of current retirees at promised levels and to pay the pensions of workers close to retirement who do not have time to accumulate savings under the privatized system for retirement. These problems are less acute for nations in which the average age of workers is relatively low.

[1]See U.S. Department of Health and Human Services, Social Security Administration, *Social Security Programs throughout the World* (Washington, D.C.: U.S. Government Printing Office, periodically issued).

Other Pension Income and the Well-Being of the Elderly

As of 2010, Social Security pensions accounted for 42.5 percent of income for people over the age of 65 in the United States. These pensions on average are the largest source of income for the elderly. As individuals over the age of 65 grow older, they tend to rely more and more on Social Security as a source of income. In 2010 one-third of the persons in the United States over the age of 80 relied on Social Security pensions for 90 percent of their income. Private pension and annuity income amount to 14.4 percent of the income of those over the age of 65 on average in 2010, while income from earnings accounted to 19.7 percent of income and investment earnings accounted for 19.7 percent of income on average. For retirees with the lowest income levels (in the bottom fifth of the income distribution), Social Security pensions accounted for nearly 90 percent of their incomes in 2010.[4]

Those retirees who enjoy the benefits of a private pension achieve replacement rates at retirement that exceed those they have under Social Security alone.

[4]See Employee Benefit Research Institute, *EBRI Databook on Employee Benefits*, November 2011.

However, the number of workers covered by defined-benefit, private pension plans in which the worker is guaranteed a pension based on a formula depending on earnings and years of service has been declining. In 1980 about 40 percent of jobs in the private sector offered private pensions. By 2005 only about 20 percent of jobs in the United States offered private pensions and that number has continued to decline between 2005 and 2009. On average in 2011 only about 20 percent of individuals over the age of 50 in the United States received private pension or annuity income. And there have been some notable bankruptcies of large firms in the private sector in which businesses have been unable to deliver the pensions promised to retirees. In the future if they wish to supplement their Social Security pensions to enjoy higher replacement rates, retirees will have to rely more on defined contribution pensions plans, in which pension benefits depend on worker and employer contributions and uncertain rates of return on the balances in the individual accounts as well as private savings. As of 2012, less than half of American workers were participating in a private retirement plan.

The economic status of the elderly has improved substantially since 1967. Median income of the elderly has risen significantly faster than that of the rest of the population. The growth of Social Security pensions and increases in the replacement rates for those pensions during that period have helped improve the economic status of the elderly in the United States. After adjustment for size of household and other factors that affect the budgets of the elderly relative to the rest of the population, many studies conclude that, on average, the elderly in the United States are now at least as well-off as the nonelderly, using income as a measure of well-being. However, low-income retirees are particularly dependent on Social Security pensions, which amount to 90 percent of their income. *Over half of retirees would be below poverty without Social Security.*

Cost-of-Living Adjustments

Since 1972, the Social Security pensions received by retired workers have been directly indexed to consumer prices. Retirement benefits of the elderly are protected against erosion by inflation. This implies that, unless the method of calculating benefits is changed, the retiring worker will have the NRR obtained in the year of retirement maintained in real terms over the full period of retirement. Nominal benefits will increase with the rate of inflation.

The method of indexing retirement benefits is often criticized as being overgenerous, because many claim the Consumer Price Index (CPI) is based on a basket of goods more typical for young rather than elderly households. In particular, changes in mortgage interest rates—included in the index as an estimate of housing costs—might have little impact on the elderly. The index currently used to adjust Social Security pensions for inflation is the Bureau of Labor Statistics' Consumer Price Index for Urban Wage Earners and Clerical Workers (CPI-W).

Other sources of income to the elderly are also likely to vary with the price level. For example, the value of government-provided medical care through the Medicare program also increases with inflation. Further, some private pensions are indexed for inflation, and for elderly homeowners, inflation increases the return on their investments in their homes. In short, inflation erodes very little of the income of the elderly.

In 1997, a special government commission studying the way inflation is measured in the United States concluded that the CPI overstates inflation by about 1.1 percent. If this is the case, then the indexation of Social Security benefits by means of the CPI

P U B L I C   P O L I C Y   P E R S P E C T I V E

Social Security and the Family: Some Anomalies in the Modern Age

Social Security laws were enacted in the 1930s when divorce was relatively rare and when the norm was a single-earner family in which the breadwinner was male. Labor force participation among women was low at the time, and most women were dependent spouses engaged primarily in household activities and child-rearing. Today the family is quite different. More than one out of every three children in the United States is now born out of wedlock. Divorce is commonplace and remarriage rates are falling. The percentage of single-person households is growing. At the beginning of the new millennium, 44 percent of adults in the United States were unmarried compared with 32 percent in 1970 and nearly one-quarter of adults today have never been married.

Anomalies are created by the way Social Security provides benefits to dependent spouses and surviving spouses. When a worker with a dependent spouse reaches retirement age, the spouse when reaching full retirement age also is entitled to 50 percent of the breadwinner's pension (spousal retirement benefits are also available to those between 62 and full retirement age but at less than the 50 percent rate). Thus, a dependent spouse who has never worked outside the household and has never paid any Social Security payroll tax is automatically eligible for a Social Security pension. Further, when a retiree with a dependent spouse dies, the surviving spouse continues to receive the retiree's entire pension (the amount the retiree would obtain individually not including the 50 percent increment for the dependent).

The spousal benefit creates situations that many consider inequitable. In effect, the benefit reduces the net return to work for many spouses who pay Social Security taxes. A worker who would otherwise be a dependent spouse pays full Social Security taxes but for that payment receives benefits that total only the excess over the 50 percent of the breadwinner's pension. For example, take two households with the same lifetime annual income equal to twice the average income of workers—say $60,000. In one household, the husband is the sole breadwinner and earns the entire $60,000, while the wife does not work outside the home. In the second household, the income is derived from equal earnings of the husband and wife ($30,000). Suppose the breadwinner in the single-earner household retires in 2032. He would be eligible for a pension of about $25,000 per year under current rules. Because he has a dependent spouse his wife will get a Social Security pension of $12,500 at her full retirement age. The total Social Security pension income of the household will therefore be $37,500. If the retired breadwinner in the single-earner household dies, the surviving dependent spouse will continue to receive his $25,000 pension for the remainder of her life.

The two-earner household also retires in 2032 and each spouse gets a Social Security pension of about $17,000 based on their own earnings record.

has been, on average, increasing the real value of pensions to the elderly, not just compensating them for the effects of inflation on the purchasing power of their pensions.

Criticism of the accuracy of the CPI-W in measuring the impact of inflation on the elderly is leading many economists and politicians to push for adjustments in the formula for indexing Social Security pensions. Naturally, the elderly, and special-interest groups that represent them, such as the American Association of Retired Persons (AARP), oppose such changes.

If the rate at which pension benefits is indexed is reformed, the elderly would still be compensated for inflation but at a lower rate. Initially, the change would be small. For example, if current inflation is 3 percent, then a 1.1 percent decline in the indexing rate would mean that pensions would increase by only 1.9 percent annually to adjust for inflation. The average monthly pension check would decline by $8. However, over time, the reduced rate of indexation would compound.

Their total pension benefits will be $34,000—about $3,500 less per year than the single-earner family! In effect, this family is receiving a negative reward for its additional lifetime of work by one of the spouses! The two-earner household receives a lower pension than the equal-income, single-earner household. In effect, the system favors dependent spouses (the exception rather than the rule today) over working spouses.

The anomalies are even more pronounced between unmarried female workers and dependent spouses. A dependent spouse married to a man earning $55,000 in 1999 who retired in 2000 is entitled to a spousal benefit of $8,500 and a survivors' benefit of $17,000 per year should her husband die. A single mother who raised two children on an income of $15,000 per year would get a pension of about $8,000 if she retired in 2000 and no survivor's benefit. The single mother's pension is $500 less than the spousal benefit of the dependent spouse and ends up being $9,000 per year less than the pension of the dependent spouse should she be widowed![1] Given the growing numbers of single mothers in the nation, this anomaly is likely to create lots of complaints in the future because Social Security definitely short-changes unmarried women working outside the household.

Divorce also creates some absurdities under current Social Security rules and regulations. Social Security provides both spousal benefits and survivor's benefits to divorced dependent spouses *provided that they were married to a retiree for at least ten years.* If the primary worker remarries, the divorced dependent spouse still is entitled to benefits. However, if the previously dependent spouse remarries she (or he) is no longer entitled to benefits. This means that a divorced dependent spouse who was married for 9 years and 11 months to a retiree gets zero benefits while the divorced dependent spouse who was married ten years exactly gets full spousal and retirement benefits. A divorced or widowed dependent spouse will be discouraged from remarrying if remarriage means significant loss in spousal benefits from her previous husband.

Divorce can get expensive for Social Security. Suppose Murry gets married every ten years—taking his first bride at age 15. None of his wives work outside of the household. He retires at age 65, happily married to his fifth and final wife, Marlene. Naturally, Marlene receives a spousal benefit. However, Murry's four previous unremarried wives will also get a spousal benefit each equal to one-half of the pension Murry gets! And, if after the first year of blissful retirement with Marlene, Murry expires, then Marlene and the previous four wives will get a survivor's benefit equal to Murry's pension! Naturally, taxpayers will foot the bill for these pensions. Fortunately for Social Security's budget, polygamy is illegal in the United States. Also fortunately for Social Security, marriages that end in divorce in the United States average only seven years in duration.

[1]See The Urban Institute, *Social Security: Out of Step with the Modern Family* (The Retirement Project, The Urban Institute 1999).

Assuming steady 3 percent inflation, reduction in the annual indexation rate by 1.1 percent would reduce the average check by $100 compared to what it would otherwise be in ten years. In other words, reducing indexation is a way to reduce the replacement rate for pensions.

Another way to reduce replacement rates for Social Security pensions is to change the method currently used to determine the *initial* monthly pension by changing the way either AIME or PIA is calculated by the Social Security Administration. Currently AIME is calculated by multiplying wages earned before age 60 by an index computed as the ratio of average wages in the year the worker reaches age 60 to average wages in the year of earnings. Once AIME is calculated, dollar "bend" points are determined each year to calculate PIA. If instead of wage indexing, a price index were used to calculate AIME, the growth of PIA would fall in the future. This is because prices tend to rise more slowly than wages.

Alternatively, the dollar value of the bend points could be indexed to inflation or the percentage applied to the bend points reduced. Any one of these methods would ultimately reduce replacement rates substantially in the future by slowing the growth of future pension benefits.[5]

CHECKPOINT

1. How is the gross replacement rate calculated? What does GRR measure?
2. How is the net replacement rate calculated? How does NRR differ from GRR?
3. How do net and gross replacement rates of Social Security pensions vary with the preretirement income?

THE RETURN TO WORKERS: HOW DO PENSION BENEFITS COMPARE WITH THE TAXES THAT WORKERS PAY?

What is the rate of return to retirees who pay Social Security taxes over their lifetimes? In other words, if the total Social Security taxes paid by the worker and his or her employer had been invested, what rate of interest would produce the stream of retirement benefits for which the retiree is eligible? This return varies from worker to worker, depending on the worker's earnings history and personal circumstances. However, it is interesting to perform this calculation in the aggregate to see how the ability of a pay-as-you-go retirement system, which pays benefits in excess of the taxes paid by workers, depends on certain economic variables.

To calculate the average rate of return to retirees as a percentage of their taxes requires a number of simplifying assumptions. First, assume that the payroll tax rate on workers' wages is fixed over time. Also assume that the size of the workforce is constant. Finally, assume that the rate of inflation is zero.

In a pay-as-you-go system, the taxes paid by workers in any one year go directly into the pockets of retired workers. Given the assumptions, the annual increase in aggregate taxes collected, and therefore total pensions paid, equal the annual growth of labor earnings subject to the Social Security tax. This is because in any given year revenue available to pay benefits will be tW, where t is the Social Security tax rate and W is total aggregate labor earnings subject to the tax. With t fixed, revenues available to pay pensions will increase only if W increases. The growth of revenues depends on the annual rate of growth of labor earnings subject to taxation.

Adjusting for inflation, the rate of growth of wages per worker in the United States has averaged about 2 percent per year since the Social Security system has been in operation. This is the average return on taxes paid that workers can expect, provided that the size of the workforce and tax rates are fixed. Because net

---

[5]See Julia Lynn Coronado and Paul A. Smith, "Social Security at 70: Principles, Issues and Alternatives," *National Tax Journal* 58, 3 (September 2005): 505–522.

replacement rates (NRRs) vary with preretirement income, some workers receive a higher return and some a lower return.

However, until the late 1970s, retiring workers were able to enjoy a much higher average return on the taxes they paid during their lifetimes because during that period the number of workers paying Social Security payroll taxes steadily increased. In addition, the tax rates paid by workers were steadily increased by Congress. From 1950 to 1975, the segment of the U.S. population older than 16 rose at an annual rate of 1.4 percent, labor force participation rates of workers increased, and Social Security taxes were levied on workers in many new industries and jobs and on the self-employed as these workers were made eligible for pension benefits.

Until the late 1970s, on average, workers who were retiring under the Social Security system received a relatively high return on their taxes paid compared with what they could have earned, on average, had their Social Security taxes been invested in a fully funded system. More generous Social Security benefits, and their indexing for inflation, were enacted into law in the 1970s and financed by a growing amount of taxable wages earmarked to finance benefits and only modest increases in tax rates paid by workers.

From 1950 to 1975, the average return that a conservative portfolio manager could have earned, in real terms, on a fully funded pension system was about 5 percent. This is based on real (adjusted for inflation) yields of about 8 percent on common stocks and 3 percent on high-grade corporate bonds. A less conservative portfolio (one subject to more risk) could have earned considerably more. A common estimate of the postwar real rate of return in the corporate sector is about 12 percent through 1976.[6]

Martin Feldstein has estimated that the real rate of Social Security tax receipts (excluding the portion of the tax used to finance health benefits for the elderly) grew 10.4 percent per year from 1950 to 1975.[7] This compares very favorably with the 12 percent achievable on a conservative portfolio in the corporate sector over the same period. (Social Security taxpayers bore little risk over this period, because they were guaranteed a pension by the taxing power of the federal government.)

This favorable past performance of the Social Security system is not likely to be repeated in the future. Any future increase in Social Security receipts to pay pensions over and above the value of taxes paid will be limited to the annual growth rate of real wages. This is because taxable wages are no longer growing through increases in the number of workers covered. Most economists predict that this rate will be no more than a mere 2 percent in real terms. Of course, stock market returns can fall as well. During the financial crisis of 2008 and the first three months of 2009 major stock market indices plummeted nearly 40 percent. This reduced the four-year return stocks to a negative return of 11 percent unadjusted for inflation. This makes a 2 percent real return look pretty good! Stock prices could easily move up again over time (as they did in the last nine months of 2009) and investment yields could return to long-term average rates in the next ten years. Further, productivity growth, the major determinant of the annual growth in real wages, could be either greater or lesser than forecast.

---

[6]Martin Feldstein, "Facing the Social Security Crisis," *The Public Interest* 47 (Spring 1977): 88–100.
[7]*Ibid.*, 91.

Intergenerational and Distributive Effects of Social Security

An interesting intergenerational aspect of Social Security benefits is the inevitable result of starting up a pay-as-you-go retirement system. Workers who reached retirement age in the early years of the Social Security system received a better deal than do workers currently retiring and those who will retire in the future. This is because the first workers who received pensions had not paid Social Security taxes over their entire working lives. For example, Ida Fuller of Brattleboro, Vermont, the first Social Security pension recipient in the United States, paid approximately $22 in Social Security taxes over her lifetime. Fuller died at the ripe old age of 99, after collecting a grand total of approximately $20,000 in Social Security benefits—not a bad return on $22!

Workers who retired through 1990 paid taxes over a long period when tax rates under Social Security were quite low. For example, workers who had median earnings and who had retired in 1971 earned pension benefits three times greater than they could have enjoyed had their Social Security taxes paid over their lifetimes been returned to them at 6 percent interest on retirement.[8] A middle-income person who retired in 1970 with no dependents received a pension with a discounted present value of $25,000 more than the taxes paid during the retiree's lifetime—a good deal! However, a person in the exact same circumstances retiring in the year 2020 will pay $88,000 more in taxes over a lifetime of work than the discounted present value of the Social Security pension received at that time—a bad deal![9] Workers who are entering the labor force now will pay high tax rates earmarked for current Social Security benefits during their entire careers. In addition, some of those taxes will be used to build up the trust fund to prepare for the increase in Social Security outlays in the future, as the proportion of retirees in the population increases. This makes the Social Security system a much poorer deal on average for workers today than it has been for their parents and grandparents.

Finally, the way in which Social Security gross replacement rates (GRRs) vary with family status and income also affects the benefits received by retired workers. In general, as the analysis of replacement rates has shown, Social Security retirement benefits compared with taxes paid are a better deal for low-income workers than for upper-income workers. In addition, married workers with dependent spouses are better off than single workers or workers with employed spouses eligible for their own Social Security benefits.

The Social Security system affects the distribution of income by transferring income from workers to retirees, from single workers to married workers with dependent spouses, and from high-income workers to low-income workers.

DEMOGRAPHIC CHANGE AND THE FUTURE OF SOCIAL SECURITY

Maintenance of gross replacement rates (GRRs) at legislated levels has required sharp increases in payroll tax rates since 1970 to provide the revenue for current and future pensions. The tax increases will result in the Social Security trust fund

---

[8]Donald Parsons and Douglas Munro, "Intergenerational Transfers in Social Security," in *The Crisis in Social Security*, ed. Michael J. Boskin (San Francisco: Institute for Contemporary Studies, 1977).

[9]See Michael D. Hurd and John B. Shoven, "The Distributional Impact of Social Security," in *Pensions, Labor, and Individual Choice*, ed. David A. Wise (Chicago: University of Chicago Press, 1985): 193–215.

growing until the end of the first quarter of the 21st century. This means that the Social Security system will be less of a pay-as-you-go system for current workers, who will pay taxes not only to finance the pensions of current retirees but also to accumulate reserves that will pay some of their own pensions. However, as the second half of the 21st century approaches, the Social Security trust fund will be drawn down rapidly, because payroll tax revenues will fall short of expected outlays for pensions at that time. By the mid-21st century, the fund is forecast to have a large negative balance, which could require that more tax revenues be devoted to paying pensions at that time.

The basic problem is that the proportion of retirees relative to the working population has been, and will continue to be, increasing. Since 1957, the birthrate in the United States has fallen. In 2000, there were nearly five workers for each retiree. Demographic projections by the Social Security Administration indicate that by the year 2050 there will be only fewer than three workers for each retiree. After 2050 the number of workers per retiree could fall to fewer than two!

From 1967 to 1973, changes in legislation sharply increased Social Security benefits by more than 70 percent. The expansion of Social Security benefits paid to retirees led to concerns that the system would have difficulty meeting its future commitments. But given the political popularity of the system and the fact that the system's ability to pay benefits is based on the taxing power of the federal government, fears of the system's collapse are unwarranted.

The solution was new legislation that sharply increased both the maximum taxable wages per worker and the tax rate applied to wages for the collection of the Social Security payroll tax. In 1977, Congress passed a number of significant amendments to the Social Security Act, allowing these tax increases along with certain changes in the way that Social Security benefits will be calculated in the future, to reduce replacement rates. Additional reforms enacted by Congress in 1983 accelerated the rate of increase of Social Security taxes; increased the tax rates applied to self-employment income; and placed new federal employees under coverage of Social Security, thereby subjecting these workers' wages to Social Security taxes. In addition, the changes decreased the benefits to early retirees and increased the bonus paid to workers delaying retirement. The retirement age at which the retiree is eligible for full benefits is being raised gradually to 67.

The intergenerational aspects of a Social Security retirement system can be understood better with the analysis of some basic accounting relationships involved in a pay-as-you-go retirement system. This analysis also shows clearly how aging of the population affects the tax rate necessary to finance Social Security pensions on a pay-as-you-go basis.

In any given year, the tax rate, t, applied to taxable wages must be sufficient to pay the benefits promised to retirees based on existing replacement rates that year. Assume that each year the system taxes wages so as to generate just enough to pay pensions and neither accumulate a surplus in the trust fund nor run a deficit. It follows that the tax rate must equal the ratio of Social Security pensions paid that year to total wages subject to taxes that year.

Total Social Security benefits can be thought of as average Social Security benefits per recipient, B, multiplied by the number of Social Security recipients, R. Total taxable wages are average taxable wages, W, multiplied by the number of workers in the labor force, L.

Total revenue collected at tax rate, t, is therefore tWL. For a pay-as-you-go tax financed pensions system total revenue must equal total Social Security pension benefits each year:

$$tWL = BR \qquad (8.4)$$

Solving for t:

$$t = BR/WL \qquad (8.5)$$

$$t = B/W \times R/L. \qquad (8.6)$$

The fraction B/W is the average level of Social Security benefits divided by average wages, a measure of the average replacement rate for current retirees. The fraction R/L, the ratio of the number of retirees to the labor force, is the *dependency ratio* for the nation—a measure of the number of retirees who must be supported, on average, by each worker:

$$t = \text{Average Replacement Rate} \times \text{Dependency Ratio.} \qquad (8.7)$$

In the early years of the U.S. Social Security system up to the mid-1960s, both the average replacement rates and the dependency ratio were low compared to current levels. Consequently, Social Security pensions could be financed with relatively low tax rates compared to current levels. As replacement rates rose in the 1970s and demographics worked to increase the dependency ratio, tax rates had to rise to continue to finance Social Security benefits promised to retirees. As dependency rates rise dramatically in the next century, tax rates for a pay-as-you-go system of financing Social Security pensions will also have to rise to maintain benefits at constant replacement rates.

The dependency ratio as of 2000 in the United States was 0.2. By the year 2050, the dependency ratio is expected to be less than 0.4, meaning that there will be fewer than three workers for each retiree in the nation. Given current replacement rates, this implies that the combined employee-employer tax rate allocated to pay Social Security pensions, which was about 12 percent (excluding the Medicare portion of the payroll tax) in 2009, would have to rise to 17 percent by the year 2030 and could climb to as much as 20 percent by the year 2070!

Further, as we have shown, the equilibrium average rate of return on a worker's Social Security taxes in the future will be equal to the real rate of growth of real wages, projected to be between 1 and 2 percent. If tax rates to finance Social Security pensions grow, then the return to workers will fall still more. The *money's worth ratio* for Social Security is the ratio of the discounted present value of pension benefits for workers to the discounted present value of taxes paid. When this ratio falls below one, then Social Security will cost workers more than they will get from it. The money's worth ratio for U.S. workers retiring in the early 21st century will be less than one for all but the lowest-income workers.[10] For individual workers, the burden of paying taxes for the pensions of retirees will exceed their own benefits for all except the lowest-wage workers. If the tax rate is increased as the dependency ratio increases, the money's worth ratio will continue to fall so that Social Security will become a "bad deal" for all younger workers. As this occurs, conflicts between the old and the young could develop, and unless the system is reformed, support for Social Security will decline. This is why reform of the Social

---

[10]See Edward M. Gramlich, "Different Approaches for Dealing with Social Security," *Journal of Economic Perspectives* 10, 2 (Summer 1996): 55–66.

Security system is becoming urgent. Given projected dependency ratios, tax rates will have to rise substantially in the future, or government budget deficits will have to increase, unless replacement rates are lowered. It remains a political choice to be made either today or in the future as to whether or not we wish to allocate more of our resources than we do today to pay pensions of the elderly.

Rise of Social Security Tax Rates

Both Social Security tax rates and the maximum level of wages per year subject to those tax rates have already been increased substantially since 1983. Unless reforms are enacted, these rates will have to rise still more in the future as the population ages and dependency ratios increase if the Social Security trust fund is to continue to raise enough funds each year to pay at least that year's pension benefits.

Table 8.2 shows the tax rate schedule and maximum taxable wages per worker for selected years from 1937 to 2012. The combined employee–employer tax rate has nearly doubled since 1966, totaling 15.3 percent in 2012. This tax rate includes a 2.9 percent combined employer–employee tax that finances health insurance for the elderly (Medicare). The maximum taxable wages per worker for OASDI have increased from $3,000 in 1937 to $110,100 in 2012. Starting in 1991, the maximum taxable wages for the health insurance tax (HI) was increased above that for OASDI. Beginning in 1994, *all labor earnings*, without limit, are subjected to a 2.9 percent HI tax. The maximum taxable wages per worker are indexed with the rate of inflation. The sharp tax increases are designed to ensure that the Social Security Administration can continue to pay benefits based on existing replacement rates. Beginning in 2013, an additional HI tax of 0.9 percent will be applied to earned income exceeding $200,000 for individuals and $250,000 for married couples filing joint federal income tax returns. Some high-income individuals will also have to pay a 3.8 percent HI tax on investment income.

Table 8.2 shows the combined maximum tax paid by both employees and employers. The employer's share of tax is paid out of compensation that the worker could otherwise receive as wages. Almost all of the portion of the tax paid by employers represents a cost in terms of forgone wages to employees. The combined employee–employer tax of a worker earning $110,100 in 2012 was $16,845.30. A married couple with each spouse earning the maximum taxable wages will have their salaries generate more than $33,000 in payroll tax revenue in 2012—enough to pay the Social Security pension of a typical high-income worker in that year! The Medicare (HI) tax has no limit.

If demographic and economic growth projections are correct and if replacement rates for Social Security pensions remain as currently legislated, then the proportion of GDP devoted to Social Security pensions will increase through the first half of the 21st century. The initial Social Security legislation was passed during the height of the Depression of the 1930s. Economic conditions and the general quality of life in the United States have changed drastically since that time. In view of the financial problems anticipated by the Social Security retirement system in the future, many economists have begun to reassess some of the basic assumptions underlying government-supplied retirement benefits financed by compulsory taxation.

Government-supplied retirement systems can be viewed as a means of forcing citizens to save for their own retirement. By forcing workers to pay Social Security taxes in exchange for the promise of retirement benefits at some point in the future, the government in effect assures the public at large that the elderly will have at least

TABLE 8.2   Social Security Tax Rates, Maximum Taxable Wages, and Taxes, Selected Years, 1937–2012

YEAR	BASIC OASDHI TAX RATE	COMBINED EMPLOYER–EMPLOYEE TAX RATE	MAXIMUM TAXABLE WAGES PER WORKER ($)	MAXIMUM TAX BASED ON COMBINED TAX RATE ($)
1937	1.00%	2.00%	3,000	60.00
1957	2.25	4.50	4,200	189.00
1967	4.40	8.80	6,600	528.00
1977	5.85	11.70	16,500	1,930.50
1978	6.05	12.10	17,700	2,141.70
1979	6.13	12.26	22,900	2,807.54
1981	6.65	13.30	29,700	3,950.10
1983	6.70	13.40	35,700	4,783.80
1984	7.00	14.00	37,800	5,292.00
1985	7.05	14.10	39,600	5,583.60
1987	7.15	14.30	43,800	6,263.40
1988	7.51	15.02	45,000	6,759.00
1990	7.65	15.30	51,300	7,849.90
1997	7.65	15.30	65,400[a]	10,006.20[b]
2000	7.65	15.30	76,200[a]	11,658.60[b]
2001	7.65	15.30	80,400[a]	12,301.20[b]
2003	7.65	15.30	87,000[a]	13,311.00[b]
2006	7.65	15.30	94,200[a]	14,412.60[b]
2009	7.65	15.30	106,800[a]	16,340.40[b]
2012	7.65	15.30	110,100[a]	16,845.30[b]

[a]Automatically adjusted upward each year. Excludes earnings subject to additional HI tax.
[b]Does not include HI tax (2.9 percent) levied on earnings in excess of $65,400 per year in 1997, $76,200 per year in 2000, $80,400 in 2001, $87,000 in 2003, $94,200 in 2006, $106,800 per year in 2009, and $110,100 in 2012. Starting in 2013, an additional HI tax of 0.9 percent will be applied to earned income exceeding $200,000 for individuals and $250,000 for married couples filing joint federal income tax returns. These limits are not indexed after 2013.
Source: Social Security Administration.

some minimal means of support after their working years. This frees children from the necessity and worry of supporting their parents in their old age and reduces the probability that the elderly will require additional government assistance. An underlying presumption behind this justification for the Social Security system is that a substantial number of workers will fail to set aside an adequate amount of savings to support themselves in their old age.

If current replacement rates are maintained, many workers at or below the median income level might find that at retirement their real income rises relative to their wages earned when they were 30 to 50 years old. This might seem a pleasant state of affairs if it were a costless development. However, workers typically have more expenses in their middle years, when they are raising families and furnishing households. Many workers might not realize how high the replacement rates are and how much the increased tax burden that they bear to finance Social Security benefits to others reduces their own real incomes during their working years.

Changes in the replacement rates are likely to be unpopular with persons who are approaching retirement. The elderly are a potent and effective political force. Elderly people have more leisure time and probably are more likely to vote than younger citizens. They also have more time to inform themselves about current political issues. In future years, demographic change will result in the elderly constituting an ever-increasing percentage of the total population, as the children of various postwar "baby booms" reach old age. This effect might be even more pronounced if the life span of the elderly is lengthened as a result of medical advances. As the median voter ages, political support for reducing Social Security benefits might prove difficult to pass by majority rule. Some nations, such as Chile, have privatized their social security systems to deal with the problem of an aging population (see Global Perspective box).

PROPOSALS TO REFORM SOCIAL SECURITY: MAINTAINING BENEFITS VERSUS PARTIAL PRIVATIZATION

In January 1997, the Advisory Council on Social Security, appointed in 1994, issued a report on the long-range financial status of the U.S. Social Security pension system. Although members of the commission agreed that something must be done to prepare for the flood of retirees expected by the mid-21st century, they could not agree on a single solution. Instead, they offered three alternative policies for improving the finances of the system. Still other critics have offered other solutions. Whatever is done—and something will have to be done—there will be a difficult trade-off between providing existing benefits to those already retired and attempting to continue providing benefits to those who will retire in the future without raising taxes to outrageous levels or running catastrophic budget deficits. As of 2012, 15 years after issuance of the Advisory Council on Social Security report, no action has been taken by the Congress to reform the Social Security pension system. As the federal government budget deficit grows and the population relentlessly ages, the pressures for reform will be even greater.

The proposals to reform the system represent various mixes of reforms that could allow portions of Social Security payments by workers to be invested in corporate stocks while retaining portions of the existing system. A key issue in implementing any reform is transition to the new system. The Social Security system is now based on workers paying taxes to support retirees receiving Social Security pensions. If current workers are allowed to divert some of what they would otherwise pay in taxes to their own individual investment accounts to provide retirement income for themselves based on the performance of these investments, there will be fewer funds to pay the pensions of existing retirees. Because Social Security is on a pay-as-you-go basis, any reallocation of existing tax collections at current tax rates to individual retirement accounts means less available to pay current pensions. This trade-off implies that transforming Social Security from a government-financed, pay-as-you-go, *defined-benefit* plan to a privatized *defined-contribution* plan will leave some middle-aged workers out in the cold. These workers would not have time to build up their own accounts before retiring and would also lose the benefit of taxation of current workers to pay their pensions.

Let's look at the three options proposed by the Advisory Council.

Option 1: Maintain Benefits

The least radical proposal is to preserve Social Security in its current form with only slight reductions in replacement rates for retirees by more inclusive taxation of Social Security benefits along with large-scale investment of Social Security tax proceeds in corporate stocks. Currently, 50 to 85 percent of Social Security benefits are taxed for taxpayers with incomes above certain amounts. This proposed system would fully tax the portion of Social Security benefits in excess of previously paid employee payroll taxes.

This plan also recommends investing up to 40 percent of Social Security tax collections in the stock market in an attempt to raise the rate of return on the system above the projected rate of growth of wages of between 1 and 2 percent per year. This plan would help the system if the real return on stocks, which historically has been much higher than 2 percent, remains at those levels. The funds would be invested in an enormous index-type mutual fund that invests in a bundle of stocks, such as those represented by the Dow Jones Average, to prevent political manipulation of the funds. Such a fund would eventually have a trillion dollars invested. This option is probably not going to be particularly attractive given the performance of the stock market between 2008 and early 2009 and the realization that investments in stocks are inherently risky.

Finally, the proposal recommends an increase in the payroll tax of 1.6 percentage points in 2045 to keep the tax collections from Social Security sufficient to pay the pensions of the large cohort of retirees expected at that time.

This plan addresses the long-term problems of Social Security without radically changing the pension system or substantially cutting the replacement rates for current and future retirees. It will generate additional funds to pay pensions only if the return on stocks substantially increases the income of the Social Security trust fund.

However, the commission may have underestimated the necessary tax increase required to avoid benefit cuts. As of 2005 it was estimated that an immediate 1.92 percentage point increase in Social Security payroll taxes would allow the system to continue operating over a 75-year period without reductions in replacement rates or shortfalls of revenue after the Social Security trust fund is exhausted. However, each year an increase in tax rates is not enacted by Congress, the greater the tax rate increase that will be necessary in the future to keep the system operating on a pay-as-you-go basis. Current projections indicate that if there were no payroll tax increase until 2041, the payroll tax would have to increase by 4.26 percentage points to keep the system operating over a 75-year period from that point. If nothing were done until 2079, the corresponding required tax increase would be 5.7 percentage points. If no tax increases were enacted and the system remained operating on a pay-as-you-go basis, then benefits would have to be cut by 26 percent in 2041 and 32 percent in 2079.[11]

---

[11]See Julia Lynn Coronado and Paul A. Smith, "Social Security at 70: Principles, Issues and Alternatives," *National Tax Journal* 58, 3 (September 2005): 505–522.

Option 2: Individual Accounts

This option raises the retirement age at which full benefits can be claimed under Social Security and reduces the replacement rate for upper-income workers. This approach would create individual accounts equal to 1.6 percent of covered payrolls under Social Security. These accounts would be held and administered by the Social Security system, and individuals would be free to choose how to invest the funds in these accounts among stock and bond mutual funds. The pensions that individuals would receive from the individual accounts would be based entirely on the amounts they contributed and the investment performance of their funds. The remainder of the pensions would come from regular Social Security formulas. This approach amounts to a 1.6 percent increase in taxes on payrolls to finance defined-contribution retirement accounts that would then supplement regular Social Security pensions, whose replacement rates would decline, especially for upper-income workers. The plan would also accelerate the increase in the retirement age at which full Social Security pensions are paid and would adjust this retirement age in the future with changes in longevity of the population.

This plan would give individuals some additional control over their Social Security retirement pensions and possibly allow them to get higher returns to improve the money's worth of the program. It would, however, raise tax rates to accomplish this objective.

Option 3: Personal Security Accounts

This is the most radical proposal. It would move more in the direction of privatizing Social Security than the individual account approach. Under this option, the 10 percentage points of the payroll tax that are allocated to finance retirement benefits would be split. The portion paid by employers, amounting to 5 percent of taxable payrolls, would be allocated to a Social Security trust fund dedicated to pay a guaranteed flat benefit to all retirees amounting to about two-thirds of the poverty threshold income (about $400 per month). In effect, this would guarantee all workers a minimal tax-financed pension. The 5 percentage points of payroll paid by employees would be allocated to an individual "personal security account" for each employee. This proposed account would be managed privately through investment companies in the same way that individual retirement accounts and other defined-contribution pension plans are managed by the private sector today. The accounts would provide retirement support to workers that would vary with the amount contributed and the performance of their investments over time. When a worker retires, the fund's assets would be his or her personal property to do with as chosen: Provide an annuitized retirement income, liquidate in a lump sum, or leave as part of an estate. The retirement age at which full benefits could be claimed would be increased and thereafter adjusted for changes in longevity.

The problem with this approach is one of transition. As the 5 percentage points of tax are removed from financing current pensions to provide future individual retirement income, a large deficit in the ability to finance the pensions of current retirees would develop. Those at or near retirement age would be in trouble because they would have paid payroll taxes at high rates all their working lives to finance Social Security pension for their parents while their children would have the bulk of their payroll taxes allocated to pay for their own retirement!

To prevent some retirees from falling through the cracks, a transition scheme would have to be developed for which all workers close to retirement (say, age 55 and above) would be covered by the rules of the present Social Security system while all workers under the age of 25 would be on the new system, where their pension would consist of a future flat benefit plus the return on their personal security accounts. Workers between the ages of 25 and 55 could then have pension benefits based partly on the present system and partly on the return from their own personal security accounts. This complicated scheme would probably require a supplementary tax to finance the retirement benefits of workers over the age of 55 at the time the plan is enacted. The transition would be complete sometime in the 21st century, and then the transition tax could be eliminated.

The advantage of the privatization scheme is that it could increase the return to Social Security tax payments from the current implicit rate of about 2 percent to as much as 9 percent if the historical differential between the return on stocks and other assets holds up in the future. This means that a given amount of taxes paid would generate higher pension levels to future retirees. However, some analysts dispute whether this return would hold up, given the flood of new money into the stock market, and also argue that the high cost of administering the small accounts could reduce their net return substantially. The sharp decline in stock values during 2008 and 2009 also emphasizes how stock returns are inherently unstable particularly in the short run and that long-run returns can be difficult to forecast.

However, there remain many problems with personal accounts for Social Security old-age pensions, and the experience with the accounts in the United Kingdom has been riddled with controversy. Errors by financial service providers in that country caused losses to workers that were subsequently reimbursed by the financial providers. The number of British workers participating in the private account system has declined substantially since 1993, and a national commission on pensions in the United Kingdom has recommended abolition of the accounts for workers.

Private retirement accounts are a better deal for upper-income workers than for lower-income workers. The current Social Security retirement system provides a reasonably good return for lower-income workers because of the relatively high replacement rates available to lower-income workers compared to higher-income workers. Also, upper-income workers tend to be more educated in the economics of finance necessary to earn high returns on investment portfolios. If upper-income workers can earn higher returns on individual private retirement accounts than lower-income workers and have longer life expectancy (as is the case), then the shift to private accounts would allow upper-income workers to earn higher returns for longer periods. The private accounts scheme is therefore likely to redistribute retirement income from lower-income groups to upper-income groups.[12]

Given the risks associated with making investments privately, the administrative costs of small individual private accounts, and the costs of administering annuitization of those accounts into pensions at retirement, it is not clear that workers on average will increase the return they get from paying payroll taxes for regular Social

---

[12]For a complete analysis of the effects of a shift to individual accounts, see John Turner, *Individual Accounts for Social Security Reform: International Perspectives on the U.S. Debate* (Kalamazoo: W.E. Upjohn Institute, 2006).

Security pensions. Except for the higher-income workers with the lowest replacement rates under existing Social Security pension formulas, the risks of private accounts could result in many workers becoming worse off at retirement than they would be under the current system.

The reduction in payroll tax revenues resulting from diversion of those tax revenues to private accounts would require the treasury to borrow funds to pay promised Social Security benefits to other retired workers in the future. This increase in debt coupled with the implicit debt workers incur through a reduction in future Social Security tax-financed pensions could contribute to a decline in national savings.

Any full or partial privatization scheme will be successful in alleviating the problems of Social Security only if it ultimately raises the rate of national saving. The current system is likely to require a payroll tax in the year 2045 that is as much as 5 percentage points higher than the one we have today. To prevent high future tax increases, the nation must either increase the return to national saving in Social Security assets, reduce the number of eligible beneficiaries for full pension benefits (by raising the retirement age), or reduce the replacement rate for retirees (for example, cost-of-living adjustments could be reduced). All these are likely to be tough political choices that we will have to confront soon.

CHECKPOINT

1. What influences the average rate of increase in funds collected to pay Social Security pensions?
2. Why are Social Security pensions on average a much worse deal for workers who will be retiring in the next ten years than they were for their parents?
3. Why are demographic change and declining economic growth rates likely to increase the share of GDP allocated to pay Social Security pensions throughout the first half of the 21st century?

THE IMPACT OF SOCIAL SECURITY ON SAVINGS AND WORK INCENTIVES

Among the issues of greatest concern in the recent upsurge of criticism against the Social Security system is the impact of government-supplied retirement benefits on incentives to save and work. This is an area of considerable controversy and disagreement. Although economic theory suggests that a pay-as-you-go system of retirement distorts both savings and work choices, no conclusive evidence confirms this nor does any measure the actual effect. The impact of Social Security retirement benefits on economic incentives is the combined effect of its influence on the choices of both recipients of benefits and those who finance the benefits. Those who pay the payroll taxes to finance Social Security pensions and other benefits will have their economic choices influenced by Social Security taxes. Those already receiving Social Security benefits, or who are close to receiving such benefits, likewise have their choices influenced by the system. The analysis of work incentives in this chapter considers only the effect of Social Security benefits on the work incentive of the elderly eligible for pensions.

GLOBAL PERSPECTIVE

Social Security Pensions in the European Union

After the end of World War II many European nations began to increase social insurance benefits available to citizens. Over time these benefits, particularly, for social security pensions, became more generous with some nations offering very high average replacement rates and retirement ages for full pensions benefits that were relatively low compared to other nations. The period 1960–1990 was favorable for expansion of these benefits because most of the European nations were experiencing rapid economic growth and had a relatively low dependency ratios due to an expanding labor force and few citizens eligible for retirement pensions.

In recent years conditions have changed drastically as European populations have aged and growing government budget deficits and sovereign debt in some of the nations (particularly Greece) have made it clear that the ability to finance the pay-as-you-go pensions at their current levels is not feasible. Public spending on pensions in 15 European Union nations averaged 10.2 percent of GDP in 2010. Although some reforms have already been made to reduce spending on pensions as a share of GDP in these nations, current projections by the European Commission indicate that the share of GDP allocated to social security pensions will rise to 12.6 percent mainly as a result of aging of populations and longer life expectancy for retired workers. There is considerable variation in the pension systems of the European Union nations with some nations projected to have pensions as a share of

GDP rising faster than average. Greece currently allocates 11.7 percent of GDP to public pensions but if steps are not taken to reform their systems, the share of GDP absorbed by these pensions is projected to increase to 24.1 percent by 2060. Luxembourg, currently allocating 8.7 percent of GDP to pensions, is projected to have that allocation increase to 23.9 percent by 2060. In Italy, where some reforms have already been enacted, such as increases in the retirement age, the share of GDP allocated to pensions is projected to decline from 14 percent to 13.6 percent by 2060.

The following table shows full retirement ages and median replacement rates for 15 European Union nations.

Social Security Pension System Characteristics in 15 European Union Nations (2010)

NATION	FULL RETIREMENT AGE	MEDIAN REPLACEMENT RATE (PERCENTAGE)
Austria	65*	76.6
Belgium	60	42.6
Denmark	65	84.7
Finland	65	57.8
France	61	49.1
Germany	65	42.0
Greece	57	95.7
Ireland	65	34.9
Italy	59	64.5

Work Incentives

Social Security affects the size of the workforce by influencing the willingness of workers and spouses to participate in the labor force and by controlling the age of retirement. Social Security benefits reduce the incentive that older workers might have to work beyond the age at which they can begin collecting benefits. In many cases, net replacement rates (NRRs) for workers with dependent spouses are more than 85 percent of previous earnings and tend to be supplemented with benefits from private pensions. Little financial incentive to work beyond the age of 65 exists for workers who realize NRRs close to 100 percent. Since 1961, male workers have had the option to retire at age 62 with reduced benefits. Women have had this option since 1956. Many workers have taken advantage of this alternative since it was first introduced, apparently because they value the three extra years of benefits and leisure time more than the reduction in annual benefits.

NATION	FULL RETIREMENT AGE	MEDIAN REPLACEMENT RATE (PERCENTAGE)
Luxembourg	60	90.3
The Netherlands	65	89.1
Portugal	65	54.4
Spain	65	81.2
Sweden	65	53.8
United Kingdom	65*	37.0
EU-15 Average	63.1	53.8

*60 for Women

Source: OECD.

In 2010 the full retirement age in all the nations listed in the table was below that of the United States. Some of the European nations (for example, France, Greece, Luxembourg, Portugal, and Sweden) allowed early retirement at reduced benefits at ages as low as 50 (Greece). The full retirement age in the United States is now over 66 and will soon approach 67.

The European replacement rates are higher than those in the United States. The replacement rate for the average earner retiring under Social Security in the United States at full retirement age is 42.5 percent compared with a European average of 53.8 percent. In Greece the median replacement rate in 2010 was 95.7 percent for public pensions! This combined with Greece's low full retirement age largely explains why public pensions will account for nearly one-quarter of GDP in that country unless steps are taken soon to reform the system. Very high median replacement rates in excess of 75 percent are also currently provided in Austria, Denmark, the Netherlands, and Spain.

Given the high levels of debt in nations such as Greece, Portugal, Spain, Italy, and Ireland, growing shares of GDP absorbed by tax-financed pensions are unlikely to be sustainable without cutting other government spending severely or increasing taxes. Because high debt levels and the risk of default on sovereign debt are already making it difficult for these nations to borrow to finance public expenditures and causing interest rates to rise, increased deficit finance is not likely to be an option. All these nations are under pressure from the European Union to reduce their budget deficits in exchange for bailouts of billions of Euros to help finance debt.

Reforms are already in place to slow the growth of public pensions as a share of GDP in some nations. Denmark and the United Kingdom will increase the full retirement age to 67 by 2040. Italy has recently passed legislation to increase the full retirement age from 59 to 65 by 2040. However, in nations where replacement rates are well above the EU-15 average, it is clear that replacement rates will have to be reduced to avoid default on debt, severe cuts in other government spending or crippling tax increases.

Some countries have also introduced structural reforms to supplement public pensions with defined contribution pension plans to cushion any future reductions in public pension replacement rates. In some nations these supplementary accounts are mandatory (a form of forced saving for retirement) but in most cases the accounts are optional. Several nations require the accounts to be converted to an annuity at retirement based on life expectancy to supplement reductions in future public pensions.

Also, an annual earnings test for retirees below full retirement age can affect the amount of benefits received, regardless of the amount to which the retiree is entitled. Although the reduction of Social Security retirement benefits, with earnings, had been moderated somewhat since the passage of the 1977 and 1983 amendments, the effects still can significantly influence the older worker's incentive to work.

For example, in 2012, most retired workers aged 62 to full retirement age could earn $14,640 per year with no reduction in benefits. The amount of retiree earnings exempt of the earnings test is indexed with the rate of inflation. After the maximum earnings of $14,640 are achieved, retirees' Social Security benefits will be reduced by $1 for each $2 of earnings for those below full retirement age. The earnings test is not applied to workers who reach full retirement age. Retired workers also must pay Social Security payroll tax and federal and state income taxes on their earnings.

FIGURE 8.2   Social Security Pensions and the Work-Leisure Choice

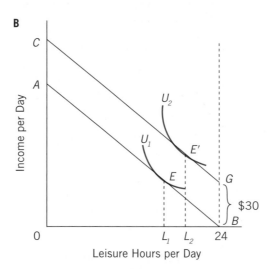

The worker whose budget line and indifference curves are shown in **A** is subject to the earnings test. This worker encounters a substitution effect when he works more than five hours per day. Given his preferences, he is in equilibrium at point *H*. The worker whose choice to work is shown in **B** is not subject to the earnings test. His work-leisure choice is not affected by a substitution effect unfavorable to work.

© Cengage Learning

Figure 8.2 shows the impact of Social Security pensions and the earnings test on workers' incentives. Worker's leisure time per day is plotted against income, given the wage rate per hour for the worker. Each graph shows a retired worker's indifference curves for income and leisure and the income-leisure budget line. The slope of the income-leisure budget line is equal to w, where w is the net wage that the worker can earn.

In Figure 8.2A, the distance BG represents the worker's daily pension benefits, which for a worker with average income would be approximately $30 per day. This would be his income if he took 24 hours per day in leisure. Assume that a typical worker could earn on average up to $30 per day without being subject to the earnings test. Assuming that the worker could find employment at $6 per hour, on average he could work five hours per day without having his pension reduced. This would occur at point *H*, which corresponds to 19 hours of leisure and 5 hours of work per day. Daily income at point *H* will be $60, which equals $30 in wages and approximately $30 of pension benefits. If the worker works more than an average of five hours per day, his Social Security pension, *BG*, will be reduced by $1 for each $2 of earnings. If, for example, *BG* = $30 per day, the worker who earns $90 per day would have his Social Security pension reduced to zero. This is because after the $30 per day not subject to the earnings test is deducted, the worker would have $60 in earnings. This would reduce his pension by the full $30 per day. Because this worker who earns $6 per hour would have to work 15 hours per day (leaving only nine hours of leisure per day) to have his pension benefits reduced to zero, it is unlikely that the worker would lose all of his pension. If the worker chose to work a standard eight-hour day, he would earn $48 per day, on average. Because these earnings are $18 more than the wages not subject to the earnings test, his pension would average $(30 − 18/2) = $21 per day, and his gross daily income would average $48 in earnings plus $21 in pension benefits, or $69. The number of hours of work that would reduce the worker's pension to zero would be less if the worker's hourly wage were higher.

Pension benefits allow the worker some income equal to the distance *BG* even without work. This results in an income effect that increases the demand for leisure. In addition, after a certain point the earnings test reduces the net wage that the retiree can earn until (24 − *L**) hours per day are devoted to work. This decrease in the net wage results in a substitution effect that is also unfavorable to work. In Figure 8.2A, the worker is in equilibrium when eligible for pension benefits at point *H*. At that point, the worker takes 19 hours in leisure and works, on average, only five hours per day, up to the point at which the earnings test begins. This result depends on worker preferences and wage rates. A worker with weaker preferences for leisure or a higher net wage works more hours even though additional work will reduce Social Security benefits. Finally, a worker with strong desires for leisure might be in equilibrium at point *G*. This worker would drop out of the labor force and enjoy 24 hours per day of leisure.

Naturally, the number of hours of work per day at which the pension benefits will fall to zero depends on the worker's pension per day relative to the wage the worker can earn. For workers with low pensions relative to their hourly wages, the point *F* in Figure 8.2A would lie further to the right and would correspond to more leisure and less work per day. Workers with strong desires for work or money income might actually be in equilibrium on the section *AF* of the budget line, at which they forgo their Social Security pension completely and remain in the labor force working full time.

Figure 8.2B shows the impact of Social Security pensions on the work choices of a retiree older than the normal retirement age, not subject to the earnings test. The worker is in equilibrium at point *E* prior to retirement. When this worker retires, the budget line shifts up, parallel to itself, from *AB* to *CG*. The worker's income is increased by the same amount, *BG*, independent of the hours worked. Here there is only an income effect, which is unfavorable to work. Because there is no substitution effect, the worker has greater incentive to work, other things being equal, than would be the case if the earnings test applied. The worker is in equilibrium at point *E′*, at which he continues to work (24 − *L*₂) hours per day. Workers with stronger preferences for leisure might choose to drop out of the labor force.

Participation of the elderly in the labor force has declined since 1940, when 59.6 percent of men aged 65 to 69 were in the labor force. In 2003, 31 percent of men in the 65 to 69 age group and only 18 percent of all men aged 65 or older were still in the labor force. Clearly, the decline was influenced by the increased availability of private pensions and the general trend since 1940 to increasing real income. It is likely, however, that Social Security pensions and other benefits played a significant part in the reduced work incentive of the elderly. A number of empirical studies have provided some evidence of the effect of Social Security benefits on retirement choices and labor force participation. These studies have indicated a very strong negative relationship between labor force participation and the availability of Social Security benefits.[13] Similarly, others have found strong association between increased Social Security benefits and coverage and the declining labor force participation of older workers.[14] However, labor force participation of the elderly has risen significantly since 1990. In that year approximately 16 percent of all 65- to 74-year-olds were in the labor force. Since 1990 labor force participation of this age group has risen steadily, and according the Bureau of Labor Statistics' estimates, in 2005, 22.8 percent of persons age 65 to 74 were in the labor force. The U.S. Bureau of Labor Statistics forecasts that labor force participation of the elderly will continue to grow, and by 2017 it is expected that 27 percent of men age 65 or more will be in the labor force.

The average age of retirement for both men and women as of 2012 is very close to 62 in the United States. One way to further encourage increased labor force participation of the elderly is to raise the minimum age of eligibility for Social Security retirement pensions from 62 to 65. Those who do retire at age 62 receive 25 percent less Social Security pension benefits per year than they would have received had they deferred retiring until they reach their full retirement age. Discouraging early retirement in this way would result in higher annual pension incomes for those who are capable of working after they reach age 62. Studies by the Congressional Budget Office and the Government Accountability Office indicate that as many as 85 percent of those who retire at age 62 do not do so because of health issues that make it difficult or impossible for them to work.

The U.S. income tax system also results in high rates of taxation for persons older than the full retirement age who choose to continue working. In addition to being subjected to the earnings test, which results in a reduction in Social Security pension benefits to retirees younger than the full retirement age, retirees who work also must pay payroll taxes and regular income taxes on their earnings. In addition, elderly workers whose income is more than $25,000 if they are single, or $32,000 if they are married, who have Social Security pensions will pay income tax on one-half to 85 percent (depending on their total income, including one-half of their Social Security pension) of their Social Security benefits. For some retired workers, a dollar of earnings will result in both taxes and loss of Social Security benefits that will exceed the dollar of earnings! This results in very little incentive for the elderly to work. Only those elderly who enjoy working and are willing to work for much less than their gross compensation actually choose to remain in the labor force.

---

[13]Joseph F. Quinn, "Microeconomic Determinants of Retirement: A Cross-Sectional View of White Married Men," *Journal of Human Resources* 12 (Summer 1977): 329–346.

[14]Michael J. Boskin, "Social Security and Retirement Decisions," *Economic Inquiry* 15 (January 1977): 1–25.

Saving Incentives

Among the most serious criticisms of the Social Security system is the assertion that it significantly reduces the rate of saving and capital formation in the economy. This could reduce both economic growth and the potential of the economy to provide jobs and raise incomes. The basic concern is that a pay-as-you-go system of retirement pensions has created the illusion that the tax contributions are placed in a trust fund and invested to provide retirement benefits to workers who belong to the system. As previously emphasized, the tax contributions of workers have been paid by and large directly to existing retirees until recently. The opportunity cost of such a system of paying pension benefits is the forgone return to capital that could have been earned had the taxes collected been invested in a true trust fund.

In effect, those who pay Social Security taxes receive as their return a claim not against any capital asset but against the earnings of future workers who will finance the current worker's pension when they retire. This line of reasoning remains correct even though the Social Security trust fund will grow substantially in the future, because much of the growth of the trust fund will be interest credited to its account by the U.S. Treasury. This interest will not constitute net income to the federal government because the credit of interest income to the fund will be offset by a debit of interest to the Treasury. When, however, the interest buildup is drawn on to pay cash benefits to retirees, the Treasury will have to use general fund revenues to pay out the benefits. Unless economic growth permits such revenues to be allocated without a general tax increase, the federal government might have to choose between increasing tax rates, cutting other government programs, or cutting Social Security replacement rates to meet its commitments.

Although the effects of Social Security retirement benefits on saving are not clear cut even in theory, the worker's incentive to save is affected in two ways. First, the promise of a pension ensures an income for the worker's retirement years, thereby reducing the necessity of saving for old age. Second, by enabling the worker to retire earlier and discouraging work after retirement, Social Security increases the retirement years of the worker. This provides incentives to save more in order to provide the resources to finance various activities associated with a greater period of nonwork and more leisure time.[15] In the United States since the end of World War II, the percentage of national income saved (in the aggregate) has been remarkably stable. Evidence is still scanty and somewhat conflicting, so no consensus has yet emerged among economists as to the actual effects of the Social Security system on saving.

The most controversial of the studies was conducted by Martin Feldstein and first published in 1974.[16] Feldstein's empirical work showed a significant impact of Social Security "wealth" (current value of promised pensions) on the rate of saving. Subsequent research by Leimer and Lesnoy found an error in Feldstein's calculation and concluded that the impact of Social Security wealth on saving could not be verified.[17]

---

[15]Another effect also might increase saving. If Social Security retirement benefits did not exist, and if the law provided for public assistance to the elderly poor, incentives might exist to avoid saving for one's old age so as to be eligible for a means-tested poverty benefit at the time of retirement. The existence of Social Security pensions offsets the incentive to avoid saving so as to be eligible for public assistance at retirement.

[16]Martin Feldstein, "Social Security, Induced Retirement, and Aggregate Capital Accumulation," *Journal of Political Economy* 92 (September–October 1974): 905–926.

[17]Dean R. Leimer and Selig D. Lesnoy, "Social Security and Private Saving: New Time-Series Evidence," *Journal of Political Economy* 90 (June 1982): 606–629.

The Asset-Substitution Effect

The promise of a Social Security pension results in what Feldstein calls an **asset-substitution effect**, reducing the incentive to save. In addition, the Social Security tax directly reduces the worker's income so that the ability to save is reduced, and this, in turn, lowers the rate of saving still further.

Figure 8.3 illustrates the asset-substitution effect for two cases. In Figure 8.3A, a worker's indifference curves for consumption per year prior to retirement and consumption per year after retirement are drawn. If no government retirement system exists, the worker must save to provide retirement income. The line AB shows the worker's opportunity to give up annual preretirement consumption for annual postretirement consumption. The slope of the line reflects the rate of interest that the worker can earn. In the absence of a retirement system, the worker whose indifference curve U_1 is illustrated in Figure 8.3A is in equilibrium at point E. At that point, he gives up CB of annual preretirement consumption each year, which is saved to provide annual postretirement consumption of R per year.

Now suppose the government institutes a payroll tax of T dollars per year and promises the worker a pension of G per year at retirement. Assume that this tax is less than the amount the worker would otherwise save annually for retirement ($S = CB$). The distance DB represents the tax T. The payroll tax reduces the maximum amount of current annual consumption to $0D$ per year but guarantees the worker an annual pension at retirement of $0G$ even if the worker does not save. The worker's opportunity to trade current consumption for saving for retirement is now described by AFD. The worker whose indifference curves are illustrated in Figure 8.3A is still in equilibrium at point E. However, he now is saving only CD per year. The reduction in saving from CB to CD represents the asset-substitution effect. The worker saves less because he is promised a pension of G even in the absence of any saving. In addition, the payroll tax reduces the person's current income, further reducing the ability of the worker to save. However, this worker is no worse off because he still enjoys $0C$ of current consumption and postretirement annual consumption of $0R$. The annual retirement income is equal to the government pension plus GR, from the worker's annual savings of CD.

Figure 8.3B shows the case of a worker who is made worse off as a result of the Social Security system. This worker would be in equilibrium at point E, where S per year is saved to provide postretirement annual consumption of R_2. For this worker, the annual payroll tax, T, exceeds the amount that she normally would save for retirement. However, this tax guarantees the worker a pension of G_2 per year, which is greater than the R_2 income her savings would have financed. The worker's opportunities for allocating consumption between preretirement and postretirement years are now represented by AFD. The government pension system does not give the worker the opportunity to give up part of her pension for more current consumption. The worker's highest level of well-being is now at point F, at which she receives utility level U_1, less than the U_2 that would be possible without Social Security benefits. This worker's saving falls to zero because the payroll tax of T per year and the overgenerous government pension (relative to the worker's preferences) remove both the capacity and the incentive to save for retirement. Also, an excess burden exists in this case due to the distortion between preretirement and postretirement consumption. This distortion results in the loss in well-being, from U_2 to U_1, for the worker.

The Asset-Substitution Effect

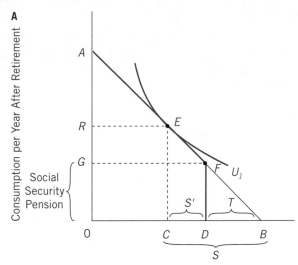

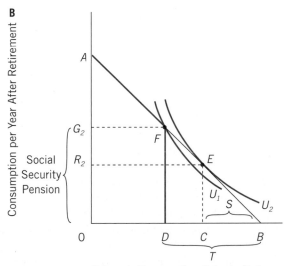

In **A**, the annual Social Security tax, reduces annual savings from *S* to *S'*. In **B**, the annual Social Security tax exceeds annual saving. For this worker, saving falls to zero. He is worse off than if no Social Security system existed and he were allowed to retain enough current income to save for retirement. His utility level is reduced from U_2 at point *E* without Social Security to U_1 at *F* with Social Security.

© Cengage Learning

In both cases, the reduction in saving by workers causes a decline in the rate of saving in the economy. This is because a pay-as-you-go government pension system does not replace lost private saving with government saving. Instead, the payroll taxes collected from individual workers are used to finance the postretirement consumption of retired workers. The result is a net reduction in savings.

The Induced-Retirement Effect

The negative impact of the asset-substitution effect on saving could be offset, however, by other possible effects of the Social Security retirement system. The **induced-retirement effect** results from the fact that Social Security benefits and the earnings test for such benefits tend to provide incentives for early retirement and less work during retirement years. This, in turn, provides incentive for workers to save more for a more lengthy period of retirement.

Feldstein has argued that the asset-substitution effect outweighs the induced-retirement effect. If this is true, the resulting reduction in saving reduces investment and tends to make capital scarcer than it would otherwise be. The scarcity of capital results in workers having fewer machines and other tools to work with than they would otherwise have. This reduces their productivity and results in lower wages than they would otherwise be earning.

It now is generally agreed that Feldstein's original model overestimated the reduction in saving caused by the asset-substitution effect of Social Security wealth. Subsequent research by Alicia Munnell found the induced-retirement effect for increased saving being roughly offset by the asset-substitution effect of Social Security wealth on reduction in saving. Munnell points out, however, that participation of the elderly in the labor force might increase in the future; this would result in a decrease in the reliance on saving to finance retirement. This could increase the relative importance of the asset-substitution effect and cause a net reduction in saving attributable to the existence of Social Security pensions.[18]

The Bequest Effect

Further analysis by Robert J. Barro suggests a theoretical basis for believing that Feldstein's asset-substitution effect is offset by still another influence of Social Security pensions on saving incentives.[19] Barro argues that strong incentives exist for parents to leave bequests to their children. This is the **bequest effect**. Social Security is, in effect, an agreement between generations to finance retirement by taxes on the working population. The transfer from the working population to the retired population, inherent in tax-financed Social Security benefits, increases the capability of the retired generation to put aside funds for bequests to their children. Barro believes that the existence of Social Security pensions provides incentives for the elderly to increase their saving to provide bequests to their children. He has also argued that Social Security pensions decrease the need for children to make payments to support their retired parents. This tends to increase their saving over their working life.[20]

Others have argued that the uncertainty over the future of the Social Security system due to its financial difficulties and the decline in the expected return on tax contributions is likely in the future to increase incentives to save for retirement. To the extent to which the yield on Social Security wealth declines in the future and market interest rates rise above the return on Social Security, increased saving will result. The net effect of the existence of government-supplied retirement benefits on saving remains indeterminate.

---

[18]Alicia H. Munnell, *The Future of Social Security* (Washington, D.C.: The Brookings Institution, 1977), Chapter 6.

[19]Robert J. Barro, "Are Government Bonds Net-Worth?" *Journal of Political Economy* 82 (November/ December 1974): 1095–1117.

[20]Robert J. Barro, *The Impact of Social Security on Private Saving* (Washington, D.C.: American Enterprise Institute, 1977).

1. How are Social Security pensions affected when retirees younger than full retirement age have earnings from work?
2. Explain why both the income and substitution effects of Social Security pensions are unfavorable to work incentives.
3. Why is it difficult to predict the effect of Social Security pensions on saving?

HEALTH INSURANCE FOR THE ELDERLY: MEDICARE

The elderly have had government-supplied health insurance benefits since 1965, when amendments to the Social Security Act were passed. Under this health insurance plan, called **Medicare**, the elderly are covered by hospitalization insurance, which is financed by a special payroll tax amounting to a combined rate of 2.9 percent for employees and employers in 2012 on all labor income. As part of the provisions of the *Patient Protection and Affordable Care Act of 2010*, beginning in 2013 an additional tax of 0.9 percent will be applied to labor income exceeding $200,000 for individuals and $250,000 for married couples filing joint federal income tax returns. Some high-income individuals will also have to pay an additional tax earmarked for Medicare on their investment income.

Medicare is a program of health insurance for eligible persons older than 65 who, in general, have worked in qualified employment subject the HI taxation for a period of ten years, and some disabled workers. Medicare also pays for dialysis and kidney transplants for victims of renal disease no matter what their age. Part A of Medicare is a program of hospital insurance financed by a special payroll tax, the proceeds of which go into the Medicare Hospital Insurance (HI) Fund. Hospital benefits are subject to a deductible and cover only services that are considered medically necessary. Only reasonable charges are paid, and in some cases, Medicare patients end up paying part of the costs of covered services. Part B of Medicare is supplementary medical insurance for doctor's services, diagnostic tests, and some home health care services. Part C, which is also called Medicare Advantage, is a system of private health insurance plans that provide Part A, Part B, and usually prescription drug benefits, to Medicare beneficiaries who choose to enroll in it. As of 2012, about 27 percent of Medicare beneficiaries were enrolled in Part C.

The supplementary medical insurance program under Part B is voluntary and is available to all Americans older than 65 who can purchase the coverage at subsidized rates that vary with incomes of enrollees.. The program pays 80 percent of covered services with certain maximum payments per medical service. In 2006 a new Medicare Part D optional prescription drug program was introduced. This plan provides financial assistance to the elderly to purchase medicines and is administered by private insurance plans. This plan and other aspects of Medicare in the United States will be discussed in detail in Chapter 9.

Why should government provide medical insurance to the elderly? One reason is the "adverse selection problem." *Adverse selection* is a process by which persons who have the greatest probability of obtaining benefits seek to obtain insurance and conceal information about their adverse conditions. In general, insurance companies can pool risks to avoid large payouts due to adverse selection by covering large groups rather than by offering their services to individuals. However, individuals who are no longer employed or do not belong to a clearly definable, insurable group will have to pay higher premiums, because insurance companies must protect themselves from high payouts that might result from adverse selection. Private insurance companies might be reluctant to provide health insurance to the elderly on an individual basis because of the adverse selection problem. This provides a basis for government to pool insurance risks by providing compulsory insurance for a large group, such as the elderly, and financing the costs through taxation. The argument for government supply of medical insurance is based on the presumption that government can provide such coverage to large groups at a lower cost than can be achieved if the insurance were provided through the market.

Expenditures under Medicare were 3.6 percent of GDP in 2010. Medicare expenditures are projected to rise to 5.5 percent of GDP by 2035, and to about 6.2 percent of GDP by 2085. A modest amount of deductible expense must be incurred by the recipient before benefits are paid. Hospitalization benefits are paid for stays of up to 90 days for each benefit period. In effect, Medicare operates like a private health insurance program, providing benefits to all its enrollees independent of their ability to pay for medical services.

Medicare, like its companion program for the poor, Medicaid, discussed in Chapter 7, encourages the consumption of medical services by reducing the price of such services to patients. The effects of government subsidization of consumption of medical services are analyzed in Chapter 7. As pointed out there, upward pressure on the price of medical services to those not covered by the public health plan can result from medical subsidies, and an excess burden will arise from the subsidy when it induces recipients to consume medical services beyond the point at which marginal benefit equals marginal cost.

The Medicare program and other issues in government provision of health care are discussed in greater detail in Chapter 9.

UNEMPLOYMENT INSURANCE

Benefits from **unemployment insurance**, which provides income support for those temporarily out of work because they have been laid off or have lost their jobs for reasons other than misconduct or a labor dispute, are managed by individual states. Each state has its own separate trust fund; however, tax collections to support the program, as well as the trust funds, are managed by the federal government. Unemployment insurance was enacted into law as part of the original Social Security Act of 1935. Unemployment insurance is financed by a federal payroll tax levied entirely on employers on taxable wages up to a maximum of $7,000 per worker. The tax rate paid by each employer is based, in part, on the firm's layoff experiences, with firms that have relatively higher numbers of layoffs paying higher tax rates. This tax is collected by the federal government, but most of the funds are returned to the states, which administer the unemployment insurance program. The individual states levy their own unemployment taxes on wages. The taxable wage base varies by state, but in no case is it less than the federal taxable wage base of $7,000 per year. In

2012, only two states, Arizona and California, had a taxable wage base equal to the federal minimum. In other States the taxable wage base ran from $7,700 per employee to as much as $38,200 per employee. State unemployment tax rates also vary considerably.

Unemployment insurance benefits vary from state to state. The average weekly benefit in 2009 was $410 per week. However, some states, for example Massachusetts, were paying benefits as high as $900 per week to some recipients of unemployment insurance in that year. Maximum weekly unemployment insurance compensation ran from a low of $230 per week in Mississippi to over $900 per week with several states paying maximum benefits of more than $500 per week. Typically, in nonrecession periods benefits have a maximum duration of 26 weeks. In periods when the economy is doing well most unemployed workers find new jobs and go off unemployment insurance compensation within 15 weeks. Congress typically extends benefits beyond the basic 26 weeks during periods of high unemployment. During periods of high unemployment, the "Extended Benefits Program" provides a further 13 to 20 weeks of unemployment compensation to jobless workers in states with very high unemployment rates. The additional 13 weeks is allowed when the unemployment rate exceeds 6.5 percent but is less than 8 percent. When the unemployment rate reaches 8 percent in a state, an additional 20 weeks of eligibility is allowed. Usually the cost of these extra benefits is split between state governments and the federal government. However, during the period 2009–2010 the federal government paid all of these additional costs. Congress often extends benefits beyond that for the long-term unemployed. In 2009 Congress enacted the Emergency Unemployment Compensation Program that allowed as much as 53 extra weeks of unemployment insurance benefits when unemployment rates in a state were at least 8.5 percent allowing maximum possible duration of benefits of 99 weeks in states with very high unemployment rates.

The average duration of benefits in 2009 was close to 70 weeks and some states with very high unemployment rates paid benefits for a maximum of 79 weeks to eligible recipients. The Emergency Unemployment Compensation Program was extended through 2012 to assist the long-term unemployed in states still recovering slowly from the 2007–2009 recession.

The average gross replacement rate as of the period 2007–2009 was close to 50 percent of lost earnings for the average worker collecting unemployment insurance. Gross replacement rates have been increasing in recent years and during periods of recession. Also as a result of new legislation, more workers are eligible for unemployment insurance benefits. The 2009 *American Recovery and Reinvestment Act* allocated $7 billion to states for reforming their unemployment insurance systems and expanding eligibility for benefits. As of 2011, 36 states had enacted reforms. Some states now allow part-time workers to receive unemployment insurance benefits provided that they are willing to seek a new part-time job. In addition, some workers who leave their jobs for certain compelling family reasons are eligible for unemployment insurance benefits. Finally, workers in approved training programs can qualify for an additional six months of unemployment insurance benefits and some workers with dependents will receive additional benefits.

Unemployment insurance benefits vary from state to state, with some states paying dependent allowances. However, in recent years benefits paid have been declining and now average only 33 percent of previous earnings, not keeping pace with inflation rates. Gross replacement rates (GRRs) have declined on average from

50 percent to the current average of 33 percent. Unemployment insurance mainly benefits workers who are laid off or who lose their jobs when businesses shut down or reduce the scale of their operations. Unemployment insurance benefits are not available to new entrants or reentrants into the labor force. For example, a college student who graduates and enters the labor force to look for a job is classified as unemployed until he or she finds a job. However, even if it takes this new entrant a year to find the job, the graduate is not eligible for unemployment insurance benefits.

Unemployment insurance is one of the automatic stabilizers in the federal budget. Its designers expected the system to maintain aggregate demand in periods of recession, when the demand normally falls due to unemployment.

Unemployment benefits are available to all workers who are covered by unemployment insurance, which includes virtually all full-time workers and some part-time workers. The benefits received are positively related to previous earnings. Since 1986, unemployment insurance benefits have been fully taxable as personal income under the federal income tax.

In recent years, the proportion of the unemployed actually receiving unemployment insurance benefits has declined substantially. For example, in early 1990, a recession year, only about one-third of the unemployed was collecting unemployment insurance benefits. In 1975, on average, three-quarters of the unemployed collected such benefits. The reason for the decline is that the contemporary economy includes more service workers and part-time workers, and many of these workers change jobs frequently. The workers do not stay in one job long enough to become eligible for unemployment insurance benefits. In addition, state governments now require workers to work longer and earn more wages before they can collect benefits. Even though nearly all workers are covered by unemployment insurance benefits, the proportion of workers who actually work in covered jobs long enough to get those benefits has been declining. At the beginning of the 2007–2009 recession somewhat less than 40 percent of unemployed workers were collecting unemployment insurance benefits. However, the proportion of the unemployed receiving benefits rose in 2010 as more workers lost their jobs as a result of layoff and the average period of unemployment increased.

Research on the economic effects of unemployment insurance has concentrated on its impact on the duration of unemployment. Some have argued that the availability of generous unemployment insurance benefits subsidizes unemployment and job search by workers who lose their jobs, and therefore this availability lengthens the period of unemployment desired by workers.

As was the case for Social Security retirement benefits, the net replacement rate is a key factor influencing the choices of those receiving unemployment insurance benefits. One study found that a 10 percentage point increase in the replacement rate increased the duration of unemployment by 1½ weeks.[21]

Although unemployed workers are required to register for employment at local offices of the various state employment services, they cannot lose their unemployment benefits unless they refuse the offer of a suitable job. It is, however, difficult to force unemployed workers to accept jobs that pay considerably less than their previous jobs or that have substantially poorer working conditions. Workers have some control over the amount of time they remain unemployed. Their incentives to

---

[21]See Bruce D. Meyer, "Unemployment Insurance and Unemployment Spells," *Econometrica* 58, 4 (July 1990): 757–789.

search for work and to accept lower-paying jobs depend on their replacement rates, the duration of unemployment insurance, and the availability (during their unemployment) of such subsidiary benefits as Supplemental Nutrition Assistance, relative to what they could earn on a new job. The decline in replacement rates since 1970 is likely to have increased incentives for the unemployed receiving unemployment insurance benefits to search for new jobs. The length of the period of job search associated with unemployment, however, has some positive aspects in that in many cases it allows workers to find higher wages and more stable employment.[22] We cannot therefore conclude that reduction in the duration of unemployment is necessarily a good thing.

During the recession that began in late 2007 in the United States, the share of the unemployed receiving unemployment benefits varied widely from state to state from a low of 19 percent to a high of 67 percent. In general, in states where labor unions were strong or where wages were relatively high, workers were more likely to be receiving unemployment insurance benefits. From 2007 to 2009 the number of households receiving unemployment insurance benefits increased from 4.1 to 9.6 percent of all households. Over the same period as a result of longer periods of unemployment and higher weekly benefits the average annual amount received by recipients on unemployment insurance benefits increased from $4,400 to $8,340.

There is also a trend toward workers simply leaving the labor force after losing a job, particularly if they have a disability. In 2010 more that 10 million people were receiving disability pension benefits from the Social Security Administration. Of these recipients, 80 percent were disabled workers and 20 percent were the workers' dependents and payments under the program in 2010 amounted to more than $100 billion. Since 1990, the number of persons receiving disability pension benefits in the United States has more than doubled. One theory for the increase in enrollment is that as wages for skilled workers and unemployment insurance benefits have declined, more workers with mild disabilities have chosen to apply for disability benefits. These workers would have normally worked despite injuries and chronic pain. However, many of these workers, who lack college education and qualify only for low-paying jobs, find that the benefits they qualify for are a better alternative to the wages they can earn in the labor market.

CHECKPOINT

1. How does the Medicare program operate in the United States?
2. Why does "adverse selection" make it difficult or expensive for the elderly to obtain private health insurance?
3. How does the unemployment insurance system operate in the United States? Why has the proportion of the unemployed who actually receive such benefits been declining in recent years?

---

[22]For a review of studies on the effects of unemployment insurance, see Anthony B. Atkinson and John Micklewright, "Unemployment Compensation and Labor Market Transitions: A Critical Review," *Journal of Economic Literature* 29 (December 1991): 1679–1727.

SUMMARY

The Social Security Act of 1935 is the basis for most forms of social insurance in the United States today, including government-supplied retirement benefits, disability and survivors' insurance, health insurance for the elderly, and unemployment insurance. Social insurance is more comprehensive in many European countries, where health insurance, family allowances, and maternity benefits are supplied to all residents and financed through tax contributions.

The Social Security retirement system is tax financed and has been designed on a pay-as-you-go basis. Benefits are financed by a payroll tax on both employees and employers on wages paid up to a certain maximum amount per worker. The gross replacement rate (GRR) measures the percentage of preretirement earnings replaced by pension benefits. This rate tends to decline with preretirement income. The net replacement rate (NRR) is the percentage of preretirement after-tax earnings replaced by pension benefits.

Demographic changes anticipated in the 21st century have necessitated increases in Social Security taxes to finance benefits to future retirees at existing replacement rates. The amendments to the Social Security Act, passed by Congress in 1977 and 1983, scheduled significant increases in the payroll tax that will finance Social Security retirement benefits.

The return earned on Social Security by retirees, given rates of taxation to finance benefits, depends on the rate of growth of the taxable wages. In turn, the growth of taxable wages depends on the growth of the labor force subject to Social Security taxes and the growth of real wages, with the latter being dependent on productivity. Little growth is expected in the labor force during the next few years and the rate of productivity growth is

forecast to be no more than 2 percent. Given the increased ratio of retirees per worker expected in the future and the indexing of retirement benefits with the rate of inflation, payroll tax rates have risen to finance current and future Social Security pensions.

Considerable concern has been expressed about the impact of Social Security retirement benefits on incentives to work and save. The availability and structure of Social Security benefits can discourage the elderly from working. The earnings test for retired workers between the ages of 62 and the full retirement age reduces retirement benefits by one dollar for every two dollars earned, after a certain allowable amount of earnings.

The effect of Social Security retirement benefits on saving is controversial. Because Social Security guarantees workers a pension, the incentive to save for retirement is diminished. On the other hand, insofar as Social Security benefits enable the worker to retire early, the incentive to save, and thus to provide for a longer period of retirement, is increased. The net effect on saving is indeterminate. The actual impact of the Social Security system on saving has not been unequivocally determined by empirical research.

Other forms of social insurance in the United States include health insurance for the elderly and unemployment benefits for workers. Medicare subsidizes medical expenses incurred by people age 65 and older. Unemployment insurance is available to workers who are laid off from their jobs. The replacement rate averages about 33 percent of previous wages. Because unemployment insurance subsidizes those workers who are between jobs, concern has been expressed about its impact on the length of unemployment desired by workers.

LOOKING AHEAD

Chapter 9 presents a discussion of health and medical expenditures and discusses the role of government in providing health benefits. The current system of provision of

health insurance is discussed and the costs and benefits of an expanded government role in the provision of health insurance services are analyzed.

KEY CONCEPTS

Asset-Substitution Effect

Average Indexed Monthly Earnings (AIME)

Bequest Effect

Earnings Test

Fully Funded Pension System

Gross Replacement Rate (GRR)

Induced-Retirement Effect

Medicare

Net Replacement Rate (NRR)

Old-Age, Survivors, and Disability Insurance (OASDI)

Pay-as-You-Go Pension System

Social Security and Insurance Programs

Tax-Financed Pension System

Unemployment Insurance

REVIEW QUESTIONS

1. What are the basic distinctions between social insurance and government assistance programs for the poor?

2. How do Social Security benefits increase the incomes of low-income workers relative to upper-income workers? Discuss the distinction between the net and gross replacement rates for workers. What does a NRR of 100 percent imply about the standard of living of a retiree relative to preretirement earnings?

3. What are the fundamental differences between fully funded and pay-as-you-go tax-financed retirement systems? How can the Social Security system continue to pay pension benefits even if its trust fund is depleted?

4. Under what conditions will the growth of tax revenues to pay Social Security benefits equal the rate of growth of labor earnings in the economy? Why have payroll tax rates been increased in recent years?

5. How can lowering replacement rates or increasing the retirement age affect the Social Security tax rate?

6. Many economists assert that Social Security pensions redistribute income from single workers to married workers with dependent spouses and from high-income workers to low-income workers. Why is this likely?

7. Use indifference curve analysis to show how the availability of Social Security pensions and the application of the earnings test are likely to decrease hours worked and labor force participation of the elderly.

8. Use indifference curve analysis to show how a pay-as-you-go Social Security retirement system can decrease a worker's savings per year from a positive amount to zero. Under what circumstances will the system make a worker worse off than would be the case if there were no such system?

9. In what sense are Social Security pension benefits based on "need"?

10. How can the bequest effect and the induced-retirement effect offset the asset-substitution effect?

PROBLEMS

1. A middle-income worker with a dependent spouse older than the normal retirement age retired in January 2004. In the year prior to retirement, her gross monthly earnings are $1,500. Her Social Security pension benefit is $1,000 per month. Prior to retirement, she was subject to total taxes on her labor earnings amounting to 20 percent. Calculate her gross and net replacement rates. Suppose the cash value of Medicare subsidies that she expects to receive during retirement amount to $2,000 per year. Recalculate the replacement rates, including the Medicare benefits.

2. Suppose the real rate of growth of wages subject to Social Security taxes is expected to average 1 percent per year during the next 40 years. Assuming that the Social Security tax rate remains constant, prove that the average return on Social Security taxes paid into the Social Security trust fund also will be 1 percent. Explain why workers with high incomes can expect negative returns on their Social Security taxes during this period.

3. Use the data from Problem 1 to plot the worker's daily money income–leisure trade-off line. To do so, calculate her daily pension and assume 150 working hours in a month. Assume that the worker is allowed to earn $8,000 per year before her Social Security benefits are reduced by $1 for each $3 of labor earnings. Show how it is possible for the retiree to be indifferent between not working at all and working enough to give up all her Social Security benefits.

4. Use indifference curve analysis to show how the Social Security pension system can reduce annual consumption for some workers who have strong preference for current versus future consumption. What factors will influence the effect of the Social Security system on an individual's well-being and savings rate?

5. Suppose the average Social Security benefits in the nation are $12,000 per year. The number of Social Security pension recipients is currently 50 million. There are 150 million workers in the workforce this year and the average taxable wage per worker is $25,000 per year.
   a. Calculate the dependency ratio for the nation.
   b. Calculate the average replacement rate for Social Security retirees.
   c. Calculate the tax rate on wages necessary to pay Social Security benefits this year assuming the system is operating on a pay-as-you-go basis.
   d. Suppose the number of retirees is expected to increase to 75 million in the next ten years while the labor force remains at 150 million. Assuming nothing else changes, calculate the tax rate necessary to pay promised benefits on a pay-as-you-go basis. What can be done to lower this tax rate?

ADDITIONAL READINGS

Aaron, Henry J. "Social Security Reconsidered." *National Tax Journal* 64, 2 (June 2011): 385–414. Analysis of ways to reform the U.S. Social Security system while maintaining its basic pay-as-you-go framework, restoring fiscal balance, and improving its social insurance functions by adjusting benefit structures to reflect demographic changes since the system was first developed such as the growth of two-earner families.

Clements, Donna A. *Guide to Social Security*. 41st ed. Louisville, Ky.: Mercer, 2013. A concise booklet explaining the nuts and bolts of the Social Security system. Revised annually.

Cordes, Joseph J., and C. Eugene Steurle. *A Primer on Privatization*. The Retirement Project Occasional Paper Number 2. Washington, D.C.: The Urban Institute, November 1999. A discussion of issues and problems relating to privatization of Social Security in the United States.

Diamond, Peter A. "Proposals to Restructure Social Security." *Journal of Economic Perspectives* 10, 4 (Summer 1996): 67–88. Extensive discussion of issues in Social Security reform, including analysis of reforms in Chile, Sweden, and other nations.

Favreault, Melissa M., Frank J. Sammartino, and C. Eugene Steuerle, eds. *Social Security and the Family*. Washington, D.C.: Urban Institute Press, 2002. A collection of essays analyzing how changes in the structure of the American Family have affected the way Social Security pensions serve the elderly. Reforms in the system of spousal and survivors' benefits are discussed.

Kotlikoff, Laurence J. "Fixing Social Security—What Would Bismark Do?" *National Tax Journal* 64, 2 (June 2011): 415–428. Discusses a radical reform of the U.S. Social Security system to reduce its complexity and its possible adverse affects on saving and intergenerational equity. Advocates a "Personal Security System" designed to increase national savings rates, reduce future budget deficits, and achieve a higher return on retirement saving.

Rejda, George E. *Social Insurance and Economic Security*. 6th ed. Englewood Cliffs, N.J.: Prentice-Hall, 2000. A comprehensive analysis of the many social insurance programs commonly provided by industrial nations.

Stein, Bruno. *Social Security and Pensions in Transition*. New York: The Free Press, 1980. A comprehensive analysis of both government and private pension systems. Discusses the history of the Social Security system, development of private pensions, and basic problems faced by both types of retirement systems. The book is written well and does not require a strong background in economics.

U.S. Congress of the United States, Congressional Budget Office. *Baby Boomers in Retirement: An Early Perspective*. Washington, D.C.: U.S. Government Printing Office, September 1993. An analysis of how the baby-boom generation is likely to fare in retirement compared with their parents.

U.S. Congress of the United States, Congressional Budget Office. *Social Security: A Primer*. Washington, D.C.: U.S. Government Printing Office, September 2001. An informative overview of the Social Security program, focusing on some of the challenges the system will face as the population ages.

INTERNET RESOURCES

http://www.ssa.gov

This is the home page of the Social Security Administration. You can browse this site to obtain data on current Social Security programs, including pensions, disability insurance, and other programs. With proper personal identification, you can even obtain information on your own payment of Social Security taxes (the Social Security Administration might refer to these as "contributions" but they are simply payroll tax payments made by you and your employers). If you are close to retirement, the site can also provide information on your prospective retirement benefits.

http://www.dhhs.gov

This is the home page of the Department of Health and Human Services. If you access the Health Care Financing Administration, you can obtain data and information on both the Medicare and Medicaid programs.

http://www.urban.org

This is the home page of the Urban Institute, which is sponsoring "The Retirement Project." You can access papers and information about Social Security at this site.

Chapter 9

GOVERNMENT AND HEALTH CARE

LEARNING OBJECTIVES

After reading this chapter, you should be able to:

- Explain the unique features of the market for health care in the United States and how these impair efficiency of operation of the market.

- Discuss trends in health care spending in the United States.

- Analyze how third-party payments for health care services affect incentives to purchase and provide such services.

- Evaluate the role of government in regulating and providing health care services.

- Discuss the basic benefits of the Medicare and Medicaid programs.

- Analyze alternative government policies for controlling the growth of health care costs and extending health insurance coverage to all citizens of a nation.

In the United States, we spend much more per person for health care than do citizens of other nations—twice as much as a share of our GDP as Denmark, Japan, and the United Kingdom, and one third more as a share of GDP compared to most industrial nations. As of 2010, the United States was allocating nearly 18 percent of its GDP to health care, while most other industrial nations were allocated between 6 and 12 percent of their respective GDPs. Projections by the Centers for Medicare and Medicaid Services indicate that unless reforms are enacted, health care spending in the United States will approach 20 percent of GDP by 2020 and amount to more than nearly $14,000 per person at that time! Yet despite the high spending on health care, dissatisfaction with the system is widespread. Other nations, particularly those in Europe, spend less on health care as a share of their GDP, provide universal coverage of health benefits to all their citizens, and produce better health care outcomes such as lower rates of infant mortality, higher survival rates for heart attacks, and longer life expectancy. Rapidly rising prices for medical services are a serious concern—during the 1980s, prices for medical services rose at more than twice the rate of prices for other goods and services on average. As of 2009, inflation for medical services was running at 4 percent per year, while prices on average for all consumer items were falling. In 2014, Center for Medicare and Medicaid Services projects that health spending will grow 8.3 percent. The projected acceleration in the growth rate, up from 5.5 percent in 2013, is the result of expansion of health insurance coverage expected as a result of recent legislation.

Governments are playing an increasingly active role in the finance of health care in the United States. Federal, state, and local governments paid 44 percent of health care bills incurred by Americans in 2010. The federal government's budget is allocating more and more funds to finance health care expenditures. In 1970, the federal government allocated 7.1 percent of its budget to health care spending; by 2010, it allocated 25 percent of its budget to health.

In 2010, after a long political battle, President Obama signed new and controversial legislation designed to reform the system of health care in the United States. The *Patient Protection and Affordable Care Act of 2010* will have a major impact on the markets for health care and health insurance as its provisions are phased in through 2018. This new legislation is designed to provide health insurance coverage to American citizens previously without such coverage. The Act includes a mandate requiring many of the currently uninsured to obtain health insurance along with a host of provisions to subsidize the costs of insurance for many of these people and new regulations and taxes designed to reform the health insurance markets and finance the costs of the program.

In this chapter, we examine the market for health care in the United States with special emphasis on the role of government in that market. We examine how a system of third-party payments for medical services affects incentives to consume and supply such services. We then examine mechanisms and policy alternatives that can result in a more efficient allocation of resources to health care and stem the growth of rising health care expenditures. Finally, we look at alternative means of financing and rationing medical and health care services, including universal entitlement, national health insurance, and government-provided health care.

CHARACTERISTICS OF THE U.S. MARKET FOR HEALTH CARE

Buying health care is not like buying pizza or jeans. Purchases of most medical services are not made to provide immediate gratification or to satisfy a person's desire to accumulate possessions. By and large, medical services are purchased when a person is ill or injured. A great deal of uncertainty surrounds an individual's own demand for medical services because no one can predict an illness or an injury. However, when such services are needed, the individual can expect potentially high treatment costs—in some cases of catastrophic illness or injury, these costs could exceed the ability of the individual to pay and force the person into bankruptcy. Because of both the uncertainty and potentially high cost, individuals rationally seek to purchase insurance for their health care costs.

The system that has evolved in the United States is one in which health insurance is provided as part of the compensation of most employees, whereas the elderly and the poor who qualify are covered under Medicare and Medicaid—government-provided health insurance programs. Those who do not receive health insurance benefits from their employers, or do not qualify for either Medicare or Medicaid, can purchase health insurance in the marketplace if they choose to do so.

As of 2010, some form of health insurance covered 84 percent of the U.S. population. An estimated 50 million Americans lacked such insurance in that year. Health insurance has become the ticket for health care services in the United States. Those without health insurance coverage run the risk of being refused service by medical providers when they need it unless it is an emergency or unless they pay for the service in advance. The *Patient Protection and Affordable Care Act of 2010* will reshape the market for health care in the next few years by sharply reducing the number of uninsured and increasing government subsidies for health insurance through tax credits and expansion of eligibility for Medicaid.

The insurance-dominated market for medical care has reduced the price consciousness of the public. On average, consumers of medical care pay 14 percent of the market price of services they consume. This encourages both the provision and consumption of medical services. The bulk of our bills for medical services is paid for by insurance, and the premiums we or our employers pay are not necessarily related to the quantity of such services we as individuals consume. However, as we all consume more services and are offered better-quality (and therefore higher-cost) services, our health care spending rises. And as spending on health care increases, so do insurance premiums. In other words, the insurance-based payment system for medical services has impaired the ability of prices to ration medical services efficiently, and this, in turn, has increased insurance premiums so that many individuals choose not to purchase insurance. Many employers, especially those who employ unskilled workers, find that to offer health insurance to their workers would raise their labor costs enough to impair their competitiveness in their product markets. Therefore, under the current system, many small firms often choose not to include health insurance as part of the compensation of their workers.

The host of other imperfections in markets for medical services includes problems of dispersing accurate information to consumers, a tax system that has encouraged some large employers to compensate workers with general health insurance plans while making it difficult for small businesses to get insurance for their employees, and an array of private and government insurance plans that pay different prices for the same medical services, thereby affecting the incentives of medical providers. All these imperfections naturally result in demands for government action to alter both the function and outcomes in the market for medical services and health care.

Before we examine the role of government in this market, we must examine how some of its unique features affect the way it functions. Let's first examine spending trends in the market for health care services and then look at some of the possible explanations for these trends.

Health Care Spending in the United States

Expenditures on health care in the United States have been rising rapidly. In 1960, we allocated only 5.3 percent of the value of our national production to health care. In 2010, total national spending, including hospital care, professional services, drugs, and a variety of other health services such as research and the construction of medical facilities, amounted to 17.9 percent of GDP. The share of GDP allocated to health care has more than tripled since 1960. Figure 9.1 shows how health care spending has increased as a percentage of GDP since 1960. Between 1993 and 1998, health care spending in the United States stabilized at around 13.5 percent of GDP. Health care expenditures have risen rapidly since 2000 and are projected to grow as a share of GDP approaching 20 percent by 2020.

FIGURE 9.1   U.S. Health Expenditures as a Percentage of Gross Domestic Product, 1960–2010

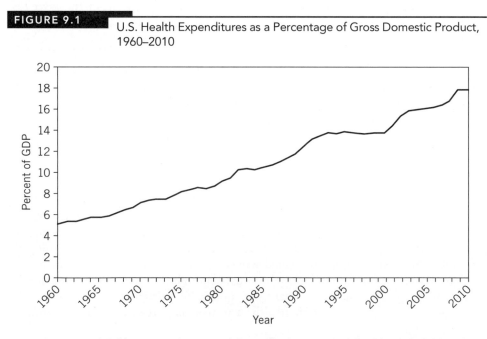

Expenditures on health care in the United States have risen rapidly since 1960, absorbing 17.9 percent of GDP in 2010.

Source: Centers for Disease Control and Prevention, National Center for Health Statistics, Health, United States.

FIGURE 9.2 Financing Health Care Expenditures in the United States, 2010

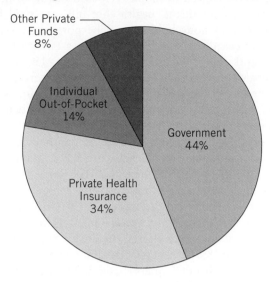

Source: "Centers for Medicare & Medicaid Services, Office of the Actuary, National Health Statistics Group." Percents in the pie chart have been rounded to full numbers.

The pie chart in Figure 9.2 shows how total health expenditures in the United States were financed in 2010. Of the total amount spent in 2010, 43.8 percent was paid for by governments, with the federal government accounting for the largest share (about 70 percent) of total federal, state, and local government spending on health care. The strong government presence in the market for these services has been growing at a rapid rate as has the overall rate of increased spending on health care in the nation. However, expenditures by governments in the United States are low compared to health care spending by governments in other industrialized nations. Most European nations have extensive government provision of health care, and governments typically foot 77 to 90 percent of the health care bill and finance those costs with taxes. For example, Norway has an extensive publicly financed system of health care and pays 97.6 percent of all the health expenditures of Norwegians. Yet at the same time, Norway allocates only 9.6 percent of its GDP to health care compared to 17.9 percent in the United States as of 2010. Most European nations devote less than 10 percent of their GDP to health expenditures. Health expenditure per capita in the United States is more than double that of most European nations.

As of 2010, according the U.S. Department of Census Current Population Survey, only about 31 percent of the population is enrolled in the two major government health insurance programs: Medicare and Medicaid. However, those enrolled in these programs—the elderly, the poor, and the disabled, as well as those in these groups receiving services in nursing homes—tend to consume large amounts of medical care. For this reason, these programs absorb a disproportionate amount of total medical costs relative to the numbers enrolled.

Even though 64 percent of the American population in 2010 was enrolled in private health insurance plans, these plans absorbed only 34 percent of total health care costs. This is because many of those enrolled in such plans are relatively young and healthy members of the workforce.[1] As of 2010, about 55 percent of the people in the United States were covered by employer-based health insurance.

Only 13.7 percent of Americans' health care bills are paid for directly by the individuals as out-of-pocket household costs. The portion of health care expenses directly paid for by Americans has been declining as a result of increased insurance coverage of major and minor health problems since 1965. In that year, out-of-pocket costs of health care to individuals financed 46 percent of expenditures in the United States. We have been spending less and less of our own funds on health care during the past 30 years, with more of our medical bills being paid for by various insurance programs. This is a very significant factor in the rise of health care spending in the United States that we analyze in depth in this chapter. Even in recent years, out-of-pocket costs for medical care have fallen from 17 percent of total expenditures in 1998 to 13.7 percent in 2010. Since 2010 the out-of-pocket cost of health care has risen as private and government insurance plans have increased insured's co-payments and deductibles for health expenditures.

Total spending on health care per person in the United States amounted to $8,402 in 2009. Government expenditures for health care in the same year were $1,138 billion, with nearly 80 percent of that amount accounted for by Medicaid and Medicare. As pointed out in Chapters 7 and 8, Medicaid provides health insurance mainly for the poor and Medicare for the elderly and the permanently disabled.

Per capita spending for health care by governments was more than $3,680 in 2009—and rising rapidly. Expenditures for health care in the United States include hospital services; professional services such as those of physicians, dentists, and nurses; drugs; health care equipment and buildings; the cost of administering the system; and the cost of research.

Asymmetric Information

One possible explanation for rising health care spending concerns the methods of providing information in the marketplace for medical services. The market for medical care is one of *asymmetric information* in which the sellers of medical care are better informed about cost and quality than are the buyers with whom they trade. Usually, consumers of medical care are patients whose only source of information on the benefits of medical procedures and products is the medical care providers, mainly physicians. Often, information on the costs of treatments, especially emergency treatment, is difficult or impractical to obtain in advance. In effect, patients allow physicians to make decisions for them. The physician in most cases is trained to and has the incentive to maximize the quality of care provided to the patient.

However, medical care, like any other good or service, is provided in efficient amounts only when it is consumed to the point at which its marginal benefit to the consumer falls to equal its marginal cost to the provider. The problem under asymmetric information in the market for health care is that the consumer must rely on the provider for information on both the marginal benefit and the marginal cost of the health care. If the marginal benefit of medical procedures is overstated or if physicians, in their attempt to provide the highest-quality care, prescribe procedures

---

[1]Sherry A. Glied and Dahlia K. Remler, "What Every Public Finance Economist Needs to Know about Health Economics: Recent Advances and Unresolved Questions," *National Tax Journal* 55, 4 (December 2002): 772.

for which marginal benefits fall short of marginal costs, then more than the efficient amount of resources will be devoted to medical care.

Some evidence indicates that asymmetric information does lead to overspending on health care. For example, a study of Medicare patients who underwent a procedure to remove plaque from their carotid arteries to avoid blockage found that one-third of the operations involved costs that exceeded benefits. The problem was that patients were not adequately informed about the complications possible from the procedure, such as the risk of stroke. In fact, about 10 percent of the people undergoing the procedure died within a month after the surgery!

Similarly, many life-lengthening procedures for terminally ill patients could cost more than their benefits to patients. Remember that physicians are trained to provide benefits to their patients. The weighing of the benefits of such life-lengthening procedures against the costs can be done only by the patient receiving the benefits. Further, under an insurance-based health care system, the patient rarely bears the full cost of such procedures. Instead, the costs are shared by many individuals to the extent to which services to individuals increase health care spending and insurance premiums.

Risk and the Market for Health Insurance

In a risky world, individuals desire health insurance to cushion the costs of unplanned and uncertain medical expenses. Private insurance companies can provide such coverage for individuals while earning profit because they are able to pool the risks incurred by a large group of individuals. Because you do not know in advance that you might be unfortunate enough to become ill or have an accident that forces you to incur very high medical bills for the year, you are likely to seek insurance. Most people are risk averse, meaning that they prefer to incur a certain modest cost for insurance rather than to risk high costs as a result of an unforeseen prospect. For example, you might be perfectly healthy this year and incur no medical expenses at all. On the other hand, suppose there is a 1 percent probability that you will contract a major illness that requires you to spend $100,000 in medical bills. The expected costs of your medical expenses are $1,000. A risk-averse person prefers the certain outcome of spending $1,000 or even more for $100,000 of health insurance as opposed to running the risk of getting ill and having to pay $100,000 for treatment.

Companies that provide health insurance to a large and diverse group of clients, on the other hand, can easily predict their expenses. If they know the historic probabilities of recent diseases and other medical problems, they can charge premiums that cover the costs of the medical expenses they insure and can add on additional administrative costs for processing claims and still make a profit by selling the policies to risk-averse consumers. For example, if the company provides $100 million worth of insurance per year for which the average probability of payout is 1 percent, then it can finance payouts if it collects premiums from enrollees of $1 million per year. To cover administrative costs and earn a profit, the company will charge a bit more, say, 10 percent.

The system of health insurance in the United States does not, however, insure only against low-probability medical expenses. Instead, virtually all expenses are covered up to certain limits after patients meet their deductibles. Our insurance system insures against low-cost treatment as well as high-cost treatment. By insuring treatment of high-probability expenses, such as treatment of minor ailments, including the common cold and most routine visits to a physician for minor health problems, health insurance in the United States has reduced price consciousness of the public and has impaired the ability of the marketplace to ration health care services. Many employer-provided health insurance plans also pay for routine dental expenses and eyeglasses.

The extension of health insurance to cover both high-probability and relatively low-cost risks has resulted in high insurance premiums. The coverage costs more simply because more is being covered. In addition, the risks associated with the sale of private health insurance have made health insurance providers more cautious when taking on new business. In deciding to provide insurance to a group of individuals or an employer, insurance firms weigh the marginal cost of providing that insurance against the marginal return. If the marginal revenue from the sale of the policy falls short of the marginal cost, the insurance firm will not sell the insurance. Given the rising cost of health care and the high expenditures associated with major illnesses, many health insurers have been reluctant to expose themselves to the risk of high payouts. The insurers have moved from "community rating," which charges premiums based on the expected costs of serving a population, to "experience rating." Under experience rating, insurance firms base premiums for a group on the expected costs of serving *that particular group*. Under this method of pricing, relatively healthy groups pay low prices for health insurance. On the other hand, a group with a poor experience rating, or for which one member has incurred very high medical expenses during the year because of an illness, will pay much higher premiums than would be the case if community rating was used.

Third-Party Payments

The system of health care that has evolved in the United States is based mainly on private provision of services with a mix of private and government health insurance programs reimbursing health care providers for their services. Those who have health insurance pay only a small portion of their health care bills. Instead, most medical and health care costs are paid for by an insurance company or a government program such as Medicare or Medicaid on behalf of the patients. As of 2011, average annual premiums for employer-provided health insurance policies were $5,429 for coverage of individuals and $15,000 for policies that covered workers and their families. On average, employers paid 82 percent of the cost of coverage for individual workers and 72 percent of the cost of policies that covered workers and their families (based on the Kaiser/HRET Survey of Employer-Sponsored Health Benefits, 2011).

The system of health care provision in the United States is financed by **third-party payments,** where the third party is neither the purchaser nor the seller of the service. Third-party payments have important effects on the incentives of patients to use medical services and on the incentives of health care providers to supply those services. When an insured person needs health care services, all but a small portion of the bill is typically paid by the insurer. The typical insurance plan requires patients first to incur a certain amount of health care expenditures, called the **deductible,** before the plan starts paying benefits. After this initial amount is paid by the patient, the plan takes care of most of the additional expenses incurred during the year up to a certain maximum that varies from plan to plan. The amount paid as an out-of-pocket cost by the individual is called **coinsurance** and varies from plan to plan, but is typically 20 percent of the cost. After a patient incurs the deductible expense of the plan, the insurance plan pays the remaining 80 percent of covered expenses.

The system of third-party payments increases the incentive to both consume and provide health care services. Figure 9.3 shows that having health insurance increases spending on health care. The graph shows both the demand and supply curves for health care services. Without health insurance, each patient would have to pay his or her own medical bills, the equilibrium price of health care services on average would be P^*, and the equilibrium quantity sold per year would be Q^*. Assuming that the demand for health care services reflects the marginal social benefit of such services and the supply reflects the marginal social cost, the efficient quantity of these services would be produced, because at P^* the marginal social benefit of health care equals its marginal social cost. However, with both private and government-provided health insurance, the price per unit of health care services will be lower than P^*. The explanation is that after patients meet their deductible, they pay only a small fraction of the actual charge for various health care services, including surgery, hospital stays, and prescription drugs. Suppose that on average, availability of health insurance reduces the price per unit of service from P^* to P_1 to patients. As a result of the price decline in out-of-pocket costs, the quantity of health care service demanded increases from Q^* to Q_1. As the quantity demanded

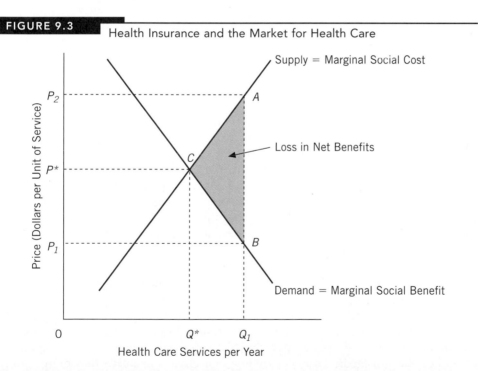

FIGURE 9.3   Health Insurance and the Market for Health Care

The third-party payment mechanism of health insurance lowers the out-of-pocket cost of health care to insurees. The price of health care is effectively reduced to consumers from P^* to P_1. As the quantity demanded increases from Q^* to Q_1, the price to health care providers must rise to P_2 to prevent shortages in the market. Third parties pay the difference between the price to buyers and the price received by providers. The system encourages an overallocation of resources to health care beyond the point at which the marginal social benefit of such services falls to equal the marginal social cost.

© Cengage Learning

increases, the quantity supplied also must increase to prevent shortages in the market. However, to attract the additional resources required to increase the availability of medical services, the price paid to the supplier must increase. As shown in Figure 9.3, the price to medical providers per unit of service on average must increase from P^* to P_2 to induce providers to make Q_1 units of service available per year. The system of third-party payments has both reduced the price of services for patients and increased the price of services received by health care providers while increasing the amount of resources devoted to health care!

The system reduces people's incentive to economize on the use of health care services. The quantity of services demanded does not increase because people are becoming ill more often. It increases because individuals visit physicians more often for minor ailments they might choose to treat themselves if they had to pay the full price for such services. In addition, because physicians and other medical practitioners know that patients pay only a fraction of the price for services, they prescribe more tests and other services than they would otherwise. Naturally, because the price paid per unit of services to providers increases as a result of health insurance while the quantities demanded and supplied also increase, total expenditures on health care also increase. As shown in Figure 9.3, total expenditures per year on health care services increase from P^*Q^* to P_2Q_1. Health insurance therefore increases spending on health care. Total out-of-pocket expenditures by consumers are, of course, much lower after health insurance—an amount represented by the area $0P_1BQ_1$ in the graph. However, the bulk of the expenditures for health care is paid directly to medical providers by the private and government health insurers. The amount paid by third parties is represented by the area P_1P_2AB. These expenditures are financed by the health insurance premiums employers and their employees pay for coverage and the taxes that finance the government insurance programs of Medicare and Medicaid.

As a result of third-party payments, more than the efficient amount of health care services is provided in the marketplace. Health insurance results in Q_1 units of health care demanded per year. At that level of consumption, the marginal social cost of health care services exceeds the marginal social benefit of such services to consumers. The marginal social cost of the services at point A is P_2, while the marginal social benefit of Q_1 units of service per year (see point B on the demand curve) is only P_1. The marginal social cost of the services exceeds the marginal social benefit by an amount equal to the distance AB, which represents the average portion of services paid by third parties.

The area ABC represents the loss in net benefits from resource use resulting from overallocation of resources to health care production beyond the point at which MSB falls to equal MSC.

The **moral hazard of health insurance** is the increase in the incentive to consume and supply health care services that results from the reduction in price to consumers when third parties pay the bulk of medical expenses. Because out-of-pocket costs for medical services are low to insured consumers, they more readily agree to more procedures and prescriptions than they would in the absence of insurance. Another reason for the increase in the quantity demanded is that coverage by insurance reduces incentive to take adequate precautions against incurring an insured expense. For example, those with theft insurance might take few precautions (such as locks and burglar alarms) to discourage thieves than would be the case if no insurance was available. People with health insurance might take fewer precautions to protect their health than they would if they had to pay the full price of medical care resulting from illnesses that they could avoid through changing their lifestyle. The magnitude of the moral hazard of health insurance would depend on the elasticity of demand for health care services. The more elastic the demand, the greater is the magnitude of the moral hazard. Based on an estimated price elasticity of demand for medical care of –0.2, one ballpark estimate of the efficiency loss of health insurance is quite high—amounting to between 8 and 28 percent of total national health expenditures.

Concern about the moral hazard problem associated with reduced-price provision of a good that is price excludable, such as medical care, has resulted in the development of various schemes to make consumers more price conscious. The deductible amount of an insurance policy, as previously discussed, requires a certain amount of expense to be incurred for health care before the company will start to pay benefits. Deductibles for many private health insurance plans run between $150 and $1,000 per year. The deductible reduces the incentive to seek medical care for minor problems. Because consumers who do not exceed the deductible in medical care costs will pay the full price of service, they must compare the marginal benefit of such services with the marginal social cost of the services. These individuals will be more careful in planning their health care expenditures than other individuals whose expenditures exceed the deductible.

Coinsurance, as mentioned earlier, requires consumers to pay some share of the price of the health care services they consume while the remainder is paid by the insurance company. Coinsurance is commonly used together with deductibles to make insured consumers more price conscious.

Finally, insurance companies often limit their payments to fixed amounts for certain services. If this amount does not cover the full cost, the insured has to make up the difference or the provider will have to absorb the difference. This technique of limiting payout provides incentives for both the consumers and providers of medical care to economize on the quantity and quality of services they consume. Sometimes health insurance companies reimburse providers for "usual, customary, and reasonable" charges for certain medical procedures. The patient has to pay any differences between these charges and actual charges.

However, health care providers can be expected to respond to limits in payment. One obvious response is to refuse service to those whose insurance plans do not reimburse providers at acceptable rates. Often a provider must sign a contract with insurance firms and agree to accept a stipulated fee as payment in full without the option of charging the patient the difference. Under these circumstances the provider might refuse to accept patients with such insurance.

Providers often respond to limits in reimbursement by increasing the volume of services sold to patients in the insurance plan. This might include more (and possibly unnecessary) tests, extra visits to check on progress, and other services providing little or no benefit to the patient. In the case of health maintenance organizations (HMOs), integrated delivery and finance systems for healthcare, and managed care facilities where providers receive a fixed fee per patient regardless of the volume of services, the impact on incentives could be to reduce volume of service per patient. The physician in the practice might also seek to discourage unhealthy patients from enrolling in the HMO because of high costs. They could also limit tests and cut back on referrals to specialists for fear that the insurance company might not reimburse them for costs. So limiting payments to HMOs could provide incentives to cut services rather than to become more efficient and contain costs.

Other Features Contributing to Inefficiency and High Medical Costs

Malpractice Insurance   Another factor influencing the cost of medical services has been the soaring cost of malpractice insurance for physicians in recent years. These costs have, in part, been passed on to patients as higher fees. To reduce their risks of malpractice suits and to keep their malpractice insurance premiums under control, many physicians have resorted to more testing of patients, more office visits, and maintaining more extensive records to protect themselves in case of a malpractice suit. Furthermore, high malpractice insurance rates and the effect of malpractice suits on those rates have also resulted in some physicians refusing to treat high-risk patients or perform high-risk procedures.

Service to Uninsured Patients   Another important characteristic of the market for health care is that many health care facilities, such as community hospitals or nursing homes, are nonprofit institutions or are run by governments. Many of these institutions are obligated to serve uninsured patients who cannot afford to pay for their health care. Naturally, the costs incurred on behalf of these uninsured patients must be covered to prevent the institution from suffering losses. Providers of medical care often cover their losses while providing services to the uninsured by charging higher prices to the insured. This "cross-subsidization" of patients unable to pay by those who can pay through health insurance and out of their own pockets implies that health insurers pay more as the cost of treating the uninsured is transferred to the insured. Because the insured consumers of health care pay only a small share of the price of those uninsured, the higher prices do not substantially reduce the quantity of health care demanded. However, the higher medical expenses of the insurance firms are transferred to employers and other providers of health insurance through higher insurance premiums. In effect, when nonprofit institutions treat uninsured patients who cannot pay their own bills, health insurance costs for all of the insured rise, meaning that the insured end up paying for the treatment of the uninsured.

Technological Advances and Lack of Price Competition   Rapid technological change in health care has certainly improved the quality of service to patients. However, because third-party payments encourage overuse of new technology, new technology has likely been overdeveloped beyond the point at which its marginal benefit equals its marginal cost. If new technology is developed and utilized beyond the efficient level, then more than the efficient amount of capital will be employed in the health care industry. In fact, hospitals often compete to attract patients by offering the latest technologies and comfortable rooms. They seek to attract patients by capital investments that improve the quality of care (and contribute to higher cost) rather than seeking to economize on costs and keep prices for services down to the minimum possible.

An eagerness on the part of physicians to supply and prescribe the wonders of modern technology has also contributed to rising health care expenditures in the United States. The system of third-party payments for medical treatment in the United States encourages doctors and their patients to utilize the new technology. As new technological equipment and procedures are disseminated through the marketplace, their very existence provides incentives for the owners (often physicians themselves) to utilize the equipment. Many small hospitals in the United States

Why Worry about Growth in Health Care Costs?

Why should public policy be affected by the fact that health care spending in the United States has absorbed sharply increasing shares of our GDP since 1960? As we devote increasing shares of our resources to health care, less will be available to spend on alternative goods and services. In other words, the opportunity cost of spending more on health care is a decrease in alternative goods and services. Health care spending in the United States is likely at a point at which the marginal costs of health care exceed the marginal benefits, and still further increase in the allocation of resources to health care will add to the inefficiency with which resources are used. For this reason, many are demanding more government intervention in the market for health care to control growth in spending.

The rising cost of health insurance policies provided by employers has probably resulted in lower money wages and less generous nonmedical benefits to workers in the United States. Between 1972 and 2011, average weekly real wages paid to workers in the United States have fallen 14 percent but the share of worker's compensation accounted for by health insurance benefits has been rising. Much of this is the result of the favorable tax treatment of health insurance benefits that has encouraged corporations to overallocate resources to health insurance. The growth in worker money pay has consequently lagged behind the growth in payments for their health insurance. Bidding up of health care prices and an increase in prescribed treatments as a result of the growth of third-party payments also have pushed the price of health insurance policies beyond the ability to pay of many individuals who do not receive such benefits from their employers.

Other labor market effects of the system of health insurance also have evolved. In general, skilled high-wage employees of large companies tend to be the beneficiaries of good employer-provided health insurance while those without

health insurance benefits are low-wage unskilled workers employed by small firms and who often drift in and out of the labor force. For low-wage workers, the cost of health insurance is a higher proportion of their money wage than for high-wage workers. Many employers avoid putting low-wage workers on their full-time payroll to avoid having to pay health insurance benefits for them. When added to low wages, health insurance premiums often make the labor more expensive than it is worth to the firm. Some firms hire independent contractors that employ low-wage workers without health insurance benefits to do janitorial work and other low-skill jobs. The employer-provided health insurance system also impairs the fluidity of labor markets by reducing the incentive to change jobs as workers often fear that they will lose their health insurance or not be covered for preexisting illness if they move to a better-paying or more suitable job than the one they currently hold.

From the government's point of view, rising health care costs cause more difficulty in balancing budgets or funding other programs. Unless other programs are cut to finance increasing government spending on health care, we can expect higher taxes.

In short, imperfections in the market for health care probably result in more than the efficient allocation of resources to its provision. Our institutions for financing health care spending have caused health insurance premiums to increase, which has put such insurance out of the financial reach of many Americans and has contributed to increased government spending to finance Medicare and Medicaid. Real wages have not grown as employers compensate workers with funds to pay their health insurance, and labor market fluidity has been impaired. We are giving up more than the efficient amount of other goods and services for health care. Correcting these inefficiencies will cause pressure for government intervention in the market for health care in the years to come.

obtain equipment and finance its costs easily through third-party payments on behalf of insured patients. The abundance of such marvels of medical technology as open-heart surgical units in the United States has led to a vast demand for use of these facilities not only by Americans but by foreigners as well, many of whom (such as those from Canada) live in nations where governments, rather than the marketplace, determine the allocation of resources to new medical technology. The scarcity of the new medical technology in many countries results in long waiting periods for patients to use the facilities.

Abundance of new technological marvels does not necessarily imply efficiency in their use. When the facilities are purchased in numbers for which their marginal benefits exceed marginal costs, more than the efficient amount of resources is utilized in providing the services of these new facilities. The third-party payment system encourages exactly such an overuse of all medical services.

In nations where government controls limit the spending for and availability of new technologies, as in Canada and the United Kingdom, there are long waiting lists for access to the marvels of modern technology. The U.S. system encourages overuse of new technology and more than the efficient number of facilities; however, those insured patients who require access to the new technology can generally be accommodated without delay. If you require special medical equipment, you can get it readily in the United States. However, the opportunity cost of this abundance is a reduction of the availability of alternative health services (such as preventive care) or expenditures on other goods and services for which the marginal social benefit might be higher.

CHECKPOINT

1. What are some of the unique features of the market for health care in the United States that contribute to overallocation of resources to medical services?
2. How does the system of third-party payments through health insurance affect the market for health care?
3. What is the moral hazard of health insurance?

GOVERNMENTS AND HEALTH CARE: COMPENSATING FOR MARKET FAILURE

Imperfections in the markets for health care services result in demands for government activity in such areas as research, provision of information, and the distribution of services.

Certain aspects of the provision of health care often are difficult to sell. Pure medical research with no ready or current commercial application could be underfunded by organizations that seek profits from their operations. For this reason, many argue that medical research should be like a public good, financed by government and made freely available to all who seek to use it. This view would prevent the patenting of basic medical advances resulting from pure research. By preventing ownership of and the right to charge royalties for the use of basic advances in medical knowledge, the cost of new medical technology and procedures would be lower.

Also, some positive externalities are associated with reducing contagious diseases. To internalize these externalities, it is reasonable to subsidize the provision of vaccines. The Public Health Service of the U.S. government monitors contagious diseases and has the power to enforce regulations pertaining to vacci-nations and quarantining individuals with contagious diseases. The service also provides information on the health effects of such activities as smoking and drink-ing. In recent years, the Public Health Service also has been active in providing information about AIDS and encouraging personal health practices that limit the spread of AIDS.

The general belief that individuals tend to underconsume medical services because they have inadequate information also has led to government subsidization of medical expenditures through tax exclusion of employer-provided health insur-ance benefits. However, as our analysis in this chapter has shown, the system of health care provision in the United States leads to an overconsumption rather than underconsumption of medical services because of reduced price consciousness on the part of consumers.

The government also plays an active role in helping protect patients. Physicians must be licensed by state governments and doctors must pass a test and go through a number of procedures to assess their professional skills. The federal government also assists in assessing and guaranteeing the competency of physicians through a process of peer review of physicians who treat Medicare patients. Physicians whose competency is in question can be denied reimbursement under Medicare.

Income Inequality and Health Care

Assuring access to medical services to all citizens irrespective of their ability to pay or employment status is viewed by many as a desirable government function. According to this view, health care should be a guaranteed right, equally available to all as if it were a public good. For example, those who support this view would argue that it is acceptable for lack of income or wealth to prevent a person from buying a luxury car but that same lack of ability to pay should not prevent indivi-duals from receiving a needed heart transplant. Under the current health care system in the United States, ability to pay is chiefly determined by health insurance coverage rather than income. Some insurance plans do cover expensive procedures such as transplants while others do not. The ability of a given patient to obtain expensive care that will prolong life depends not only on whether the patient has insurance but also on the extent of that insurance. Insurance companies have also been criticized for denying insurance to applicants who have preexisting conditions, leading for calls for government to guarantee the right to health insurance for all citizens regardless of the state of their health.

A system of free access to medical care has existed in the United Kingdom since the end of World War II. Such a system provides health care benefits to all, rich or poor, at zero price. The government system shifts the responsibility of rationing medical services from the market, where ability to pay (determined mainly by health insurance coverage) would determine priorities, to committees that decide who should obtain treatment and the priority list for deciding who gets the treat-ment first. The system is more equitable than that in the United States, but it still does not prevent those with higher incomes from consuming more or better-quality medical services because those individuals can purchase such services in either the domestic or international marketplace. However, such rich people would pay the full marginal cost of such services out of their own pockets.

As an alternative to equal care for all, many individuals argue that all citizens should be guaranteed a minimum level of health care regardless of their income.

The Medicaid program is designed to achieve such a goal by guaranteeing medical care at zero price to the poorest members of society. However, many of the near-poor do not qualify for Medicaid, and others qualify only after they have exhausted the bulk of their income or assets as a result of catastrophic medical expenditures. Governments can extend health insurance to many of the near-poor as well by provide health insurance to those workers who are not covered by employer-provided health insurance policies. These people could be provided with health insurance similar to that available through employers with a certain deductible and a reasonable rate of coinsurance. The cost of the insurance could be financed by taxes on employers through a payroll tax or out of general tax revenue.

Because many of the uninsured are employed, one way to accomplish this would be to mandate that all employers provide health insurance. This method could, however, be particularly burdensome to small firms where insurance premiums based on experience ratings are very high. Mandating insurance as a fringe benefit by these firms could make it impossible for them to operate profitably and force them out of business. Mandated insurance could also be a great burden for firms that employ unskilled workers. Unskilled workers typically earn relatively low wages. For these workers, health insurance payments would be a substantial portion of the wage bills—about $5,000 per year—to employers. The $5,000 per employee bill amounts to only 10 percent of the wage bill of a $50,000 per year worker but is 25 percent of the wage bill for a $20,000 per year worker. The increase in the cost associated with employing these unskilled workers could reduce employment opportunities for them. This insurance could be financed by increased payroll taxes. However, if the payroll taxes are levied on the employers, the effect will still be to increase the cost of labor, and this could still reduce the quantity of labor employed.

The *Patient Protection and Affordable Care Act of 2010* does use mandates to extend health insurance to the uninsured. However, to avoid many of the problems discussed earlier for mandates to businesses, the new law applies mainly to individuals and sets up health insurance exchanges to pool many applicants and reduce the risk associated with adverse selection. Small businesses with fewer than 50 employees will be exempt from mandates under the new law. Many of the uninsured will also become eligible for Medicaid under the new legislation and many of those who do not will receive tax credits to help them buy health insurance.

Finally, another proposal is for the government to provide catastrophic health insurance. This type of insurance could supplement private health insurance by kicking in only after patients have exhausted any private health insurance benefits they have and after they have paid a certain amount of medical expenses out of their own pockets. In effect, this would be insurance with a very large out-of-pocket deductible. The deductible could vary as a percentage of household income.

Because the incidence of catastrophic medical expenses is of low probability and quite predictable from year to year for the whole population, this type of insurance could be provided at relatively low cost per person for all and financed through taxation. By establishing an insurance pool of the entire nation, the government could provide this coverage to all at low cost and fill a gap in the insurance protection of most Americans, including Medicare enrollees, who are not insured against catastrophic medical expenses.

GOVERNMENT SPENDING ON HEALTH CARE IN THE UNITED STATES

Governments are directly involved in medical and health research and also provide some funding for the construction of such medical facilities as hospitals. You should be familiar with the work of the surgeon general of the United States, who supervises the Public Health Service and occasionally publishes reports on health issues and provides information about contagious diseases such as AIDS. However, it might surprise you that the bulk of government expenditures for health care is made through direct payments to physicians, hospitals, and other health care provided through the country's two major public health insurance programs. Medicaid along with the Child Health Insurance Program (CHIP) and Medicare accounted for about 80 percent of all government spending on health care in the United States in 2009. Medicare is the largest program and accounts for 45 percent of total government health care spending, mainly in the form of reimbursement to health care providers who treat the elderly. Medicaid, which assists the poor in meeting health care expenditures, accounts for about 35 percent of government health expenditures.

Governments also pay medical expenses of disabled workers through various worker's compensation programs provided by governments and provide medical services to military personnel and veterans. State and locally run hospitals and their activities are subsidized through government payments financed by taxes.

Table 9.1 summarizes public expenditures for health care in 2009 and shows that the bulk of these expenditures is accounted for by government-financed health insurance programs. Like overall spending for health care, government spending in this field has been rising at a very rapid rate since 1965, when Medicaid and Medicare were introduced as government health insurance programs. Figure 9.4 shows how government expenditures for health care have grown since 1965.

The federal government also provides health benefits to veterans at hospitals run by the Veterans Administration. The cost of providing medical services to veterans has been increasing as those who served in World War II have aged and as veterans of the wars in Iraq and Afghanistan have needed treatment.

Medicare

Much of the growth of federal spending is accounted for by the largest federal health program, Medicare. Medicare reimburses health care providers for much of

TABLE 9.1	Total Government Health Care Spending, 2009 (Billions of Dollars)
Medicare	502.3
Medicaid CHIP	385.0
Other[a]	250.7
Total	1,138.0

[a]Includes the Public Health Service, worker's compensation medical payments, Veteran's, defense, and state/local government hospitals and medical expenditures, medical research, and medical facility construction.

Source: U.S. Bureau of the Census, Statistical Abstract of the United States, 2012.

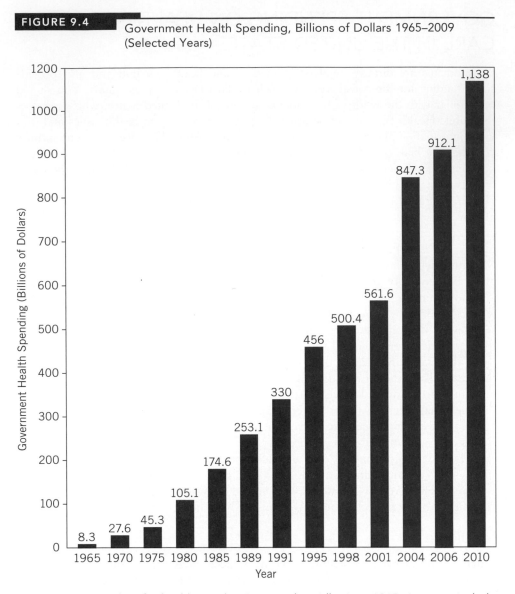

FIGURE 9.4   Government Health Spending, Billions of Dollars 1965–2009 (Selected Years)

Government spending for health care has increased rapidly since 1965. Amounts include government spending for research and medical facilities.

Source: U.S. Department of Commerce.

the medical costs incurred by those older than 65 and some disabled people in the United States. The elderly comprise about 85 percent of enrollees in Medicare. A person becomes eligible for Medicare at age 65 if he or she has paid health insurance (HI) payroll taxes for a period of at least ten years. People under the age of 65 can become eligible for Medicare benefits if they are disabled or if they have end-stage renal disease or amyotrophic lateral sclerosis (commonly known as "Lou Gehrig's disease). Medicare will pay for kidney transplants for those with end-stage renal disease. As of 2011, 47.7 million people were enrolled in the Medicare program—15 percent of the U.S. population. As pointed out in Chapter 8, Medicare is a government entitlement program available to all those eligible regardless of their income. All eligible people receive hospital insurance through Medicare and all are eligible for Medicare's supplementary medical insurance, which makes payments to physicians and other medical providers. Those enrolled in the supplementary insurance program pay a monthly fee. The amount collected from these fees is not sufficient to cover the costs of the supplementary health insurance so the difference is made up with government funds obtained through taxation. In other words, Medicare's supplementary health insurance is heavily subsidized. However, Medicare benefits are subject to strict limits that are less generous than most private health insurance programs. For example, Medicare does not cover long-term care for the elderly in nursing homes and provides only optional and limited coverage for prescription drugs under Medicare Part D. Many individuals older than 65 in the United States also are covered by private health insurance plans to fill in the gaps of their Medicare coverage. Although Medicare is primarily thought of as a health insurance program for the elderly, it also provides benefits to the disabled. In 2011, disabled people accounted for 16 percent to total Medicare enrollment.

Aging of the population has contributed to rising Medicare spending. A number of steps have already been undertaken or proposed to keep the costs of the Medicare program down. Since January 1992, reimbursement to physicians under the program has been based on a Medicare fee schedule (MFS) that sets payments according to the time, skill, and intensity of the service rendered. The fee reimbursement schedule for physicians is based on complicated formulas designed to limit payments. The system is designed to reimburse physicians on the basis of the value of resources that go into the services they provide to Medicare patients. Under the MFS system, the reimbursement rate for a service can increase only if the cost of providing it goes up. Some critics of the system fear that if MFS rates lag behind reimbursement rates paid by private insurers, the quantity of medical services provided to Medicare patients will decrease.

Medicare limits payments for specific hospital providers to certain amounts independent of the actual costs of the procedures. The current law pays hospitals a flat fee for illnesses classified into Diagnosis Related Groups (DRGs). Under the DRG system, payment for a medical procedure is the same regardless of any complications that might develop during the medical procedures. For example, a hospital treating a heart-attack patient will be eligible for a certain flat fee no matter how much is actually spent caring for the patient. Some argue that the system provides incentives for hospitals to keep costs down so as to maximize profit. However, the DRG system does not completely curb the incentive to cut costs, because doctors and hospitals can charge the elderly who are able to pay for those services that are not covered by Medicare. This means that the elderly end up paying more for their medical care. The DRG system has not been politically popular among the elderly. Some also fear that the DRG system could result in a reduction in the quality of medical care to the elderly who lack the ability to pay for services not covered by Medicare.

Like any third-party payment system, even one with co-payments, Medicare encourages the consumption of medical services beyond the efficient level (see the analysis of the Medicaid program in Chapter 7). The federal government has chosen to limit the incentives to overconsumption mainly through programs that place limits on reimbursement to medical providers. Medicare increases the quantity of medical services demanded by the elderly. The DRG system acts to limit the quantity of medical services supplied to the elderly by capping the price per unit of service to medical providers.

In recent years the annual rate of growth of Medicare spending has slowed to 2 percent and is now growing more slowly the spending under private insurance plans. A change in the way physicians and hospitals are paid moving away from "fee-for-service" toward bundled payments designed to increase incentives to economize on medical resources is further expected to slow the rate of growth of Medicare spending. This new system of payment is being phased in as part of the *Patient Protection and Affordable Care Act of 2010.*

Given the aging of the population, the Medicare program remains a source of concern. Addition of prescription drug coverage to Medicare as Part D in 2006 increased the share of GDP accounted for by Medicare spending.

Medicare Financing and Spending

Like the Social Security program, Medicare is basically a pay-as-you-go social insurance program. There is a trust fund that has a slight surplus that is expected to be depleted by 2024. The legislation enacted in 1997 will help keep Medicare functioning without the need for tax increases until the second quarter of the 21st century. However, after that time, as the ranks of the portion of the population over the age of 65 begin to swell, spending will increase at a rapid rate as the baby boomers become eligible for Medicare. Currently, Medicare is financed by a 2.9 percent tax on payrolls and by modest fees levied on beneficiaries. Effective 2013, the tax base for the 2.9 percent Medicare tax will be broadened and some upper-income taxpayers will be subject to an additional 0.9 percent Medicare tax on labor income and a 3.8 percent Medicare tax on some investment income. When the Medicare trust fund is depleted, tax rates will have to increase or other sources of financing will have to be found to prevent outlays from exceeding revenues unless benefits are cut.

Much of the problem is Part A of Medicare, which is hospital insurance financed by the 2.9 percent payroll tax. Part A covers inpatient hospital services, care at skilled nursing facilities, home health care, and hospice care. Projections by the trustees of the Medicare program indicate that, based on policies in place as of 2011, the expenditures under Part A will increase from 1.7 percent of GDP in 2011 to 2.24 percent of GDP in 2070. Total spending under all parts of Medicare was 3.65 percent of GDP in 2011 and is projected by the Actuary of the Medicare system to rise to 6.2 percent of GDP by 2070.

Part B of Medicare, which is primarily a program covering physician and out-patient hospital services to beneficiaries, is largely financed out of general federal revenues. The premiums paid by enrollees cover only about 25 percent of the costs of the program. Growth in Part B spending increases federal outlays and contributes to increases in the federal budget deficit. Beginning in 2006 Medicare offered optional prescription drug insurance coverage under Medicare Part D. Spending under Medicare Part D accounted for 0.44 percent of GDP in 2011 and is projected to rise to 1.7 percent of GDP by 2085.

Limits in reimbursement encourage providers to seek out more cost-effective delivery of health care. It is crucial to control spending per beneficiary under the program in the future as the number of beneficiaries begins to swell due to the aging of the U.S. population. Since Medicare constitutes such a large share of demand for medical services in the United States, its policies affect both medical service prices and the use of those services. Because it is difficult to forecast the demand for services by the elderly in the future, it is much more difficult to come to grips with the growth in spending for Medicare than it is for the growth in spending for Social Security pensions. Over the long run, eligibility for Medicare and a change in the structure of its benefits are likely to be required to avoid sharp increases in tax rates to finance the medical expenditures of an aging nation.

Up to now, the major tool used to control Medicare spending has been limits on payments to providers through the prospective payment system and other limits on how much Medicare will pay for certain procedures. Such methods reduce the incomes of health care providers but do not necessarily reduce quality of service to patients if providers use medical resources more efficiently as a result of reduced reimbursement. However, this system has its limits because it could eventually affect the willingness of providers to accept Medicare patients. The Medicare payment system, in some cases, has perverse effects that actually increase spending. For example, the prospective payment system limits the amounts that Medicare pays for hospital stays. In doing so it has encouraged hospitals to transfer patients quickly to skilled nursing facilities or to long-term care facilities where Medicare is obligated to pay on a fee-for-service basis, thereby contributing to increased costs.

Over the long run, increases in fees paid for coverage under Part B of Medicare are likely. Other alternatives that could reduce the growth rate of spending include raising the age of eligibility from, say, 65 to 67. The Congressional Budget Office estimates that phasing in an increase in the eligibility age from 65 to 67 would reduce Medicare enrollment by 9 percent and reduce spending by 5 percent by 2025.

Finally, costs could be reduced sharply by increasing deductibles and coinsurance payments for those covered by Medicare. This would increase the portion of medical expenses borne by patients themselves, and as the analysis later in this chapter will prove, would decrease the quantity of such services demanded. The annual medical deducible for physician services and for hospital stays under Medicare has been quite low compared to those of private insurance plans. And many Medicare patients have private "medigap" insurance that pays for these noncovered charges. Medicare combined with medigap often reduces the out-of-pocket cost per service to patients to zero, thereby encouraging consumption beyond the point at which marginal benefit falls to marginal cost.

An extreme type of reform could cap Medicare spending by turning it into a "defined-contribution" health insurance subsidy plan. One suggested approach for accomplishing this is to give each recipient a voucher each year to purchase health insurance in a competitive market equal to net spending for each Medicare enrollee in the year 2000. This amount would increase each year with the rate of inflation. Medicare would then be transformed into a health insurance plan on a premium basis that would compete with private insurance plans offering health care insurance to the elderly. This approach would effectively cap federal health care cost but, depending on the amount of the subsidy and the health insurance that could be offered on the market for that amount, there would probably be an increase in the out-of-pocket cost of health care to the elderly.

Prescription Drug Coverage under Medicare Part D

In November 2003, Congress passed historic new legislation to provide citizens over the age of 65 with subsidized prescription drug insurance. The *Medicare Prescription Drug and Modernization Act of 2003* provides Medicare beneficiaries with an optional drug purchase insurance plan known as *Medicare Part D*. This insurance coverage is provided through subsidized private prescription drug insurance plans available to Medicare enrollees in a given geographic area. The subsidized prescription drug coverage began on January 1, 2006. Participation in the plan is voluntary and enrollees pay a premium that pays part of the cost of the plan. The new Part D also provides subsidies to cover the costs of prescriptions for some low-income Medicare enrollees who previously had their drugs covered under Medicaid.

Medicare beneficiaries who choose to enroll in the plan pay a premium set by the private provider of the plan they choose. About 75 percent of the cost of the insurance is subsidized by the federal government and financed through taxes. Private insurance companies administer the plan under contract with the federal government. There is a standard benefit, but private insurance companies negotiate with pharmaceutical providers to keep the prices of prescriptions low. The insurance companies do not offer each brand of specific drugs to enrollees or might offer some particular drugs at lower prices than alternatives, depending on deals they make with pharmaceutical firms.

The plans cover prescription drugs using a deductible and coinsurance. After beneficiaries incur a "deductible" of $320 in 2012 of expenses for prescription drugs each year, the Medicare Part D insurance plan pays 75 percent of drug costs up to a maximum of $2,950 in 2012 per year. The "coinsurance" for the plan up to this level of expenditure in excess of the deductible is therefore 25 percent.

After the $2,950 coverage is exhausted, there is no coverage for drug costs between $2,950 and $4,700 per year in 2012. However, when drug costs for an enrollee reach $5,100, the plan covers 95 percent of expenditures in excess of that amount. The intent of this part of the plan is to cover "catastrophic" drug expenses. The gap in coverage up to this amount (popularly called the "donut hole") is an attempt by Congress to keep the costs of the plan down. The *Patient Protection and Affordable Care Act of 2010* will phase out the "donut hole" gap in coverage until it is completely eliminated by 2020.

Some low-income enrollees are not required to pay either the premium or the deductible and are exempt from the coverage gap. It is difficult to determine the net benefit of this aspect of the plan, because some of these low-income elderly enrollees could have previously been receiving benefits under Medicaid.

One of the difficulties in gaining political support for Medicare drug coverage was the fear that some retirees who already had prescription drug coverage through their employer-provided health insurance could be made worse off. To discourage employers from terminating their prescription drug coverage for retired workers the legislation provides tax-free subsidies, to employers who maintain drug coverage for retirees after the Medicare plan became effective in 2006. Those retirees whose drug coverage under private health insurance plans is superior to that provided by Medicare can retain coverage and choose not to enroll in the Medicare plan.

Part of the costs of Medicare Part D is offset by higher premiums for Medicare Part B out-of-hospital health insurance enrollees. The premium increases began in 2007. As of 2012, the monthly premium for Part B was $99.90 for single enrollees with income less than $85,000 per year and enrollees filing joint tax returns with income less than $170,000 per year. Premiums are then adjusted upward with income with the highest income enrollees paying $319.70 per month in 2012.

As of 2011 there were 35 million beneficiaries enrolled in Medicare Part D. Government spending for the plan as of 2011 had been much less than originally forecast when the plan was first introduced in 2006.

Medicaid

Medicaid is also an entitlement program that is available to many low-income people who meet eligibility criteria. Unlike Medicare, which is run by the federal government, Medicaid is administered by state governments under federal guidelines. The states have considerable flexibility to design their own Medicaid programs and eligibility standards. On average, states pay about 43 percent of the costs of the program with the federal government paying for the remainder through grants to the states. About two-thirds of Medicaid enrollees obtain medical services through managed care provider networks. Enrollees generally do not pay health insurance premiums and have little or no co-payments for services they consume. Eligibility for Medicaid varies from state to state, as do the benefits provided to those who are eligible. Like Medicare, Medicaid operates basically like an insurance program, reimbursing hospitals and those providing medical and health services to individuals enrolled in the program according to guidelines and limits that vary from state to state. In recent years, the costs of the Medicaid program, like the costs of most other health insurance programs, have been soaring. Many state governments have reacted to the increases by sharply reducing benefits available to Medicaid patients. The Medicaid program was designed to guarantee a minimum level of health care primarily to those in poverty (see Chapter 7). Medicaid also can be considered an insurance program that is part of a "safety net" for all. After an individual's income and assets are literally exhausted by an illness or other catastrophic health problem, that person can become eligible for Medicaid. Medicaid finances both medical expenses and nursing home care to those who qualify. However, many of those classified as poor are not eligible for Medicaid. About one-third of Medicaid outlays are for people with disabilities. Medicaid accounts for about one sixth of health care spending in the United States with the bulk of that spending concentrated on the elderly and the disabled.

The Medicaid program is designed to make sure that the poor and those who become poor because of catastrophic medical expenses will be able to obtain medical care. Much of the cost of the Medicaid program is paid for by state governments, many of which have experienced severe financial problems in recent years. As Medicaid absorbs an increasingly large share of state government budgets, the states are seeking ways to control expenditures by reducing benefits they pay on behalf of Medicaid patients.

Medicaid is the health insurer of last resort—it takes many of the cases that no other insurance program pays for: crack-addicted babies, the homeless with disabilities, and AIDS patients who run out of private insurance and exhaust all other financial means of paying medical bills. Medicaid also pays for long-term care for elderly patients who can no longer take care of themselves and have used up all their savings. In fact, one of every three dollars spent under Medicaid pays for health care for the elderly. Many elderly Americans are becoming skilled in concealing their financial assets from government authorities so they can get their medical and nursing home bills paid through Medicaid before they go broke! Medicaid spending is counter-cyclical. When the economy falls into recession, unemployment increases and incomes decline, resulting in more people qualifying for Medicaid. The recession of 2007–2009 resulted in spending increases under Medicaid. During the period 2008 to 2011, the federal share of Medicaid spending was increased under provisions of the *American Recovery and Reinvestment Act*. This extraordinary funding for the program expired in 2012 putting increased pressure on state budgets and resulting in efforts by the states to cut Medicaid spending.

Enrollment in the Medicaid program has been soaring in recent years. The rise in spending comes at the same time states have been cutting their reimbursement rates to hospitals and physicians in an attempt to control the rising costs. Because of reduced reimbursement rates, many physicians refuse to treat Medicaid patients. Even though we are spending more for Medicaid, more impoverished patients are finding it harder to obtain medical care from physicians and must resort to hospital emergency rooms for routine medical problems.

Like Medicare, expenditures under Medicaid are likely to soar as the U.S. population ages. This is mainly because Medicaid pays for nursing home care for the elderly with low incomes and few assets. As the population ages, so will the demand for long-term care services. By 2050, a higher percentage of the population will be over the age of 65, and they will live longer than they do today. As a consequence, people over the age of 65, now 10 percent of the U.S. population, will constitute a projected 22 percent of the population by the year 2050! Because the very old are likely to live in nursing homes and exhaust their private assets, expenditure for Medicaid will soar under current rules. To keep costs under control, many have advocated a shift to private insurance plans to pay for the long-term care of the elderly in the future.

How State Governments Are Trying to Control Medicaid Costs

State government spending under the Medicaid program has been increasing on average at an annual rate of between 8 and 13 percent since 2001. In some states the rates of increase are astounding: Arizona, Mississippi, New Mexico, North Carolina, and Washington experienced rates of growth in 2002 between 30 and 50 percent. Almost all states are taking measures to stem the rate of growth of spending in this entitlement program.

Although increased caseloads in 2002, in part due to the effects of a recession, contributed to the rising costs, price increases, particularly for prescription drugs, were also responsible for the rising expenditures. From 2000 to 2001, spending on outpatient drugs under Medicaid has been increasing at an annual rate of 18 percent. However, nursing home and long-term care are also increasing spending under Medicaid. A majority of states are finding that they have inadequately budgeted for Medicaid. Shortfalls in 2001 averaged 6.2 percent of costs for the states, with some states experiencing shortfalls approaching 30 percent of costs. In 2004, the rate of growth in Medicaid spending declined somewhat to 8 percent, due in part to cost containment efforts by state governments. The recession of 2007–2009 contributed to increased spending under Medicaid. Over the period of 2007–2010 total Medicaid enrollment increased 19 percent. Although total spending under the program increased by 24 percent during this period, spending per enrollee increased by 4 percent reflecting cost control measures undertaken by the states.

State governments are taking steps to reduce the rate of growth of spending under Medicaid. A common strategy has been to reduce reimbursement rates to Medicaid providers. Because pharmaceuticals are a major factor in higher costs, many states are restricting reimbursement rates to providers of prescription drugs, requiring special authorization for use of the drugs, and even requiring the Medicaid recipients to pay some of the costs of the drugs and other services. Some states are negotiating special arrangements with medical providers and pharmaceutical companies to reduce prices or to receive special quantity discounts.

As of 2011, Medicaid was consuming 23.6 percent of state general fund budgets. Medicaid costs were still rising more than twice the rate of general inflation in the United States. Some states are actually placing limits on how much they will pay for Medicaid recipients' medical costs. Other states are making it more difficult for low-income people to qualify for Medicaid, and as a result hundreds of thousands of individuals are losing their Medicaid health insurance. These cuts have been especially severe in Florida, Vermont, and Tennessee.

New federal legislation has allowed states to start charging premiums and co-payments for Medicaid recipients and have made it more difficult for some people to qualify for Medicaid coverage of nursing home care. For example, the state of Missouri in 2005, faced with a budget shortfall, lowered eligibility for Medicaid from 75 to 22 percent of the federal poverty line. This meant that a family of three would qualify for Medicaid only if its annual income was a mere $3,504 excluding some child care costs. As a result more than 100,000 people in Missouri lost coverage of Medicaid health insurance. In 2008 Medicaid rules were changed again to allow state governments to charge premiums and higher co-payments for Medicaid. Under the new rules Medicaid recipients are expected to pay an estimated $1.3 billion in co-payments from 2008 through 2012. The resulting decrease in quantity of medical services demanded by Medicaid patients is expected to reduce health care spending under Medicaid by the federal and state governments by an estimated $2.5 billion. The new rules permit a sliding scale for co-payments with upper-income Medicaid patients paying more but limit the sum of premiums and co-payments to a maximum of 5 percent of a family's income. Because of actions by the state governments, Medicaid spending per enrollee actually rose more slowly than the increase in spending per enrolled under employer-provided health insurance over the period 2007–2010.

Many states are also taking action to reduce cost for long-term care services for the elderly. Such services for elderly and disabled beneficiaries are extremely expensive. It has been estimated that the 4 percent of Medicaid beneficiaries who receive long-term care count for as much as 50 percent of the costs for Medicaid nationally! So cuts for long-term care services will go a long way in reducing expenditures under Medicaid.

Indirect Government Finance of Health Care

Thus far, we have discussed only the direct government expenditures for health spending—those that involve outlays of funds by governments. However, a surprisingly large amount of health care spending is financed by indirect government subsidies to private health insurance. Instead of involving spending by governments, these subsidies take the form of reduced revenues through favorable tax treatment of employee and employer contributions for private health insurance.

Employer-sponsored health insurance programs cover about 60 percent of Americans and pay about one-third of all medical expenditures. Federal, state, and local governments give favorable tax treatment to employee compensation in the form of health insurance premiums paid by employers. The amount that employers pay for health insurance to employees is neither taxable as payroll nor is it considered part of the taxable income of employees. Also, in many cases when employees themselves pay a portion of their employer-provided health insurance premiums for themselves or their dependents, they receive favorable tax treatment for those expenditures. Under current tax rules, many employers set up special plans that allow their employees to exclude the amount they pay for health insurance for themselves and their dependents from their taxable income.

By excluding employer-paid fringe benefits in the form of medical insurance premiums from the taxable income of employees, governments forgo the opportunity to collect taxes on this income. The reduced income tax collections constitute a government subsidy to private health insurance. Exclusion of employer-paid health insurance benefits from the taxable incomes of employees cost the federal government nearly $177 billion in revenue in 2011. Additional losses accrued to state and local governments.

This subsidy encourages employers to provide employees compensation in the form of health insurance as opposed to cash income. The health insurance is worth more to employees than the cash income because it is available tax-free. In other words, the employee can get health insurance at a lower price than using taxable income to reimburse employers for the costs. For example, suppose that on each extra dollar of earnings an employee pays income taxes amounting to one-third of earnings. Assume that the cost of employer-provided health insurance is $150 per month for this employee. If the employer, instead of directly providing the insurance at no charge, charged the employee $150 for it each month and increased the employee's salary by the same amount, the employee would be worse off, assuming that she still wanted to purchase $150 worth of insurance. This is because the $150 would be taxable, and the tax due would be $50. If the employee wanted to buy the $150 of coverage, she would have to earn more than $150 in money income to pay the bill! The employee would have to earn $225, which, after paying one-third of that in taxes, would provide after-tax income of $150 that could be used to buy health insurance from the employer at the rate of $150 per month. In effect, the special tax treatment of employer-provided health insurance lowers the price of the insurance to employees and increases the quantity of health insurance demanded as a form of labor compensation.

For example, suppose your health insurance policy costs your employer $5,000 this year. Let's also assume that your combined federal and state income tax rate that would be paid on an additional $5,000 earnings is 35 percent. An additional $5,000 earnings would also be subject to payroll tax withholding of 7.65 percent. The total tax rate applied to the $5,000 would be 42.65 percent. If your employer paid you an additional $5,000 instead of using the money to buy health insurance for you, you would receive only $2,867.50 after taxes. If you intended to get a $5,000 health insurance policy anyway, you are clearly better off having your employer provide it as a nontaxable fringe benefit instead of earning more cash and then buying the policy yourself out of taxable earnings!

The federal government also allows limited deductions for direct out-of-pocket medical and long-term care expenses paid by individuals. Taxpayers can deduct medical expenses in excess of 7.5 percent of their adjusted gross income from their taxable income. This preferential tax treatment of medical expenses was estimated to cost the federal government $9.5 billion in revenue in 2011, which is only a small fraction of the amount given up from nontaxation of insurance premiums. Additional revenue is lost through exclusion of Medicare benefits to the elderly as part of their taxable income.

Figure 9.5 shows that the preferential treatment of health insurance premiums by the U.S. tax system increases the quantity of employer-provided health insurance services demanded. The figure shows the demand curve for health insurance in the nation. Suppose that on average employers can make employees as well-off by giving

FIGURE 9.5   The Effect of Preferential Tax Treatment of Employer-Provided Health Insurance

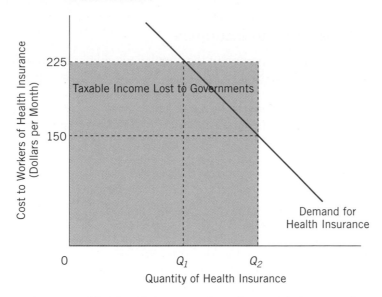

Excluding employer-provided health insurance from the taxable income of employees increases the quantity of health insurance demanded by lowering the effective price to both employers and their employees.

© Cengage Learning

them health insurance that costs $150 per month instead of paying them $225 in money wages before taxes. The employer can save $75 per employee per month in wages by providing health insurance instead of the money income. In effect, by reducing the price of health insurance to the employee, when it is provided by the employer, and by making it cheaper for employers to compensate employees in health insurance, the tax system encourages (and subsidizes) employer health insurance.

The graph shows that the tax treatment of insurance affects the quantity of health insurance demanded. In this case, the employee gets health insurance as a nontaxable $150 per month fringe benefit. The average employee would have to earn $225 per month to pay for the policy if it were purchased from the employer for $150. The effective reduction in price from $225 to $150 for workers increases the quantity of insurance demanded. The income corresponding to the shaded rectangle in the graph that represents the taxable wages that would have been otherwise paid to workers to buy the same amount of health insurance provided tax-free by employers is not taxed.

If the tax exemption of health insurance premiums paid by employers were terminated, it is likely that a substantial number of firms would choose to stop offering health insurance to employees. One study concluded that 14 percent of firms currently offering this fringe benefit would have dropped it if it became taxable. This would have resulted in an additional 22 million workers without employer-provided health insurance.[2]

---

[2]See Jonathan Gruber, "Taxes and Health Insurance," in *Tax Policy and the Economy*, Vol. 16, James Poterba (Cambridge, Mass.: NBER and MIT Press, 2002): 32–66.

The lost revenue from tax exemption of health insurance premiums paid by employers and portions paid by employees should be added to direct government spending on health care.

Employer-Based Health Insurance

Between 1997 and 2010, the portion of the population without any health insurance rose from 12.9 to 16 percent. Smaller firms have been less likely to offer health insurance than larger firms. Even in firms offering health insurance, about 20 percent of workers on average have been ineligible for such benefits because they have not been on the job long enough or because they were part-time workers. People without employer-based health insurance must often pay higher (nongroup) rates for insurance if they desire to have it. Also, because employed workers tend to be healthy, insurers presume that those not employed are more likely to have higher medical costs and price their policies accordingly. In effect, the employment-based system tends to raise the price of insurance for those who are not in the workforce.

The employment-based system of health insurance also has reduced worker mobility and can result in workers delaying retirement to avoid losing health insurance benefits before they qualify for Medicare. Workers have often refrained from changing jobs even if they can get health insurance in a new job because a new health insurance plan might not cover preexisting conditions and will require delays before full benefits become available. The *Patient Care and Affordable Care Act of 2010*, to be discussed later in this chapter, when fully effective is designed to alleviate many of the problems associated with employer-based health insurance.

As the cost of health care has increased, many employers have also cut back on the generosity of their plans. Deductibles and coinsurance paid by workers have been increasing by close to 30 percent in recent years. Partly as a result of the recession of 2007–2009 and its aftermath of high unemployment, the portion of the population with employer-based health insurance decreased somewhat to 55 percent since 2007.

CHECKPOINT

1. How much of the GDP in the United States is allocated to health care?
2. Who pays the U.S. health care bills?
3. What are the major government programs of health care finance in the United States? How do governments indirectly subsidize private health insurance in the United States?

HEALTH CARE REFORM: ISSUES AND POLICIES

In the United States, the controversy over health care reform and the role of government in that process has centered around two issues:

1. Controlling the growth of health care spending to prevent health care from absorbing ever-increasing shares of our GDP.
2. Moving toward universal coverage for Americans by making health insurance a government-guaranteed right for all citizens.

The desire to control the rate of growth of spending on health care is getting stronger and stronger. Some critics of the U.S. health care system argue that increased government participation in the market for health care is desirable both to curb the growth of spending and remove inequities from the system. The problem is not only to control the growth of spending but also to improve efficiency within the mix of services provided by the system. Health care providers often favor certain costly treatments that are covered by insurance over less expensive alternatives that involve greater out-of-pocket expenses to patients. For example, coverage of inpatient psychiatric costs and exclusion or limited coverage of outpatient psychiatric visits encourage hospitalization of people with psychiatric problems. The exclusion of preventive measures and tests such as mammograms from insurance coverage in many insurance programs discourages patients from taking these tests, often at the risk of much higher third-party payments on their behalf at a later time. Finally, the fragmented nature of the health insurance system in the United States involves high administrative costs that could be reduced with centralized claims processing. In Canada, where claims processing is handled by the government and is more centralized than the U.S. operations, administrative costs are only 2.5 percent of health care spending as opposed to 5 percent in the United States.

Increasing the Price of Health Care to Consumers: Coinsurance and Deductibles

The most obvious way for controlling health care spending is to increase the out-of-pocket price of those services to the individuals who consume them. By increasing the price of medical care to consumers, the quantity demanded will decline. Increased cost sharing of medical costs by patients will provide incentives for economizing on the use of health care services. The declining share of medical costs paid by consumers of these services has, in fact, been a major cause of the increase in prices and increase in volume of medical services consumed. A classic study of health care spending by the Rand Corporation in the late 1970s and early 1980s found that spending per person for health care was 45 percent higher in insurance plans that required no cost sharing compared to an alternative plan that required 95 percent cost sharing (meaning that health insurance paid only 5 percent of the medical bills of insurees) up to an annual maximum of $1,000.

Increased cost sharing in both private health insurance plans and such government plans as Medicare and health care benefits for veterans, in which the policy holders have the ability to pay (as opposed to Medicaid, in which the recipients of services are indigent and presumably incapable of paying), has great potential for reducing health care spending. However, for such plans to be effective, governments will have to ban the development of supplementary health insurance (such as the medigap policies purchased by Medicare enrollees) that will turn the patient's share of costs into a third-party payment. In other words, increased cost sharing will have to be made mandatory and apply to all insurance plans— public and private. This would require increased government regulation of the health insurance industry.

Two ways exist to increase consumer cost sharing. One is to increase the deductible amounts that consumers must incur before they become eligible for insurance payments. This would make consumers who are relatively healthy, and therefore incur health care costs less than the deductible, more price conscious.

These consumers would presumably compare their marginal health benefits with the marginal cost and consume health care services up to the point at which their marginal benefits equal the marginal social cost of health care services. One disadvantage of increasing the deductible amount is that it could discourage patients from seeking early medical care or tests for symptoms, and this could result in high medical costs in the future.

Another way to reduce the incentive to consume medical services is to increase the coinsurance rate paid by consumers. As this is done, the quantity of medical services demanded will decrease as will the quantity supplied. The effect of increasing the coinsurance rate is illustrated in Figure 9.6. Suppose the coinsurance rate is initially set at 20 percent after the deductible is met. At that level of coinsurance, third-party payers absorb 80 percent of the price of medical services for the insurees. If the coinsurance is increased to 40 percent, the quantity of medical services demanded will decline, thereby reducing the quantity supplied. The share of the price of the services absorbed by third parties will be reduced to 60 percent. As a result of the increased coinsurance, the market price of medical services on average will also decline.

FIGURE 9.6   How an Increase in Coinsurance Can Reduce Health Care Spending and Improve Efficiency in the Market for Health Care Services

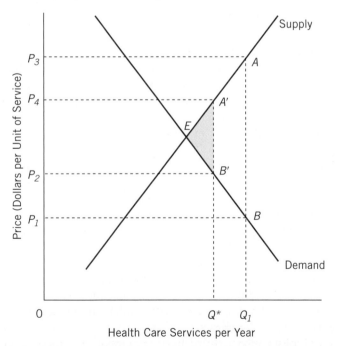

Increasing the coinsurance rate for insurees increases the price from P_1 to P_2 to patients and results in a decrease in the quantity of medical care demanded. As this occurs, the price to providers also declines from P_3 to P_4. The reduction in both the quantity consumed and the price paid to providers decreases expenditures on health care. This reduces the overallocation of resources to health care, and the loss in net benefits from this overallocation declines from the amount represented by the triangle *ABE* to the amount represented by the smaller triangle *A'B'E*.

Both the decline in the quantity of medical services demanded and the decline in price contribute to a decline in health care expenditures, causing a reduction in the overallocation of resources to medical services. The loss in net benefits from inefficient use of medical services will decline from an amount represented by the area ABE to an amount represented by the smaller area $A'B'E$.

Managed Care: HMOs and Other Means of Limiting Freedom of Health Care Providers to Prescribe Services and Patients Choosing Providers

Another way to control the rate of increase of medical services is to intervene in the decisions of medical care providers and patients directly through a system of managed care. Under managed care, the decisions of physicians and other health care providers are reviewed to determine whether they are appropriate for the patient. The patients themselves are required to purchase health care services from a specified network of providers and their freedom of choice in both treatments and physicians is limited. Finally, the means of paying the providers is often specified by the insurance firms sponsoring the managed care facilities. Patients often are charged no direct price for the services they consume. However, the providers frequently receive **capitation payments**, which are fixed amounts per patient per year. This fixed amount encourages providers to economize their use of medical resources. Their profits are higher when they do not prescribe inappropriate procedures or procedures for which the marginal benefit to the patient exceeds the marginal cost. A number of studies of medical procedures have provided evidence that insurance plans using a capitation fee have lower rates of hospitalized surgical procedures than insurance plans providing similar coverage but reimbursing physicians on a fee-for-service basis.[3]

HMOs usually receive capitation payments from the health insurers with whom they contract. For the fixed fee per patient, the HMO provides comprehensive medical care for those it serves. Because the HMO's profit is the difference between capitation payments and the cost of its services, it has a financial incentive to minimize the cost of medical care.

Some holders of traditional health insurance plans obtain medical services from a Preferred Provider Organization (PPO), for which coinsurance payments by the patient are lower than with other health providers. PPOs still operate on the basis of fees for services and their patients are free to choose their own health care providers. However, the services provided by PPOs are monitored by the health insurance company, thereby giving it some control over services prescribed.

HMOs are apparently effective in reducing use of medical care. However, such organizations tend to have higher administrative costs because of the process of reviewing the decisions of health care providers. Although transfer of patients to HMOs does reduce the overall cost of health care at the time the transfer is made, the growth of spending on health care through HMOs has been as rapid as overall growth of health care spending.[4]

---

[3]See Paul J. Feldstein, *Health Care Economics*, 6th edition (Clifton Park, N.Y.: Delmar, 2005).

[4]See Congressional Budget Office, *Rising Health Care Costs: Causes, Implications, and Strategies* (Washington, D.C.: Congress of the United States, Congressional Budget Office, 1991).

Regulation of Pricing, Competition, and Reimbursement of Hospitals and Physicians

The most direct and drastic ways of government intervention in the market for health care services to control expenditures are direct controls on prices and regulation of the volume of services supplied. Direct controls set limits on the amount of reimbursement to physicians for the services they provide. Private insurance companies typically limit reimbursement to physicians for procedures provided.

Unless implemented by all third-party payers and accompanied by controls on the ability of health care providers to increase the quantity of procedures supplied, price controls are not very effective in limiting the growth of spending. During the 1984–1986 period in which physician reimbursement rates were frozen by Medicare, the rate of physician expenditures per enrollee continued to increase at a rate of about 10 percent. Apparently, physicians were able to increase the volume of services they supplied to Medicare patients to offset the effect of the price freeze on their incomes.

Medicare has also experimented with some innovative pricing mechanisms designed to economize on the use of hospital facilities. The **Prospective Payment System** used by Medicare gives hospitals a fixed payment per patient for the expected costs of treating patients with specific illnesses. The fixed payment, known as DRG charges and discussed earlier in this chapter, does not vary with length of stay in the hospital, thus giving hospitals the incentive to discharge patients as soon as it is medically advisable. During the first five years of this payment system, the average length of hospital stay for Medicare patients declined by 10 percent. The system is supplemented with a hospital utilization review process that limits admission of Medicare patients to hospitals. In 1992, Medicare extended this payment system to physicians and limits reimbursement to them on the basis of estimates of reasonable costs and charges associated with given diagnoses.

The Medicaid program also has limited reimbursement to hospitals and physicians on behalf of patients in the program. State governments limit their reimbursement to hospitals for Medicaid patients to covering the minimum possible average cost of hospital services. The average reimbursement rate under Medicaid is about 80 percent less than hospital costs of services. Physicians who provide services to Medicaid patients are also reimbursed at lower rates.

Unfortunately, low rates of reimbursement under Medicaid have reduced access to medical care for those enrolled under the program. Many doctors are unwilling to accept Medicaid patients and some hospitals are reluctant to admit them. Because of difficulties in finding physicians to treat them, Medicaid patients often seek treatment at hospital emergency rooms, where cost of treatment is more expensive to third-party payers.

To be effective, price controls and review procedures have to be instituted on a national basis and apply to all third-party payers. In nations with government-provided health insurance, such as Canada, health care providers are reimbursed on a fee-for-service basis with fees negotiated by the government authorities who administer the health plan. All providers are paid according to the same schedule for all patients so no incentive exists to refuse to treat patients as is the case under Medicaid price controls.

CHECKPOINT

1. How would the market for health care be affected if the federal government required all health insurance companies to increase their coinsurance rates from current levels by 50 percent?
2. How do capitation payments affect the incentive of suppliers to provide health care services?
3. What techniques have been used by the Medicare and Medicaid programs to control the growth of health care expenditures?

UNIVERSAL COVERAGE

In light of what we now know about the market for health care services and how incentives to consume health care services are influenced by the price system, health care providers themselves, and the institutions for paying for health care services, we can examine alternative means of extending guaranteed health care to all. Any plan of universal coverage must involve more extensive government intervention in the market for health care than has prevailed in the United States. First, let's examine the gaps in coverage in the United States.

Gaps in Health Insurance Coverage

The U.S. health insurance system provides health insurance benefits to the bulk of the employed, the indigent, and the elderly. However, there have been significant gaps in coverage. As of 2010, it was estimated that 50 million people younger than 65 had no health insurance. This total amounted to 16.3 percent of the U.S. population. This gap in health insurance coverage is a matter of serious concern. Naturally, those without insurance face the prospect of financial ruin if they are struck by a major illness. However, because many of the uninsured will obtain treatment in nonprofit hospitals, the costs of the treatment will be borne by the rest of the population because hospitals cover their losses by increasing fees paid by insured patients. Finally, some of these uninsured could be reduced to poverty status as a result of illness or other medical problems. If this is the case, their health care will be paid for by others through higher taxes as these people become eligible for the Medicaid program.

One cause of the decline in coverage has been a reduction in the number of employees who are covered with health insurance by their employers. The shift in jobs to the service sector of the economy accounts for most of the decline because service workers are less likely to enjoy coverage than industrial workers.

About one-half of the uninsured younger than 65 have had jobs and relatively low incomes, but their income levels are not low enough to qualify them for Medicaid benefits. Another 30 percent of the uninsured are dependents of uninsured workers. Many of those who lack health insurance coverage have been part-time workers and young adults. Workers employed by smaller firms are less likely to have health insurance than workers employed by large firms. Almost all U.S. firms with 100 or more employees provide health insurance. However, less than half of the firms with fewer than 25 employees provide their employees with health insurance.

GLOBAL PERSPECTIVE

National Health Insurance and Health Services in Great Britain and Canada

Government plays a much more active role in the provision of health insurance and health care in many foreign nations than is the case in the United States. All these nations have national or regional budgets for health care that attempt to cap or at least target total annual health care spending. Most of these nations also limit the supply of health care provided through their budgets and limit the acquisition of medical equipment and facilities. Also, review systems are in place to monitor and control the supply of medical care to keep costs down.

Let's examine the role of government in health insurance and health care in two nations with extensive government participation in health care: Great Britain and Canada.

Great Britain

Perhaps the most famous government health insurance system is the British National Health Service (NHS). In Britain, the government operates and supplies the bulk of health care services produced in the nation. The NHS provides universal coverage for physician and hospital services, long-term care, and prescription drugs, and funds those services almost entirely through taxes, which pay for 97 percent of NHS services. British citizens pay little or no fees directly for the health care services they consume.

Private health insurance is also available in Great Britain to finance elective surgery and nursing home care that is not covered by the NHS. But only a bit more than 10 percent of British citizens carry private insurance. Some private provision of hospital services is available. However, the NHS has a virtual monopoly on the supply of hospital services, accounting for nearly 80 percent of the hospital beds in the nation.

British citizens have very little choice among health care providers. To obtain health care services, a British citizen must register with a general practice (GP) physician who is currently accepting patients. The GP serves as the patient's access to the health system in much the same way as GPs control access to health care services in an HMO in the United States. GPs refer patients to specialists who can order tests and admit patients to hospitals. Once hospitalized, a patient is treated by salaried NHS specialists on the staff of the hospital.

GPs receive capitation payments for their patients. This practice provides incentives to economize on the use of medical services because each physician receives a fixed payment from the NHS per patient regardless of the number and kind of services provided to the patient. NHS specialists are salaried government employees of regional health authorities. However, some physicians do receive fee-for-service payments for such services as preventive medicine and family planning services. Physicians who serve private hospitals also are paid on a fee-for-service basis.

Budgeting for capital expenditures is done by the government. Regional boards participate in decisions to acquire such new equipment as CT scanners. The budgetary limits on capital expenditures and payments to physicians often result in shortages of services and long waiting lists. Typically, getting emergency care in Great Britain is no problem, but long waits (weeks and even months) to obtain an appointment with a specialist are common. Doctors classify patients according to their needs for hospitalization and surgery, and the classification system determines their place in line to be admitted to hospitals. It typically takes about a year to get to the top of the list for such common operations as hernia repair, varicose veins, hip replacements, and cataract removals. Limitations on the hospital budgets to pay surgeons have resulted in the waiting lists growing.

Many British citizens are frustrated by waiting to obtain services and often choose to go to private hospitals for operations, where they must pay the full cost of the services. Britain spends about 9 percent of its GDP on health care—a bit more than half the amount spent in the United States. However, there are not enough services to go around, and the services are rationed by long waiting lists. The services are free to all but are not readily available. The NHS physicians control access to health care for the bulk of the population, while the rich who can afford to pay the full price of medical services can purchase those services at private hospitals.

Canada

Unlike the British, the Canadians do not operate the health care system. Instead, each province administers its own health insurance plan under a system of universal health insurance and federal Canadian guidelines. The system has been in operation since 1972. The provincial insurance plans guarantee minimum standards of health care for all Canadians and are financed, in part, by federal income taxes. Most provinces finance the remainder of the costs of the plans with their own tax revenues.

The Canadian health care plans cover physician and hospital services in much the same way that private health insurance plans do in the United States, but do not cover prescription drugs and long-term care. However, most provinces do have their own plans that pay the bills for these uncovered services for the elderly and the poor. Private health insurance provides benefits for services not covered by the provincial health care plans. Most of the health care bills of Canadians are therefore paid by governments. Because the Canadian provinces act as the health insurers in Canada, the administrative costs of the system are lower than those in the United States, where there are many private insurers, each with its own claims-processing facility.

Governments budget for health care in Canada. Many Canadian provinces establish expenditure targets for physician services and adjust the fees to physicians downward if the targets are exceeded. Physicians in Canada are reimbursed on a fee-for-service basis, which is negotiated with the provincial governments that are in effect the single purchasers of physician services. The fees are also, in effect, controlled by the provinces. Hospitals face stiff budgetary constraints under the Canadian system and receive fixed annual allocations that vary with such criteria as the number of hospital beds and the types of services provided. The federal government also places limits on its own annual health spending. These federal limits have in recent years increased the share of health care costs borne by the provinces.

Hospitals in Canada must request funding for capital acquisitions—including those for new structures, equipment, and other capital outlays—from a provincial ministry of health. Most of the new funding of capital equipment comes from the provincial governments, but hospitals also bear some of the costs. In addition, Canadian provinces have committees to review physician patterns and budgets and limit the number of physicians available to the public. As is the case for the British system, shortages of medical services and facilities in Canada are common, resulting in long waiting lists for medical procedures and hospital beds.

Problems with National Health Plans

In recent years there has been increased dissatisfaction with national health insurance both in the United Kingdom and in Canada. Budget constraints have been severe in the United Kingdom, making many services that we take for granted in the United States difficult to obtain. These constraints have capped health care spending but at the expense of reducing the quality of health care. Waiting times for elective surgery are much longer in the United Kingdom than in other countries. Even more disturbing is the fact that survival rates following cancer treatment are much lower in that country than in other industrial nations. This has led many citizens to seek treatment from private providers.

Efforts have been made in the late 1990s to reform the NHS through quasi-marketlike arrangements designed to improve quality while keeping prices low for services. The results were mixed, and high administrative costs for the reform led to its abandonment in 1997. The system is still struggling to improve quality of treatment and is trying to meet the demand for service by encouraging specialist doctors to treat patients after normal NHS hours.

Similar problems prevail in Canada's system. Shortages of services and limits on prescription drugs lead some Canadians to travel over the border to the United States for treatment by private physicians.

As of 2005, Canadians had to wait an average of about eight weeks for an appointment with a specialist after a referral from a family physician. After seeing a specialist, Canadians had to wait an average of a bit more than nine weeks to actually receive treatment. As of 2006, Canada remained the only major industrial nation that officially outlawed private supply of basic medical services. However, this law is rarely enforced, and many private clinics have been operating in the country to treat patients who find it difficult or impossible to obtain timely treatment from the national public health system. Court challenges to public monopoly on health care are expected.[1]

[1]See Clifford Krauss, "Canada's Private Clinics Surge as Public System Falters," The New York Times, February 28, 2006.

Even in large firms, substantial numbers of employees are not eligible for employer-provided health insurance. Part-time workers, who make up about 20 percent of the U.S. labor force, generally are not eligible for employer-provided health insurance even in large firms. New employees typically have to wait for a period before they become eligible for employer-provided health insurance coverage. Workers who change jobs frequently and work only for a short time at a job, even one in a large firm, often are without health insurance coverage for long periods.

The uninsured are generally quite sensitive to the price of medical services because they pay the full costs of such services out of pocket. Those without health insurance are generally more reluctant to use physician services and much less likely to use inpatient hospital services than the insured.[5] Physicians and hospitals also are less likely to provide the uninsured with expensive medical procedures that are readily available to the insured.

Although Medicaid covers virtually all the costs of its beneficiaries, Medicare pays only 45 percent of the total health costs of the aged and disabled eligible for coverage. Also, many private insurance plans place annual limits on out-of-pocket costs once an enrolled individual has incurred a certain amount of medical expenditures, but Medicare patients have no such cap. Medicare enrollees are at much greater risk than the rest of the U.S. insured population for the effects of catastrophic medical expenses. About 80 percent of Medicare enrollees, however, have supplementary health insurance either from their former employers or through a medigap policy purchased from a private insurer. Medicare patients who are medically indigent also are eligible for benefits under the Medicaid program.

Finally, employer-based health insurance does not provide benefits for long-term nursing home care. **Long-term care services** are medical, support, and rehabilitative services for patients who have functional limitations or chronic health problems and need daily assistance with the normal activities of living. Most private insurance and Medicare do not cover long-term care services. Currently, governments pay half the total cost of long-term care through the Medicaid program. However, this provides little protection for the average family because to be eligible for such payments, it must first be literally bankrupted by its long-term care expenditures. In view of the aging U.S. population, increased demands are likely for insurance coverage for long-term care or through Medicare or other means. Projections indicate that nursing homes in the United States will have more than 5 million residents by the year 2050, three-fifths of whom will be over the age of 85!

Eliminating the Gaps in Health Insurance Coverage and Reforming Health Insurance Markets: *The Patient Protection and Affordable Care Act of 2010*

On March 23, 2010, President Obama signed the *Patient Protection and Affordable Care Act of 2010*. This legislation is a comprehensive and controversial attempt to reform the system of health care provision in the United States. The Act will result

---

[5]See S. Long and J. Rodgers, *The Effects of Being Uninsured on Health Care Service Use: Estimates from the Survey of Income and Program Participation* (Bureau of the Census, SIPP Working Paper #9012, 1990).

in government mandates to extend health insurance and therefore improved access to health care to more than 30 million people by 2019 who have been unable to easily obtain such coverage at reasonable rates of payment. The provisions of this legislation are being phased in through 2018 and, unless Congress modifies the new law, will become fully effective by 2019.

The legislation provides subsidies through tax credits to help individuals who do not receive health insurance from an employer defray some of the costs of paying for the policies. Some small businesses will also receive tax credits to help them provide health insurance for their employees. To improve the market for health insurance new "health insurance exchanges" will be set up in each state to help make affordable and flexible coverage available to individuals and small businesses. In addition, eligibility for Medicaid will be adjusted so that many Americans with relatively low incomes who previously could not qualify for this program of government-provided health insurance will now be able to obtain coverage.

To pay for federal government expenditures under the legislation new taxes, fees, regulations limiting certain tax deductions or exemptions, and penalties for those who do not obtain mandated health insurance coverage are also being phased in through 2018.

Major Provisions

1. **Mandated Health Insurance for Individuals:** Effective 2014, all persons who are not covered by Medicaid, Medicare, or an employer-provided health insurance program (with some exceptions for religious or financial reasons for those for which health insurance premiums would exceed 8 percent of monthly income) must obtain an approved private health insurance policy or pay a penalty. The penalty will be $95 or 1 percent of income, whichever is greater in 2014 but will rise to $695 or 2.5 percent of income by 2016 with some exemptions permitted. Health insurance exchanges will be set up in each state to improve the market for coverage by encouraging competition among private providers and allowing a variety of plans some of which would receive government subsidies to be made available to individuals through the market place rather than by government provision. The exchanges will create groups of enrollees from individual applicants thereby allowing pooling of risk and reducing the problem of adverse selection. The will permit the insurance providers to sell policies at lower premiums than would be the case if they sold to individual applicants.

2. **Expanded Medicaid Eligibility:** All individuals and families with adjusted gross income up to 133 percent of the poverty level will become eligible for Medicaid and easier access to CHIP, the child health insurance program. More than half of the 32 million people expected to become insured by 2019 will obtain their insurance because of the expansion of Medicaid eligibility. The federal government will finance roughly 95 percent of the cost of this extended Medicaid coverage during the period 2014 to 2019. This means that the costs to state government would amount only to 5 percent of the additional coverage cost over this period but that share will likely increase starting in 2020. Initially the legislation stipulated that states refusing to provide the additional coverage would lose all of their Medicaid funding. However, a Supreme Court ruling in June 2012 held that portion of the law unconstitutional. State governments can choose not to provide the additional coverage to those with up to 133 percent of the poverty level and face no loss of funds. For political reasons

or because of concerns about higher state share of Medicaid costs in the future, 14 states (as of March 2013) have chosen not to expand Medicaid eligibility.

3. **Tax Credits for Health Insurance Premiums:** Those with incomes up to 400 percent of the federal poverty income level will receive subsidies, with amounts depending on their actual incomes, to offset some of the cost of mandated health insurance purchased through health insurance exchanges. Families with the lowest income levels will have their out-of-pocket payments limited to 2 percent of their income while those with incomes at 400 percent of the poverty level will have the income share for such premiums limited to 9.5 percent of their income. Given the 2011 poverty income level of $22,350 for a family of four, this means that such families with incomes as high as $89,400 in 2011 dollars are eligible for such tax credits beginning in 2014. Certain small businesses are eligible for two years of tax credits starting in 2014 to offset the costs of providing health insurance for their employees. Employers of early retirees with heavy medical expense not yet qualifying for Medicare will receive subsidies to help reinsure these retirees.

4. **Minimum Standards:** All health insurance policies will be required to meet new federal government guidelines. Annual and lifetime caps on coverage will be banned. Adults with preexisting conditions cannot be denied health insurance coverage nor, beginning in 2014, can they be charged higher premiums based on such conditions. Nor can higher premiums be based on gender. Certain preventive care services will become available at no out-of-pocket cost to insured patients. Dependent children up to their 26th birthday are now permitted to remain on their parents' health insurance plan and insurers are not permitted to cancel the policies on individuals after they become ill.

5. **Changes in Medicare:** The new law will change the way physicians are reimbursed for treating those covered by Medicare to move away from "fee-for-service" to a new "bundled payment" plan designed to reduce expenditures per patient. New research on the effectiveness of certain treatments can also result in reduced reimbursement. Medicare patients will also receive improved coverage under Medicare Part D through elimination of the "doughnut hole" gap in coverage for expenditures on pharmaceuticals. The elimination of this gap will be phased in through 2020. New preventive care services will also be available to Medicare patients at zero co-pay.

6. **Miscellaneous Provisions:** Many other provisions of the law will impact markets for health care. Attempts will be made to address shortages of health care personnel in certain areas. Incentives will be established for primary care providers to locate in underserved areas. Physicians and hospitals will be provided with incentives to improve the quality of care while reducing average cost of treatments. Fraud in Medicare, Medicaid, and private insurance claims will be subject to a crack down. Certain individuals who remain without health insurance coverage after the law is fully phased in may be offered a catastrophic-only health insurance plan to cover major medical costs of a debilitating disease or accident but with very high copayments for noncatastrophic health problems.

Funding to Finance Tax Credits and Other Government Health Subsidies

1. **Medicare Tax:** The tax base for the 2.9 percent Medicare Tax has been broadened effective 2013 to allow an additional 0.9 percent levy on the wages of individuals and the self-employed with adjusted gross incomes of more than

$200,000 per year for single taxpayers and $250,000 per year for married tax-payers filing joint returns. Certain high-income individuals will also have to pay a 3.8 percent Medicare tax on investment income.

2. **An Excise Tax on High Value Health Insurance Policies:** To discourage employers from compensating employees with overly generous (and tax exempt) health insurance policies, effective 2018 a 40 percent excise tax will be levied on the excess above premiums of $10,200 for individuals and $27,500 for families. The tax will also be applied to amounts in excess of $11,850 for individual retirees and $30,950 for retirees with family coverage. These amounts will be indexed with the rate of inflation.

3. **Other Revenue:** Fees will be levied on health insurance providers and manufac-turers and importers of branded drugs. An excise tax of 2.3 percent will be levied on certain medical devices. The floor at which medical expenses can be deducted before computing taxable income will be raised from 7.5 percent of adjusted gross income to 10 percent of adjusted gross income.

Impact of the Act on Health Insurance Coverage, Market Imperfections, Health Outcomes, and Federal Budget Balance Estimates by the Congressional Budget Office suggest that the number of uninsured individuals in the United States will decline by approximately 32 million by 2019. Allowing dependents ages 19–25 to remain on their parents' health insurance already has contributed to a substantial decline of individuals in this age group without health insurance. However, a sub-stantial number of individuals will remain without health insurance at that time. Those will mainly include illegal immigrants who are expected to account for about one-third of about 23 million individuals without health insurance in 2019. Others without insurance are expected to include those eligible for coverage under Medicaid who do not enroll, those who opt out of the mandate to purchase health insurance and choose to pay the penalty, and those whose cost of health insurance coverage would exceed 8 percent of their income and choose not to buy insurance but would be exempt from any penalties. It remains to be seen how many healthy citizens will choose to pay the penalty rather than purchase health insurance they still consider "a bad deal." It is not clear how the penalty will be enforced. Further, in the past if someone waited until he or she were sick to buy insurance he or she often found that no company would sell it to him or her because of a preexisting condition. However, the new law makes it illegal to refuse insurance coverage to those with preexisting conditions. Under those circumstances it might seem rational for many to pay the penalty until they become sick and then purchase insurance.

Offsetting the incentive to opt out is the fact that insurance has become the ticket to health care. Those without insurance may find it difficult to find health care providers to serve them unless they pay high prices for service in advance. Because being without health insurance tends to have adverse affects on access to medical care, it can adversely affect the health of the uninsured. In addition, lack of health insurance can increase financial risk. It is therefore likely that expanding availability of health insurance will both improve health status of those previously uninsured and decrease their risk of financial loss due to high medical bills.

The rationale behind the mandate to purchase insurance is to reduce imperfec-tions in the health insurance markets, such as adverse selection, that make it difficult, costly, or impossible for individuals who lack coverage from an employer or under Medicaid or Medicare to obtain health insurance. When persons apply for insurance individually instead being a part of a large group, there is a tendency for those who know they will need expensive medical care to demand the insurance while healthy individuals will decide to do without insurance. Because insurers are aware of this adverse selection, they raise premiums to cover the high expected outlays under individual policies. This makes insurance still more expensive to those who are healthy leading to still more concentration of high-cost individuals in the group and still higher premiums. Eventually, insurance companies decline to sell health insurance to individuals because of this adverse selection.

The new legislation mandates insurance coverage, in part, to correct for the market failures involved in covering individuals and small groups by creating a larger group to spread the risk and requiring healthy individuals to purchase insurance. This reduces the adverse selection problem and ultimately will lower insurance premiums to all those in the group. It will also encourage more insurance companies to offer insurance to individuals and small groups and therefore increase competition in the health insurance markets. The legislation also helps reduce the adverse selection problem through a risk adjustment process that will transfer funds from insurers with relatively healthy enrollees (and therefore low-cost in terms of payouts for claims) to those with enrollees in poorer health (therefore requiring relatively more medical expense).

Currently, in many states, the health insurance market is dominated by three or four large insurance companies giving them the potential to exercise monopoly power. Making it easier to obtain insurance coverage and making it difficult for insurance companies to terminate coverage to sick people or not insure those with preexisting conditions can also improve the function of labor markets by reducing the probability that people will stay on a job they are not suited for just to retain their health insurance.

Another reason individuals do not purchase insurance is that they expect that hospitals and health care providers (or other charitable givers) might help them with medical expenses when they are sick or injured. When hospitals and health care providers forgive bills of those who are unable to pay, they often transfer those costs to those with insurance thereby contributing to higher premiums for the insured. Mandating health insurance coverage will help reduce the impact of charity on insurance premiums. Those who are already insured could see their premiums decline as the cost of providing uncompensated care to the uninsured is reduced.

Although health insurance premiums are expected to rise as a result of increased demand by the previously uninsured, those falling in that group will also largely benefit from tax credits and other subsidies that will lower their net cost per policy. Total health care expenditures in the nation are also likely to increase partly as a result of expanded health insurance coverage. Other measures are still needed to control and reduce the rate of growth of heath care expenditures as a share of GDP.

The Act will have little impact on large employers and their employees. Currently in the United States virtually all employers with 200 or more employees provide health insurance. Large groups of enrollees for these firms are often not given the option of refusing health insurance or can only sign up during certain designation periods so the problem of adverse selection is not usually present for these groups. Such groups are not formed for the purpose of seeking health insurance so there is no problem of adverse selection. Similarly, 95 percent of employers with between 50 and 199 employees also provide health insurance as a fringe benefit. The *Affordable Care Act* imposes a $2,000 per full-time worker penalty on firms with 50 or more workers who do not offer health insurance. Employees who do not get employer-provided health insurance could raise costs to the federal government by obtaining tax credits to purchase insurance on their own through insurance exchanges effective 2014. It is expected that few firms will be affected by this provision because well over 95 percent already provide health insurance to their employees. Business with fewer than 50 employees will not be subject to this penalty but will, in fact, be encouraged to provide insurance to their workers because they will be eligible for tax credits and their workers can be insured through a larger pool of enrollees established by the insurance exchanges.

The *Affordable Care Act* both increases government spending and raises more revenue mainly through tax increases. Initial analysis of the fiscal impact of the Act on the federal budget balance by the Congressional Budget Office indicated that revenues will exceed expenditures as the provisions of the legislation is phased in over a ten-year period. However, such estimates are notoriously inaccurate and the impact of the new legislation on the federal budget will depend on how expenditures change as new incentives are provided to individuals and how taxpayers react to the new levies.

SUMMARY

Health care expenditures have been claiming an increasing share of GDP in the United States in recent years. Governments have been playing an increasingly active role in the financing of health care expenditures in the United States since 1965. Federal, state, and local governments currently pay more than 45 percent of the health care bills of Americans, mainly through Medicaid and Medicare, the two major government health insurance programs. Governments also indirectly subsidize private health insurance by excluding employer-provided health insurance from taxation.

The system of health insurance in the United States is a mix of government and private insurance programs. Under the U.S. health insurance system, most Americans pay only a small portion of the price of medical services. Out-of-pocket costs for health care services cover less than one-fifth of the costs. Third-party payments by private insurance firms and the government cover the bulk of health care costs. Because the third-party payments reduce the price of medical services to consumers, the quantity demanded increases. The price of health care services must rise to increase the quantity supplied, assuming an upward-sloping supply curve. Third-party payments contribute to an increase in the quantity of medical services demanded and the price of those services, thereby increasing health care expenditures. The moral hazard of health insurance is the increase in the quantity of health care demanded that results when insurance companies pay most of the bills of consumers.

Health care expenditures are difficult to control because health care providers can influence the demand for such services. Health insurance seeks to control expenditures by establishing deductibles and coinsurance to make consumers more price conscious. Some insurance companies provide service through HMOs, where the physicians receive capitation payments that vary with the number of patients rather than services provided. The capitation payments provide incentives for the providers to economize on the use of health care resources.

In other nations, national health insurance schemes provide universal health insurance coverage and finance the coverage through taxation. In those nations, governments budget for health care spending and control reimbursements to hospitals and physicians to achieve spending targets. Control of spending for capital facilities in most nations with national health insurance limits access to these facilities and often results in long waiting lists for admission to hospitals and for surgical procedures.

LOOKING AHEAD

Taxation is the major means of financing government expenditures. Part III develops techniques to analyze the economic effects of taxes. Chapter 10 discusses taxation and alternative methods of financing government goods and services.

KEY CONCEPTS

Capitation Payments

Coinsurance

Deductible

Long-term Care Services

Moral Hazard of Health Insurance

Prospective Payment System

Risk Averse

Third-Party Payments

REVIEW QUESTIONS

1. How are health care expenditures financed in the United States?
2. What is the role of governments in providing health insurance and financing health care in the United States?
3. What are third-party payments and how do they result in an overallocation of resources to the provision of health care?
4. Show how the moral hazard of health insurance varies with the coinsurance rate. How can an increase in deductibles reduce the moral hazard of health insurance?
5. What are capitation payments? How can capitation payments of HMOs help control health care spending?

6. Discuss some of the major aspects of the Medicaid and Medicare systems and techniques used by these programs to control government health care spending in recent years.
7. What are some of the problems involved with providing health care as a public good free of charge and in equal amounts to all consumers?
8. Which groups in the United States are not covered by health insurance? How does the lack of health insurance affect those who are not covered and those who are?
9. How are health care services rationed in Great Britain and Canada, where universal health insurance is available?
10. How is health care spending controlled in Great Britain and Canada?

PROBLEMS

1. The current tax rate paid by employees in a company on their income is 30 percent. Currently, the employer provides workers with a health insurance policy that is worth $3,000 per year.
   a. Assuming that the company has 1,000 workers, what is the indirect government subsidy for health insurance for workers in the company?
   b. Suppose that instead of providing the workers with health insurance as a fringe benefit, the employer sold them the policy for a $3,000 annual premium. How would this change affect the typical worker, assuming that he or she still wants $3,000 worth of insurance under the new arrangement?
2. The graph on the right shows the supply and demand for health care in the nation. The demand curve reflects the marginal social benefit of health care, while the supply curve reflects the marginal social cost.
   a. What is the efficient amount of health care expenditures?
   b. Suppose that under current arrangements health insurance reduces the price of health care to the population from an average of $100 per unit to $20 per unit. Show how third-party payments

will affect the market for health care by affecting the quantity demanded and quantity supplied. Assuming that the price must increase $150 to accommodate the new quantity demanded, calculate the increase in expenditures for health care. Is efficiency now attained in the market?

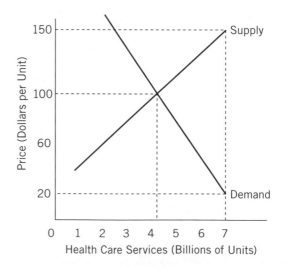

3. Use the graph from Problem 2 to show the loss in efficiency that results from third-party payments. Show how the loss in net benefits from overallocation of resources to health care can be reduced by increasing coinsurance from $20 per unit of health care services to $50 per unit.

4. How do health care providers control the demand for health care? Suppose reimbursement rates to physicians under all payers is limited by law. Use supply and demand analysis to show how the limit in reimbursement need not decrease expenditures for health care if health care providers succeed in increasing the demand.

5. One method commonly used by both governments and private health insurers to control the growth in health care spending is to limit reimbursement to providers. How can these limits to reimbursement be viewed as the exercise of monopsony power? To prevent health care providers from prescribing more services it is often common to limit approval of services to health care recipients. How is this practice affecting recipients of Medicaid and Medicare?

ADDITIONAL READINGS

Feldstein, Paul J. *Health Care Economics*. 7th ed. Clifton Park, New York: Delmar Learning, 2011. A textbook covering the major economic issues in health care, including health insurance and health care financing.

Glied, Sherry A. and Dahlia K. Remler. "What Every Public Finance Economist Needs to Know about Health Economics: Recent Advances and Unresolved Questions." *National Tax Journal 55*, 4 (December 2002): 771–788. A review of issues and problems regarding the market for provision of medical services, and the role of economic policy in influencing health care.

McClellan, Mark. "Medicare Reform: Fundamental Problems, Incremental Steps." *Journal of Economic Perspectives* 14, 2 (Spring 2000): 21–44. A discussion of the Medicare system as it has evolved in the United States and analysis of options for reform to control costs in the future. This article is one of several relating to Medicare in the same issue of the journal.

McGarry, Kathleen. "Public Policy and the U.S. Health Insurance Market: Direct and Indirect Provision of Insurance," *National Tax Journal 55*, 4 (December 2002): 789–827. A comprehensive review of the system of health insurance in the United States. Discusses the history of U.S. health insurance, direct and indirect subsidies for health insurance, and the impact of the system on incentives, prices, and the distribution of well-being in the United States.

Moon, Marilyn. *Medicare: A Policy Primer*. Washington, D.C.: Urban Institute Press, 2006. An analysis of the Medicare system in the United States, how it works, its problems, and challenges.

Phelps, Charles E. *Health Economics*. 3rd ed. Upper Saddle River, N.J.: Prentice Hall, 2010. An analysis of issues in health economics.

INTERNET RESOURCES

http://www.cms.hhs.gov

The home page of the Centers for Medicare & Medicaid Services of the Department of Health and Human Services contains a wealth of information on government health care programs. Data about national expenditure on health care, as well as details about the Medicare and Medicaid programs, can be obtained from this site.

http://www.ebri.org

This is the home page of the Employee Benefit Research Institute. Information about health insurance coverage of Americans can be obtained here.

http://www.kff.org

This is the home page of the Kaiser Family Foundation. Information and data on private and public health insurance plans, including the Employer Health Benefits Annual Survey and data on both the Medicare and Medicaid programs, can be accessed at this site.

PartThree

FINANCING GOVERNMENT EXPENDITURES

Chapter 10

INTRODUCTION TO GOVERNMENT FINANCE

LEARNING OBJECTIVES

After reading this chapter, you should be able to:

- Discuss alternative means of financing government expenditures, the effects they have on the economy, and issues relating to the distribution of the burden of government finance.

- Understand the basic terminology used to analyze the impact of taxes on the economy,

including the tax base and the tax rate structure.

- List the criteria used to evaluate alternative means of financing government expenditures.

- Examine alternatives to taxation as means of government finance.

F ederal, state, and local governments in the United States spent close to $5.5 trillion in 2012. To raise the funds necessary to finance their expenditures, governments tax economic activities, including income-earning activities and consumption of goods and services. Those who own homes and other property also are taxed according to the value of their property. The average U.S. worker allocates more than four months of annual earnings to pay federal, state, and local taxes. You name it, some government taxes it—everything, including gasoline, alcoholic beverages, jewelry, electricity, not to mention your earnings from work and savings, and, if you are fortunate enough to own one, your home!

Although taxation is the main source of revenue for governments in the United States, governments obtain some funds from fees and charges, including tolls, and tuition charges at state-run colleges and universities. Governments also raise funds from enterprises they operate, such as public utilities (water, gas, and electricity) and the liquor stores operated by many state governments. State governments even operate gambling enterprises that raise revenue from lotteries and legal off-track horse race betting! Governments must borrow funds when they cannot cover all their expenditures from tax and nontax receipts.

This chapter begins an exploration of the means and consequences of government finance. We develop the vocabulary necessary to analyze tax systems and such alternatives to taxes as user charges for government-provided services and borrowing. We also discuss the criteria used to evaluate systems of government finance. In most cases, funds to pay for government-provided goods and services are obtained in a way that is fundamentally different from that used to finance goods and services in markets. Buyers and sellers interact in markets to establish prices that provide sales revenue to pay the costs of making goods available. The prices simultaneously ration the goods and services and provide the revenue necessary to finance the costs that sellers incur in providing the goods to consumers. Taxes do not ration goods and services in this way because payment of taxes is not a prerequisite for enjoying the benefits of most government-supplied goods and services. So although these benefits are financed by taxes, the absence of a direct link between taxation and enjoyment of government-provided goods and services complicates the analysis of government finance.

PURPOSE AND CONSEQUENCES OF GOVERNMENT FINANCE

Government activity requires the reallocation of resources from private to government use. To accomplish this, individuals must be induced to surrender their right to command resources for their own private uses so that government authorities can then obtain those rights for the purpose of providing goods and services.

The particular method of finance that is either proposed for a community or actually used can affect a number of important economic and political variables. These include the following:

1. **The Political Equilibrium.** The equilibrium quantity and mix of government-provided goods and services depend on the distribution of tax shares per unit of those goods and services, because citizens' tax shares influence their voting choices.

2. **Overall Market Equilibrium and Efficiency with Which Resources Are Employed in Private Uses.** The particular method of finance used can distort the prices of goods and services in ways that prevent competitive markets from achieving efficiency.

3. **The Distribution of Income.** Alternative financing schemes affect the distribution of income by reducing the income that people have to spend on private goods and services and by influencing prices and the amounts of private goods exchanged in markets. In fact, many citizens advocate the use of particular methods of public finance precisely for the purpose of redistributing income.

The impact of the method of finance on political equilibrium is discussed in the chapters on public goods and choices. This chapter and those to follow concentrate on the impact of government finance on private choices and on the distribution of income.

PRINCIPLES OF TAXATION

What Are Taxes?

Taxes are compulsory payments associated with certain activities. Revenues collected through taxation are used to purchase the inputs necessary to produce government-supplied goods and services or to redistribute purchasing power among citizens.

Taxation reallocates resources from private to government use in two distinct steps. First, the ability of individuals to command resources is reduced, because taxation reduces income for spending on market goods and services. Second, the revenues collected by government then are used to bid for resources necessary to provide government goods and services and to provide income support payments to recipients of government transfers such as Social Security pensions. For example, a family whose annual income is $70,000 and who pays $14,000 in taxes must necessarily curtail either annual consumption or saving. The $14,000 could have been used to purchase home furnishings or to help finance private investment. The private goods and services that could have been bought with the $14,000 is the opportunity cost of government-supplied goods and services for this particular family.

Under tax financing, resources released and made available to government as a result of taxes do not always correspond to resources required to produce the politically chosen government-provided goods and services. In such cases, government demands on resources, coupled with the reduction in private demands caused by the taxes themselves, cause the relative prices of some inputs to change. For example, if taxation results in a reduction in the demand for blue-collar workers while government spending increases the demand for white-collar workers, the net effect will be an increase in the wages of white-collar workers relative to those of blue-collar workers if full employment is to be maintained.

A single-step alternative to taxation is the use of government power to acquire resources directly. The most common example of this is the military draft. When resources are acquired directly, their owners bear the cost of finance by losing the opportunity to use them in the way that maximizes their income or satisfaction.

Tax Base

The **tax base** is the item or economic activity on which the tax is levied. The most commonly used tax bases can be grouped into three broad categories: income, consumption, and wealth. These are economic bases; their values depend on decisions made by individuals. For example, individuals make daily choices that affect their income. They also can control the allocation of their income between saving and consumption. Because most individuals must save to accumulate wealth, their decisions regarding consumption also affect their wealth.

A person's income is the sum of the value of his or her annual consumption of goods and services and annual saving. Income is often regarded as a good index of the ability to pay taxes. Total annual income in a nation is equal to the value of the total consumption and saving of all people and organizations in the country. A person's annual consumption is his or her annual income less the amount of that income saved that year. Finally, wealth represents the value of a person's accumulated savings and investments at any point in time. The annual flow of income from the stock of accumulated wealth in a nation is the annual return to saving.

The three major tax bases are related. Consumption is the portion of income that is not saved, while wealth is the net value of a person's stock of accumulated savings or investments.

Because income is believed to be a good index of the ability to pay taxes, many economists use this broad economic base as a benchmark for evaluating the fairness of taxes. The amount of taxes paid is generally computed as a percentage of annual income. The way a particular tax varies as a percentage of income per year is often used to make judgments about the fairness of the distribution of taxes among taxpayers.

Taxes on economic bases can be general or selective. A **general tax** is one that taxes all of the components of the economic base, with no exclusions, exemptions, or deductions from the tax base. For example, a general income tax would tax all sources of income and would not allow any sort of deduction from total income in computing tax liability. All income, irrespective of its source or use, would be taxable. Similarly, a general wealth tax would tax all forms of holding wealth.

A **selective tax** is one that taxes only certain portions of the tax base, or it might allow exemptions and deductions from the general tax base. For example, an **excise tax** is a tax on the manufacture or sale of a particular good or service. Excise taxes are selective taxes on production or sales. Similarly, a tax on real estate is an example of a selective tax on a particular form of wealth. A tax on profits is a selective income tax, because it taxes only a particular form of income.

Tax Rate Structure

The **tax rate structure** describes the relationship between the tax collected during a given accounting period and the tax base. In evaluating taxes on such economic bases as income, the tax rates are calculated as the ratio of taxes paid to the various values of the base. The **average tax rate (ATR)** is simply the total dollar amount of taxes collected divided by the dollar value of the taxable base:

$$ATR = \frac{\text{Total Taxes Paid}}{\text{Value of the Tax Base}}. \qquad (10.1)$$

The **marginal tax rate (MTR)** is the additional tax collected on additional dollar value of the tax base as the tax base increases:

$$MTR = \frac{\Delta \text{ Total Taxes Paid}}{\Delta \text{ Value of the Tax Base}}. \qquad (10.2)$$

A **proportional tax rate structure** is one for which the ATR, expressed as a percentage of the value of the tax base, does not vary with the value of the tax base. For example, an income tax of 20 percent would tax all income at 20 percent.

Thus, a person with an income of $10,000 and a person with an income of $100,000 would each be subject to the same rate of taxation. The tax on $10,000 at 20 percent would be $2,000, and the tax on $100,000 of income at 20 percent would be $20,000. Under proportional taxation, the ATR, but not the amount of tax, is independent of the size of the base. A tax with a proportional rate structure is sometimes called a **flat-rate tax.**

For a proportional tax rate structure, both the average and marginal rates of taxation are the same. Because the rate of taxation does not vary with the annual value of the base, additional increments in the tax base, such as additional earnings under an income tax, are taxed at the same rate as that applied to previous values. This is illustrated in Figure 10.1.

When a **progressive tax rate structure** is used, the ATR increases with the size of the base. The larger the tax base, the larger the MTR applied. The **tax bracket** gives the increment of annual income associated with each MTR. The MTRs and associated tax brackets for a progressive income tax are illustrated in Figure 10.2.

For progressive taxation, the marginal rate of taxation eventually exceeds the average rate of taxation as the MTR increases. The dichotomy between the two rates is important, because the MTR is more crucial in determining behavior changes that can cause losses in efficiency than is the average rate. Therefore, when the average and marginal rates of taxation vary from each other, it is necessary to carefully delineate the two in order to ascertain properly the effect of the tax on individual behavior. For example, if a person is deciding to work more hours, the net gain for doing so would be the net income he or she can keep after taxes. If the person's income is subject to a 50 percent MTR, he or she will be able to retain only half of his or her extra income. However, because only income after a certain amount is subject to the 50 percent rate, the person's ATR will be lower than 50 percent. The difference between average and marginal rates of taxation for a typical progressive tax is illustrated in Figure 10.2.

Table 10.1 shows the marginal and average tax rates on which the graph in Figure 10.2 is based. All income up to $4,000 per year is subject to a zero marginal and average tax rate. This is the first tax bracket. Income between $4,000 and

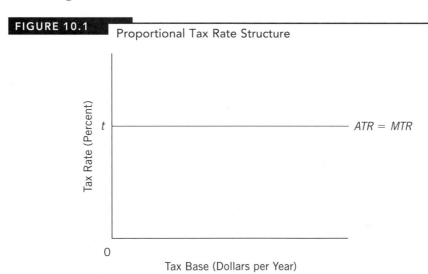

FIGURE 10.1   Proportional Tax Rate Structure

Tax Rate (Percent)

t ———————————————— $ATR = MTR$

0

Tax Base (Dollars per Year)

The tax base is subject to a flat rate of t percent at all annual values. Under a flat-rate tax, the average tax rate (ATR) is always equal to the marginal tax rate (MTR).

FIGURE 10.2 Progressive Tax Rate Structure

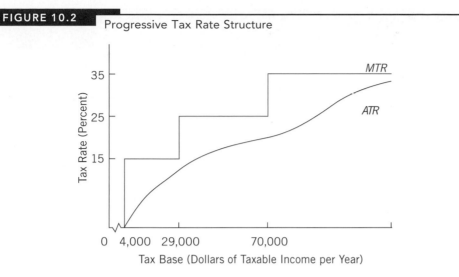

Under a progressive tax rate structure, the ATR increases with the size of the tax base. The MTR exceeds the ATR after a point. These curves are based on Table 10.1.

© Cengage Learning

TABLE 10.1 An Example of a Progressive Tax Rate Structure

TAX BRACKETS (TAXABLE INCOME)	MARGINAL TAX RATES (MTR)	AVERAGE TAX RATES (ATR)	
		BEGINNING OF BRACKET	END OF BRACKET
0–$4,000	0%	0%	0%
$ 4,000–$29,000	15%	0%	13%
$29,000–$70,000	25%	13%	20%
Above $70,000	35%	20%	34%[a]

[a]Calculated for $1,000,000 annual income.

© Cengage Learning

$29,000 per year is subject to a 15 percent MTR. Income between $29,000 and $70,000 per year is subject to a 25 percent rate. Finally, all income greater than $70,000 per year is subject to a 35 percent MTR. These are the MTRs for each *bracket* of income.

Table 10.1 shows the ATRs for income at the beginning and end of each tax bracket. For example, a taxpayer with a $4,000 annual income would pay a zero ATR, because only income greater than $4,000 would be taxable. A taxpayer with income at the end of that bracket would pay 15 percent on the amount of income greater than $4,000. This will be 15 percent of $25,000, which is $3,750 per year. Dividing this by that taxpayer's $29,000 annual income gives an ATR of 13 percent, which is less than the 15 percent MTR.

In each tax bracket, the ATR would steadily rise. Thus, a taxpayer just entering the $29,000 to $70,000 bracket would be paying an ATR of slightly more than 13 percent. A taxpayer with a $70,000 annual income pays nothing on the first $4,000 of income, 15 percent on all income from $4,000 to $29,000, and 25 percent

GLOBAL PERSPECTIVE

Taxes and Tax Rates throughout the World

You might think that taxes take a big bite out of incomes in the United States. However, taxes are a relatively small share of aggregate income in the United States compared to other industrial nations of the world. As of 2010, total federal, state, and local taxes in the United States amounted to about only 24.8 percent of U.S. gross domestic product (GDP). The share of GDP allocated to pay taxes provides a rough indication of the ATR for all taxes expressed as a percentage of aggregate domestic income. As of 2010, taxes as a share of GDP in the United States was among the lowest of all the 34 member nations of the Organization of Economic Cooperation and Development (OECD) where taxes averaged about 33 percent of GDP. Only Chile and Mexico had taxes as a share of GDP lower than that of the United States.

The chart shows average tax rates measured by tax revenues as a percentage of GDP for major industrial nations in 2010. Almost all industrial nations had average tax rates in the aggregate of at least 30 percent of GDP. The highest tax rates were in the Scandinavian nations, which have extensive social programs administered by the government sector of the economy. Tax revenues amounted to more than 40 percent of GDP in Denmark, Sweden, Belgium, France, Norway, Italy, Finland, and Austria. Canada allocated 31 percent of its GDP to taxes in 2010. Only Japan, Korea, and the United States had revenues amounting to less than 30 percent of GDP. The only OECD nations with average tax rates less than 25 percent are the United States, Chile, and Mexico.

Most tax revenues in industrial nations come from taxes levied on both personal and corporate incomes, from taxes on payrolls used to finance social security programs, and from taxes on goods and services. The United States, Canada, and Australia rely heavily on the income tax base as a source of revenue. For example, more than 50 percent of tax receipts in the United States come from taxes on personal and corporate income. France and Italy, on the other hand, rely more heavily on consumption taxes and high payroll taxes. Canada relies very heavily on consumption as a tax base and has relatively low payroll taxes.

Average Tax Rate by Nation Measured by Revenues as a Percentage of GDP, 2010.

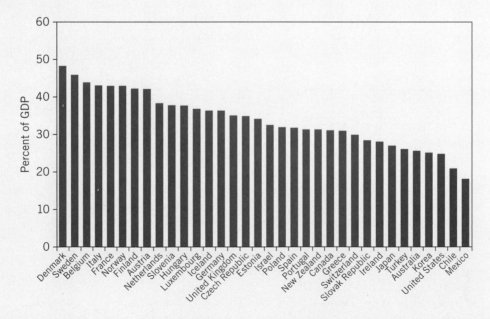

Source: Organization for Economic Cooperation and Development (OECD), 2011 Tax Statistics. Note: Data for Australia, Japan, Netherlands, Poland are for 2009.

on income greater than $29,000 up to $70,000 per year. The total tax is $3,750 + 0.25 ($70,000 − $29,000) = $14,000. The ATR for a taxpayer with $70,000 annual income would be 20 percent. For the final tax bracket, which is open-ended, the table shows the ATR for a taxpayer with $1,000,000 annual income. The ATR for taxpayers with higher annual income would rise steadily and approach, but never equal, the MTR. In Figure 10.2, a line is traced through the corresponding points on the ATRs within brackets to show how ATRs vary. Notice that the ATR is always less than the MTR at all levels of income.

Finally, taxes may have a **regressive tax rate structure** in which the ATR declines as the size of the tax base increases. In a regressive tax rate structure, the MTR is less than the ATR for all those brackets above the lowest. A regressive income tax results in a lower annual ATR as income rises. More productive individuals would be rewarded with lower tax rates as they produced and earned more. However, the opposition to such a method of taxation is strong because it violates the widely held belief that ability to pay increases with income. However, in many cases, a regressive tax rate structure can result in upper-income people paying higher dollar amounts of taxes than lower-income people.

An example of a tax with a regressive rate structure is the payroll tax used to finance Social Security pensions and Medicare. In 2006, the combined employee–employer tax rate was 15.3 percent, levied on labor earnings up to a maximum of $94,200 per year (this amount is adjusted for inflation each year). Labor earnings in excess of $94,200 were taxed at a 2.9 percent rate without limit. This is a two-bracket regressive tax rate structure, as illustrated in Figure 10.3. A worker earning $94,200 in 2006 would generate tax revenue of $14,412.60 = (0.153 × $94,200) from this payroll tax. The MTR would be 15.3 percent, which would also be the ATR for all workers earning $94,200 or less in that year.

FIGURE 10.3   Example of a Regressive Tax Rate Structure

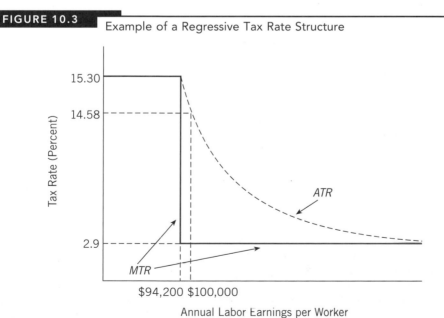

This is the tax rate structure used for the Social Security payroll tax for 2006. It is a two-bracket regressive rate structure.

Workers earning more than $94,200 would be subject to an MTR of only 2.9 percent on earnings in excess of this amount under this payroll tax. For example, suppose you were fortunate enough to earn $100,000 in 2006. You would pay $14,412.60 on $94,200 of your earnings plus an additional tax equal to 2.9 percent of the difference between $100,000 and $94,200. This additional tax would be $168.20. Your total tax would be $14,580.80 and your ATR would be this amount divided by your $100,000 labor earnings or 14.58 percent. Your ATR is therefore lower than the 15.3 percent paid by workers with earnings of $94,200 or less. Figure 10.3 shows how the ATR would continually decline for earnings in excess of $94,200.

Sales taxes in the United States are often labeled regressive by critics. Strictly speaking, the retail sales tax as used by most state and local governments is basically a tax with a proportional rate structure applied to the consumption base. However, because consumption as a percentage of income tends to fall as income rises, the proportional tax on consumption could be regressive with respect to income (depending on the actual details of the tax). Thus, those who argue that sales taxes are regressive are evaluating the taxes with respect to a base different from that on which the tax is actually levied. This is commonly done. They, in fact, believe that sales taxes are regressive with respect to the income base.

CHECKPOINT

1. What is a tax base? List three major classes of tax bases, and give an example of a particular type of tax levied on each of the three major bases.
2. What is a general tax? How does a general tax differ from a selective tax?
3. How does the relationship between the marginal tax rate (MTR) and the average tax rate (ATR) vary, depending on whether a tax rate structure is proportional, progressive, or regressive?

HOW SHOULD THE BURDEN OF GOVERNMENT FINANCE BE DISTRIBUTED?

A basic problem in government finance is to distribute among citizens the burden of financing the costs of government-supplied goods and services. No way of distributing these costs will satisfy all citizens. However, some clearly defined principles, or "philosophies," have been developed regarding the ways of distributing the costs of financing government-provided goods and services. Two major approaches to use as principles in determining the distribution of the burden of government finance are discussed in this section.

Benefit Principle

The **benefit principle** argues that the means of financing government-supplied goods and services should be linked to the benefits that citizens receive from government. From the point of view of those who favor the benefit approach, fees and charges are ideal forms of government finance. Charges, like prices, distribute the costs of goods and services among those who consume them.

A major advantage of the benefit approach is that, if successfully implemented, it links the cost per unit of government-provided services with the marginal benefits of those services. A distribution of tax shares per unit of a pure public good that reflects marginal benefits received by taxpayers induces individual citizens to vote for the efficient output of that good. Taxing all citizens according to their marginal benefits results in a Lindahl equilibrium, provided that the free-rider problem does not exist.

Most government-provided goods and services result in collectively consumed benefits that are difficult to assign to individuals. The only way to determine such benefits would be to ask individual citizens how much extra units of the good or service are worth to them. If individuals know that their share of the financial burden depends on their declaration of benefits, they might have little or no incentive to declare their true benefits. Only in communities that are fairly small, where individuals know each other's tastes, can a voluntary benefit approach work easily and without compulsion.

In some cases, the benefits from government-provided services can be correlated with a particular economic activity, which is taxed so that the amount paid varies according to benefits received by taxpayers. For example, the linking of gasoline taxes and road construction can be thought of as an attempt to apply the benefit principle by earmarking a particular tax for a particular use. The presumption behind the use of the gasoline tax to finance roads is that the benefits of road use vary directly with the consumption of gasoline. Most user charges, such as tolls for road and bridge use, fares for use of public transport, and admission fees for use of recreational and cultural facilities, are based on the benefit principle.

Ability-to-Pay Principle

The **ability-to-pay principle** maintains that taxes should be distributed according to the capacity of taxpayers to pay them. Citizens with greater ability to earn income, for example, should be taxed more heavily than those with less capacity to earn. Using this approach, the problem of distributing tax shares is viewed as independent of individual marginal benefits received from government activities. The implementation of a tax system based on the ability to pay requires some collective agreement concerning an equitable distribution of the taxes among citizens. Individual evaluations of the ability to pay are likely to differ among citizens whose preferences differ. In the United States, general consensus holds that the ability to pay varies with income.

Related to the ability-to-pay principle are the notions of horizontal equity and vertical equity. **Horizontal equity** is achieved when individuals of the same economic capacity (measured, for example, by income) pay the same amount of taxes per year (or over their lifetimes). **Vertical equity** is accomplished when individuals of differing economic ability pay annual tax bills that differ according to some collectively chosen notion of fairness. Both these concepts are subjective and are difficult to administer. Insofar as individual assessments of economic capacity differ, no consensus concerning horizontal equity is likely—and vertical equity requires judgments on income distribution that are even more subjective than those associated with horizontal equity.

Let's consider a few examples to illustrate the difficulties involved in determining whether a tax system achieves horizontal or vertical equity. The application of the principle of horizontal equity requires agreement on some measure of equality between individuals. For example, you might argue that two people who earn exactly the same income each year be considered equal for the purpose of deciding how much tax to pay. Suppose that both Mary and John earn $50,000 per year.

However, John also owns a house valued at $500,000 that he was fortunate enough to inherit from a rich uncle, has no debts, and has $100,000 in the bank. Mary, by contrast, rents a small apartment, owns no property, and has little savings in the bank. Are these two people really equal in the sense that they have the same economic capacity to pay taxes? Although they have the same money income, John has more wealth (property and financial assets) than Mary and really has more capacity to pay taxes than does Mary.

Consider another example: Suppose two physicians have exactly the same training and capacity to earn income. However, one physician, Dr. Jones, values her leisure time more than Dr. Smith and spends more time on the golf course and on vacations. Because Dr. Jones spends less time in the office than Dr. Smith, she has less income. If you use income as the basis for determining horizontal equity, we would argue that it is all right for Dr. Jones to pay less taxes than Dr. Smith. However, if we use earning capacity rather than actual income earned as our measure of the ability to pay taxes, the two physicians should both pay the same tax even though their incomes differ.

Vertical equity is even more difficult to establish than horizontal equity. Even if a tax system is generally agreed to have satisfied criteria for horizontal equity, say, because people with equal income pay equal amounts in taxes, it might not satisfy everyone's ideal of how people of different economic capacity pay different amounts in taxes. For example, suppose you think that a tax system achieves vertical equity if all taxpayers make an equal sacrifice to pay for government services. But you might also reason that equal sacrifice does not mean that all taxpayers pay the same number of dollars in taxes. It is reasonable to assume that the marginal benefit of a dollar to a person varies with the number of dollars that person earns each year and the number of dollars stored up as wealth. Accordingly, a dollar might be worth a whole lot to a person with little income and little wealth, such as a single mother with no savings or property, who works in a factory for $8 an hour and supports two children. That same dollar might be worth much less to a billionaire like Donald Trump, who has a lot of income and wealth. Most people would argue that equal sacrifice requires that the rich pay more dollars in taxes each year than the poor. But how much more should they pay? If, for example, both the working mother and Donald Trump paid the same percentage of their income in taxes, Trump would pay more dollars in taxes because a fixed percentage of several billion dollars will be more money than the same percentage of a modest annual income of say $20,000. But for many, this would not be sufficient to achieve vertical equity. Because the marginal benefit of a dollar falls with income, to achieve equal sacrifice of the benefits of income, a person as rich as Trump should pay a *higher percentage* of income in taxes than people with lower incomes. But how much higher a percentage should it be? We all might have different ideas about this, based on our own assessments of the way the marginal benefit of a dollar will vary with the person's income and wealth.

It is possible to derive technical rules for vertical equity by making specific assumptions about the way the marginal benefit of income declines as income (or wealth) rises.[1] To derive these rules, we also would have to make interpersonal

---

[1]See Joseph J. Thorndike and Dennis J. Ventry, Jr., *Tax Justice* (Washington, D.C.: The Urban Institute Press, 2002). The problem of equal sacrifice in taxation was considered in great detail by the English classical economist John Stuart Mill in his *Principles of Political Economy*, ed. W. I. Ashley (London: Longmans, 1921). For technical derivations of such rules, see Richard A. Musgrave, *The Theory of Public Finance* (New York: McGraw-Hill, 1959), Chapter 5. Also see Martin Feldstein, "On the Theory of Tax Reform," *Journal of Public Economics* 6 (July–August 1976): 77–104. Feldstein argues that the principle of horizontal equity requires that the posttax utilities of two people with the same pretax utility levels be the same.

comparisons of well-being among taxpayers—something that is difficult to do. You might think that a dollar to someone with $100,000 annual income is worth less than half as much as that to a person with only $25,000 annual income, but how do you really know? The person with the larger income might be ill and expect sharp declines in the future income because of inability to work and therefore values current income very highly. Determining the precise number of dollars that each taxpayer would have to pay for equal sacrifice is a very difficult task.

Nonetheless, despite our inability to determine a precise rule for vertical equity, the consensus in the United States appears to be that the poor should pay less in taxes than the rich. For example, the federal income tax has provisions that keep the tax burden of the lowest income groups at or close to zero, while tax rates are designed to increase as income increases to achieve vertical equity.

Actually assessing the fairness of tax systems according to the way tax burdens vary with ability to pay also is complicated by the fact that taxes affect prices and quantities of both inputs and outputs sold. Taxes affect incomes in very complex ways. For example, a sales tax on boats might raise the price of the product, reducing the real income of people who buy it. But the tax would not raise the price of the boat by the full amount of the tax per boat. Therefore, after selling the boat and paying the tax, the boat builder would have less revenue per boat. For example, imagine a $5,000 tax on a $100,000 boat. If the price of the boat rises to $102,000 after the decrease in supply that results from the tax, the net revenue per boat taken in by the builders after paying the tax will be only $97,000—that is, $3,000 less than before the tax. The boat builders also are made worse off. The price increase caused by the tax also will reduce the quantity of the product demanded, reducing revenue taken in by sellers. As this occurs, the sellers use less input to produce the product. If workers and owners of capital who must find alternative uses for their resources because of the tax cannot do so for the same rates of pay, their incomes will decline as a result of the tax. If skilled boat builders who lose their jobs because of the tax cannot find work that pays wages as high as they earned in boat building, their incomes will fall.

We need to trace out all the effects of a tax on prices and the quantities of outputs and inputs sold before we can accurately assess how much of it is directly and indirectly paid by different individuals. Once we have this information, we can then use it to determine whether taxes vary according to commonly held notions of ability to pay.

CRITERIA FOR EVALUATING ALTERNATIVE METHODS OF GOVERNMENT FINANCE

No single criterion exists by which to evaluate alternative means of government finance. In reality, the system of government finance that emerges is one that makes trade-offs among such normative criteria as

1. **Equity.** The distribution of the burden of government finance should coincide with commonly held notions of fairness and the ability to pay.

2. **Efficiency.** The system of government finance should raise revenues with only minimal loss in efficiency in the private sector.

3. **Administrative Ease.** A government finance system should be relatively easy to administer in a consistent manner, without excessive costs to collect, enforce, and comply with taxes and tax laws.

All these criteria must be considered in evaluating taxes. It is unlikely, however, that all can be achieved simultaneously. Efficient taxes are likely to be considered inequitable by many citizens, but equitable taxes might be costly to administer and could entail losses in efficiency.

Equity versus Efficiency

Government finance often has significant and complicated effects on the private choices made by citizens. Taxes can affect the willingness of individuals to produce and invest. User charges affect the levels of consumption of those goods and services on which they are levied, with subsidiary effects on the consumption of substitutes for and complements to government-supplied goods and services. The use of debt finance can affect the market equilibrium rate of interest and the willingness of investors to make private investments.

Because the main function of government finance is to reallocate resources away from private use and toward government use, government must reduce private consumption and investment to accomplish its objective. The main concern in evaluating the efficiency of proposed taxes and methods of finance is the impact of any financial scheme on the total income and wealth available. Two alternative methods of financing a given dollar amount of government-provided goods and services can result in different levels of national income and well-being. The most efficient means of government finance raises that given level of revenue while at the same time it minimizes the loss in well-being from market production and exchange.

The goals of efficiency and equity in the distribution of taxes among citizens are likely to conflict. Methods of government finance that minimize losses in efficiency in markets are not always considered desirable by all citizens. Those who subscribe to the ability-to-pay approach, or who believe that the system of government finance should be used to redistribute income, often oppose taxes that involve minimal losses in efficiency on the grounds that the distributive effects are undesirable. For example, strong support for progressive income taxes exists in industrial nations mainly because many citizens believe that a progressive tax rate structure applied to income correlates taxes with the ability to pay.

The trade-off between an equitable and an efficient system of government finance must be resolved through political interaction. In reality, under a system of compulsory finance, such as taxation, the resulting structure of government finance likely will be neither efficient nor equitable from the point of view of all citizens. In particular, unless a general consensus exists on what is a fair and equitable distribution of taxes among taxpayers, a given system of finance will be unlikely to satisfy all citizens.

For most democratic nations, the tax systems that tend to emerge are full of exemptions and deductions that grant special favors to particular groups for a variety of reasons. Many economists have argued that tax systems should be as efficient as possible and that the questions of income redistribution should be treated separately through a system of transfers independent of the tax system.

Equity remains a subjective concept, and the economist's judgments are no better than anybody else's. The economist, however, can generate information on how taxes affect the distribution of income in a community. Quite often, taxes have rather subtle effects on relative prices that might not be immediately obvious to citizens when they are considering the impact of a proposed tax. The economist's estimates of effects that alternative taxes have on relative prices, incomes, and efficiency are useful for citizens in evaluating any particular tax in relation to their own concepts of equity or fairness. Such estimates permit more-informed collective choices by participating citizens.

Tax Compliance and Evasion

A tax system must have rules for payment that are easily understood by citizens and are enforceable at low cost. **Tax evasion** is noncompliance with the tax laws by failing to pay taxes that are due. The question of tax compliance and evasion is essentially a legal problem with economic aspects. In the absence of strong moral constraints against noncompliance with tax laws and payment of government charges, the incentives for evasion by individuals depend on the costs and benefits expected from noncompliance. The benefits of evasion tend to increase with the amount of tax, or money in general, saved by not complying with the rules. This, in turn, tends to increase with the MTR and the amount of tax owed.[2]

The costs of tax evasion vary with the penalties involved and the probability of being caught by the authorities. Additionally, individuals consider the probability that they actually will be convicted of a crime after being caught, along with having to bear any costs of legal action necessary to defend themselves.

From the legal point of view, a distinction exists between the concepts of tax evasion and tax avoidance. **Tax avoidance** is a change in behavior to reduce tax liability. Taxpayers respond to the changes in prices caused by taxes by rearranging their personal affairs. High taxes on labor income might induce workers to refuse overtime work. Similarly, taking advantage of special provisions (sometimes called loopholes) in the tax code that reduce tax liability constitutes tax avoidance. Tax evasion is illegal, whereas tax avoidance merely involves adjusting the extent to which one engages in a taxed activity in response to the rate at which that activity is taxed. Tax avoidance is not illegal. However, tax avoidance is socially wasteful in that it results in distorted choices made on a basis other than the marginal social cost and benefit of an economic activity.

To ensure proper compliance with a system of government finance, an administrative mechanism must be established to collect the tax and to enforce penalties against noncompliance. This involves hiring personnel, establishing offices, acquiring such capital equipment as computers, building toll booths, and so on. To ensure low-cost administration, the taxed activity should be easily measurable, and the costs of collecting that information should be low. For example, the computerized system of tax withholding from employees' wages, so prevalent in many nations using the income tax, constitutes a simple and very inexpensive way of ensuring tax compliance.

Tax evasion has become a serious problem in the United States. Noncompliance with tax laws reduces revenues collected for any given tax rate structure. The greater the noncompliance, the higher the tax rates necessary to raise any given amount of revenues per year. Honest taxpayers have to pay higher tax rates than would otherwise be the case. The Internal Revenue Service (IRS) estimated that revenue loss from noncompliance with the tax laws was $450 billion in 2006.

---

[2]For a comprehensive analysis of factors affecting tax compliance and tax evasion, see James Alm, "Tax Compliance and Administration." In W. B. Hildreth and J. A. Richardson (eds.), *Handbook on Taxation* (New York: Marcel Dekker, Inc., 2000): 741–768 and Joel Slemrod and Shlomo Yitzhaki, "Tax Avoidance, Evasion, and Administration." In Alan J. Auerbach and Martin Feldstein (eds.), *Handbook of Public Economics* (Amsterdam, The Netherlands: Elsevier Science Publishers B.V., 2002): 1423–1470.

The $450 billion in 2006 is called the "gross tax gap." The overall voluntary compliance rate implied by the tax gap is 83 percent, which means that 17 percent of tax due was not collected in 2006. The bulk of the tax gap (about 90 percent) is due to underreporting and underpayment of tax due both on individual and corporate tax returns. After IRS enforcement efforts and late payments that year, the IRS collected an additional $65 billion resulting in a net tax gap of $385 billion.[3] Total tax revenue collected by the IRS in 2011 amounted to $2.5 trillion dollars. The gross tax gap in 2006 amounted to 16.9 percent of total revenue collected that year. If we project the IRS 2006 findings to 2011, assuming that the gross tax gap remains the same, the loss of revenue to the U.S. Treasury in 2011 would have amounted to approximately $480 billion in that year.

Understanding the incentives for tax evasion provides a useful starting point to the development of policies to fight it.[4] Assume that all taxpayers seek to maximize their expected income after taxes. To do so, other things being equal, they seek to minimize their tax payments. They are willing to take the risk of not complying with tax laws if the gains for doing so outweigh the expected costs. This, of course, is a simplification because some citizens feel that it is their duty to comply with the tax laws. However, many citizens reason that if they reduce their tax payments through noncompliance, the quantity and quality of government-supplied services that they receive will not be affected.

Both costs and benefits are associated with tax evasion. The benefit to the taxpayer is the reduction in taxes. The costs are the penalties, both monetary and otherwise, that the taxpayer will incur if caught.

For the taxpayer, the marginal benefit of tax evasion is the dollar amount of taxes not paid. This depends on the taxpayer's MTR. Assume that the taxpayer is subject to a progressive tax rate structure, as is the case under the personal income tax. In this case, the marginal benefit of a dollar of tax evasion declines as more taxable income is not reported, because tax evasion pushes the taxpayer into lower tax brackets. The MTR, and thus the marginal benefit in terms of taxes saved, declines as more taxable income is not reported. This is shown in Figure 10.4A, where the marginal benefit of tax evasion is plotted against the amount of taxable income not reported.

The expected marginal cost of tax evasion is likely to rise, because taxpayers are likely to reason that both the probability of detection and the penalty will increase as more taxable income is not reported each year. Assuming that the taxpayer has no moral compunction against tax evasion, the optimal amount of tax evasion in the form of unreported income (shown in Figure 10.4A) corresponds to the point at which the marginal cost of tax evasion to the person equals the marginal benefit. This occurs when D^* dollars per year are not reported.

A reduction in MTRs, such as that which resulted from changes in the U.S. tax law in 1986 and 2001, reduces the marginal benefit of tax evasion. As shown in Figure 10.4B, this will result in a downward shift in the MB curve and a decrease in unreported income. Increasing moral pressures against tax evasion also could shift the MB curve down. In Figure 10.4B, tax evasion declines from D_1^* to D_2^* as MB_1 shifts to MB_2.

---

[3]See "Tax Gap for Tax Year 2006: Overview," January 6, 2012, www.irs.gov

[4]See Ann D. Witte and Diane F. Woodbury, "The Effect of Tax Laws and Tax Administration on Tax Compliance: The Case of the U.S. Individual Income Tax," *National Tax Journal* 38 (March 1985): 1–13.

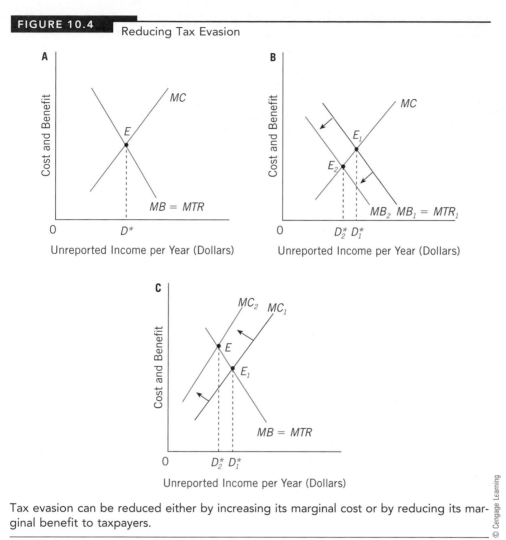

FIGURE 10.4 Reducing Tax Evasion

Tax evasion can be reduced either by increasing its marginal cost or by reducing its marginal benefit to taxpayers.

Increases in the marginal cost of tax evasion also will reduce the amount of tax evasion. This can be done by either increasing the probability of detection or increasing the penalties to taxpayers who are detected. This is shown in Figure 10.4C. After the marginal cost curve shifts from MC_1 to MC_2, tax evasion declines from D_1^* to D_2^*. If the probability of detection were 100 percent, or if the penalties were severe, the optimal amount of tax evasion to any citizen could fall to zero.

One study of tax compliance for the income tax suggests two effective ways to decrease tax evasion: (1) increase the probability of IRS tax audits for taxpayers and (2) increase the requirements for reporting income to the IRS and for withholding taxes from earnings. The researchers also conclude that much of the increase in tax evasion in the United States during the 1970s was accounted for by a reduction in the probability of audits of tax returns during that period.[5] However, little progress was made in increasing audits during the 1980s. In 1987, the IRS examined

[5]See Witte and Woodbury, "The Effect of Tax Laws," 9–10.

42 percent fewer returns than it did in 1978. In 2011, only 1.1 percent of returns filed were audited compared with 2.3 percent audited in 1978.

CHECKPOINT

1. What are the two major "philosophies" of taxation used to guide the way the burden of government finance is distributed?
2. What are some of the difficulties involved in determining whether a tax meets criteria of horizontal or vertical equity?
3. How could tax evasion in the United States be reduced?

ALTERNATIVES TO TAXATION

Although taxation is the dominant form of government finance, other alternatives are used, including debt finance, government-induced inflation, donations, user charges, and government-run enterprises such as state lotteries.

Debt Finance

Debt finance is the use of borrowed funds to finance government expenditures. Those who lend funds to the government for the purpose of financing government expenditures usually do so under their own free will. In return for the funds that they lend to the government, they receive a bond, or some other note of government indebtedness, that embodies the promise of the government to repay the loan with interest at some future date. Presumably, the interest payment received by these individuals adequately compensates them for the consumption and alternative private investments that they could have enjoyed had they chosen not to buy the government securities. On the other hand, as the debt is paid off by the government, some form of alternative finance is necessary, unless the government decides to retire the debt through issuance of additional debt. If taxes are used in future periods to pay off the debt, citizens will be forced in those future periods to reduce their consumption and saving to compensate those who voluntarily gave up their income in the past to buy the government securities. In other words, debt finance can be used to postpone the burden of taxation.

Government borrowing often is used to finance capital expenditures made by government authorities. Under those circumstances, borrowing by government authorities allows the financing of projects with benefits that will accrue in the future, without excessive reduction in the purchasing power of citizens in the current period. For example, construction of a major public facility, such as a hospital or a road, can take years. If these facilities were to be financed immediately by taxation, individuals would be forced to forgo consumption and saving opportunities equivalent to the entire capital cost of the facility, without any benefits accruing until the facility was fully constructed and functioning. The use of debt finance allows government authorities to tax citizens in the future, as the facility is being constructed and after it is completed. This, in effect, spreads the costs over time and allows citizens to pay for the facility as it is being used, rather than at the initial point of construction. If debt finance is used prudently, it can improve the efficiency of the use of resources for the economy by linking the tax cost of public investments to the stream of benefits produced by those investments.

The implication for the use of debt finance by government on the distribution of well-being among generations is an issue of controversy among economists. In view of the importance of debt finance by central governments in the United States and other nations, the debate on its effect on intergenerational equity has taken on added significance. Chapter 12 provides a detailed analysis of the issues involved in determining the burden of the government debt.

Inflation as a Means of Finance

Government-induced inflation is a sustained annual increase in prices caused by expansion of the money supply to pay for government-supplied goods and services. Government authorities simply can print money to pay for costs of government-provided goods and services or take other measures to expand the money supply.

The net effect of such continual increases in the money supply is, of course, sustained increases in the general level of prices—in other words, inflation. Increases in the market prices of goods and services caused by expansion of the money supply force citizens to curtail their consumption and saving, which in turn finances the reallocation of resources to public use over the long run. The burden of government-induced inflation varies according to the extent to which individuals succeed in adjusting their money incomes and assets, along with the rate of increase of retail prices.

Any increase in the money supply to finance government expenditures can result in inflation. If the central bank cooperates with government authorities by increasing the monetary base in response to government credit requirements, inflation is likely to result. An increase in the monetary base by the central bank is the equivalent of printing money. The impact of increased government borrowing to finance deficits on the rate of inflation is complex. Among the various factors that influence the effect of increased borrowing on the price level are (1) the extent to which the monetary reserves are increased by the central bank, (2) the maturity structure of the government debt, (3) the extent to which citizens substitute new government debt for existing private debt and consumption, and (4) the effect of government borrowing on the velocity of circulation of money.[6]

As illustrated in Figure 10.5, the use of inflationary finance can be considered an attempt to move outside the production-possibility curve. For example, creating money in times of war to increase the annual output of military goods, such as guns, is an attempt to increase their output with no reduction in annual output of such civilian goods as butter. In other words, inflationary finance attempts a move from point A to point I in Figure 10.5. The result is inflation, which moves the economy to a point such as C, where the increased annual output of guns causes a reduction in the annual output of butter to B_2. The higher prices effected by inflationary finance cause consumers to reduce their consumption of civilian goods. Inflation also can decrease the real value of accumulated savings held by citizens, thereby decreasing their wealth.

---

[6]For an outstanding discussion of inflation as a means of public finance, see Stanley Fisher, "Towards an Understanding of the Costs of Inflation: II." In Karl Brunner and Alan Meltzer (eds.), *The Costs and Consequences of Inflation* (Carnegie-Rochester Studies on Public Policy 15, 1981): 5–42. Also see G. Thomas Woodward, "Inflation Tax." In Joseph Cordes, Robert D. Ebel, and Jane G. Gravelle (eds.), *The Encyclopedia of Taxation and Tax Policy*, 2nd edition (Washington, D.C.: The Urban Institute Press, 2005): 203–204.

FIGURE 10.5   Inflationary Finance

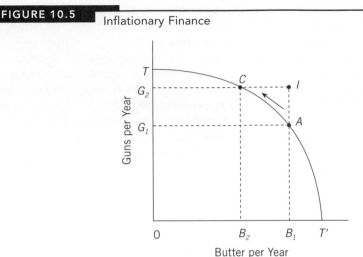

Using inflation as a way of financing government-supplied goods, such as guns for national defense, is an attempt to increase the output of these goods without decreasing the output of such private goods as butter. The government attempts to move to point I, but the increase in the price level decreases consumption of private goods, and the economy actually moves from point A to point C. The annual output of butter must decline to release the resources necessary to increase the annual output of guns.

© Cengage Learning

Inflation induced by the government's expansion of the monetary base reduces the purchasing power of money held by the public. The reduction in the real value of money is the "inflation tax" that ultimately reduces command over resources in the private sector and transfers resources to government use. The more money that is created to finance government purchases, the greater is the burden in terms of inflation and reduction in private-sector purchasing power.

Inflationary government finance can be used only for short periods of time. Eventually individuals will develop techniques to avoid holding domestic money. They could use foreign currency for transactions or develop techniques to minimize the amount of money they hold. If this occurred, the government would have to issue more and more money to meet its expenses and the inflation rate would have to increase accordingly. The eventual result is hyperinflation where inflationary expectations are constantly increasing. Efforts to unload money balances quickly cause rapidly increasing inflation rates. The ever-higher inflation is also likely to cause declines in both saving and investment within a nation. Individuals try to acquire foreign currencies and export capital. This often leads to political instability and "austerity programs" that sharply reduce government spending and borrowing. In short, it is prudent for governments to avoid using inflation as a means of financing their expenditures.

Donations

Donations are voluntary contributions to governments from individuals or organizations. These occasionally are used to finance particular programs. For example, governments might set up special funds to finance aid to victims of natural disasters and other individuals in difficulty, perhaps asking citizens to send contributions to such funds. In wartime, citizens of many nations have been invited to contribute both materials and their time in support of the war effort. Similarly, in peacetime, organizations such as the Peace Corps have been set up to induce individuals to volunteer their time, with little or no monetary remuneration, for providing specific public services for certain groups of individuals. Governments also could encourage businesses and individuals to provide public goods such as roads, sewers, and parks that would otherwise be provided by government.[7]

In communities where individuals have similar tastes or commonly shared goals, voluntary contributions of both funds and productive inputs might work well as a means of finance. However, such community consciousness or patriotism tends to diminish as the diversity of preference and population increases. In the United States, voluntary finance has been used extensively in the past in small communities, particularly in rural areas, for financing such services as fire protection, transportation of ill people to hospitals, and police protection. In many small towns today, a common form of supplying and financing fire protection is the volunteer fire department. Even in large cities, many individuals volunteer their time to serve as nurses' assistants in hospitals and convalescent institutions. However, voluntary donations remain only a minor source of finance in most nations.[8]

Grants from one level of government to another are similar to donations. However, these grants are financed by taxes levied on citizens of the grantor government. For example, federal grants to state and local governments financed 23 percent of expenditures of those governments in the United States in 2011. Of course, those who pay federal taxes finance the costs of these grants. Grants are not really an alternative to taxation. The impact of grants on recipient governments is discussed in the last part of this book.

User Charges

User charges are prices determined through political rather than market interaction. These charges can finance government-supplied goods and services only when it is possible to exclude individuals from enjoying their benefits unless they pay a fee. User charges often help to finance such government-supplied services as highways, bridges, and recreational facilities. Tolls for the use of superhighways and bridges are common in the United States and in many other nations. One advantage of user charges is that they make those who directly consume the services pay for at least part of the costs of producing those services, forcing individuals at least to compare some of the benefits of using the public services with the costs imposed by the user charge. In addition, user charges ration the use of public facilities in such a way as to avoid congestion.

User charges can take such forms as (1) direct prices associated with the consumption of particular goods and services, (2) fees for the option to use certain facilities or services provided by the government, (3) special assessments on privately held property, (4) licenses or franchises, and (5) fares or tolls. The distinction between such charges and market prices is that user charges do not necessarily reflect the interplay of supply and demand in markets. They reflect political and other forces.

---

[7]Corporate philanthropic contributions and provision of charitable services have received some analysis. See Ferdinand K. Levy and Gloria M. Shatto, "The Evaluation of Corporate Contributions," *Public Choice* 33 (1978): 19–28.

[8]For a formal analysis, see Clarence C. Morrison, "A Note on Providing Public Goods through Voluntary Contributions," *Public Choice* 33 (1978): 119–123.

PUBLIC POLICY PERSPECTIVE

User Charges and Efficient Allocation of Resources to Transportation Infrastructure

There is a rising tide of demands for increased spending on such transportation infrastructure as roads and airports. If you have driven the nation's congested interstate highways or have missed a connection at a congested airport because of delays during periods of peak travel, you might well agree that we need more roads and airports. However, the demand for new roads and airport facilities depends, in part, on the prices charged for use of existing facilities. One economist has argued that our worn and congested roads and runways are partly a result of underpricing. If the marginal costs of road use and congestion costs were charged to users, not only would they generate a lot of revenue to help pay for new facilities, but they also would help ration the use of these facilities so as to reduce wear and tear and the funds required to replace or expand the facilities.[1]

Clifford Winston argues that "the belief of most economists that public infrastructure spending should be substantially increased is not based on efficient pricing and investment principles."[2] We often demand more and wider roads because the use of existing roads is free. When new roads are built and congestion is reduced, it encourages more traffic from other routes. The road inevitably fills again at peak-use periods because congestion costs are rarely priced. Winston argues that efficient pricing based on marginal cost would decrease the demand for new transportation infrastructure and generate sufficient revenue to finance improvements on roads where congestion is a problem without the need to dip into tax funds.

An efficient pricing mechanism must calculate the marginal cost of using a facility based on both congestion and wear. For example, wear of a road varies with the vehicle weight per axle. A truck of a given weight with four axles does less damage to a road than one of equal weight with only two axles. Trucks therefore should be charged tolls to use roads and bridges according to their "equivalent standard axle loads," where the standard axle is one of 18,000 pounds. Currently, some roads and bridges that do charge tolls charge vehicles according to the number of axles, thereby discouraging truckers from adding more damage-averting axles per vehicle! Similarly, the fuel tax discourages truckers from adding axles because trucks with more axles get fewer miles

Earmarked taxes are special taxes designed to finance specific government-supplied services. These taxes are similar to user charges. For example, the gasoline tax in the United States is a levy on the consumption of gasoline, the proceeds of which are used exclusively to finance roads and alternative public transport facilities. Although earmarked taxes do not serve the same rationing function as user charges, they can make it easier for citizens to compare the benefits of specific government-provided services with the taxes they pay for those services. If the tax scheme is designed well, it can link tax payments with benefits received by taxpayers.

Typically, user charges are less than the average cost of providing the good or service. The difference between the average cost and the charge is a subsidy to users that is financed by taxes. It is often possible to arrange the subsidies of such goods in a way that varies the charge for use with the income of the consumer. Examples of government-supplied goods and services for which user charges are levied to at least partially finance consumption benefits include public housing; public transit; educational services; public recreational facilities; sewer and water services; and such public health services as inoculations, ambulance transport, and various hospital services.

per gallon. Winston also estimates that if road surfaces were built thicker and truckers were charged tolls according to the pavement wear damage they do, the result would be a sharp reduction in the rate at which roads wear out. According to Winston, a $1.2 billion investment in thicker road surfaces would yield an annual maintenance cost reduction of nearly $10 billion if coupled with axle-based tolls that would encourage truckers to distribute their loads on more axles. The higher tolls also would result in higher truck shipping charges, which would encourage more rail shipping and a reduction in truck traffic on the nation's roads.

Winston also points out that modern electronics can be used to vary toll charges with congestion on roads. Congestion charges can work to decrease demand for road use during peak-use periods, thereby reducing both congestion and wear and tear. The charges also would generate much revenue in tolls that could be used to finance road maintenance and improvements. There are automatic toll roads in use in Canada and the United States.

A similar problem exists for the way airports charge for the use of their services. Currently, airports charge fees to land aircraft based, in part, on aircraft weight. This means that the fee to land a large, fully loaded Boeing 747 is much higher than the charge to land a small, two-seat aircraft. However, the congestion cost of landing the small plane can be quite high if it delays a fully loaded large plane. If airports were to charge landing fees based on marginal congestion costs instead of aircraft weight, they could generate enough revenue to finance expansion by building additional runways. Passengers would enjoy fewer delays as a result of less airport congestion and the value of their time saved would be $8 billion annually, according to Winston. Winston argues that airfares would actually fall under a congestion fee because landing fees would actually be lower after funds collected were invested in new runways. Passengers would benefit from both lower fares and fewer delays with congestion-based landing fees used to finance new runways. However, the big loser in the shift to the congestion-based fees would be general aviation, as the small planes would see their landing fees skyrocket.

---

[1]See Clifford Winston, "Efficient Transportation Infrastructure Policy," *Journal of Economic Perspectives* 5, 1 (Winter 1991): 12–127.
[2]*Ibid.*, 114.

Charges often do cover the full costs of providing certain government-supplied services. This is often the case for water and sewer charges levied by municipal governments. The administrative costs for such services as processing applications (for example, for passports) are often financed by fees. In some European countries, citizens are required to purchase special stamped paper when making applications or inquiries to government authorities. The price of the paper is intended to cover some of the administrative costs of processing the citizens' requests.

A common criticism of user charges is that they prevent the poor from using government-supplied services. For example, many argue that publicly supplied cultural and recreational facilities should be made available free of charge to all citizens so as not to prevent those who are unable to pay from enjoying these services. One problem with this argument is that if such services are made available to all free of charge, a subsidy accrues not only to the poor who use the service but also to the rich. Thus, tax financing of parks, museums, and concerts, with free admission, provides few benefits to poor people if attendance by people who can afford to pay is heavy. In fact, if the tax system is such as to weigh heavily on the poor, it is possible that such free admission policies could redistribute income from the poor to the rich. For example, insofar as demands for use of public library and museum facilities are income elastic, and taxes used weigh heavily on low-income groups, tax financing will redistribute income from the poor to the rich.

Special reductions in user charges always can be allowed for low-income people or for other groups singled out for special treatment, such as children or the elderly. The reduction in the cost accruing to these groups might take the form of direct price reductions upon presentation of a special document. This technique allows a user charge to generate revenue while still permitting those least able to pay to enjoy the services of such government-supplied facilities as museums and parks.

User Charges and Efficiency

Creative use of user charges as an alternative to tax financing improves the efficiency of use of productive resources and lowers the annual tax bills of citizens. In many cases, the goods provided by governments that are, in fact, price excludable generate external benefits. For example, goods and services such as schooling, inoculations, and cultural events are commonly believed to generate external benefits. The problem is one of determining whether it is desirable to charge users for at least some portion of their private benefits.

The problem of determining the appropriate user charge for a government-supplied good or service with external benefits is similar to that of determining a corrective subsidy. Figure 10.6 shows the marginal social cost and marginal

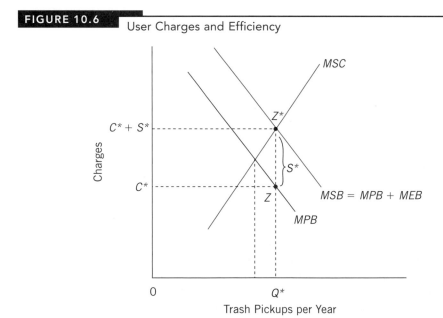

FIGURE 10.6   User Charges and Efficiency

The efficient user charge is C^* per trash pickup. However, because this does not cover the marginal social cost of pickups at the efficient level of Q^*, a subsidy of S^* per pickup must be provided by the government and financed by taxes.

social benefit of trash pickups in a city. The marginal social benefit has two components: a marginal private benefit for trash pickup service, *MPB*, and a marginal external benefit, *MEB*, to others. The external benefit could be in reduced risk of disease or simply a cleaner city. This is a public benefit that all citizens in the city enjoy. The efficient number of trash pickups per year, Q^*, corresponds to point Z^* at which $MSB = MSC$. This level could be attained by charging C^* per pickup. At that price, citizens demand Q^* pickups per year. This corresponds to point Z on the graph. However, a user charge of C^* per pickup falls short of the marginal social cost of that number of pickups per year. The difference must be made up by a subsidy of S^* per pickup. Taxpayers pay S^* for each pickup per year, while the citizens who order each pickup pay C^* per pickup.

User charges also can help in attaining efficiency if the benefits of government-supplied goods and services are subject to congestion. For example, if a road is subject to congestion, additional use of the road after the point of congestion decreases the benefits that all consumers obtain from the road. To attain the efficient level of traffic on the road, its services should be priced according to the marginal social cost imposed at any given level of traffic. A zero price is desirable only when the level of traffic is below the point of congestion. This is illustrated in Figure 10.7. If the road is a congestible public good, the marginal social cost of accommodating additional users falls to zero after the first user enters the road but eventually becomes positive. In Figure 10.7, the point of congestion occurs where the traffic on the road is 100 vehicles per mile per hour. If the demand curve for road use were D_1, a zero user charge would be efficient. This is because at zero price, the

FIGURE 10.7   User Charges for a Congestible Government-Supplied Service

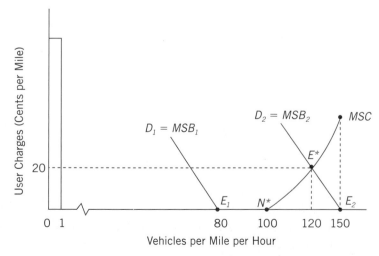

If the demand for road services is D_1, the efficient toll is zero. However, if demand increases to D_2, the efficient toll per mile is 20 cents. If a zero toll were charged when demand is D_2, equilibrium would be at point E_2, at which $MSB > MSB_2$.

© Cengage Learning

equilibrium would be at point E_1, at which $MSB_1 = MSC = 0$. This follows because the level of usage at E_1 is 80 vehicles per mile per hour, which is below that point of congestion, at N^*. If, however, the demand for road services were to increase to D_2, a zero user charge would no longer lead to efficiency. At zero price, the equilibrium would be at point E_2, at which 150 vehicles per mile per hour would be using the highway. Because the marginal social cost at that level of usage exceeds the marginal social benefit ($MSC > MSB_2$), more than the efficient amount of traffic would prevail per hour.

The efficient level of traffic corresponds to point E^* for which $MSB_2 = MSC$. This corresponds to 120 vehicles per mile per hour. To attain that level, government could impose a user charge of 20 cents per vehicle per mile.[9] Thus, a user charge of 20 cents per mile would serve to decrease traffic on the road to its efficient level while raising government revenues.

GOVERNMENT ENTERPRISE

Governments often run enterprises, selling private goods and services, to raise revenues. The difference between the revenues that are taken in by such enterprises and the costs can be used to reduce reliance on taxes. Many governments sell gambling services through the operation of state lotteries and betting games. This type of government enterprise is quite popular in Latin America and also is used in the United States. When a monopoly does not exist, governments must provide prizes and "odds" that are attractive enough to compete with the private supply of gambling. In addition, the amount of net revenues that the government unit collects from the lottery is limited by the demand for gambling services in the area.

Many government units also engage in retail sales of private goods, and some actually produce the private goods offered for sale. An example is the liquor stores run by many states. The profits of such stores often provide a significant amount of revenues to local government units. The markup on liquor by government-operated stores is equivalent to a tax on liquor.

Pricing the Output of Government Enterprise

Whatever the justification might be for government ownership of enterprises that produce items having the characteristics of private goods, the problem faced by government authorities is to price their output to cover costs in a collectively agreed-upon manner. At the extreme, the services of the public facility can be priced at zero, as is the case for most road services provided by state and local governments. The costs can be completely financed through taxation or the use of such earmarked taxes as the gasoline tax. Alternatively, prices can be set equal to average costs, including a normal return on the capital invested in the government-owned facility, with no taxes imposed on the public.

[9]The toll could be set on the basis of the weight or horsepower of vehicles, as is common. Trucks therefore would pay a higher toll than passenger vehicles.

The traditional normative approach to public finance argues that the output of public enterprises must be priced at its marginal cost in order to achieve efficiency. To implement marginal cost pricing correctly, all costs involved in using the facility, including congestion costs, must be measured. For example, once a road or bridge has been constructed, the capital costs that went into its construction budgets will not vary with traffic and will not be figured into the marginal costs. Therefore, marginal cost will be very low relative to the average cost per mile traveled. However, if the price for using the facility is placed at zero, or an amount close to zero, overuse of the facility can occur if congestion exists.

In applying the principle of marginal cost pricing, the incremental cost in supplying additional facilities when demand increases must be considered. A problem with various government-supplied facilities is that investments can be made only in large lumps. It is true that capital costs do not vary with output once a facility, such as a road, actually opens. However, future capital costs involved in expanding capacity can be considered as long-run marginal costs. Therefore, long-run marginal cost should include funds for expansion of units of capacity after the facility reaches that point of congestion. Marginal cost should include a capital recovery cost, which can be used to finance extra units of capacity.

The U.S. Postal Service: A Government Enterprise with a Large Growing Deficit

The U.S. Postal Service is a government enterprise that has been producing mail delivery services in the United States for over 200 years. Although the Postal Service has a monopoly on first-class mail delivery to mail boxes, it faces a great deal of competition in the modern digital age. As a quasi-government agency, it is also at the mercy of Congress in any plans it might have to change its business model. Since 2005 mail volume has fallen by nearly 25 percent as the postal service faces competition from such private carriers as FedEx and UPS for packages and parcels. In addition, first-class mail has fallen considerably as more people use e-mail for communication and computer access to bank accounts to pay their bills.

The Postal Service lost $8.5 billion in 2010. Because this loss adds to the federal government budget deficit, taxpayers are, in effect, subsidizing the service. Without legislative change, there is little prospect for the Postal Service to generate enough revenue in the future to cover its costs. If it were a private enterprise, it would have to go out of business unless it can figure out ways to raise more revenue or cut its costs.

In 2011 the Postal Service reduced its contribution to postal workers defined benefit retirement plan as a stop-gap measure to save about $800 million that year. However, with no prospect of mail volume increasing in the future, it is clear that the only way the Postal Service can return to profitability is by restructuring its operations by closing down facilities and reducing the size of its work force or finding new products to sell to the public. The Postal Service would like to eliminate Saturday mail delivery to cut costs by about $3 billion annually but this has been opposed both by postal workers and many politicians.

In a recent report the U.S. Government Accountability Office (GAO) outlined some actions to help restore the Postal Service to financial solvency.[10] These included allowing the Postal Service to sponsor its own health benefit plan and increasing employee and retiree contribution rates rather than being part of the federal government's health plan. A surplus estimated at $6.9 billion in funding for the Postal Service retirement plan would be reimbursed to help offset operating losses. Most importantly, it was recommended the service be downsized with mail processing plants and retail service facilities being closed. Such closures would of course mean reducing the Postal Services work force by an estimated 125,000 career employees by 2015. All these changes would require Congressional approval and is likely to meet stiff opposition by unionized postal workers and the patrons of the Postal Service who would suffer service reductions. Postal workers are federal government employees and the Postal Service is the government's largest civilian employer with a workforce of more than 650,000. From 1999 to 2011 the Postal Service has actually reduced the size of its workforce by 235,000 through attrition. However, future reductions are likely to require layoffs of career workers. Layoffs would require Congressional approval through new legislation and would also involve renegotiation of collective bargaining agreements with major postal worker unions.

Any closure of facilities could be subject to an appeals process that could be time consuming and make it difficult for the Postal Service to reduce its losses. Allowing the Postal Service to sell other products such as Internet access or cell phones could also meet with opposition from other retailers whose businesses could be affected adversely.

The plight of the U.S. Postal Service illustrates many of the difficulties in dealing with government enterprises. Although the outputs of these organizations are subject to changes in market conditions, they cannot respond in the same way that private business firms can. Service levels are often influenced by political considerations. For example, rural delivery services are more expensive to provide than urban delivery where population density is higher. However, alternatives to rural delivery that would require the rural postal client to travel to pick up their mail rather than have their mail delivered is likely to be opposed and receive enough political support to prevent reform. Changes in pricing and output levels must be politically approved through Congress rather than just being a business decision. And the U.S. Postal Service cannot simply go out of business without an act of Congress!

CHECKPOINT

1. What are some of the problems that result when a government prints money rather than raises taxes to pay its expenses?
2. Give some examples of donations used to finance public goods and services.
3. How should user charges for government-provided goods and services be set to achieve efficient outputs and usage rates of such products?

---

[10]See GAO, "U.S. Postal Service: Actions Needed to Stave Off Financial Insolvency," Statement of Phillip Herr, Director Physical Infrastructure Issues, September 6, 2011, GAO-11-926T.

P U B L I C   P O L I C Y   P E R S P E C T I V E

State Lotteries—A Government Enterprise with a Hidden Regressive Tax on Gambling

Government-run lotteries were used in the United States in colonial and revolutionary periods to raise funds for such purposes as the Jamestown settlement, the Continental Army, and to finance infrastructure, including bridges and schools. However, in the post–Civil War era, Congress enacted a series of restrictive rules on the use of the mails to conduct lotteries and barred lottery activity in interstate commerce. From 1895 to 1963, every state prohibited lotteries and shunned them as a source of revenue. Then, in 1963, New Hampshire reintroduced the state lottery as a government enterprise and source of revenue. As of 2012, 43 states and the District of Columbia were running lotteries.[1]

Lotteries are a form of government enterprise. In most states, the government-run lottery is a monopoly on large-scale organized gambling. The only legal competition is often the lotteries of other state governments. Lotteries are profit-making enterprises that most states run like any business, with heavy advertising and innovation in products to generate sales. The modern lottery offers instant-win game tickets, a computerized numbers game that allows players to pick their own numbers, and lotto—a game with long odds and enormous jackpots.

In fact, lotteries are very profitable for state governments; their net revenue generates enough funds to account for more than 3 percent of state revenue on average. The percentage of lottery revenues that are returned as prizes is extremely low relative to commercial gambling. For example, horseracing and slot machine operations both return more than 80 percent of the revenue collected as prizes. The payout rate for states' lotteries average only slightly more than 50 percent. After deduction of the costs of operating the lottery, including commissions to retail sales agents, most states' lotteries generated net revenue (profit) that averaged a whopping 40 percent of sales! The low odds of winning in state lotteries contribute to the high profits of the enterprises.

The state profit from operating the lotteries really can be regarded as a tax on the tickets sold to the more than 60 percent of adults in a lottery state who pay to play the games. If the average 40 percent profit is deducted from the price of a ticket, and the tax collected is expressed as a percentage of expenditures net of the revenues that are returned to the

state treasuries, the effective tax rate on lottery tickets is 66 percent! Those who buy lottery tickets therefore pay high taxes on their purchases in return for pretty low odds of winning! Also, evidence suggests the lottery is a regressive tax when expressed as a percentage of the income of those who play it. Much of the revenue generated from the lottery comes from the most active 10 percent of players who account for about half of the receipts. The average amount spent on lottery tickets by households making $10,000 is pretty much the same as that spent by households earning $60,000. Because expenditures on lottery tickets do not vary much with income, the implicit "lottery tax" is a smaller percentage of the income of upper-income groups than it is of the income of lower-income groups.[2]

Analysis of lotteries in Texas, where lotteries were introduced in 1992, concluded that the games there amount to a highly regressive tax. It was estimated that lottery games in Texas amounted to a 38 percent tax on gambling services provided by the state, and revenues collected from lotteries amounted to about 4 percent of general revenue in the mid-1990s. People with lower education levels, older people, and members of minority groups in Texas purchased proportionately more of games offered by the state with very high implicit regressive taxes. One of the games offered by Texas was found to be an inferior good—one whose consumption decreases as income increases.[3]

In states with lotteries, there is also evidence that spending on the state-sponsored gambling results in an approximate 2.4 percent decline in other household nongambling consumption. The fall in consumption of other goods in the state results in a decline in tax revenue collected from state sales and excise taxes.[4]

---

[1] See Charles T. Clotfelter and Philip J. Cook, "The Economics of State Lotteries," *Journal of Economic Perspectives* 4, 4 (Fall 1990): 105–119. The information presented here is based on research by Clotfelter and Cook.

[2] *Ibid.*, 112.

[3] See Donald I. Price and E. Shawn Novak, "The Tax Incidence of Three Texas Lottery Games: Regressivity, Race, and Education," *National Tax Journal* 52, 4 (December 1999): 741–751.

[4] See Melissa Schettini Kearney, "State Lotteries and Consumer Behavior," *Journal of Public Economics* 89, 11–12 (December 2005): 2269–2299.

SUMMARY

Government finance transfers use of productive resources from individuals and business firms to the government. Taxes are the major method of government finance. However, governments also can obtain resources through the use of police power to acquire resources directly and through user charges, inflation, and borrowing. Donations also can be used to obtain revenues.

The method of government finance used can have an impact on political and market equilibrium and on the efficiency with which resources are employed in the private sector. Different means of government finance have different effects on the distribution of income.

A basic problem in government finance is the distribution of the costs of financing public goods among citizens. No one best way of accomplishing this exists that will satisfy all citizens. The benefit approach argues that taxes should be distributed according to benefits received from government expenditures. The ability-to-pay approach argues that taxes should be dependent on one's economic capacity. As a matter of practice, application of these two concepts is difficult not only because of data problems but also because of disagreement on what constitutes the most applicable index of the ability to pay.

In addition to affecting the political equilibrium, the method of government finance chosen often has significant and complicated effects on the private choices made by citizens. In particular, taxes and other means of finance can affect production incentives in such a way as to impair the efficiency with which resources are used in the private sector.

LOOKING AHEAD

Chapter 11 develops techniques of analysis for determining the impact of taxes on market prices, income distribution, and the efficiency with which resources are used in the market. These techniques are applied in later chapters to evaluate specific taxes on economic bases of income, consumption, and wealth.

KEY CONCEPTS

Ability-to-pay Principle

Average Tax Rate (ATR)

Benefit Principle

Debt Finance

Donations

Earmarked Taxes

Excise Tax

Flat-rate Tax

General Tax

Government-induced Inflation

Horizontal Equity

Marginal Tax Rate (MTR)

Progressive Tax Rate Structure

Proportional Tax Rate Structure

Regressive Tax Rate Structure

Selective Tax

Tax Avoidance

Tax Base

Tax Bracket

Tax Evasion

Tax Rate Structure

Taxes

User Charges

Vertical Equity

REVIEW QUESTIONS

1. In what important ways do taxes differ from prices as a means of finance and as a means of rationing goods and services?
2. How does government finance affect both political and market equilibrium?
3. How does the ability-to-pay principle of taxation differ from the benefit principle? What problems are encountered in implementing both these tax philosophies?

4. What is the difference between horizontal equity and vertical equity?
5. A tax rate schedule for the federal income tax is usually included with its instruction packet. Identify the MTRs associated with each tax bracket. Plot the MTRs associated with the taxable income in each tax bracket. Compute the ATR associated with the income corresponding to the beginning and end of

each tax bracket. Plot the ATRs and MTRs associated with the ends of each tax bracket.
6. What is a flat-rate tax? Plot the MTRs and ATRs associated with a flat-rate tax of 5 percent on sales.
7. How can inflation be viewed as a form of taxation?
8. List alternatives to taxation as a means of financing government expenditures. Give an example for each alternative.

9. What are user charges? How can user charges be used to both finance government-supplied services and ration their use? How can user charges help achieve efficiency for consumption of price-excludable, government-provided goods?
10. What criteria can be used to price the output of government enterprises?

PROBLEMS

1. Suppose you currently earn taxable income of $100,000 per year. You are subject to an MTR of 50 percent. Currently, your ATR is 35 percent. Calculate your annual tax. Calculate the extra tax that you would pay per year if your annual income increased to $110,000. What is your ATR when your annual income is $110,000?
2. The payroll tax for unemployment insurance in a certain nation taxes all wages up to a maximum of $30,000 per worker at a 5 percent flat rate. What are the marginal and average tax rates on the wages for each of the following three workers?
   a. A restaurant worker with annual wages of $18,000.
   b. An assistant bank manager with wages of $35,000 per year.
   c. A corporate CEO with an annual salary of $500,000.
3. A large city currently provides free water service to residents. The marginal social cost of making a gallon of water available per month is estimated to be 5 cents no matter how much water is used. Currently, city residents consume 500,000 gallons of water per month. The costs of making the water available are financed by a local tax on city residents.

a. Draw a graph to show that the current monthly consumption of water is not efficient.
b. Show the net gains in well-being possible by applying a user charge of 5 cents per gallon to residential users. Assume that monthly consumption declines to 400,000 gallons after the user charge is imposed. Calculate the tax revenues that can be freed for other uses each month (including a reduction in taxes to local residents) after the user charge is imposed.
4. Indicate whether you agree with the following statement, and give your reasons for doing so: "If the beltline surrounding the city of Raleigh were a pure public good, efficiency would require that the price to use the road be zero. However, during rush hour congestion, the road cannot be regarded as a pure public good and a toll should be charged for its use."
5. If an automated vehicle identification system (AVI) were established for residents of the metropolitan area around Raleigh who use the beltline, how would you set tolls to achieve efficient use of the road? The AVI system would allow you to send a bill to each user of the road each month based on miles traveled on the road and the price you charge, which could vary by time of day.

ADDITIONAL READINGS

Brunoir, David. *State Tax Policy*. Washington, D.C.: The Urban Institute Press, 2001. An analysis of issues confronting state governments in formulating tax policy.

Cordes, Joseph, Robert D. Ebel, and Jane G. Gravelle (eds.). *The Encyclopedia of Taxation and Tax Policy*, 2nd edition. Washington, D.C.: The Urban Institute Press, 2005. The complete source for looking up tax terminology and issues. This encyclopedia has short articles on hundreds of topics relating to taxation and tax policy. If there is something you need to know about taxes, this is where to find it.

Groves, Harold. *Tax Philosophers*. Madison: University of Wisconsin Press, 1974. A review of various philosophies of taxation as articulated by economists from Adam Smith to J. M. Keynes and J. K. Galbraith.

Musgrave, Richard A. *The Theory of Public Finance*. New York: McGraw-Hill, 1959. Chapters 4 and 5. A classic technical analysis of alternative philosophies of taxation.

Slemrod, Joel and Jon Bakija. *Taxing Ourselves*, 4th edition. Cumberland, R.I.: The MIT Press, 2008. An analysis of issues and recent developments in tax policy in the United States and how taxes affect the daily lives of citizens.

Thorndike, Joseph J., and Dennis J. Ventry Jr., (eds.). *Tax Justice*. Washington, D.C.: The Urban Institute Press, 2002. A collection of essays on issues relating to distributive justice in taxation. Theoretical issues relating to distributive justice are discussed along with analysis of the U.S. tax system and proposals to reform the system.

U.S. Congress of the United States, Congressional Budget Office. *The Growth of Federal User Charges*. Washington, D.C.: U.S. Government Printing Office, August 1993. Analysis of the types of user charges used by the federal government, the growth of these as a means of finance, and issues relating to the charges.

INTERNET RESOURCES

http://www.oecd.org
Information on tax rates and tax policy in member nations of the Organization for Economic Cooperation and Development is available at this address.

http://www.cbo.gov
This is the home page of the Congressional Budget Office where you can access CBO studies on the budget, the deficit, tax rates, and tax policy.

http://www.taxanalysts.com
This site offers up-to-date information on current issues relating to federal, state, local, and international taxation by tax analysts. Much of the material is available free. More specialized information designed for tax professionals requires a subscription fee. This site has good links to other resources on tax information and policy.

http://www.ncsl.org
At the home page of the National Conference of State Legislatures you can access information on policy and tax issues relating to state and local governments. Links to every state legislature are provided so you can find out what your elected representatives in your own state are up to.

Chapter 11

TAXATION, PRICES, EFFICIENCY, AND THE DISTRIBUTION OF INCOME

LEARNING OBJECTIVES

After reading this chapter, you should be able to:

- Define a lump-sum tax and explain why it is used as the benchmark standard against which other taxes are compared when analyzing the effects of taxation on resource use.

- Explain the concepts of excess burden of a tax and use indifference curve analysis to compare the effects of a lump-sum tax and a price-distorting tax on decisions and well-being of an individual.

- Use supply and demand analysis to show the effects of unit and ad valorem taxes on equilibrium prices and quantities of goods or services traded in markets and to show how

the total excess burden of a tax varies with the unit tax or tax rate and the price elasticities of supply and demand of the taxed item.

- Calculate the efficiency-loss ratio of a tax.

- Describe how taxes are shifted, how the shifting of a tax affects its incidence, and how the incidence of a tax depends on the price elasticities of supply and demand of the taxed item and the extent of competition in the market.

- Use a general equilibrium analysis to evaluate the total excess burden of several taxes and the incidence of taxes.

Taxes affect the decision to buy and sell products and inputs. By shifting market supplies or demands of goods and services, taxes inevitably change their prices and thereby influence the pattern of resource use. However, the effects of taxes on prices are often quite misunderstood. For example, many motorists line up at the gas pumps to fill their tanks before a new gasoline tax increase goes into effect. A good understanding of the economics of taxation would tell these people that it is unlikely that a gasoline tax increase would increase the price of gasoline by the full amount of the tax. Some of the tax would be absorbed by sellers as a reduction in the net price received after paying the tax.

Taxes can cause a loss in efficiency in private use of income and resources. When taxes influence the prices of goods and services traded in competitive markets with no externalities, losses in efficiency are likely to result. This is because, as demonstrated in this chapter, prices that are distorted by taxes no longer simultaneously reflect the marginal social costs and benefits of goods and services. Simple techniques are developed in this chapter to measure the losses in well-being when taxes prevent the attainment of efficiency through market interaction.

No person enjoys paying taxes. Taxes, however, do provide revenues to finance government-supplied goods and services, which, in turn, benefit taxpayers. Although this is true, the impact of taxes on the well-being of those who pay them can be analyzed independently of the benefits received from the uses of tax revenues. This is the approach that is usually pursued in the economic analysis of taxes.

Finally, to evaluate the fairness of taxation, it is necessary to determine the actual impact of taxes on the incomes of citizens. This is no easy task. The people from whom taxes are collected are not necessarily those whose incomes are reduced by taxation, because the impact of taxes on prices can result in a transfer of the payment of a tax from those groups from which the tax is collected. For example, an excise tax on gasoline is commonly collected from distributors of that product. However, if the tax has the effect of decreasing the supply of gasoline, it will increase the market price of that product. By doing so, the tax will make consumers of gasoline worse off by decreasing their real incomes. The analysis in this chapter shows how changes in prices caused by taxes can be considered to determine the distribution of taxes paid among buyers and sellers of goods. The techniques and terminology developed here are used to discuss important current issues in tax policy in Part 4.

LUMP-SUM TAXES: A BENCHMARK STANDARD FOR COMPARISON

A **lump-sum tax** is a fixed sum that a person would pay per year, independent of that person's income, consumption of goods and services, or wealth. The fixed annual payments by people to government authorities do not depend on any controllable variable. Imposition of these taxes would reduce the ability of consumers to purchase market goods and services and to save. But these taxes influence choices only through income effects. As shown in this chapter, no substitution effects result from a lump-sum tax. (See the appendix to Chapter 1 for a definition of income and substitution effects.) Therefore, a lump-sum tax does not provide any opportunity or incentive to substitute one activity for another.

Lump-sum taxes, however, do force those bearing the burden of taxation to reduce consumption, saving, or investment. Yet they accomplish this objective without distorting prices in ways that prevent marginal social costs of goods and services from being set equal to their marginal social benefits. For this reason, the lump-sum tax is used as the benchmark against which the effects of price-distorting taxes are compared. Lump-sum taxes do not prevent the attainment of efficiency in markets.

Lump-sum taxes are likely to affect the distribution of income; therefore, they move the economy to a new efficient allocation of resources consistent with the pattern of demand that results from the new income distribution. A **head tax** is an example of a lump-sum tax that would require all adults to pay an equal amount each year to governing authorities. In no way could taxpayers rearrange their economic affairs to avoid or reduce the tax burden.[1] A head tax would not distort any prices in ways that prevent markets from achieving efficiency. Nevertheless, when a head tax is used, the after-tax distribution of income will be less equal than the before-tax distribution of income. Such a tax would necessarily be regressive with respect to income, because the tax, as a percentage of income, would fall as income rose.

For example, total revenues raised by the federal government in the United States in 2011 were $2.5 trillion. If there are 200 million adults, raising that amount with a head tax would have required each of them, without exception, to pay a tax of $13,000 per year. The average tax rates (ATRs) would amount to 50 percent for a person whose annual income was $26,000 but only 10 percent for a person whose annual income was $130,000. The ATR would decline with a person's annual income. The marginal tax rate (MTR) associated with a lump-sum tax is *always* zero. Regardless of any change in a person's income, consumption, or wealth, a lump-sum tax causes no change in the tax due.

Lump-Sum versus Price-Distorting Taxes: Indifference Curve Analysis

A **price-distorting tax** is one that causes the net price received by sellers of a good or service to diverge from the gross price paid by buyers. Indifference curve analysis can be used to compare the effects of a lump-sum tax and a price-distorting tax, each collecting the same amount from a person. Suppose a price-distorting tax is imposed on some good, for example, gasoline, the proceeds of which are used to finance government-supplied services. In Figure 11.1, the tax is assumed to increase the current market price of gasoline, which swivels the consumer's budget constraint line from AB to AB'. The amount of tax paid by the person whose indifference curves are drawn in Figure 11.1 is influenced by the quantity of gasoline purchased per year. The gross price paid by the buyer includes the tax. The net price received by sellers is the gross price minus the tax. The tax-induced price increase affects the consumer's choice of consuming gasoline or spending available income on other goods. The consumer enjoys an annual income represented by the distance $0A$. This gives the dollar amount of expenditures on goods other than gasoline that the consumer could buy if he or she purchases no gasoline in one year.

The consumer is initially in equilibrium at point E, consuming Q_1 gallons of gasoline per year and spending Y_1 on all other goods per year. The amount spent

---

[1]This assumes that migration to another country to avoid the tax is impossible or that a person migrating would have to pay the discounted present value of future tax liabilities under the head tax before being permitted to migrate.

FIGURE 11.1   A Price-Distorting Tax versus a Lump-Sum Tax

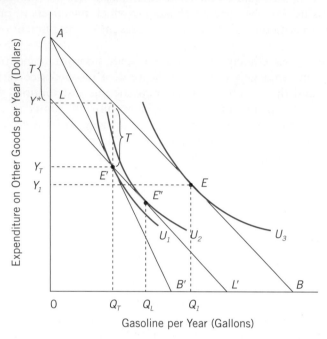

A lump-sum tax that collects *T* in taxes from a person allows that person to attain higher level of well-being than a price-distorting tax that collects the same amount. The loss in well-being due to the substitution effect of the price-distorting tax is its excess burden.

© Cengage Learning

on gasoline per year prior to the tax is AY_1. This is the difference between his or her total annual income and his or her annual expenditure on other goods. The tax-induced price increase causes movement to a new equilibrium at E', where annual consumption of gasoline is reduced to Q_T gallons. The person now spends AY_T on gasoline each year at the price including the tax, leaving Y_T to spend on other goods each year. If the tax were not present, he or she would have to give up only AY^* of expenditure on other goods to obtain the same amount of gasoline per year. Of the total expenditure on gasoline, the distance $Y_T Y^* = T$ represents the annual gasoline tax payments. This equals the difference between the amount of income he or she must give up to buy Q_T gallons of gasoline per year when the price includes the tax and the amount that he or she would give up for Q_T gallons in the absence of the tax. T is also the difference between the amount sellers receive for the Q_T gallons, AY^*, and the amount the consumer actually spends, AY_T. The effect of the tax is to reduce the consumer's utility from U_3 to U_1, reduce consumption of gasoline from Q_1 to Q_T gallons per year, and reduce annual after-tax income from $0A$ to $(0A - T)$.

If T per year were collected from this person as a lump-sum tax, neither the price of gasoline nor the price of any other good would be distorted. No difference would result between the gross price paid by the buyer and the net price received by the seller. The lump-sum tax merely would reduce the income of the taxpayer by shifting the budget constraint line down, parallel to itself, from AB to LL'.

All points along LL' collect T in tax by reducing the consumer's income by that amount, independent of the amount of gasoline purchased per year.

Figure 11.1 shows that the person is better off under the lump-sum tax than under the price-distorting tax if both collect T per year. With the lump-sum tax, the taxpayer attains an equilibrium at point E'', where he or she achieves utility level U_2 and consumes Q_L gallons of gasoline per year. Provided that gasoline is a normal good, the decrease in income caused by the lump-sum tax results in a decline in its consumption. However, because $Q_L > Q_T$, he or she consumes more gasoline per year than when he or she paid the price-distorting tax. Although the lump-sum tax reduces the taxpayer's income, it causes no substitution effects, because it does not affect the relative price of gasoline or any other good or service. The taxpayer consumes more gasoline than under the price-distorting tax, because the price paid is lower under the lump-sum tax. Because the consumer has the same disposable income under the two taxes but consumes more gasoline per year under the lump-sum tax, it follows that he or she must be better off when paying T in annual taxes under the lump-sum tax. This is shown in Figure 11.1, in that the level of well-being at E'' under the lump-sum tax is $U_2 > U_1$. Thus, provided both taxes collect the same amount from the taxpayer, the lump-sum tax will be preferred by the taxpayer.

GLOBAL PERSPECTIVE

The Lump-Sum Tax Takes Its Lumps in the United Kingdom

It caused riots in Trafalgar Square and was instrumental in the fall of the reign of Margaret Thatcher as prime minister. What was it? Simply a lump-sum tax—the paragon of efficiency in raising revenue for government!

In the 1980s, Thatcher's government replaced a local property tax with a form of lump-sum tax called "the community charge." The tax was supposed to be a means of financing local government services (such as schools and streets) and facilities that fell equally on all taxpayers, irrespective of their personal income or property holdings. The level of the tax was set by each local council and was a fixed amount per adult taxpayer. The tax varied considerably among jurisdictions, but because it was a fixed lump sum per taxpayer, it amounted to a higher percentage of the earnings of low-income than high-income taxpayers in each jurisdiction.

The tax was enormously unpopular in the United Kingdom. It was quickly dubbed a poll tax even though it was not a requirement for voting. Some 15 million Britons, including members of Parliament, actually refused to pay the tax, and local governments estimated that they were only able to collect slightly more than 50 percent of the tax due. The very efficient lump-sum tax was viewed as so unfair by such a large percentage of taxpayers that they were willing to break the law and risk imprisonment by refusing to pay it.

By 1991, Prime Minister John Major's government threw in their hats and developed a plan to replace the hated poll tax with a new package of local taxes including increased sales taxes and increased central government responsibility for the financing of education.

The British version of the lump-sum tax and their problems with it illustrate the inevitable trade-off between equity and efficiency in tax policy. Although the lump-sum tax does not distort prices and does not impair efficient operation of markets, it results in a regressive distribution of tax burden with respect to income. Very regressive taxes, such as the lump-sum community charge, have proved to be politically unpopular. One politician in Great Britain estimated that three-quarters of the British public opposed the tax. The political opposition to the tax ultimately led to its rescission.

The loss in well-being of the taxpayer when she pays T in taxes under the price-distorting tax instead of under the lump-sum tax is the **individual excess burden of a tax**. The excess burden measures the loss in well-being to a taxpayer caused by the substitution effect of a price-distorting tax. The excess burden of the price-distorting tax is the reduction in well-being of the taxpayer from U_2 to U_1 when the price-distorting tax is used instead of the lump-sum tax.

CHECKPOINT

1. What is a lump-sum tax?
2. What are the desirable and undesirable aspects of using a lump-sum tax to finance government expenditures?
3. What is the excess burden of a price-distorting tax for an individual taxpayer?

THE IMPACT OF TAXES ON MARKET PRICES AND EFFICIENCY

A Unit Excise Tax: Impact on Market Equilibrium

Suppose a good such as gasoline is traded in a competitive market and that no externalities are associated with market exchange of gasoline. Under these conditions, market exchange of gasoline results in the efficient output of this good. This is illustrated in Figure 11.2, with a market price of gasoline at $1 per gallon. The demand curve, D, reflects the marginal social benefit of the good, while the supply curve, S, reflects its marginal social cost. The market equilibrium at point B corresponds to the efficient amount of gasoline per year. At the output Q^*, the marginal social benefit of gasoline is equal to its marginal social cost. The $1 price of gasoline equals both the marginal social cost and marginal social benefit of gasoline ($P = MSB = MSC$).

A **unit tax** is a levy of a fixed amount per unit of a good exchanged in a market. Suppose that a unit excise tax of 25 cents per gallon of gasoline is levied on the sellers of gasoline. This fixed tax due on each gallon sold is independent of the price of gasoline. If the price of gasoline were to rise, the tax would not collect any more revenue per gallon. Taxes that are a percentage of the price of a good or service are analyzed later in this chapter.

When the tax is imposed, the marginal cost of selling gasoline increases by 25 cents per gallon because of the tax. In addition to covering all other variable costs of production, sellers must cover the tax to avoid losses when selling gasoline. This shifts the supply curve (which is the marginal cost curve under perfect competition) upward, from $S = MSC$ to $S_T = MSC + 25$ cents at each level of annual output. The effect of the tax is equivalent to an increase in the marginal cost to sellers that decreases the market supply of gasoline.

The decrease in supply results in a new posttax equilibrium at C, implying that the quantity sold decreases to Q_1 and that the equilibrium price rises to $P_G = \$1.15$. The price P_G is the new market price paid by consumers of gasoline. This is the gross price received by sellers. The sellers, however, must pay 25 cents of the gross price received as a tax. Their net price, P_N, is only 90 cents per gallon

FIGURE 11.2 Impact of a Unit Tax on Market Equilibrium

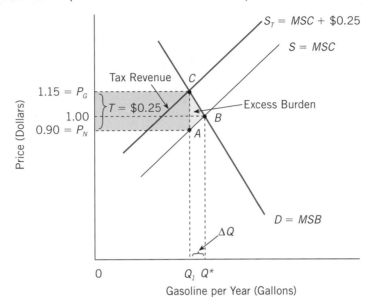

A unit tax of 25 cents on gasoline collected from sellers decreases the market supply of the good and increases the price. The market price, P_G, paid by buyers increases from $1.00 to $1.15. After payment of the tax, the net price received by sellers falls to 90 cents. If ΔQ is the reduction in output due to the substitution effect of the tax, then the area ABC measures the excess burden of the tax.

after payment of the tax. In general, if T is the unit tax, the relationship between the gross price and the net price, P_N, received by sellers is

$$P_N = P_G - T. \tag{11.1}$$

The amount of revenue collected from the tax by the government is the amount of gasoline sold after the tax multiplied by the tax per unit, TQ_1. This is represented by the rectangle $P_N P_G CA$ in Figure 11.2. The total revenue of producers is simply $P_N Q_1$. For example, if Q_1 is 10 million gallons of gasoline per year, the tax would collect $2.5 million annually. Total revenue taken in by sellers after paying the tax would be $9 million per year.

Excess Burden of a Unit Tax

When the excise tax of $0.25 is imposed, buyers and sellers then base their decisions on their differing views of the price of gasoline. Buyers decide how much to buy by comparing P_G, the gross price, with their marginal benefit. Sellers, however, decide how much to sell by comparing their net price, P_N, with their marginal cost. In the absence of any externality, the marginal cost and benefit reflect marginal social cost and benefit. The tax prevents market interaction among buyers and sellers from automatically equating marginal social cost and marginal social benefit, as is required to attain efficiency. Because $P_G > P_N$ after the tax, it follows that $MSB > MSC$ at Q_1, as shown in Figure 11.2. As a result of the tax, less than the efficient annual output, Q^*, of gasoline will be sold in the market.

The **total excess burden of a tax** is an additional cost to society over and above the amount of dollars that citizens pay in a tax. The *excess* burden measures the loss in net benefits from private use of resources that results when a price-distorting tax prevents markets for taxed goods and services from attaining efficient output levels.

The total excess burden of a unit tax is the loss in well-being to buyers and sellers in a market over that which they would suffer if a lump-sum tax were used to collect the revenues. A lump-sum tax would not prevent the attainment of efficiency in markets because it causes no substitution effects. If this benchmark type of tax were used, no difference would result between the price paid by buyers and that received by sellers.

Figure 11.2 shows how the excess burden of the unit tax can be measured. Assume that the income effect of the tax-induced price increase on the consumption of gasoline is negligible. This implies that the observed reduction in the quantity of gasoline consumed entirely reflects the substitution effect of the tax-induced price increase. The efficient output is Q^*. This means that increasing output from Q_1 to Q^* would allow increments in well-being that exceed the incremental social costs. The price-distorting excise tax prevents the achievement of net gains, represented by the difference between the marginal social benefits and the marginal social costs of $\Delta Q = Q^* - Q_1$ gallons of gasoline. The total excess burden of the price-distorting tax can be represented by the area of the triangle ABC in Figure 11.2. This area represents the net loss in well-being to buyers and sellers of gasoline due to the substitution effect of the tax.[2] It is a measure of the loss in efficiency in the gasoline market attributable to the price-distorting gasoline tax.

When the excess burden is positive, the total burden of a tax on buyers and sellers in a market exceeds the tax revenues collected. Even if the total tax revenues collected were returned to buyers and sellers of gasoline as a lump-sum payment of TQ_1 (represented by the area $P_N P_G CA$ in Figure 11.2), the excess burden would not be recovered. For this reason, the total excess burden of a tax sometimes is called a *deadweight loss*. It is a loss in efficiency that cannot be regained even if tax revenues collected provide benefits equal in dollar amount to the amount paid by citizens in taxes.

Call W the area of triangle ABC. The area W is

$$W = \frac{1}{2}T\Delta Q,$$ (11.2)

where T, the tax per unit, is the base of triangle ABC, and ΔQ, measuring the decrease in the consumption of gasoline because of the substitution effect of the tax-induced price increase, is its height. For example, if ΔQ is 2 million gallons per year, the excess burden of the tax would be $250,000 per year.

Excess Burden, Unit Taxes, and Price Elasticities

The excess burden actually varies more than proportionately with the unit tax, T, because ΔQ depends on the increase in price, ΔP, caused by the tax. Because ΔP depends on the amount of the tax per unit, ΔQ also depends on T. The higher the

[2]When the income effects of tax-induced price changes cannot be ignored, ΔQ must be estimated along a compensated demand curve. The relationship between price and quantity demanded for which the income effect of price changes has been removed is the compensated demand curve. The appendix at the end of this chapter shows how compensated demand curves are derived.

unit tax, other things being equal, the greater is the annual reduction in gasoline (or any taxed good) sold. The reduction in output that results from the substitution effect of a price-distorting tax can be predicted with estimates of the price elasticities of demand and supply of the taxed goods.

A bit of algebraic manipulation (see the appendix at the end of this chapter) can show how the excess burden of a tax depends on the unit tax, initial prices and quantities traded, and price elasticities of supply and demand. As derived in the appendix, the resulting formula for the excess burden of a unit tax is

$$W = \frac{1}{2}T^2 \frac{Q^*}{P^*} \cdot \frac{E_S E_D}{E_S - E_D},\tag{11.3}$$

where E_S is the price elasticity of supply, E_D is the price elasticity of demand, Q^* is the pretax quantity, and P^* is the pretax market price of the taxed good. Because the price elasticity of demand is a negative number, the change in well-being that results from the excess burden will be equal to or less than zero, indicating a loss.[3]

According to Equation 11.3, the excess burden of a tax varies quadratically with the unit tax. If the unit tax on a good, such as gasoline, were to double from 25 to 50 cents, the loss in well-being from the excess burden of a tax could be expected to increase fourfold! Other things being equal, the losses due to the excess burden of a tax increase at a faster rate than the rate of increase of a tax. The formula for the excess burden also indicates that, other things being equal, the more elastic the demand for the good, the greater the loss in well-being due to the excess burden of a tax. Similarly, other things being equal, the greater the price elasticity of supply, the greater is the loss due to the excess burden of a tax. Assuming that income effects are negligible, any commodity for which either $E_S = 0$ or $E_D = 0$ has a zero efficiency loss. The most efficient taxes are those levied on commodities or inputs that are in inelastic supply, demand, or both. In general, to minimize the excess burden of a tax, goods and services for which minimal substitution effects are likely should be taxed.

The algebraic result is in accord with commonsense reasoning. The less the opportunity or willingness to substitute other goods and services for those that are taxed, the less is the distortion introduced into the economy with respect to resource allocation. On efficiency grounds, the best taxes are those levied on goods that have few substitutes in either production or consumption.

The graphs in Figure 11.3 show that the excess burden of a tax would be zero if either the demand or supply of a tax product were perfectly inelastic. In the case of a perfectly inelastic demand shown in Figure 11.3A, the tax causes the price to rise, but because the quantity demanded is not reduced, the change in output is zero and the excess burden is also zero. The more inelastic the demand for a taxed good or service, the smaller the area of the triangle that represents the excess burden of the tax.

In Figure 11.3B, the tax is represented by a decline in the net price received by sellers and is subtracted from the price paid by buyers, which is represented by the market demand curve. When the market supply is perfectly inelastic, sellers suffer a net reduction in the price received for the item they sell, but they do not alter the quantity supplied in response. As a result, their net revenue from selling the product falls, but no change occurs in the quantity of the product made available to buyers.

---

[3]The elasticities must be based on changes in output due only to the substitution effects of tax-induced price increases in cases for which income effects of the price increases are not negligible.

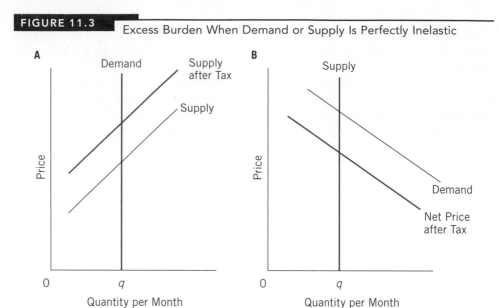

FIGURE 11.3   Excess Burden When Demand or Supply Is Perfectly Inelastic

The more inelastic the demand or the supply of a taxed item, the lower the excess burden. As either the price elasticity of demand or the price elasticity of supply approaches zero, the excess burden of the tax approaches zero because the reduction in quantity sold as a result of the tax approaches zero.

Also, the excess burden is zero because the change in the amount of the product sold as a result of the tax is zero. In general, the more inelastic the supply of an item, other things being equal, the smaller the reduction in the quantity sold after the tax and the smaller the excess burden.

The Efficiency-Loss Ratio of a Tax

To compare the relative loss in efficiency of various taxes, economists often calculate the excess burden *per dollar of tax revenue*. The ratio of the excess burden of a tax to the tax revenue collected each year by that tax is called the **efficiency-loss ratio** of the tax (W/R):

$$\frac{W}{R} = \frac{\text{Excess Burden}}{\text{Tax Revenue}}. \tag{11.4}$$

An efficiency-loss ratio of 0.2 means that the excess burden of a tax is 20 cents for each dollar of revenue raised per year. The efficiency-loss ratio of a tax sometimes is called the *coefficient of inefficiency* of the tax.

Estimates of the efficiency-loss ratios of different kinds of taxes are extremely useful in achieving the goal of minimization of the total excess burden of taxation. By reducing use of taxes with high excess burdens per dollar of revenue while increasing use of taxes with lower excess burdens per dollar, the total excess burden of the tax system can be reduced without sacrificing revenues. For example, suppose that the efficiency-loss ratio for taxes on interest income is estimated to be 0.35, while the efficiency-loss ratio for taxes on gasoline is only 0.1. Each extra dollar of revenue gained from increasing gasoline taxes results in an excess burden of

10 cents. On the other hand, each dollar increment in revenue obtained from taxes on interest income is associated with an increase of 35 cents in excess burden. It follows that, on the margin, each dollar reduction in taxes on interest made up by a dollar increase in taxes on gasoline results in a *net reduction* of total excess burden equal to 25 cents. Estimated efficiency-loss ratios for taxes thus can be used to recommend policy changes that will result in net gains in well-being.

One study of the U.S. tax system estimated that the excess burden per dollar of tax revenue ranged from 13 to 24 cents per dollar of revenue in the mid-1970s and was running at about 18.5 cents in the mid-1980s.[4] Based on the tax laws and the tax rates effective in 1973, Ballard, Shoven, and Whalley concluded that the present value of the gain in well-being that would have been possible by replacing the tax system of 1973 with a system of lump-sum taxes would have been between $1.86 trillion and $3.36 trillion! The range of their estimates varies with assumptions made about price elasticities in their various simulations of the impact of taxes on the economy.

They found that the taxes on interest and investment income caused the greatest distortion in 1973. The average rate of taxation of capital income was about 45 percent in that year. Since that time, taxes on capital income have been reduced substantially compared with the levels that prevailed in 1973. Depending on the assumption made about the interest elasticity of supply of savings, the efficiency-loss ratio for taxes on industrial capital income in 1973 ranged from 15 to 35 cents per dollar of revenues collected.

The researchers concluded that savings would be 80 percent higher if a lump-sum tax collected the same revenue as that collected by the U.S. tax system in 1973. This estimate is based on tax rates of 1973 and on an interest elasticity of saving supply of 0.4. In their simulations, over 100 years the higher savings would increase the ratio of capital to labor in production by 31 percent. This would contribute to higher labor productivity and higher wages for workers.

A study by the Joint Economic Committee staff of the U.S. Congress in 1999 concluded that the marginal efficiency loss of federal taxation in the United States as of the late 1990s was in the range of 25–40 cents for each additional dollar of federal revenue raised.[5] The researchers also concluded that the federal tax system was biased against saving and investment. As was the case in the 1970s, the U.S. tax system still taxes saving and investment more heavily than consumption. The efficiency loss of taxes on capital is higher than that on consumption because of the higher rates of taxation.

Research on the excess burden of taxation by Martin Feldstein takes a more inclusive approach to the concept and finds much higher excess burden at tax rates prevailing in the United States as of the mid-1990s. Feldstein argues that the excess burden stems for reallocation of resources away from taxed activities toward untaxed activities. For example, tax rates can influence occupation choices by discouraging people from taking high-wage jobs because of the high tax rates on that income. High tax rates on money income also encourage workers to seek

---

[4]Charles L. Ballard, John B. Shoven, and John Whalley, "The Total Welfare Cost of the United States Tax System: A General Equilibrium Approach," *National Tax Journal* 38 (June 1985): 125–140. Also see Don Fullerton and Diane Lim Rogers, *Who Bears the Lifetime Tax Burden?* (Washington, D.C.: The Brookings Institution, 1993): 163–170.

[5]U.S. Congress, Joint Economic Committee Study, *Tax Reduction and the Economy* (July 1999). Also see Richard Vedder and Lowell Gallaway, *The Size and Function of Government and Economic Growth*, Joint Economic Committee (April 1998).

compensation, such as good working conditions, and more fringe benefits, such as health insurance. When tax rates are high, some people might choose to retire earlier than they would under lower tax rates.

For tax-deductible activity, taxpayers are encouraged to engage in those activities beyond the point at which their marginal benefit falls to their marginal cost. For example, if a person is subject to a 40 percent marginal tax rate (MTR) on income, and if interest on borrowing money to buy a home is tax deductible (as it is in the United States), then this person is encouraged to borrow until the marginal benefit of doing so falls to 60 cents per dollar borrowed. This $1 of interest paid will cost only 60 cents after taxes are reduced by the remaining 40 cents. Although the marginal cost of the borrowing remains $1, the individual rationally continues to borrow until the marginal benefit falls to 60 cents—the net price after tax. The tax system induces you to give up a dollar for something that is only worth 60 cents—an excess burden of 40 cents on the dollar.

Feldstein argues that the excess burden of taxation depends on the elasticity of demand for tax-favored goods (those activities that reduce your tax bill if you engage in them) with respect to the net of tax price. With estimates of these relevant elasticities, Feldstein concludes that the excess burden per additional dollar of tax revenue raised for the U.S. tax system in 1994 was $1.65. With a marginal excess burden of $1.65, the total cost of raising a dollar of tax revenue would be $2.65: $1.00 for the tax and an additional $1.65 in lost net benefits as the higher tax rates induce greater pursuit of activities for which marginal benefit falls short of marginal cost.[6]

Incidence of a Unit Tax

As illustrated in Figure 11.2, a unit tax can cause the market price of the taxed good to change. Tax-induced price change reduces the real incomes of groups other than those from whom the tax is collected. The **shifting of a tax** is the transfer of the burden of paying a tax from those who are legally liable for it to others. When a tax is shifted, those liable for its payment succeed in recouping some of the reduction in their income caused by tax payments through changes in the prices of items that they either buy or sell. These changes in prices are caused by tax-induced shifts in either supply or demand.

Forward shifting of a tax is a transfer of its burden from sellers who are liable for its payment to buyers as a result of an increase in the price of the taxed good. For example, in Figure 11.2, the price of gasoline increases as a result of a tax levied on sellers, thereby shifting part of the burden to buyers. **Backward shifting** of a tax is a transfer of its burden from buyers who are liable for its payment to sellers through a decrease in the market price of the taxed good. For example, if employers are liable for payroll taxes on wages paid to workers, they will succeed in shifting part of the burden of the tax to sellers of labor services (workers) if wages decline as a result of the tax. The **incidence of a tax** is the distribution of the burden of paying it.

In Figure 11.2, the market price of gasoline increased from $1.00 per gallon to $P_G = \$1.15$ per gallon at the posttax market equilibrium. As a result, sellers succeeded in shifting 15 cents of the tax of 25 cents per gallon to consumers. The remaining 10 cents of the tax per gallon was borne by sellers, as the net price P_N that they received declined from $1 to 90 cents per gallon. The incidence of the

---

[6]See Martin Feldstein, "How Big Should Government Be?" *National Tax Journal* 50, 2 (June 1997).

tax per gallon was shared by buyers and sellers of gasoline. Although the entire tax of 25 cents per gallon is collected from sellers, they recoup 15 cents of the tax per gallon through the increase in the market price of gasoline. The total tax revenues collected can be represented by the rectangle $P_N P_G CA$. The upper portion of the rectangle represents the part of the total tax revenues that, in effect, is paid by buyers of gasoline. This is the 15-cents-per-gallon portion of the unit tax that is shifted to buyers multiplied by the annual consumption of gasoline. If after the tax is imposed and 10 million gallons of gasoline are sold per year, consumers pay $1.5 million of the $2.5 million in tax revenue. The remaining $1 million per year is paid by sellers.

Ad Valorem Taxes

Ad valorem taxes are levied as a percentage of the price of a good or service. For example, retail sales taxes are ad valorem taxes levied as a certain percentage of the price received by sellers of a good. Similarly, the payroll tax is an ad valorem tax because it is levied as a percentage of wages paid by employers. The higher the price of the taxed good or service, the greater is the amount of the tax per unit under ad valorem taxation.

The preceding analysis for a unit tax is easily applicable to ad valorem taxes. Suppose consumers must pay a certain percentage of the market price of gasoline as a tax. In this case, the amount of tax collected *per unit of output*, T, is the tax rate, t, multiplied by the gross price paid by consumers of the product:[7]

$$T = tP_G = \text{Tax Revenue per Unit of Output,} \tag{11.5}$$

where P_G is the gross price paid by consumers. For example, if a flat-rate tax of 10 percent were levied on gasoline, the amount collected would be 10 cents *per gallon* if the market price of gasoline paid by buyers were $1 per gallon. However, if the market price paid by buyers were $2 per gallon, the same tax of 10 percent would collect 20 cents per gallon. An ad valorem tax automatically collects more revenues per unit of the taxed item when the market price of that item increases.

Substituting Equation 11.5 for the tax per unit in Equation 11.3 for the excess burden of a unit tax gives

$$W = \frac{1}{2} t^2 P_G^2 \frac{Q^*}{P^*} \cdot \frac{E_S E_D}{E_S - E_D}. \tag{11.6}$$

For taxes that result in very small changes in price so that the difference between the initial market price, P^*, and the posttax market price, P_G, is negligible, the excess burden of the tax can be approximated by the following equation, which is derived from Equation 11.6, by setting $P_G = P^*$:

$$W = \frac{1}{2} t^2 (P^* Q^*) \frac{E_S E_D}{E_S - E_D}. \tag{11.7}$$

$P^* Q^*$ is the total expenditure on the taxed commodity prior to the tax. Economists often use a formula like this one to estimate the excess burden that results from ad valorem taxes levied on the sale of goods or services.

---

[7]In many cases, the tax is levied on the net price, P_N, received by sellers. For example, under a retail sales tax, the actual gross price paid by consumers includes the tax that is levied as a percentage of the net price received by retailers. In such cases, $T = tP_N$.

As with the unit tax, the loss due to the excess burden of an ad valorem tax varies with the square of the tax rate. To predict the loss due to the excess burden of an ad valorem tax, Equation 11.7 requires estimates of the relevant price elasticities of supply and demand of the taxed item and data on current expenditures on the item to be taxed.

Ad Valorem Taxes on Labor

Figure 11.4 shows the impact of an ad valorem tax on market equilibrium. Suppose all wages earned are subject to a flat-rate tax of 20 percent deducted from the wages of workers. The tax is collected from workers rather than employers. The tax can be thought of as a reduction in the gross wage received by workers for each hour of work. This is similar to the payroll tax used to finance Social Security benefits.

In Figure 11.4, the actual demand curve for labor indicates the gross wage that employers would pay for each yearly amount of labor hours. The pretax equilibrium is at point E, where workers of a given skill earn $5 per hour and Q^* labor hours are employed per year. A tax of 20 percent would reduce the net wage received for any amount of work per week to 80 percent of the gross wage that employers actually pay. In Figure 11.4, the curve labeled "Net Wage" shows the actual wages received by workers after the tax has been deducted from the gross wage paid by employers. The tax per labor hour is represented by the difference

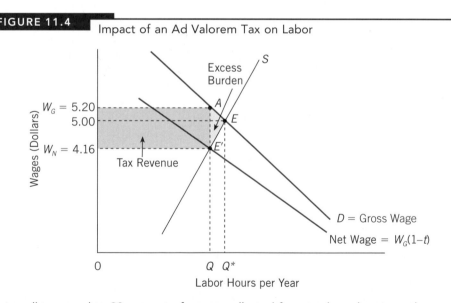

FIGURE 11.4   Impact of an Ad Valorem Tax on Labor

A payroll tax equal to 20 percent of wages collected from workers decreases the wages received by workers from W_G to $W_N = W_G (1 - t)$ for each hour worked per year. Workers respond to the reduction in their take-home wage by reducing the quantity of labor hours supplied per year. Part of the tax burden is shifted to employers as the market wage increases from $5.00 per hour to $5.20 per hour.

between the gross wage curve and the net wage curve. In general, the following relationship exists between the gross wage, W_G, at any level of employment and the net wage, W_N:

$$W_N = W_G(1 - t), \tag{11.8}$$

where t is the tax rate. As the gross wage increases, the actual tax per labor hour paid, tW_G, increases. This is why the difference between the gross wage curve and the net wage curve increases as gross wage increases. For example, if the market wage were only \$2 per hour, the tax collected per labor hour would be only 20 cents under a tax rate of 10 percent. At a wage of \$10 per hour, the same tax rate would collect \$1 per labor hour at the same rate of 10 percent.

Workers base their work-leisure choices on the net wage; employers decide how much labor to hire on the basis of the gross wage. The posttax market equilibrium corresponds to point E', at which the quantity of labor that workers are willing to supply based on their net wage equals the quantity of labor that employers are willing to hire based on the gross wage. At the posttax equilibrium, the market wage, W_G, increases to \$5.20 per hour but the net wage received by workers, W_N, is only 80 percent of that amount, or \$4.16 per hour. The quantity of labor hired declines from Q^* to Q_1 hours per year. Because workers decrease the quantity of labor hours supplied per year as a result of the tax, they succeed in shifting part of its burden of payment forward to employers as the market wage rises to \$5.20 per hour.

The loss due to the excess burden of the tax could be estimated as the area of the triangle AEE' in Figure 11.4. Actual estimate of the tax would require an estimate of the reduction in hours worked due to the substitution effect of the tax-induced wage reduction.

CHECKPOINT

1. What influences the magnitude of the total excess burden of a tax?
2. What is forward shifting of a tax? What is backward shifting of a tax?
3. How does an ad valorem tax differ from a unit tax?

FURTHER ANALYSIS OF TAX INCIDENCE

Tax Incidence Is Independent of Legal Liability for Taxes

The final incidence of a tax is independent of whether the tax is collected from buyers or sellers of goods and services. To see this, suppose the unit tax on gasoline discussed earlier in this chapter were collected from buyers instead of sellers. This would be the case if the tax were added on to the market price of gasoline. Buyers would pay the market price plus the tax for each gallon purchased. The tax can be thought of as being deposited in a box near each gas pump to be picked up each day or week by the tax authorities. The tax is the legal liability of buyers, not sellers.

When the tax is collected from buyers in this way, the marginal cost to sellers does not increase. Instead, the tax is subtracted from the marginal benefit that consumers get from each gallon of gasoline. Therefore, the maximum price that any buyer would pay for a gallon of gasoline, no matter how much was available, would fall by exactly 25 cents. Assume that the marginal benefit received by consumers also equals the marginal social benefit of the good.

Figure 11.5 shows that the demand curve D would shift downward to $MSB - T$. Subtracting T from the marginal social benefit of each quantity gives the net marginal benefit that consumers would get from gasoline after paying the tax. They now base their decision to buy gasoline on their net marginal benefit.

The pretax market equilibrium corresponds to point B. The decrease in demand caused by the tax results in a new market equilibrium corresponding to point A. At that point, the market price of gasoline falls to 90 cents per gallon. This is now the gross price received by sellers, because they are not liable for the tax. This is exactly the amount that sellers received per gallon, after taxes, when they were liable for the tax (see Figure 11.2)! However, the total amount paid by buyers for each gallon is $1.15, because in addition to paying the market price of 90 cents per gallon, they have to pay the tax of 25 cents on each gallon that they purchase. This corresponds to point C on the original demand curve, D. The total amount that buyers pay per gallon, including the tax, is exactly the same as the market price of gasoline that would prevail if the tax were collected from sellers!

FIGURE 11.5   Incidence of a Tax Collected from Buyers

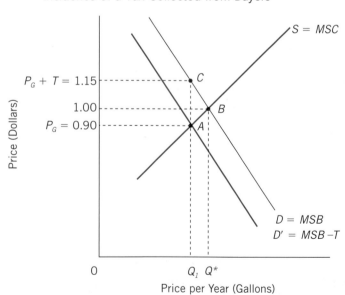

The incidence of a tax is independent of whether it is collected from buyers or sellers. Here, a 25 cent unit tax on gasoline is collected from buyers. This causes a decrease in the demand for the good. The market price received by sellers falls to 90 cents per gallon. The total price paid by buyers, including the tax, goes up to $1.15. This results in exactly the same distribution of tax burden that prevailed when the tax was collected from sellers.

When the tax is collected from buyers, the decrease in demand for gasoline caused by the tax results in backward shifting from buyers to sellers as the market price of gasoline declines. However, the distribution of the burden of the tax between buyers and sellers is exactly the same as when sellers were liable for the tax.

Tax Incidence and Price Elasticities of Demand and Supply

Other things being equal, the more inelastic the demand for a taxed good or service, the greater is the portion of the tax borne by buyers. This is shown in Figure 11.6. The demand curve labeled D' is more inelastic at any price than the demand curve labeled D at each price. However, D' intersects the pretax supply curve, S, at point B. Therefore, the pretax price would be the same no matter which demand curve prevailed. Suppose the taxed good is once again gasoline. When the demand curve D prevails, a 25 cents per gallon tax increases market price to $1.15 and results in a 90 cent net price to sellers. The same tax of 25 cents per gallon that is collected from sellers would result in a sharper increase in market price when the more inelastic demand curve D' prevails. The posttax market equilibrium would correspond to point E when the market demand curve is D'. The market price paid by buyers would be $1.20 per gallon under those circumstances. The net price that sellers would receive would be 95 cents per gallon. The more inelastic demand allows the sellers to shift 5 cents more of the tax per gallon to buyers than they could when demand was D, because buyers are less responsive to price

FIGURE 11.6   The More Inelastic the Demand, the Greater the Portion of a Tax Borne by Buyers

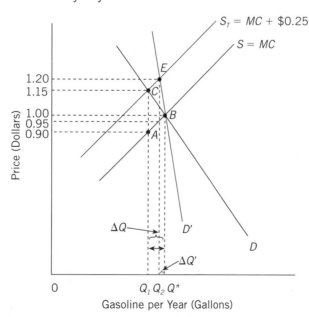

The demand curve D' is more inelastic than the demand curve D at each possible price. As a result, the same unit of tax of 25 cents would result in a greater increase in market price, when demand is D'. More of the tax is shifted to buyers when the more inelastic demand prevails.

increases when demand is more inelastic. In Figure 11.6, $\Delta Q'$, the reduction in quantity demanded due to the tax when the demand curve is D', is less than ΔQ, the corresponding reduction when the demand curve is D.

Also, other things being equal, the more elastic the supply of a taxed good or service, the greater is the portion of a tax borne by buyers. Suppose a tax is levied on the sale of a good that is so elastic in supply in the long run that the supply curve is indistinguishable from a horizontal line. For example, suppose housing services can be produced under conditions of constant costs in the long run. Under those circumstances, the supply of housing services will be infinitely elastic.

Figure 11.7 shows the demand and supply for housing services. This indicates that the marginal cost of producing housing in the long run is constant and equal to the long-run average cost. In Figure 11.7, the pretax market equilibrium corresponds to point E, where rent is 50 cents per square foot; so a 600-square-foot apartment would rent for $300 per month in the absence of any taxes on housing.

Now suppose a tax of 10 cents per square foot is levied on sellers of housing services. This would shift the supply curve up, from MC to $MC + T$, where T is the 10 cent tax. The new market equilibrium will be at point E', at which the equilibrium quantity falls from Q^* to Q_1 square feet rented per month. The gross price paid by buyers of housing services rises from 50 to 60 cents per square foot. The sellers of housing services succeed in shifting the entire tax of 10 cents per square foot to buyers. Suppose the market price did not increase by the full amount of the tax. The net price received by sellers then would be less than 50 cents per square foot per month; that is, the net price would fall below the average costs of production. Firms would leave the industry, and the quantity supplied would decrease until the market price rose enough to eliminate the losses. If price were to rise more than 10 cents per square foot per month, firms would earn economic profits,

FIGURE 11.7   Impact of a Tax on a Good with a Perfectly Elastic Supply

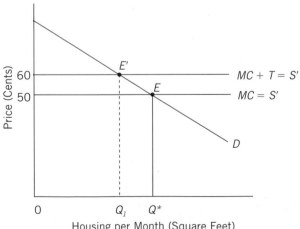

A tax on a good in perfectly elastic supply collected from sellers is fully shifted to buyers.

and new firms would enter the industry. This would increase the quantity supplied until market price once again was 60 cents per square foot. This would return the net price received by sellers to 50 cents per square foot after paying the tax. If this were the case in the housing market, the tax of 10 cents per square foot would raise the monthly rental rate on a 600-square-foot apartment from \$300 to \$360.[8]

Generally, the supply of most goods and services is much more elastic in the long run than in the short run. In other words, buyers are likely to pay more of a tax in the long run regardless of whether that tax is levied on buyers or sellers in a market. Industries in which resources can easily be shifted to other use over a long period will have supply that is close to infinitely elastic over the long run, and prices will eventually rise by the full amount of taxes levied on the products of those industries. If the labor and capital employed in production can be reemployed easily elsewhere in the economy with no reduction in price received, then little backward shifting of taxes to suppliers of resources will occur. Therefore, for industries of constant costs, in the long run it is quite likely that the prices of taxed products will rise to reflect the entire tax while the equilibrium output of the taxed products will decline.

Suppose the supply of a taxed good or service were so unresponsive to changes in its price that its supply could be regarded as perfectly inelastic. For example, if the supply of labor hours were perfectly inelastic, the amount of labor hours supplied per year would be fixed. Figure 11.8 illustrates the impact of a flat-rate tax, such as a payroll tax, on wages under these conditions in a competitive labor market.

As was shown in Figure 11.4, a tax on labor services deducted from the wages of workers causes the net wage received by workers to fall below the gross wage paid by employers. The flat-rate payroll tax on wages reduces the gross wage by tW_G for any given amount of labor hours supplied per week. The net wage is $W_G(1 - t)$. Because the supply of labor hours per week is perfectly inelastic, workers do not respond to the tax-induced wage reduction by varying the amount of hours worked per week. Workers cannot shift the burden of the tax backward to employers. The quantity of labor hours supplied must decline to result in an increase in the gross, or market, equilibrium wage paid by employers. In other words, the tax must have the effect of making labor scarcer for shifting to occur. As shown in Figure 11.8, the tax has no effect on either the market equilibrium quantity of labor hours per week or the wage. The pretax equilibrium wage is W_G^*. The posttax equilibrium wage is also W_G^* because the equilibrium quantity supplied remains Q^* hours per week. The entire tax per labor hour is borne by workers as a reduction in the wages received per hour to $W_N = W_G^*(1 - t)$.

Shifting under Monopoly

A monopolist maximizing profits will choose that output level corresponding to the point where marginal revenue is equal to marginal cost. The marginal revenue curve for a monopolist is steeper than the average revenue (or demand) schedule

---

[8]This conclusion holds as well for an ad valorem tax on sellers of housing services. This is because $P_N = MC = AC$, where P_N is the net price received by sellers in long-run equilibrium. An ad valorem tax on P_N increases MC to $MC' = MC + tP_N$ at all quantities. This will shift up the supply curve parallel to itself, because $P_N = MC = AC$. In the posttax equilibrium, $P_G = (1 + t)P_N$. Because $P_N = MC$ under constant costs, it follows that the posttax market price is $P_G = (1 + t)MC$. When an ad valorem tax is levied on P_G, market equilibrium price in posttax equilibrium is $P_G = MC/(1 - t)$ because $P_N = MC = (1 - t)P_G$.

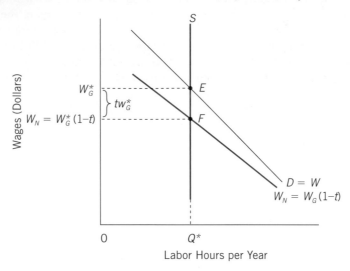

FIGURE 11.8   Tax Incidence When Market Supply Is Perfectly Inelastic

If the supply of labor hours were perfectly inelastic, a payroll tax would decrease the net wage by the full amount of the tax per hour.

and falls below the average revenue curve. A unit excise tax on output produced by a monopoly increases marginal cost at each level of output by an amount equal to the unit tax. However, in this case the effect on price is somewhat more complex.

To understand this, consider a perfectly competitive industry that has been transformed into a cartel and behaves as if it were a monopolist. This is illustrated in Figure 11.9. The demand curve for the industry's output is D, and the marginal revenue schedule corresponding to this demand is MR. The curve MC is the initial marginal cost schedule, while $MC + T$ is the marginal cost schedule after the imposition of the excise tax. If the industry were perfectly competitive, the initial price would be P^*, and the quantity sold would be Q^*. These are the price and quantity corresponding to the intersection of the MC curve and the demand schedule. But, under monopoly, the equilibrium price and quantity correspond to the intersection of the marginal revenue and marginal cost curves. The monopolist or cartel would produce $Q_M < Q^*$ at price $P_M > P^*$. Accordingly, the cartel initially produces less than the perfectly competitive industry, and it charges more.

Now the tax increases marginal costs from MC to $MC + T$ at all levels of output. Under conditions of perfect competition, the effect of the tax would be to reduce quantity sold from Q^* to Q_T^* and raise consumer prices from P^* to P_T^*. But under monopoly, the effect of the tax is to reduce quantity sold by an amount less than the reduction that would prevail under perfect competition when the demand curve is linear. Thus, in Figure 11.9, when the monopolist readjusts output after the tax is imposed, output falls to Q_{MT}, and price rises to P_{MT}. The reduction in monopolistic output, ΔQ_M, due to the tax is less than the reduction in output, ΔQ^*, that would prevail for the same tax levied on a competitive industry. This is because the marginal revenue schedule is steeper than the demand schedule. The price rise to consumers as a result of the tax is less than that which would occur under perfect competition, because the reduction in quantity supplied as a result of

FIGURE 11.9 Shifting under Monopoly

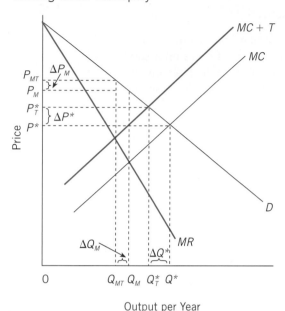

A monopolist would shift less of a given unit tax forward than would be the case if the same output were produced by a competitive industry assuming a linear demand curve.

© Cengage Learning

the tax is less.[9] Therefore, in Figure 11.9, $\Delta P_M < \Delta P^*$. Less forward shifting occurs under monopoly than under perfect competition. This, however, is not really good news for consumers, because they pay a higher price for the commodity under monopoly in the first place! As can be seen in Figure 11.9, consumers still pay a higher price for the commodity in the taxed monopoly relative to the taxed perfectly competitive industry ($P_{MT} > P_T^*$).

Under monopoly, the degree to which taxes are shifted in the long run also varies with the cost structure of the monopolistic firm. The greatest forward shifting is likely to occur under conditions of constant long-run average costs, because the marginal cost curve would be horizontal under those circumstances. In general, the greater the rate of increase of marginal costs with output for a monopolistic firm, the smaller is the portion of a unit or ad valorem tax shifted forward to buyers.

CHECKPOINT

1. What factors influence the incidence of a tax?
2. Why is the incidence of a tax independent of legal liability for the tax?
3. Under what circumstances can a tax on a product cause the market equilibrium price of the product to increase by the full amount of the tax per unit?

---

[9]For complete analysis of shifting under monopoly, see Elchanan Cohn, "A Reexamination of the Price Effects of a Unit Commodity Tax under Perfect Competition and Monopoly," *Public Finance Quarterly* 24, 3 (July 1996). This helps us obtain a more realistic picture of the impact of taxes on resource use and provides insights to help reduce the efficiency loss from taxes.

GENERAL EQUILIBRIUM ANALYSIS OF THE EXCESS BURDEN AND INCIDENCE OF TAXES

In our discussion of the excess burden and incidence of taxes, we have thus far examined only the impact of taxes on a single market. In reality, a system of taxes affects many markets and results in resource flows among many sectors of the economy. A general, or multimarket, analysis of excess burden and tax incidence helps us obtain a more realistic picture of the impact of taxes on resource use and provides insights to help reduce the efficiency loss from taxes.

An economy is composed of complex interrelated markets. This implies that the effect of a tax in any one market is not likely to be confined to that market alone. Instead, repercussions are likely in related markets, along with possible feedback effects in the market initially taxed.

For example, a tax on the consumption of electric power affects not only the price of electricity but also the demand for various electrical appliances and for natural gas for cooking and heating. These secondary shifts in demand affect the prices of these substitutable and complementary activities. This, in turn, might result in feedback effects on both the demand and the supply of electricity. Because electricity is used as an input in most productive processes, one also might expect that the goods that require proportionately more electricity than others for production likewise will rise in price relative to those others. Tracing the full multimarket, or general equilibrium, effect on a tax on electricity is difficult because of the large number of markets likely to be affected.

Minimizing the Excess Burden of Sales and Excise Taxes

Suppose tax authorities wish to minimize the excess burden associated with a system of sales and excise taxes. Surprisingly, they must tax various goods at differing rates rather than at uniform rates to accomplish this. To see why this is so, take two goods, for example, food and clothing. Assume that the demand for food is more inelastic than the demand for clothing and that the demand for each of these goods is independent of the price of the other. Accordingly, when the price of either good changes, the demand curve for the other does not shift.

Figure 11.10 shows the demand curves for food and clothing. Assume that income effects of price changes for these goods are negligible so that the resulting changes in quantities demanded reflect only the substitution effects caused by the taxes. The curves have been drawn under the presumption that, at any given price, the demand for food is more inelastic than the demand for clothing. Now suppose a flat-rate sales tax of t percent is levied on both of these goods. Prior to the tax, the price of food is P_F and the price of clothing is P_C. Assume that the supply of both of these goods is infinitely elastic in the long run so that ultimately the tax raises the price of each of these goods by t percent.

Because the demand for food is more inelastic than the demand for clothing, the excess burden in the clothing market exceeds that in the food market. The excess burden in the food market is the triangular area AE_2E_1 in Figure 11.10A. The excess burden in the clothing market is the triangular area BE_2E_1 in Figure 11.10B. The excess burden is higher in the clothing market because the substitution effect of the tax is greater there than in the food market.

This analysis suggests a way to minimize the excess burden associated with any system of sales or excise taxes. The total excess burden associated with the sales tax

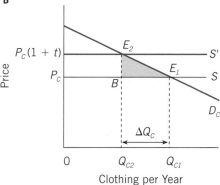

FIGURE 11.10 Multimarket Analysis of Excess Burden

A flat-rate sales tax of *t* percent levied on both food and clothing results in greater excess burden in the clothing market as shown in **B** than in the food market as shown in **A**. Total excess burden can be reduced by increasing the tax rate on food and lowering the tax rate on clothing until the marginal increase in the excess burden in the food market equals the marginal decrease in excess burden in the clothing market.

© Cengage Learning

could be reduced if the tax rate were raised in the food market and lowered in the clothing market. By adjusting the tax rates in the two markets until the marginal reduction in the excess burden in the clothing market is balanced by the marginal increase in the excess burden in the food market, the total excess burden can be minimized.

The implication of this analysis is that efficiency loss can be minimized if, other things being equal, goods are taxed at rates that decrease with the elasticity of demand. The more inelastic the demand, the higher is the tax rate necessary to ensure minimization of efficiency loss.[10] Such a tax rate structure will ensure that the percentage reduction in the quantity demanded due to the substitution effect of the tax-induced price increase is equal for each good.

An efficient system of sales and excise taxes is likely to face considerable political opposition if it is regarded as unfair. In fact, the demand for such necessities as food and housing is likely to be more inelastic than the demand for luxury goods. Therefore, a system of excise taxes that minimizes excess burden is likely to call for higher tax rates on the consumption of necessities. This will bear more heavily on the incomes of the poor relative to the rich.

---

[10]For any two goods F and C, the following condition minimizes the total excess burden:

$$t_F E_F = t_C E_C,$$

where t is the tax rate for each good (indicated by the subscript) and E is its price elasticity of demand. This is sometimes called *Ramsey*'s rule, which states that the percentage reduction in the quantity demanded of each of the goods must be equal. To see this, note that t_F and t_C are the percentage changes in the prices of food and clothing, respectively. Therefore,

$$t_F \frac{\Delta Q_F / Q_F}{t_F} = t_C \frac{\Delta Q_C / Q_C}{t_C}.$$

Therefore, $\Delta Q_F / Q_F = \Delta Q_C / Q_C$. Given E_C and t_C, the lower the E_F, the higher is the tax rate on food necessary to achieve this condition. For a more advanced analysis, see Agnar Sandmo, "Optimal Taxation—An Introduction to the Literature," *Journal of Public Economics* 6 (July–August 1976): 37–54.

Multimarket Analysis of Incidence

Some of the basic ideas of a multimarket analysis of tax incidence can be illustrated simply by expanding the analysis to deal with two markets. Assume, for example, that the economy produces only two goods, food and clothing, and that a tax is levied on the sale of clothing but not on food. The resource flows induced by taxation and consequent effects are illustrated in Figure 11.11.

The tax on clothing acts to decrease the supply of clothing, with a consequent increase in its market price from P^* to P_G and a reduction in quantity demanded from Q^* to Q', as shown in Figure 11.11A. The reduced production of clothing caused by the tax frees productive resources from clothing production for alternative use. If these resources are used to produce government-supplied services, they will be reemployed in the government sector. However, if government does not require the same resources directly freed by the tax, or if the tax revenues are used to finance transfers, the productive resources that are released would have to find employment in alternative industries.

The tax can cause the price of specialized inputs used in the production of the taxed good to fall. This will reduce the incomes of owners of these inputs, thereby forcing them to bear a portion of the incidence of the tax. This is because the reduction in output in the taxed industry results in suppliers of input to that industry seeking work in other industries where their specialized skills are worthless.

The tax on clothing shifts the supply curve from S to S', raises the price of clothing to P_G, as shown in Figure 11.11A, and releases inputs from clothing production. The flow of resources from clothing to food production results in a shift in the supply curve of food to S' and a decrease in the price of food from P_F to P'_F, as shown in Figure 11.11B.

The determination of the incidence of the tax is now more complex. Although the tax causes the price of clothing to increase, it indirectly causes the price of food to decrease. From the point of view of consumers, the increase in clothing prices is

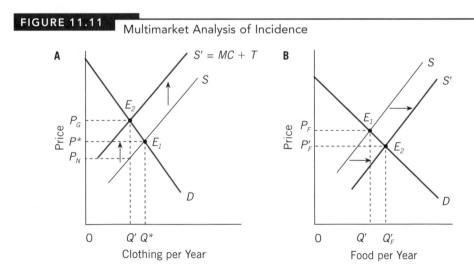

FIGURE 11.11   Multimarket Analysis of Incidence

A tax on output in one market can affect prices in other markets. Here, the tax-induced increase in the price of clothing causes inputs to flow into the food industry. This increases the supply of food and decreases its market price.

balanced to some extent by a corresponding decrease in the price of food. If, on average, the impact of the increase in the price of clothing is exactly offset by the decrease in the price of food, consumers are made no worse off by the tax. The tax is borne by owners of all specialized inputs in clothing production as a reduction in income. If, for example, machine operators who have special skills and who are freed to transfer to food production for employment receive lower wages now, they will be worse off as a result of the tax. Consumers who spend relatively more on clothing than on food also suffer a decrease in real income.

A single-market, or partial equilibrium, analysis often gives a good approximation of the incidence of the tax. If the resources that seek alternative employment as a result of tax-induced decreases in production in one market are absorbed in many markets, little effect on input and output prices in other markets is likely. This is because the amount of resources freed will be small relative to the total supplies of those resources. If these inputs are not specialized, they can be reemployed in other industries, with no decrease in their prices or those on the outputs that they produce. The extent to which the results of a multimarket analysis differ from a single-market analysis depends on the degree to which tax-induced resource flows are concentrated in particular markets and the extent to which displaced inputs have specialized uses in the taxed industry.

The situation is more complex still if the possibility of overall changes in the aggregate supplies of particular inputs as a result of the tax is considered. If workers or owners of capital decide to work or invest less as a result of the lower returns available after taxation, further changes in input prices will occur.

TAXES, GOVERNMENT EXPENDITURES, AND THE DISTRIBUTION OF INCOME

Policy makers and citizens must have reasonably accurate information concerning the effect of government activity on the distribution of well-being among households in the community. Insofar as a household's well-being is correlated with its real income, changes in the distribution of welfare can be approximated by measuring changes in the distribution of disposable income. Predictions of the effect of proposed tax and expenditure policies on the distribution of income can permit more-informed collective choices on the extent and nature of government activities. Quantitative estimates of the extent and nature of government expenditures and tax policies help voters compute their true cost shares of collectively supplied services relative to the net benefits that they receive from government activities.

The incidence of a specific government policy refers to the resulting change in the distribution of income available for private use attributable to that policy.[11] To determine the incidence of a policy, no other factors can be attributable to, say, other policies simultaneously affecting the distribution of income. This implies that other variables that affect income distribution (for example, other government policies) must be held fixed in order to obtain a meaningful measure of the incidence of any specific policy.

---

[11]For a classic study of this topic, see Musgrave, *Theory of Public Finance* (New York: McGraw-Hill, 1959): 207–208.

With that caution in mind, three concepts of incidence that relate to government taxes *and* expenditures can be distinguished:

1. Budget incidence
2. Expenditure incidence
3. Tax incidence

Budget and Expenditure Incidence

Budget incidence evaluates the effects of both government expenditure and tax policies on the distribution of income in the private sector. A comprehensive analysis of budget incidence in the United States would generate data relative to the influence of governments (federal, state, and local government activities) on the distribution of income. Alternatively, the incidence of a change in the size of the government budget could be evaluated. This would analyze the effects on the distribution of income of a particular increase in government expenditures accompanied by increases in taxes.[12]

Expenditure incidence evaluates the effects of alternative government expenditure projects on the distribution of income. To be sure that only the expenditure project being evaluated is affecting the distribution of income, all other possible influences on the distribution of income must be held fixed. This implies that the total level of expenditure is held constant in real terms and that the particular project being evaluated is substituted for some other project or group of projects. At the same time, we must adjust for any change in the tax structure that alters the distribution of income. This *differential* approach to the incidence of expenditures allows the economist to generate data concerning the relative redistributive effects of alternative expenditure policies alone.[13] It allows policy makers and citizens to evaluate the relative redistributive effects of alternative expenditure policies. The determination of expenditure incidence remains difficult because of the inherent problems involved in imputing the collectively consumed benefits of government-provided goods and services to specific households and business firms.

Differential Tax Incidence

Differential tax incidence is the resulting change in the distribution of income when one type of tax is substituted for some alternative tax, or set of taxes, yielding an equivalent amount of revenue in real terms, while both the mix and level of government expenditures are held constant. Because any given level and mix of government expenditures can be financed through alternative tax schemes, the concept of differential tax incidence enables one to determine the relative redistributive impact of alternative taxes and tax structures. An analysis of differential tax incidence attempts to delineate all direct and indirect effects of the substitution of one tax for another. This includes all secondary shifts in relative prices that result from tax shifting, as well as direct transfers of income.

However, the concept of differential incidence ignores the interdependence between the revenue and expenditure sides of the budget. Because alternative tax schemes, other things being equal, do have varying effects on the distribution of

---

[12]Musgrave calls this "balanced-budget incidence." See *Theory of Public Finance*, pp. 214–215.

[13]See Musgrave, *Theory of Public Finance*, pp. 212–225, for a more extensive discussion of differential incidence.

income in the private sector and on tax shares, the assumption of holding the level and mix of government expenditures constant is questionable. The reason is that changes in the distribution of income and tax shares are likely to change the demand pattern for public services. The willingness to vote approval on specific projects is, in part, a function of tax shares.

The Lorenz Curve

The effect of taxes on income shares can be partially tabulated by using Lorenz curves. A **Lorenz curve** gives information on the distribution of income by size brackets. A hypothetical Lorenz curve is plotted in Figure 11.12. The horizontal axis gives the percentage of households ranked in terms of their income, while the vertical axis measures the percentage of income. The line $0E$ is called the *line of equal distribution*. An economy whose income distribution is measured along line $0E$ has a perfectly uniform distribution of real income. To understand why this is so, consider the percentage of income going to the lowest 10 percent of households (the bottom decile) for an economy with a Lorenz curve of $0E$. Because $0E$ is at a 45-degree angle to the horizontal axis, the lowest decile of households ranked in terms of income size has 10 percent of the nation's real income. Similarly, the lowest 90 percent of households has 90 percent of the nation's income. The top 10 percent of households ranked in terms of income (the top decile) also has 10 percent of the nation's income. Any decile rank chosen has 10 percent of the nation's total real income. Income would be equally distributed.

No nation has a Lorenz curve such as $0E$. Significant degrees of income inequality exist. For example, the income distribution might be measured by the Lorenz curve $0xyE$ in Figure 11.12. Such an income distribution implies that the bottom decile of households ranked in terms of income has only 3 percent of

---

FIGURE 11.12 A Lorenz Curve

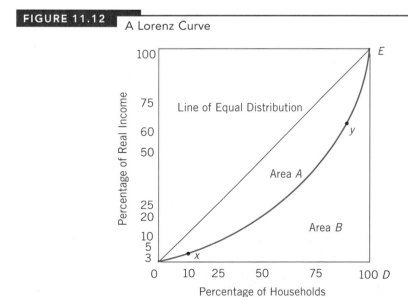

A Lorenz curve shows how a nation's actual income distribution deviates from a perfectly equal income distribution.

the nation's real income, at point *x*, while the top decile of households has 40 percent of the nation's real income, at point *y*.

Now consider the effect of taxation on the distribution of income. After all changes in input and output prices and direct reductions of income have been determined, along with changes in quantities purchased and sold by households, and the new data can be tabulated by income size brackets and plotted in Figure 11.12 as a new Lorenz curve. This permits comparison of the new income distribution by size classes with the income distribution that existed before the policy change. However, insofar as households trade places within the income distribution, with no change in the degree of income inequality, the Lorenz curve does not reflect the change in the distribution.

Measuring Income Inequality: The Gini Coefficient

A summary index of the information contained in a Lorenz curve is a **Gini coefficient**, which measures the degree of inequality for any income distribution by calculating the ratio of the area between the Lorenz curve corresponding to that distribution and the 45-degree line to the total area under the 45-degree line. Thus, in Figure 11.12, call *A* the area between the 45-degree line and the Lorenz curve, and call *B* the area under the Lorenz curve; then, the Gini coefficient, *G*, is

$$G = \frac{\text{Area } A}{\text{Area } A + \text{Area } B}.$$ (11.9)

If the Gini coefficient were equal to zero, the Lorenz curve would be the 45-degree line. The closer the Gini coefficient is to zero, the more equal is the income distribution. Gini coefficients are often calculated for pretax and posttax income distributions. If the Gini coefficient is lower for the posttax distribution of income, then taxes have served the function of reducing income inequality. The Gini coefficient provides only a rough index of income inequality. It is of limited usefulness when changes in income distribution, induced by taxes or other policies, result in new Lorenz curves that intersect the initial Lorenz curve and when the ranking of households changes.[14] To the extent to which the Gini coefficient corresponding to posttax income is less than that corresponding to pretax income, taxes have served to decrease income inequality as measured by the Gini coefficient.

A study of the incidence of the overall 1980 tax structure (all federal, state, and local taxes) in the United States concluded that, except for those with very high incomes and very low incomes, the overall distribution of the tax burden is roughly proportional to income.[15] Joseph A. Pechman, in a major study done at the Brookings Institution, concluded that, based on 1980 effective tax rates, the Gini coefficient of the pretax income distribution was reduced by taxation by no more than 2.5 percent. Using the Gini coefficient as a rough index of income inequality, this implies that the overall combined effect of federal, state, and local taxes on the income distribution was negligible in that year. A similar study by the Congressional Budget Office for federal taxes alone concluded that federal taxes reduced the Gini coefficient by between 4 and 5 percent based on the tax law prevailing in 1988.[16] Taken by

[14]More refined measures of the degree of progressiveness of taxes are possible. For outstanding examples, see Daniel B. Suits, "Measurement of Tax Progressivity," *American Economic Review* 67 (September 1977): 747–752.

[15]Joseph A. Pechman, *Who Paid the Taxes: 1966–1985?* (Washington, D.C.: The Brookings Institution, 1985).

[16]U.S. Congress, Congressional Budget Office, *The Changing Distribution of Federal Taxes: 1975–1990* (Washington, D.C.: Congress of the United States, October 1987): Appendix C.

TABLE 11.1	Effective Tax Rates for All Federal Taxes, 1998 and 2003	

	EFFECTIVE TAX RATE (PERCENT)	
INCOME CATEGORY	**1998**	**2003**
Lowest Quintile	4.5	4.8
Second Quintile	13.3	9.8
Third Quintile	18.9	13.6
Fourth Quintile	22.1	17.7
Highest Quintile	28.7	25.0

Source: Congressional Budget Office.

themselves, federal taxes contribute more to reducing income inequality than do taxes levied by all levels of government in the United States.

Analysis of the federal tax structure after tax reforms that went into effect in 1997 and after tax cuts that went into effect in 2003 indicates that the federal tax structure is quite progressive with respect to income. According to estimates by the Congressional Budget Office, the average tax rate (ATR) for all federal taxes was 23.8 percent after the *Taxpayer Relief Act of 1997*. After tax cuts resulting from the *Economic Growth and Tax Relief Reconciliation Act of 2001* became fully effective in 2003, average tax rates for all federal taxes fell to 20.7 percent. Table 11.1 shows the effective tax rates for each quintile of households ranking according to the amount of annual income earned from all sources adjusted for household size in 1998 and 2003 after the changes in the tax code went into effect.[17] Given the progressive nature of federal taxes overall, they are likely to shift the Lorenz curve inward and contribute to reducing income inequality in the United States.[18]

Reforms enacted in 2001 reduced income tax rates substantially. These reforms reduced effective income tax rates for all taxpayers except those in the lowest quintile of the income distribution. These taxpayers experienced a slight increase in the effective tax rate from 4.5 to 4.8 percent. However, the overall incidence of the federal tax system remains progressive. Looking at the difference between the second and fifth quintiles, the effective tax rate in the highest quintile was 2.5 times higher than in the second quintile in 2003. This difference is actually greater than was the case in 1998 when it was only a bit more than two times higher. Between 2003 and 2011 there have been no major changes in federal tax policy, so the effective tax rates shown in Table 11.1 as estimated by the Congressional Budget Office are probably reasonably close to those which prevailed in 2011. However, despite clear evidence that federal taxes are progressive with respect to income there are political pressures to increase effective tax rates on upper income groups in the United States.

---

[17]See Congress of the United States, Congressional Budget Office, *Economic Analysis of the Taxpayer Relief Act of 1997* (April 2000) and *Historical Effective Federal Tax Rates: 1979 to 2003* (December 2005). See these publications for additional information on techniques used by the CBO to measure income and adjust for household size.

[18]Analysis of the distributional effects of taxes is more of an art than a science. Such studies typically must make many simplifying assumptions and guesses about the effects of taxes on incomes to calculate effective tax rates. See Congress of the United States, Joint Economic Committee, *A Guide to Tax Policy Analysis: Problems with Distributional Tables* (January 2000) for an analysis of some of the technical issues involved in measuring the incidence of taxation.

1. Explain why minimizing the excess burden from a state sales tax would require that products with inelastic demand be taxed at higher rates than products with elastic demand.
2. Explain how a tax on one product, such as gasoline, can cause the price of other products to decline.
3. What is differential tax incidence? How can a Gini coefficient be used to determine whether a substitution of one tax for another results in a more equitable income distribution?

SUMMARY

Taxes can affect prices of outputs and inputs, causing losses in efficiency by preventing prices from accurately reflecting marginal social costs and benefits of goods and services. Price-distorting taxes induce individuals to take actions with lower social value than they would choose if no such tax existed. The excess burden of a tax is a measure of the tax-induced loss in efficiency in private use of resources due to the substitution effects of taxes.

The standard of comparison for measuring losses associated with price-distorting taxes is the lump-sum tax, which does not prevent prices from being equal to the marginal social cost and marginal social benefit of goods and services. Such a tax transfers resources from private use to government use without offering any opportunity or incentive to substitute one private activity for another. Lump-sum taxes result only in income or wealth reductions; they do not cause losses in the efficiency with which private resources are used.

Price-distorting taxes act as wedges in markets, making prices paid by buyers diverge from net prices received by sellers. This prevents competitive markets from automatically equating marginal social costs and marginal social benefits. The result is a loss in efficiency. Efficiency loss, or excess burden, depends on the tax rate, the expenditure on the taxed good, and its price elasticities of demand and supply. Excess burden varies quadratically

with the tax rate. Excess burden is minimized when taxing activities for which substitution effects of price changes are close to zero.

The burden of paying a tax can be shifted from people who are liable for the tax to other groups. This occurs when prices change as a result of a tax. The incidence of a tax measures the distribution of the burden of paying a tax among people. In general, other things being equal, the more inelastic the demand for a taxed good or service, the greater is the portion of the tax paid by buyers of the item. Similarly, other things being equal, the more inelastic the supply of a taxed good or service, the greater is the portion of the tax paid by sellers.

A multimarket analysis of incidence considers the effect of tax-induced resource flows on the prices of inputs and outputs in markets other than those directly taxed. The determination of incidence in such cases is more complex. Input prices often fall, and prices of goods produced with inputs released by taxation also fall.

Data on income shares by income class can be tabulated with a Lorenz curve, which plots the percentage of households ranked according to income against their share of income. A Gini coefficient, which summarizes information contained in a Lorenz curve, provides a rough index of income inequality. The smaller the Gini coefficient, the more equal the income distribution.

LOOKING AHEAD

Chapter 12 discusses the government budget balance and budget deficits. Borrowing to cover government expenditures raises questions about the implications of government

debt on resource use and the distribution of well-being between present and future generations.

KEY CONCEPTS

Ad Valorem Taxes
Backward Shifting

Budget Incidence
Compensated Demand Curve

Compensated Supply Curve

Differential Tax Incidence

Efficiency-loss Ratio

Expenditure Incidence

Forward Shifting

Gini Coefficient

Head Tax

Incidence of a Tax

Individual Excess Burden of a Tax

Lorenz Curve

Lump-sum Tax

Price-distorting Tax

Shifting of a Tax

Total Excess Burden of a Tax

Unit Tax

REVIEW QUESTIONS

1. Why are most taxes likely to cause losses in efficiency? Be sure to relate your answer to the impact of taxes on prices.
2. Why should the excess burden of taxation be added to revenue collected from taxes in order to accurately measure the opportunity costs of government-supplied goods and services?
3. Explain why lump-sum taxes will not cause any losses in efficiency. Are lump-sum taxes feasible? Lump-sum taxes do not result in substitution effects, but they do affect prices. Is this a contradiction?
4. Show how a gasoline tax of 10 cents per gallon collected from sellers affects the market equilibrium for gasoline. Assume that the demand curve for gasoline is downward sloping and that the supply curve is upward sloping. Show the excess burden of the tax on your diagram. What is the incidence of the tax between buyers and sellers? How would your answer be affected if the tax were collected from buyers instead of sellers?
5. The price elasticity of demand for automobiles is -2 and the price elasticity of supply is 3. Expenditure on automobiles after imposing a sales tax of 2 percent is $5 billion. Calculate the excess burden of the

tax, assuming that automobiles are sold in perfectly competitive markets. Assume that the price elasticities given are based on the substitution effect of the tax and that the difference between pretax and post-tax prices of cars is very small.
6. Why would a national land tax be likely to have zero excess burden? Show the incidence of a tax on land between landlords and tenants. In answering this question, assume that the supply of land is perfectly inelastic.
7. Suppose the efficiency-loss ratio of taxes on capital income is 30 percent. The capital income taxes currently collect $50 billion of revenue per year. What would be the gain in well-being if a lump-sum tax replaced the current taxes on capital income?
8. Under what circumstances does a single-market analysis of tax incidence give a good approximation of the multimarket incidence?
9. How would the differential tax incidence of replacing an income tax with a lump-sum tax be determined?
10. What is a Gini coefficient? How can this coefficient be used to determine the impact of taxes on income distribution?

PROBLEMS

1. The annual demand for liquor in a certain state is given by the following equation:

$$Q_D = 500{,}000 - 20{,}000P$$

where P is the price per gallon and Q_D is quantity of gallons demanded per year. The supply of liquor is given by the equation:

$$Q_S = 30{,}000P.$$

Solve for the equilibrium annual quantity and price of liquor.

Suppose that a $1-per-gallon tax is levied on the price of liquor received by sellers. Use both graphic and algebraic techniques to show the impact

of the tax on market equilibrium. Calculate the excess burden of the tax, the amount of revenues collected, and the incidence of the tax between buyers and sellers.
2. Figure 11.11 shows that a tax on clothing can reduce the price of food. Suppose that after the tax on clothing consumption is imposed, another tax is levied on the consumption of food. For example, the consumption of both commodities could be subject to a tax of 5 percent. Show how the conclusions of the analysis in the text are modified when the same tax is present in both markets. Analyze the incidence of the tax. In your answer, assume that the tax revenue is returned in equal lump-sum transfers to all citizens.

3. The price elasticity of demand for wine is estimated to be −1 at all possible quantities. Currently, 200 million gallons of wine are sold per year, and the price averages $6 per bottle. Assuming that the price elasticity of supply of wine is 1 and the current tax rate is $1 per bottle, calculate the current excess burden of the tax on wine. Suppose the tax per bottle is increased to $2 per bottle. What will happen to the excess burden of the tax as a result of the tax increase? Under what circumstances can a doubling of the tax on wine actually improve resource use in the United States, despite the increase in the excess burden of the tax?

4. Suppose you had to design a system of taxation for a republic of the former Soviet Union that was transforming its economy into a modern Western-style mixed economy. What criteria would you consider to minimize the excess burden of the system of taxation? Why would a uniform system of sales taxes likely have a higher excess burden than a system of excise taxes in which tax rates varied among taxed products? What would be the possible distortions resulting from a tax system that only taxed consumption of goods and services and did not tax leisure activities? Why would a very efficient tax system be unlikely to gain broad political support in the republic?

5. Suppose the supply of housing construction is infinitely elastic at a price of $150 per square foot. Currently 1 million square feet are built per month. If the price elasticity of demand for housing is −1, calculate the monthly excess burden of a 10 percent tax on housing construction. (Hint: Go to the appendix at the end of this chapter and read the discussion on taxation of constant cost industries.) What is the monthly excess burden if the tax is 20 percent? Who will bear the incidence of the tax?

ADDITIONAL READINGS

Dahlby, Bev. *The Marginal Cost of Public Funds*. Cumberland, R.I.: The MIT Press, 2008. An analysis integrating excess burden of taxation and tax policy to calculate measures of the marginal cost of public funds. The results are applied to a variety of tax issues and problems in a number of nations.

Fullerton, Don, and Diane Lim Rogers. *Who Bears the Lifetime Tax Burden?* Washington, D.C.: The Brookings Institution, 1993. An innovative extension of incidence analysis that examines tax burdens over the lifetime of individuals. Much of the analysis in this book is quite technical.

Harberger, Arnold C. *Taxation and Welfare*. Boston: Little, Brown, & Co., 1974. A collection of classic articles by Harberger that develop techniques for measuring efficiency loss.

Miezkowski, Peter. "Tax Incidence Theory: The Effect of Taxes on the Distribution of Income." *Journal of Economic Literature* 7 (December 1969). An outstanding review of basic incidence theory.

Salanie, Bernard. *The Economics of Taxation*. Cambridge, Mass.: The MIT Press, 2003. A comprehensive exposition of theories of taxation, the impact of taxes, and analysis of the design of tax systems.

Slemrod, Joel. "Optimal Taxation and Optimal Tax Systems." *Journal of Economic Perspectives* 4, 1 (Winter 1990): 157–178. A readable discussion of theoretical and practical issues in designing tax systems based on normative criteria including efficiency and various concepts of horizontal and vertical equity.

Slemrod, Joel, and Jon Bakija. *Taxing Ourselves: A Citizen's Guide to the Great Debate over Tax Reform*, 2nd edition. Cambridge, Mass.: The MIT Press, 2000. An overview of the U.S. system that discusses its economic effects and the distribution of its burden along with analysis of proposals for reform.

Steurle, C. Eugene. *Contemporary U.S. Tax Policy*. Washington, D.C.: Urban Institute Press, 2008. A overview of public decision making about taxes and tax policy in the United States from the post–World War II era to George W. Bush's second term as president.

INTERNET RESOURCES

http://www.cbo.gov
This is the home page of the Congressional Budget Office (CBO). The CBO conducts ongoing studies of the federal tax system to keep the Congress and the public informed on the effect of the tax system on economic decisions and income distribution. You can access CBO studies and reports at this site.

http://www.jec.senate.gov
This is the home page of the Joint Economic Committee of Congress. The committee's research staff provides Congress and the public with analysis of the federal tax system and its economic effects. Click on Issues or Resources to access studies, charts, and data related to taxation.

THE EXCESS BURDEN OF TAXATION: TECHNICAL ANALYSIS

DERIVATION OF THE FORMULA FOR THE EXCESS BURDEN OF A UNIT TAX

It is easy to show that the excess burden of a unit tax varies with the square of the tax per unit, T. Begin with the formula for the area of the triangle representing the loss in well-being attributable to the excess burden of the tax:

$$W = \frac{1}{2} T \Delta Q. \tag{11A.1}$$

where ΔQ is the change in the sale of the good or service due only to the substitution effect of the tax-induced price increase. The unit tax, T, can be expressed as the difference between the gross price paid by buyers and the net price received by sellers:

$$T = P_G - P_N \tag{11A.2}$$

The change in the gross price paid by buyers is

$$\Delta P_G = P_G - P^*, \tag{11A.3}$$

where P^* is the pretax market equilibrium price.

The change in the net price received by sellers is

$$\Delta P_N = P_N - P^*. \tag{11A.4}$$

The change in price to buyers is positive, whereas the change in the net price received by sellers is negative.

The price elasticities of demand and supply at any price and quantity, P, Q, are

$$E_D = \frac{\Delta Q/Q^*}{\Delta P_G/P^*} \tag{11A.5}$$

and

$$E_S = \frac{\Delta Q/Q^*}{\Delta P_N/P^*}, \tag{11A.6}$$

where Q^* is the initial equilibrium quantity. When the elasticities are based on changes in quantities due only to substitution effects, they are called compensated elasticities. Substituting Equations 11A.3 and 11A.4 into 11A.5 and 11A.6 gives the following:

$$E_D = \frac{\Delta Q}{Q^*} \cdot \frac{P^*}{P_G - P^*} \tag{11A.7}$$

and

$$E_S = \frac{\Delta Q}{Q^*} \cdot \frac{P^*}{P_N - P^*}. \tag{11A.8}$$

Solving for P_G and P_N

$$P_G = \frac{\Delta Q P^*}{Q^* E_D} + P^* \tag{11A.9}$$

and

$$P_N = \frac{\Delta Q P^*}{Q^* E_S} + P^*. \tag{11A.10}$$

Substituting Equations 11A.9 and 11A.10 into 11A.2 yields

$$T = \frac{\Delta Q P^*}{Q^*} \cdot \frac{E_S - E_D}{E_S E_D}. \tag{11A.11}$$

Solving Equation 11A.11 for ΔQ gives

$$\Delta Q = T \frac{Q^*}{P^*} \cdot \frac{E_S E_D}{E_S - E_D}. \tag{11A.12}$$

Finally, substituting Equation 11A.12 in the expression for W gives

$$W = \frac{1}{2} T^2 \frac{Q^*}{P^*} \cdot \frac{E_S E_D}{E_S - E_D}. \tag{11A.13}$$

This is the formula used in the text for determining the loss in well-being from the excess burden of a unit tax. The price elasticity of demand, E_D, is a negative number; therefore, the value of W is negative, indicating a loss.

EXCESS BURDEN OF AN AD VALOREM TAX WHEN THE TAXED GOOD OR SERVICE IS PRODUCED UNDER CONDITIONS OF CONSTANT COSTS

If a good is produced under conditions of constant costs, its long-run supply curve will be infinitely elastic. Remember, if the difference between the pretax and posttax price is small, the excess burden of an ad valorem tax can be approximated by

$$W = \frac{1}{2} t^2 (P^* Q^*) \frac{E_S E_D}{E_S - E_D}, \tag{11A.14}$$

which can be written as

$$W = \frac{1}{2} t^2 (P^* Q^*) E_D \frac{E_S}{E_S - E_D}. \tag{11A.15}$$

The horizontal supply curve associated with constant costs implies an infinite elasticity of supply. As E_S approaches infinity, the value of the ratio $E_S/(E_S - E_D)$ approaches one. The formula in Equation 11A.15 therefore reduces to

$$W = \frac{1}{2} t^2 P^* Q^* E_D. \tag{11A.16}$$

Thus, under conditions of constant costs, calculation of the excess burden requires an estimate of the price elasticity of the taxed good and an estimate of current expenditures of the good. The more inelastic the demand for the good, the lower is the excess burden.

Suppose the supply of new housing is infinitely elastic in the long run. If the total annual revenue of the housing industry is currently $50 billion in new home sales, a tax of 2 percent of new home sales would result in an annual excess burden of $10 million per year in the long run when the compensated price elasticity of demanded is equal to −1.

INDIVIDUAL LOSSES IN WELFARE UNDER CONDITIONS OF PERFECT COMPETITION

It is often useful to calculate the excess burden borne by certain groups in the economy. If the taxed output or input is traded under conditions of perfect competition, owners can sell as much as they like at the going market price. This implies that, from their point of view, the demand curve that they face is perfectly elastic at the going market price. In this case, the price elasticity of demand relevant for computing the excess burden is infinite. Substituting an infinite E_D in Equation 11A.14 for the excess burden of an ad valorem tax gives

$$W = \frac{1}{2}t^2(P^*Q^*)E_S. \tag{11A.17}$$

For example, a formula like the one in the previous equation could be used to calculate the excess burden associated with each marginal tax rate, t, on labor income for the personal income tax. The amount of income in each tax bracket would correspond to P^*Q^* in the formula because labor income represents the product of wages and labor hours per year. An estimate of the price elasticity of supply of labor based on the substitution effects of tax-induced wage changes then would be required to calculate the excess burden for each tax bracket. The total excess burden could be obtained by summing the excess burden associated with each tax bracket.

COMPENSATED DEMAND CURVES

The price elasticities of demand of taxed outputs used to calculate excess burden are based on the substitution effects of price changes. These are calculated from points on a compensated demand curve. A **compensated demand curve** of a good shows the relationship between the price and the quantity demanded of a good due only to substitution effects of price changes.

Figure 11A.1 shows that the compensated demand curve for a normal good can be derived from a regular demand curve. Consumption of a normal good increases as income increases and decreases as income decreases. Compensated demand curves do not include any of the effects of changes in well-being for consumers that result from price changes. Each time a price increases, consumers would have to be given a compensating increase in income to offset the decrease in well-being caused by the income effect of the price rise. Similarly, the consumer would have to be compensated by decreases in income each time prices fell to adjust for the increase in real income. The adjustments in income remove the income effects of price changes.

In Figure 11A.1, the current market price of gasoline is P_1. Suppose the price increases. If gasoline is a normal good, the income effect of the price increase will reduce its consumption. This is because the increase in price reduces consumers'

FIGURE 11A.1   Regular and Compensated Demand Curves for a Normal Good

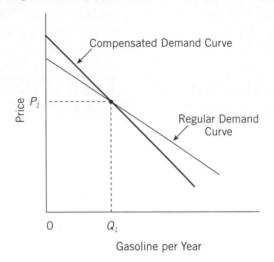

Compensated demand curves remove the income effects of price changes from demand responses. The compensated demand curve in the graph shows the substitution effects for all price changes above and below the initial price, P_1. The compensated demand curve for a normal good is more inelastic than the regular demand curve at any given price above or below the initial price.

© Cengage Learning

real income. When income is reduced, consumers reduce the consumption of a normal good such as gasoline. If consumers were given a compensating increase in income to make them as well-off as they were before the price increase, they would consume *more* than otherwise would be the case. It follows that removing the income effect of price increases would increase the consumption of gasoline. Therefore, points on a compensated demand curve reflecting *only* the substitution effects of price increases would lie to the right of points on the regular demand curve for prices higher than P_1.

Similarly, price decreases below P_1 would make the consumer better off. The increase in real income would result in an income effect that would increase the consumption of a normal good such as gasoline. Removing the income effect by decreasing consumers' income would decrease the quantity demanded in response to the price decline. Points on a compensated demand curve below P_1 would lie to the left of points on the regular demand curve.

Points on compensated demand curves for normal goods tend to have lower price elasticity than points corresponding to the same price on regular demand curves. The difference between the compensated and regular demand curves depends on the size of the income effects of price changes. When these income effects are relatively small, using price elasticities based on the regular demand curve will give a good approximation of the excess burden of a tax.

Figure 11A.2 shows that a compensated demand curve can be used to determine the excess burden of a tax on gasoline when the income effect of the tax-induced increase in market price is not negligible. Assume that gasoline is a normal good. The supply curve of gasoline is labeled S on the graph. The regular,

FIGURE 11A.2 Using a Compensated Demand Curve to Isolate the Substitution Effect of a Tax-Induced Price Increase

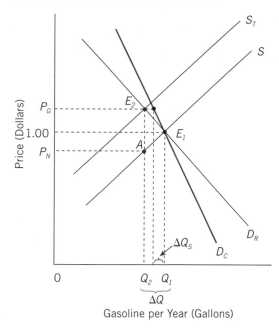

A tax on gasoline raises the market price from $1 per gallon to P_G. The corresponding reduction in quantity demanded, ΔQ, is the combined income and substitution effects of the tax-induced price increase. The compensated demand curve is used to show the substitution effect of the price increase, ΔQ_S. Using the actual reduction in quantity demanded overestimates the excess burden if the taxed item is a normal good.

or market, demand curve for gasoline is labeled D_R. The initial market equilibrium corresponds to point E_1, at which the regular market demand curve and the market supply curve intersect. The equilibrium quantity sold per year is Q_1 and the equilibrium price is $1. The imposition of a unit tax on gasoline shifts the supply curve upward from S to S_T. The new market equilibrium corresponds to point E_2, at which the market price of gasoline increases to P_G, and the net price received by sellers corresponds to P_N. The equilibrium quantity of gasoline demanded per year declines to Q_2. The total decline in the annual consumption of gasoline of ΔQ gallons per year reflects the combined income and substitution effects of the tax-induced price increase.

The compensated demand curve, labeled D_C, is used to isolate the substitution effect of the tax-induced price increase. Along the compensated demand curve, quantity demanded declines by the amount ΔQ_S in response to the tax-induced price increase. The excess burden then can be calculated from the formula $\frac{1}{2}T\Delta Q_S$. The substitution effect can be predicted by using a compensated price elasticity of demand calculated for points along a compensated demand curve. Measuring the excess burden as the area of the triangle AE_2E_1 overestimates the actual excess burden when the income effect of a tax-induced price increase is not negligible.

FIGURE 11A.3   A Compensated Supply Curve for an Input

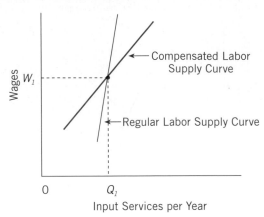

A compensated supply curve for an input, such as labor services, removes the income effect of price changes from the input owner's decision to offer input services for sale.

COMPENSATED SUPPLY CURVES

The price elasticities of supply used to calculate the excess burden of taxes on input services are based on price elasticities of supply that reflect only the substitution effects of changes in wages and other input prices. The **compensated supply curve** of an input is one that reflects only the substitution effects of input price changes. Compensated supply curves for input services can be derived by eliminating the income effects of input price changes on the supply decisions of sellers.

For example, a labor supply curve shows that labor hours supplied vary with wage changes. An increase in wages results in a substitution effect that not only encourages people to work more but also causes an income effect. The income effect of an increase in wages increases the demand for normal goods. If leisure is a normal good, the income effect serves to reduce hours worked. Removing the income effect of a wage increase therefore increases the labor supply response of workers to wage increases.

Similarly, removing the income effect of wage decreases dampens the labor supply response of workers, because a wage decrease decreases income and therefore decreases the demand for leisure, assuming that it is a normal good. As a result, the income effect encourages workers to work more when wages decline. Removing the income effect of wage declines results in less work than otherwise would be the case. Compensated labor supply curves are more elastic than regular labor supply curves, as shown in Figure 11A.3. In Chapter 13, compensated labor supply curves are used to determine the excess burden of taxes on labor income.

Chapter 12

BUDGET BALANCE AND GOVERNMENT DEBT

LEARNING OBJECTIVES

After reading this chapter, you should be able to:

- Discuss the federal government budget deficit or surplus and issues involved in measuring the budget balance and its impact on interest rates, national saving, economic growth, and resource use.

- Define the net federal debt and explain how growth of the debt is related to the federal budget balance.

- Describe the ownership pattern of the national debt and the distinction between external and internal debt, and the burden of the debt.

- Examine economic issues relating to borrowing by state and local governments.

Governments can spend more than they collect from taxes and other sources of revenue by borrowing. By running up the public debt, governments can put off the burden of taxation to the future. When government spending exceeds revenues, the result is a budget deficit. Budget deficits have been common for the federal government in the United States since 1960. State and local governments by and large are required by state law to keep their budgets in balance and borrow only to finance capital expenditures. Since 1960, it has been common for state and local governments to run modest budget surpluses. However, unanticipated declines in revenue can result in deficits for state and local governments that require rebalancing of their budgets. The recession that began in late 2007 resulted in sharp declines in revenues for most state governments in 2008 and 2009. Several states had budget deficits amounting to more than 20 percent of their planned expenditures. The deficits forced these state governments to cut expenditures, layoff or furlough state employees, and increase tax rates to bring their budgets back into balance.

The recession had a major impact on the federal government's budget balance in 2009. Revenues declined in that year and expenditures for transfer programs such as unemployment insurance increased, while extraordinary expenditures were incurred to cope with a financial crisis and stimulate an economy with an unemployment rate approaching 10 percent. By 2009, the federal budget deficit was moving in the range of an unprecedented $1.4 trillion—an amount equal to 10.1 percent of GDP! Projections by the Congressional Budget Office in 2012 indicated that based on likely scenarios for federal spending and tax collections, the federal budget was likely to continue to be in deficit through 2022, although the share of the deficit as a percentage of GDP was likely to decline significantly after 2012 to a range between 1 and 6 percent of GDP. In the future, most of the growth of federal spending contributing to future deficits, other than interest on the federal debt, will result from three major entitlement programs: Medicare, Medicaid, and Social Security. Expenditure for these programs will result mainly as a result of aging of the population. This chapter will discuss why there is good reason to be concerned about negative economic effects of chronic government deficits. To control those deficits in the future will require initiatives that reduce the rate of growth of entitlement programs contributing to the deficit.

Borrowing by the federal government to finance public expenditures has been the rule rather than the exception in the United States since 1960. The brief four-year period of federal budget surpluses between 1998 and 2001 demonstrated that budget surpluses, just like deficits, can be used to finance government expenditures or tax rate reductions. A surplus gives politicians the opportunity to fund new programs without increasing taxes or to slash taxes without cutting back on public expenditure. The federal budget surplus that prevailed from 1998 to 2001 was dissipated over a four-year period, in part, due to a recession in 2001 and slowdown in the economy's rate of growth that cut tax collections. However, tax cuts enacted in 2001 along with increased demands for spending for national defense and homeland security also contributed to the demise of the surplus. If surpluses are allowed to persist, they can be used to pay off and reduce the federal government's debt. Used in this way, budget surpluses increase national saving and make more funds available in credit markets. The increase in national saving could lower real interest rates, contribute to more investment, and thereby increase the economy's rate of economic growth. This faster growth would increase the tax base and mean that a given amount of government spending could be financed with lower tax rates in the future. The opposite is true if budget deficits are allowed to persist. Budget deficits absorb funds from credit market and contribute to declines in national saving. The decline in national saving can increase real interest rates, reduce private investment, reduce economic growth, and decrease future living standards.

This chapter examines the federal budget balance and the role that both borrowing and budget surpluses play in public finance. We look at effects on interest rates, saving, investment, and future living standards. We also analyze the federal debt and its effect on the economy along with the consequences of reducing the debt.

THE FEDERAL BUDGET BALANCE

Why all the concern about the federal budget balance (deficit or surplus) and the government debt? What, if anything, is wrong with government borrowing as a means of financing its activities? What should be done with a government budget surplus? Should the budget always be balanced with neither a deficit nor a surplus in any year? In 2009 and 2010, a huge federal budget deficit emerged as spending was increased and tax revenues declined. The deficit in that year helped to stabilize an economy in recession. However, the size of the federal budget deficit (or surplus) can have long-term effects on saving, investment, and the nation's rate of growth. Fiscal policy, the use of the government budget to stabilize the economy, can help move the economy back to full employment during recessions, but long-term concerns about the impact of a deficit on national saving and future living standards must also be considered. The federal budget deficits since 1980 have been mainly structural in the sense that they represented basic imbalances between federal revenues and spending. These deficits would have persisted even if the economy were at full employment. For example, the U.S. economy was operating at close to full employment in 1996 when the unemployment rate was below 5.5 percent for most of the year. However, during that year the federal government incurred a deficit of $107 billion. Similarly, in 2005, when the economy was also running close to full employment with an unemployment rate of 5.1 percent, the federal government ran a deficit of $318 billion.

When a recession hits, such as the major recession that began in late 2007 in the United States, the deficit tends to grow as both revenues decline, in response to the decline in economic activity, and expenditures for entitlement programs grow, as more citizens become eligible for transfers as a result of declines in employment and income. The financial crisis that triggered the recession also resulted in emergency spending by the federal government to assist businesses in the financial and automotive sectors of the economy and prevent the undesirable effects of their economic failure. A stimulus bill designed to increase employment during the recession also added to federal spending causing the federal deficit to run up to levels unseen since World War II.

Rather than looking at the dollar amount of a deficit or surplus, most economists prefer to measure it as a share of GDP. GDP is a measure of the aggregate income generated from domestic production of goods and services. When we view a deficit as a percentage of GDP, we get a picture of the burden of federal borrowing as a share of aggregate income of the nation. In 2005, the federal budget deficit amounted to 2.6 percent of GDP and in 2004 it was 3.6 percent of GDP.

This means that the federal government borrowed an amount equivalent to 2.6 percent of the nation's aggregate income in 2005 and even more than that in the previous year. By 2009, the federal budget deficit was approaching 10.1 percent of GDP! This means that in that year the federal government was borrowing the equivalent of about 10.1 percent of the nation's domestic income to finance federal expenditures. Much of that borrowing was financed by foreigners purchasing federal government securities. As the deficit grows, so does the federal debt held by the public and foreigners. The very large deficits in 2009 and 2010 caused the federal government debt to the public to grow from 40 percent to over 60 percent of GDP and also result in federal interest payments on the debt increasing from 1 percent of GDP in 2008 to 1.4 percent of GDP by the end of 2012. The share of interest payments on the federal debt in GDP would have been even higher had not interest rates in the United States fallen to historically low levels over the same period.

Borrowing is an alternative to current taxation as a means of financing government expenditures. A **budget deficit** is the excess of government outlays over receipts taken in from taxes, fees, and charges levied by government authorities. A **budget surplus** is the excess of government receipts over government outlays. Figure 12.1 shows how the federal budget balance as a percentage of GDP has been negative, signifying a budget deficit, in most years over the period 1962–2012. Federal outlays have exceeded receipts in every year since 1962 except for 1969 and the period 1998–2001 when the balance was positive, indicating a budget surplus.

From a public finance point of view, using borrowing to finance government expenditures implies lower current taxes for citizens in the year deficits are incurred, but that greater portions of future tax revenue must be used to pay

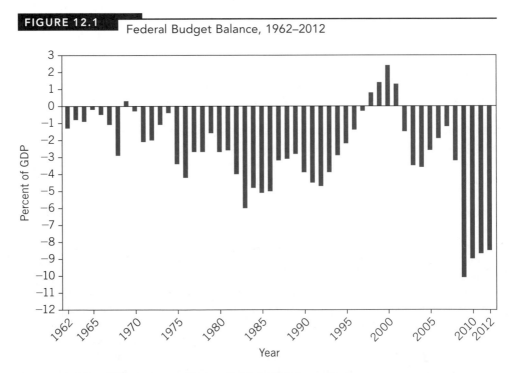

FIGURE 12.1   Federal Budget Balance, 1962–2012

Source: U.S. Office of Management and Budget. Deficit for 2012 is an estimate.

interest on debt instead of providing government services. If budget deficits persist for many years, current generations of taxpayers will shift the burden of taxation for government goods and services they enjoy to future generations of taxpayers. As you will soon see, the deficits also can reduce living standards of future generations by contributing to reduced industrial investment and lower economic growth.

As shown in Figure 12.1, the federal budget deficit remained between 2 and 6 percent of GDP over the period 1975–1985. Although the deficit declined as a percentage of GDP between 1983 and 1989, it began to rise as a share of GDP again in 1990. However, as a result of a growing economy and new legislation, the deficit declined from 1993 to 1999. From 1998 through 2001 there was a budget surplus. However, the surplus offered opportunities for government to fund new programs or reduce current taxes. Many politicians and economists argued that the surplus should be "saved" for future use particularly by retiring outstanding government debt. However, President George W. Bush argued that the surplus should be used to reduce tax rates. By 2002, the federal budget balance returned to deficit in part as a result of tax cuts enacted by Congress in 2001. Between 2001 and 2008, the deficit fluctuated between 1 and 3.6 percent of GDP before climbing to about 10.1 percent of GDP in 2009 as a result of the recession in that year. Slow economic growth in 2010 and 2011 continued to adversely affect both federal government expenditure and revenues, so despite the end of the recession in 2009, the deficit has persisted at high levels running between 8 and 9 percent of GDP.

State and local government budgets typically are in balance or run at a small surplus. However, because of unanticipated shortfalls of revenue, state and local government budgets in the aggregate had a small deficit in 2000 and 2001. The total government budget balance is obtained by adding state and local government budget balances to the federal deficit or surplus. Over the period 2002–2005, state and local budgets were in balance with neither a surplus nor a deficit. In 2009, most state governments were struggling to balance their budgets to eliminate deficits caused by the recession-induced decline in revenues. In some states, the deficits were running between 20 and 40 percent of current outlays, and rebalancing of the budgets required major cuts in state government services and painful increases in taxes. Since 2009, many state governments have still been in fiscal distress as tax collections lagged because of a sluggish recovery from the recession of 2007–2009, and as a result state government spending has not returned to its prerecession levels.

The High-Employment Deficit or Surplus

The size of the federal budget deficit or surplus in any given year is influenced by the fluctuations in economic activity normally associated with the business cycle. Federal government expenditures, such as those for unemployment insurance and public assistance to the needy, increase when unemployment rates go up. Tax revenues automatically increase with increases in employment and GDP. Corporate income tax collections are particularly sensitive to fluctuations in economic activity. Personal income tax collections based on a progressive rate structure also fluctuate with the level of economic activity.

The advantage of the automatic changes in the budget balance with the level of economic activity is that they help stabilize the economy. They do so by directly adding to the demand for goods and services when unemployment rates increase. Tax revenues decline more than proportionately with increases in unemployment, thereby maintaining disposable income. Similarly, unemployment insurance payments enable workers who are laid off to maintain their spending until they go back to work.

In any given year, the budget deficit or surplus reflects *both* the level of economic activity in that year and the structural imbalance between revenues and expenditures. It is possible to adjust for the influence of fluctuations in economic activity by computing the **high-employment deficit or surplus**. This calculation estimates the budget deficit or surplus that would prevail at a certain designated level of unemployment in the economy. The standardized level of unemployment is usually set between 5 and 6 percent. To estimate this deficit, receipts and expenditures are adjusted accordingly to reflect their levels if 94–95 percent of those in the labor force were actually employed. The benchmark level of unemployment is selected arbitrarily; some might argue that other levels should be used as the benchmark to calculate the deficit. In any event, after removing the impact of the deviations of economic activity from the benchmark high-employment level, any remaining deficit reflects a basic structural imbalance between government revenues and expenditures.

From 1960 to 1980, the high-employment budget deficit averaged less than 2 percent of GDP. In 1988, the economy was close enough to full employment so that the actual deficit could be viewed as the high-employment deficit. In that year, the deficit amounted to 3 percent of GDP. A positive high-employment deficit indicates that increases in the level of economic activity alone are not sufficient to eliminate the deficit. In 1995, an estimate of the high-employment deficit by the Congressional Budget Office placed its value at 1.9 percent of GDP, indicating that the deficit was not the result of the sluggish economy, and the deficit was providing considerable spending power to support economic activity at a time when the U.S. economy was expanding. Clearly, the federal deficit has been used in the United States primarily as a means of financing government expenditures rather than a means to stabilize the economy.

By 1999, when the federal government ran a budget surplus, the Congressional Budget Office estimated, using a 5.2 percent standardized level of unemployment, that, at high employment, the surplus was close to zero. Even though the dollar amount of the surplus was $126 billion, the actual unemployment rate was below the standardized level that year. Accordingly, the Office adjusted revenues downward and expenditures upward to a recalculated high-employment surplus of only $11 billion that year. In 2005, the CBO estimated that the U.S. economy's actual GDP was slightly below the high employment level of GDP and calculated a standardized federal budget deficit of $226 billion, which was below the actual deficit of $318 billion. In 2009, the economy was in a major recession with an unemployment rate close to 10 percent. The actual federal deficit that year of about $1.4 trillion was much higher than that which would have prevailed had the economy been at full employment that year with a standardized level of unemployment of between 5 and 6 percent. Because the unemployment rate remained abnormally high in 2010 and 2011, the federal budget deficit in those years was also greater than the high employment deficit and provided stimulus for the economy as well as financed federal expenditures.

Measuring the Budget Balance

Measurement of the federal government's budget deficit or surplus is complicated by the fact that some receipts and expenditures of the federal government operate through trust funds that are officially "off budget." The two main government operations treated in this way are Social Security and the U.S. Postal Service. In recent years, the Social Security trust funds have run a substantial surplus (in 2008 it was $180.2 billion), and so has the U.S. Postal Service, although its surplus was small (in 2008, it amounted to $3 billion). Even though trust funds are budgeted for separately, their revenues and expenditures affect the federal government's overall borrowing demands on the credit markets. When the Social Security trust funds run a surplus, the surplus is lent to the Treasury and reduces the Treasury's demands on the credit markets. Since 2008, the surplus from off-budget trust funds and the postal service has declined substantially to $67 billion as the small surplus from the postal service has turned into a deficit and the Social Security trust fund surplus has declined.

The *unified budget balance* is the difference between all federal government expenditures and all federal government revenues, be they "on budget" or "off budget." A unified budget deficit is the best measure of the amount of the funds that the federal government must borrow in any given year. However, from the point of view of measuring the long-term impact of a deficit or surplus on the economy, the unified budget has some shortcomings. The net economic effect of the budget depends entirely on the negative or positive saving it generates. In some cases, federal government's borrowing has been to cover existing debts of government insurance programs such as those for bank deposits and natural disasters. Such borrowing merely assumes old debt and reflects past obligations of the government that should have been included in past deficits but were not.

The *NIPA budget balance* is the official measure of the federal deficit in the National Income and Product Accounts (NIPA). The NIPA budget deficit or surplus does not include any transactions that finance preexisting debts, such as outlays for deposit insurance. The NIPA budget is the best measure of the net new debt that results from the federal budget deficit. For this reason, the NIPA budget is most often used to gauge the long-term impact of changes in the budget balance.

Like most economic magnitudes, the federal government deficit or surplus can be adjusted for inflation. The **real budget balance** is a measure of the change in the federal debt after adjustment for the effects of inflation and changing interest rates on the real market value of the outstanding net debt. Like all debtors, the federal government benefits from inflation because a rising price level causes the real value of its previously issued outstanding debt to decline. Fluctuating interest rate levels also affect the market value of outstanding debt in a given year. When interest rates rise, the market value of outstanding debt issued at lower interest rates tends to fall. Similarly, decreases in market interest rates tend to increase the market value of outstanding debt previously issued at higher interest rates. It follows that rising interest rates contribute to decreases in real debt while falling interest rates contribute to increases in real debt.

Analysis by the Congressional Budget Office suggests that unadjusted *changes* in the surplus or deficit as a percentage of GDP provide a reliable measure of the impact of the federal budget on the performance of the economy.[1] In particular, the CBO concludes that changes in the unadjusted deficit *as a percentage of GDP* provide a good indication of the burden of deficit finance on the public. An increase

---

[1]See U.S. Congress, Congressional Budget Office, *The Federal Deficit: Does It Measure the Government's Effect on National Saving?* (Washington, D.C.: U.S. Government Printing Office, March 1990).

P U B L I C   P O L I C Y   P E R S P E C T I V E

How Did the Deficit Get So Big in 2009? The Impact of Recessions and Public Policies

In 2001, the federal government was running a surplus equal to 1.5 percent of GDP and was paying down the federal debt as it had been doing since 1998. Then beginning in 2002 the red ink started to flow and deficit finance became the norm again. By 2009, the deficit had grown to more than 10 percent of GDP, and there seemed to be little chance that the federal government would balance its budget any time soon.

How did we return to deficit finance so quickly after a four-year interval of surpluses? The growth of the deficit has its roots partially in the business cycle—recessions in 2001 and 2007–2009—but public policy also plays a part. Tax cuts and a ramping up of military spending during the administration of George W. Bush after 2001 contributed to growth in the deficit. Debt was incurred to finance both the increased military spending and extension of Medicare pharmaceutical benefits to the elderly. During the Bush administration, a new Medicare prescription drug benefit (Medicare Part D) was enacted that increased health care spending. And as a result of aging of the population, spending for all parts of Medicare and Medicaid has increased. Extension of health insurance benefits to the uninsured is likely to also increase health care spending.

Military operations by the United States in Iraq and Afghanistan increased defense expenditures. Increased spending in 2008 and 2009 to stimulate the economy in the throes of a recession also added to the red ink and a likely growth in government spending for health care and Social Security in the future is likely to further widen the gap between federal outlays and revenues.

The business cycle plays an important role in influencing the deficit. The recession of 2001 reduced tax collections for the federal government and increased spending for transfer programs. Slower growth after the recession also caused revenues to grow more slowly than previously forecast. The effect of the recession from 2007 to 2009 sharply reduced revenues again and increased spending for safety net programs such as unemployment insurance and aid to the poor.

In October of 2008, the Congress enacted the *Emergency Economic Stabilization Act of 2008* in response to a financial crisis. This legislation was primarily designed to provide funds to financial institutions that had incurred losses as a result of the decline in the value of mortgage-backed securities. The Act authorized the U.S Secretary of the Treasury to inject up to $700 billion into the economy over

in the deficit implies an increase in the share of GDP that is borrowed by the federal government, while a decrease in the deficit or an increase in the surplus signals a decrease in the share of GDP that is borrowed by the federal government. The next step is to examine the impact of government borrowing or saving on national saving and the current, and more importantly, future performance of the U.S. economy.

CHECKPOINT

1. From a public finance point of view, what are the implications of a government budget deficit or a budget surplus?
2. How does the high-employment deficit or surplus differ from the actual deficit or surplus?
3. What is the real deficit or surplus?

several years to purchase illiquid assets through the Troubled Assets Relief Program (TARP) and prop up distressed banks by purchasing their corporate stock, thereby giving the federal government an ownership share in the financial institutions. A sum of $250 billion of the total was made available immediately upon enactment of the legislation with the remainder to be spent after a detailed plan was submitted by the president for approval by the Congress.

The purpose of the legislation was to prevent erosion of confidence in the United States financial system, reduce the risk of the failure of depository institutions, and restore the health of other financial intermediaries vital to the functioning of credit markets. The assets acquired by the government under this program could eventually be resold at a later date thereby offsetting some of the $700 billion cost to taxpayers with future revenue from asset sales and contributing to a reduction in the deficit. The legislation also increased deposit insurance on individual accounts at federally insured U.S. banks from $100,000 to $250,000, which could increase federal spending in the future if bank failures increase. Although the spending authorized by this legislation was primarily directed toward financial institutions, the goal was to improve the flow of credit to individuals and businesses thereby stimulating private spending and reducing foreclosures of

mortgages on private homes so as to prevent further erosion in home values and tax collections.

In the first weeks of the Obama presidency, Congress enacted the *American Recovery and Reinvestment Act of 2009* (ARRA). This legislation was intended to stimulate the U.S. economy with a combination of federal tax cuts, increases in transfer payments, such as unemployment insurance benefits and other social insurance, assistance to state and local governments, and an increase in federal government spending over several years in such areas as infrastructure (including roads and bridges), education, health care, and energy.

The increase in federal spending authorized under both these Acts was unprecedented in amount. Combined with estimated losses in revenue the federal government's budget deficit ballooned into the range of 10–11 percent of GDP.

The deficits of recent years have therefore resulted in part from increased spending and tax cuts. We have simply been financing basic federal government expenditure by borrowing. Although a fall in tax revenue and an increase in federal spending to stimulate the economy in 2009 might account for as much as 40 percent of the $1.4 trillion deficit in that year, the remainder is a result of the federal government systematically using the deficit as a means of finance.

ECONOMIC EFFECTS OF THE FEDERAL BUDGET BALANCE

A Deficit and Political Equilibrium

The mix and quantity of government services and investment depend, in part, on the means used to finance such government expenditures. By borrowing rather than using taxes to finance government activities, politicians can influence the willingness of voters to vote for increased spending. In other words, the political equilibrium quantity of government spending can be affected when we use deficit as opposed to tax finance. Deficits can affect both resource allocation (by influencing the types of government spending) and the overall size of the government sector in the economy. They also can influence prices and interest rates, thereby affecting the distribution on income.

By using deficit finance, we can keep taxes lower than they otherwise would be and still enjoy a given quantity and mix of government services. However, deficit finance also can allow higher government spending either for transfers or for purchases of goods and services without raising taxes. In fact, the federal deficits of the 1970s and 1980s were, in part, used to finance investments in military technology. However, much of the growth in federal spending during that period (as shown in Chapter 1) is accounted for by an unprecedented increase in transfers both in kind and as income support, mainly to the elderly.[2]

Because borrowing to finance deficits postpones the burden of taxation to the future, it makes sense to use deficits to finance government investments that will provide a stream of future benefits. This is efficient because taxes will then be distributed among future generations who will share the benefits of such government investments as roads, structures, transportation and communication networks, and environmental protection. Traditionally, nations have relied heavily on borrowing to finance wars and investments in military technology and equipment under the presumption that the removal of a threat to national security will provide future benefits for which future taxpayers should pay.

However, the deficits of the 1970s and 1980s were not incurred in a period of war or a period of significant increased national investment in infrastructure. Instead, much of the growth of spending that, in effect, was financed by the deficit was in the form of transfers of income and services (especially medical services) to the poor and the elderly. These federal expenditures mainly financed consumption as opposed to investment. The ratio of taxes to GDP remained quite stable during this period at around 20 percent of GDP, while federal outlays increased to 25 percent of GDP. The growing deficits of the 1970s and 1980s could be viewed as the outcome of a political system that satisfied the demand for increased federal transfer programs (many of which benefited the elderly) while preventing federal average tax rates (ATRs) from increasing significantly. It is possible that this growth in transfers could not have been approved through the political system if it were financed by increased taxes (or cuts in other types of spending) rather than by borrowing. Of course, it is difficult to pin down exactly what the deficit financed during this period because borrowing is not earmarked to any specific purpose. For example, use of the deficit also made it easier for both the Carter and Reagan administrations to gain political approval for increased government purchases for programs of investment in military technology.

A surplus also affects political equilibrium. Surpluses can be used to finance new government spending or tax rate reductions. A surplus can be maintained over the long term only if it does not give rise to political forces to spend it. During the presidential election of 2000, a major issue was what to do with the growing budget surplus. Some politicians advocated returning the surplus to "the people" through reduction in income tax rates targeted to benefit families. Others argued that the surplus should be saved to bolster the economy's future growth rate. The surplus was used, in part, to finance tax cuts enacted in 2001.

Between 2001 and 2005, deficit finance was once again employed to finance increased military expenditures for the war in Iraq and to defend the nation against terrorism. Both tax cuts and increased spending for social insurance, such as extension of Medicare coverage for prescription drugs, contributed to increased deficit spending. In 2006, the deficit moderated somewhat as the economy boomed but

---

[2]During the 1980s, when federal deficits were increasing as a share of GDP, spending on the elderly continued to grow, and it now absorbs nearly one-half of noninterest domestic spending by the federal government. See Rudolph G. Penner, "Federal Government Growth: Leviathan or Protector of the Elderly?" *National Tax Journal* 44, 1 (December 1991): 437–450.

as the recession began in 2007 deficit finance was once again employed to finance aid to financial institutions holding troubled assets, to assist the automotive industry, and to finance the ARRA of 2009 to stimulate the economy. Between 2011 and 2012, the budget deficit remained high as a share of GDP mainly as the result of a sluggish economy and extension of tax rate cuts to stimulate the economy.

Effect of a Deficit on Credit Markets

The economic effects of a federal budget deficit on the economy also depend on how it affects interest rates, national savings, and investment. The influence of a deficit on these economic variables is contingent on how the federal deficit influences the demand and supply of loanable funds in credit markets. A federal budget deficit adds to the national debt and, by doing so, increases the future interest costs to the federal government. Therefore, each year more and more tax revenues must be devoted to paying interest on the national debt instead of providing goods and services to citizens. Net interest paid by the federal government has increased from 6.8 percent of total expenditures in 1959 to 15 percent of expenditures in 1999. Since 1999, net interest has fallen to 6.4 percent of federal outlays in 2011 as interest rates have declined. The increase in the federal deficit beginning in 2009 is projected to increase net interest costs for the federal government to 12.5 percent of federal outlays by 2017, and this could even be higher if interest rates rise more than anticipated in the forecasts.

The traditional view of the economic effects of federal government budget deficits hypothesizes that, other things being equal, the deficit contributes to higher interest rates. By doing so, the deficit can choke off private investment, thereby slowing the real rate of economic growth for the nation. Figure 12.2 shows that an increase in demand for loanable funds by the government to finance a deficit can increase market interest rates. The market demand for loanable funds is composed of the demand for credit by households, business firms, state and local governments, and the federal government. When the federal government increases the demand for funds, it can bid up interest rates because it borrows a significant amount of the total available funds per year. The initial equilibrium is at point E, where the interest rate is i_1 and the total quantity of funds borrowed is L_1.

As shown in Figure 12.2, an increase in government demand for funds shifts the market demand curve from D_1 to $D_1 + \Delta D_G$ and results in a new market equilibrium at E'. The market rate of interest increases to i_2, and the quantity of loanable funds supplied increases to L_2. The increase in the market rate of interest decreases the quantity of loanable funds demanded by business firms for investment. It also chokes off some borrowing by households to finance acquisition of such durable goods as automobiles and homes. At the same time, higher interest rates encourage more saving, thereby decreasing private consumption in the current year.

The budget deficit can be represented by the distance BE' in Figure 12.2, which is the difference between private borrowing, L, and total borrowing L_2 after the government finances its deficit. Part of the budget deficit is financed by an increase in the quantity of loanable funds supplied to the markets represented by the distance L_1L_2. The remainder of the budget deficit is financed by a reduction in borrowing for private investment represented by the distance L_1L. This is a reduction in the quantity of loanable funds demanded to finance private investment that results from the increase in the market equilibrium interest rate from i_1 to i_2. These funds are then reallocated to buy government securities that finance the deficit.

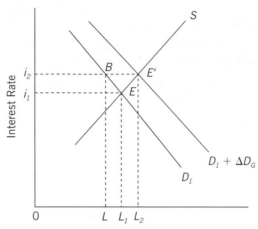

FIGURE 12.2 Government Demand for Loanable Funds and the Market Rate of Interest

An increase in government demand for loanable funds to cover budget deficits shifts the demand curve from D_1 to $D_1 + \Delta D_G$. This increases the equilibrium market rate of interest from i_1 to i_2. The higher interest rate increases the quantity of loanable funds supplied to the market but also "crowds out" some private borrowing that would have otherwise occurred. As the quantity of funds demanded for private investment falls, these funds are reallocated to finance the deficit.

© Cengage Learning

Many, but not all, economists attribute the high real interest rates of the mid-1980s in the United States to the effect of the budget deficit on the demand for credit.[3] High interest rates hurt consumers by making it more difficult to borrow funds to purchase homes and other durable goods. They harm workers by decreasing the quantity of annual investment. This, in turn, decreases job opportunities. Reduced private investment also contributes to lagging worker productivity, resulting in lower wages than otherwise would be the case. Higher interest rates also increase the demand for U.S. dollars by foreigners who seek to invest dollars earned from foreign trade. This bids up the price of dollars compared with other currencies and makes U.S. goods less competitive in international markets.

The idea that the federal deficit can increase interest rates and choke off investment is not accepted by all economists. The classical economists of 19th-century

---

[3]See Laurence H. Meyer, (ed.), *The Economic Consequences of Government Deficits* (Boston: Kluwer-Nijhoff Publishing, 1983). Some research, however, indicates little relation between government deficits and interest rates. One such research study on the impact of federal borrowing on short-term interest rates found that increased borrowing had little effect on the market interest rates. See Gregory P. Hoelscher, "Federal Borrowing and Short-Term Interest Rates," *Southern Economic Journal* 50 (October 1983): 319–333. For more recent analysis of the impact of deficits on long-term interest rates see William G. Gale and Samara R. Potter, "An Economic Evaluation of the Economic Growth and Tax Relief Reconciliation Act of 2001," *National Tax Journal* 55 (March 1, 2002): 133–186. Recent analysis does indicate that deficits do increase long-term interest rates and reduce national saving. See William G. Gale and Peter R. Orszag, "Budget Deficits, National Savings, and Interest Rates," *Brookings Papers on Economic Activity* (September 2004). Their empirical analysis suggests that each percentage of GDP in current deficits reduces national saving by 0.5–0.8 percent of GDP. Each percentage of GDP in projected future-unified deficits raises forward long-term interest rates by 25–35 basis points, and each percentage of GDP in projected future primary deficits raises interest rates by 40–70 basis points.

England believed that interest rates, current economic activity, and economic growth would be unaffected by the way the government financed its expenditures. David Ricardo, the famous English classical economist (1772–1832), argued that increased government borrowing can result in increased saving by forward-looking taxpayers. These taxpayers know that the government will have to raise taxes in the future to pay back what it borrowed and the interest on those funds. To prepare for the higher future tax burdens, Ricardo argued that they will increase their current saving by an amount exactly equal to the deficit. When the government runs a deficit, according to Ricardo, households will cut their consumption so they can save more and prepare for the higher future taxes they know will come.

If an increase in government borrowing to finance a deficit causes a sufficient increase in private saving to keep the level of interest rates in the economy fixed, **Ricardian equivalence** prevails. According to the idea of Ricardian equivalence, both tax finance and deficit finance have the same impact on current aggregate spending and future economic growth. If Ricardian equivalence prevails, an increase in government borrowing will be exactly offset by an equal reduction in consumption as households seek to save to finance higher future taxes. The result is no increase in aggregate current spending, no effect on interest rates, no crowding out of private investment, and therefore no reduction in future economic growth.[4] The idea of Ricardian equivalence has been advanced in recent years by the American economist Robert Barro of Harvard University.

It is easy to see why increased private saving as a result of deficit finance can offset the impact of increased demand for funds on interest rates as the government borrows more to finance its deficit. The graph in Figure 12.3 shows that the increase in government borrowing to cover the deficit increases the demand for loanable funds. However, as a direct result of this borrowing, the supply of savings increases from S to S' to provide funds for higher taxes anticipated in the future. The increase in the supply of loanable funds results in a new equilibrium at point E. At that point, an additional ΔL dollars of loanable funds are made available per year for financing future taxes resulting from the deficit. The equilibrium amount of loanable funds is now L_3 dollars per year. If these extra funds exactly equal the amount of funds required to finance the deficit, the interest rate under the equilibrium is i_1, the initial level.

Thus, this view concludes that government borrowing to cover deficits does not increase the market rate of interest. It causes no crowding out of private investment or of consumer borrowing for durable goods. The deficit does not matter according to this view.[5] This means that changes in the deficit will not affect aggregate demand, because changes in government borrowing will be offset by changes in private saving.

Empirical research on the impact of deficits on saving suggests that an increase in saving occurs as a result of budget deficits in the United States. However, the research also indicates that the increase in saving does not appear to offset exactly the increase in government borrowing, which implies that upward pressure on

---

[4]For a rigorous discussion of Ricardian equivalence, see John J. Seater, "Does the Government Debt Matter? A Review," *Journal of Monetary Economics* 16 (July 1985): 121–131. Also see Roberto Ricciuti, "Assessing Ricardian Equivalence," *Journal of Economic Surveys* 17 (2003): 55–78. Available at SSRN: http://ssrn.com/abstract=377104.

[5]Considerable empirical evidence supports this view. See Charles I. Plosser, "Government Financing Decisions and Asset Returns," *Journal of Monetary Economics* 9 (May 1982): 325–353; and John J. Seater and Roberto S. Mariano, "New Tests of the Life Cycle and Tax Discounting Hypothesis," *Journal of Monetary Economics* 15 (March 1985): 195–215.

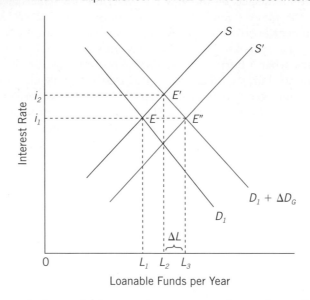

FIGURE 12.3   Ricardian Equivalence: Deficits Do Not Affect Interest Rates

Under Ricardian equivalence, the increase in government borrowing to finance the deficit is exactly offset by an increase in annual private savings to pay the taxes necessary in the future to retire the debt. Consequently, the interest rate does not increase above its initial level, i_1.

© Cengage Learning

interest rates is likely a result of government deficits.[6] Increased private saving caused by government deficits can lead to increased bequests, or intergenerational transfers, between citizens who are living now and their heirs. The increased saving by those who currently pay taxes that results from deficit-induced saving allows them to increase their own voluntary private bequests to their children beyond the amounts that would be possible if tax finance were used. These bequests help the future generation to pay the higher taxes that will be necessary to cover the interest payments on the debt in the future. Similarly, the reduced tax burden on the current generation, made possible by debt finance, decreases the likelihood that these tax-payers in their old age will need transfers from their children. The compensating intergenerational transfer therefore decreases the burden of the debt on the future generation.[7]

Effect of a Budget Surplus on Credit Markets

When the federal government's budget is in balance or in surplus, naturally there is no need for the government to enter the credit markets as a borrower. A balanced budget or a budget in surplus implies that the market demand for credit is equal to the private demand for credit. However, when the government runs a surplus, it can

[6]See Michael J. Boskin, "Consumption, Saving, and Fiscal Policy," *American Economic Review* 78, 2 (May 1988): 401–407.

[7]See Robert J. Barro, "Public Debt and Taxes," in *Federal Tax Reform*, Michael J. Boskin, (ed.), (San Francisco: Institute for Contemporary Studies, 1978).

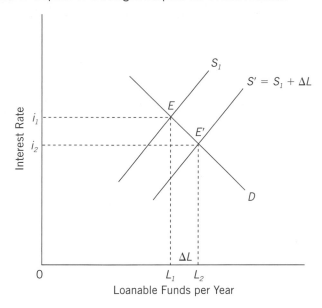

FIGURE 12.4   Impact of a Budget Surplus on Credit Markets

An increase in supply of loanable funds results from using a surplus to repay existing federal debt. By repaying the debt, the federal government adds loanable funds to the credit markets. The increase in supply lowers market interest rates and encourages more investment.

affect the supply of loanable funds available for private investment in the credit markets. Figure 12.4 illustrates the possible effect of a surplus used to retire outstanding government debt on the credit market and the equilibrium market interest rate.

If the budget is balanced so that there is neither a surplus nor a deficit, the demand for credit will be D and that demand will be equal to private demand for credit. The market equilibrium interest will be i_1. If the government runs a surplus and uses that surplus to retire existing debt, then the supply of credit will increase from S_1 to S' where S' is equal to $S_1 + \Delta L$, and ΔL is the amount of government debt that is retired. By retiring the debt, the federal government exchanges bonds for cash, thereby increasing the supply of loanable funds. Other things being equal, this increased supply of loanable funds causes the market equilibrium interest rate to decline from i_1 to i_2. The lower interest rate increases the quantity of loanable funds demanded for investment and other private borrowing from L_1 to L_2. The increased investment contributes to increases in future worker productivity and can increase future income and living standards.

If instead of being dedicated to retiring existing debt, the surplus is used as a source of public finance and therefore allows taxes to be reduced, the effects are likely to be different. If the surplus is used for tax reductions, then it supplies funds to consumers as well as investors. If households decide to use the extra funds they receive from tax cuts for consumption instead of saving, then there will be no increase in the supply of loanable funds and no decline in real interest rates. Given the meager saving rates of U.S. households (in the range of 1 percent of disposable income), the most likely scenario for tax cuts is, in fact, increased consumption and no increase in savings rates. Because it is saving and investment that contributes to economic growth, many economists and politicians would like surpluses to be used to retire the debt.

Of course, other things can offset the potential increase in supply of loanable funds resulting from use of surpluses to retire debt. The Federal Reserve could offset the effects in credit markets with restrictive monetary policy. It is also possible that higher savings rates by government could be offset by lower savings rates by households (although this cannot get much lower), businesses, and foreigners in the United States.

Budget Balance, National Saving, and Economic Growth

A nation's rate of economic growth, the expansion of its potential to produce goods and services, depends on investment. Investment requires a sacrifice of current consumption so that the resources used to produce goods for today can be reallocated to the production of capital goods. When we save more, we can allocate more resources to the development of new technology, production of new machinery, and investment in people through education. The more we save today, the greater our future rate of growth of output. Conversely, the less we save, the smaller our future potential to grow.

National saving is the sum of personal saving by households, business saving, and saving by the government sector. The government sector contributes to an increase in national saving when it spends less than it takes in. In other words, for government to help increase national saving, it would have to run a budget *surplus*. When the government sector runs a deficit, it spends more than it takes in and therefore must borrow instead of save.

The net contribution of the government sector to national saving is the combined deficit or surplus of the federal government and all state and local governments. When the government sector runs a deficit, it contributes to a decline in national saving. In effect, a government deficit amounts to negative saving that absorbs loanable funds rather than making them available for investment. When the government sector runs a surplus, more revenue is taken in during the year than is spent. Just like you save when your income exceeds your expenses, so does the government sector save when revenues exceed outlays. In such cases, as explained earlier, the government sector surplus adds loanable funds to credit markets.

Figure 12.5 shows the gross national saving rate and its components from 1964 to 2012. Gross national savings declined from more than 20 percent of aggregate income to less than 11 percent in 2009. Negative saving by government in the form of deficits contributed to a decline in the national savings rate in the 1980s and the first half of the 1990s, and between 2001 and 2005, government saving fell substantially in 2008 after the recession began. Gross business savings, which consists of capital consumption allowances and undistributed corporate profits, is fairly stable and runs between 12 and 15 percent of gross national income. Personal savings of households fell precipitously between 1990 and 2007 from 6 percent of gross national income to zero. Personal saving rose in 2008 after the recession began. Since 1999, national saving has fallen to 13 percent of gross national income and government saving has plummeted from 5 percent of gross national income to −5 percent.

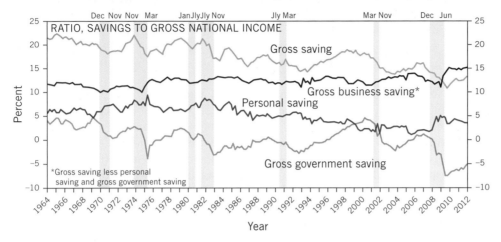

National saving in the United States as a percentage of gross national income fell substantially between 1998 and 2009. Since 2009 national saving has risen from 10 percent of gross national income to nearly 14 percent as business and personal saving has increased and government borrowing has declined.

Source: Department of Commerce; Bureau of Economic Analysis.

For most of the period between 1980 and 1995, government saving was negative. Government saving is the sum of saving by federal, state, and local governments. The major cause of negative saving by the government sector during this period was the federal budget deficit. During this same period, state and local governments in the aggregate actually ran surpluses, thereby contributing to national savings. From 1996 to 2001, government saving had been positive, thanks to a federal budget surplus and an equally strong surplus position for most state and local governments. However, by 2002 government saving had moved into negative range again because of the recurrence of deficits. As a result of budget surpluses run by state and local governments, saving moved into positive territory between 2005 and 2007. However, government saving plummeted in 2008 as a result of sharply increased federal government deficits. Between 2009 and 2011 negative saving by the government sector moderated from −8 percent of gross national income to −5 percent of gross national income.

Why worry about reduced savings? A reduced supply of savings can contribute to higher real interest rates and lower economic growth. If we save less, we will devote less of our current production to investment, which is the driver of future economic growth. Lower economic growth causes a slowdown in the rate of improvement of living standards. U.S. savings rates have been much lower than those of other industrial nations in recent years.

The federal deficits averaged 4.5 percent of net national product (which is gross national product (GNP) less depreciation) in the 1980s. In the 1970s, the federal deficit averaged only 2 percent of net national product. The rising share of GDP absorbed by the government deficit reduces national saving and lowers future living standards, other things being equal. Federal budget deficits averaged 9 percent of GDP between 2009 and 2011.

By absorbing saving that could otherwise be used for private investment, a federal deficit can slow economic growth and reduce the rate at which our standards of living improve.

The Incidence of Deficit Finance

What is the incidence of deficit finance? If, as many economists believe, deficit finance bids up real interest rates and contributes to both a reduction in national saving and a reduction in national investment, then deficit finance contributes to a slowdown in capital formation and economic growth. This, in turn, implies that the rate of growth of income will be slower in the future so that future taxpayers (younger people) will have lower future incomes than otherwise would be possible. Unfortunately, these young people also will be subject to higher taxes and greater portions of their tax payments are being used to finance interest costs of growing federal debt. Thus, deficit finance is likely to redistribute the burden of financing government outlays from the current generation to future generations of taxpayers. If, on average, these taxpayers have lower income than the current generation, in part, because of the undesirable effects of taxes on economic growth, then this incidence could be regressive.

However, to get a full picture of the incidence of deficit finance, we also need to look at possible offsetting effects. One possible effect is suggested by the hypothesis of Ricardian equivalence. If the current generation of taxpayers realizes that deficit finance implies higher taxes for themselves and their descendants, they could increase their current saving. This increase in saving increases the supply of loanable funds in credit markets and could offset both the negative saving of the deficit itself and any possible crowding out of private investment.

It also is possible that deficit finance permits a change in political equilibrium so that more government spending is allocated to investment in infrastructure and other spending that will yield a stream of benefits to future generations. Under these circumstances, even if private investment is crowded out as a result of higher interest rates, future economic growth rates need not decline as long as the government investment is at least as productive as the private investment that it displaces.

Government deficits also can contribute to increased government purchases that keep the economy from having severe recessions and help keep it on a steady path of economic growth near its potential. If this is the case, the deficit can actually increase private investment by contributing to economic stability. A stable economy with few severe downturns not only encourages investment by domestic producers but also can encourage inflow of foreign saving and investment.

Unfortunately, the federal deficits in the 1970s and 1980s in the United States appear to have allowed growth in federal transfers (mainly to people older than 65) that encouraged consumption rather than investment. Therefore, unless a significant increase in national saving has occurred as a result of the deficit (which does not seem to be the case), the incidence of deficit finance will be on future generations.

The incidence of a surplus also depends on how it is used. If the surplus is used to retire debt, it will contribute to lower interest rates. If those lower interest rates result in increased investment, the effects could be felt throughout the economy as increased productivity contributes to higher worker incomes. If instead the surplus is used to lower taxes, it could benefit upper-income households disproportionately. This is because the upper-income groups in the United States pay proportionately more in taxes than lower-income groups and are more likely to benefit from tax cuts.

CHECKPOINT

1. How can a government budget deficit cause the level of interest rates to rise for an economy? How can a budget surplus cause interest rates to fall?
2. What is Ricardian equivalence, and what does it imply about the impact of a government budget deficit on the economy and the desirability of borrowing versus raising taxes to finance government expenditures?
3. What is national saving, and how does the government sector of the economy affect the national savings rate?

GOVERNMENT DEBT

As of mid-2012, the gross public debt of the U.S. Treasury amounted to $15.7 trillion. The debt of state and local governments amounted to an additional $3 trillion. Borrowing has been a major source of government finance despite the controversy that surrounds its use. By far, the major share of controversy concerns the federal debt rather than the debt of state and local governments. This is not merely because the federal debt is larger than the debt of state and local governments but also because of the real economic differences in the use, funding, and ownership pattern of the securities that are issued by federal governments and by state and local governing bodies. The problem of the federal, or central, government use of debt is considered next, followed by a discussion of the use of debt as a means of finance for state and local governments.

Magnitude and Structure of Federal Debt in the United States

The **net federal debt** is that portion of the debt of the federal government held by the general public, excluding the holdings of U.S. government agencies, trust funds, and the Federal Reserve banks. As of June 2012, the net debt totaled about $11 trillion, representing 70 percent of GDP. Between 1950 and 1970, however, the net federal debt, when expressed as a percentage of GDP on a fiscal year basis, declined steadily, from about 75 percent to approximately 22 percent. From 1970 to 1980, the monetary amount of debt outstanding rose astronomically, but debt as a percentage of GDP remained more or less constant. Mainly as a result of the recession of 2007–2009 and other policies that increased the federal budget deficit to help stimulate the economy, the net federal debt nearly doubled in the four-year period from mid-2009 to mid-2012.

Figure 12.6 shows the net federal debt from 1790 to 2011. Federal debt held by the public declined after World War II from more than 100 percent of GDP to 20 percent of GDP in the mid-1970s. The deficits of the last quarter of the

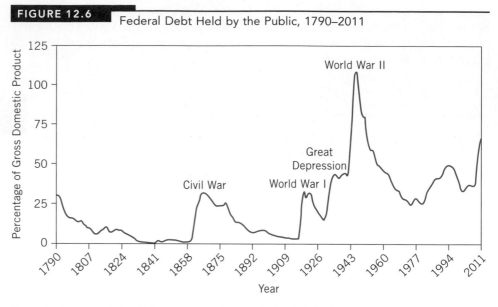

FIGURE 12.6   Federal Debt Held by the Public, 1790–2011

Over the history of the United States, the net federal debt has fluctuated typically rising during wars and recession periods. The federal debt held by the public reached a peak of over 100 percent of GDP during World War II. By 1977, much of that debt was paid off, and the net federal debt declined to 25 percent of GDP. The debt rose substantially as a share of GDP during the 1980s as a result of large federal budget deficits and peaked at 50 percent of GDP in 1994. Strong economic growth and a brief period of federal budget surpluses contributed to a decline in the net federal debt as a share of GDP from 1995 to 2001. Since the recession of 2007–2009 the debt has more than doubled as a share of GDP.

Sources: Congressional Budget Office; Office of Management and Budget.

20th century contributed to an increased net public debt share of GDP. After peaking at 50 percent of GDP in 1995, the debt has declined as a share of GDP. Since 2001, the debt as a share of GDP has risen to nearly 75 percent of GDP.

Unless changes are made soon in the federal budget that cut spending or raise taxes, the Congressional Budget Office projects that the federal debt could rise to over 175 percent of GDP by 2035—a level that would eclipse that which prevailed at the end of World War II.

The total volume of the gross federal government debt outstanding at any point in time reflects the previous and current budget deficits and the accumulated interest burden on the securities issued to cover those deficits. To retire the public debt—that is, to allow existing issues of securities to be paid off at their maturity without replacing them with additional debt obligations of the federal government—would require that the federal government budget be operated at a surplus for a considerable number of years.

Ownership Pattern of the Federal Debt

To help evaluate the costs of the debt, it is useful to study the structure of the federal debt in terms of its ownership pattern. Table 12.1 presents data on the gross federal debt of the U.S. Treasury by type of holder as of June 2012. As of that

TABLE 12.1	Gross Public Debt of the U.S. Treasury by Holder, June 2012	
HOLDER	**AMOUNT OF DEBT (TRILLIONS OF DOLLARS)**	**PERCENTAGE OF TOTAL**
U.S. Government Agencies, Trust Funds, and Federal Reserve Banks	4.9	31
Private Investors	11.0	69
Total	15.9	100.0

Source: U.S. Treasury, Bureau of Public Debt.

date, the total federal debt outstanding was $15.9 trillion, of which 31 percent was held by government agencies, trust funds, and the Federal Reserve banks. The remaining 69 percent was held by various financial institutions and private investors and represents the net debt of the U.S. Treasury. The federal debt held by the Federal Reserve banks represents acquisitions of such securities as part of the Federal Reserve's open market activities. Such holdings represent an exchange of interest-bearing securities of the U.S. government for noninterest-bearing dollars. The Federal Reserve System purchases such securities in exchange for deposits in the various Federal Reserve banks, which become part of the commercial banking system's reserve base.

Table 12.2 shows the ownership pattern of the net debt outstanding as of June 2012. Depository institutions (banks) in the United States held 3.25 percent of the debt at that time while 9.2 percent was held by mutual funds, 5.5 percent by state and local governments, 8.5 percent by pension funds, and 57 percent by foreigners or in international accounts. The remainder was held mainly by various types of individual investors and businesses.

The portion of a government's indebtedness owed to its own citizens is an **internal debt.** Repayment of internal debt represents a redistribution of purchasing power from certain groups of citizens who pay taxes and other citizens who in the past

TABLE 12.2	Net Public Debt of the U.S. Treasury by Holder (Percentage Distribution), June 2012
HOLDER	**PERCENTAGE OF TOTAL**
Depository Institutions	3.25
Mutual Funds	9.22
Insurance Companies	2.76
Pension Funds	8.47
State and Local Governments	5.54
Foreign and International Accounts	56.62
Other Investors	14.13
Total	100.00

Source: U.S. Department of Treasury.

have been creditors of the federal government. When a central government borrows mainly from its citizens, the opportunity cost is forgone consumption and investment in this country rather than from foreign sources. More than half of the net debt outstanding as of the end of June 2012 represented funds, or **external debt**, borrowed from abroad. When external debt is repaid, resources necessarily flow out of the nation, with a consequent loss in productive opportunities. The external debt varies with interest rates in the United States relative to those that can be earned on funds abroad and the U.S. balance of international trade with the rest of the world.

When much of the U.S. debt is an internal debt, many argue that repayment will not involve export of economic resources. Those who hold this view further argue that only little concern is justified about the total volume of the debt and its interest charge because any refunding or payment of interest on the debt at maturity involves merely a redistribution of purchasing power among citizens.

However, the portion of debt actually held by foreigners has grown rapidly since 1970, and as of the end of June 2012, nearly 60 percent of the debt was held by foreigners. It could grow even faster in the future if the United States continues to run balance-of-trade deficits, which put dollars into the hands of foreigners, and if interest rates increase significantly above those available on competing securities (both foreign and domestic). Conversion of the national debt into one that is increasingly more external can have serious consequences for future growth opportunities in the United States if taxes must be raised to pay foreigners for past loans to the federal government. Under such circumstances, paying off the debt would involve outflows of funds and real losses in productive opportunities rather than mere redistributive effects. There is also concern that heavy reliance on foreign borrowing can cause real interest rates to rise in the United States if foreigners become concerned about the foreign exchange rate of the dollar. If the dollar falls in value, the investment income return to foreign holders of the debt denominated in dollars will be worth less in foreign currency. If foreigners become reluctant to acquire U.S. debt for that reason, then interest rates would have to rise to compensate them for foreign exchange risks. The higher interest rates could reduce real private domestic investment thereby slowing future growth in the United States.

BORROWING BY STATE AND LOCAL GOVERNMENTS

The ability of central, or federal, governments to print money as a last resort makes the risk of default on the securities of such governments virtually nil (unless the government is overthrown). However, federal debt does remain subject to the risk of reduced value due to inflation. On the other hand, state and local governments, because they cannot monetize their debt, conceivably can default on their debt obligations. As a result, from the point of view of investors, state (or provincial) and municipal securities are inherently more risky than federal government securities. The interest that state and local governments must pay on their various security issues depends not only on the maturity of such issues but also on the risks of default as well as the risks of inflation.

Typically, the debt issues of various state and local governments are evaluated by private bond-rating services according to their riskiness based on past repayment history. If a state or local government defaults on repayment of a security issue, its bond rating would be unfavorably affected. This will result in higher risk premiums, causing the cost of borrowing to that particular government to rise. Any given state or local government borrows such a small amount in the markets for loanable funds at any given time that it cannot influence interest rates as can the federal government.

Characteristics of State and Local Government Debt

Because the debts of state and local governments are marketed nationally, the particular governing body that issues the securities has no control over who purchases them. Much of the holdings of the debt of any particular state or local government is likely to be in the external debt category; that is, it is held by people not residing in the government jurisdiction. This implies that issuance of the debt allows importation of funds, but repayment necessarily will involve a significant drainage of purchasing power out of the government jurisdiction in question. Thus, undue reliance on debt finance can result in a significant redistribution of future income away from residents of the locality, as tax revenues are used to pay creditors who reside in other jurisdictions. This makes borrowing by state and local governments somewhat similar to private borrowing by individuals, unlike borrowing by the federal government.

State and Local Debt Management

State and local government authorities must concern themselves with minimizing the interest burden on their debt and with the risk of default. State and local governments issue two broad types of securities to cover their debt: general obligation bonds and revenue bonds.

General obligation bonds are backed by the taxing power of the government that issues the securities, whereas **revenue bonds** are backed by the promise of revenue to be earned on the facility being financed by the bonds. Revenue bonds typically are used to finance roads and bridges and other facilities (such as sports stadiums) that will generate revenue through tolls and other forms of user charges. Investors often consider general obligation bonds to be safer than revenue bonds; as a result, general obligation bonds often can be floated at interest rates lower than those on revenue bonds of similar maturity for the same government unit. Nevertheless, some inherent risk does exist for investors in that even general obligation bonds are subject to default risk. This is because reductions in state or local economic activity could make it difficult for these government units to raise the tax revenues necessary to repay their debts.

Long-term debt financing by state and local governments can be justified on the basis of the benefit principle for financing capital projects. Because capital expenditures by state and local governments involve the construction of facilities (roads, public institutions, and other structures) that will provide a stream of public services to future citizens of the state or municipality, it is reasonable to finance such expenditures through debt. This postpones the burden of taxation to future taxpayers, making particular sense in a community where citizens are mobile. Financing capital expenditures through current taxation results in the taxation of current residents who often will not be residents of the taxing jurisdiction when the capital facilities are completed. For this reason, debt finance allows collective approval for projects that will benefit future citizens, even though those citizens are not present to vote at the time of approval. Spreading the cost over time induces current residents to consider voting affirmatively for projects that they would not support if they knew they were to be taxed for the full cost in one year. Many state and local governments have separate capital budgets that involve projects financed exclusively by public borrowing.

BURDEN OF THE DEBT

Debt financing implies the sale of a security that bears the promise to pay interest over a given number of years and to return the principal loaned at the end of the given time period. No compulsion is involved in the sale of such securities. Instead, governments compete with other borrowers in the market for loanable funds. The government pays the going market rate of interest, adjusted for risk and maturity characteristics of the obligation that it issues. Accordingly, the issuance of government debt is similar to the sale of services that have the regular characteristics of private goods. Governments sell securities of various types and maturities (for example, savings bonds or U.S. Treasury bills) that compete with various private securities, such as savings deposits and corporate bonds.

A great deal of controversy exists concerning the appropriateness of debt finance by the various levels of government in the United States. What is the *burden* of the debt, and what are the relative advantages of debt financing compared with tax financing?

Burden of the Debt and Income Redistribution

The **burden of the debt** is the redistributive effect of debt financing. Consider the impact of debt financing in elementary terms. When governments obtain funds to finance public expenditures by issuing debt, no compulsion is involved, unlike tax financing. Instead, securities issued by government authorities are purchased voluntarily by individual citizens, financial institutions, and other private economic units.

The individuals who purchase such securities surrender present consumption opportunities for future consumption opportunities, or they substitute public debt for private securities in their portfolio. They make this voluntary sacrifice because the return that they expect to receive on their forgone consumption exceeds their subjective estimate of the cost of sacrificing current consumption opportunities. At the same time, debt financing makes it unnecessary to increase current taxes, thereby avoiding the need to force citizens to curtail current consumption and saving. Under debt financing, private investment is "choked off" only to the extent to which increased government borrowing causes, by increasing the demand for credit, the general level of interest rates to rise. Thus, compared with tax financing, debt financing allows the current generation more private consumption opportunities over its lifetime than could be enjoyed if taxes were used.

To pay interest on the debt and return the principal, the government usually increases taxes. If so, other things being equal, taxpayers in the future undergo reductions in consumption or saving. The increased tax revenues necessary to pay interest on the debt redistribute income from the taxpayers to the holders of public debt. Because about 43 percent of the federal debt in the United States is owed to U.S. citizens, its retirement would not represent a complete drain of resources from the country; therefore, much of the effect of such retirement would be to redistribute income among citizens.

Impact of Debt on Future Generations

Some economists argue that the burden of the debt cannot be transferred to future generations but must be borne by the present generation, because resources are withdrawn from the private sector at the time the debt is created. This definition of burden implies that debt creation merely involves forgone private consumption in the current period. It neglects the fact that this sacrifice of consumption is completely voluntary on the part of the private economic units and is compensated by greater opportunities for future consumption as a result of interest payments on government securities.[8]

Under the assumption that the future generation must be taxed to pay the interest burden on the debt, that generation must undergo a real reduction of income, without the compensation of increased future consumption. In this sense, the burden of the debt does fall on the future generation; it bears the brunt of compulsory taxes. The burden of the debt is a reduction in welfare for future taxpayers who do not hold or inherit government securities that are paid off in the future.[9] Future generations will pay more in taxes to pay interest instead of receiving government goods and services in return for those taxes. Interest amounted to about 15 percent of federal expenditures in the 1990s, so 15 cents of each dollar taxpayers paid were used to pay interest to holders of the net federal debt rather than to provide such services as roads and education. By 2008, interest on the federal debt had fallen to 8.5 percent of federal spending. As a result of historically low interest rates in 2011, interest payments fell to less than 7 percent of federal expenditures in that year. However, unless the outstanding amount of debt is reduced, interest payments are likely to increase substantially as a share of federal spending in the future especially if market rates of interest start rising.

Future generations also will suffer a reduction in their living standards as a result of the federal debt if past deficits cause interest rates to rise and reduce private investment. A reduction in private investment implies that the capital stock of the nation will grow more slowly than it would have otherwise. The effect will be slower economic growth for the economy. Because workers in the private sector will have less capital to work with than they otherwise would have, productivity and therefore their incomes also will be lower. This implies a growing national debt and a reduction in future living standards. This burden, however, can be offset if increased saving by the current generation of taxpayers results from the use of deficit financing. According to this view of government deficits, this is a likely outcome and will result in increased bequests to future taxpayers that offset the burden of the debt.

The burden of the debt can also be offset if the revenue obtained from the issuance of public debt is used to finance projects that yield future benefits. On the basis of the benefit principle, it might be viewed as efficient to transfer the burden of present expenditures to future generations if it can be demonstrated that particular expenditures will benefit them. For example, it is reasonable to postpone until the future the burden of taxes for financing war, because the benefits of a successfully completed (that is, won) war will accrue to those living in the country in the future.

---

[8]See James M. Buchanan, "The Italian Tradition in Fiscal Theory," *Public Debt and Future Generations*, James M. Ferguson, (ed.), (Chapel Hill: University of North Carolina Press, 1964): 48–49.

[9]The interpretation has been emphasized by James M. Buchanan in *Public Principles of Public Debt* (Homewood, Ill.: Richard D. Irwin, 1958).

GLOBAL   PERSPECTIVE

Consequences of Uncontrolled Budget Deficit Growth: The Case of Turkey

Turkish citizens have much of the taxes they pay to the government allocated to pay interest on an enormous government debt that resulted from uncontrolled deficit financing of government expenditures in the 1990s. In the early 1990s the Turkish government financed salary increases to government workers and transfers to state-owned enterprises with borrowing. In 1992, the government budget deficit was approaching a whopping 20 percent of GDP in Turkey! The central bank of Turkey assisted in the process by expanding the money stock in line with the government borrowing, and by mid-1993, inflation rates in Turkey were running at around 75 percent. A whole slew of economic problems resulted from the out-of-control fiscal situation. As investors tried to put their funds into assets denominated in foreign currencies, the exchange rate of the Turkish lira on the foreign exchange market fell precipitously, and Turkey's government debt was downgraded. By 1994, the Turkish government was forced to take draconian measures to deal with the fiscal crisis by cutting back government spending and eliminating transfers to state enterprises. Taxes were increased and a pledge was made to privatize many of the state-run enterprises. The measures designed to reduce the deficit then plunged the Turkish economy into a deep recession.

Turkey is still suffering from the consequences of the enormous budget deficits of the 1990s. Between 1994 and 2004, government debt as a percentage of GDP grew from less than 15 percent to nearly 60 percent. The increased debt along with increases in domestic interest rates meant the Turkish taxpayers would see higher percentages of the tax monies used to pay interest on the government debt instead of being used to supply government services and transfers to citizens. In 2001, the Turkish government underestimated interest payments because of an unexpected increase in market rates of interest and had to borrow to finance the gap between appropriated funds for interest payments and actual payments. Borrowing to cover the costs of past deficits pushed up interest rates and resulted in more deficit spending! Interest payments by the Turkish government rose from about 7 percent of GDP in 1995 to 23 percent of GDP in 2001. Between 2001 and 2004 interest payments as a share of GDP declined to about 13 percent.

Interest payments accounted for more than half of the Turkish government's outlays in 2001 compared to 20 percent of outlays in 1990. By 2004, interest outlays still accounted for about 40 percent of government spending. Turkish citizens continue to pay the price of past uncontrolled deficit finance by being forced to have large portions of their tax payments allocated to providing interest income to the government's creditors. The huge government debt in Turkey resulting from deficit finance contributed to inflation, recession, and a government sector that finds it difficult to finance government spending for public goods and social insurance because of a huge interest burden that is likely to remain with it for many years. All citizens of governments that rely too heavily on budget deficit finance should learn a lesson from the Turkish economy. There is a heavy price to pay in the future for borrowing recklessly.

Unfortunately, the federal deficits of the 1970s and 1980s were not accompanied by new government investment. Instead, they helped finance federal entitlement programs, including Social Security pensions, Medicare, and Medicaid. These programs have important social benefits but they finance mainly consumption expenditures.

Use of Borrowing to Finance Capital Expenditures by Nonfederal Governments

The transference of the burden of finance to the future has particular relevance for capital expenditures undertaken by state and local governments because the makeup of the population in these areas changes over time. Such changes are due not solely to the life cycle of individuals but also because individual citizens move in and out of the area. This implies that the population that receives the benefits of current capital expenditures (for example, a new sewer system or a new school) might be in the future a completely different aggregation of people compared with those who currently live in the area.

Therefore, on the basis of the benefit principle, it is legitimate to finance projects that yield the bulk of their benefits in the future, and in a particular local area, through borrowing. The taxes levied to pay the interest and principal on the debt can coincide more or less with the benefits flowing from the project. Those actually receiving the benefits—the individuals of the future tax base—also will bear the tax cost of financing the projects. The postponement of taxes as a result of debt issue is often referred to as "pay-as-you-use" finance. Citizens are taxed for capital expenditures at the time the expenditures yield benefits, not at the time the capital expenditures are initiated. The principle underlying this method of finance is similar to that of financing an automobile or a home through a loan. Many local governments have special capital budgets that list expenditures to be financed by the issuance of public debt.

CHECKPOINT

1. What is the net federal debt, and how much of it is an external debt?
2. What is the possible future burden of the net federal debt?
3. Under what circumstances can borrowing by state and local governments contribute to improved resource allocation?

SOVEREIGN DEBT: DEFAULT RISK, INTEREST RATES, AND AUSTERITY

Sovereign debt is the net debt of a national government. In most cases such debt issued by governments to the public in the form of securities of various maturities (bills, notes, and longer-term bonds ranging from a 5-year maturity to 30 years or longer) is viewed as relatively free of the risk of default. This is because a national government can always print money to repay the debt or it can use its powers of taxation to raise funds to repay the debt. Private issuers of debt do not have such options and therefore private debt has a much higher default risk. Of course, all securities have market risks associated with holding such assets because the price of the securities can fall if interest rates rise and the value of the currency of the nation issuing the debt can lose purchasing power because of inflation (especially if it creates money to pay its debt). However, the probability of default is not zero even for sovereign debt if political and economic forces make it difficult or impossible for a nation to pay its debt by raising taxes or printing money.

In recent years, the risk of sovereign debt default has increased, particularly for nations in the euro zone such as Greece, Spain, Ireland, Portugal, and Italy. The euro zone nations use the euro as a common currency. Each nation can issue its own debt denominated in euros. When the nations run budget deficits to finance government expenditures, their sovereign debt increases. Because the euro zone nations do not have their own currency, they lack the ability to print money to pay off or refinance the debt. Thus, these nations must rely on their ability to tax or issue more debt to avoid default. If anything impairs the ability of a nation to borrow or use its taxing power effectively to pay off its sovereign debt, then default becomes a distinct possibility.

The nation's taxing authority and its ability to print money back the sovereign debt of the United States. In the past, federal government debt has generally been viewed as free of default risk. However, Congress sets a debt ceiling that limits the amount the U.S. Treasury can borrow. Once that ceiling is reached, the Treasury can no longer borrow funds to finance government expenditures or refund debt that has reached maturity and has to be paid off. Congress has routinely increased the debt ceiling before it was reached. However, during the summer of 2011 political gridlock in Congress resulted in delays in raising the debt ceiling. At that time, partly as a result of the aftermath of the recession of 2007–2009, the federal government was relying on borrowing to finance about 40 percent of federal government spending. Had Congress and the president not reached an agreement on conditions for increasing the debt ceiling, federal spending would have had to be cut (perhaps by as much as 50 percent) or else the Treasury would not have had the tax revenue to refund maturing debt. Such a condition would have resulted in a failure to pay interest and principal on the nation's sovereign debt on time therefore putting the nation in default. Although an agreement was reached to raise the debt ceiling, one credit rating agency downgraded the quality of U.S. debt citing risks of future political battles that might prevent the debt ceiling from being increased as needed or a lack of willingness by Congress to use the nation's taxing authority to refund the debt held by the public.

Ultimately, markets determine the risk of default through the willingness of lenders to supply funds to sovereign governments entering the market as borrowers. In the case of the United States, the aftermath of the debt ceiling battle was that lenders continued to view U.S. government securities as free of default risk and safe allowing the federal government to continue to borrow at historically low interest rates.

The situation regarding default risk for the sovereign debt of some euro zone nations is much different than that of the United States. Although these nations do not face debt ceilings, their ability to borrow has been limited as lenders in credit markets view the risk of default as high. As a result nations, such as Greece, are already effectively shut out of international credit markets, and other nations find that the interest rates that they must pay to borrow have increased to cover default risk. In most cases, the risk of default stems from the inability of nations to reliably increase tax revenues sufficiently to refund existing debt. In Ireland and Spain, sovereign debt increased as their central governments assumed the debt of banks whose assets dwindled as a result of the collapse of a real estate bubble. In Greece, generous tax-financed pensions along with a bloated and inefficiently run public sector and high wages for government workers caused deficits and debt to soar. Growing sovereign debt was underreported by Greece. As recession set in, tax revenues declined and deficits soared. Banks holding Greek sovereign debt agreed to a write off of slightly more than half the amount held—in effect resulting in a default on much of the debt. European authorities set up a fund to provide bailouts for the economies of Ireland, Greece, and Spain to prevent further defaults and help finance essential public services. In exchange for the funds, recipient nations were required to institute "austerity programs" to increase taxes and reduce government spending so that government deficits and debt burdens reduced. Unfortunately, these austerity programs also contributed to declines in economic activity and soaring unemployment rates in the countries that instituted them. However, over the

TABLE 12.3	Deficit and Net Public Debt as a Percentage of GDP in Selected Euro Zone Nations, 2011	
NATION	GOVERNMENT DEFICIT	NET CENTRAL GOVERNMENT DEBT
Greece	9.2	170.0
Ireland	13.0	114.1
Spain	9.3	75.3
Italy	3.8	119.7
Portugal	4.2	117.6
France	5.2	100.1
Germany	1.0	87.2

Source: OECD Economic Outlook, No. 91, June 2012.

longer run it was hoped that reduction in structural budget deficits would ultimately result in stronger economies. Table 12.3 shows debt levels and deficits as a share of GDP of selected euro zone nations.

High deficits or net public debt as a share of GDP does not necessarily imply risk of default. The capacity of a nation to refund its debt depends on its capacity to raise revenue or its ability to monetize the debt. For example, in 2011 Japan had a government deficit of 9.5 percent of its GDP and its net public debt was 205.5 percent of its GDP, yet there was virtually no risk of default and the Japanese government was able to borrow funds in credit markets at very low interest rates. Similarly, the U.S government budget deficit was 9.7 percent of GDP (greater than that of Greece or Spain) in 2011 and its net debt was 75 percent of GDP—about equal to that of Spain. However, markets viewed default risk on U.S. debt at virtually nil, and the federal government could borrow at very low interest rates. Spain, on the other hand, was viewed at high risk of default and interest rates on its debt were approaching 7 percent in 2011.

SUMMARY

A budget deficit or surplus reflects an imbalance between expenditures and revenues. Deficits increase the federal debt and also can contribute to higher market interest rates and increased inflation. Borrowing to finance public expenditures postpones the tax burden to the future. A budget surplus adds to national savings and can lower interest rates and increase investments. As deficits and debt increase, more tax revenue must be allocated to paying interest on the debt rather than providing government goods and services.

Because state and local governments lack the power to create money, the securities of these governments are inherently more risky to investors than are those of the federal government. State and local debt holdings are likely to be more external to the issuing jurisdiction than are federal debt holdings, implying that repayment of such debt might withdraw significant amounts of resources to other jurisdictions.

The burden of the government debt can be defined as the decrease in well-being of citizens who are taxed to pay off the principal and interest on past debt. It can be argued that no burden is incurred until the debt is repaid, because purchasers of government securities lend money to the government voluntarily, without compulsion. Presumably, they are compensated for any lost consumption or investment opportunities by the rate of interest that they receive. The burden of the debt on future generations can be offset if current taxpayers increase saving to pay taxes anticipated in the future as a result of the deficit. More than half of the U.S. net federal debt is owned by foreigners and is therefore an external debt that could drain resources from the nation when it is repaid.

LOOKING AHEAD

Part 4 considers tax theory and tax structure in detail. Major forms and methods of taxation in the United States are analyzed and detailed. Before beginning Part 4, students should be certain that they have mastered the analysis in Part 3.

KEY CONCEPTS

Budget Deficit

Budget Surplus

Burden of the Debt

External Debt

General Obligation Bonds

High-Employment Deficit or Surplus

Internal Debt

Net Federal Debt

Real Budget Balance

Revenue Bonds

Ricardian Equivalence

REVIEW QUESTIONS

1. Explain why a budget deficit in a given year when the unemployment rate is 10 percent could be, in fact, a surplus in that year if the unemployment rate were 5 percent.
2. Why do some economists argue that budget deficits contribute to increased market rates of interest and reduced private investment?
3. What is Ricardian equivalence? Why does it imply that budget deficits cannot influence interest rates?
4. What is the significance of the distinction between internal debt and external debt?
5. Why is the actual net liability of the federal government much less than the gross public debt? How do increases in market rates of interest and increased inflation affect the burden of the debt?
6. In what sense does repayment of the federal debt constitute a redistribution of income among citizens?
7. How can deficit finance influence political equilibrium? Has deficit finance been associated with increased federal investment in the United States?
8. Why is repayment of state and local government debt more likely to drain purchasing power from citizens of state and local governments?
9. What are some of the advantages of financing capital expenditures with debt for governments with mobile populations?
10. In what sense does the use of debt financing by a national government impose a burden on the future generation? How does debt financing increase the "wealth" of the current generation compared with tax financing? Under what circumstances will the burden of the debt on future generations be offset?

PROBLEMS

1. The current market rate of interest is 8 percent. At that rate of interest, businesses borrow $500 billion per year for investment and consumers borrow $100 billion per year to finance purchases. The government is currently borrowing $100 billion per year to cover its budget deficit. Derive the market demand for loanable funds, and show how investors and consumers will be affected if the budget deficit increases to $200 billion per year. Show the impact on the market rate of interest, assuming that taxpayers do not anticipate any future tax increases. How would your conclusion differ if taxpayers fully anticipate future tax increases?
2. Suppose 90 percent of the net federal debt was acquired by foreign investors. How would this affect the burden of the debt for U.S. citizens?
3. The classical economists argued that budget deficits would not affect current spending. Suppose the federal government increases its purchases of goods and services by $100 billion this year. Classical economists who believe in the idea of Ricardian equivalence would argue that the increase in federal spending would have no effect on aggregate spending in the economy and no effect on private investment. Explain how a $100 billion increase in spending financed by a deficit can have no effect

on the economy other than a reallocation of resources from private to government use.

4. Trace the implications of a government budget surplus on the following:
   a. National saving
   b. Interest rates
   c. Private investment
   d. Economic growth
   e. Future living standards

   When tracing the effects of the budget surplus, list the assumptions you are making.

5. Suppose gross saving in the United States is 20 percent of gross national product (GNP). If business saving is 15 percent of GNP and government saving is 4 percent of GNP, what percentage of GNP is personal saving? Explain why a federal budget surplus increases national saving while a budget deficit decreases national saving. How can a federal budget deficit increase market equilibrium interest rates and reduce private investment and future economic growth?

ADDITIONAL READINGS

Barro, Robert J. "Public Debt and Taxes." In *Federal Tax Reform*, edited by Michael J. Boskin, 189–209. San Francisco: Institute for Contemporary Studies, 1978. A readable summary of some of Barro's ideas on debt versus taxes.

Buchanan, James M. *Public Principles of Public Debt*. Homewood, Ill.: Richard D. Irwin, 1958. A classic analysis of the burden of debt.

Schultze, Charles L. "Of Wolves, Termites, and Pussycats or, Why We Should Worry about the Budget Deficit." *The Brookings Review* (Summer 1989): 26–33. A good review of arguments on the pros and cons of reducing a federal budget deficit.

U.S. Congressional Budget Office. *The Budget and Economic Outlook*. Washington, D.C.: U.S. Government Printing Office. Published annually. Find out in this report what the current federal budget deficit (or surplus) is now and what it is likely to be in the future.

INTERNET RESOURCES

http://www.publicdebt.treas.gov/

At the home page of the U.S. Bureau of the Public Debt, you can watch the national debt grow and get information on the ownership of the debt. A useful FAQ link answers questions about the debt.

http://www.whitehouse.gov

Click on The Administration and then click on Executive Office of the President to find the home page of the Office of Management and Budget. From this site you can search the federal budget to get information about the budget balance, the federal debt, and a host of other issues relating to government finance.

http://www.concordcoalition.org

The Concord Coalition monitors government budget issues with particular emphasis on Social Security and Medicare. This nonpartisan institution compiles information on the government budget deficit.

PartFour

TAXATION: THEORY AND STRUCTURE

Chapter 13

THE THEORY OF INCOME TAXATION

LEARNING OBJECTIVES

After reading this chapter, you should be able to:

- Discuss the concept of comprehensive income and how it is measured using the Haig-Simons definition.

- Show how a comprehensive income tax affects the work-leisure choice and labor markets.

- Analyze the excess burden and incidence of a general proportional tax on comprehensive income.

- Discuss the relationship between income tax rates, saving, and investment.

When you mention taxes, what immediately comes to mind to most Americans is "April 15." That is the date the federal income tax returns and income tax returns for most states become due. Taxes on personal income represent the dominant source of revenue for the federal government in the United States. Personal income taxes accounted for 42 percent of federal revenue in 2011. Since 1960, personal income taxes have become an increasingly important source of revenue for state governments. As of 2011, all but seven states used a personal income tax levied on individual incomes, and income from personal income taxes accounted for 34 percent of state government tax revenue. The personal income tax has enjoyed strong political support in the United States.

Direct taxation of personal income is a relatively new phenomenon in the United States. Prior to 1913, the major source of revenue for the federal government was the customs duty, or tariffs. Although an income tax was utilized briefly from 1861 to 1872 on the national level as an emergency measure during the Civil War, it did not become a permanent feature of the federal tax structure until 1913. An attempt in 1894 by President Grover Cleveland to introduce the income tax on the national level failed when the U.S. Supreme Court declared the enacted law unconstitutional. In 1913, a constitutional amendment was adopted that empowered Congress to levy taxes on both personal and business incomes. The initial income tax passed under the new amendment exempted the first $3,000 of income from taxation for a single person and the first $4,000 for a married couple. All income above this exemption up to $20,000 was taxed at the proportional rate of 1 percent, with surcharges ranging as high as 7 percent for higher levels of income. The highest tax rate was applied to taxable income in excess of $500,000. The newly enacted income tax provided a significant amount of revenue to finance military expenditures for World War I.

At the state level, experience with an income tax had been unfavorable prior to the early 20th century. Although six states had experimented with income taxation in the 19th century, the tax proved both unpopular and difficult to administer. The first successful state income tax was instituted by Wisconsin in 1911. The Wisconsin tax law featured improved administrative techniques that facilitated equitable collection of the tax. The income tax was soon adopted by other states.

Complexities of the tax code are not discussed in this chapter. Instead, the chapter defines income from an economic point of view and assumes that *all income, regardless of its source or use, is taxed at the same rate.* The consequences of a flat-rate, or proportional, income tax in labor markets and markets for investible funds are traced. It is assumed that taxes on personal income are the only taxes being utilized by government authorities and that a fixed, proportional rate of taxation is applied to income, with no exclusions, exemptions, or deductions allowed from the tax base.

COMPREHENSIVE INCOME: THE HAIG-SIMONS DEFINITION

Two preliminary steps are necessary before any comprehensive definition of income can be developed. First, the taxpaying unit must be selected. In the case of a personal income tax, that unit must be the individual. All individuals who earn income, regardless of age or the amount of income earned, will be subject to the tax. No separate tax on business income is necessary. All businesses are owned by individuals. Business income, in one form or another (profits, dividends, retained earnings), accrues to the person(s) who own the businesses. In the case of corporate income, a comprehensive personal income tax would require that all income of the corporation be allocated to shareholders in proportion to their ownership of shares.

The second step is to define the time period relevant for measuring personal income. The concept of income is meaningless unless a time period is specified. Income is a flow over time and will vary in amount with the time interval chosen. It makes no sense to say that an individual's income is $10,000, for this might mean $10,000 per hour, per day, per month, or per year. Income can even be defined over a person's lifetime. For tax purposes, the income of an individual is usually specified per year. A yearly accounting of income causes few problems in a system of income taxation that has a fixed, proportional rate, invariable over time.

In an economic sense, income is usually viewed as a measure of a person's power to purchase goods and services in a given year. As defined by Henry Simons, income is an indicator of "the exercise of control over the use of society's scarce resources.[1] Income can be spent, thereby converting purchasing power into consumption, or it can be stored for future use.

Income can be measured according to its sources or its uses. Sources of income, calculated from the beginning to the end of the accounting period, are earnings from the sale of productive services; transfers from either government or individuals; and increases in the value of assets owned by the individual. Uses of income include consumption, or purchase, of goods and services; taxes; donations; and saving. Increased holdings of assets over liabilities constitute saving. Positive saving in a given year stores income for future consumption. Saving represents an increase in a person's net worth. **Net worth** is the value of a person's assets held at any point in time less the value of a person's liabilities, or debts. A person's net worth at any point in time can be positive or negative.

In a given year, an individual might save negatively by borrowing funds or by liquidating some assets into cash and spending the cash on consumption items. Also, in a given year, the dollar value of income received from sources must equal the dollar value of all uses of income.

Comprehensive income is the sum of a person's annual consumption expenditures and the increment in that person's net worth in a given year:

$$I = C + \Delta NW, \tag{13.1}$$

where I is annual income, C is annual consumption, and ΔNW is annual change in net worth. If people save more than they borrow in a given year, the increment in net worth will be positive. It will be negative if they draw on accumulated savings and spend the funds or if they borrow more than they save in a given year. Comprehensive income must be adjusted for inflation to accurately measure increases in potential purchasing power. As will be shown, inflation creates significant problems for administering an income tax. The concept of comprehensive income is also called the *Haig-Simons definition of income*.[2] Consumption includes all voluntary expenditures, including donations to charity and gifts.

Comprehensive income can also be defined in terms of its sources. Income is any payment or increment in a person's net worth that increases that person's ability to purchase or use goods and services in a given year. Table 13.1 shows

---

[1]Henry Simons, *Personal Income Taxation* (Chicago: University of Chicago Press, 1938): 49.

[2]See Simons, *Personal Income Taxation*, 49. Also see Robert Murray Haig, "The Concept of Income: Economic and Legal Aspects" in *The Federal Income Tax*, ed. Robert Murray Haig (New York: Columbia University Press, 1921): 7, reprinted in *Readings in the Economics of Taxation*, eds. Richard A. Musgrave and Carl S. Shoup, American Economic Association (Homewood, Ill.: Richard D. Irwin, 1959): 59.

TABLE 13.1   An Income Statement

SOURCES	USES
Earnings from Sale of Productive Services	Consumption
Transfer Payments Received	Taxes, Donations, and Gifts
Capital Gains (or Losses)	Savings (Increases in Net Worth)

Sources = Uses

Earnings +   Consumption +

Transfer Payments = Taxes, Gifts, and Donations

\+ Capital Gains   + Savings

© Cengage Learning

three major sources of personal income: earnings from the sale of productive services, transfer payments received from government and private organizations or people, and capital gains on existing assets currently held. **Capital gains** are increases in the value of assets over the accounting period.

Earnings include both income from labor and income from capital. Labor income is measured by wages and salaries from the sale of labor services; capital income represents the sum of interest and dividends and rents. Transfers are payments for which no good or service is received in return. Gifts are transfers, as are government payments to individuals such as cash assistance to the poor.

Comprehensive income measures capital gains on assets as they accrue regardless of whether the asset is sold or exchanged; that is, it includes both realized capital gains and unrealized capital gains. *Realized capital gains* result when an asset is sold for cash or exchanged for another asset. *Unrealized capital gains* are increases in the value of assets in a given year that accrue on assets that are not sold for cash or exchanged for other assets. An example of an unrealized capital gain is the increase in the value of a corporate stock over a year that is not converted into cash by selling the stock or not exchanged for another asset. The logic behind including unrealized capital gains in income is that any increase in the value of assets, be it converted to cash or not, increases the individual's potential to purchase items in a given year. *Net capital gains* are capital gains minus capital losses. Comprehensive income deducts the transactions costs incurred in earning income. Thus, brokerage fees, costs of tools, uniforms, travel, and other costs of acquiring income would be the only legitimate deductions from the comprehensive tax base. Sources and uses of income are as follows:

$$\text{Sources} = \text{Earnings} + \text{Transfers} + \text{Net Capital Gains}$$
$$- \text{Cost of Acquiring Income,} \tag{13.2}$$
$$\text{Uses} = \text{Consumption} + \text{Gifts and Donations} + \text{Savings}$$
$$- \text{Cost of Acquiring Income.} \tag{13.3}$$

Sources are always equal to uses. A comprehensive income tax is levied on all income irrespective of its use or its source.[3] Table 13.1 summarizes the alternative ways of measuring comprehensive income. It also includes taxes as one of the uses of income. Of course, taxes represent compulsory payments that reduce a person's spendable income.

---

[3]For a more detailed analysis of the comprehensive base, see David F. Bradford and the U.S. Treasury Tax Policy Staff, *Blueprints for Basic Tax Reform*, 2nd edition (Arlington, Va.: Tax Analysts, 1984). This classic monograph discusses issues in measuring comprehensive income and basic issues in income taxation.

Let's use a numerical example to illustrate how comprehensive income would be computed. Suppose in a given year a person earns $20,000 from the sale of labor services and also earns $1,000 in interest from certificates of deposit, which represent funds loaned to a bank. His total annual earnings equal $21,000. He also receives $2,000 as a gift from his parents that year to help with his expenses. In addition, he was unemployed for one month during the year, so he received $800 in unemployment insurance payments from the government. Both the $2,000 gift and the $800 unemployment insurance payments would be regarded as transfers and would be included in his comprehensive income. His total transfer income would be $2,800. In addition, he earns capital gains of $1,500 and incurs $600 in capital losses from stock market transactions. His net realized capital gains are $900 that year.

Suppose the value of the stock he owns, but does not sell, falls by $500. He would incur unrealized capital losses of that amount on unsold stock. Over the same year, market appraisal indicates that the value of his home has increased by $2,000. The net unrealized capital gains would be $2,000 − $500 = $1,500. Adding all the sources of his income indicates that his comprehensive income is $26,200. This example assumes that the costs of earning income have already been netted out of earnings and capital gains.

The uses of his annual income also must be $26,200. Suppose he pays $2,500 in taxes and saves $2,500 of his income. Assuming that he does not give monetary gifts to other people and that his donations to charity are also zero, his consumption this year will be $21,200.

Problems of Measurement

A means of measuring income, either from the sources side or the uses side, must be developed before any income tax can be implemented. Most systems of accounting use the sources side as the base for measurement. The Haig-Simons definition of income would require that both realized and unrealized capital gains be included in income; a mechanism would have to be developed to measure increments (and decrements) in the value of all capital assets held by individuals as these gains or losses accrue. Whatever system might be developed also has to adjust these gains for inflation so that only real increases in the potential to consume would be included in income. Although measurement of unrealized gains might be relatively easy for assets that are traded frequently in secondary markets, such as stocks and bonds, administrative problems would make it difficult to measure such gains for all types of assets. For instance, devising an equitable system that could accurately measure annual gains and losses on such assets as real estate, antiques, jewelry, and livestock is probably impossible.

Another set of problems stems from adequately defining and delineating costs of earning income. Such expenses are analogous to the costs of running a business and might include such items as tools, work clothes, union dues, child care expense, and such legitimate travel expense as commuting costs to and from work. In other words, all those expenditures that are made neither for consumption nor for adding to net worth would be deductible, as expenses, from income.

Some tools that an individual uses in work might also be used for personal purposes and would be considered consumption. The acquisition of skills in training programs or in continued education adds to the individual's human capital. Thus, expenditures for such activities might be legitimately deducted from income insofar as they will result in higher earnings that will be subject to taxation. However, education that produces human capital for home use is not legitimately deductible if the increased consumption enjoyment stemming from taking crafts courses and various "how-to-do-it" courses escapes taxation. Many arbitrary judgments would have to be made to decide which expenses are legitimate costs of earning income and which should be considered consumption or increases in net worth. One common method of avoiding these problems is to allow all taxpayers to take a lump-sum deduction designed to cover basic expenses involved in commuting to work, buying work clothing, and so on.

As previously indicated, a comprehensive income tax would eliminate the need for a separate tax on corporate business income. In individual proprietorships and partnerships in the United States, business income is already declared as part of the owner's personal income. A comprehensive income tax would attribute all corporate income to shareholders in proportion to their ownership of stock in the corporation, thereby eliminating the need for a separate corporate income tax.

Income-in-Kind

Income-in-kind is income in the form of goods and services rather than cash payments. One of the most serious problems involved in administering any type of income tax is the treatment of nonmonetary transactions. Difficult problems arise in measuring and tracing various forms of income-in-kind. Nonmarket transactions that increase consumption without increasing monetary earnings result in income-in-kind. For reasons of administrative feasibility, most tax codes make only feeble attempts to tax various forms of income-in-kind.

Income-in-kind often results from home production of goods and services. In this case, people make things for themselves or provide themselves with services rather than purchasing those goods and services from others in markets. Individuals who build additions to their own homes, sew for their family, or provide such basic homemaking functions as cooking and cleaning produce valuable services that accrue to members of their households and that usually escape taxation. A comprehensive income tax base would include these services.

Similarly, individuals who own their own homes receive income-in-kind in the form of imputed rent, which represents a flow of housing services that the individuals, in effect, sell to themselves insofar as they are both landlord and tenant. Failing to subject such income-in-kind to taxation indirectly subsidizes activities that generate such income and can result in more than the efficient amount of resources allocated to the activities. As a matter of administrative practicality, however, the inclusion of all types of income-in-kind is infeasible. The ultimate line between what is or is not income is likely to be drawn by arbitrary decisions. One type of income-in-kind that is fairly easy to tax is fringe benefits provided by employers for their employees. These include such compensation to employees as medical and life insurance, use of vehicles for personal purposes, and free meals. Recent tax reform proposals have advocated taxing noncash employee fringe benefits by estimating the market value of these benefits and including it in the employee's taxable income.

Nonpecuniary returns associated with various occupations are yet an additional aspect of the income-in-kind problem. *Nonpecuniary returns* represent satisfaction that individuals receive from their employment that is not reflected in their wages.

For example, some occupations allow workers flexible hours and freedom from pressures. Wages in those occupations are likely to be lower than in occupations that require the same level of skills but stricter scheduling of worker time. Two occupations with the same required skills might be able to attract workers at differing wages, depending on the extent to which they offer nonpecuniary returns. The job with better nonpecuniary benefits will pay less, and the actual wage differential will reflect the value of the nonpecuniary returns.

To the extent that nonpecuniary returns are not taxed, the attractiveness of jobs that provide such benefits increases relative to other jobs. This affects occupational choice. Thus, when income-in-kind for various jobs escapes taxation, the tax system encourages individuals to enter those jobs, and it encourages employers to provide nonpecuniary benefits in lieu of taxable monetary benefits.[4]

CHECKPOINT

1. What is comprehensive income?
2. How would capital gains be treated under a comprehensive income tax?
3. What is income-in-kind? What are some of the difficulties involved in including income-in-kind in a measure of comprehensive income?

A GENERAL TAX ON COMPREHENSIVE INCOME: ECONOMIC EFFECTS OF A FLAT-RATE INCOME TAX

Everyone complains about the complexity of the U.S. income tax code. Reformers have suggested that the tax system would be a lot more efficient if we had a flat-rate income tax. However, any tax involves distortions—even a flat tax. In this section, we examine the economic effects of a flat tax on income, concentrating on the way taxes affect choices between work and leisure and between present and future consumption. Once you understand the economic effects of such a tax, you will be in a better position, especially after reading Chapter 14, to evaluate the pros and cons of such a flat tax.

A general proportional tax on comprehensive income is a flat rate on all income regardless of its source or use.[5] The analysis in this chapter presumes that all earnings are either wages or interest and that the costs of earning income are zero. Because all income is taxed at the same rate regardless of its source, the ratio of the price of labor to the price of capital is not distorted by the tax. Similarly,

---

[4]For an analysis of in-kind compensation of employees (nontaxable fringe benefits), see Charles R. Clotfelter, "Equity, Efficiency, and the Tax Treatment of In-Kind Compensation," *National Tax Journal* 32 (March 1979): 51–60. Also see Anne Beeson Royalty, "Tax Preferences for Fringe Benefits and Worker's Eligibility for Employer Health Insurance," *Journal of Public Economics* 75 (February 2000): 209–227.

[5]If some initial amounts of income, say, $5,000 per person, were tax exempt, as is the case in many proposals for a flat-rate tax, the tax really would have a two-bracket progressive rate structure, with a zero marginal tax rate in the first bracket.

because taxes paid are independent of the uses to which income is put, the comprehensive income tax does not distort the relative prices of consumption of goods and services. The tax neither will distort choices in the income-producing activities in which individuals engage nor will it distort the pattern of consumption of taxpayers in ways that prevent attainment of efficiency.

Although no loss in efficiency will occur in the way individuals spend their income or earn it, the tax is likely to distort the choices that are made concerning the allocation of time between work and leisure and between consumption and saving or productive investment. The flat-rate tax on comprehensive income can therefore prevent labor markets and investment markets from attaining efficiency.

Taxation of Labor Earnings and the Work-Leisure Choice

By far, the major source of income in the United States today is wages. Income from the sale of labor services accounts for more than 60 percent of gross income. Labor income is a dominant component of comprehensive income. Efficiency losses caused by taxation of labor income are of serious concern because of the importance of wages as a percentage of national income. This section analyzes the impact of the portion of a flat-rate comprehensive income tax that is levied on wages.

The impact of income taxation on the choice to work cannot be predicted unequivocally. The tax sets up both income and substitution effects; these work in opposite directions on workers' choices to work. Given preferences between work and income on the one hand and the market wage rate on the other, each worker is presumed to allocate time between work and leisure to maximize utility. The equilibrium allocation of time depends on individual preferences and the wage a worker can earn per hour.

Figure 13.1 shows a typical worker's indifference curves for money income from work and leisure. In drawing the curves, it is assumed that leisure is a normal good for the worker. The indifference curves exhibit diminishing marginal rates of substitution of leisure for income. Twenty-four hours are available each day to allocate between gainful employment and all other activities for which the worker is not paid. Leisure is a catchall term for any activity other than work for an employer. You can think of leisure as a nonmarket activity, including home production activities, such as cooking, cleaning, and engaging in do-it-yourself projects.

The line *HJ* represents the opportunities for the individual to trade leisure for money income through the sale of labor services to an employer. Nonlabor income is presumed to be zero in Figure 13.1. If the worker chooses not to work at all, her income is zero in this simple model. This is illustrated at point *H* in the figure. At that point, the individual spends 24 hours per day in leisure activity and would earn zero money income. For any other point along *HJ*, the individual's income can be expressed as

$$I = w(24 - L), \tag{13.4}$$

where L is the amount of hours of leisure per day and w is the wage per hour. The variable L is best thought of as the average amount of leisure per day over a year. The maximum income that the individual can earn in this case is $0J$ dollars per day. This is her income when she chooses to work 24 hours per day and enjoys zero leisure hours per day.

FIGURE 13.1   Impact of a Flat-Rate Income Tax on the Work-Leisure Choice

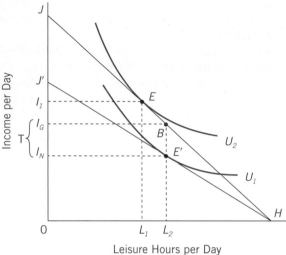

The income tax reduces the slope of the worker's wage line. As a result, the worker moves from point E to point E'. In this case, leisure per day increases. The tax results in a decrease in hours worked per day on average over the year.

Under the assumption of a diminishing marginal rate of substitution of leisure for income, neither the extreme J, no leisure, nor H, no work, is a likely choice. Instead, the worker is likely to maximize her utility at some intermediate point on the line HJ. In Figure 13.1, this occurs at point E, where the indifference curve U_2 is tangent to the wage line HJ. At that point, the slope of the indifference curve, $-MRS_{LI}$, is equal to the slope of the line HJ. But from Equation 13.4, the slope of HJ is simply $-w$, the rate of return from work effort. Because both slopes are negative, the equilibrium condition for the utility-maximizing allocation of time between work and leisure is

$$w = MRS_{LI} \tag{13.5}$$

The introduction of a flat-rate tax on the worker's labor income of t percent reduces the return to work effort at all levels of work. Assuming no change in the gross, or market, wage paid by an employer, the net wage received by the worker after payment of the income tax is now

$$w_N = w_G(1 - t). \tag{13.6}$$

This rotates the line that depicts the market possibilities for transforming leisure into income through work effort from HJ down to HJ'. The equation for this line now becomes

$$I = w_G(1 - t)(24 - L). \tag{13.7}$$

The new equilibrium for the worker now occurs at point E'. The new equilibrium condition is

$$w_G(1 - t) = MRS_{LI}. \tag{13.8}$$

For the individual whose indifference curves are depicted in Figure 13.1, the proportional income tax has the following effects:

1. A reduction in utility from U_2 to U_1. (This ignores any benefits from government expenditures accruing to the individual.)

2. An increase in leisure hours per day from L_1 to L_2. This worker chooses to work fewer hours per day as a result of the tax on labor earnings.

3. A consequent reduction in actual labor earnings per day from I_1 to I_G because of the reduction in hours worked. Because taxes are levied on I_G, net income available to spend falls to I_N.

The government collects $E'B = T$ dollars per day of this individual's income in taxes. This represents the difference between gross daily wages paid by employers, I_G, and net wages per day received by the worker, I_N, after payment of taxes. Net income after taxes is $I_N = I_G - T$. In this case, the tax has been detrimental to work effort. The individual reduces her hours worked per day by L_1L_2 as a result of the income tax.

For example, suppose $w_G = \$5$ per hour. If $t = 0.2$, the net wage declines as a result of the tax to \$4 per hour. If hours worked are $(H - L_1) = 8$ hours on average over the year, suppose that the tax decreases average hours worked per day to $(H - L_2) = 7$ hours. Gross daily labor income will fall from \$40 per day to \$35 per day after the tax. Net daily income will be \$28 per day. The total tax per day will be \$7.

Income and Substitution Effects of a Tax on Labor Earnings

The impact of the tax on work effort of any worker depends on the income and substitution effects of the tax-induced reduction in the wages received by individual workers. The tax can be viewed as lowering the opportunity cost of an hour of leisure by reducing the wages that workers receive from w_G to $w_G(1 - t)$. In effect, the tax lowers the implicit price of leisure by reducing the return from work effort, which is the opportunity cost of leisure.

The income tax results in a substitution effect that is unfavorable to work effort. The tax reduces the return from work effort, thereby making work less remunerative. This, in turn, makes leisure more attractive. The incentive is to substitute leisure for work effort because the per hour opportunity cost of leisure (the net hourly return from work effort) has fallen as a result of the introduction of the income tax. Thus, the substitution effect induced by the income tax tends to increase the consumption of leisure by the individual. This substitution effect represents a potential loss of output of goods and services due to the reduction in the incentive to work.

An income effect also results from the tax-induced decline in the net wage. The income effect tends to be favorable to work effort, provided that leisure is a normal good. The income tax reduces income at all levels of work. Even if the individual chooses to work the same number of hours as he did prior to the imposition of the tax, he earns less income after taxes than he did previously. The effective reduction in income results in a decrease in the consumption of all normal goods. Because leisure is likely to be a normal good for most people, the income effect results in a decrease in leisure consumption by the individual. If the worker reduces consumption of leisure per day, then it follows that hours devoted to work per day must increase. Thus, the income effect of taxation provides an incentive to increase work effort when leisure is a normal good. In a sense, the individual tends to work harder to maintain his previous income level.

The actual effect on individual work effort depends on the relative magnitudes of the income and substitution effects. If the substitution effect outweighs the income effect, the individual tends to consume more leisure and consequently works less as a result of the tax. This is evidently the case for the individual whose indifference curves are depicted in Figure 13.1. If, however, the individual's preferences are such that the income effect outweighs the substitution effect, the result of the tax-induced wage reduction is a decrease in the daily consumption of leisure and a consequent increase in work per day.

Graphic Analysis of Income and Substitution Effects of Tax-Induced Wage Decreases

Figure 13.2 shows how the substitution effect of a wage reduction caused by the income tax can be separated from the income effect. As a result of the tax, the worker's wage declines, thereby shifting the budget line from HI to HI'. The actual worker equilibrium shifts from the allocation of time corresponding to point E_1 to that corresponding to point E_2.

To isolate the substitution effect of the reduction in the wage, the worker would have to be given a compensating increment in average daily income to make her as well-off as she was before the tax reduced the wage. Suppose the worker were given $BH = CI'$ dollars per day, as shown in Figure 13.2, after the tax is imposed on wages. This is a lump-sum daily payment that shifts the leisure-income line upward,

---

FIGURE 13.2   Income and Substitution Effects of a Tax-Induced Wage Decline

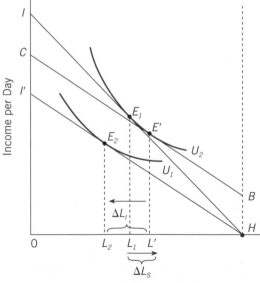

Leisure Hours per Day

The substitution effect is separated from the income effect by giving the worker a compensating variation in income equal to an average of BH dollars per day over the year. In this case, the income tax results in an increase in work effort because the income effect, ΔL_I, outweighs the substitution effect, ΔL_S.

parallel to itself, from $I'H$ to CB. Now, she has BH dollars per day of nonlabor income. This is exactly enough to return her to indifference curve U_2, which is the level of well-being that she enjoyed before the tax. If it were possible to make such a compensating variation in her income, the resulting change in the allocation of time observed would represent the substitution effect. This is the change in the daily number of hours of leisure only due to the decrease in the net wage caused by the tax.

The worker would be in equilibrium at point E' if the income effect could be removed by such a compensating increase in income. The substitution effect is the increase in leisure per day from L_1 to L', labeled ΔL_S in Figure 13.2. The convexity of the indifference curves for income and leisure guarantees that the substitution effect will increase leisure hours per day. This is because the lower wage caused by the tax means that the slope of the line CB is less than the slope of the original leisure income line IH. The tangency at E' must be to the right of the tangency at E_1, as long as the marginal rate of substitution of leisure for income declines. It follows that the substitution effect of a tax-induced wage decrease always serves to decrease the number of hours worked per day (or per month or per year).

If the compensating increase in income were taken away from the worker, the resulting change in the allocation of time between work and leisure would represent the income effect. Taking away BH dollars per day from the worker returns the worker to E_2. If leisure is a normal good, this will reduce the hours of leisure chosen per day. In Figure 13.2, the income effect is the reduction of leisure hours from L' to L_2, labeled ΔL_I. The income effect is opposite in direction to the substitution effect if leisure is a normal good. In this case, the income effect is actually stronger than the substitution effect. As a result, the wage reduction caused by the tax results in the worker whose indifference curves are drawn in Figure 13.2 choosing to work more hours per day. Compare this with the case of the worker whose indifference curves are drawn in Figure 13.1. In that graph, the substitution effect of the tax-induced wage decrease outweighs the income effect for that worker because she chooses to work fewer hours per day after the tax. Similarly, it is possible to envision a case in which the income and substitution effects are equal in magnitude and thus cancel one another. Under those circumstances, the observed labor supply would be perfectly inelastic.

LABOR MARKET ANALYSIS OF INCOME TAXATION

The impact of taxes on labor income, market wages, net wages, and efficiency depends on the responsiveness of workers to tax-induced wage declines. The analysis to follow considers two broad cases. The first case assumes that the market supply of labor is perfectly inelastic. The second case assumes that the elasticity of supply of labor exceeds zero. In both cases, the demand for labor is presumed to be downward sloping.

Case 1: Perfectly Inelastic Labor Supply

The total excess burden of the comprehensive income tax on labor income depends on the substitution effect of the tax-induced net wage decline and the tax rate. All taxes, including lump-sum taxes, result in income effects that, other things being equal, make taxpayers worse off. Therefore, the tax-induced distortion in the work-leisure choice used to measure the excess burden of the tax must be based only on the change in work hours due to the substitution effect caused by the tax. Thus, the labor supply response of workers must be adjusted to remove the income effect of the tax-induced wage change. A curve that shows how hours worked per day (or per year) vary with wages when the income effect of wage changes is removed is called a **compensated labor supply curve**. Such a curve reflects only the substitution effects of wage changes. (See Appendix 11 for a more detailed analysis of compensated supply curves.) Statistical techniques are used to remove the income effect from labor supply responses to estimate labor supply curves. Points on such supply curves can be used to measure the excess burden of a tax on labor income.

Even if the regular, or uncompensated, market supply curve of labor is perfectly inelastic, the excess burden of the tax will not be zero. In Figure 13.3A, the regular market supply curve of labor is assumed to be perfectly inelastic. The demand curve, D, is based on the gross wage, W_G, that employers must pay to attract any given number of labor hours per year. The impact of a tax on labor income is to reduce the wages received by workers from W_G to $W_N = W_G (1 - t)$ for any amount of hours supplied. This is reflected by the gross wage curve, W_G, swiveling down to W_N. The extent of the reduction in wages at any given level of employment depends on the flat-rate tax rate, t. Workers respond to the net wage in deciding how many hours of work to supply per year. However, because the market supply of labor is perfectly inelastic, the tax-induced reduction in wages received by workers does not result in any reduction in the quantity of labor hours supplied. No change occurs in the initial market wage of W_G^*. Net wages received by workers therefore fall by the full amount of the tax per hour of labor to $W_N = W_G^* (1 - t)$. Under these circumstances, the income tax is borne entirely by workers in the form of a reduction in wages.

Recall that the substitution effect of a wage decline always causes a worker to reduce hours worked per year. The perfectly inelastic supply curve of labor in

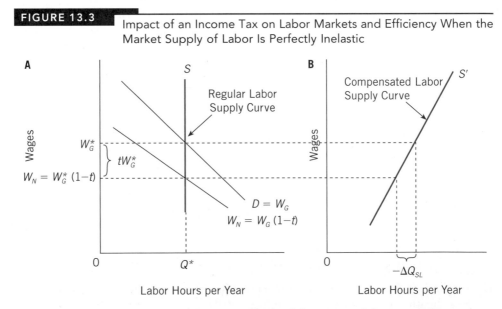

FIGURE 13.3   Impact of an Income Tax on Labor Markets and Efficiency When the Market Supply of Labor Is Perfectly Inelastic

An income tax on labor reduces net wages by the full amount of the tax per hour when the supply of labor is perfectly inelastic, as shown in **A**. However, the excess burden of the tax is not zero because the substitution effect of the tax reduces labor hours supplied per year. If a lump sum were used, workers would work more hours per year. **B** shows that the compensated labor supply curve is upward sloping.

Figure 13.3A indicates that the substitution effect is exactly offset by an equal and opposite income effect, assuming that leisure is a normal good. Removing the income effect of the wage changes from the market supply curve results in the upward-sloping compensated labor supply curve, as shown in Figure 13.3B. The tax-induced decline in net wages received by workers is tW_G^* when the market supply curve is perfectly inelastic. This decline in wages received results in a substitution effect of $-\Delta Q_{SL}$ hours per year, as shown in Figure 13.3B. The excess burden of the tax equals $\frac{1}{2}(tW_G^*)\Delta Q_{SL}$. One study has concluded that the excess burden per dollar of taxes on labor income based on the tax rate structure prevailing in the United States in the mid-1970s would have been 8.1 cents even if the market, or uncompensated, elasticity of supply of labor were zero.[6]

Also, when the supply of labor is perfectly inelastic, the incidence of taxes on labor will be borne entirely by workers. This is because the net wage falls by the full amount of the tax per labor hour.

Case 2: The Elasticity of Supply of Labor Exceeding Zero

Now suppose the market supply curve of labor is upward sloping. When the income effect of the tax is believed to be small, the regular labor supply curve could be used to approximate the excess burden of the tax. Otherwise, a compensated labor supply curve is necessary to estimate the substitution effect of the tax-induced wage decline.

In Figure 13.4, the pretax equilibrium is at point A. At that point, the wage is W_1, and Q_1 hours per year are supplied. The tax reduces the net wage for any number of hours worked per year from W_G to $W_G(1-t)$. The new equilibrium is at point B, where the net wage is $W_N^* = W_G^*(1-t)$. As a result of the tax, hours worked per year decline from Q_1 to Q_2. The gross, or market, wage increases from W_1 to W_G^*. Net wages received by workers decline to $W_N^* = W_G^*(1-t)$. In this case, workers succeed in shifting a portion of the tax to employers. Wages do not decline by the full amount of the tax, tW_G^*, paid per hour. The increase in wages reduces the profits of employers or results in higher market prices of goods and services, as marginal costs of production increase. This results in some shifting of the tax burden to groups other than workers.

If the reduction in hours worked, ΔQ, were entirely attributable to the substitution effect, the triangular area BCA could be used to estimate the excess burden of the tax. If this is not the case, a compensated supply curve must be used. When leisure is a normal good, the compensated supply curve is more elastic at any wage level than the regular supply curve (see Appendix 11). In Figure 13.4, the compensated supply curve is labeled S_C and the regular supply curve is labeled S_R. As shown on the graph, the reduction in net wages caused by the tax, ΔW, would result in a reduction in hours worked equal to ΔQ_{SL} as hours worked per year decline to Q_3 when the income effect of the tax-induced wage change is removed. The change in hours worked due to the substitution effect, ΔQ_{SL}, exceeds ΔQ, the uncompensated response. Using the area of the triangle BCA to measure the excess burden will underestimate the actual excess burden when income effects are not negligible.

When the supply of labor is not perfectly inelastic, workers can shift the tax to other groups. In addition, the excess burden of the tax will be greater than when the supply of labor is perfectly inelastic.

---

[6]Charles L. Ballard, John B. Shoven, and John Whalley, "The Total Welfare Cost of the United States Tax System: A General Equilibrium Approach," *National Tax Journal* 38 (June 1985): 125–140.

FIGURE 13.4   Effect of Income Taxes on Labor Markets When the Supply of Labor Is Responsive

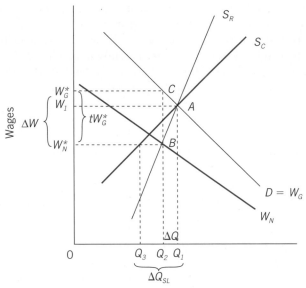

If the supply curve of labor is not perfectly inelastic, a tax on labor income increases market wages and decreases the quantity of labor hours supplied per year. If a regular supply curve, S_R, is used to estimate the excess burden of the tax, the burden will be underestimated. The compensated supply curve, S_C, must be used to estimate the substitution effect of the tax, ΔQ_{SL}.

Empirical Evidence on Labor Supply

The excess burden of a tax on labor income depends on total labor income, the tax rate, and the willingness of workers to substitute leisure for work. The substitution effect depends on the elasticity of supply of labor along the compensated labor supply curve.

Empirical evidence on labor supply suggests that for males between the ages of 25 and 55, the income effect of wage changes is roughly equal to the substitution effect. The observed responsiveness of males in this age range to changes in tax rates is quite low because the overall wage elasticity of labor supply with respect to the wage is close to zero. A zero overall elasticity of labor supply suggests that the incidence of a comprehensive income tax on labor income is borne by workers as a reduction in net wages.

However, some empirical research has suggested that the substitution effect of wage reductions caused by income taxes is fairly large but is offset by an equally large income effect.[7] This is consistent with low labor supply responses to changes in tax rates. Because the substitution effects of wage changes are of relevance in calculating the excess burden of the income tax, this implies that the income tax can result in fairly large losses of efficiency in labor markets, even though the overall wage elasticity of supply of labor is close to zero.

---

[7]See Jerry A. Hausman, "Labor Supply," in *How Taxes Affect Economic Behavior*, eds. Henry J. Aaron and Joseph J. Pechman (Washington, D.C.: The Brookings Institution, 1981).

Using econometric techniques, it is possible to remove the income effect from estimated market labor supply elasticities to derive a compensated elasticity of supply that reflects only the substitution effect of tax-induced wage changes. Empirical evidence indicates that the efficiency-loss ratio of taxes on labor income in the United States in the 1970s was in the range of 5 to 30 cents of revenues collected. For example, one study concluded that in the tax system of the 1970s, the efficiency-loss ratio for the average married male was 22 percent. This implies that taxes on married males in the 1970s in the United States caused distortions in resource use resulting in an excess burden of 22 cents for each dollar of revenue collected. Estimates based on the income tax laws prevailing in 1988, which had much lower marginal tax rates than those of the 1970s, suggest that a dollar of revenue raised by taxes on labor income in 1988 resulted in only 13.5 cents of excess burden. The reduction in excess burden is due entirely to lower tax rates because both the 1970s and 1988 estimates were based on the same labor supply elasticities.[8] However, analysis of the economic effects of the tax rate reductions of the Tax Reform Act of 1986 now suggests that there was very little increase in labor supply as a result of the tax declines. There were only modest increases in hours worked in response to reductions in marginal tax rates that averaged about 8 percent. One study concluded that males increased labor hours by about 1 percent as a result of the tax cuts and female workers increased labor hours worked only by about one-third of 1 percent in response to the lower marginal tax rates. The greatest response to the lower tax rates appeared to have been by married females subject to the highest tax rates, whose labor supply increased by about 18 percent. The general conclusion of analysis of the effects of the Tax Reform Act of 1986 on labor supply is that such effects were not significant.[9] However, it is possible that the tax rate changes were not large enough in many cases to induce a response.

In a more recent study, Ziliak and Kniesner used sophisticated econometric techniques to estimate life cycle labor-supply tax effects. They considered the impact of the income tax on both labor and interest income and took a more long-range look at the way income tax affects work decisions. This study picked up a larger effect of tax rate reductions on labor supply than previous analyses. The researchers concluded that the tax reforms of the 1980s, which reduced the income tax rate, stimulated male labor supply in the United States by about 3 percent and reduced the excess burden of income taxation by about 16 percent. Their estimated compensated wage elasticity of labor for prime-age males was 0.15. They also estimated that hours worked by prime-age males would fall by 0.05 percent in the short run in response to a 10 percent increase in marginal income tax rates. Their research suggests that completely eliminating income taxes would lead prime-age married males on average to work 4 percent more hours. Those males in the highest income quartile of the population would work 7 percent more hours.[10]

[8]See Jerry A. Hausman and James M. Poterba, "Household Behavior and the Tax Reform Act of 1986," *Journal of Economic Perspectives* 1, 1 (Summer 1987): 101–120.

[9]For a summary of recent studies on the impact of tax rates on labor supply, see Alan J. Auerbach and Joel Slemrod, "The Economic Effects of the Tax Reform Act of 1986," *Journal of Economic Literature* 26, 2 (June 1997): 589–632.

[10]James P. Ziliak and Thomas J. Kniesner, "Estimating Life Cycle Labor Supply Tax Effects," *Journal of Political Economy* 107, 2 (1999): 326–359.

PUBLIC POLICY PERSPECTIVE

The Incidence of Payroll Taxes in the United States

Most workers pay a payroll tax on their earnings of 7.65 percent of wages they earn in the United States. The taxes are deducted from their pay by their employers. Employers pay an additional 7.65 percent tax on the wages they pay. The taxes are levied on worker earnings up to a maximum amount, which was set at $110,100 in 2012 in most cases.[1] The total combined tax rate was 15.3 percent for workers earning $110,100 or less in 2012. The payroll tax has been the fastest-growing tax in the United States in recent years. Many workers with moderate earnings now pay more in payroll taxes than they do in federal income taxes! A worker earning $50,000 would have $3,825 withheld from his or her earnings to pay the tax, and the worker's employer would pay an additional $3,825 so that the wages of a worker earning $50,000 would generate $7,650 in payroll taxes earmarked to pay Social Security benefits—mainly to retirees!

Although only half the total Social Security payroll tax is withheld from workers' wages, there is good reason to believe that the incidence of the payroll tax falls entirely on workers because the supply of labor is close to perfectly inelastic in the United States. Actually, it makes no difference whether the tax is collected from employees or employers. If the supply of labor is very inelastic, the bulk of the tax will be borne by workers no matter how its collection is split between the two groups. Most empirical evidence suggests that labor supply on average is very unresponsive to changes in tax rates in the United States.[2] The following graph analyzes the impact of the U.S. payroll tax on labor markets, assuming a perfectly inelastic supply of labor.

If the supply of labor is perfectly inelastic, a payroll tax collected from both employers and employees would be fully borne by workers as the hourly wage falls by the full amount of the tax per labor hour.

The Payroll Tax

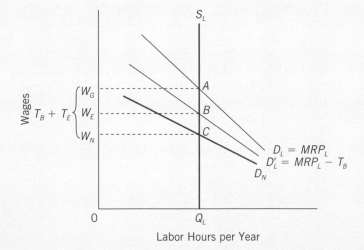

If the supply of labor is perfectly inelastic, a payroll tax collected from both employers and employees would be fully borne by workers, as the hourly wage falls by the full amount of the tax per labor hour.

The gross wage before the introduction of the payroll tax is W_G. Assuming a perfectly competitive labor market, this equilibrium wage is equal to the marginal revenue product of labor, MRP_L. Now assume that a payroll tax is levied on all wages. This tax will be split between employees and employers so that each pays an equal amount per hour of labor.

The introduction of the payroll tax reduces the demand for labor from D_L to D'_L. This is because the employer's part of the tax is subtracted from MRP_L at any point. Employers make their hiring decisions on the basis of MRP_L minus the tax T_B per hour of work they must pay. A worker's contribution to a firm's revenues now is less at any point, because the employer's portion of the tax must be deducted from the revenues generated by workers as more are hired. The decrease in the demand for labor by employers caused by the tax decreases the equilibrium market wage received by employees from the initial level, W_G, to W_E, in the accompanying figure.

The portion of the tax paid by employees will be deducted from the market wage, W_E, that they receive. This reduces the net wage received by employees at all hours of work. The curve labeled D_N in the figure gives the net wage for workers. The net wage received by employees in equilibrium is $W_E - T_E$, where T_E is the workers' share of the tax per hour of work.

If the total labor hours employed per year were Q_L, the total tax deducted from workers' labor earnings would be $T_E Q_L$. This tax is represented by the area $W_E BCW_N$. But is this all the tax borne by workers?

The answer is no, because the tax also has reduced the market wage received by employees from W_G to W_E. If the supply of labor were perfectly inelastic, the entire portion of the employer's tax would be shifted backward to workers. The market wage received by employees falls by the full amount of the tax per hour of work paid by employers, T_B. The portion of the tax collected from employers is $T_B Q_L$ per year, represented by the area $W_G ABW_E$. That entire amount is the annual reduction in the payroll paid to workers due to the tax-induced reduction in the market wage from W_G to W_E. This result is independent of how the nominal collection of the payroll tax is split between the employer and the employee. If the entire tax were levied on the employer, the result would be exactly the same. In that case, the market demand would fall to D_N, and the gross market wage received by workers would decline to W_N.

The payroll tax also might have an effect on labor market behavior due to some of the peculiarities of its application. In particular, the labor force participation of family members other than the major breadwinner can be affected. This is because in many cases spouses who work would have their wages reduced by the tax without any real expected benefits, inasmuch as most Social Security benefits already accrue to them from the package made available to the main breadwinner in the family. For example, a dependent spouse over retirement age is entitled to 50 percent of his or her retired spouse's Social Security pension when he or she reaches full retirement age.[3] This pension benefit is independent of whether the dependent spouse has paid Social Security taxes. The net benefit of paying taxes is reduced accordingly for dependent spouses who seek work. This, in turn, can affect their willingness to find work outside the home. This phenomenon might also provide incentives for workers to engage in work at home "off the books," either for themselves or for others, in order to avoid the payroll tax. This contributes to the development of the so-called underground economy.

---

[1]Workers with earnings in excess of this limit, which is indexed with the rate of inflation, are subject to a 2.9 percent tax on their earnings without limit.

[2]See Hausman and Poterba, "Household Behavior and the Tax Reform Act of 1986," for a review of these studies.

[3]Some evidence indicates that high net payroll taxes in the United States discourage labor force participation of many married women. See Therese A. McCarty, "The Effect of Social Security on Married Women's Labor Force Participation," *National Tax Journal* 43, 1 (March 1990): 95–110.

The many econometric studies of the impact of income taxation on labor supply generally conclude that income taxes have little effect on labor supply decisions of workers who provide the main source of income to a household. However, the impact of income taxes on the labor supply of spouses, partners, and other household members appears to be significantly greater. The impact of income taxes on labor earnings can result in household members who are not the main breadwinner deciding not to participate in the labor force at all.[11] Estimates of the effect of income taxes on efficiency of use of labor remain controversial. The overall effect in labor markets requires estimates of compensated labor supply elasticities of various demographic groups. Income taxes can affect household labor supply by influencing labor supply decisions of spouses.[12] Income taxes can also affect labor supply by influencing retirement decisions, intensity of work, willingness to acquire skills that increase labor income, and choice of occupation.

CHECKPOINT

1. What effects will a comprehensive income tax have on the incentive to work?
2. Why is it difficult to predict whether work effort will increase or decrease as a result of an income tax?
3. Why do many economists believe that the excess burden of the income tax in labor markets is low and that the tax on labor income is borne fully by workers?

TAXATION OF INTEREST INCOME AND ITS EFFECT ON SAVING

The taxation of interest income also results in both income and substitution effects. Taxation of interest income lowers the return to saving but can either increase or decrease the actual amount of saving observed. Considerable controversy surrounds the interest elasticity of supply of savings. Many economists believe that its value is close to zero. Others believe that this elasticity is greater in magnitude than the low wage elasticities of work previously discussed.[13] The

---

[11]Although several studies have found that married women are sensitive to the impact of taxes on after-tax wages and salaries and tend to respond by working less, recent empirical analysis suggests that in recent years the labor supply of married women has become less sensitive to tax-induced reduction in wages and salaries. See Francine Blau and Lawrence Kahn, "Changes in the Labor Supply Behavior of Married Women," *National Bureau of Economic Research (NBER) Working Paper 11230* (Cambridge, Mass.: NBER, 2005).

[12]See Robert K. Triest, "The Effect of Income Taxation on Labor Supply in the United States," *Journal of Human Resources* 25, 3 (Summer 1990): 491–516. Also see Thomas MacCurdy, David Green, and Harry Paarsch, "Assessing Empirical Approach for Analyzing Taxes and Labor Supply," *Journal of Human Resources* 25, 3 (Summer 1990): 415–490.

[13]For a discussion of the impact of taxation on savings see B. Douglas Bernheim, "Taxation and Saving" in A. J. Auerbach and M. Feldstein (eds.), *Handbook of Public Economics*, Vol. 3 (Amsterdam: Elsevier Science Publishers, 2002), Chapter 18, pp. 1173–1249. Also see Michael J. Boskin, "Taxation, Saving, and the Rate of Interest," *Journal of Political Economy* 86 (April 1978): S3–S28. Boskin's estimate of the interest elasticity of supply of saving is 0.4. Critics of Boskin's work argue that his methodology was flawed and that when properly estimated, changes in interest rates in the United States do not affect saving and investment. See Allan S. Blinder and Angus Deaton, "The Time Series Consumption Function Revisited," *Brookings Papers on Economic Activity* 2 (1985): 465–511. Research by Bernheim and Shoven suggests that rising real interest rates actually seem to decrease saving. See D. Bernheim and J. Shoven, "Pension Funding and Saving," *NBER Working Paper 1622* (Cambridge, Mass.: National Bureau of Economic Research, May 1985). Also see Jonathan Skinner and Daniel Feenberg, "The Impact of the 1986 Tax Reform on Personal Saving," in *Do Taxes Matter: The Impact of the Tax Reform Act of 1986*, ed. Joel Slemrod (Cambridge, Mass.: The MIT Press, 1990).

impact of a tax on interest income on choices can be understood with a simple intertemporal analysis of consumption in two periods. The allocation of a given amount of income over the two periods depends both on individual tastes and the interest rate that a saver can earn.

Graphic Analysis of Taxation of Interest Income

Figure 13.5 uses indifference curve analysis to analyze an individual's choice between consumption and saving. In effect, by saving, a person forgoes present consumption in exchange for more future consumption. The two variables in the analysis are consumption in the current period, C_1, and consumption in the second period, C_2. The individual's willingness to forgo present consumption for future consumption is, in part, a matter of taste.

The **marginal rate of time preference** (**MRTP**) is the slope of an indifference curve for present and future consumption multiplied by −1. It is a measure of the willingness of savers to forgo current consumption in exchange for future consumption. A high marginal rate of time preference implies that the individual strongly prefers current consumption to future consumption (he is impatient). It is generally presumed that the marginal rate of time preference for most people exceeds 1. In other words, it would require more than a dollar of future consumption to compensate the person for giving up a dollar of present consumption out of current income and still be at the same level of utility.

The opportunity to transform present consumption into increased future consumption depends on the market rate of interest, r. If the individual's income is

---

Income Taxation and Intertemporal Choice

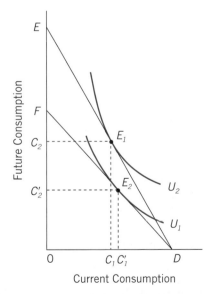

The income tax reduces the net interest earned by savers. This shifts the intertemporal budget line downward from *ED* to *FD*. In this case, the substitution effect of the tax-induced decline in net interest received increases current consumption out of income and therefore reduces savings.

fixed at I in the beginning of the current period and is zero in the second period, future consumption of current income will be equal to

$$C_2 = (1 + r)S, \tag{13.9}$$

where S is the amount of current income saved. For example, suppose the person's income is \$30,000, and he saves \$5,000 in year one. He will be able to consume \$5,500 in year two if the interest rate is 10 percent.

S can also be expressed as the difference between income and current consumption:

$$S = I - C_1. \tag{13.10}$$

The equation of transformation line ED therefore is

$$C_2 = (1 + r)(I - C_1). \tag{13.11}$$

The slope of the line is $-(1 + r)$. The individual maximizes utility by allocating income between present and future consumption until the transformation line ED is tangent to an indifference curve. This occurs where the slope of the indifference curve, $-MRTP$, is equal to the slope of the transformation line, $-(1 + r)$:

$$MRTP = (1 + r) \tag{13.12}$$

The introduction of a tax on interest income reduces the net return obtained from saving. In this analysis, it is assumed that the market rate of interest paid by borrowers, r, is unchanged when the tax is introduced. If the tax is levied at a rate t, the net yield after payment of the tax becomes $r(1 - t)$. This reduces the slope of the transformation line, and it swivels downward to FD, which, in turn, moves the individual to a new equilibrium in response to the lower return to savings. The new equilibrium is at point E_2, where the individual adjusts his allocation of income between present and future consumption to reduce his marginal rate of time preference so as to make it equal to the new lower return to saving:

$$MRTP = [1 + r(1 - t)]. \tag{13.13}$$

As shown in Figure 13.5, this results in an increase in current consumption from C_1 to C_1' and a consequent reduction in saving. The actual impact on saving for any individual represents the combined income and substitution effects of the tax-induced reduction in the net interest rate. It is not possible to predict unequivocally the impact of the tax on savings.

The income effect of the reduction in the interest rate savers receive from r to $r(1 - t)$ provides incentive to reduce consumption of all normal goods in the current period and in the future. However, the tax reduces consumption of all goods in the second period, through the reduction in interest income. The only way that consumption can decline in the current period is for saving to increase. The income effect of the tax provides an incentive for the person to save more so as to make up for the reduction in second-period consumption due to the tax-induced decline in interest income.

The substitution effect of the decrease in the net return to savings caused by the tax increases current consumption and results in less saving. The decline in the interest rate raises the implicit price of future consumption by increasing the amount of current consumption that must be given up to obtain any dollar amount of future consumption. This provides incentives to save less.

The actual effect on saving is the combined effect of the opposing income and substitution effects forces and cannot be predicted by theory alone. Insofar as savers seek to save specific amounts, or "target" levels of saving, the income effect of the tax dominates, and savers actually may increase their rates of saving to offset the effect of the tax on their net returns.

MARKET ANALYSIS OF TAXATION ON INTEREST AND INVESTMENT INCOME

Excess Burden

Figure 13.6 shows the impact that a tax on interest income has on market saving and investment. The initial equilibrium is at point A, at an interest rate of r_1, which results in an efficient allocation of resources by equating the marginal social cost of saving with the marginal social benefit of investment. The introduction of the tax inserts a wedge between the interest received by savers and paid by investors and other borrowers, causing a loss in efficiency. Investment and saving fall from their initial equilibrium level, S_1, to a reduced level, S_2.

The tax lowers the return to saving at all levels from r_G to $r_G (1 - t)$, thereby swiveling down the net interest at all levels, resulting in the curve r_N. The consequent reduction in the quantity of saving raises the market interest rate to r_G^* but

---

FIGURE 13.6 Impact of an Income Tax on Investment Markets and Saving

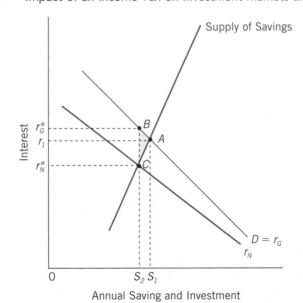

An income tax reduces annual saving and investment when the supply of saving is responsive to changes in net interest. If income effects of tax-induced interest charges are negligible, the area *ABC* can be used to approximate the excess burden of the tax.

© Cengage Learning

leaves the net interest received by savers below its initial level, r_1. Net interest now equals $r_N^* = r_G^* (1 - t)$. To measure the excess burden of the tax, the reduction in savings due only to the substitution effect of the tax must be measured. This would require measuring the reduction in saving, S_1S_2, along a compensated supply curve of savings.

The excess burden of the tax is approximated by the area of the triangle *ABC* if income effects of tax-induced interest rate changes are negligible.[14] The excess burden depends on the tax rate applied to interest income and on the interest elasticity of supply of savings. Quite a controversy has risen over the interest elasticity of the supply of savings in the United States. Some research studies have indicated that the (uncompensated) interest elasticity of the supply of savings was about 0.4 in the late 1970s.[15] Under those circumstances, the excess burden of taxes on capital income would have been more than $50 billion, or more than 30 cents per dollar of revenue. Some economists, however, maintain that the actual interest elasticity is, in fact, much higher than 0.4 in this country.[16] Studies based on this higher elasticity indicate that the excess burden of the tax could be three times higher than estimates based on the 0.4 elasticity. However, still other studies provide evidence that the interest elasticity of supply of savings is quite low.[17] Thus, economists disagree on the actual value of the interest elasticity of supply of savings and on the excess burden of taxes falling on capital income.

As in the case of taxes on labor income, most studies find little response of savings supply to changes in tax rates. Studies of the tax rate reductions of the Tax Reform Act of 1986 were unable to detect any significant increase in savings attributable to the tax rate declines. However, the changes in the tax law at that time had only a mixed effect on the incentives to save and did not reverse the long-term decline in the personal savings rate that began in the 1970s in the United States.[18] There is, however, evidence of significant effects of taxation of capital on incentives to invest. Taxes on investment income increase the cost of capital. Recent studies suggest that these taxes do reduce investment.[19]

Incidence of Taxes on Interest Income

The value of the interest elasticity of supply of saving is also crucial for the determination of the degree of shifting of the tax on interest income. If the annual amount

---

[14]Feldstein has argued that the excess burden of taxation of income from saving and investment is more appropriately thought of as a distortion in the timing of consumption over the life cycle rather than as a decrease in saving. Even if the amount of saving is unaffected by a tax on interest income (because of perfectly inelastic supply), future consumption will fall as a result of the tax-induced decline in net interest. A decline in the interest rate, in effect, raises the "price" of future consumption by increasing the amount of present consumption that must be given up to get any dollar amount of future consumption. Using a methodology to calculate the efficiency loss in capital taxation in this way, Feldstein calculates the cost at 0.5 percent of national income when the amount of saving is unaffected by the tax. See Martin Feldstein, "The Welfare Cost of Capital Income Taxation," *Journal of Political Economy* 86, pt. 2 (April 1978): S29–S51.

[15]Boskin, "Taxation, Saving, and the Rate of Interest," S11–S28.

[16]Lawrence H. Summers, "Capital Taxation and Accumulation in a Life Cycle Growth Model," *American Economic Review* 71 (September 1981): 533–544.

[17]Irwin Friend and Joel Hasbrouck, "Savings and After-Tax Rates of Return," *The Review of Economics and Statistics* 65 (November 1983): 537–543. See also Blinder and Deaton, "The Time Series Consumption Function."

[18]See Auerbach and Slemrod, "The Economic Effects of the Tax Reform Act of 1986," 589–632.

[19]For a summary of these studies, see Eric Engen and Jonathan Skinner, "Taxation and Economic Growth," *National Tax Journal* 49, 4 (December 1996): 617–642.

P U B L I C   P O L I C Y   P E R S P E C T I V E

The Supply-Side Tax Cuts of the 1980s

Instead of lowering tax revenue, can decreases in income tax rates increase tax revenue by causing the amount of work and investment to increase? This was the basic idea of the supply-side approach to economic policy that was put forth by the Reagan administration in the 1980s. Reagan put his ideas into force with a major tax decrease—the *Economic Recovery Tax Act of 1981* (ERTA). This new law resulted in a 25 percent across-the-board reduction in tax rates. The top marginal tax rate applied to nonlabor income was reduced from 70 percent to 50 percent and was accompanied by a series of special tax breaks designed to encourage saving and investment.

The 1981 tax rate cuts *did not* increase tax revenues as the supply-siders maintained it would. However, in response to the declines in marginal tax rates, federal revenues did not decrease by as much as most non-supply-siders thought would be the case. This implies that workers and investors respond to tax rate cuts but not by enough to offset the negative effect of tax rate cuts on revenue collected.[1]

Declines in income tax rates can increase tax revenue only if the rate reduction causes taxable income to increase by a greater percentage than the percentage reduction in tax rates. In such cases, the negative effect of the reduction in tax rates on tax revenue is offset by the positive effect on revenue of increased work and investment that increase both labor and capital income subject to tax. Taxable income did not increase enough in response to the 25 percent cut in tax rates in 1981 to prevent revenue from declining.

However, in one case that tax cut did increase revenue in the 1980s. Realization of capital gains is apparently quite elastic with respect to the tax rate in the short run. When tax rates on realized capital gains were cut significantly in 1982, the amount of taxable capital gains realized in that year by taxpayers increased by a greater percentage than the percentage of decline in tax rates. Because the dates of capital gain realizations can be controlled and because accrued unrealized capital gains are not taxable, the reduction in the tax rates in 1982 released a tide of selling of assets to take advantage of the lower tax rates.[2] The very elastic capital gains tax base caused tax revenues from taxation of realized capital gains to increase despite the lower tax rates. However, this was a one-time effect. Other portions of the income tax base, namely labor and forms of capital income other than capital gains, were not elastic enough to result in increases in tax revenue.[3]

The general consensus among economists is that both work effort and investment, which provide the bulk of income, are highly unresponsive to changes in tax rates. Apparently this was the case for the United States in the 1980s because the ERTA tax cuts did not increase income enough to cause revenue to increase.

---

[1]See Martin Feldstein, "Supply-Side Economics: Old Truths and New Claims," *American Economic Review* 76, 2 (May 1986): 26–30.
[2]See Lawrence B. Lindsey, "Capital Gains Rates, Realizations, and Revenues," in *The Effects of Taxation on Capital Accumulation*, ed. Martin S. Feldstein (Chicago: University of Chicago Press, 1987): 69–97.
[3]For a discussion of the general effect of tax cuts on capital gains see Jane G. Gravelle, "Economic and Revenue Effects of Permanent and Temporary Capital Gains Tax Cuts," Congressional Research Service, September 2001.

---

of saving is responsive to tax-induced declines in net interest payments, the tax can be shifted from savers to borrowers through an increase in the market rate of interest. In Figure 13.6, the market interest rate rises from r_1 to r_G^* as a result of the total reduction in the quantity of savings supplied because of the tax on interest. Higher interest offsets some of the tax burden on savers, but it increases production costs and results in some of the tax being shifted to consumers in the form of higher prices for goods and services. This means that part of the incidence of the tax is shifted to people who are not savers.

Decreased investment also results in slower growth of the capital stock of a nation. Workers will have less capital to work with than would be the case if a lump-sum tax, which did not influence the interest rate, were used. Because a lower ratio of capital to labor decreases labor productivity, the implication is that in competitive labor markets, where the marginal product of labor is a crucial determinant of the wage, wages would be lower than if there were no tax on interest income. The tax on interest income could be shifted, in part, to workers in the form of lower wages when market interest rates rise. Under these circumstances, removal of taxes on interest earnings in the United States would result in decreases in the market rate of interest and eventual increases in wages. Therefore, workers as well as savers would benefit from a reduction in the tax rate applied to interest income. Of course, the lower the reduction in actual savings as a result of taxes on interest income, the less the increase in the market rate of interest. At the extreme, if the interest elasticity of supply of savings were actually zero, the market rate of interest would be unaffected by the income tax. Under such circumstances, only savers would benefit from reduction in the tax on interest income. Only when the interest elasticity of supply of savings is zero will a tax on interest income be borne exclusively by savers. In other cases, the incidence of the tax will be shared by savers and others who do not save any of this income.

CHECKPOINT

1. Why is it difficult to predict the effect of a comprehensive income tax on saving?
2. Why is there a controversy about the excess burden of the income tax in investment markets?
3. How can the income tax decrease future living standards?

SUMMARY

Taxes on personal income account for over 40 percent of federal government revenues in the United States. Income is viewed by many as an appropriate index of ability to pay taxes.

For tax purposes, income is usually measured as an annual flow of earnings. The economist's definition of income is, however, an annual accretion of purchasing power. This is known as comprehensive income and is measured as the sum of annual consumption and increased net worth. Consumption represents spent purchasing power, while increases in net worth represent purchasing power stored for future use. Sources of income include earnings from the sale of productive resources, transfer payments received, and net capital gains accrued. Uses of income include consumption of goods and services, taxes, and saving, or increases in net worth. Comprehensive income includes unrealized capital gains and allows deductions for the costs required to earn income.

Among the problems encountered in implementing a tax on comprehensive income are (1) measuring the value of income-in-kind and other nonmarket transactions, (2) measuring unrealized capital gains, and (3) determining what constitutes a cost of earning income. Under a comprehensive income tax, income of corporations would be allocated to individuals according to the proportion of their share in ownership of the corporation, with no separate corporate income tax.

A general tax on comprehensive income would tax all income at the same rate regardless of its source or use. Although such a tax does not distort choices concerning sources of income or consumption expenditures, it will distort choices between work and leisure and between present and future consumption.

The tax on comprehensive income causes wages, as seen by employers and employees, to diverge. This results in an efficiency loss in labor markets. The actual effect of the tax on hours worked depends on income and substitution effects; it cannot be predicted by theory alone. Empirical estimates of the excess burden of taxes on labor income range from 5 to 29 percent of revenue collected.

Taxation of interest income causes the interest rate paid by investors to diverge from that received by savers. The result is a loss in efficiency in markets for loanable funds used to finance investment and accumulation of assets. Most evidence appears to indicate that savings is quite unresponsive to changes in the market rate of interest. When interest rates change, income and substitution effects influence both current and future consumption, making it difficult to predict the effect of the change in the interest rates on saving. Although some empirical studies have suggested that saving is somewhat responsive to change in interest rates, most economists believe that the effect, if any, is small—implying that taxation of interest income has little effect on savings rates in the United States.

LOOKING AHEAD

Chapter 14 continues the analysis of income taxation by considering the basic provisions of the personal income tax in the United States. In practice, income taxes do not tax all income regardless of its source or use at the same rate. This results in distortions in resource use that would not prevail under a comprehensive income tax. In Chapter 14, these additional distortions are discussed and proposals for tax reform are reviewed.

KEY CONCEPTS

Capital Gains

Compensated Labor Supply Curve

Comprehensive Income

Income-in-Kind

Marginal Rate of Time Preference (MRTP)

Net Worth

REVIEW QUESTIONS

1. What is comprehensive income, and how is it related to an individual's command over resources? Explain how income can be measured from either the sources or the uses side.
2. Why would a comprehensive income tax eliminate the need for a separate tax on corporate income?
3. Why is income-in-kind often excluded from income in implementing an income tax? What are some major forms of income-in-kind, and what are the economic consequences of excluding such items from taxation?
4. What distortions are introduced by a general tax on comprehensive income that taxes all income regardless of its source or use?
5. What is the major source of income in the United States?
6. How does a proportional income tax introduce a wedge between the gross wage paid by employers and the net wage received by workers? Explain how this tax wedge results in efficiency losses in labor markets.

7. Why must the substitution effect be separated from the income effect of tax-induced wage reductions to measure the excess burden of a comprehensive tax on labor income? Draw a graph that shows how the excess burden of the tax can be measured. Explain why it is impossible to predict the effect of an income tax on labor hours worked using theory alone.
8. What is the consequence of a highly responsive supply of labor hours for the excess burden of an income tax on wages? Show that a low elasticity implies that workers bear most of the income tax on wages.
9. How does a tax on interest income influence a person's willingness to save? Can the impact of the tax on saving be unequivocally predicted from theory? Explain why or why not.
10. Under what circumstances will the supply of savings be unresponsive to changes in interest rates? Why does a perfectly inelastic supply of savings not imply zero excess burden from income taxes on interest income?

PROBLEMS

1. Mary has earnings of $50,000 this year. She also has been fortunate because the market value of the condominium she purchased this year for $100,000 has increased by 5 percent. Assuming that the rate of inflation is 3 percent, and that Mary has neither capital losses or other earnings, and receives no transfers, calculate Mary's comprehensive income. If she were subject to a comprehensive income tax

at a 20 percent flat rate, what would her tax liability be for the year?

2. An estimate of the efficiency-loss ratio of taxes on labor income is 15 percent. The efficiency-loss ratio of taxes on capital income is estimated to be 45 percent. Assuming that these estimates are accurate, calculate the change in well-being that would result from a $10 billion reduction in taxes on capital income, accompanied by a $10 billion increase in taxes on labor income.

3. Suppose the current market rate of interest is 8 percent. John is subject to a 31 percent marginal tax rate on his interest income. What is John's equilibrium marginal rate of time preference? Suppose the marginal tax rate John is subject to decreases to 20 percent. Can you predict the effect of the decrease in marginal tax rates on John's current saving?

4. Suppose leisure is an inferior good for a worker. Set up this worker's indifference curves for money income and leisure, and derive the income and substitution effects of a tax-induced wage decline. Derive the compensated labor supply curve for this worker, and explain how it differs from the compensated supply curve of a worker for whom leisure is a normal good.

5. Empirical studies show that the market labor supply of prime-age males (between the ages of 25 and 55) in the United States is close to perfectly inelastic with respect to the labor compensation. If this is the case, explain why it does not imply that the excess burden of a tax on the labor income of prime-age males is necessarily zero. What does a perfectly inelastic market labor supply imply about the incidence of taxes on labor income? Why is there reason to believe that the overall market labor supply is not perfectly elastic when groups other than prime-age males are considered? What possible problems exist in empirical studies of the response to taxes on labor income that might make it difficult to estimate actual labor market responses?

ADDITIONAL READINGS

Aaron, Henry J., Leonard E. Burman, and C. Eugene Steurle, eds. *Taxing Capital Income.* Washington, D.C.: The Urban Institute Press, 2007. Analysis of taxation of capital income on tax rate progressivity and saving.

Aaron, Henry J., and Joseph A. Pechman, eds. *How Taxes Affect Economic Behavior.* Washington, D.C.: The Brookings Institution, 1981. A collection of research studies on the impact of income taxes on labor supply, investment in equipment, stock prices, saving, and other economic variables. Bosworth, Barry, and Gary Burtless. "Effects of Tax Reform on Labor Supply, Investment, and Saving." *Journal of Economic Perspectives* 6, 1 (Winter 1992): 3–25. An analysis of the effects of tax reforms in the 1980s on resource use in the United States.

Bovenberg, A. Lans. "Tax Policy and National Saving in the United States, a Survey." *National Tax Journal* 62, 2 (June 1989): 123–138. A good analysis of the possible ways the U.S. tax system affects saving.

Cordes, Joseph, Robert D. Ebel, and Jane G. Gravelle. *The Encyclopedia of Taxation and Tax Policy*, 2nd ed. Washington, D.C.: The Urban Institute Press, 2005. Everything you want to know about taxation and tax policy (even if you were afraid to ask) is available in this encyclopedia. It contains articles on major topics in taxation and income taxation by 150 tax experts.

McClure, Charles E. Jr., and George R. Zodrow. "The Study and Practice of Income Tax Policy." In *Modern Public Finance*, edited by John M. Quigley and Eugene Smolensky, 165–212. Cambridge, Mass.: Harvard University Press, 1994. A review of theoretical issues and research on the economics of income taxation.

INTERNET RESOURCES

http://www.irs.gov
Access this site for information on U.S. income taxes.

http://www.ntanet.org
This home page of the National Tax Association can be used to access studies on income taxation and details of the U.S. tax system.

http://www.cato.org
The home page of the Cato Institute—a think tank that analyzes public policy and tax issues.

Chapter 14

TAXATION OF PERSONAL INCOME IN THE UNITED STATES

LEARNING OBJECTIVES

After reading this chapter, you should be able to:

- Define adjusted gross income and taxable income, and describe how personal exemptions and various deductions influence the portion of a household's income actually subject to tax in the United States.

- Discuss the tax rate structure of the U.S. personal income tax and the degree of progressivity of taxation.

- Explain how tax preferences can distort choices and prevent efficiency from being attained in markets.

- Analyze the possible effects of major tax preferences in the United States on decisions and resource use.

- Discuss major issues relating to economic effects of income taxation in the United States.

Even if you file the simplest of tax forms, you might be bewildered by the complexity of the U.S. income tax rules. The income tax in the United States is almost continually being reformed in the hopes of simplifying it. However, to the consternation of everyone involved—including the Internal Revenue Service (IRS), whose officials and agents must administer and enforce the tax laws—it seems to get ever more complex after each round of reform enacted by Congress. The Tax Reform Act of 1986 was supposed to be the definitive income tax overhaul of the 20th century. This reform of the U.S. personal income tax sharply reduced tax rates and the number of tax brackets for the federal personal income tax while eliminating many of the deductions, exclusions, and exemptions from income that influence how much of a person's income is actually subject to tax. Then, in 1990, under pressure to raise revenue to cope with a growing federal deficit, the president and Congress tinkered with the income tax once more, changing both the tax rate structure and some of the rules that determine how much of a taxpayer's income is subject to tax. In 1993, to cope with the budget deficit, President Clinton proposed higher marginal tax rates (MTRs) on upper-income groups and additional reforms of the income tax. Congress responded in that year with legislation that reversed the trend toward lower MTRs.

In 1997, Congress and the president collaborated to enact the *Taxpayer Relief Act of 1997*—a package of tax reductions for middle-income taxpayers with children and for investors in homes and other assets earning long-term capital gains. The resulting income tax changes included tax credits to families with children, tax credits for college tuition expenses, and new incentives to save for retirement. Most of these changes have affected the distribution of tax burden somewhat while probably increasing both the complexity of the U.S. tax code and the excess burden of the tax system on the economy.

In 2001, Congress enacted the *Economic Growth and Tax Relief Reconciliation Act* (EGTRRA). The cornerstone of this new tax legislation was a reduction in MTRs for all brackets. The top MTR, which was set at 39.6 percent in 2000, was reduced to 35 percent. In addition, many other changes were made in the tax law, including a reduction in the so-called marriage penalty that was phased in beginning in 2005 to be fully effective in 2009. There were also increases in tuition credits, child credits, and in allowable contributions to tax-deferred retirement accounts. In 2003, in response to strong pressure from the president to stimulate a sluggish economy, Congress enacted the *Jobs and Growth Tax Relief Reconciliation Act of 2003*. This legislation accelerated many of the provisions of EGTRRA to make them effective for 2003 and 2004. It lowered MTRs for these two years and also accelerated the marriage penalty relief for 2003 and 2004. The legislation also reduced tax rates applying to capital gains and dividends and enacted special provisions to encourage business investment.

In 2009, some special tax cuts were incorporated into the *American Recovery and Reinvestment Act of 2009* (ARRA) and did become effective in that year. These special emergency tax benefits were designed to encourage spending for such items as homes and automobiles so as to stimulate sectors of the economy where economic activity was depressed as a result of a major recession.

The basic tax rate reductions embodied in EGTRRA along with the subsequent cuts enacted by Congress between 2002 and 2009 were originally set to expire at the end of 2010 to be replaced with the tax rates and all the other provisions of the federal income tax code that prevailed in the year 2000. However, because of the effects of the recession of 2007–2009 on the economy, Congress extended the tax cuts through the end of 2012. At the end of 2012, Congress enacted the *American Taxpayer Relief Act of 2012* (ATRA). Without this new legislation a massive automatic increase in tax rates would have taken effect at the beginning of 2013 with the marginal tax rates in all tax brackets reverting to the much higher levels that applied in the year 2000 before EGTRRA was enacted. The new legislated made permanent EGTRRA marginal tax rates for all but the highest income taxpayers. Beginning in 2013 individual taxpayers with taxable income above $400,000 per year ($450,000 per for married couples) will once again pay a top MTR of 39.6 percent. Taxpayers with income above these amounts will also pay higher taxes on their capital gain and dividend income beginning in 2013.

Congress has a habit of tinkering with the tax code. The tax code is fluid and has been persistently revised, sometimes for the better—and sometimes for the worse—over the years. Strong pressures still exist for reforming the tax code, including movement to a flat tax and further exemption of savings from taxation. Significant declines in revenues due to slower than expected growth can also result in tax rate increases as can pressures for increased military or social spending by the federal government. Reductions in federal government spending could, on the other hand, allow Congress to reduce federal income tax rates without increasing the budget deficit. Many politicians would like to see more progressivity restored to the rate structure. Do not be surprised if some of these tax reforms are further revised as the forces affecting political equilibrium shift. There is also likely to be dissatisfaction with the fact that proliferation of tax credits available to middle-income taxpayers will subject more and more of them to the alternative minimum tax, thereby increasing their effective average tax rates (this will be discussed later in this chapter).

Because of the special provisions of the income tax, taxpayers can influence their annual tax bills by controlling the sources and uses of their income. The tax code is a very complicated set of rules. Only a portion of the comprehensive Haig-Simons definition of income is actually subject to tax in the United States. Issues in tax policy and tax reform often relate to questions concerning the degree of progression of the tax rate structure and the impact of adjustments that reduce gross income, tax credits, as well as deductions, exemptions, and exclusions from the tax base on market efficiency and the distribution of the tax burden. Because of the complexity of the tax code, the income tax results in losses in efficiency as taxpayers consider the tax as well as the social benefits of their decisions. The income tax in the United States not only distorts choices regarding use of labor and capital, but it also distorts choices regarding the sources and uses of income. In this chapter, we examine the personal income tax in the United States based on laws prevailing as of 2012. Changes in the personal income tax code effective in 2013 as a result of provisions of ATRA will also be discussed.

THE TAX BASE: BASIC RULES FOR CALCULATING TAXABLE INCOME AND WHY MUCH OF INCOME IS UNTAXED

If you are like most American adults, you are required to file a federal (and state) income tax return by April 15 of each year. The amount of tax you pay depends on how much income you have received during the year from earnings and other sources subject to tax, the deductions and exemptions you are entitled to, and the tax rate to which you are subject.

Taxable income is the portion of income received by individuals that is subject to the personal income tax. In practice, taxable income is considerably less than the Haig-Simons definition of comprehensive income discussed in Chapter 13. This section shows how taxable income in the United States is calculated.

The first step in calculating taxable income is to list the basic sources of income subject to taxation. **Gross income** is all income received during the year from taxable sources. Included in gross income are wages and salaries, interest income from taxable sources, dividends, rental income, and profits from business activity. Also included in gross income, under rules prevailing in 2012, are realized capital gains from sale or exchange of securities and other property. However, long-term capital gains and capital gains on sales of personal residences are subject to preferential treatment and lower tax rates. Unemployment compensation received from government is subject to tax, and upper-income retired taxpayers are required to pay tax on part of their Social Security pensions. Among the miscellaneous income that is subject to tax under the provision of the U.S. income tax code are prizes and awards, royalties, a portion of private pension benefits, alimony, and net gambling gains. Even income illegally obtained by criminals is subject to tax in the United States when the authorities are successful in getting crooks to report their earnings! For example, a convicted embezzler is required by law to pay taxes on his embezzlements! Table 14.1 shows the components of gross income based on tax rules prevailing in 2012.

Once gross income has been computed, certain adjustments are permitted. **Adjusted gross income (AGI)** is gross income minus any allowable adjustments. Adjustments to gross income include subtraction of worker moving expenses, contributions made to special retirement plans, expenses for health insurance paid by self-employed individuals, penalties for early withdrawal of savings, some education expenses, and alimony paid.

After AGI is computed, personal exemptions and deductions are subtracted from it to obtain taxable income. A **personal exemption** is a certain sum of money that a taxpayer is allowed to deduct from AGI that varies with the number of dependents claimed on the return. In 2012, most taxpayers were allowed a $3,800 personal exemption for themselves and each dependent. A personal exemption could not be claimed by a person who was claimed as a dependent on another taxpayer's return. For example, if you have a part-time job and your parents still claim you as a dependent on their income tax return, you *cannot* claim a personal exemption for yourself on your tax return.

The final step in calculating taxable income is to make additional deductions from AGI allowable under the law. Taxpayers can either take the **standard deduction**, which is a fixed dollar amount that is adjusted for inflation each year and varies with the filing status of the taxpayer, or itemize their deductions. The base standard deduction established in 2012 was $5,950 for a single taxpayer. Based on provisions of legislation enacted in 2003, married taxpayers filing jointly are allowed a standard deduction of twice that of single taxpayers ($11,900) in 2012.

Taxpayers also have the option to itemize specific allowable tax-deductible expenses *instead* of taking the standard deduction. **Itemized deductions** are expenses that can be legally deducted as an alternative to the standard deduction from adjusted gross income in figuring taxable income. Persons whose itemized deductions exceed the standard deduction to which they are entitled can obtain a lower taxable income by itemizing their deductions on a special form (Schedule A).

| TABLE 14.1 | Calculating Taxable Income under the U.S. Personal Income Tax System (Based on Rules Prevailing in 2012) |

Sources of Income Subject to Tax:

    Wages and Salaries

    Interest Income Received

    Dividends

    Rental Income

    Profits from Noncorporate Business Activity

    Taxable Pension Benefits

    Realized Capital Gains (Special Tax Rates Apply in Many Cases)

    Unemployment Compensation and a Portion of Other Government Payments to Individuals

    Alimony Received

    Miscellaneous Income (e.g., Awards and Prizes)

Total Equals: Gross Income

Less Adjustments to Gross Income:

    Moving Expenses Relating to Start of Work

    Contributions to Special Retirement Plans and Medical Savings Accounts

    Penalties for Early Withdrawal of Savings

    Alimony Paid

    A Portion of Self-Employment Tax and Heath Insurance

    Miscellaneous Costs for Employees and Businesses

    Miscellaneous Education Expenses

Equals: Adjusted Gross Income

Less Exemptions and Deductions (Either Standard or Itemized)

Equals: Taxable Income

© Cengage Learning

Taxable income in the United States is less than half of *personal income*, which is a measure of income available for persons to spend before personal taxes.[1] This suggests that the U.S. income tax is far from comprehensive in that it allows a substantial portion of personal income received each year to escape taxation. The fact that individuals can control their taxable income, and therefore the amount of tax they pay by controlling the sources and uses of their income, results in distortions in economic choices.

Tax Rate Structure

Once taxable income has been computed, the next step is to calculate tax liability. To do this, taxpayers use a tax rate schedule that applies to them. Different tax rate

---

[1]Internal Revenue Service, *Statistics of Income, Individual Income Tax Returns*, and U.S. Department of Commerce.

schedules apply to different taxpayers, depending on their filing status. One tax rate schedule applies to single taxpayers, another to married taxpayers filing joint returns, a third to married taxpayers filing separate returns, and yet a fourth to taxpayers filing as head of household.

A **tax bracket** is a range of income subject to a given marginal tax rate. Before 1987, the tax schedule contained as many as 16 different tax brackets, each with its own MTR. In 1980, the top marginal tax rate applied to nonlabor income in the highest tax bracket was 70 percent! As of 2012, the schedule contained only six tax brackets for taxpayers with taxable income, and the highest MTR was 35 percent.

Figure 14.1 shows how MTRs vary with taxable income based on the tax rate schedule that prevailed in 2012. In 2012, the 10 percent marginal tax bracket applied only to taxable income up to a maximum of $8,700 for single taxpayers and $17,400 for married taxpayers filing jointly. Thus, a married couple earning only $17,400 taxable income in 2012 would have paid $1,740 in income tax. Income above $8,700 for single taxpayers ($17,400 for married couples filing jointly) is taxed at 15 percent up to $35,350 ($70,700 for married couples filing jointly). Remember, these are MTRs that apply only to income in the designated bracket. As a taxpayer's income rises, the extra income is taxed at a higher rate only if it is beyond the bounds of the previous tax bracket. The graph shows how MTRs increase with taxable income. There are also tax rate schedules with brackets adjusted for heads of household and married taxpayers filing separately. The schedules for these two classes of tax filers are not shown in Figure 14.1.

FIGURE 14.1   Statutory MTRs for the U.S. Personal Income Tax, 2012*

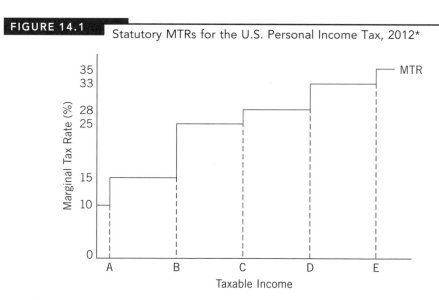

The U.S. personal income tax has a six-bracket progressive rate structure.
A = $8,700 for single taxpayers, $17,400 for married taxpayers filing jointly.
B = $35,350 for single taxpayers, $70,700 for married taxpayers filing jointly.
C = $85,650 for single taxpayers, $142,700 for married taxpayers filing jointly.
D = $178,650 for single taxpayers, $217,450 for married taxpayers filing jointly.
E = $388,350 single taxpayers, $388,350 for married taxpayers filing jointly.

*Intervals on the Horizontal axis are not drawn to scale.

Remember, taxable income is always less than gross income. If you are a single taxpayer who claimed one personal exemption worth $3,800 on your tax return in 2012 and took the standard deduction of $5,950 and made no adjustments to your gross income, then if your gross income were $25,000, your taxable income would be $25,000 − $9,750 = $15,250. The first $8,700 of this taxable income would be taxed at 10 percent. The $6,550 above the $8,700 would be taxed at 15 percent. Total tax would be $870 + $982.50 = $1,852.50. The ATR would be $1,825.50/ $15,250 or 12 percent of taxable income. Taxes paid are 7.3 percent of gross income.

Taxation of Low-Income Households

The income tax system has certain provisions that minimize the tax burden for low-income families and actually provides negative tax payments to some low-income workers. First of all, the personal exemptions and standard deduction imply that a substantial portion if not all of the gross income of low-income taxpayers is non-taxable. For example, suppose a low-income family of four, consisting of a married couple and two children, had a gross income of $27,100 in 2012 and takes the standard deduction. The family will be entitled to four personal exemptions worth $3,800 each and a standard deduction of $11,900 from income. The family deducts $15,200 in personal exemptions from its gross income, which when combined with the $11,900 standard deduction would result in $27,100 in deductions from gross income. The family's taxable income therefore would be zero!

In addition to benefiting from the personal exemptions and a standard deduction that are high proportions of a low income, those low-income taxpayers with dependent children and some workers without children are eligible for a special payment from the government if they work. The **Earned Income Tax Credit (EITC)** is a payment from the IRS to workers with dependent children and some single workers equal to a certain percentage of wage and salary income to those eligible. *In effect, the EITC is a tax refund to persons who do not owe any tax!* The credit amounts to a negative tax, or a subsidy, to the working poor. The EITC offsets the payroll tax on wages for many low-income workers. A certain maximum EITC per family applies, and the amount actually received depends on the family's actual earnings. The credit rises with wage and salary income at first and then is eventually phased out as income increases. The EITC provides income support to the working poor who are not eligible for federal income support through other programs and also supplements the income of part-time workers (see Chapter 7 for a discussion of EITC).

Changes in the Tax Base and Tax Rate Structure Beginning in 2013

The *American Taxpayer Relief Act of 2012* will result in changes in the way the tax base is calculated and in the tax rate structure beginning in the 2013 tax year. A seventh tax bracket is effective in that year with a marginal tax rate of 39.6 percent starting at $400,000 taxable income for single taxpayers and $450,000 for married taxpayers filing joint returns. Taxpayers with incomes above these levels will also pay a 20 percent tax personal income tax rate on their long-term capital gain and dividend income, which is up from the 15 percent tax rates that were applied under the provisions of EGTRRA. There is also a limitation on itemized deductions and a phaseout of personal exemptions under the provisions of ATRA starting in 2013.

Single taxpayers with threshold adjusted gross income of $250,000 per year and married couples filing jointly with AGI of $300,000 will see their otherwise allowable itemized deductions reduced by 3 percent of the dollar amount their actual AGI exceeds the applicable threshold level with a maximum reduction of 80 percent of itemized deductions. Also for taxpayers exceeding these threshold levels of income, their personal exemptions claimed will be reduced by 2 percent for each $2,500 their AGI exceeds the threshold level. Very high-income taxpayers can therefore lose the entire dollar amount of their personal exemptions when computing their taxable income.

CHECKPOINT

1. How is taxable income derived from gross income under the U.S. income tax code?
2. Why can't the U.S. income tax be regarded as a comprehensive income tax?
3. Describe the rate structure of the U.S. federal income tax.

TAX PREFERENCES

Still more complexity results from the federal income tax because individuals can, in part, control their taxable income by varying the sources and uses of their gross income. Let's now analyze how the rules and regulations of the income tax affect individual choices and the functioning of the economy.

Tax preferences are exclusions, exemptions, and deductions from the tax base. Tax preferences in the U.S. income tax code account for differences between taxable income and comprehensive income. Tax preferences can be thought of as subsidies—intentional or unintentional—to certain economic activities. Tax preferences are sometimes referred to as *tax loopholes*, but this term implies that they enter the tax code by accident, when, in fact, only a minority of the existing deductions and exemptions are present unintentionally. In any event, the existence of tax preferences changes the behavior of taxpayers so that they can avoid or manage their tax burden by taking advantage of the special provisions. Since tax preferences reduce the size of the tax base, their elimination would increase the amount of revenue that a given tax rate structure can collect. Tax preferences also affect the distribution of the tax burden and influence equity aspects of taxation.

Justification for Tax Preferences

Tax preferences are justified on various grounds: (1) administrative difficulty in taxing certain activities, (2) improving equity, and (3) encouraging private expenditures that generate external benefits. Whatever the justification, the existence of tax preferences has consequences both for the efficiency with which private resources are used and for the distribution of income.

Such exclusions from income as income-in-kind and unrealized capital gains represent tax preferences and often are allowed because of administrative difficulties in measuring their values. It would be difficult to develop a method of taxing all forms of income-in-kind in a consistent and equitable manner. Enforcement costs could be very high in administering a tax on these items, given the difficulties involved in measuring such items accurately. Similarly, it would be hard to measure unrealized capital gains or losses on such assets as owner-occupied homes that are infrequently sold.

Many exemptions and deductions from the tax base are justified in terms of equity considerations. For example, the basic personal exemption in the income tax varies with family size. It is based on the notion that it is equitable for families who have more children to pay less in taxes than families who have the same income but fewer children. In effect, this provides a subsidy for children. Similarly, deductions for medical expenses and casualty losses are based on the presumption that a loss in well-being occurs when either medical expenses or casualty losses resulting from theft or disaster over a certain percentage of income are not compensated with insurance reimbursement. Thus, individuals with high expenses of this type essentially are viewed as being less capable of paying taxes than are individuals who have the same income but no losses or medical expenses.

Finally, tax preferences are justified to encourage particular activities. For example, deductions from AGI for charitable donations constitute subsidies to charitable giving.[2] When tax preferences serve to encourage expenditures that generate positive externalities, they act as proxies for corrective subsidies. As such, these tax preferences could serve to help achieve efficiency. When viewed as corrective subsidies, tax preferences must be evaluated in terms of their costs (revenues sacrificed), the extent to which they internalize externalities, and their impact on the distribution of both the tax burden and income.[3]

Excess Burden of Tax Preferences

Tax preferences can distort the relative prices of items and activities that can be excluded, exempted, or deducted from taxable income in ways that lead to efficiency losses in markets. The **marginal tax benefit** of an activity is the extra tax reduction that results when an individual engages in it. For example, when an individual is allowed to deduct the interest on a mortgage, then his or her decision to obtain a mortgage to buy a home depends not only on the marginal social benefit from doing so but also on the marginal tax benefit (a reduction in taxes) that results. The marginal tax benefit results in efficiency losses when it causes persons to make decisions that result in divergences between marginal social benefits and marginal social costs of activities. Unless marginal tax benefits are balanced by marginal external benefits, tax preferences decrease efficiency by encouraging more than the efficient amount of an activity to be undertaken.

Let's assume a perfectly competitive market and also that as more of the activity is demanded, its market price remains unaffected. This assumption implies a perfectly elastic supply curve of the activity. This activity could be one that provides income from a certain source that is eligible for exclusion or exemption from

---

[2]For an analysis of the impact of tax preferences on charitable giving, see Charles T. Clotfelter, "The Impact of the Tax Reform on Charitable Giving: A 1989 Perspective," in *Do Taxes Matter?* ed. Joel Slemrod (Cambridge, Mass.: The MIT Press, 1990).

[3]Feldstein has argued that it might be desirable in certain cases to subsidize activities through tax preferences. See Martin Feldstein, "Contribution to the Theory of Tax Expenditures: The Case of Charitable Giving," in *The Economics of Taxation*, eds. Henry J. Aaron and Michael J. Boskin (Washington, D.C.: The Brookings Institution, 1980): 99–122. Also see Gerald E. Auten, Holger Sieg, and Charles T. Clotfelter, "Charitable Giving, Income, and Taxes: An Analysis of Panel Data," *American Economic Review*, 92 (March 1, 2002): 309–385.

taxable income. It could also be an activity, such as charitable donations or payment of interest on mortgages, that is tax deductible. The supply curve of the activity for the taxpayer is a horizontal line reflecting the marginal social cost of the activity, as shown in Figure 14.2. The efficient output, Q^*, assuming no externalities, corresponds to point A. At that point, the marginal social cost of the activity equals its marginal social benefit. The market price of the item is P_G.

Now assume that good X is an item for which annual personal expenditures can be deducted before computing personal income. This has the effect of decreasing the price of the preferred item to certain taxpayers according to their marginal tax rate, t. The effect is to lower the net price, as seen by those taxpayers, from P_G to

$$P_N = P_G(1 - t). \tag{14.1}$$

The decrease in the price to P_N is only for those taxpayers eligible for the tax preference, and it varies with the MTR. In the case of tax preferences from deductions, taxpayers who do not itemize their deductions would still pay P_G, the gross price of the good. For example, assume that the tax-preferred activity is borrowing money to finance the purchase of a home. Suppose a taxpayer who is subject to a marginal tax rate of 28 percent borrows money at 12 percent interest. If interest is tax deductible for this person, the net interest rate is

$$i_N = 12\%(1.0 - 0.28) = 8.64\% \tag{14.2}$$

By lowering net prices in this way, tax preferences increase the annual amount of the tax-preferred item or activity from Q^* to Q_1. There is an efficiency loss measured by the excess of the marginal social cost over the marginal social benefit of

FIGURE 14.2 Tax Preference and Efficiency

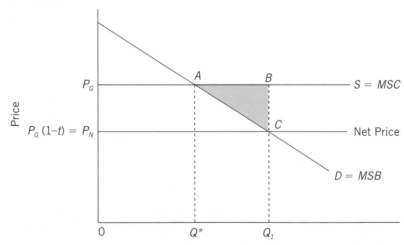

Tax preferences reduce the net prices of engaging in tax-preferred activities. The efficient output corresponds to the point at which $MSC = MSB$. The tax preference reduces the net price of purchasing or supplying tax-deductible or other tax-preferred activities. As a result, annual output increased from Q^* to Q_1. The loss in efficiency is represented by the shaded area ABC.

the good. For the taxpayer whose demand curve is illustrated in Figure 14.2, the social loss in net benefits due to the tax-induced increase in resources used in the annual amount of the tax-preferred activity is the area ABC.

Notice that the excess burden of a tax preference depends not only on the number of persons who qualify for it or take advantage of it but also on the MTR. Figure 14.3 shows the impact of MTRs on tax preference activities. Suppose an upper-income taxpayer is subject to a 50 percent MTR. The price of engaging in the tax-preferred activity is P_G. In the absence of any tax preference, the individuals would choose Q^* units of the preferred activity. This is the amount for which the marginal social cost of the activity equals its marginal social benefit. Under a 50 percent marginal tax rate, this person engages in Q_1 units of the tax-preferred activity per year. The excess burden of the tax preference is represented by the area of the triangle ABC. Assume that this person is now subject to a 28 percent MTR. The price of the tax-preferred activity is now $0.72\ P_G$. The increase in the net price in engaging in the activity decreases the annual amount from Q_1 to Q_2. The corresponding decrease in the excess burden is $B'BCC'$. For example, mortgage interest deductions, tax-free interest income from municipal bonds, and charitable contributions all will be worth less to taxpayers as a result of the decrease in MTRs. In general, this would imply a decrease in the volume of activities that are still tax preferred.

The excess burden of existing tax preferences depends in part on the MTR paid by those who can engage in them. When MTRs decline on average, the excess burden of existing tax preferences also will fall as the incentive to engage in them diminishes. Conversely, when MTRs increase, the excess burden of tax preferences will go up.

FIGURE 14.3   Decrease in Excess Burden of Tax Preferences

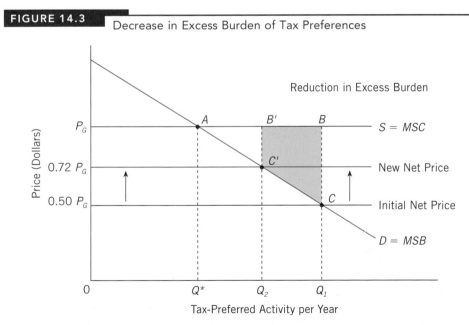

A decrease in the MTR results in a decrease in the excess burden from tax preferences. The area $B'BCC'$ represents the gain in net social benefits as a result of the reduction in the MTR.

1. What are tax preferences?
2. What is the marginal tax benefit of an activity?
3. How do tax preferences result in inefficient resource use?

TAX PREFERENCES UNDER THE U.S. INCOME TAX SYSTEM

We can now examine major tax preferences in the tax code that account for differences between taxable income and a comprehensive measure of income and discuss their economic effects. Tax preferences can be divided into three major categories: exclusions from income, itemized deductions from adjusted gross income, and tax credits.

Exclusions from Income

1. **Income-in-Kind and Imputed Housing Rental Income** Much of income-in-kind, such as that stemming from do-it-yourself activities, is simply difficult to measure. These items typically are excluded from taxable income. It is unlikely that any consistent and equitable manner could be devised to measure and tax this form of income. Other types of income-in-kind, such as imputed rentals on housing, conceivably could be measured and taxed. For example, some European countries do tax the imputed rentals on owner-occupied homes, and data from the local property tax on housing values conceivably could be used to derive a consistent and reasonably equitable measure of imputed rent.

   Exemption of imputed rentals on owner-occupied homes gives considerable subsidy to home ownership in the United States. Some of this subsidy, however, might be offset by the impact of local property taxes on the cost of home ownership. Homeowners in owner-occupied homes essentially rent their homes to themselves. Because no market transaction takes place and no cash is exchanged, the housing services thus obtained escape taxation. However, the value of housing services homeowners receive, less the costs of home ownership, is part of their comprehensive income. The exclusion of imputed rentals on owner-occupied homes is a subsidy to home ownership that encourages more than the efficient amount of resources to be allocated to the production of housing. The Office of Management and Budget estimated that the value of this subsidy to homeowners in fiscal year 2012 amounted to a bit more than $50.6 billion. Because taxpayers with higher incomes are more likely to own rather than rent their homes and tend to live in bigger more valuable homes, this subsidy tends to accrue disproportionately to upper income groups.

   One estimate of the distortion in the choice between renting and owning homes, due to the exclusion of imputed rent and other preferential treatment of housing in the tax code, suggests that one-fourth of the U.S. growth in the proportion of home ownership from World War II through the 1970s is traceable to such preferential tax treatment.[4] In general, tax reform proposals have rarely suggested broadening the tax base by trying to tax nonmonetary rents, because it would be hard to accurately measure these rents. It is also likely that such a proposal would be politically unpopular with homeowners. If imputed rents were taxed and the mortgage interest deduction eliminated, De Leeuw and Ozanne estimate that the price of a typical home would fall by more than 14 percent.[5] However, the reduction in marginal tax rates (MTRs), particularly for upper-income taxpayers since 1980, has reduced the value of the exclusion of imputed rentals significantly. The reduced tax benefit of home ownership implies a reduced demand for homes, particularly expensive homes, which can downward pressure on home prices.[6] The values of homes in many areas of the nation declined in the early 1990s, due in part to changes in the tax law.

2. **Fringe Benefits** Workers are typically compensated in forms that supplement their wages and salaries and are excluded from current taxable income. For example, if you have a pension or retirement plan at your job, it is likely that your employer contributes to this plan. Although employer contribution to pension or retirement plans constitutes part of the compensation of workers, and certainly adds to employees' net worth, these contributions are excluded from current gross income under the present-day U.S. tax laws.

   Similarly, employer contributions for employees' insurance is another fringe benefit that is part of a worker's income and is also excluded from gross income. Group-term life insurance, health insurance, educational benefits, legal services, and child care provided by employers are really forms of income-in-kind that are excluded from income.

   Self-employed workers also can defer taxation on pension contributions by deducting as an adjustment to gross income their contributions to special retirement plans they can set up under current law. However, retired workers receiving pensions do pay taxes on the portion of their pensions that was excluded from their income during their working years. The exclusion of pension contributions and medical insurance premiums from current gross income of workers results in a loss of income tax revenue to the government amounting to more than $315 billion in 2012, according to estimates by the Office of Management and Budget.

3. **Transfers** Most government transfers to individuals are excluded from gross income. Government transfers may be either in the form of government income support or in the form of social insurance payments to individuals. Private transfers also exist in the form of private charity or gifts. Under a comprehensive income tax, transfers represent taxable income for the recipient.

   The U.S. federal tax code does not treat transfers consistently. Gifts and inheritances are excluded from the income of the recipient under the presumption that,

---

[4]Harvey S. Rosen and Kenneth T. Rosen, "Federal Taxes and Homeownership: Evidence from Times Series," *Journal of Political Economy* 88 (February 1980): 59–75.

[5]See Frank D. De Leeuw and Larry O. Ozanne, "Housing," in *How Taxes Affect Economic Behavior*, eds. Henry J. Aaron and Joseph A. Pechman, 29.

[6]See James M. Poterba, "Taxation and Housing Markets: Preliminary Evidence," in *Do Taxes Matter? The Impact of the Tax Reform Act of 1986*, ed. Joel Slemrod (Cambridge, Mass.: The MIT Press, 1990): 141–161. For recent analysis, see Edward L. Glaeser and Jessie M. Shapiro, "The Benefits of the Home Mortgage Interest Deduction," in *Tax Policy and the Economy*, James M. Poterba (ed.), vol. 17, pp. 37–82 (Cambridge, Mass.: The MIT Press, 2003).

as income to the donor, they already have been taxed. There are, however, gift and inheritance taxes separate from the income tax that are discussed in Chapter 17. In most cases, a gift cannot be deducted from the income of the donor unless it is a charitable contribution. According to the Haig-Simons definition, a gift qualifies as a use of income to the donor and represents a form of consumption to the donor that would be included in income. Similarly, because a gift increases the donee's command over resources, it is technically part of his or her income as well. Although this subjects a gift to double taxation, it is a consistent way of treating the tax base, which is defined on an individual basis.[7] An exception to this rule is alimony, which the tax code treats as taxable income to the recipient but constitutes an adjustment subtracted from the gross income of the person who pays it. However, child support payments are not included in the income of the recipient, nor are they deductible as an adjustment to income for the person paying them.

No attempt is made to tax such transfers-in-kind as Supplementary Nutrition Benefits, Medicare and Medicaid payments, and such other subsidies as public housing, even if these subsidies accrue to individuals whose annual income exceeds any basic tax-free allowance. Even if these items were to be included in the income of the recipients, it is unlikely that they would be taxable because of the fact that personal exemptions and the standard deduction remove most persons in poverty from the tax rolls. Unemployment compensation is, however, now included in gross income and fully taxable. Social Security retirement benefits are partially taxable for persons with incomes above certain levels. As much as 85 percent of the Social Security pensions of those with relatively high incomes can be subject to tax under rules prevailing in 2012.

4. **Capital Gains and Dividends** Perhaps the most controversial area in defining taxable income is the treatment of capital gains. *Only realized capital gains are included in taxable income.* A realized capital gain is one that is obtained when an asset is sold for cash or exchanged for another asset. In 2012, realized short-term capital gains on most assets were taxed as ordinary income. Long-term capital gains (those on qualified assets sold at least one year after purchase) are taxed at 15 percent for most taxpayers with some taxpayers with low incomes exempt from taxes on capital gains. Based on provisions of the *American Taxpayer Relief Act of 2012* upper-income taxpayers with more than $400,000 taxable income ($450,000 if married filing jointly) will pay a 20 percent income tax rate on their realized long-term capital gains starting in 2013.

Net positive capital gains, adjusted by an index of the price level, do constitute an increase in a person's potential purchasing power. The federal income tax code currently does not adjust capital gains for inflation.[8] In this sense, much of the tax on capital gains is not levied on increased purchasing power.[9] Some economists have argued that preferential tax treatment of realized capital gains is justified in the United States to compensate for the fact

---

[7]Gift and inheritance taxes do subject the donor or his or her estate to taxes. These are property transfer taxes, which are discussed in Chapter 17.

[8]For a discussion of issues involved in indexing capital gains for tax purposes, see U.S. Congress, Congressional Budget Office, *Indexing Capital Gains* (Washington, D.C.: U.S. Government Printing Office, August 1990).

[9]See Martin Feldstein and Joel Slemrod, "Inflation and the Excess Taxation of Capital Gains on Corporate Stock," *National Tax Journal* 31 (June 1978): 107–118.

that such gains are not indexed for the rate of inflation. Failure to adjust capital gains for inflation creates serious problems in tax equity and efficiency. This is considered later in this chapter.

Exclusion of unrealized capital gains from taxation makes those who have such gains better off. This is because they can defer the tax on any gains that they do not convert into cash. For example, if a person buys $5,000 worth of corporate stock and the value of that stock increases to $10,000 over the year, he or she will have earned $5,000 in capital gains. If all his or her capital gains, realized and unrealized, are subject to a tax of 20 percent, he or she would have a tax liability of $1,000 on the gain. If only realized gains are taxed, he or she can postpone the tax by holding on to the stock and not converting it to cash. This makes his or her better off because he or she can earn interest, and possibly additional capital gains, on the $1,000 that he or she otherwise would have had to pay in taxes that year.

Under current rules, capital gains are not taxed at death. This means that unrealized capital gains can escape taxation completely if they are held until death. Investors therefore can leave more to their heirs by not cashing in their capital gains before they die.

Some evidence indicates that exclusion of unrealized capital gains from taxation does discourage investors from selling assets on which they have accumulated gains. This is sometimes called the lock-in effect, resulting from the exclusion of unrealized capital gains from taxation. One study found that a reduction in actual capital gains tax rates would be likely to increase turnover of assets.[10] A number of studies have found that capital gains realizations are very sensitive to the tax rate applied to realized capital gains.[11]

Very liberal provisions exist for excluding long-term capital gains on owner-occupied housing. Married couples can earn up to $500,000 in capital gains exempt from tax from the sale of their principal residence. Single taxpayers can exempt $250,000 capital gains from the sale of their homes.

The controversy over tax treatment of capital gains continues, with some arguing that exclusion of a portion of realized capital gains from taxation can increase the return to investment and encourage the start of new businesses. However, preferential treatment of capital gains also can encourage conversion of other forms of income into capital gains. For example, a lower tax applied to capital gains could encourage corporations to reduce payout of dividends. Instead, the corporations would take income normally used to finance dividends and use it as a means of increasing their acquisition of capital. This would provide shareholders with income in the form of capital gains, which then would be taxed at a lower rate than dividend income. Based on legislation enacted in 2003, dividends received by individual shareholders from domestic and qualified foreign corporations are taxed at the same rate as long-term capital gains. This legislation is designed to encourage investment in corporate assets.

---

[10]Gerald E. Auten and Charles T. Clotfelter, "Permanent versus Transitory Tax Effects and the Realization of Capital Gains," *The Quarterly Journal of Economics* 97 (November 1982): 613–632.

[11]For a summary of these studies, see U.S. Congress, Congressional Budget Office, *How Capital Gains Tax Rates Affect Revenues: The Historical Evidence* (Washington, D.C.: The Congress of the United States, March 1988). Also see Alan Auerbach and Jonathan Siegel, "Capital Gains Realizations of the Rich and Sophisticated," *American Economic Review*, 90 (May 2000): 275–282 and Zoran Ivkovic, James Poterba, and Scott Weisbenner, "Tax Motivated Trading by Individual Investors," National Bureau of Economic Research (NBER) Working Paper 10275 (Cambridge, Mass.: NBER, 2004).

5. **Interest on State and Local Government Bonds** Exclusion of interest earned on state and local government bonds from taxable income represents a subsidy to these governments. This tax preference subsidizes state and local governments by allowing them to borrow money at lower rates than would be the case if purchasers of their bonds had to pay tax on their interest earnings. The attractiveness of such bonds to holders depends on their net yield (which, in turn, depends on the taxpayer's marginal tax rate) and the interest spread between municipal bonds and securities with similar risk and return attributes but a yield that is subject to taxation. For example, an investor who is in a 33 percent tax bracket and who can earn 14 percent on a fully taxable bond would require a yield of at least 9.38 percent on a municipal bond of equal riskiness to be induced to buy it. This is because his after-tax return on the taxable bond is 9.38 percent, which is equal to $14(1 - 0.33)$ percent. An investor in a 15 percent marginal tax bracket, however, would earn 11.90 percent after taxes on the 14 percent bond. This investor would not buy the municipal bond unless it returned at least 11.90 percent. The actual interest rate paid by local governments depends on the demand and supply of their bonds. However, the more bonds they must sell to investors in tax brackets below 33 percent to obtain their required funds, the higher the interest rate that state and local governments must pay to attract funds.

   The subsidy to state and local governments is measured by the yield spread between the interest rate at which they can borrow and the rate at which they would have to borrow in the absence of the exclusion. This second rate can be approximated by the rate on taxable securities of similar maturity and risk. The cost of the subsidy to the federal government is measured by the loss in tax revenues from excluding the interest from taxable income.

   Suppose state and local governments save on average about 20 percent on their interest rates, because they have to make their bonds attractive to taxpayers with MTRs below 33 percent to raise enough funds. They might pay 8 percent instead of the 10 percent that corporations pay on average. Suppose, however, the federal government loses on average 30 percent of the interest rate. This is because many investors with MTRs in excess of 30 percent buy the bonds. The market interest rates for the bonds must be high enough to make them attractive to at least some investors in the lower tax brackets. For example, if $5 billion in interest is earned on tax-exempt bonds, the government would lose 30 percent of this amount, or $1.5 billion per year in revenues. The savings to state and local governments are only $1 billion, or 20 percent of the $5 billion interest costs. The subsidy costs more than it is worth. In other words, those who pay federal taxes would be better off, and local governments could be as well-off, if the federal government made payments to local governments equal to the interest spread that prevails under exclusion instead of excluding the interest from taxation.

6. **Miscellaneous Exclusions and Adjustments** Scholarships and fellowships are excluded from income for degree candidates only. However, these sources of income are excluded only to the extent to which they do not exceed tuition and other course-related expenses. Amounts for room, board, and other incidental expenses are not excluded from gross income.

   Saving for retirement in special accounts is an adjustment to income. Individuals with incomes below a certain level and others who are not active participants in an employer-maintained retirement plan can deduct limited amounts of saving from their gross income when computing adjusted gross income. Employees also can exclude some of their income from taxation by contributing to special retirement plans called 401(k) and 403(b) plans, which are permitted by these numbered sections of the Internal Revenue Code. Finally, self-employed persons can also deduct retirement contributions made to special "Keogh," "SIMPLE," and "SEP" plans as adjustments to their gross income.

Adjustments to income for retirement saving are designed as a subsidy to saving that allows amounts deposited in such accounts along with accrued earnings tax-free status until withdrawn as retirement income after the worker reaches a certain age, usually 59½. Exclusions from and adjustments to gross income give taxpayers taking advantage of such provisions ample opportunity to "defer" taxable income. **Deferral of taxable income** means that income that is ordinarily taxable can be excluded or deducted from gross income in the current year but will be taxed eventually along with the accrued interest and capital gains. Deferral of tax liability makes taxpayers better off by allowing them to earn both interest and possible capital gains on the amount they would have paid in taxes.

The advantage of postponing tax liability can be enormous. For example, suppose you are self-employed and put $10,000 this year into an SEP retirement plan. Also assume that you are in the 28 percent marginal tax bracket. This means that of the $10,000 saved, $2,800 would have been paid in taxes. In effect, you would be saving $7,200 of your own income and $2,800 in taxes. Assume that you hold this money in an account that earns 10 percent annually for 20 years and that you remove the principal and accumulated interest from the account and pay the regular 28 percent tax on the sum after 20 years. When saving that was previously tax deferred is removed from an account, it is taxed as if it were current income.

As the $10,000 is held in the account, the interest income accrues *tax-free*. After 20 years, assuming annual compounding, the $10,000 will be worth

$$\$10,000(1 + 0.10)^{20} = \$67,000 \tag{14.3}$$

The net income over the 20-year period would be $57,000. When the asset is cashed in, a tax liability of 28 percent of the net income *and* the $10,000 principal will be incurred of $0.28(\$67,000) = \$18,760$. The net income earned over the 20-year period after taxes would be $57,000 − $18,760 = $38,240.

If instead the $10,000 saving was *not allowed to be deducted* from gross income, then, by saving, the taxpayer would not reduce his tax liability by $2,800 in the year the $10,000 is saved. Therefore, after deduction of $2,800 of taxes due on the $10,000 of taxable income saved, the net saving will be only $7,200. Further, if the interest on the saving is treated as normal income, it will be taxed as it accrues because it will no longer be in a special tax-deferred account. The *after-tax* interest rate will be

$$10(1 - 0.28)\% = 10(0.72)\% = 7.2\%. \tag{14.4}$$

After 20 years, the net saving of $7,200 will be worth

$$\$7,200(1 + 0.072)^{20} = \$28,944. \tag{14.5}$$

The net income after taxes in 20 years will be $28,944 minus $7,200, or $21,744. This is substantially less than the net income of $38,240 that can be obtained after taxes when saving is deductible as an adjustment to income and the interest accrues tax-free until the funds are removed from the account. Tax deductibility of funds put into special savings accounts and deferral of taxes on interest and other earnings on those accounts therefore represent a substantial subsidy to saving.

Itemized Deductions from Adjusted Gross Income

Taxpayers have the option of itemizing deductions. When the itemized deductions a taxpayer can claim exceed the standard deduction entitled to the taxpayer, then it pays to itemize. By increasing the standard deduction substantially indexing it for inflation, the Tax Reform Act of 1986 increased the threshold over which itemized deductions must pass to make it worthwhile. As a result, the number of taxpayers itemizing deductions has declined. In 2012, the standard deduction for married taxpayers filing joint returns was $11,900. This means that a household filing a joint return would effectively reduce its taxes by itemizing its deductions only if the total amount of deductions exceeded $11,900. The standard deduction for a single taxpayer was $5,950 in 2012. Nonetheless, upper-income taxpayers still take advantage of itemization, and their choices are strongly influenced by the rules governing what is or is not deductible.

The major tax-deductible expenses are reviewed in this section. Remember that the benefit of a tax deduction varies with the taxpayer's marginal tax rate. If a person subject to an MTR of 33 percent obtains a mortgage of 10 percent and can deduct all interest payments, his or her *net interest* is only $10(1 - 0.33)\%$, or 6.7 percent, after the benefit of the tax deduction is considered. A person who is subject to a marginal tax rate of 15 percent and who can deduct interest payments would pay a net interest of $10(1 - 0.15)\%$, or 8.5 percent, on a loan at 10 percent after the tax deduction. Of course, one who does not itemize deductions does not enjoy any tax-induced price reduction on borrowed funds. Tax deductibility of an expense provides a reduction in the net price of the associated activity available to those who itemize deductions according to the taxpayer's marginal tax bracket. Discussions of the major tax-deductible expenses follow.

1. **Medical Expenses** Unreimbursed medical expenses in excess of 7.5 percent of AGI were tax deductible in 2012 (starting in 2013 only medical expenses in excess of 10 percent of AGI will be deductible). The floor in medical expense, before deductibility is allowed, can be viewed as consistent with the notion that a certain minimal amount of medical expense increases individual well-being and does not decrease the ability to pay taxes. The generalization that all medical expenses greater than the minimal amount decrease well-being and the ability to pay is somewhat broad. Elective cosmetic surgery and voluntary psychiatric treatment are examples of chosen medical expenditures that are likely to increase well-being.

   The result of allowing individuals to deduct a portion of their medical expenses is that the federal government pays part of the medical bills of certain households. After an individual who itemizes deductions incurs medical expenses in excess of 7.5 percent of AGI, the federal government, in effect, pays a portion of any additional bills according to the taxpayer's MTR. For example, if the taxpayer is subject to a 33 percent MTR, then after incurring a certain amount of expense, the federal government ends up paying one-third of this person's out-of-pocket additional medical bills in excess of 7.5 percent of the taxpayer's adjusted gross income. This subsidizes medical services above the tax deductibility threshold. Taxpayers also can be induced to adjust the timing of some out-of-pocket medical expenses so that they are lumped in a single year and will exceed 7.5 percent of AGI.

2. **State and Local Income and Property Taxes** Certain taxes, including income and property taxes, paid to state and local governments are tax deductible. These deductions constitute indirect subsidies to those governments, encouraging them to adjust their tax structures to include more types of taxes that are deductible from AGI under the federal income tax. These subsidies occur because the deductions reduce the tax burden to taxpayers in states and localities, making it easier to gain collective approval on extensions of local public spending. The benefit of this provision varies from taxpayer to taxpayer according to the marginal tax bracket, but it might be offset by higher federal tax rates to compensate for the resulting loss in federal revenues. In addition, citizens in states or localities with above-average tax rates or income levels gain as a result of this provision relative to citizens in other areas.

   Some reform proposals have recommended the elimination of these tax deductions, which would cut the subsidies to state and local government expenditures. The argument is that services supplied by state and local governments provide benefits to citizens exactly as private goods do; therefore, they should be viewed analogously. Also, subsidies accrue more than proportionately to high-tax, urban states. In addition, high-income taxpayers subject to high MTRs receive proportionately more of the benefits. Eliminating the deductibility of state and local taxes would make it more difficult for state and local governments to raise revenues. The Tax Reform Act of 1986 removed the deductibility of state and local sales taxes, but income and property taxes levied by state and local governments are still included in federal itemized deductions.

3. **Interest Payments** Certain interest payments made by households are tax-deductible. Interest on mortgages of a taxpayer's first and second home is deductible. Interest incurred to make financial investments, such as to buy stock on margin, is deductible but is limited to total investment income. No deduction, however, for such personal interest expense as car loans, credit cards, or other personal loans, including educational loans, is permitted.

   Interest on mortgage debt incurred to buy, build, or improve a main or second home in excess of $1 million of mortgage debt is not deductible. And mortgage interest on mortgage debt greater than $100,000 is not deductible if that debt was incurred on the main home for a purpose other than to buy, build, or improve a home. However, special deductibility limits are available for homeowners who refinance their mortgages and obtain line-of-credit mortgages.

   The deduction of mortgage interest is based on an analogy between the business firm and the household, arguing that interest is a cost of production. The difference between household mortgage credit and business credit is important. Firms borrow to finance their productive operations; income from production is then subject to tax. Individuals who receive credit to finance homes obtain assets or consumer services that produce income-in-kind, which is not subject to taxation. Using a comprehensive definition of income, deduction of interest would be warranted as a cost of earning income only to the extent to which income-in-kind, stemming from expenditures made possible by borrowing, were taxed.

Another problem with the mortgage interest deduction stems from the fungibility of money. Money can be used for a multitude of purposes. By limiting interest deductions to mortgages, Congress hoped to discourage borrowing for consumer purchases like vacations, stereos, cars, and other consumer durables. However, when a person borrows to finance a home, it frees income to be used for other purchases. Some taxpayers now may choose to borrow more than they would have otherwise on their homes—or build or buy more expensive homes. The resulting increases in their cash balances enable them to buy more consumer items without incurring debt specifically for those purchases. Banks and financial institutions realized this quickly and developed "line of credit home equity loans" that enabled consumers who owned homes to use their homes as collateral for credit. The limits on deductibility of interest imposed by Congress are designed to limit the incentive to use mortgages in place of consumer credit.

Evidence of the impact of the limitations on deductibility of interest from adjusted gross income suggests that although the limits did reduce taxpayer reliance on personal borrowing, it was not effective in reducing overall borrowing. The wealthier taxpayers who owned homes and itemized deductions consolidated and reshuffled their personal debts into home mortgage loans, leaving total credit extended unchanged.[12] The mortgage interest deduction subsidizes home ownership in the same way as the exemption of imputed rents on owner-occupied homes. It encourages investment in housing and, because under current law, the deduction is allowed on mortgage loans up to $1 million in value, and on second homes it is likely to accrue disproportionately to upper-income households. Critics of the mortgage interest deduction and other aspects of the tax code that subsidize home ownership argue that the indirect subsidy to housing diverts capital from other uses that would increase worker productivity and long-term economic growth and that it encourages wealthy taxpayers to build large and expensive homes. The Congressional Joint Committee on Taxation estimated that in 2004, 55 percent of the benefit of the mortgage interest tax preference accrued to only 12 percent of taxpayers. That 12 percent consisted of upper-income households with incomes in excess of $100,000 per year. Because most lower income households choose to take the standard deduction rather than itemizing deductions when they file their income tax returns, they get no benefit from the interest deduction.

To correct for these perceived inequities from the mortgage interest deduction, a 2005 report by a presidential commission on tax reform recommended converting the deduction to a tax credit that would be available to all homeowners whether or not they itemized their deductions and to limit the amount that can be claimed to much less than the current amounts. Curtailing the mortgage interest deduction and other tax preferences in the tax code that subsidize home ownership would likely decrease the demand for homes while

---

[12]See Jonathan Skinner and Daniel Feenberg, "Impact of the 1986 Tax Reform on Personal Saving," in *Do Taxes Matter?* ed. Slemrod, 50–79.

increasing the demand for rental housing and other investments. It would likely result in a fall in the market equilibrium price of single-family and vacation homes that would decrease the value of a principal asset in most families' portfolios: their homes. Expensive homes are likely to be most affected. However, for modest homes typically purchased by lower-income households who do not itemize deductions, prices could conceivably rise if the tax credit increases demand for these homes.

4. **Charitable Contributions** As discussed previously, deductibility of charitable contributions, including those made in-kind, constitutes a subsidy to private transfers to charitable and other nonprofit organizations, including educational institutions. A number of studies have provided evidence indicating that charitable giving is highly responsive to tax deductibility.[13] The tax deduction decreases the "price" of charitable giving by the giver's MTR. For example, a taxpayer subject to an MTR of 33 percent really gives only 67 cents each time he or she donates $1 to charity. The other 33 cents is represented by a reduction in tax revenues to the federal government. If charitable donations are elastic with respect to tax deductibility, the percentage increase in giving that results from the tax deduction exceeds the percentage reduction in taxes paid. This means that the 33 cents of lost revenue to the Treasury from the tax deduction results in *more* than 33 cents worth of additional giving. For this reason, the tax deduction for charitable contributions seems to be a very effective means of encouraging donations. This could even act to reduce government expenditures if the private giving made it possible for the government to devote less of its resources to helping the poor than it would otherwise.

   Research on the impact of reduced MTRs since 1986 has provided evidence that the reductions in the marginal tax rates did result in a fall of charitable contribution by taxpayers for which the "price" of giving was increased.[14]

5. **Miscellaneous Deductions** Employees who incur unreimbursed business expenses, including those for travel, can deduct those expenses but only to the extent to which they exceed 2 percent of AGI. However, attendance at conventions or seminars is not deductible unless it is for trade or business purposes, and only 50 percent of meals and entertainment expenses are tax deductible.

Tax Deductions versus Tax Credits

Tax credits instead of tax deductions have been available for such activities and expenses as child care. The difference between a tax credit and a tax deduction is that credits are based on a certain percentage of the expense incurred, and this percentage is fixed for all taxpayers regardless of their income and

---

[13]See Charles T. Clotfelter and C. Eugene Steurle, "Charitable Contributions," in *How Taxes Affect Economic Behavior*, eds. Aaron and Pechman, 403–446. Also see Gerald E. Auten, Holger Sieg, and Charles T. Clotfelter, "Charitable Giving, Income, and Taxes: An Analysis of Panel Data," *American Economic Review*, 92 (March 1, 2002): 309–385.

[14]See Charles T. Clotfelter, "Impact of Tax Reform on Charitable Giving: A 1989 Perspective," in *Do Taxes Matter?* ed. Slemrod, 203–235.

MTRs and whether they itemize deductions. The value of tax deductions, on the other hand, varies with the taxpayer's marginal tax bracket in terms of the reduction in taxes that the deductions entail. They give more benefit, in monetary terms, to upper-income taxpayers, who are subject to higher MTRs. Those who favor an increase in the progressivity of the federal tax rate structure generally favor tax credits over tax deductions. Another advantage of credits to lower income tax is that individuals get a tax reduction from engaging in the activity for which a credit is provided even if they do not itemize their deductions. Because most low-income taxpayers do not itemize, this is of considerable benefit to them.

The *Taxpayer Relief Act of 1997* sharply expanded the scope of tax credits available to families with children. These credits accrue mainly to lower- and middle-income households and are phased out for upper-income households according to a complex formula. As of 2012, the maximum credit per child was $1,000, which was directly deductible from the taxpayer's tax liability. The credit is generally available to households with children under the age of 17 and is phased out for households with more than a certain amount of adjusted gross income ($110,000 for couples, $75,000 for single parents). In addition, the EGTRRA increased the maximum amount available for the child and dependent care credit to $3,000 for a single qualifying dependent and $6,000 for two or more dependents.

Tax credits (called "hope" and "lifetime learning" credits) are also available to taxpayers with expenses for higher education. These tax credits are available mainly to lower- and middle-income taxpayers paying higher education expenses for students (either for themselves, a spouse, or dependents). The amounts available are limited and are phased out (reduced) as taxpayer income rises above certain limits. As of 2012, most single taxpayers with adjusted gross income between $52,000 and $62,000 ($104,000 and $124,000 if married and filing jointly) had their benefits reduced below the maximum amounts available. In 2012, taxpayers with adjusted gross incomes in excess of $62,000 ($124,000 if married and filing jointly) generally were not eligible for higher education tax credits. As of 2012, the maximum hope credit was $2,500 per eligible student and the maximum lifetime learning credit was $2,500 per tax return. These tax credits can be viewed as subsidies to both child rearing and higher education.

Tax Expenditures

Tax preferences not only cause losses in efficiency but also result in reduction in revenue collection by decreasing the size of the tax base. **Tax expenditures** are losses in tax revenues attributable to tax preferences. The Office of Management and Budget is required to compute tax expenditures annually and submit them to Congress as part of the president's budget. Tax expenditures also are estimated by the Joint Committee on Taxation of the U.S. Congress, which publishes five-year projections of tax expenditures for use by Congress. Tax expenditures provide a useful starting point for evaluating tax preferences in terms of the loss in tax revenues.

Elimination of tax preferences broadens the tax base and allows lower rates of taxation without reducing revenues collected. However, the elimination would increase the net price of engaging in tax-preferred activities and reduce the levels of such activities. Taxable income would not increase by the full amount of income on which tax expenditures are calculated. Elimination of certain tax preferences would cause persons to adjust their behavior to decrease tax-preferred activities and to increase the amount of activities that still receive preferential treatment for tax purposes. Therefore, it is likely that gains in revenue to the Treasury due to the elimination of tax preferences are overestimated. In effect, the Treasury, in computing tax expenditures, assumes that all activities are perfectly inelastic with respect to their tax-preferred treatment and that elimination of any one tax preference does not affect the value of any other tax preference.

Table 14.2 shows the major tax preferences of the personal income tax and the projected revenue losses for fiscal year 2012. The largest tax expenditure item

---

TABLE 14.2   Major Tax Expenditures Resulting from the U.S. Income Tax, Fiscal Year 2012

PROVISION	REVENUE LOSS, 2012 (MILLIONS OF DOLLARS)
Exclusion of Employer Contributions for Medical Insurance Premiums and Care	170,650
Deductibility of Mortgage Interest Owner-Occupied Homes	86,910
Net Exclusion of Pension Contributions and Earnings: Employer Plans	44,490
Net Exclusion of Pension Contributions and Earnings: 401(k) Plans	60,090
Capital Gains (Reduced Tax Rates)	66,210
Deductibility of State and Local Taxes Other Than on Owner-Occupied Homes	33,180
Deductibility of Charitable Contributions Other Than Education and Health	33,290
Step-Up Basis of Capital Gains at Death	19,940
Exclusion of Interest on Public Purpose State and Local Bonds	29,080
Exclusion of Interest on Life Insurance Savings Child Credit	23,570
	24,470
Capital Gains Exclusion on Home Sales	16,040
Net Exclusion of Pension Contributions and Earnings Individual Retirement Accounts	15,410
Exclusion of Social Security Benefits for Retired Workers	25,970
Deductibility of State and Local Property Tax on Owner-Occupied Homes	16,150

Source: Office of Management and Budget.

in the tax code is exclusion of employer contributions for medical insurance and health care from taxable income. This tax preference was projected to result in a loss of more than $170 billion in revenue for the Treasury in 2012. Deductibility of mortgage interest on owner-occupied homes cost the Treasury over $87 billion in 2012. Several provisions excluding pension contributions and earnings together reduced revenue by over $100 billion. Similarly, as the table shows, the Treasury forgoes billions of dollars of revenue from exclusion of Social Security benefits from taxation, deductibility of state and local income and property taxes, deductibility of charitable contributions, exclusion of capital gains from home sales, exclusion of capital gains at death, and many other provisions not included in Table 14.2.

The Alternative Minimum Tax (AMT)

Concern that many high-income taxpayers could pay little or no income tax by taking advantage of tax preferences led Congress to enact the Alternative Minimum Tax (AMT) in 1969. Although originally conceived as a way to make sure that a few wealthy tax filers paid a reasonable amount of tax on their gross income, the AMT has been increasing tax liability of many middle-income taxpayers in recent years. The reductions in MTRs resulting from EGTRRA did not significantly alter the provisions and tax rates under the AMT. Unlike the regular income tax rate structure, the tax brackets under AMT are not indexed for inflation and, as a result, more and more households will pay higher tax rates as incomes rise over time.

The AMT is set up as a shadow tax rate structure that applies to taxpayers who have significant amounts of certain tax preferences. The provisions of the AMT are complex and require those subject to its provisions to calculate their tax liability in two ways. First they use the regular income tax rules to figure the tax liability. Then they must calculate tax liability again using the special rules that apply under the AMT. If the tax is higher under AMT rules, taxpayers must pay the difference between their regular tax and the tax due under the AMT rules. The AMT is, in effect, a surcharge on regular income tax that applies to certain taxpayers. If this sounds complicated, it is because the rules are, in fact, exceedingly complex and unfortunately many taxpayers will be paying the AMT unless Congress acts to change the law.

The tax base under AMT rules adds "exemption preferences" to taxable income. This includes such items as personal exemptions, the standard deduction, and itemized deduction for state and local income taxes, certain tax-exempt income, and miscellaneous deductions. Middle-income taxpayers with large families and those living in states with relatively high personal income taxes are likely to have large dollar amounts of these exemption preferences. There are also "deferral preferences" that put off tax liability under the regular income tax or delay the taxability of the income to later years. These include such items as accelerated depreciation. Items included in this category are likely to be tax preferences used by high-income taxpayers.

Only 3 percent of households were subject to the AMT in 2011, partly because the amounts of income exempt from the special tax were temporarily increased between 2003 and 2011. The special AMT relief was scheduled to expire at the end of 2011. The Congressional Budget Office has estimated that by 2012 as many as 18 percent of households would be paying the AMT. As of

2011, the exemption was 74,450 for married couples and $48,450 for single taxpayers. After the exemption is deducted, the sum calculated is subject to the following tax rate schedule:

1. The first $175,000 of net income calculated for purposes of the AMT is subject to a tax rate of 26 percent.

2. Amounts over $175,000 are subject to a 28 percent tax rate.

3. The AMT exemption is phased out for upper-income taxpayers, which, in effect, increases the effective AMT tax rate above 28 percent for these tax filers.

Middle-income taxpayers subject to the AMT of 26 percent will find that their MTR is higher than what they would pay under the regular income tax. Compliance costs will also be higher because many taxpayers will be forced to compute their tax liability twice. Because eliminating the AMT would reduce federal tax collections significantly, it is unlikely that the tax will be abolished without finding some alternative source of revenue to replace it. However, because many politicians and their constituents regard the AMT as both inefficient and unfair, there is very likely to be pressure to eliminate or modify it soon.

As of 2006, half the people subject to the AMT were residents of California, Massachusetts, New Jersey, or New York, states with relatively high income and property taxes. With no changes in the AMT, the taxes collected under this parallel tax system will soon exceed those collected by the regular progressive income tax. There is enormous political pressure from residents in these high tax states to have the AMT repealed. If it is not, state and local governments will have difficulty raising state and local income and property taxes and might be pressured by their residents to reduce reliance on these taxes. In November 2005, the President's Advisory Panel on Federal Tax Reform recommended elimination of the AMT. However, because it generates so much revenue for the federal government, any reduction in the AMT will have to be offset by tax increases or other changes in the tax code that will generate more revenue.

American Taxpayer Relief Act of 2012 changed the provisions of the AMT for the 2012 tax year and for future tax years by increasing the exemption amounts to $50,600 for single taxpayers and $78,750 for married taxpayers filing jointly. These amounts will now be indexed for inflation in future tax years. Beginning in 2012 all tax credits claimed by taxpayers will be allowed to offset the AMT amount due. These changes will substantially reduce the number of taxpayers subject to the AMT in 2012 and subsequent years.

CHECKPOINT

1. List some major exclusions from income under the federal income tax, and explain how they can affect resource use.
2. What are the major deductions allowed from adjusted gross income? How do these deductions affect resource use? How do tax credits differ from tax deductions?
3. What are tax expenditures?

ISSUES IN INCOME TAX POLICY

The income tax in the United States is perennially subject to reform. Some issues, such as the comprehensiveness of the tax base and the tax rate structure, are discussed in this and the previous chapter. In general, because the excess burden of the tax in labor and capital markets as well as the distortions caused by tax preferences depend on marginal tax rates, we can always reduce the excess burden of the tax by reducing MTRs. However, reductions in MTRs imply losses in revenue. To prevent losses in revenue, tax rate reductions can be balanced by base broadening through the elimination of tax preferences. However, the politics of income taxation often make it difficult to gain agreement on broad elimination of such time-honored deductions as deductibility of mortgage interest.

In this section, we look at a selection of issues in income taxation.

The Flat Tax

Everyone complains about the incredible complexity of the federal income tax code. The *Tax Reform Act of 1986* was a major effort to simplify the tax code by eliminating many tax preference items. However, since 1986 the Congress has increased the number of tax brackets, tinkered with MTRs, and enacted many new tax laws and special provisions that are phased out as income rises. The result is that the income tax code is as complex, and perhaps even more complex, than ever. Passage of the *Tax Relief Act of 1997* sent the stocks of tax information and preparation companies, such as H&R Block, soaring because the complex provisions of the new law were expected to send more and more taxpayers to professional services to prepare their tax forms!

EGTRRA added to the complexity of the tax code in 2001 by increasing the likelihood that more taxpayers would be subject to the AMT. Intelligent people are often baffled by the complex instructions for tax forms. Not only are the income tax forms often confusing, but they are also costly to prepare, and it is costly to keep records to comply with the tax code. Taxpayers spend millions of dollars paying professional tax preparers, accountants, and lawyers to help them comply with taxes. They also spend hours of their time if they file taxes on their own. The Tax Foundation (a nonprofit, nonpartisan research and public education organization) estimates the total cost incurred by individuals, businesses, and non-profit organizations of complying with the federal income tax code (including corporate income taxes) at $409.5 billion in 2012 or 21.5 percent of tax revenue collected. This is the estimated value of 5.8 billion hours of time necessary to keep records and file tax forms.[15] Businesses bear about 53 percent of this cost and the remainder is borne by individuals.

In addition to the excess burden of the personal income tax code resulting from distortions in resource use, we must add the compliance costs to measure the resource cost of collecting taxes. The Tax Foundation's estimates indicate that for each dollar of revenue collected by the federal income tax in 2012 we must add 21.5 cents of compliance cost. The compliance costs also appear to be regressively

---

[15]See J. Scott Moody, "The Cost of Complying with the Federal Income Tax," *Tax Foundation, Special Report No. 114* (Washington, D.C.: The Tax Foundation, July 2002).

distributed with lower-income taxpayers paying more in compliance cost as a percentage of their income than upper-income taxpayers.

As a result of the costs of complying with the complexity of the tax code and the many distortions caused by tax preferences in the personal income tax, there are perennial political calls for tax simplification. A flat tax would be similar to the type of rudimentary income tax we discussed in Chapter 13. It would, in theory, be a general tax on a comprehensive income tax base with no exemptions or deductions. Such a tax would still have economic effects because it would affect the work-leisure and saving-investment choice. However, because most studies show that these effects are minimal, few would disagree that movement to a flat tax would reduce excess burden of the income tax by eliminating the distortions that arise from tax preferences.

However, proposals for a flat tax rarely encompass a full comprehensive income tax base. At a minimum, for equity reasons, most proposals would exempt some low-income households from taxation. An additional problem in actually implementing the tax is that wholesale elimination of tax preferences would be an enormous shock to the economy. People have been making economic decisions partially on the basis of the tax preferences of the income tax for many years. For example, many who buy their own homes do so because of the tax benefits of home ownership, such as deductibility of mortgage interest and nontaxation of imputed rents. If these benefits were eliminated, the demand for homes would plummet. All those who currently own their own homes would find the prices of their homes falling as the playing field between renting and owning is leveled. As this occurs, many people would find their wealth reduced and would certainly complain to their representatives in Congress. Similarly, eliminating the tax-exempt status of state and local public-purpose bonds would increase the interest rates that these governments must pay to borrow, which could increase state and local tax rates. The price changes resulting from the shift to a flat tax would likely cause a storm of political protest that would make it difficult to enact a truly comprehensive income tax. The fact is that some people benefit from special deductions and exemptions from the tax code, and these benefits are capitalized into the prices of many assets. Unless taxpayers gain more from the lower tax rates over time than from their loss in benefits and loss in value from assets and changes in other prices for things they buy and sell, they will oppose the shift to a flat tax on a comprehensive base.

To be revenue neutral, a flat tax would have to be set at a tax rate that allows the federal government to collect the same amount of revenue as it does under the current complex tax structure. This will inevitably imply that some taxpayers will have to pay higher tax rates while others will pay lower rates. For example, suppose the existing progressive rate structure is replaced with a 15 percent flat tax. This would mean the upper-income taxpayers who are subject to marginal and average tax rates higher than this will gain. However, lower-income taxpayers whose marginal and average tax rates are lower than 15 percent would lose. There would be distributive effects of the flat tax that many would find undesirable—the rich would gain at the expense of the poor.

It is difficult to predict whether shifting to a flat tax would increase work effort or savings because it would have complex effects on incentives for taxpayers depending on their income and what happens to their average and marginal tax rates as a result of the shift. For example, consider an upper-income taxpayer now subject to the 35 percent maximum marginal tax rate (MTR) who pays 30 percent of his total income in federal income tax. If this taxpayer were subject to a 15 percent flat tax, both his marginal and average tax rates would fall.

Analysis of the Shift from a Progressive to a Flat-Rate Tax

Proposals for a flat-rate tax argue that a reduction in the high MTRs of the current rate structure would reduce the efficiency loss from the current tax system. At the same time, they argue that lower MTRs would reduce incentives for tax evasion. Moving to a flat-rate tax also would reduce the incentive to shift income among family members to take advantage of lower tax rates that children, for example, might enjoy relative to their parents. Finally, the flat-rate tax would diminish the problems that occur as a result of widely fluctuating personal income. For example, under a progressive tax, a person who has an income of $100,000 in one year but zero in the four preceding years would pay a much higher tax on his overall five-year income than a person who earns $20,000 per year over a five-year period. However, adopting a flat-rate tax also would result in a significant redistribution of the tax burden from upper-income to lower-income groups.

The flat-rate tax would tax all taxable income at the same rate. The tax rate could be chosen to generate the same amount of revenue that is currently generated under the existing progressive tax rate structure. The actual rate would depend on whether a zero bracket would be included. If it is, the flat-rate tax actually would be a two-step progressive rate, with the first, say, $15,000 of income subject to a zero rate. Most proposals for the flat-rate tax recommend retention of a zero bracket amount and increased personal exemptions, say, to $5,000 per taxpayer and dependents, to ease the burden of the shift to low-income groups. Ideally, a flat-rate tax would tax all income, irrespective of its source or use. It would have effects similar to the comprehensive income tax discussed in Chapter 13.

Suppose a flat-rate tax of 15 percent on comprehensive income could raise the same revenue as the current progressive tax rate structure. What would be the effects of substituting the flat-rate tax for the progressive tax on work effort, saving, and the distribution of the tax burden?

Progressive taxation implies an increase in average and marginal rates of taxation as income increases. Economic theory can be used to compare incentives to earn income under proportional and progressive tax rate structures that raise equal revenues. Assume that the flat rate (or the reduction in tax preferences) is adjusted to assure equal revenues.

The average tax rate (ATR) indicates the extent to which a tax reduces income. Changes in ATRs therefore result in income effects. The MTR measures the extent to which the tax reduces the return to extra work and saving and therefore is indicative of the substitution effects caused by tax rate changes.

Assume that the same level and mix of government expenditures is financed by both types of rate structures. Under those circumstances, the effects of the change of the rate structure on incentives to work and save can be isolated and analyzed.

The change from a progressive to a flat-rate tax structure would change the distribution of the tax burden. Under the flat-rate tax, the rate of taxation, t, is both the average and marginal rate of taxation at all levels of income. Under progressive taxation, taxpayers pay more on the last dollar of income that they earn than the average amount of taxes that they pay on total income. Taxpayers can be divided into three groups according to their taxable income so that the effects of the two equal-yield rate structures can be compared.

Low-income groups are harmed by the substitution of the flat-rate tax for the progressive tax by having both their average and marginal rates of taxation increased. The increase of the average rate of taxation decreases their after-tax income and is indicative of the income effect. If leisure is a normal good, this effect is unfavorable to leisure and favorable to work. Similarly, the decrease in income caused by a shift to the flat-rate tax also tends to increase saving when present consumption is a normal good. As a practical matter, low-income groups save very little, so the increase in saving caused by this effect might be negligible. On the other hand, the increase in the marginal rate of taxation means that the taxpayer retains less of the income earned from extra work and savings. This decreases the net wage and interest after taxes on the margin and is indicative of the substitution effect which is unfavorable to work and saving. The actual effect on the amount of hours worked by taxpayers and on saving in this group is indeterminate and depends on the relative magnitudes of the income and substitution effects, which work in opposite directions.

For middle-income taxpayers, the average rate of taxation increases as a result of the shift to a flat-rate tax, but their marginal tax rates fall. The increase in the ATR is favorable to work effort and saving because of the resulting income effect of the increase in after-tax income. The decrease in income after taxes decreases leisure and current consumption per year, provided that these are normal goods. The decrease in the MTR to these middle-income taxpayers results in substitution effects that also act to increase annual work and saving. This is because the introduction of the flat-rate tax lowers the marginal tax rate for these taxpayers and increases the rewards for work and saving on the margin. In this case, for this group of taxpayers, the effect of the shift to the flat-rate tax can definitely be predicted to increase hours worked and the amount saved per year. Since the majority of taxpayers are likely to fall in the middle-income group, these effects on work and saving could be substantial.

Upper-income taxpayers have both their average and marginal rates of taxation reduced as a result of the shift to the proportional tax rate structure. The decrease in the average rate of taxation results in an increase in income after taxes. This results in an income effect that increases desired leisure and current consumption per year, provided that these are normal goods. As a result of the decrease in the ATR, work effort and saving decrease for these upper-income groups, provided that leisure and current consumption are normal goods. There is, however, also a substitution effect that results from the decrease in the marginal rate of taxation. This substitution effect is the result of the increase in net wage and net interest on the margin after taxes, made possible by the decrease in the MTR. This substitution effect tends to increase work and saving for the upper-income group. The net effect on hours worked and saving for upper-income taxpayers depends on the size of the income effect compared to the substitution effect and is indeterminate.

Only the middle-income group can be predicted unequivocally to work and save more as a result of the shift to the flat-rate tax. The aggregate effect on hours worked cannot be predicted. The actual result depends on the number of taxpayers

PUBLIC POLICY PERSPECTIVE

Reforming the Income Tax: Some Recent Proposals

In January 2005, President George W. Bush established the "President's Advisory Panel on Federal Tax Reform." This panel was charged with recommending options to simplify the federal income tax code and change the tax system to encourage economic growth. The commission issued its report in November of 2005. Its basic recommendations were controversial and both the president and the Congress were not eager to even discuss the panel's proposed options. Tax reform is a very difficult process because it will inevitably produce gains for some people and businesses and losses for others.

The president's panel targeted many tax preferences for removal, including very popular ones such as deduction for mortgage interest, state and local income taxes, and property taxes, as well as other long-standing deductions. In general, the panel argued that the function of the tax system should be to raise revenues rather than encourage individuals to favor one activity over another through tax preferences. In an attempt to improve efficiency the panel recommended elimination of these tax preferences, a change in the progressive tax rate structure, and elimination of the Alternative Minimum Tax (AMT).

Let's take a look at the recommendations and their possible impact on the economy, efficiency,

and tax revenue. The plans proposed were designed to be tax neutral. Loss in revenue from lower tax rates and elimination of the AMT had to be accompanied by other changes that would raise revenue. The panel also sought to simplify the complex income tax system in the United States. Their report claimed that the 75-line form 1040 could be reduced to only 32 lines if their reforms were to be adopted.

The panel recommended reducing the number of tax brackets in the personal income tax from six to four. The current six-bracket system has rates that range from 10 to 35 percent. The panel's recommendation is for a 15 percent bracket, a 25 percent bracket, a 30 percent bracket, and a 33 percent bracket. In effect, this new progressive rate structure is likely to increase marginal tax rates for all but the highest-income taxpayers. However, the proposal will also eliminate the AMT, which would cause revenues to fall but could reduce the marginal tax rate for many taxpayers. The higher tax rates would be necessary to offset the loss in revenue from elimination of the AMT.

A major goal of the tax reform proposals was to increase incentives to save and invest. Several of the proposals were designed to encourage individuals to supply funding for new capital

in each of the three groups and the amount of income that they actually earn. The result also depends on the preferences between work and leisure of lower- and upper-income taxpayers.

Inflation and the Cost of Capital

Inflation can change income tax rates without an act of Congress! Inflation implies that nominal income increases faster than real income. **Bracket creep** is an increase in the effective rates of taxation of real taxable income when the tax rate schedules are based on nominal values of income rather than real values. Bracket creep was a serious problem in the late 1970s when inflation was very high. During that period, inflation eroded the real value of personal exemptions, the standard deduction, and some itemized deductions. At the same time, bracket creep pushed taxpayers into higher tax brackets as their nominal income increased at a faster rate than their real income. Nominal income in tax brackets as well as personal exemptions and the standard deduction are now indexed to the rate

investment by corporations. The panel proposed that 75 percent of the capital gains from sale of corporate stocks held longer than one year be exempt from taxation. It also proposed that dividends on corporate stock be exempt from personal income taxation. These two proposals would cut in half the current tax rates for dividends and long-term gains on stock sales for upper income taxpayers from the current 15 to 8.5 percent. Capital gains from sale of other assets, including businesses, art, and farmland would be taxed at the same rate as ordinary income. These changes would direct investment toward corporations but could also discourage entrepreneurship by reducing the return to investment in smaller non- incorporated business.

To offset revenue losses from the AMT, the panel proposed eliminating deductions from state income taxes and local property taxes. The home mortgage interest deduction would be sharply curtailed. The deduction would be eliminated and replaced with a tax credit of 15 percent of mortgage interest paid on a principal residence. The tax credit would be limited to an amount that would vary with the maximum value mortgage loan that the Federal Housing Administration would insure in a region. Shifting to a tax credit from a tax deduction would allow lower-income taxpayers who do not typically itemize their deductions to benefit from the tax preference for home ownership. Currently all mortgage interest on loans of up to $1 million is tax deductible. The proposal would limit the loan amount eligible for the interest tax credit to an amount that would vary between $244,000 and $312,895 in 2005 dollars depending on housing costs in a region. Deductions for interest paid on home equity loans and second homes would no longer be allowed. These new proposals would be phased in over a period of five years to minimize disruptive effects on housing markets. The amount of capital gains from home sales that is exempt from taxation would rise from the current $500,000 to $600,000.

To encourage savings the panel recommended increasing the amounts that households could save with earnings on those savings free from federal income tax. The panel would continue to allow deductions for charitable contributions but only to the extent that those contributions exceed 1 percent of adjusted gross income. This deduction would be available to all taxpayers, not just those who itemize deductions.

There were many other recommendations for changes in the federal tax code. It remains to be seen whether any of the panel's recommendations will be acted on by Congress.

of inflation. However, because many believe that the Consumer Price Index (CPI)—used to index tax brackets, personal exemptions, and the standard deduction—overstates inflation by as much as 1.1 percentage points, indexation is likely to reduce real tax burdens over time. A reform to change the way the CPI is computed would solve this problem.

Although indexation of tax brackets can prevent bracket creep, inflation can still cause serious distortions in taxation of capital income. Inflation creates serious problems in accurately measuring interest income and capital gains. In the case of interest income, the problem is obvious. At 10 percent inflation, a yield on savings deposits of 5 percent implies that the saver is losing a net 5 percent of the value of savings. Although interest accrues at 5 percent at the end of the year, the value of the dollars in the account, including the interest accrued, is worth 10 percent less. However, the tax system taxes nominal interest as it accrues, with no adjustment for inflation. Savers who earn negative rates in real terms pay positive taxes on those negative returns. This, in turn, reduces the return to saving still further and is likely to result in a decline in annual saving.

Similar problems occur for interest deductions allowed in computing taxable income. The interest deductible is based on the nominal balance outstanding. However, during inflation, debtors benefit because their outstanding balances on any loans decrease in real terms. Put differently, they pay off their loans in dollars that are worth less than those they borrowed. Allowing an interest deduction on the basis of the nominal interest paid on the outstanding balance overstates the real value of that deduction and decreases the tax liability of debtors relative to other taxpayers. To adjust for inflation, the deduction should be in terms of real interest paid.

Finally, the tax system taxes nominal capital gains without adjustment for inflation. This can create serious problems in capital mobility and incentives to make investments. The argument here is similar to the one made for other types of income. However, since capital gains are taxed only as they are realized, there are some additional problems that stem from the fact that taxpayers can postpone or avoid the tax by continuing to hold the asset. By holding the asset and avoiding annual payment of taxes on accrued gains, taxpayers can increase their net return over the life of the asset by earning gains both on the value of the asset and the value of the amount of tax that they would have paid on the gains had they been taxed on accrual.[16] As discussed previously, if a person holds an asset until death, his or her unrealized gain escapes taxation completely.

Taxation of the nominal gain on an asset means that the effective rate on the real gain is much higher than indicated by the rate schedule. This reduces the net return to capital and can adversely affect savings and capital accumulation. The gain itself is only taxable on realization. Because annually accrued gains escape taxation, the tendency is for the tax to "lock in" investors, as pointed out earlier in this chapter. This discourages shifts in investment portfolio composition in response to changing market conditions and impairs the efficiency in the operation of capital markets.

Martin Feldstein and Joel Slemrod have estimated that individuals paid more than $500 million extra tax on corporate stock capital gains as a result of inflation in 1973. Their research also indicates that 40 percent of the capital gains taxes paid in 1973 would not have been due had the nominal gains been adjusted for inflation.[17] Other research by the same authors provides some evidence that the "lock-in effect" of the capital gains tax is indeed significant, and it does decrease capital mobility.[18] One research study on the effect of a significant reduction in the tax rate on capital gains realizations concluded that a tax cut on capital gains in 1982 increased realizations to such a degree that more revenue was collected by the Treasury despite the lower tax rates.[19] These distortions are often used to justify the lower tax rate on realized capital gains.

More general analysis of the effect of expected inflation on the relative income from capital, compared to labor, concludes that inflation causes nominal capital income to grow more rapidly than labor income. The reason for this is that

---

[16]For proof of this, see Shoven, "Inflation," in *Federal Tax Reform*, ed. Michael J. Boskin (San Francisco, Calif.: Institute for Contemporary Studies, 1978): 177.

[17]Feldstein and Slemrod, "Inflation," 110–113.

[18]Joel Slemrod and Martin Feldstein, "The Lock-in Effect of the Capital Gains Tax: Some Time Series Evidence," *Tax Notes* 7 (August 7, 1978).

[19]See Lawrence B. Lindsey, "Capital Gains Rates, Realizations, and Revenues," in *The Effects of Taxation on Capital Accumulation*, ed. Martin S. Feldstein (Chicago, Ill.: University of Chicago Press, 1987): 69–97.

inflation increases both the return to investment (the nominal interest rate) and the value of capital assets. As these two separate effects compound, the rate of growth of nominal capital income exceeds that of wages when wages are adjusted for inflation. Thus, inflation biases the nominal income of capital relative to the nominal income of labor, and therefore results in increased nominal rates of taxation on capital relative to labor.[20]

The Taxpaying Unit: Does the Tax System Discriminate against Married Couples?

The tax rate structure applied to taxable income depends on the status of the tax-paying unit. Separate rate schedules apply to single, married couples filing jointly, married couples filing separately, and head-of-household taxpayers. In all cases, the schedules are defined according to the MTRs that apply to various brackets of income. The standard deduction amount differs, depending on filing status.

Two single people who earn the same income and live together have paid lower rates of taxation than a married couple, other things being equal, if each spouse earns the same income as each of the single persons. The joint rate schedule, in effect, has provided benefits to taxpayers only to the extent to which the income of one of the spouses is significantly higher than the other's. This is the so-called *income-splitting effect*, which divides the income of both taxpayers equally between them in computing taxes and pulls the income of the spouse who earns the higher income into a lower tax bracket under progressive taxation. If, for example, a husband with a dependent spouse earns $50,000 per year and his wife has no taxable income, $50,000 would be taxed as if the husband earned $25,000 per year and the wife earned $25,000 as well. This income splitting, which is built into the tax rate schedule for those who are married but filing jointly, lowers the marginal tax rate of the single-earner couple. As the incomes of the two spouses become equal, the benefit disappears. This is the so-called *marriage tax*, which has been present in the tax structure since 1969, when a reform designed to reduce the rate of taxation on single taxpayers resulted in this quirk: The rate for equal-income married taxpayers rose above the corresponding rate for two single taxpayers with the same income.

For example, suppose your taxable income was $50,000 in 2000. If you were single, your tax liability based on tax rates prevailing in 2000 would have been $10,587. If instead you were married *and your spouse had no taxable income*, your tax liability would have been only $8,299. By marrying someone with no taxable income, you would save $2,288 in 2000 taxes over what you would pay as a single taxpayer. However, if you were to file a "married filing separately" return rather than a joint return after you married, your tax bill would be $11,150—an increase of $563 over the single rate. This is because the tax rate schedule for a married person filing separately has tax brackets that result in relatively higher tax rates applied to a given income compared to single taxpayers. In addition, by filing separately, all the $50,000 is taxed as your income

---

[20]For proof, see Peter A. Diamond, "Inflation and the Comprehensive Tax Base," *Journal of Public Economics* 4 (August 1975): 227–244. For a comprehensive analysis of taxation of capital income, see Jane G. Gravelle, *The Economic Effects of Taxing Capital Income* (Cambridge, Mass.: The MIT Press, 1994).

instead of being allocated half to you and half to your spouse. Naturally, assuming you are rational, you would choose to file jointly with your spouse after marrying.

The situation differs if you marry a person who earns the same taxable income as you. Two single persons earning $25,000 taxable income each per year in 2000 would have paid $3,750 each in taxes for a total tax of $7,500. If these two were to marry and file jointly, their tax bill would be $8,299, an increase of $799 over what they would have paid together on single returns. Reduction of the MTRs and the degree of progression of the income tax rate structure have reduced the marriage penalty somewhat for lower-income taxpayers.

EGTRRA addressed concern about the marriage penalty. The standard deduction for married couples was increased to equal twice that of the standard deduction for single taxpayers. Also by 2009, the interval for the 15 percent tax bracket for joint returns was adjusted to twice as large as the bracket that applies to single returns. These changes eliminated most of the marriage penalty for middle-income taxpayers. The boundaries for the new 10 percent tax bracket established by EGTRRA also has intervals that are twice as high for married joint filers as they are for single filers providing additional relief from the marriage penalty. However, no changes were made in the bracket structures for MTRs above 15 percent, so the marriage penalty will not be entirely eliminated. The marriage penalty is worse for upper-income taxpayers. Effective 2013 single taxpayers pay a MTR of 39.6 percent on taxable income over $400,000. Married taxpayers filing jointly with taxable income of $450,000 also fall into this tax bracket. This means that a couple living together unmarried each earning $400,000 will not pay the higher MTR until their combined taxable income exceeds $800,000 per year. However, a married couple, each earning only $225,000 taxable income, each start paying the 39.6 percent MTR when their joint taxable income rises above only $450,000!

As an additional benefit for low-income married taxpayers, EGTRRA changed the structure of the EITC to reduce benefit losses to married couples with children. The income levels for married couples at which the EITC is phased out were increased significantly. This will provide more incentive for low-income couples to marry without fear of significant reduction in payments they receive under the EITC.

Removing Savings from the Tax Base: The Consumption Tax

The personal income tax code has a number of provisions that encourage saving, including deductions for amounts deposited into IRAs, Medical Savings Accounts, employer-sponsored retirement accounts (such as 401K and 403B plans), and plans for self-employed workers (SIMPLE and SEP retirement accounts). As discussed earlier in this chapter, all these plans allow both capital gains and investment income to accrue tax-free as long as the funds are kept in the account. When the funds are withdrawn for the purpose intended (such as to provide retirement income), they are then taxed as ordinary income.

To encourage saving, many reformers have argued in favor of allowing all taxpayers to deduct saving for any purpose from their taxable income. Any withdrawal of saving (or negative saving in the form of loans) would be added to income. Such a tax would, in effect, be a tax on consumption rather than income. Income is the sum of consumption plus saving. By exempting all saving, the tax base becomes consumption. We will analyze the effect of such a tax in detail in Chapter 16. However, at this point we briefly point out some of the advantages and disadvantages of such a tax in comparison with the standard income tax.

If exempting savings from taxation actually increases savings rates, it will increase the supply of loanable funds in credit markets and lower interest rates. This will have the effect of stimulating investment. Higher investment rates will improve future living standards by increasing productivity and income growth. There is, as we have pointed out previously, considerable disagreement about the

G L O B A L   P E R S P E C T I V E

Income Taxes and Economic Growth

How do taxes affect economic growth? Many economists have argued that tax systems that are heavily weighted toward income taxes and taxes on capital are less desirable than those that are heavily weighted toward taxes on consumption. Higher tax rates can adversely affect growth by reducing investment rates through their influence on the net return to investment. Higher tax rates also can affect labor supply by encouraging substitution of leisure for work and influencing the choice of occupation. The tax system also can distort investment choices away from high-return projects. By influencing both the supply of resources and their allocation among alternative uses, taxes can adversely affect growth.

A number of studies have examined the relationship between taxation and economic growth through statistical analysis of taxation and growth in a cross-section of nations.[1] One study of a sample of member nations of the Organization for Economic Cooperation and Development found a strong negative effect of personal income tax rates on output growth between 1960 and 1985.[2] Another study for the same group of nations also suggests that income taxation is more harmful to economic growth than broad-based consumption taxes.[3] Taxes on both labor income and capital income tend to be inversely related to growth rates among nations. Taxes on capital income are also negatively associated with investment rates. Analysis suggests that a 10 percent reduction in tax rates on profits could increase investment by 2 percent.[4] This implies that shifting to a broad-based

consumption tax (one that exempts saving from taxation) could improve economic growth rates, other things being equal.

It does appear that tax policy can affect economic growth. Engen and Skinner conclude, based on a variety of studies, including cross-country studies, that a major reduction in all MTRs of 5 percent and of ATRs by 2.5 percent could increase long-term growth rates by between 0.2 and 0.3 percentage points. Although this is a small increase in the growth rate, it can make enormous differences in living standards over time. Over a 35-year period, such a small increase in the growth rate could increase real gross domestic product by 7.5 percent compared to what would be the case 35 years from now if there were no increase in the growth rate.[5] However, lower tax rates will not generate enough increase in economic activity to prevent revenue from falling. If this is the case, nations that reduce tax rates must take care not to reduce those components of public spending that increase productivity in the private sector or to increase their deficits. Both of these consequences could negate the benefits of lower tax rates.

---

[1]For a review of these studies, see Eric Engen and Jonathan Skinner, "Taxation and Economic Growth," *National Tax Journal* 49, 4 (December 1996): 617–642.
[2]See Steve Dowrick, cited in Engen and Skinner, 626.
[3]Enrique G. Mendoza, Assaf Razin, and Linda L. Tesar, cited in Engen and Skinner, 626–628.
[4]Ibid., 633.
[5]Engen and Skinner, 636.

responsiveness of savings to changes in the tax rate. However, there is a growing body of evidence that suggests that complete exemption of savings from taxation does increase savings rates.[21] Full exemption of saving could therefore substantially increase savings rates.

Because an increase in national savings and investment is crucial to improving future living standards, increasing the wherewithal to pay for retirement and medical benefits to the elderly in the future, further exemption of saving from taxation is a likely avenue of tax reform. Because higher incomes are correlated with higher savings rates, such a switch will benefit upper-income groups at least in the short run more than middle- and lower-income groups. We will also show in Chapter 16 that exemption of saving from the tax base will shift the burden of taxation away from owners of capital toward workers. Over the long run, however, if economic growth is stimulated as a result of exemption of savings from taxation, all will benefit in the form of high wages and improved job opportunities.

CHECKPOINT

1. How would a flat tax affect incentives to work and income distribution if it were substituted for the existing progressive income tax?
2. How can inflation affect income tax rates?
3. What are some of the advantages of excluding saving from the income tax base?

Tax goal

- Efficiency of growth

Tax efficiency

HOW PROGRESSIVE ARE FEDERAL INCOME TAXES? EFFECTIVE AVERAGE AND MARGINAL TAX RATES

Everyone knows that the rate schedule for the federal income tax is progressive when viewed against **taxable income**. But, as you know from the analysis of income measurement, taxable income is much less than comprehensive income because of exemptions, deductions, and exclusions from the tax base. How progressive is the federal income tax when tax burdens are calculated using a more comprehensive measure of gross income? Does the effect of other federal taxes diminish the progressivity of the personal income tax?

To answer these questions, the Congressional Budget Office (CBO) has used a broad measure of family income calculated as the sum of wages, salaries, business income, rents, interest, dividends, realized capital gains, cash transfer payments, payroll taxes paid by employers, other business payments that can be reflected in household income such as contributions to retirement plans, and

---

[21]See, for example, R. Glenn Hubbard and Jonathan S. Skinner, "Assessing the Effectiveness of Savings Incentives," *Journal of Economic Perspectives* 10, 4 (Fall 1996): 73–90 and James M. Poterba, Steven F. Venti, and David A. Wise, "How Retirement Saving Programs Increase Savings," *Journal of Economic Perspectives* 10, 4 (Fall 1996): 91–112.

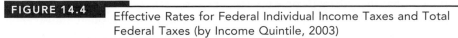

FIGURE 14.4 Effective Rates for Federal Individual Income Taxes and Total Federal Taxes (by Income Quintile, 2003)

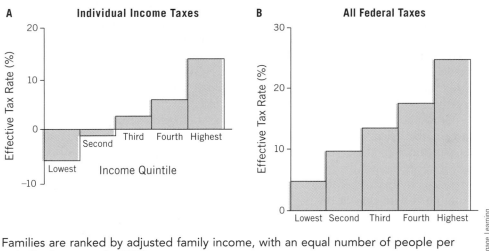

Families are ranked by adjusted family income, with an equal number of people per quintile. Rates are for 2003.

© Cengage Learning

cash pension benefits.[22] It then divided families in the United States into five groups of equal number ranked according to their income. An estimate of taxes paid, based on the tax law prevailing in 2003, by each of these groups was then made and divided by the gross income of each group. The results show the estimated **average effective tax rate**, which are actual taxes as a percentage of a measure of gross (rather than taxable) income for each group.

The bar graph **A** shown in Figure 14.4 demonstrates that average effective income tax rates for the U.S. individual income tax did rise as gross income increased in 2003. The federal income tax really does distribute the burden of taxation in a progressive manner. The lowest-income group had a *negative effective tax rate* of about 5.9 percent of its income. In other words, on average, this group receives an amount equivalent to 5.9 percent of its earnings as a transfer from the federal government. Effective tax rates increase with income steadily and the effective income tax rate on the highest-income group is 13.9 percent. The highest-income earners pay the highest effective average tax rates. The CBO estimates that those with the highest incomes in the United States corresponding to the top 1 percent of families ranked according to their income pay effective average tax rates of 20.6 percent.

[22]See Congressional Budget Office, "Historical Effective Federal Tax Rates," www.cbo.gov. This measure is less than comprehensive income because it excludes unrealized capital gains, employer contributions to pension funds, and in-kind income. In the estimates presented here, corporate income tax paid by households is assumed to vary with a family's capital income. Payroll taxes are included in family income. For details of the calculations, see U.S. Congressional Budget Office, *The Changing Distribution of Federal Taxes*, 1975–1990 (Washington, D.C.: U.S. Congress, October 1987): Chapter V, 42–48. See Congress of the United States, Congressional Budget Office, *The Economic and Budget Outlook: Fiscal Years* 1995–1999 (Washington, D.C.: U.S. Government Printing Office, January 1994): 52–57 for estimates of progressivity of the U.S. income tax in 1994. Also see Congressional Budget Office, "An Economic Analysis of the Taxpayer Relief Act of 1997," April 2000.

It is clear that the federal income tax remains progressive with respect to a broad measure of household income. The tax reforms under the Bush administration have reduced tax rates in all income quintiles. On average, effective tax rates fell 1.2 percentage points between 2002 and 2003. The lowest-income quintile, whose negative tax rate is largely due to the impact of the Earned Income Tax Credit, did not see a change in their effective tax rates. However, those in all other quintiles did see their effective tax rates fall in 2003, with the highest quintile seeing effective income tax rates fall from 15.5 to 13.9 percent. In 2002, those in the top 10 percent of the income distribution paid an effective tax rate of 17.9 percent. That tax rate was reduced to 16 percent in 2003 after EGTRRA became effective.[23]

What about the effect of other federal taxes on the distribution of income? For example, the federal government also relies heavily on payroll taxes, and many families pay more in these social insurance taxes than they do in income taxes. The payroll tax is essentially a tax on labor income. A more complete picture of income tax progressivity can be obtained if the impact of the federal income tax on income is combined with that of the payroll tax.

The CBO also has estimated the progressivity of federal taxes when payroll taxes are combined with the federal income tax and federal excise taxes. Their estimates indicate that when all these taxes are taken into account, effective tax rates in 2003 ranged from 4.5 percent for the 20 percent of the population with the lowest incomes to 25 percent for the portion of the population with the highest incomes. The bar graph **B** in Figure 14.4 shows the average effective federal tax rates for 2003. Notice that low-income families pay significant amounts in both payroll and excise taxes that offset the positive effects of the EITC on their incomes. However, overall the federal tax structure was quite progressive in 2003.

Estimates of the distribution of tax burden for both income and payroll taxes for 2012 also suggest that the burden of federal income taxes and combined federal income and payroll taxes are distributed in a progressive manner. Table 14.3 shows the CBO's estimates of the distribution of tax burden for 2012 for single taxpayers and for a married couple with two children.

Also shown in Figure 14.5 and Figure 14.6 are schedules for effective marginal tax rates for 2005. Effective MTRs differ from the statutory rates in that they reflect phaseouts of various credits, exemptions, and deductions that are built into the tax code. The impact of these phaseouts depends on family circumstances. Figure 14.5 shows MTRs for a single taxpayer. Figure 14.6 shows MTRs for a married couple with two children. The graphs reflect phaseins and phaseouts of benefits for the EITC, the child credit, education credits, and phaseouts of personal exemptions and itemized deductions according to the law that prevailed in 2005 which is very similar to the law prevailing in 2012. As you can see, the actual effective schedule is a lot more complex than the statutory schedule because of the effect of the various phaseins and phaseouts of special benefits and phaseouts of exemptions and deductions. The actual schedule is more like a roller-coaster ride with both ups and downs. MTRs are negative for the lowest-income groups who are eligible for the EITC. However, MTRs increase sharply for these groups as the EITC is phased out.

With the combined effects of both personal income taxes and phaseouts of credits, deductions, and exemptions, taxpayers with the highest incomes were subject to between 35 and 36 percent MTR in 2005. Lower-income groups are also

---

[23]For methods of measuring tax progressivity, see Michael D. Stroup, "An Index for Measuring Tax Progressivity," *Economics Letters*, 86 (2005): 205–213.

| TABLE 14.3 | Distribution of Federal Tax Burden, 2012 |

A. INDIVIDUAL INCOME TAX AS A SHARE OF INCOME (PERCENTAGE), 2012

INCOME LEVEL	SINGLE TAXPAYER	MARRIED COUPLE WITH TWO CHILDREN
Half the Median	−1	−10
Median	6	4
Twice the Median	9	13
Four Times the Median	14	20

B. INDIVIDUAL INCOME AND PAYROLL TAXES AS A SHARE OF INCOME (PERCENTAGE), 2012

INCOME LEVEL	SINGLE TAXPAYER	MARRIED COUPLE WITH TWO CHILDREN
Half the Median	8	−1
Median	17	14
Twice the Median	21	25
Four Times the Median	25	29

Source: Congressional Budget Office, *The Long Term Budget Outlook*, June 2012.

subject to high MTRs as their tax credits are phased out, but after a while, as their income increases, their MTRs fall sharply. For the highest-income groups, no relief is available from the high MTRs!

We can conclude that the federal income tax of 2003 by itself was quite progressive. The entire federal tax system, despite heavy reliance on payroll taxes, also is progressive with respect to income. However, marginal effective tax rates vary in a way that reflects the complexity of the federal tax code itself. These changes in MTRs are likely to have complex effects on labor supply decisions of individuals. Because the federal tax system in 2012 was basically the same as that prevailing to 2003 the foregoing conclusion is valid for that year as well. In 2013, the addition of the 39.6 percent tax bracket increases marginal tax rates applying to those with the highest incomes. This will make the tax system even more progressive.

Effective Marginal Tax Rates on Labor and Capital Income

It is possible to estimate the marginal tax rate applying the each extra dollar of labor and capital income on average for the economy as a whole. Because marginal tax rates are the key determinant of the excess burden of the tax system, these estimates are useful both in computing excess burden and in forecasting whether the excess burden will change in the future.

The effective marginal tax rate on labor income is the share of the last dollar in earnings that is taken by federal income and payroll taxes. The Congressional Budget Office estimates that the marginal tax rate on labor income in 2012 was 28 percent. The effective marginal tax rate on capital income is the share of the last dollar of capital income that is taken by federal individual and corporate income taxes.

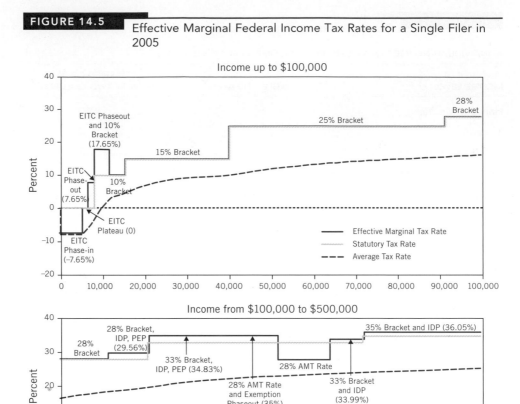

FIGURE 14.5 Effective Marginal Federal Income Tax Rates for a Single Filer in 2005

Note: This example assumes that the taxpayer has no dependents, that all income is from wages, and that the taxpayer has itemized deductions worth 18 percent of income and claims the greater of those deductions or the standard deduction. (Forty percent of the itemized deductions are assumed to be state and local taxes, and the rest are charitable contributions and mortgage interest.) ETIC = earned income tax credit; IDP = itemized-deduction phaseout; PEP = personal-exemption phaseout; AMT = alternative minimum tax.

Source: Congressional Budget Office.

The Congressional Budget Office estimates that marginal tax rate on capital income was 15 percent in 2012.

Of course, change in the tax rate structure or an overall increase in tax rates in the future to reduce the budget deficit would result in either higher or lower marginal tax rates. Higher marginal tax rates mean more excess burden from the tax system depending on the responsiveness of labor and capital to those higher rates.

State Income Taxes

As of 2012, all but seven states (Alaska, Florida, Nevada, South Dakota, Texas, Washington, and Wyoming) used personal income taxation as a major source of revenue. Most states have progressive rate structures, but California, Massachusetts, Michigan, and Pennsylvania use a flat-rate proportional rate structure. In

FIGURE 14.6   Effective Marginal Federal Income Tax Rates for a Married Couple
with Two Children in 2005

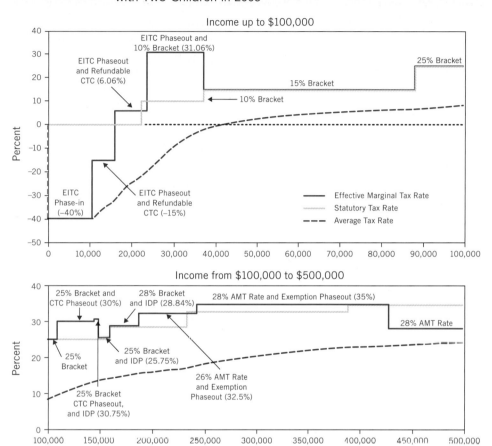

Note: This example assumes that the taxpayers are a married couple filing jointly with
two dependents. All of the couple's income is from wages earned by one spouse. The
couple has itemized deductions worth 18 percent of income and claims the greater of
those deductions or the standard deduction. (Forty percent of the itemized deductions
are assumed to be state and local taxes, and the rest are charitable contributions and
mortgage interest.) ETIC = earned income tax credit; CTC = child tax credit; IDP =
itemized-deduction phaseout; AMT = alternative minimum tax.

Source: Congressional Budget Office.

New Hampshire and Tennessee, the state income tax is limited to dividend and interest income only. On average, taxes on personal income generate nearly 30 percent of
revenue each year for state governments. In several states personal income taxes
account for more than 50 percent of revenue. Income taxes have surpassed sales
taxes to become the most important source of revenue for state governments.

Most states have linked their personal income tax to the federal income tax in
one way or another. This practice, called "conforming," simplifies tax administration at the risk of abrupt changes in revenue when federal tax law changes (as it
often does). For the vast majority of states, the starting point for figuring the tax
base is federal AGI. However, many states simply ask taxpayers to report their

P U B L I C   P O L I C Y   P E R S P E C T I V E

Measuring the Progressivity of the Federal Personal Income Tax

How progressive are federal income taxes? Has progressivity increased or decreased in recent years? To answer these questions Professor Michael D. Stroup of the Stephen F. Austin State University in Texas has developed an index of progressivity for the federal income tax. The index takes on a value of zero for a proportional income tax and increases to a maximum of one. If the index were equal to one, it would imply that the richest person in the nation would be paying all the income tax and everyone else would pay nothing.[1]

Stroup used data from the Internal Revenue Service that have been collated by the Tax Foundation on shares of adjusted gross income and shares of income tax burden for U.S. households ranked by income.[2] He then computed an index of federal personal income tax progressivity from 1980 through 2003. The index is shown in the table at right, along with a relative index that sets the degree of progressivity prevailing in 1980 arbitrarily equal to 1.000.

In general, the index shows that federal income taxes are progressive with an index that ranges from 0.2138 in 1980 to 0.3248 in 2002. The index shows that the degree of progressivity for the income tax has increased substantially since 1980. Income taxes did become less progressive over the period 1986 and 1991 after the Tax Reform Act of 1986 went into effect. However, increases in marginal tax rates for the highest income tax brackets in 1990 and 1993 resulted in increased progressivity for the federal income tax.

Expansion of the Earned Income Tax Credit in 1994, which results in the lowest-income taxpayers often paying negative tax rates, also contributed to increased progressivity. Tax cuts that became effective in 2003 resulted in a very small reduction in the progressivity index from 0.3248 to 0.3227.

The relative index of progressivity with 1980 as the base year indicates that federal income taxes

were 51 percent more progressive in 2003 than they were in 1980. Progressivity was also greater in 2003 than it was in 1998. The following graph plots the relative index of progressivity from 1980 to 2003.

Income Tax Progressivity Index

YEAR	FEDERAL INCOME TAX PROGRESSIVITY INDEX	RELATIVE INDEX 1980 = 1.00
1980	0.2138	1.000
1981	0.2003	0.937
1982	0.2050	0.959
1983	0.2133	0.998
1984	0.2169	1.015
1985	0.2204	1.031
1986	0.2409	1.127
1987	0.2347	1.098
1988	0.2351	1.100
1989	0.2235	1.045
1990	0.2227	1.042
1991	0.2325	1.088
1992	0.2498	1.168
1993	0.2666	1.247
1994	0.2679	1.253
1995	0.2746	1.285
1996	0.2840	1.328
1997	0.2841	1.329
1998	0.2934	1.373
1999	0.3014	1.410
2000	0.3031	1.418
2001	0.2997	1.402
2002	0.3248	1.519
2003	0.3227	1.510

Source: Michael D. Stroup, Stephen F. Austin State University.

There are several reasons for the increase in progressivity of the income tax. Since 1980 income tax rates have declined, but effective tax rates have declined more for the lower-income groups than the upper-income groups. Stroup estimates that since1980 the richest 1 percent of the population had their federal income tax burden reduced by 10.6 percent while the 50 percent of the population with the lowest incomes experienced a 37.5 percent decline in their federal income tax burden expressed as a percentage of their adjusted gross income. The richest taxpayers also are now earning a greater share of total income than they were in 1980, contributing to an increase in the relative share of total taxes they pay. For the lower-income groups, the reduction in tax burden is largely due to the fact that the effective federal income tax rate structure has become more progressive, especially since 1993, contributing to lower tax shares for the relatively lower-income groups.

---

[1]For details on how this index is constructed see Michael D. Stroup, "An Index for Measuring Tax Progressivity," *Economics Letters*, 86 (2005): 205–213.

[2]Tax Foundation, *Internal Revenue Service Federal Income Tax Data*, 2003, www.taxfoundation.org

---

Relative Index of Progressivity for Federal Income Tax, 1980–2003

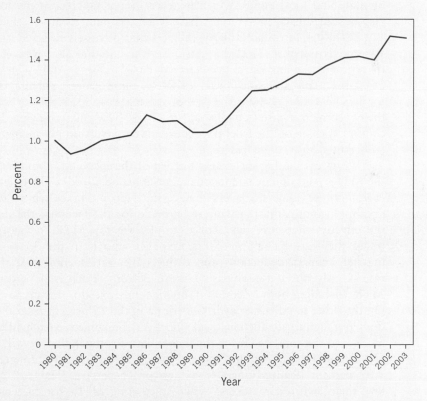

Source: Michael D. Stroup, Stephen F. Austin State University.

federal taxable income or federal tax liability as a "starting point" and then either make adjustments to arrive at their own base or levy their state tax as a percentage of the federal income tax. For example, Vermont levies its income tax as 24 percent of the taxpayer's federal tax liability under the personal income tax (making some adjustments). The linking of state income taxes to federal income taxes does create some problems for states when the federal government reduces income tax rates or changes tax provisions, as was the case under EGTRRA in 2001. Changes in federal tax legislation can cause revenue losses on the state level. Often state legislatures have to convene and modify their tax code to temper any revenue losses from changes in federal rules. There are, of course, important distinctions between state taxation of income and federal taxation. Most states do not allow preferential treatment of capital gains. When capital gains decline (or increase), the impact on state income tax collections is much more pronounced than at the federal level because those gains are typically taxed as ordinary income. During the stock market decline of 2001 and 2002 and 2007–2009, many state governments saw tax collections from capital gains decline substantially, which contributed to the budget crisis on the state level. Most states require taxpayers to add back in to the tax base any state and local income taxes that were deducted in computing their federal taxable income. Interest on state and local bonds, which is generally not taxable on the federal level, must also be added back in to the tax base when computing state taxable income.

EGTRRA introduced many changes that adversely affected tax collections for state government in 2002. Expansion in the amounts that workers can contribute to retirement plans on a tax-deferred basis reduced AGI, which is the starting point for many state income taxes. New, more generous depreciation allowances for business also reduced the size of the tax base for state governments that link their income tax base to the federal tax base. New rules allowing deduction of education expenses on the federal level even if taxpayers do not itemize deductions also contributed to revenue losses.

When calculating the excess burden of the income tax and its tax preferences, the MTRs paid under state income taxes must be added to the federal MTRs. However, because some taxpayers deduct state income taxes when computing federal taxable income, adjustment must be made for the fact that the deduction reduces the effective state tax rate. For example, the top MTR in Georgia is 6 percent under the state income tax. If a taxpayer who is in the 33 percent federal tax bracket itemizes deductions and deducts the state income tax, then the effective rate is only about two-thirds of the 6 percent which is 4 percent. The effective MTR, including both federal and state income taxes for this taxpayer, is 37 percent. On the other hand, a taxpayer in Georgia in the 15 percent federal tax bracket who does not itemize deductions will, in effect, be subject to the full 6 percent state MTR and the total MTR for the income tax for this taxpayer will be 21 percent.

Top MTRs in state income tax rate structures in 2012 ranged from a low of 3.07 percent (Pennsylvania) to a high of 11 percent (Hawaii). Many cities also levy their own income taxes. When calculating MTRs for citizens, in some states the sum of federal, state, and any city income taxes must be added in. For example, a resident of New York City will pay a maximum state MTR of 6.85 percent but will all pay a top city MTR of 3.648 percent. A high-income resident of New York City subject to a 39.6 percent federal MTR in 2013 would have an additional 10.5 percent MTR added to that resulting in a total MTR of about 50 percent before adjusting for the effect of deduction of the state and local income tax on the taxpayers federal return.

SUMMARY

Taxable income is the portion of income received by individuals that is subject to the personal income tax. Taxable income is calculated as AGI less the sum of personal exemptions and the standard deduction or itemized deductions. The U.S. income tax rate structure is progressive. Average effective tax rates rise with income. Because of generous personal exemptions, standard deductions in relation to income, and the EITC, very low-income taxpayers pay zero or negative ATRs under the personal income tax.

Tax preferences can be thought of as subsidies to certain activities, even though they are often introduced to achieve equity objectives and lower administrative costs of collecting taxes. Tax expenditures are losses in revenue attributable to tax preferences. In addition to revenue losses, tax preferences result in efficiency losses through their distorting effects on prices and incentives. Because of tax preferences, the personal income tax distorts the choice to engage in various activities in addition to distorting the work-leisure choice and savings decisions.

Although the tax brackets, standard deduction, and personal exemptions are indexed for inflation, problems remain in equity and efficiency that result when inflation increases nominal incomes. Inflation causes an increase in the rate of taxation of capital income relative to labor income; these distortions reduce the return to saving and investment.

LOOKING AHEAD

Chapter 15 discusses additional taxation of capital earnings under the corporate income tax. The corporate income tax has complex effects on the U.S. economy, affecting product prices, interest rates, and the return to investment in both corporate and noncorporate assets.

KEY CONCEPTS

Adjusted Gross Income (AGI)

Average Effective Tax Rate

Bracket Creep

Deferral of Taxable Income

Earned Income Tax Credit (EITC)

Gross Income

Itemized Deductions

Marginal Tax Benefit

Personal Exemption

Standard Deduction

Tax Bracket

Tax Expenditures

Tax Preferences

Taxable Income

REVIEW QUESTIONS

1. What is gross income? Why is gross income less than the Haig-Simons comprehensive definition of income? How does taxable income differ from gross income?
2. What are the major types of income excluded from gross income? Why are certain items excluded from AGI, even though they qualify as income under the Haig-Simons definition?
3. How does the treatment of capital gains under the federal income tax compare with the way in which capital gains would be treated under a comprehensive income tax?
4. What are tax preferences? What are major justifications for tax preferences? What are the economic consequences of tax preferences?
5. What are tax expenditures? How can tax expenditures be used to evaluate the desirability of tax preferences? Why do tax expenditures overestimate the gains in revenue that would come about from eliminating tax preferences? Explain how tax preferences distort prices and cause losses in market efficiency.
6. What are the major tax deductions from AGI that are allowed in computing taxable income? What are the economic justifications and consequences of allowing such deductions?
7. The EGTRRA of 2001 sharply reduced MTRs for most taxpayers. Explain why this reduces the excess burden of tax preferences.
8. What is bracket creep? How can indexation of tax brackets, the standard deduction, and the personal exemption eliminate bracket creep?

9. Why does inflation distort interest payments and receipts, thereby resulting in tax inequities?

10. Discuss the current tax treatment of capital gains under the personal income tax. Why do some economists argue that reduction in the rate of taxation of capital gains can actually increase tax revenue collected from such gains?

PROBLEMS

1. A taxpayer faces the following MTRs for labor income:

AVERAGE DAILY LABOR EARNINGS ($)	MTR (%)
0–20	0
20–40	20
40–80	30
80 and above	40

   The taxpayer can earn $10 per hour. In the absence of any taxes, he would work an average of eight hours a day. Show how the tax affects his income-leisure budget line and analyze the possible effects on his equilibrium allocation of time to work and leisure, assuming that leisure is a normal good.

2. Suppose the expected inflation rate is 4 percent this year and the nominal interest rate is 8 percent. Assuming that a taxpayer is subject to a 28 percent MTR, show how an increase in the rate of inflation next year to 8 percent while the nominal interest rate rises to 10 percent affects taxation of nominal interest. How does inflation affect taxation of capital gains?

3. A single worker has gross income of $40,000. She makes a $5,000 contribution to a special tax-deferred retirement plan offered by her employer. The worker claims one personal exemption for herself and has the following deductible payments: $1,000 in mortgage interest, $1,000 in state income tax, and $500 in property tax. Does it pay the worker to itemize deductions when filing her 2012 tax return? Using the 2012 tax rate schedule shown in Figure 14.1, calculate the worker's tax liability.

4. A worker lives in a state that has its own income tax. The worker is in the 31 percent federal tax bracket. In addition, he is subject to a 9 percent MTR for his state income tax. Assume that mortgage interest is deductible both on his federal and state income tax, and that state income taxes are deductible on the federal income tax; also assume that he itemizes deductions. Calculate the effective MTR the taxpayer is subject to after considering the tax deductibility of state income tax payments on the federal return. Show how the state income tax affects the excess burden of the mortgage interest deduction for the worker. Assuming that the worker also pays a 7.65 percent Social Security tax on his labor earnings, calculate the MTR for his labor earnings.

5. Suppose the current progressive income tax structure is scrapped and replaced by a 15 percent tax on all income with no exemptions or deductions allowed except that the first $10,000 of income will not be subject to taxation. Explain why this so-called flat-rate tax is really still a progressive-rate structure. How will the elimination of tax preferences affect resource allocation and prices in markets? How could the reform, if it really simplified the complexity of the tax code, save resources? What are some common objections to the flat-rate tax?

ADDITIONAL READINGS

Kiefer, Donald, Robert Carroll, Janet Holtzblatt, Allen Lerman, Janet McCubbin, David Richardson, and Jarry Tempalski. "The Economic Growth and Tax Relief Reconciliation Act of 2001: Overview and Assessment of Effects on Taxpayers." *National Tax Journal* 60, 1 (March 2002): 89–117. An analysis of the effects of tax reforms and tax rate reductions enacted in 2001.

Slemrod, Joel, ed. *Do Taxes Matter?: The Impact of the Tax Reform Act of 1986.* Cambridge, Mass.: The MIT Press, 1990. A collection of research on the impact of changes in the federal income tax on personal saving, housing markets, charitable giving, and economic decisions.

Steurle, C. Eugene. *Contemporary U.S. Tax Policy*, 2nd edition. Washington, D.C.: Urban Institute Press, 2008. Analysis of U.S. tax policy from the post–World War II era to 2008.

U.S. Congressional Budget Office. "The Economic Effects of Comprehensive Tax Reform." Congress of the

United States, July 1997. An analysis of alternatives for reforming the federal income tax, including discussion of specific proposals.

U.S. Department of the Treasury, Internal Revenue Service. *Your Federal Income Tax*. Published annually in November by the IRS, this booklet has just about everything you wanted to know but were afraid to ask about your income tax.

INTERNET RESOURCES

http://www.irs.gov

This is the glitzy home page of your friendly IRS. From this site you can find out everything you need to know about the federal income tax system. You can get IRS publications online and you can even download tax forms. The IRS also provides a number of studies on taxation and the tax system that you can download from this site.

http://www.house.gov and
http://www.senate.gov

The home pages of Congress can be used to access information on proposals for tax reform or whatever else the Congress might be up to regarding taxes and tax policy. This site is particularly useful for accessing the home pages of the Committees on Ways and Means, Budget, and Finance of the House and the Joint Economic Committee. Another source of information on income taxes is the Joint Committee on Taxation.

http://www.taxadmin.org

At the home page of the Federation of Tax Administrators, you will find information on state income taxation and comparisons among states.

Chapter 15

TAXATION OF CORPORATE INCOME

LEARNING OBJECTIVES

After reading this chapter, you should be able to:

- Discuss general issues involved in taxation of business income, including the treatment of normal profit and depreciation of capital.

- Explain how corporate income would be treated under a comprehensive income tax.

- Describe the possible economic consequences of separate taxation of corporate income.

- Analyze both the short- and long-run impacts of the corporate income tax on output, allocation of investment, and efficiency of resource use.

- Discuss the incidence of the corporate income tax, including its effect on product prices, return to investment, and wages.

If you were to operate your own business, the income that you would earn from its operations would be subject to taxation. As the sole owner of the business, you would be required to file a "Schedule C" as part of your personal income tax. After deduction of all the costs of operating your business, including the cost of materials, use of capital, and labor you hire, you would include the net profit as part of your personal income. The tax you paid on your business income would depend on the tax bracket you fell into after all your taxable income had been computed.

The income of sole proprietorships and partnerships is treated as personal income to the owners of businesses. Although sole proprietorships and partnerships account for about 75 percent of the business organizations in the United States, the bulk of business income (about 90 percent of the total) accrues to corporations in the United States. A **corporation** is a business that is legally established under state laws that grant it an identity separate from that of its owners. The law looks at the corporation *as if it were a person!* The corporation is a "legal fiction" that is granted the right to engage in litigation, to own property in its own name, and to incur debts. In the United States and in many other nations, the corporation is treated as a person from the point of view of taxation. The profits of the corporation are subject to a corporate income tax in the United States.

The owners of a corporation are its shareholders, who acquire transferable stock in the corporation. The portion of their ownership can be measured by their relative share of the value of outstanding stock. For example, if a person has stocks worth $2,000 in a corporation for which the current market value of all stock outstanding is $200,000, he or she has a 1 percent ownership in that corporation. Stockholders are protected by the provision of *limited liability* for the debts of the corporation; that is, their liability for debts incurred by the corporation is limited to the amount of funds they have invested in the corporation.

Many argue that separate taxation of corporations obscures the fact that the tax ultimately must be borne by the corporation's shareholders, by other investors, by consumers, or by workers. The ultimate incidence of the corporate income tax among these groups depends on the impact of the tax on the prices of goods and services, the return to investment, and wages. The separate taxation of corporate income is a subject of controversy.

This chapter discusses the issues involved in the taxation of corporations and business income in general. Some politicians believe that corporations should pay a larger share of taxes than they pay now. On the other hand, many have argued that the separate corporate income tax is unnecessary and that it should be abolished. Critics of the tax also argue that it causes large losses in efficiency by distorting the return to investment and by causing a reduction in investment throughout the economy.

In the modern global economy, taxation of corporations also can influence the location of multinational business organizations. If one nation taxes corporations at a higher rate than other nations, it might find that more corporations choose to locate their operations in foreign nations. The U.S. economy is part of a vast global economy in which tax rates influence not only domestic decisions but also foreign decisions regarding the location of international investment. In recent years, concern has been growing about the impact of the corporate income tax on the international competitiveness of U.S. business and the incentives to invest in the United States.

THE TAX BASE: MEASURING BUSINESS INCOME

Annual business income is measured by subtracting all business costs from business receipts over a period of one year. To calculate business income, we would first add up the receipts the business takes in from sale of its products or services. Then we would add net capital gains on all business assets held during the year to business income. After gross income was calculated, we would deduct the costs of operating the business during the year. These costs would include labor costs, interest payments, payments for materials and services purchased from other firms, and a measure of the cost of capital equipment used during the year. After deducting all business costs, we would have a measure of the profit of the business—its *net* taxable income.

As with the measurement of personal income, some discrepancies exist between the way corporate income is measured in practice and the comprehensive measure of income. From an economic point of view, both realized and unrealized capital gains should be included in the measure of the business's gross income. However, in the United States, when measuring business income, only realized capital gains are included in business income. Net realized capital gains (capital gains less an allowable portion of capital losses) are included in corporate income in the United States.

Another problem is the treatment of owner-supplied inputs. For example, in the case of a sole proprietorship operated by its owner, part of the cost of operation is the opportunity cost of the owner–operator's labor. Because the labor of the owner is not hired in the marketplace, neither payment for labor services nor deduction for that labor cost is ever recorded on the business's books. However, the owner–operator's labor is part of the opportunity cost of running the business, and it should be deducted from gross income. The opportunity cost of this owner-supplied service is not deductible in practice when computing business income for taxable purposes in the United States. This implies that business income as measured, in practice, includes both the *normal profit*, which is the opportunity cost of owner-supplied inputs, and the *economic profit*, which is the surplus of revenues over the opportunity cost of all inputs used during the year.

Everyone who works for a corporation is an employee; no owner-supplied labor exists in corporations. However, the corporation's owners—its shareholders—do supply funds to the corporation, and the opportunity cost of those funds net of any debt must be included in the costs of operating the corporation. The **equity** of a corporation is the difference between the value of its assets (including the cash that could be obtained if its equipment and real estate were sold) and the value of its outstanding debt. For example, if a corporation has equity of $1 million and shareholders on average could have earned 10 percent interest on that equity had they not invested it in the corporation, the opportunity cost of owner-supplied funds for the corporation would be $100,000. This sum must be deducted from corporate receipts to calculate economic profit of the corporation. However, this is not done in administering the corporate income tax in the United States. The corporate income tax is a tax on the sum of both normal and economic profits.

Net corporate income either can be retained by a corporation to finance expenses including the acquisition of new capital or it can be paid out as personal income to the shareholders of the corporation. The portion of a corporation's profits paid out to its stockholders is called **dividends**. The portion kept by the corporation is **retained earnings**. Corporate profits can be distributed to shareholders or can remain as undistributed corporate profits to be used for whatever purposes the corporation's managers see fit. The portion paid out as dividends is part of the taxable income of those who receive the payments.

Economic Depreciation: How the Cost of Capital Is Distributed over a Number of Years When Computing Business Income

Some of the inputs purchased by a business, such as fuel, are used up in the process of production within a short period. However, capital inputs, such as equipment and structures, are long lived. Vehicles can last 4–10 years before they need to be replaced, and structures can last for 50 years and longer. Because capital inputs are seldom consumed or used up completely in the year in which they are purchased, accountants usually distribute their purchase prices over a number of years by including a measure of the depreciation of the capital, rather than its total purchase price, in the annual costs of operating the business. Problems occur in defining the tax base treatment of the replacement cost of capital through depreciation. **Economic depreciation** measures the decrease in the market value of the durable physical capital used by firms in the productive process as that capital is "used up." Capital equipment is used up in the sense that it wears out and becomes obsolete over time as technology improves. Depreciation is sometimes referred to as a *capital consumption allowance*. Its inclusion in cost provides a means for the firm to accumulate a fund so as to recover its capital cost and replace such assets as machines and buildings when they wear out or become obsolete. Ideally, the rate at which an asset is depreciated for tax purposes should coincide with the actual useful economic life of the asset. In fact, however, depreciation rules are arbitrary, and the useful lives of assets as defined by Internal Revenue Service guidelines do not always coincide with their actual useful economic lives. This is of importance in defining the tax base and taxes due from the corporation, because the rate at which the firm is allowed to recover its initial capital cost affects the amount of taxes paid.

Accelerated Depreciation and Expensing

More rapid depreciation allowances give corporations a larger deduction in computing taxable income in early years of the asset's use. The consequent reduction in tax liability due to faster depreciation allows the corporation to earn more interest income than otherwise would be the case. **Accelerated depreciation** allows a firm to deduct more than the actual economic depreciation from its income each year. In effect, accelerated depreciation allows a firm to recover the costs of capital equipment more quickly than the equipment is actually used up.

The benefit of accelerated depreciation for tax purposes can be substantial to the corporation. For example, suppose a corporation acquires a machine that has a useful economic life of 10 years. The purchase price of the machine is $100,000. At the extreme, the firm could be allowed to depreciate the machine fully in the year of its acquisition; that is, it could deduct the *full purchase price* of the machine from its taxable income in the year that the machine is acquired. Deduction of the full purchase price of an asset in the year of its acquisition is called **expensing a capital asset**.

Suppose a firm is subject to a marginal tax rate (MTR) of 34 percent. By expensing the $100,000 machine, it reduces its tax liability by $34,000 in the year of purchase. Its after-tax income is that much greater that year. If the firm can earn a return of 10 percent by investing this $34,000, it would be able to increase its future income by $3,400 per year as a result of expensing the machine. However, it forgoes the opportunity to deduct any depreciation on the machine in following years.

Deduction of the same fraction of the cost of an asset each year over its useful economic life is called **straight-line depreciation**. Under straight-line depreciation, the firm deducts only $10,000 from revenues in the year of purchase of the $100,000 machine lasting 10 years. Assuming an MTR of 34 percent, the firm's tax liability is reduced by only $3,400 per year. The firm then is able to invest this $3,400 at 10 percent interest and earns only $340 per year.

In general, assuming a flat-rate tax, the firm's after-tax income in any given year is greater the more quickly it can depreciate its capital expenditures and the greater the proportion of the expenditures it can write off in earlier years of use.

Inflation, Depreciation, and the Cost of Capital

An additional problem in dealing with depreciation stems from the effect of inflation on the replacement costs of capital assets. Inflation increases the replacement cost of capital. However, depreciation is based on **historic cost**, or the acquisition price of the asset. There is no difference between historic cost and replacement cost when the price level is stable. However, during inflation, depreciation calculated on the basis of historic cost understates the replacement cost of capital and overstates the profits of the firm. Similar problems occur for valuing the firm's inventory in computing its profits. If inventory is valued at its acquisition costs and inflation makes it more expensive to replace that inventory, then the firm's profits would be overstated.

Inflation also benefits firms insofar as it decreases the value of their debt outstanding. In effect, they experience capital gains on their outstanding debt balances, and the real value of those balances declines with inflation. This is identical to advantages for individual taxpayers, as discussed in Chapter 14. Loans are paid off in dollars that are worth less than they were initially. The nominal interest deduction allowable to the corporation overstates the true interest cost.

Research on the effect of inflation on the corporate income tax has shown that the main effect on corporate profits stems from the understatement of depreciation and inventory costs. The researchers conclude that in 1977, a year of rapidly rising prices, inflation increased the effective taxes paid by corporations by 50 percent.[1] From the late 1990s up to 2012, inflation has been quite low and has had little impact on effective tax rates for corporations. In fact, the prices of many high technology computer equipment have actually fallen over this period, possibly contributing to lower effective tax rates on corporate income.

SEPARATE TAXATION OF CORPORATE INCOME: ISSUES AND PROBLEMS

Corporate Income as Personal Income under a Comprehensive Income Tax

Why should a separate tax be levied on the income of corporations? Although from a legal point of view a corporation is treated as though it were a person, this is not a sufficient economic reason to tax it as if it were a person. Some argue that

---

[1]Martin Feldstein and Lawrence Summers, "Inflation and the Taxation of Capital Income in the Corporate Sector," *National Tax Journal* 32 (December 1979): 445–470.

a separate corporate income tax is necessary to make corporations pay for the special privileges obtained from their corporate charters.

Under a comprehensive personal income tax, separate taxation of corporate income would not be needed. Total corporate income simply would be allocated to its shareholders on a pro rata basis according to the percentage value of outstanding stock that they owned. For example, suppose the total taxable income of the XYZ Corporation were $1 million this year and that an individual owned 1 percent of the stock of this corporation. At the end of the year, he would receive from the corporation a statement indicating that his share of corporate income this year is $10,000, or 1 percent of total corporate income. He then would be required to include $10,000 as part of his taxable income when he files his personal income tax for the year. Similarly, all the income of the corporation would be allocated to all its shareholders and would be taxed as personal income. It would make no difference if the corporation paid out its income to shareholders as dividends or retained its earnings to finance future expansion. No separate taxation of dividend income under the corporate income tax would be necessary. All income would be allocated to shareholders for tax purposes. The corporation would be treated like a partnership, with the income share of each partner being allocated according to the ownership share.

A scheme for integrating the corporate income tax with the personal income would, however, create some practical problems. For example, if realized capital gains are taxable, then unless pro rata portions of income retained by corporations are deducted from realized capital gains, such gains would be double-taxed. For example, suppose an individual purchased a share of stock for $100. She holds the stock for a year and then sells it for $150. However, during the year the corporation earns $30 per share, which she must declare as personal income. Of this $30, if the corporation retained $20 to finance expansion, then $20 of the $50 capital gain this individual would realize by selling the stock represents her pro rata share of retained earnings that *she has already been taxed on*. Therefore, the capital gain should be adjusted downward by $20 to reflect the increase in the capital value per share that results from retained earnings. The correct taxable capital gain would be $30.

Undistributed Corporate Profits, Dividends, and Interest Cost

The personal income tax base in the United States is, in fact, far less than comprehensive income. Given the tax preferences in the income tax code, separate taxation of corporate income might be necessary. The main tax preference that supports this argument is the exclusion of all unrealized capital gains from the tax base.

Assume that, given current tax treatment of capital gains and the definition of taxable income, corporate income is not subject to a separate tax. Consider the impact of this on the behavior of corporations in allocating earnings between dividend payments to shareholders each year and retained earnings for use within the corporation including investment. With no separate tax on the net income of the corporation, undistributed corporate profits would escape taxation under the personal income tax. Accordingly, the incentive for a corporation would be to plow its profits back into the business. In effect, this provides income to owners of stock in the corporation in the form of potential capital gains in lieu of dividends and keeps a substantial portion of the income tax base free of taxation because unrealized capital gains are not taxed. This reduces revenues to the U.S. Treasury from that particular source and creates inequities.

The source of the incentive to retain earnings as undistributed corporate profits lies in the way taxable income is defined under the personal income tax code. Under a comprehensive income tax base, both realized and unrealized capital gains are taxable annually. If the tax base under the personal income tax were to correspond to comprehensive income, stockholders would be indifferent to the disposition of corporate profits, inasmuch as they are divided between dividends and retained earnings. Under the definition of taxable income used in the personal income tax code in the United States, managers of corporations could help stockholders avoid taxes by retaining earnings as undistributed corporate profits.

Undistributed corporate profits are a form of corporate savings used to finance expansion of operations without borrowing or issuing more stock. Insofar as these retained earnings increase the value, or net worth, of the firm, they provide income for stockholders in the form of capital gains. Unrealized capital gains are nontaxable. Stockholders' tax liability can be reduced as more earnings are retained and less are paid out as dividends. Under the personal income tax, dividends are subject to full taxation. Thus, in the absence of either a separate corporate income tax or a method of allocating retained earnings as taxable income to shareholders, a significant amount of annual income would escape taxation.

However, this argument does not consider the important cost to shareholders when profits are retained. Under current law, when the corporation borrows funds to finance expansion, it can deduct the interest payments from its income. When undistributed profits are used to finance expansion, the firm incurs interest costs in terms of forgone interest on its retained earnings. These implicit interest costs, representing the opportunity cost of retained earnings, are *not* tax deductible. Thus, by retaining earnings instead of paying them out as dividends, the corporation's net taxable income, and therefore its annual tax bill, increases. Dividends cannot be deducted as a cost in figuring a corporation's taxable income under tax laws prevailing in 2012, but interest can be so deducted.

Double-Taxation of Dividends

The current policy of separate taxation of total corporate income and of the portion of income paid out as dividends to individuals subjects a substantial portion of corporate income to double-taxation. The reason for this is that all corporate income is subject to taxation when it is earned, and that portion of profits paid out as dividends is then subject to taxation under the personal income tax, as part of the tax liability for shareholders who receive dividend income. Such double-taxation of corporate income paid out as dividends serves to increase the effective rate of taxation on corporate investment.

If the corporate income tax were to be integrated into the personal income tax, as has been suggested by those advocating a comprehensive income tax, no such double-taxation would exist. Under comprehensive income taxation, corporate profits would be distributed to shareholders on a pro rata basis according to their share of ownership in the corporation. This reduces the rate of taxation of corporate profits due to the elimination of double-taxation of corporate income paid out as dividends. Owners of corporate stock would experience windfall gains in terms of an increase in the value of their corporate stock, but only if the value of previous excess taxation had been capitalized into reduced stock prices in the past. However, these gains, when realized, would be subject to taxation under the provisions of the personal income tax.

A Possible Bias toward Debt Finance

In recent years, some have been concerned that corporate finance has been biased in favor of debt finance because dividends cannot be deducted from a corporation's income, but interest can. Leveraged buyouts (LBOs) in corporate takeovers usually involve heavy borrowing by those who acquire the corporation that leaves the corporation heavily in debt. This gives the corporation high interest costs, which are tax deductible. In effect, a corporation can always borrow to purchase its own shares on the market. By purchasing shares, it no longer has to pay dividends to households on those shares, and it, in effect, exchanges obligations to pay dividends for tax-deductible interest costs. Shareholders who sell their shares to the corporation then receive taxable income in the form of realized capital gains, but total after-tax corporate income is higher because deductible interest costs reduce taxable income.

The corporate income tax reduces the incentive to retain income that would otherwise prevail in a system in which unrealized capital gains are not taxed as personal income. In addition, because interest, but not dividends, is tax deductible, the tax provides incentive for debt finance. For this reason, many economists argue that the corporate income tax biases corporate finance away from equity and toward debt as a means of raising funds.

This can be seen with a simple example. Take two corporations each with $1 million in assets. Assume that the first is financed entirely with equity while the second is 50 percent debt financed and that both corporations earn $150,000 operating income. Assume that both corporations are subject to a 34 percent income tax.

Table 15.1 shows the balance sheet and income statement of the all-equity and 50 percent debt-financed (leveraged) corporations.[2] Assuming that the leveraged

TABLE 15.1 Effect of Debt Financing on Returns to Equity Investment

ITEM	ALL-EQUITY CORPORATION	50 PERCENT DEBT-FINANCED CORPORATION
Beginning Balance Sheet		
Total Assets	$1,000,000	$1,000,000
Debt	0	500,000
Shareholders' Equity	1,000,000	500,000
Income Statement:		
Operating Income	150,000	150,000
Interest Expense	0	50,000
Taxable Income	150,000	100,000
Income Tax	51,000	34,000
Income after Corporate Tax	99,000	66,000
Return on Equity[a]	9.9%	13.2%

[a]Return on equity is computed as income after corporate tax divided by beginning shareholders' equity.

© Cengage Learning

[2]This example follows a similar one appearing on page 54 of *Federal Income Tax Aspects of Corporate Tax Structures*, prepared by the staff of the Joint Committee on Taxation for hearings before the Senate Committee on Finance and the House Committee on Ways and Means, January 18, 1989.

GLOBAL PERSPECTIVE

Tax Treatment of Multinational Corporations

The world is becoming smaller year by year. Improvements in communication and increased international competition have changed the face of business. More large corporations are multinational operations with foreign subsidiaries throughout the world. The foreign subsidiaries are incorporated under the laws of a foreign nation and are legally separate from the parent corporation.

Let's look at some of the issues involved in taxation of multinational corporations. Of course, when a U.S. firm invests in a subsidiary on foreign soil, it becomes liable for foreign corporate income taxation. Similarly, a foreign firm with a subsidiary in the United States is subject to U.S. corporate income taxation on the income earned in the United States. There is, however, wide variation in corporate income tax rates and the rules for treating foreign-source income in terms of domestic taxation. Usually, foreign-source income is subject to tax by the parent corporation's home nation only if the foreign income is "repatriated" to the parent corporation through payment of dividends, interest, or royalties. If the income is not repatriated, no domestic tax is due.

The United States and other nations, such as Japan and the United Kingdom, that tax on a world-wide basis do, however, allow a credit for taxes paid to foreign governments that is deducted from the repatriated foreign-source income. This credit serves to prevent onerous double-tax burdens that would decrease the incentive to invest abroad. There is, however, a limit on the credit allowed for foreign taxes paid that is usually equal to the home country tax that would have been paid on the foreign income had it been earned as domestic income. This limit comes into effect when a corporation has a subsidiary in a nation for which the corporate income tax is higher than that of the parent's home nation. In the United States, this limit to the foreign tax credit is designed to prevent foreign governments from levying very high taxes on U.S. subsidiaries that would increase foreign tax revenue at the expense of reducing U.S. tax revenue. The high taxes would not increase corporate tax liability of the U.S. corporation provided they were not greater than its total U.S. tax liability, but they would reduce federal tax collections by reducing the share of the repatriated foreign income that is subject to tax domestically. Any excess credit can be carried forward to later years. In general, however, the limit to the foreign tax credit can act to discourage investment in high-tax nations. A firm that has

corporation pays 10 percent interest, it will have $50,000 in deductible interest. The all-equity corporation will have no interest to deduct. Taxable income will be $150,000 for the all-equity corporation but only $100,000 for the leveraged corporation. The income tax paid at the 34 percent rate will be $51,000 for the all-equity corporation but only $34,000 for the leveraged one. By borrowing, a corporation reduces its taxable income and therefore its tax. The income after corporation tax is consequently higher for the leveraged corporation in that it enjoys a 13.2 percent return on the initial shareholder equity of $500,000, while the all-equity corporation registers only a 9.9 percent return on initial shareholder equity of $1,000,000.

Replacement of Equity with Debt

Because of the tax disadvantage of financing activities with equity, the trend in recent years has been for corporations to replace equity with debt. In general, when a corporation's ratio of debt to equity increases, the firm is said to become more leveraged. This has occurred through LBOs, leveraged *employee stock ownership plans (ESOPs)*, in which the company borrows to provide stock for the plan and outright exchanges of equity for debt and stock redemptions. Between 1983

excess foreign tax credits is likely to be very sensitive to differences in tax rates among nations because it will not immediately get a credit for foreign taxes it pays. Under worldwide taxation, therefore, corporate tax policies can affect industrial locations by encouraging firms to set up subsidiaries in relatively low-tax nations. In the 1990s, Belgium, Ireland, Luxembourg, and Spain had relatively low taxes on investment income, while Denmark, France, Germany, Greece, Italy, the Netherlands, and Portugal had relatively high taxes. The system of worldwide taxation of income, in effect, distorts the pattern of worldwide investment toward the low-tax nations because of the limits to the foreign tax credit.

Multinational corporations also have opportunities to control the tax allocation of total earnings between home and foreign operations. Naturally, a corporation can have higher after-tax income by shifting the source claimed for shares of income from high-tax nations to low-tax nations. The company can do this by charging off transfers of goods, services, and technical know-how as costs to the parent corporation when those items are transferred for subsidiary use in a nation with lower corporate income taxes. The income from the low-tax nation is higher because of the transfer of goods or other resources, but the cost of those resources is charged to the parent, thereby reducing taxable income in the high-tax jurisdiction. To avoid this problem of manipulating the source of income, a system of "transfer pricing" is necessary to charge goods and technical know-how received from the home against the income of the foreign subsidiary. This increases apparent domestic income while it decreases foreign source income. But how should the transfer price be established in the absence of any transaction? One way is to use the "arm's-length" rule, which treats the home office and the foreign subsidiary as two independent firms and tries to impute a price for the transfer of goods, services, or technical know-how based on what two independent firms would agree on to trade the input. Another way to allocate the cost of commonly used resources, such as technical know-how, is to divide it between the parent and the subsidiary according to sales or assets of each of the companies.

Another problem in determining the allocation of income between parents and subsidiaries of a multinational firm involves treatment of borrowing. Multinational firms have incentives to borrow in the high-tax jurisdictions because they get a bigger tax deduction in those jurisdictions from their interest payments. This makes their income in the high-tax jurisdiction appear lower.

and 1987, net corporation equity decreased by $313.3 billion while new corporate borrowing increased by $613.3 billion in the United States. By converting equity to debt, corporations swap nondeductible dividend payments for tax-deductible interest payments. In effect, this results in distribution of corporate operating income to creditors as interest instead of to shareholders as dividends.

To reduce the incentives for debt finance, recent proposals have advocated allowing at least limited tax deductibility of dividends paid before computing taxable income for a corporation. The bias against equity finance could also be reduced by limiting interest deductions. However, the latter option would increase overall financing costs for corporations, while the former would reduce such costs.

THE TAX RATE STRUCTURE

The corporate income tax rate structure as of 2012 is progressive with three brackets, as shown in Table 15.2. The maximum MTR is 35 percent applied to taxable income of more than $10 million per year. The benefits of lower MTRs for income less than $75,000 per year are phased out for corporations with annual

TABLE 15.2

Federal Corporate Income Tax Rate Structure, 2012

TAXABLE INCOME	AVERAGE TAX RATE AT BEGINNING OF BRACKET	MTR
Less Than $50,000	0%	15%[a]
More Than $50,000 but Less Than $75,000	15	25
More Than $75,000 but Less Than $10 Million	18	34
More Than $10 Million[b]	34	35

[a]Not available for corporations with annual incomes greater than $335,000.
[b]Corporations with taxable income greater than $15 million annually are subject to an additional 3 percent tax on the excess greater than $15 million up to a maximum additional tax of $100,000.

© Cengage Learning

taxable incomes greater than $335,000. In effect, most large U.S. corporations pay a flat-rate statutory tax of at least 34 percent on their taxable income, because most profitable large corporations earn more than $335,000 per year. The marginal tax rate for corporations with more than $10 million taxable income is 35 percent.

However, because the benefits of the lower tax brackets shown in Table 15.2 are phased out as corporate taxable income increases, some corporations with lower taxable income face effective marginal tax rates as high as 39 percent. There is also a corporate alternative minimum tax (AMT) that is designed to ensure that all corporations pay at least some tax on their taxable income.

The tax base for the corporate income tax is notoriously unstable, and the taxes collected can fluctuate widely from year to year. The reason for this is that corporate profits are highly sensitive to swings in the business cycle. It is not unusual for large corporations to make hefty profits in one year, only to register sharp losses in the following year if, due to an existing recession, their sales are curtailed significantly.

Effective Tax Rates

A measure of the *effective* corporate tax rate shows the tax rate paid by corporations on their *economic* profits. Effective tax rates for corporations differ from the statutory rates because real economic profits differ from taxable profits. The effect of inflation on profits subject to tax—a decrease in the real value of depreciation allowances and a reduction in real interest rates—must be accounted for in calculating effective tax rates for corporations. In addition, dividends paid out by corporations are subject to double-taxation, as discussed earlier. Inflation increases the cost of capital to the firm, and its net impact is to increase the effective rate of taxation on real economic profits. The effective tax rate is lowered by tax preferences in the corporate income tax code that allow investment subsidies, accelerated depreciation, and expensing of capital assets. In recent years, inflation has been quite low, whereas investments subsidies and more liberal depreciation rules have contributed to a decline in effective corporate tax rates.

Effective corporate tax rates in the United States have declined significantly since 1953. Over the 50-year period from 1953 to 2003, federal corporate income revenues have fallen from 5.6 percent of GDP to 1.2 percent of GDP. In 1953, the corporate income tax accounted for nearly 30 percent of federal revenues, but by

2003 the tax collected was only slightly more than 7 percent of federal revenue. The effective marginal tax rate on new corporate investment had fallen from 70 percent in 1953 to 32 percent in 2003.[3] From 2003 to 2012, federal corporate tax revenues fluctuated with macroeconomic conditions and corporate profits were within a range of 1–3 percent of GDP and between 7 and 13 percent of federal tax revenue.

The sharp decline in effective average and marginal tax rates on corporate income over the past 50 years largely reflects tax preferences in the income tax code that directly and indirectly subsidize new investment by corporations. While the effective corporate tax rate exceeded the statutory rates throughout much of the period of 1953–1982, since 1982 the effective tax rates are actually lower than the statutory tax rates. Estimates by Jane Gravelle indicate that as of 2003 the effective tax rate was 8 percentage points below the statutory tax rate. Overall since 1953 the effective federal tax rate on corporations in the United States has fallen by 66 percent. Some of this decline is due to declines in the statutory federal tax rates from 52 percent in 1953 to 34 percent in 2003. More generous accelerated depreciation rules that began in the 1980s lowered effective tax rates. The decline in inflation rates in the 1980s and 1990s also contributed to a decline in effective tax rates. Bonus depreciation through increased expensing and extra first-year depreciation allowances enacted as part of the Bush tax reductions in 2003 contributed to further declines in corporate tax rates.

It is also possible that changes in corporate behavior in the 1980s and 1990s contributed to declines in effective corporate tax rates. Since 1980 corporations have been more willing to take on debt to finance their expansion. Because interest on corporate debt is tax deductible, this has reduced taxable income and contributed to a decline in effective tax rates. Multinational corporations have also taken steps to shelter some of the taxable income by transferring income to foreign sources and reducing the portion of gross income subject to the relatively high U.S. corporate tax rates.

State Corporate Income Taxation

State governments also tax corporate income in the United States. Corporate income taxes averaged 5.3 percent of total state revenue in 2011. Corporate income tax is a major source of revenue for some states. For example, corporate income taxes amounted to 25.1 percent of revenue in New Hampshire in 2011 and over 8 percent of revenue in Alaska, Delaware, New Jersey, and Tennessee. All states except Nevada, Texas, Washington, and Wyoming had some sort of tax on corporate income as of 2011. The vast majority of states taxed corporate income at a flat rate. However, several states (Alaska, Arkansas, Hawaii, Kentucky, Louisiana, Maine, Mississippi, Nebraska, New Mexico, North Dakota, Ohio, and Vermont) used progressive-rate schedules.

The MTRs applied to corporate income by the states must be added to the federal tax rates when analyzing the impact of corporate income taxes. Also, states with relatively high corporate tax rates run the risk of losing businesses (and jobs) to other states (or nations) where the corporate income taxes might be lower.

---

[3]See Jane G. Gravelle, "The Corporate Tax: Where Has It Been and Where Is It Going?" *National Tax Journal* 57, 4 (December 2004): 903–923.

In recent years, state corporation tax revenue has declined as a percentage of state revenues and as a percentage of gross domestic product (GDP).[4] State corporate taxes have also declined as a percentage of corporate profits. A major factor in the decline in corporate tax revenues is competition among states for corporate business. In the belief that location of corporations within the state will generate jobs, income, and tax revenue, many states subsidize corporations through special tax concessions that reduce corporate tax collections. In the early 1990s, many states expanded tax concessions related to business location. Corporations commonly negotiate with state governments for tax credits, employment credits, and property tax abatements that generally reduce their tax liability to state governments. Automobile manufacturers, such as GM, Mercedes-Benz, and Hyundai, have obtained multimillion dollar tax abatements in exchange for the decision to locate their manufacturing facilities at a particular location. Alabama gave Mercedes a $300 million tax abatement package when the company agreed to locate in the state. These tax abatements have reduced tax collections. Abatements continue to grow amid increased competition among states for jobs.

As was the case for personal income taxes, many states tie their corporate tax to the federal corporate tax base. Federal corporate taxable income is the common starting point for calculating state corporate tax liability. The federal tax base is then modified with some additions and subtractions. Changes in the federal tax base over the years, including accelerated depreciation and greater use of tax sheltering by corporations, has consequently also eroded the state tax base. Corporations have also become more sophisticated in their tax planning and have used various schemes, including locating subsidiaries in low-tax states, to minimize their overall tax burdens. All these factors have contributed to declining tax revenues from business income at a time when states are facing budget shortfalls that require either cuts in spending or increases in other taxes.

CHECKPOINT

1. How is corporate income measured? How can accelerated depreciation affect the taxable income of a corporation?
2. How could corporate income be taxed under a comprehensive personal income tax?
3. How can the corporation income tax as administered in the United States affect the choice between equity and debt finance?

CORPORATE TAXATION THROUGHOUT THE WORLD: INTERNATIONAL COMPARISONS

Although effective tax rates on corporate income in the United States have declined over the past 50 years, corporate tax rates in the United States remain relatively high compared to those in foreign nations. Japan is the only nation in the world with higher tax rates on corporations than those prevailing in the United States. Many foreign nations, including Canada, Germany, Australia, Spain, and New Zealand,

---

[4]See William F. Fox and LeAnn Luna, "State Corporate Tax Revenue Trends: Causes and Possible Solutions," *National Tax Journal* 50, 3 (September 2002): 491–508.

have either lowered their corporate tax rates or are considering doing so. The lowest corporation income tax rates among OECD members have been those in Iceland and Ireland. The main reason for the trend to lower taxation of corporations is to provide incentives for increasing investment in foreign nations by U.S. multinational corporations.

The statutory corporate tax rate in the United States, when state taxes are included, averages close to 40 percent (although effective tax rates are lower). However, in many foreign nations the tax rates on corporate income are much lower than those in the United States. The average corporate tax rate in OECD nations in 2011 was 24 percent and that rate has declined substantially since 2000 with the rates being cut on average in those nations by about 15 percent between 2000 and 2011. In Ireland, for example, tax rates have declined from 24 percent in 2000 to 12.5 percent in 2011.[5] Many attribute the boom in foreign investment that Ireland has enjoyed in recent years to its relatively low corporate tax rates.

Tax competition for new corporate investment is a reality in the modern global economy. Nations with relatively high corporate tax rates can lose investment to foreign nations with lower tax rates. Countries with below-average corporate tax rates often collect higher-than-average revenue from their corporate income tax rates as the impact of the lower tax rates is offset by large increases in investment by foreign multinational corporations.[6]

Table 15.3 shows the statutory corporate tax rates as of 2011 in OECD nations. The highest corporate tax rates are in Japan, Belgium, France, and the United States.

SHORT-RUN IMPACT OF THE CORPORATE INCOME TAX

The corporate income tax is a discriminatory tax on the income of one particular form of business organization—the corporation. As such, it is expected to reduce the net return to investment in corporate businesses in the short run unless corporations are capable of making immediate adjustments to shift the tax in some way. The most obvious way of shifting the tax in the short run is to adjust output in response to the tax so as to raise prices. This would shift the burden of taxation from owners of the corporation (the stockholders) to consumers of output produced by the corporation. The ultimate impact of the corporate income tax on efficiency, and on the distribution of income, depends on whether the tax depresses the return to corporate investment in the first place. Accordingly, the question of short-run shifting of the tax is of crucial importance in determining the ultimate incidence and excess burden of the tax.

Conflicting theories, and conflicting evidence, exist on the short-run impact of the tax on output prices and on the return to capital invested in the corporate sector of the economy. The effect of the tax on prices and other variables, which potentially can be influenced by managers of the corporation in the short run, determines whether the tax is borne by stockholders in the short run. The short-run impact of the tax on stockholder income, in turn, influences the long-run adjustments that can take place.[7]

---

[5]The tax rate shown is the combined statutory central and sub-central tax rate applied to corporate income when sub-central taxation of corporate income exists in a nation.

[6]See Chris Atkins and Scott A. Hodge, "U.S. Lagging Behind OECD Corporate Tax Trends," *Fiscal Fact 55*, The Tax Foundation, www.taxfoundation.org

[7]For a review of the theories and evidence, see J. Gregory Ballentine, *Equity, Efficiency, and the United States Corporation Income Tax* (Washington, D.C.: American Enterprise Institute, 1980), Chapter 2.

TABLE 15.3	Marginal Corporate Income Tax Rates in OECD Nations, 2011[*]		
COUNTRY	CENTRAL GOVERNMENT CORPORATE INCOME TAX RATE	ADJUSTED CENTRAL GOVERNMENT CORPORATE INCOME TAX RATE[a]	COMBINED CORPORATE INCOME TAX RATE[b]
Australia	30.0	30.0	30.0
Austria	25.0	25.0	25.0
Belgium	33.0	34.0	34.0
Canada	16.5	16.5	27.6
Chile*	20.0	20.0	20.0
Czech Republic	19.0	19.0	19.0
Denmark	25.0	25.0	25.0
Estonia	21.0	21.0	21.0
Finland	26.0	26.0	26.0
France	34.4	34.4	34.4
Germany	15.0	15.825	30.2
Greece	20.0	20.0	20.0
Hungary	19.0	19.0	19.0
Iceland	20.0	20.0	20.0
Ireland	12.5	12.5	12.5
Israel	24.0	24.0	24.0
Italy*	27.5	27.5	27.5
Japan	30.0	28.0	39.5
Korea	22.0	22.0	24.2
Luxembourg	21.0	22.1	28.8
Mexico	30.0	30.0	30.0
The Netherlands	25.0	25.0	25.0
New Zealand	28.0	28.0	28.0
Norway	28.0	28.0	28.0
Poland	19.0	19.0	19.0
Portugal	25.0	25.0	26.5
Slovak Republic	19.0	19.0	19.0
Slovenia	20.0	20.0	20.0
Spain	30.0	30.0	30.0
Sweden	26.3	26.3	26.3
Switzerland	8.5	6.7	21.2
Turkey	20.0	20.0	20.0
United Kingdom	26.0	26.0	26.0
United States	35.0	32.7	39.2

*Rates shown for each nation are the highest statutory marginal tax rates applied to corporate income.
[a]This rate adjusts the top marginal rate to show the net rate if the central government allows deduction of the sub-central corporate tax paid when computing tax liability.
[b]This rate is the raw sum of the top marginal central government rate and any state, regional, or provincial tax rates applied to corporate income.

Source: www.oecd.org

Taxes on Economic Profits

Economic profits are a surplus in excess of the opportunity costs of running a business. Economic theory of the profit-maximizing firm suggests that a tax on economic profits cannot be shifted in the short run. A profit-maximizing firm adjusts output produced per year to equate marginal cost and marginal revenue. Figure 15.1 shows the profit-maximizing output of a perfectly competitive firm fortunate enough to be earning economic profits in the short run. The competitive firm's marginal revenue schedule graphs as a horizontal line. Along that line, the price of the firm's output is also equal to its marginal revenue. The firm maximizes profits by producing the output Q^*, which corresponds to the point at which $MC = MR$. The average cost of producing Q^* units per year is AC^*. The area $PEFG$ represents the firm's annual economic profits. If the industry is competitive, these profits will fall to zero in the long run. This suggests that a tax on economic profits collects revenues only during the short-run period for which the firm earns economic profits.

A tax on economic profits affects neither marginal costs nor marginal revenues. It merely reduces the firm's profits. For example, suppose the firm is subject to an effective average tax rate (ATR) of 40 percent. The tax reduces the firm's profits to 60 percent of its pre-tax amount. In general, if a firm earns X in profits, a tax rate of t percent per year would reduce those profits to $X(1 - t)$. Profits after taxes are represented by the area $ABFG$ in Figure 15.1.

Because the tax affects neither marginal revenues nor marginal costs, firms have no incentive to reduce output as a result of the tax. If the output Q^*

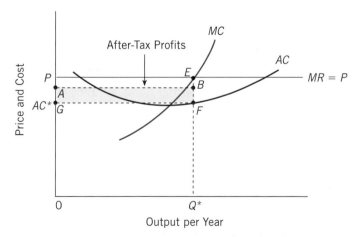

FIGURE 15.1   A Tax on Economic Profits

A tax on economic profits affects neither marginal revenue nor marginal cost—it merely takes a percentage of profits. A profit-maximizing firm has no incentive to change output. The output that maximizes total profits is the same output that maximizes profits after taxes. Because output does not change as a result of the tax, quantity supplied, and therefore price, is unaffected. The tax cannot be shifted. It is borne by owners of the firm in the short run.

maximizes total pretax profits, it also would maximize the 60 percent of pretax profits that remains after the firm pays the tax. Because the firm has no incentive to reduce output, the price of the product does not increase. The firms in the industry do not succeed in shifting the tax forward to buyers, because they cannot increase profits by reducing output in response to the tax. The short-run incidence of a tax on economic profits therefore is borne by the owners of the firm.

A Tax on the Sum of Economic and Normal Profits

As administered in the United States, the corporate income tax does not allow firms to deduct the opportunity cost of owner-supplied funds for investment. Remember, the value of assets, net of debt, is called the equity of a corporation. The opportunity cost of the equity is the normal profit. The corporate income tax is levied on the sum of normal and economic profits. Does this affect the validity of the conclusion that the tax will not affect output and will have no influence on the output price in the short run?

In the short run, the firm operates with a fixed amount of equity that it cannot control. Thus, normal profits, which are a fixed percentage of this equity, are also fixed, and the firm cannot increase its normal profits by altering the output that it produces. Because these normal profits are a fixed cost in the short run, marginal costs, which change only when variable costs change, are not affected by taxation of normal profits. It follows that even when the corporate income tax is levied on the sum of normal and economic profits, profit-maximizing firms have no incentive to adjust their output. The tax can have no effect on consumer prices in the short run and must be borne by owners of the firm in the form of decreased returns on capital invested in the corporation.[8]

Alternative Theories and Empirical Evidence

The conclusion that the corporate income tax cannot be shifted in the short run depends on the assumption that firms are profit maximizers that operate in competitive markets. More complex models, which allow explicit consideration of some of the peculiarities of oligopolistic markets and nonprofit-maximizing behavior by firms, describe situations in which firms might act to reduce output in response to the tax. Such models argue that short-run shifting of the tax in the form of higher prices can occur.[9] Empirical evidence on the short-run impact of the tax on prices is conflicting. Conclusions range from zero shifting to shifting in excess of 100 percent. Firms that use the tax as an excuse to raise prices by

[8]This conclusion must be modified by the extent to which the tax, when introduced, is capitalized into lower stock values. Under those circumstances, portfolio adjustments by investors might bid up stock prices to offset some of the initial burden on corporate stockholders. See Martin Feldstein, "The Surprising Incidence of a Tax on Pure Rent: A New Answer to an Old Question," *Journal of Political Economy* 85 (April 1977): 349–360.

[9]See, for example, Sergio Bruno, "Corporation Income Tax, Oligopolistic Markets, and Immediate Tax Shifting: A Suggested Theoretical Approach," *Public Finance* 25 (1970): 363–378.

amounts that more than cover the total tax due are said to be shifting in excess of 100 percent.[10]

LONG-RUN IMPACT OF THE CORPORATE INCOME TAX

The ultimate impact of the corporate income tax depends on its long-run influence on choices. This is dependent, as stressed previously, on the impact the tax has in the short run on the return to capital invested in corporations. Assume at first that the tax is not shifted in the short run and is borne by owners of capital in the corporate sector in the form of reduced capital income.

Long-Run Market Equilibrium

A classic model for analyzing the resource flows set up by the tax in the long run, under the assumption that it decreases the net return to capital in the corporate sector, was developed by Arnold Harberger in the early 1960s.[11] The model assumes that the economy can be thought of as being divided into two sectors: corporate sector and noncorporate sector, with the noncorporate sector being composed of alternative investments not subject to the corporate income tax. This would include housing and other investments owned by noncorporate investors. The model assumes that the corporate income tax is the only tax being used. Perfect competition is presumed to prevail in all markets. Finally, the total supply of funds for investment each year, as well as the supply of other inputs, is assumed to be fixed.

The basic reasoning of Harberger's analysis can be presented with the aid of a simple supply-and-demand analysis of the impact of a newly introduced corporate income tax on the long-run equilibrium of a two-sector economy. This is shown in Figure 15.2. The total supply of loanable funds available for investment each year is assumed to be fixed. The curve labeled S in Figure 15.2A represents the supply of savings available to finance investments in any given year. The initial total demand for funds for investment, D, is shown in Figure 15.2A. The market for loanable funds is in equilibrium at point E. The corresponding equilibrium interest rate is i_1. The corresponding equilibrium amount of dollars invested per year is the sum of I_C, corporate investment, and I_N, noncorporate investment. The equilibrium return to investment in both the corporate and noncorporate sectors of the economy must equal the equilibrium interest rate. If that were not the case, the amount

---

[10]Evidence on shifting in excess of 100 percent was found by Marion Krzyzaniak and Richard Musgrave, *The Shifting of the Corporation Income Tax* (Baltimore: Johns Hopkins University Press, 1963). Another study finding evidence of shifting in excess of 100 percent is Richard Dusansky, "The Short-Run Shifting of the Corporation Income Tax in the United States," *Oxford Economic Papers* 24 (November 1972): 357–371. A study by John Mikesell found evidence of shifting of about 58 percent by electric utilities. See John L. Mikesell, "The Corporation Income Tax and the Rate of Return in Privately Owned Electric Utilities," *Public Finance* 28 (1973): 291–300. Gregg, Harberger, and Mieszkowski found no evidence of shifting. See John G. Gregg, Arnold C. Harberger, and Peter Mieszkowski, "Empirical Evidence on the Corporation Income Tax," *Journal of Political Economy* 75 (December 1967): 811–821. A study by Oakland also found little or no evidence of shifting. See William Oakland, "Corporate Earnings and Tax Shifting in United States Manufacturing, 1930–1968," *Review of Economics and Statistics* 54 (August 1972): 235–244. For a discussion of the incidence of the corporation income tax in an open economy, see Jane G. Gravelle and Kent Smetters, "Who Bears the Burden of the Corporate Income Tax in an Open Economy?" National Bureau of Economic Research (NBER) Working Paper 86280 (Cambridge, Mass.: NBER, 2001).

[11]Arnold C. Harberger, "The Incidence of the Corporation Income Tax," *Journal of Political Economy* 70 (June 1962): 215–240.

FIGURE 15.2 Long-Run Impact of the Corporate Income Tax

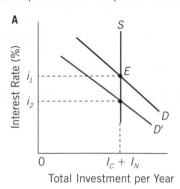

A

Interest Rate (%)

i_1

i_2

S

E

D

D'

0 $I_C + I_N$

Total Investment per Year

B

Return to Investment (%)

$MSC_C = MSR_N = S_C$

r_G^*

$i_1 = r_1$

$r_G^*(1 - t) = r_N^*$

$r_1(1 - t) = r'$

A

E_{C1}

E_{C2}

$MSR_C = D_C = r_G$

$D_C' = r_G(1 - t)$

ΔI_C

0 I_{C2} I_{C1}

Corporate Investment per Year

C

Return to Investment (%)

$S_N = MSC_N = MSR_C$

S_N'

r_1

r_2

B

E_{N1}

E_{N2}

MSR_N

ΔI_N

0 I_{N1} I_{N2}

Noncorporate Investment per Year

The corporate income tax causes a reduction in investment in the corporate sector, shown in **B**. Assuming a perfectly inelastic supply of savings, as shown in **A**, this implies an increase in the supply of investable funds in the noncorporate sector, as illustrated in **C**. This lowers the return to these investments. In the long-run equilibrium, the net return in the corporate sector is $r_N^* = r_2$, the return to noncorporate investment. The tax reduces the return to all investment.

of annual investment would change or investors would reallocate their funds between the two alternative investment sectors until the returns were equal (assuming zero transactions costs). Thus, a pretax capital market equilibrium exists when the marginal return to investment in each of the two sectors, r_1, is equal to the market rate of interest.

Initially, before the introduction of the tax, the return to investment is r_1, no matter where the funds are invested. At that equilibrium, I_{C1} per year is invested in the corporate sector, and I_{N1} per year is invested in the noncorporate sector. This is illustrated in Figure 15.2B and 15.2C. The demand for investment in the corporate sector reflects the marginal social return to investment in corporate projects, MSR_C. The supply of funds for investment in the corporate sector reflects the marginal social cost of funds used to finance that investment, MSC_C. This represents the opportunity costs of using funds to finance corporate investment *instead of* the alternative of noncorporate investment. The marginal social cost of investment in the corporate sector is the marginal social return that can be earned on noncorporate investment. If additional funds are allocated to corporate investment per year, fewer funds will be available for noncorporate investment each year. Because the marginal social return of noncorporate investment, MSR_N, increases as fewer funds are invested there, as shown in Figure 15.2B, the marginal social cost of making corporate investments increases as more are made.

The graphs in Figure 15.2B and 15.2C are mutually dependent. The sum of the annual investments in each of the two sectors must equal the fixed supply of savings each year. Increases in corporate investment imply decreases in noncorporate investment and vice versa. The marginal social cost of investing in the noncorporate sector is the forgone return on investment in the corporate sector.

The initial equilibrium allocation of investment is efficient. At point E_{C1} in Figure 15.2B, the marginal social return to investment in the corporate sector equals its marginal social cost. The efficient amount of investment is I_{C1}. Similarly, investment of I_{N1} per year in the noncorporate sector, as shown in Figure 15.2C, is also efficient because the marginal social return to that investment equals its marginal social cost at point E_{N1}.

Introduction of a corporate income tax subjects the return to funds invested in the corporate sector to a discriminatory tax that is not present in the noncorporate sector. The tax has the effect of decreasing the net return earned by investing in the corporate sector at any level of investment. This decreases the demand for loanable funds for investment in the corporate sector from D_C to D'_C, as shown in Figure 15.2B. All points along D'_C reflect the net return to investment, after payment of taxes, in the corporate sector. This net return is the gross return less the tax. If the tax is t percent of the gross return, points on D'_C would equal $r_G(1 - t)$. For example, if the tax rate were 40 percent, the net return to any investment after taxes would be 60 percent of r_G.

Initially, in the short run, the investors would not be able to reduce the amount of capital employed in the corporate sector, and the return would fall by the full amount of the tax to r' where $r' = r_1(1 - t)$. Thus, the return to corporate invest ment now would be lower than the return to noncorporate investment, since $r' < r_1$.

In the long run, fewer funds each year would be allocated to corporate investment. Instead, investors would use their funds to finance the more lucrative returns that now could be earned in the noncorporate sector. Thus, in the long run, in response to the tax, the supply of funds to the noncorporate sector would increase. This increase in supply reflects the lower opportunity cost of making noncorporate investment. Investors now forgo the lower after-tax return, $r_G(1 - t)$, instead of r_G, for corporate investment when they use their funds to finance noncorporate investment.

As shown in Figure 15.2C, the increase in the supply of funds for investment in the noncorporate sector *decreases* the equilibrium return to investment in that sector to r_2, and the new market equilibrium at E_{N2} is attained. The process of reallocation of funds for investment would continue until the return in the noncorporate sector falls to a level equal to the net return—after taxes—that could be earned in the corporate sector. When this occurs, a new general equilibrium is reached. The new equilibrium in the corporate sector corresponds to E_{C2}. At that point, investment in the corporate sector falls to I_{C2} per year. The equilibrium gross return to investment at that point is r_G^*. The net return to corporate investment is $r_G^*(1 - t) = r_N^*$. The decrease in corporate investment, ΔI_C, must exactly equal the increase in noncorporate investment, ΔI_N, because the annual supply of savings is fixed. The return now earned from noncorporate investment, r_2, must equal the net return from investment in the corporate sector:

$$r_2 = r_G^*(1 - t). \tag{15.1}$$

If this were not the case, additional reallocation of investment would occur until it was no longer possible to earn a higher return in one of the sectors.

The decrease in funds supplied to the corporate sector increases the gross return to capital there to r_G^*, but the after-tax net return is below the initial pretax return of r_1. The increased supply of funds to the noncorporate sector decreases the return there to r_2. The return to investment for the economy, as a whole, declines, as the tax decreases the return to investment earned throughout the economy. It makes no difference where, or to what use, loanable funds are put; the tax lowers their return. Thus, the corporate income tax is effectively a tax on all savings and investment income. Table 15.4 summarizes the effect of the tax on the return to investment.

Excess Burden of the Corporate Income Tax

Assuming no taxes on investments in the noncorporate sector (or that the tax on corporate income exceeds that on the income of noncorporate business), the corporate income tax distorts the pattern of investment. Less than the efficient amount of investment is in the corporate sector. Also, as a result of the tax, more than the efficient amount of investment is in the noncorporate sector. This is illustrated in Figure 15.2.

As shown in Figure 15.2B, in the long-run equilibrium in the corporate sector, there is I_{C2} of investment per year. The marginal social return to that investment is r_G^*. This exceeds the marginal social cost of investment in that sector, which is equal to r_2, the return that can be earned in noncorporate investment. Similarly, as shown in Figure 15.2C, annual investment in the long run in the noncorporate sector is I_{N2}. This is more than the efficient amount of investment because the marginal social cost, r_G^*, the return that can be earned in the corporate sector, exceeds the marginal social return, r_2, that is earned on noncorporate investment.

The excess burden of misallocation of investment in the two sectors can be measured by either of the triangular areas: $AE_{C2}E_{C1}$ in Figure 15.2B or $BE_{N2}E_{N1}$ in Figure 15.2C. These two areas are equal because $\Delta I_C = \Delta I_N$ and because the difference $(r_G^* - r_2)$ is the same in both graphs. The excess burden of the misallocation of investment between the two sectors as a result of the corporate income tax was estimated to be about 12 percent of revenues collected from the tax

TABLE 15.4	Long-Run Impact of the Corporate Income Tax	
	NET RETURN TO CORPORATE INVESTMENT	**RETURN TO NONCORPORATE INVESTMENT**
Pretax Equilibrium	r_1	r_1
Short-Run Impact of a Tax[a]	r'	r_1
Long-Run Posttax Equilibrium[b]	$r_N^* = r_G^*(1 - t) = r_2$	r_2

[a]$r' < r_1$
[b]$r_2 < r_1$

in the mid-1970s.[12] Since then, effective corporate tax rates have declined and so has the excess burden. The decline in effective marginal tax rates for the corporation income tax in the United States since 1953 has decreased the tax rate differential between corporate and noncorporate income from 33 percentage points in 1953 to 14 percentage points in 2003. Both the tax rates on corporate and noncorporate income have been reduced over this period, but the corporate tax rates still exceed the noncorporate tax rates. However, one economist estimates that between 1953 and 2003, the declines in the effective corporate tax rates eliminated 93 percent of the excess burden resulting from the misallocation of investment between the corporate and noncorporate business sectors and 88 percent of the excess burden from misallocation of capital between corporations and owner-occupied housing.[13]

This efficiency loss could be further compounded if the supply of savings in the economy is responsive to the lower return to investment induced by the tax. If the supply of savings were moderately responsive to changes in the return to investment, the conclusions of Harberger's analysis would have to be modified somewhat. The total supply of savings in Figure 15.2 now would not be fixed. As a result, as shown in Figure 15.3, the reduction in the return to investment caused by the tax would decrease savings and investment from I_1 to I_2. An additional loss in efficiency would be caused by the reduction in the growth of the capital stock. This additional excess burden is the area ABC in Figure 15.3. The added excess burden would have to be included with the intersectoral distortions in resource allocation caused by the tax. Studies of the total excess burden induced by the

FIGURE 15.3 Impact of the Corporate Income Tax When the Supply of Savings Is Not Perfectly Inelastic

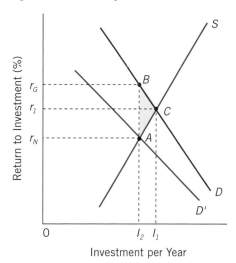

When the supply of savings is not perfectly inelastic, the corporate income tax results in a decline in annual investment from I_1 to I_2. The gross return to investment increases, whereas the after-tax return declines. The excess burden of the tax is the area ABC when income effects are negligible.

© Cengage Learning

---

[12]John B. Shoven, "The Incidence and Efficiency Effect of Taxes on Income from Capital," *Journal of Political Economy* 84 (December 1976): 1261–1283.

[13]See Jane Gravelle, "The Corporate Tax ...," *op. cit.* (December 2004).

PUBLIC POLICY PERSPECTIVE

A New Way to Tax Corporate Income—The Corporate Cash Flow Tax

A major criticism of the corporate income tax is that it distorts the pattern of investment between corporate and noncorporate uses and that it also reduces the return to capital in general, possibly reducing national investment. One way to avoid the distortions of the corporate income tax while still making corporations and their stockholders pay a fair share of taxes on corporate income is a corporate cash flow tax. This type of tax would tax the difference between a corporation's revenues and its expenditures on both current and capital inputs except that the cost of financial resources as measured by interest payments on debt would not be deductible. This simple tax eliminates the bias toward debt finance inherent in the current corporate income tax, which allows interest payments as tax deductible but not dividends paid on stock.

Let's see how the corporate cash flow tax would work. In effect, the tax would eliminate depreciation of capital acquired by corporations. Instead, all capital acquisitions would be expensed—deducted immediately as a cost of production. This, of course, would be a powerful tax incentive to encourage investment because the firms could recover part of the cost of their capital equipment as tax savings in the year they acquire the equipment rather than over a longer period. The revenue the government would forgo by not taxing a portion of the cost of capital inputs in the year they are acquired and in later years would be made up, in part, by the increase in the corporate tax base made possible by not deducting interest paid from corporate revenues. Many firms with heavy debt burdens would see their tax bills rise on average as all their interest from previous borrowings could no longer be deducted from revenue when computing taxable profits.[1]

The cash flow tax would not distort investment decisions in any way. This is because, by making an investment purchase, a corporation would be able to deduct the full cost. For example, if the corporation were subject to a 34 percent MTR, the net cost of the investment would be 66 percent of the dollar cost with the remaining 34 percent being borne by the government as a loss in current tax revenue. Then, as the investment began to yield income for the corporation, the government would collect 34 percent of the return on the investment. Because the investment is fully deductible as a cost and its return is subject to the same tax rate as the deduction, the incentive to invest is unaffected. The logic here is the same as that discussed in the text for the short-run impact of a tax on profits. The government, in effect, becomes a partner in the investment purchase by sharing a fraction of the cost and then recoups its reward of partnership with the same share of the return to the investment. In this case, the volume of investment that maximizes the gross return to the corporation is exactly the same as the volume that maximizes 66 percent of the return when the full cost of the investment is deductible.[2]

corporate income tax in the 1970s concluded that it was quite high at the time. A number of studies suggest that the excess burden of the combined distortion in the pattern of investment and reduction in total investment was between one-third and two-thirds of revenues collected.[14]

The preceding analysis presumes that the short-run impact of the tax is such as to decrease the return to capital invested in the corporate sector in the first place. If, however, the tax is shifted forward to consumers in the form of higher prices, or if it is capitalized into lower stock prices, the long-run adjustment process described by the model would not take place.

When the supply of savings is not perfectly inelastic, the corporate income tax results in a decline in annual investment from I_1 to I_2. The gross return to investment increases, whereas the after-tax return declines. The excess burden of the tax is the area when income effects are negligible.

---

[14]See Ballentine, *Equity*, Chapter 5, for a review of these studies. See, in particular, Shoven, "Incidence and Efficiency Effects."

Because a corporate cash flow tax will not impair investment decisions, it will not reduce corporate investment and will not distort the pattern of investment between corporate and noncorporate assets. Only new investment will be eligible for expensing under the tax, so no windfall gain will accrue to corporate shareholders for investment undertaken in previous years.[3] Another advantage of a cash flow tax is that inflation would no longer be a distortionary tax influence because no depreciation allowances would be eroding away with inflation, and interest payments would no longer be tax deductible.

The final remarkable fact about a corporate cash flow tax is that even though investment would be expensed, the Treasury need not necessarily suffer a reduction in tax revenue because of the shift from the existing corporate income tax. The Treasury would lose revenue from the introduction of expensing of new investments. However, it would gain revenue from discontinuing all old depreciation deductions on past investments and by disallowing all deductions for net interest paid by corporations. One study suggests that the dollar volume of corporate income subject to tax under a cash flow tax would have been greater in 1982 and 1986 than it was under the prevailing corporate income tax at that time.[4] This implies that the federal government could provide the economy with a strong growth stimulus by encouraging investment through the corporate cash flow tax while at the same time giving up but little revenue.

The President's Advisory Panel on Federal Tax Reform recommended possible options for reform of the corporation income tax in its report issued in 2005. The options for improving the environment for growth and investment suggested movement toward a corporate cash flow tax. The plan would lower statutory tax rates on large corporations from 35 to 30 percent and allow expensing of all new investment. Interest would no longer be deductible as a cost, and interest earned by corporations would no longer be taxable.[5]

[1]For a complete analysis of this type of tax, see John Shoven, "Using the Corporate Cash Flow Tax to Integrate Corporate and Personal Taxes." In National Tax Association–Tax Institute of America, 1990 *Proceedings of the Eighty-Third Annual Conference on Taxation* (Columbus, Ohio; National Tax Association–Tax Institute of America 1991): 19–27. This section is based on Shoven's analysis. The examples apply mainly to nonfinancial corporations. Financial corporations, such as banks, that deal primarily in loans and securities would have to be treated in a special way under a corporate cash flow tax.
[2]For this to hold, the government would have to allow an investment to be fully deductible, even if it results in negative net taxable income for the corporation such that firms with heavy investment in a given year could receive negative tax payments (subsidies) from the government. Measures also would have to be taken to make sure that only productive investment (as opposed to investment that is really consumption and does not yield future income) is eligible for expensing. See Shoven, p. 21.
[3]There would, of course, be some transition problems in moving to a corporate cash flow tax and some issues regarding foreign investments. Tax treatment of multinational corporations would also have to be resolved before the tax was introduced. See Shoven, pp. 25–26, for a discussion of these issues.
[4]See Shoven, pp. 24–25, for details of this calculation.
[5]See www.taxreformpanel.gov

INCIDENCE OF THE CORPORATE INCOME TAX

Impact on Output, Prices, and Wages

The tax-induced flow of investment caused by the corporate income tax can affect output prices and wages in the long run. Over time, the output produced by the corporate sector tends to fall relative to that produced by the noncorporate sector because of the reduction in investment in the corporate sector. Depending on the price elasticities of demand, these changes in the supply of goods result in an increase in the price of goods produced by the corporate sector and a decrease in the price of goods produced by the noncorporate sector. Households spending relatively large portions of their budgets on goods produced by the corporate sector experience a reduction in real income relative to other households.

The tax can also affect the wages earned by labor in the two sectors of the economy. For example, if labor and capital are used in fixed proportions in the corporate sector, it follows that when the reduction in investment reduces capital input in the corporate sector in the long run, a corresponding reduction in the amount of labor used in that sector would result. If the noncorporate sector does not employ capital and labor in the same ratio as the corporate sector, wages would have to change before the economy could return to a general equilibrium. The general level of wages in the economy might fall as a result of the tax. If the corporate sector is relatively more labor-intensive than the noncorporate sector, wages would fall to induce the noncorporate sector to absorb the labor flowing from the corporate sector. The extent of such changes in the prices of other inputs depends on the elasticities of substitution in production between capital and other factors, both in the corporate and noncorporate sectors. Thus, the corporate income tax can also affect the real income of those who own noncapital inputs.

Impact on Income Distribution

Arnold Harberger's general conclusion regarding the corporate income tax is that it is borne according to the ownership of capital. Although Harberger acknowledges that the long-run price effects of the tax are important, he presumes that individuals, on average, benefit as much by price decreases of noncorporate goods caused by the tax as they suffer from price increases for corporate goods caused by the decrease in investment in the corporate sector.

The implication of Harberger's conclusion for the evaluation of the incidence of the tax, from an equity point of view, is that its burden is distributed in a progressive manner with respect to income. This results because the distribution of the ownership of capital (wealth) in the United States is highly unequal and is concentrated in the hands of upper-income groups. If the model is correct, then the tax is paid by anyone who owns capital, including homes, human capital, consumer durables, as well as corporate stock and productive capital. The burden is spread throughout the economy according to the ownership of wealth. The inequality of the pattern of ownership of wealth ensures that the tax is progressive. It is more progressive than it would be if it were borne solely according to the ownership pattern of corporate stock, and it is certainly more progressive than it would be if it were shifted in the short run in the form of higher prices. In fact, considerable econometric analysis tends to support Harberger's conclusion.[15] A portion of the burden of the tax on capital could be shifted to workers in the form of lower wages. If this were true, the progressivity of the tax would be decreased. The shifting of the tax to workers stems from the tax-induced decline in capital formation. This decreases the amount of capital per worker and, in turn, decreases worker productivity relative to what it would be in the absence of the tax. The decline in worker productivity now that each worker has less equipment, such as machines and tools, causes a decline in wages, which in turn decreases worker income. Thus, the workers bear a portion of the tax on capital. Owners recoup part of the tax, as the tax-induced decrease in quantity of funds supplied for investment raises the market return to investment (see Figure 15.3). Estimates by Feldstein indicate that as much as 29 percent of the burden of the corporate income tax may be shifted to labor in this way.[16] Other analysis indicates that as much as 80 percent of the burden of the tax may be shifted to labor.[17]

---

[15]See Gregg, Harberger, and Mieszkowski, "Empirical Evidence," and Oakland, "Corporate Earnings."

[16]Martin Feldstein, "The Incidence of a Capital Income Tax in a Growing Economy with Variable Savings Rates," *Review of Economic Studies* 41 (October 1974): 505–513.

[17]J. Gregory Ballentine, "The Incidence of a Corporation Income Tax in a Growing Economy," *Journal of Political Economy* 86 (October 1978): 863–876. For a review of recent empirical analysis of the corporation income tax in an open economy, see Jennifer C. Gravelle, "Corporate Tax Incidence: A Review of Empirical Estimates and Analysis" Congressional Budget Office, Washington, D.C., Working Paper 2011-01, June 2011 and "Corporate Tax Incidence: Review of General Equilibrium Estimates and Analysis" Congressional Budget Office, Washington, D.C., Working Paper 2010-03, May 2010.

Thus, the incidence of the corporate income tax remains unresolved. The tax is most likely to be widely diffused in the economy. Conflicting studies indicate that the tax is shared in a complex fashion by consumers, capitalists, and workers.

CHECKPOINT

1. What effect does a tax on economic profits have on profit-maximizing a corporation's output decision in the short run?
2. Assuming that corporations maximize profits and investors maximize the return on their investments, what are the long-run effects of a corporate income tax on resource use?
3. Why does Harberger's model imply that the incidence of the corporate income tax is borne according to the ownership of capital?

SUMMARY

The corporate income tax is levied on profits of corporations and is a subject of great controversy. The actual burden of this tax appears to be diffused in a complex fashion among consumers, owners of capital, and workers.

Corporations cannot deduct the imputed interest associated with expansion financed by retained earnings. Neither can they deduct dividend payments as a cost. In consequence, many economists believe that the corporate income tax provides incentives for corporations to use debt as opposed to equity finance.

The tax base under the corporate income tax is the sum of normal and economic profits. Because the tax does not allow a deduction for the opportunity cost of capital invested in the firm, it biases financial decisions toward borrowing to finance capital expansion. The size of the tax base is influenced by allowable rules for depreciating assets.

The major controversy concerning the incidence, and other economic effects, of the corporate income tax stems from its short-run impact. Some economists believe the tax to be shifted forward immediately to consumers in the form of higher prices; others argue that its initial impact is to reduce the return to holding corporate stock. If the return to investing in corporate business is reduced as a result of the tax, a series of resource flows would be induced until a new long-run equilibrium is achieved, so that the after-tax return on corporate stock is once again equal to the return available on untaxed investment. Many believe that the net impact of this adjustment process would be such that the incidence of the tax would be borne by all investors, not only those who invest in the corporate sector. The tax also tends to cause losses in efficiency insofar as it results in a distortion in the pattern of investment between the corporate and the noncorporate sector and also reduces capital formation. Reduced capital formation reduces wages, and in this way some of the tax could be shifted to workers.

LOOKING AHEAD

Increased concern about the responsiveness of investment and saving to taxes on capital income has led to renewed interest in consumption as a tax base. Chapter 16 discusses some of the pros and cons of taxing consumption and evaluates various forms of sales taxes. Included is an analysis of the value-added tax, which is used extensively by European nations and has been proposed as an addition to the tax structure in the United States.

KEY CONCEPTS

Accelerated Depreciation

Corporation

Dividends

Economic Depreciation

Equity

Expensing a Capital Asset

Historic Cost

Retained Earnings

Straight-Line Depreciation

REVIEW QUESTIONS

1. How is business income measured? How can the tax rules for calculating taxable business income affect incentives to invest?
2. What is the "equity" of a corporation? Assuming that a corporation has $5 million in equity and that shareholders forgo a return of 9 percent by keeping their equity in the corporation, calculate the corporation's normal profit.
3. Why would expensing of capital assets for tax purposes encourage investment in new capital?
4. Explain how corporate income could be taxed under a comprehensive income tax without recourse to a corporate income tax. How can separate taxation of corporate income be justified? Given the favorable treatment of capital gains under the current rules of the personal income tax, what would be some of the consequences of eliminating separate taxation of corporate income?
5. In what sense does the corporate income tax subject corporate profits to double-taxation?
6. Why do economists argue that the tax definition of corporate profits overstates the true profits of corporations? How can this misdefinition of profit affect the financial structure of the corporation?
7. How can depreciation allowances affect the size of the tax base for the corporate income tax? How can accelerated depreciation reduce a corporation's tax

burden? What problems are caused by inflation in accurately allowing depreciation to reflect the replacement cost of capital?
8. Why is the short-run impact of the corporate income tax on prices of corporate output so crucial in determining the final impact of the tax in the long run? Explain why a profit-maximizing corporation has no incentive to adjust its short-run output in response to a tax on its profits. Who would bear the short-run incidence of the tax if the firm does not produce more or less after the tax is imposed?
9. Explain why the corporate income tax causes resources to flow out of the corporate sector when the short-run effect of the tax is to reduce the after-tax return to capital invested in the corporate sector relative to alternative investments not subject to the tax. What effect do these resource flows have on the return to capital, output prices, and the return to various factors of production?
10. Assuming a fixed aggregate supply of saving, how does the corporate income tax reduce efficiency according to the results of Harberger's model? How will further losses in efficiency result when the aggregate supply of saving is responsive to changes in its return? Assuming that the aggregate supply of saving is not fixed, how can the corporate income tax be shifted to workers in the long run?

PROBLEMS

1. A corporation has $7 million in equity. During the tax year it takes in $4 million in receipts and earns $2 million in capital gains from sale of a subsidiary. It incurs labor costs of $1 million, interest costs of $250,000, material costs of $500,000, and pays rent for structures of $250,000. Calculate the corporation's total accounting profit and, assuming that the profit is fully taxable, calculate its tax liability using the tax rates in Table 15.2. Calculate the ATR of the corporation as a percentage of its *economic* profit, assuming that the opportunity cost of capital is 8 percent.
2. A corporation has $5 million in assets and $3 million in debt. During the year it takes in $750,000 in net revenue after deduction of all costs except for interest and incurs interest expenses of $300,000. The corporation pays an ATR of 33 percent on its profit.
   a. Calculate the percentage return on equity after taxes for the corporation.

   b. Calculate the percentage return on equity for the corporation if it had the same net revenue but no debt and therefore no interest expense for the year.
3. Suppose the corporate profits are subject to a 34 percent MTR but the profits of noncorporate investment are not taxed. The gross return to corporate investment is 10 percent. Calculate the net return to corporate and noncorporate investment in the long run, assuming that the total supply of savings is perfectly inelastic for the economy. How would your answer differ if the elasticity of supply of saving were 0.5?
4. Suppose the corporate income tax were eliminated and corporate income allocated to shareholders on a pro rata basis according to their proportion of outstanding stock. How would such a change in tax policy affect the excess burden and incidence of the tax, assuming that all forms of investment income are included in a comprehensive income tax base?

5. Suppose the corporate income tax were eliminated and the revenue lost was made up by increasing the payroll tax rate on labor earnings. What would be the impact on labor and capital markets of such a shift in tax policy? What is the likely differential incidence of substituting a payroll tax for an equal-yield corporate income tax?

ADDITIONAL READINGS

Ballentine, J. Gregory. *Equity, Efficiency, and the United States Corporation Income Tax*. Washington, D.C.: American Enterprise Institute, 1980. A review of the literature on the incidence and allocative effects of the corporate income tax. Much of the analysis is nontechnical and accessible to readers with only minimal background in economics.

Gravelle, Jane G. "The Corporate Tax: Where Has It Been and Where Is It Going." *National Tax Journal* 57, 4 (December 2004): 903–923. This article examines how economic factors and changes in tax law have affected effective corporate tax rates since 1953.

Harberger, Arnold C. "The Incidence of the Corporation Income Tax." *Journal of Political Economy* 70 (June 1962): 215–240. Harberger's classic tax incidence analysis. This is a fine example of economic model building and application of economic theory to policy. This article has had considerable influence on economic thought. Requires a good background in economic theory.

Shaviro, Daniel N. *Decoding the U.S. Corporate Tax*. Washington, D.C.: Urban Institute Press, 2009. An analysis and suggestions for reform of the U.S. corporate income tax within the context of the modern global economy and political situation.

Shoven, John. "Using the Corporate Cash Flow Tax to Integrate Corporate and Personal Taxes." In National Tax Association–Tax Institute of America, *1990 Proceedings of the Eighty-Third Annual Conference on Taxation* (Columbus, Ohio: National Tax Association–Tax Institute of America, 1991): 19–27. A novel proposal to change the way corporate income is taxed while at the same time encouraging investment.

INTERNET RESOURCE

http://www.ntanet.org
The home page of the National Tax Association can be used to search for studies on business and corporate taxation and to link to other sources of information on business taxes.

Chapter 16

TAXES ON CONSUMPTION AND SALES

LEARNING OBJECTIVES

After reading this chapter, you should be able to:

- Discuss the equity aspects of direct taxation of consumption through a tax that allows households to deduct savings from their income.

- Determine the economic effects of a general direct tax on comprehensive consumption.

- Analyze the consequences for labor and investment markets of substituting a comprehensive consumption tax for a comprehensive income tax yielding the same amount of revenue.

- Evaluate alternative types of sales taxes, including retail sales taxes, excise taxes, turnover taxes, and the value-added tax.

- Explain how the value-added tax is administered in Europe through the invoice method and the advantages and disadvantages of the tax.

You are probably used to paying a sales tax because most state and many local governments rely on it as a major source of revenue. Usually the sales tax is added on to retail purchase of goods by the retail seller at the time the product is sold to a final user. Sales taxes also are widely used in Europe, but it is not so obvious to buyers that they are paying the tax. European nations rely heavily on a type of national sales tax that is included in the prices of most goods *and* services, such as hotel room rentals and transportation services. The European sales tax, called the value-added tax (VAT), is seldom itemized by the retail seller, but is included in the price of most items. Such a tax, which is currently in use by scores of nations, including Canada, has been often proposed for the United States as a sort of national sales tax to reduce the tax burden on saving.

One easy way to avoid sales taxes is not to consume. In fact, one of the advantages of taxes on consumption is that they encourage people to save because interest is not subject to sales taxes as it accrues. Taxes on consumption can be used to encourage saving. Recently, because of concerns about the long-term effects of low national saving in the United States, some congressional leaders and economists have been advocating conversion of the income tax to a tax on consumption by allowing taxpayers to deduct their savings from their income before computing their tax. This new way to have a consumption-based tax would directly tax household consumption in the same way income is currently taxed.

In this chapter, we examine the possibility of shifting to consumption rather than income-based direct taxation. We also look at the way governments tax consumption indirectly through retail sales taxes, excise taxes, and multistage sales taxes like the VAT used throughout Europe.

CONSUMPTION AS A TAX BASE

Consumption, or current expenditure, is an alternative to income as a tax base. The heavy reliance on income taxes at the federal level in the United States, however, reflects a commonly held notion that income is a superior index of the ability to pay. This notion is also reflected in economic analysis inasmuch as taxes are evaluated in terms of their effects on the distribution of income. Incidence is almost always calculated with respect to an income base. In recent years, economists' renewed interest in the consumption base reflects their persistent belief that consumption is, in fact, a good (superior, some argue) index of the ability to pay. Also, concern is increasing about relatively high efficiency losses associated with taxation of income from saving and investment. Consumption taxes are more favorable to saving and investment incentives than income taxes.

A general tax on consumption is equivalent to an income tax that allows savings to be excluded from the tax base. Annual **comprehensive consumption** is annual comprehensive income minus annual savings. This chapter discusses the feasibility of a general tax on comprehensive consumption. The advantages and disadvantages of such a tax compared with a comprehensive income tax are analyzed.

The dominant form of taxation of consumption in the United States is the retail sales tax. Used mainly by state governments in this country, retail and other general sales taxes account for approximately one-third of aggregate state government revenues. Local governments also use the retail sales tax, but revenues collected from the tax supply an average of less than 5 percent of total local government revenues. The VAT commonly used in European nations is levied on both retail and wholesale transactions, with deductions allowable for taxes paid on intermediate transactions.

The federal government taxes consumption mainly through the use of excise taxes, which are selective sales taxes levied on particular items and often collected from manufacturers. Excise taxes have accounted for less than 4 percent of total federal government revenues in recent years. Excise taxes include those levied on cigarettes, gasoline, tires, telephone services, and alcoholic beverages. Excise taxes are also used by state governments, where they account for nearly 10 percent of total revenues. State excise taxes include those on motor fuels, tobacco products, alcoholic beverages, and various miscellaneous items. The federal government also uses customs duties as a means of taxing the consumption of imported goods.

DIRECT TAXATION OF CONSUMPTION: THE EXPENDITURE TAX

The notion of directly taxing consumption in a manner similar to the way income is taxed was recommended for consideration by studies published in the United States and Great Britain in the late 1970s.[1] The method of taxation would involve annual declaration of consumption expenditures, similar to annual declarations of income, by filing annual returns on which taxable consumption would be calculated and taxed according to an appropriate rate structure. This could allow progressive taxation of consumption in a fashion similar to the way progressive rates are applied to taxable income.

Taxable consumption would be calculated directly from data on income simply by excluding that portion of income that is saved rather than spent. Although implementing such a general consumption tax poses serious problems, economists who propose its adoption argue that these problems are less serious than those that would be encountered in defining a truly comprehensive income base, because measuring annual changes in net worth would not be necessary.[2] In fact, in recent years, U.S. taxpayers have been allowed to exclude a limited amount of savings deposited in qualified retirement accounts from their adjusted gross income (AGI). Limited amounts of savings deposited in tax-deferred accounts for education and health expenditures can also be excluded from income. These savings, and the interest and other earnings accumulated in the account, are not taxable until they are withdrawn. Funds withdrawn before the taxpayer has reached the age of 59½ are subject to an additional penalty of 10 percent.

A comprehensive consumption tax, or as it is sometimes called, an *expenditure tax*, would work somewhat like an income tax that allows exclusion of retirement savings from the tax base. However, *all savings, without limit*, no matter for what purpose, would be excluded from income. No tax penalty would be incurred for withdrawing funds from savings accounts. When funds were withdrawn and

---

[1]See U.S. Department of the Treasury, *Blueprints for Basic Tax Reform* (Washington, D.C.: U.S. Government Printing Office, 1979), and Institute for Fiscal Studies, *The Structure and Reform of Direct Taxation: Report of the Committee Chaired by Professor J. E. Meade* (London: George Allen and Unwin, 1978).

[2]See, for example, Peter Mieszkowski, "The Choice of the Tax Base: Consumption versus Income Taxation," in *Federal Tax Reform: Myths and Realities*, ed. Michael J. Boskin (San Francisco: Institute for Contemporary Studies, 1978): 27–54. Also see David Bradford, "Consumption Taxes: Some Fundamental Transition Issues," in *Frontiers of Tax Reform*, ed. Michael J. Boskin (Stanford: Hoover Institution Press, 1995) and Roger Gordon, Laura Kalambokidis, Jeffrey Rohaly, and Joel Slemrod, "Toward a Consumption Tax and Beyond," *American Economic Review* 94, 2 (May 2004): 161–165.

spent, they would be taxed. In effect, such a tax allows persons to defer the tax on their savings: No tax is due on funds saved and interest earned on those funds as long as they remain in savings accounts. The tax is paid only when the funds are converted to cash and spent.

Consumption, Saving, and Economic Capacity

In 1955, Nicholas Kaldor argued that consumption is a better index of the ability to pay than income.[3] Kaldor's argument is based on the notion that personal satisfaction is obtained when goods and services are consumed. Consumption of goods and services uses up resources and prevents them from being used by others. Saving entails sacrifice and results in no increase in well-being during the current tax period.

The act of saving adds to a nation's capital stock and benefits all insofar as it allows increased future consumption. Individuals obtain direct benefits from their saving only when they liquidate their assets into cash and increase consumption. The social benefit of saving, Kaldor argues, exceeds the private benefit of consumption insofar as it adds to a nation's capital stock and improves productivity of resources.

A more modern version of Kaldor's argument is that ability to pay is more appropriately measured by a person's basic capacity to earn income. This implies that, on the basis of horizontal equity, two individuals with equal potential to earn income should pay the same amount of taxes over their lifetimes. Lifetime income depends on basic labor earnings plus a person's basic endowment of capital. To the extent that a person saves or defers consumption in other ways (such as increased time in school), he or she can increase the stock of physical or human capital. An increase in a person's stock of capital (wealth) implies increased capital income over his or her lifetime. Because an income tax includes capital income in the tax base, it tends to discriminate according to the way income is timed over a person's lifetime.

Two persons who begin life with the same endowments of physical and human capital, and therefore have the same economic capacity to pay taxes, would be taxed differently according to the way in which they differ in their tendencies to defer consumption. Quite simply, the individual who prefers to save nothing would be taxed entirely on the basis of his labor income, whereas the individual who prefers to save would pay taxes both on labor earnings and income from accumulated capital. When economic capacity is defined in terms of basic endowments of skills and physical capital, an income tax taxes savers relatively more than those who immediately consume everything they earn. A tax on consumption avoids discrimination against savers by exempting their savings and interest income from taxation until they are consumed.

Many also argue that income taxation results in double taxation of savings in the sense that the saver is taxed on her income in the year that she accumulated her savings and then is taxed again when she earns interest on her savings. Under a flat-rate tax on comprehensive income, savers would pay higher taxes over their lifetimes than individuals who consume the bulk of their income when they earn

---

[3]See Nicholas Kaldor, *An Expenditure Tax* (London: Allen and Unwin, 1955), Chapter 1. Kaldor's idea of an expenditure tax was put into practice briefly in a modified form in India and Ceylon. However, both nations eliminated the tax by 1966.

it. This results from the taxation of interest. The discrimination against savers is more acute when interest earned is not adjusted for the rate of inflation.

An Illustration: Taxation of Income versus Taxation of Consumption of "Equals"

An adult's *life cycle* can be considered to begin at age 18 and end at death. Assume that two 18-year-olds enter the labor force and begin to earn a living. They have equal levels of skill and training, with no accumulated physical capital; therefore, they have equal economic capacity. Because these two workers are viewed as having an equal ability to pay taxes, the principle of horizontal equity suggests that they could pay equal taxes over their lifetimes. Assume that they both face the same wage rates and interest rates over their lifetimes. Neither worker ever receives transfers, such as gifts, bequests, or government assistance. The only way they can obtain capital income is to defer present consumption. If one worker is unwilling to do this, he will never save. He will never accumulate savings; therefore, he will never earn interest or any return on investment. On the other hand, the other worker has a high rate of saving in her early years but then draws from the accumulated capital and interest as she ages (leaving no bequests); she will earn interest income over her lifetime in addition to her wage income. Under the income tax, the interest is taxable. The present value of taxes paid by the saver would exceed that paid by the nonsaver over the life cycle.

To see this, suppose only two tax periods occur during the life cycle. Both workers earn annual labor income of $30,000 per year in each of the two periods. One worker, A, does not save any income, consuming his entire income in each of the two periods. The second worker, B, saves $5,000 of her $30,000 income in the first period. In the second period, she liquidates her savings and spends it. The market rate of interest is 10 percent. She would have $5,500, in addition to her $30,000 income to spend in the second period.

Under a flat-rate tax of 20 percent on income, the discounted present value of income taxes (rounded to the nearest dollar) for worker A, the nonsaver, would be

$$T_A = \$6{,}000 + \$6{,}000/(1 + 0.1)$$
$$= \$6{,}000 + \$5{,}455 = 11{,}455, \tag{16.1}$$

where $6,000 is the 20 percent tax liability on labor income in each of the two years. Taxes in the second period are discounted at the market rate of interest at 10 percent.

Worker B, the saver, would pay *more* tax in the second period because of the $500 interest earnings. Total tax liability of this worker is $6,000 in the current period and $6,100 in the second period. The discounted present value of income taxes (rounded to the nearest dollar) for worker B would be

$$T_B = \$6{,}000 + \$6{,}100/(1 + 0.1)$$
$$= \$6{,}000 + \$5{,}545 = 11{,}545. \tag{16.2}$$

The discounted present value of income taxes over the two-period lifetime is $90 higher under the income tax for the saver compared with the nonsaver. In general, if interest income is taxed as it is accrued, the income tax, other things being equal, would force savers to pay more taxes than nonsavers.

If, on the other hand, the tax base were consumption, the present value of taxes paid by the two workers over their lifetimes would be equal and independent of the pattern of consumption and saving. Although the worker who saves more will consume more than her forgone consumption in later years because of the interest earned, the tax would treat them equally. The additional tax paid on interest income when it is consumed compensates for the deferral of the tax on savings. This holds, regardless of the pattern of consumption, over the life cycle. Thus, the consumption tax treats these two workers equally according to the equality of their economic capacity.

To see this, suppose both workers were subject to a 20 percent tax on consumption. As you will see, this tax will not raise as much revenue as an income tax because consumption is less than income when saving is not included in the tax base. In any given year a person's income must be equal to the sum of consumption, savings, and taxes paid. Any savings will not be subject to the tax. When the savings are withdrawn in future years to finance consumption, they will be taxed. As before, assume that the life cycle consists of two periods and that B saves $5,000 of income in the first period so that she can consume more in the second period. The market rate of interest is 10 percent.

A's tax liability will be the same in both periods because he saves nothing. First we must calculate his consumption keeping account of the fact that the sum of his consumption and the tax on that consumption (C) must exactly equal his income:

$$\text{Income} = \text{Consumption} + \text{Consumption Tax.} \qquad (16.3)$$

Because his income is $30,000 and the consumption tax is 20 percent, it follows that

$$30,000 = C + 0.2C.$$

Therefore, $C = \$25,000$ and his tax is $5,000 in both periods. The present value of his tax liability for the two periods is

$$T_A = \$5,000 + \$5,000/1.1 = \$9,545.45 \qquad (16.4)$$

For B, the saver, her consumption in year one will be C_1, which will be less than her consumption in year 2, C_2, when she can consume more than her income because she will withdraw the funds with interest she saved in the first period. In year 1, she saves $5,000. Her income must equal the sum of her consumption, consumption tax, and saving:

$$\text{Income} = \text{Consumption} + \text{Consumption Tax} + \text{Saving.} \qquad (16.5)$$

Therefore,

$$\$30,000 = C_1 + 0.2C_1 + \$5,000.$$

It follows that consumption in the first period will be $20,833.33, and the tax bill on that consumption will be $4,166.66.

In the second year, she will withdraw her savings with 10 percent interest and therefore have negative saving of $5,500. We can calculate her consumption in the second period along with her consumption tax from the following equation:

$$\$30,000 = C_2 + 0.2C_2 - \$5,500.$$

It follows that consumption in the second period must be $29,583.33, and the tax on this consumption will be $5,916.67.

Now calculating the present value of the saver's tax bill, we get

$$\$4,166.66 + \$5,916.67/1.1 = \$9,545.45.$$

This is the same amount as the discounted present value of taxes paid by the nonsaver! However, note that under the consumption tax, the 20 percent tax rate raises less revenue than it did under the income tax. When we exempt saving from taxation until it is consumed, a higher tax rate is necessary to yield the same revenue that could be obtained from an income tax of any given rate.

In effect, when a consumption tax is used, both the saver and the nonsaver are taxed only according to their labor income. Under the consumption tax, savers do not pay any tax on interest income as it accrues in their accounts, as they would under an income tax. Interest is taxed under an income tax as it accrues, reducing the net interest rate received by savers to $r_N = (1 - t)r_G$, where r_G is the gross interest earned and t is the income tax rate.

The consumption tax therefore is equivalent to a flat-rate tax on labor income alone. Interest income is not taxed as it is earned. When taxpayers spend accumulated savings and accumulated interest in future periods, the extra tax due merely represents interest on the tax that has been deferred through saving. The market rate of interest is not distorted in any way by the consumption tax.

To understand this, examine the tax paid on savings that are liquidated and spent in future periods. In effect, under a consumption tax, those who save merely *postpone* their tax liability to the future. The amount that they would have paid in taxes had they not saved can be thought of as a loan from the government. For example, under the consumption tax, a saver would save $1,000 in current taxes by deferring $5,000 of first-period consumption to the second period. When the savings are spent in the second period, the taxpayer repays the government the $1,000 in deferred taxes *plus* 10 percent interest on the deferred $1,000 consumption tax.

In general, if the interest rate is r and the tax rate is t, at the end of one year, C_1 dollars saved would be worth $(1 + r)C_1$. The tax paid would be $t[(1 + r)C_1]$ when the accumulated interest and savings are spent at the end of one year. If the C_1 dollars had been spent immediately, the tax would have been tC_1. The extra tax paid after a year of saving would be $t[(1 + r)C_1] - tC_1 = r[tC_1]$, which represents interest on the tax deferred for one year.

A COMPREHENSIVE CONSUMPTION TAX BASE

A comprehensive base for taxing consumption can be derived from the comprehensive income tax base. Comprehensive income is defined as the sum of annual consumption and increased net worth. The comprehensive consumption tax base merely excludes any change in net worth from the tax base.

Some of the advantages of the consumption tax could help solve some of the difficult measurement problems involved in administering the income tax. Only current expenditures are taxed under the consumption tax. Measuring either realized or unrealized capital gains is unnecessary. Tax administrators would not tax these until they are converted into cash and spent. Only at that point are capital gains taxable.

Inflation is no problem under the consumption tax because only current expenditures are taxed. For example, under the comprehensive income tax, taxation of capital gain would require that it be indexed for the rate of inflation. A capital gain on an asset held for many years includes the effect of inflation. However, when the gain is liquidated at any point in time, the cash obtained is also used to buy goods at the current inflated values. Therefore, adjusting the purchasing power of the gain under a consumption tax is no longer necessary—it is done automatically by current prices!

Anything that increases the net worth of the taxpayer would be excluded from the tax base. This would include all forms of saving in accounts at financial institutions and such acquisitions of income-producing physical assets as land, business inventories, and claims against income-producing assets (stocks and bonds).

Implementation of a Tax on Consumption

In treating consumption-in-kind from consumer durables, problems develop in implementing the tax base, which are similar to those encountered in defining income-in-kind. For example, the consumption of housing services flowing to occupants of owner-occupied dwellings would have to be included in the tax base if it were to be truly comprehensive. This means that an annual implicit rental must be computed to owner-occupied homes and included in the owner's taxable consumption. Similarly, all consumer durables would have to have consumption flows imputed to their use. In developing a consistent and equitable way of doing this, administrative problems could very well result in those items being excluded from the tax base, as many income-in-kind items are excluded from taxable income.

Alternatively, consumer durables could be taxed at purchase by applying the appropriate tax rate to their purchase price. This, in effect, would levy a tax on the purchaser equal to a certain percentage of the discounted present value of future service flows that stem from the asset over its useful life. For such high-priced assets as homes, this creates a liquidity problem for buyers. The problem could be solved by allowing the taxpayer to spread the tax payments over time in the form of annual installments; thus, in effect the government would lend purchasers the funds to pay the taxes on houses by allowing their amortization over time.[4] Transfers would be included in the tax base to the extent to which they were consumed. Contributions to retirement funds, including Social Security taxes, would be treated as saving and therefore excluded from taxation. Bequests at death would have to be treated as a form of final consumption at death and taxed accordingly.[5] This would prevent individuals from avoiding taxes permanently by transferring accumulated wealth at death.

An interesting difference between an income tax and an expenditure tax lies in the treatment of borrowed funds. Under the consumption tax, loans are taxed when they are spent. Under an income tax, loans are never added to the taxpayer's income, but interest payments on the loan are often deductible from taxable income. The consumption tax includes the loan proceeds in the tax base as they are spent and allows the deductions from consumption as the loan is paid off.

---

[4]See Mieszkowski, "Choice of the Tax Base," 41–51, for a discussion of some implementation problems.

[5]Alternatively, bequests could be treated as transfers and, when spent, included in the tax base of heirs. If never liquidated, the perpetual saving never would be taxed.

The Cash-Flow Tax

A modified form of a general consumption tax is the cash-flow tax.[6] Under such a tax, savers would be permitted, when computing their tax liability each year, to deduct from their income those funds deposited in "qualified accounts." Such a mechanism for deferring tax burden until funds are withdrawn from special accounts already exists as part of the federal income tax code. Currently, such deductions are allowable for special accounts—retirement plans, individual retirement accounts (IRAs), and other special tax-deferred saving—for those eligible. As discussed, the current system limits the amounts that can be deposited in these funds and imposes penalties for early withdrawal. The cash-flow tax simply would extend such treatment to a broad array of qualified accounts and allow taxpayers to withdraw and spend funds from these accounts whenever they wished, at which time they would incur a tax liability, but not a penalty.

The proposed cash-flow tax would allow taxpayers, when computing tax liability, to deduct from AGI all savings deposited in qualified accounts. When such funds and accumulated interest are withdrawn from these accounts and converted into a cash flow, they would be taxed. Taxpayers could further defer tax liability on withdrawals from existing accounts simply by redepositing the withdrawals into qualified accounts.

Under the cash-flow tax, deposits in checking accounts would not be considered qualified, because funds in checking accounts are demand deposits intended to meet transactions demand for cash rather than to provide savings. However, the cash-flow tax would not tax interest earned on checking and other nonqualified accounts. To implement the tax, important decisions would have to be made concerning which accounts would be qualified for the deduction.

Also, under the cash-flow tax, loans would be added to adjusted gross income as they are received but would be deducted from income as they are repaid. Purchases of durable assets by consumers would not be considered a form of saving, and such purchases would be subject to a tax.

The administrative mechanism already exists to implement some form of expenditure tax similar to the cash-flow tax model proposed by the U.S. Treasury study. However, important decisions would have to be made concerning the types of saving that would be deductible from income for the purpose of defining taxable consumption so as to avoid distortions in behavior. One difficult problem that would have to be resolved is the consistent and equitable treatment of saving in the form of investment in human, as opposed to physical, capital.

Some difficult transition problems could be posed in moving from an income-based to a consumption-based tax. For example, the elderly who consume all of their current income and draw down previously accumulated savings to live on could be hard hit by the shift to the consumption tax. This is because the elderly tend to consume more than their current income as they dissave.[7] The elderly would have paid income taxes on their capital income during their working years and would then have to pay the consumption tax when they liquidated their saving. Special rules to avoid double-taxing the elderly would have to be developed to avoid hitting them hard with a consumption tax.

---

[6]See U.S. Treasury, *Blueprints for Basic Tax Reform*, 113–143.

[7]For a discussion of some of the transition problems, see M. Kevin McGee, "Alternative Transitions to a Consumption Tax," *National Tax Journal* 42, 2 (June 1989): 155–166.

1. What is comprehensive consumption?
2. How would an expenditure tax work?
3. In what sense can a comprehensive consumption tax be regarded as achieving the goal of horizontal equity?

A GENERAL TAX ON COMPREHENSIVE CONSUMPTION

The advantages and disadvantages of a general tax on comprehensive consumption can be highlighted by comparing the tax with a general tax on comprehensive income. Assume that both taxes raise the same amount of revenue and finance the same mix of government services. Assume as well that both taxes are levied at a proportional rate. The consumption tax generally is more favorable to savers and is most likely to result in no efficiency loss in the allocation of resources between current and future consumption. These benefits, in turn, must be balanced by the possibility of reduced efficiency in labor markets and correspondingly higher tax burdens borne by workers.

Substituting a Flat-Rate Consumption Tax for an Equal-Yield Flat-Rate Income Tax

Consider first the efficiency effects of substituting a flat-rate comprehensive consumption tax for a flat-rate comprehensive income tax. If both taxes are to raise the same amount of revenue, and if saving in any given year is positive, then the tax rate under the consumption tax would have to be higher than the tax rate under an equal-yield income tax. This is because the tax base is smaller under a consumption tax than it would be under an income tax. Because comprehensive income is the sum of consumption and increased net worth in any given year, the exclusion of increases in net worth (saving) from the tax base requires an increase in tax rates if both taxes are to raise the same amount of revenue.[8]

If, for example, savings are 20 percent of income after the consumption tax is introduced, and income does not increase in response to the substitution of the consumption tax for the income tax, then the consumption tax rate would have to be 25 percent higher than the income tax rate to raise the same revenue. This is because with a savings rate equal to 20 percent, income is equal to 125 percent of consumption. The consumption tax taxes only 80 percent of the income base. Therefore,

$$\text{Tax Revenue} = t_I I = t_C(.8)I$$
$$1.25t_I = t_C$$

(16.6)

where t_I is the income tax rate, t_C is the consumption tax rate, and I is income.

---

[8]It is possible that lower tax rates on capital income might increase gross domestic product (GDP) and therefore increase consumption over and above what it would be under the income tax. If this were the case, the tax rate would not have to increase as much as it would if GDP did not increase. This analysis assumes that savings previously taxed under an income tax will be exempt from the consumption tax when liquidated.

Impact on Savings and Excess Burden in Investment Markets

The higher tax rate required under the consumption tax to raise the same revenue as the income tax is of no consequence for the impact of the tax on the capital market because interest income is not taxable under a consumption tax. When interest is spent, the only extra tax liability incurred by savers represents repayment of interest on deferred taxes to the government during the period the interest was being earned. The interest rate itself is not affected by the tax. Therefore, no excess burden is introduced in choices between current and future consumption as a result of the introduction of the tax.

If the taxes replace a preexisting income tax, then any excess burden existing because of tax-induced distortion in interest rates is eliminated. This is because the income tax taxes interest as it accrues and results in a loss in efficiency as individuals reallocate resources between current and future use. The removal of the tax influence on the rate of interest restores efficiency in the capital market, as the consumption tax is substituted for the income tax. This is illustrated in Figure 16.1.

Under the income tax, the net return to savings falls short of the gross return. The substitution of the flat-rate consumption tax for the income tax removes the wedge between the gross interest rate and the net interest rate. Efficiency in the market for loanable funds is restored, and the gain in well-being is approximated by the area of triangle FGE. The market rate of interest declines from r_G^* to r^*. As a result of the substitution of the consumption tax for the income tax, annual investment increases by ΔQ_I.

FIGURE 16.1   Substituting a Comprehensive Consumption Tax for a Comprehensive Income Tax: Investment Market Effects

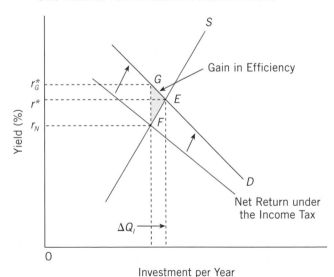

Substituting a comprehensive consumption tax for an income tax removes the tax wedge between the gross and net returns to investment. The result is a gain in efficiency in investment markets, approximated by the area. Market interest rates decline to r^*, and annual investment increases up to the efficient amount.

IMPACT ON EFFICIENCY IN LABOR MARKETS

The gains from achieving efficiency in the market for loanable funds must be balanced with the possibility of additional losses in labor markets. This is because the higher tax rate required for the consumption tax further decreases the return to work effort and induces further efficiency losses in the labor market resulting from distortion in the work-leisure choice. If, for example, the tax rate under the consumption tax must be 125 percent of the tax rate under the income tax in order to raise the same amount of revenue, workers would pay 25 percent more taxes on their wages under the consumption tax.

In Figure 16.2, the efficient allocation corresponds to point B, where wages are w_o and the quantity of labor hours is L_1. Under the income tax at rate t_I, the effective wage received by workers falls to $w_G(1 - t_I)$ at all hours of work, resulting in equilibrium at point C, where the gross wage is w_{G1} and the net wage received by workers is w_{N1}. Labor hours fall from L_1 to L_2. The loss in efficiency is measured by the triangle ABC if the reduction in labor hours reflects the substitution effect caused by the income tax.

Substitution of the consumption tax for the income tax increases the effective tax on wages and further shifts down wages received at all hours of work to $w_G(1 - t_C)$. This results in a further decline in net wages at the new equilibrium C' because t_C exceeds t_I, and a further increase in gross wages paid, as labor hours decline again to L_3. The loss in efficiency now is measured by the excess burden $A'BC'$ assuming that the reduction in hours worked does not include the income effect of the tax.

FIGURE 16.2 Substituting an Equal-Yield Comprehensive Consumption Tax for an Income Tax: Labor Market Effects

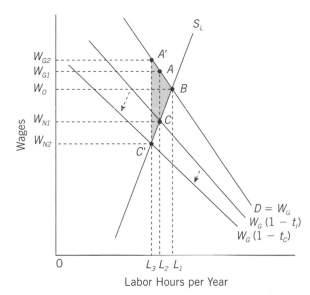

Substituting a consumption tax for an income tax increases the excess burden in the labor market, because the tax rate on labor income is higher under the consumption tax than under the income tax when the same revenue is raised under both taxes.

The substitution of the consumption tax for the income tax increases the excess burden by the area $A'ACC'$. Recall that the excess burden increases with the square of the tax rate. The increased excess burden therefore is more than proportionate to the increase in the tax rate (see Chapter 11).

The gain in efficiency introduced by a consumption tax as a result of removal of the excess burden in the capital market must be compared with the added loss in efficiency in the labor market due to the higher rate of taxation made necessary by the exclusion of savings from taxation. Even if the supply of labor hours is quite unresponsive to the wage, the added excess burden due to the higher tax on labor income could be substantial. This is because labor income accounts for more than 60 percent of all income earned in the United States; therefore, even small percentage increases in the excess burden in labor markets could involve large losses in well-being due to the large amount of earnings and dollars involved. However, if the excess burden per dollar of revenue raised by consumption taxes is lower than that per dollar of revenue raised by the income tax, as some estimates suggest, the net gain from substituting the consumption tax for the income tax would be positive.

Given reasonable estimates of the elasticities of supply of savings and labor, some research has estimated that a consumption tax would have a smaller excess burden than an equal-yield income tax. For example, one research study concluded that the efficiency gain from moving from an income tax to a consumption tax could be as much as 3 percent of GDP per year.[9] It is also possible that shifting from an income tax to a consumption tax will result in individuals paying less tax while working and more tax during retirement when savings are drawn down. The increase in saving and investment will raise the capital per labor ratio in a nation. The postponement of tax liability over the life cycle of taxpayers would therefore contribute to increased worker productivity and greater economic growth over the long run by increasing the capital per worker.[10]

Incidence of a Consumption Tax

Because capital income is excluded from taxation under the consumption tax, the tax would be borne according to labor earnings. The portion borne by labor income could be shifted to consumers if workers adjusted the quantity of hours of work supplied in response to the tax. Under the assumption of a relatively inelastic supply of labor, the portion of the tax that could be shifted to others would be small.

Assuming a relatively inelastic labor supply, as is shown in Figure 16.2, gross wages rise only slightly relative to what they would be in the absence of the tax. Thus, in Figure 16.2, under the consumption tax, wages rise from a pretax level of w_0 to w_{G2}.

Insofar as the bulk of the tax is borne according to labor income, and capital income escapes taxation, the consumption tax is likely to be more regressive with respect to income than an equal-yield income tax. However, if an expenditure tax

---

[9]See Don Fullerton, John B. Shoven, and John Whalley, "Replacing the U.S. Income Tax with a Progressive Consumption Tax: A Sequenced General Equilibrium Approach," *Journal of Public Economics* 20 (February 1983): 3–23.

[10]For discussion of these effects, see Laurence S. Seidman and Kenneth A. Lewis, "The Later You Pay, the Higher the K," *Southern Economic Journal* 69, 3 (2003): 560–577.

were used, the rate structure of the tax could be modified to achieve a collectively chosen distribution of tax burden.[11]

CHECKPOINT

1. Explain why the tax rate for a comprehensive consumption tax designed to replace an equal-yield comprehensive income tax would have to be higher than the income tax rate.
2. Why would replacement of a comprehensive income tax with a comprehensive consumption tax result in a gain in efficiency in investment markets?
3. Why would replacement of a comprehensive income tax with a comprehensive consumption tax result in a loss in efficiency in labor markets?

SALES TAXES

In practice, few sales taxes are implemented in such a way as to conform to a comprehensive consumption tax base. This is attributable to both administrative problems and political constraints. For example, many retail sales taxes are levied only on the consumption of tangible goods. The consumption of professional services (medical, legal, and educational) and such personal services as haircuts, entertainment, and transportation are usually exempt from the tax.

Perhaps the most conspicuous exemption is housing services. In addition, many states that levy retail sales taxes exempt the consumption of certain basic goods regarded as necessities from taxation in order to achieve a more equitable distribution of the tax burden. The consumption of food and grocery items was exempted or subject to lower rates in all but six of the states using the retail sales tax in 2012. Prescription drugs are exempt from taxation in every state that has a sales tax. (Illinois does not fully exempt prescription drugs but taxes them only at a 1 percent rate.) Finally, many consumption taxes are levied on the purchase of capital goods. For example, most retail sales taxes in the United States are levied on the purchases of automobiles and other consumer durables. When these durable goods that are subject to consumption taxes are purchased by business firms, they increase the marginal costs of production and are reflected in higher retail prices, which then are used as the base to apply the consumption tax all over again. This results in pyramiding taxes on taxes and consequently a higher tax rate to be borne by consumers.

Retail Sales Taxes

A **retail sales tax** usually is an ad valorem levy of a fixed percentage on the dollar value of retail purchases made by consumers. A true retail sales tax is levied only on consumption at its final stage and is collected from business establishments

---

[11]Over the long run it can be shown that a consumption tax when substituted for an equal-yield income tax will raise the economy's capital/labor ratio no matter what the interest elasticity of supply of savings. See Laurence S. Seidman and Kenneth A. Lewis, "The Consumption Tax and the Saving Elasticity," *National Tax Journal* 52, 1 (March 1999): 67–78.

that make retail sales. The tax usually is added on to the retail price of goods and services. Thus, retailers merely act as intermediaries between consumers and the government in collecting the tax. However, as the previous discussion has indicated, in many instances, the tax exempts personal services and basic food items from the tax base. Furthermore, the tax sometimes is applied to purchases by business firms that intend to use them for further production, such as office furniture, automobiles, fuel, and other equipment. Therefore, in practice, the retail sales tax cannot be considered either a general tax or one that is levied solely on final consumption.

As it is implemented in the United States, the retail sales tax is a state and local fiscal instrument rather than a national one. Its merits must be discussed as a locally administered tax within the framework of the federal system. Sales taxes are utilized as a major source of revenue in state governments. In addition, many local governments use retail sales taxes as revenue sources. Sales taxes were first enacted on the state level in the 1930s in response to the need for a more stable revenue source in the face of falling incomes and property values. The first local sales tax was enacted by the city of New York in 1934. Currently, many local governments utilize retail sales as a tax base. Most state and local retail sales taxes are collected from retailers; therefore, much of the administrative cost of the tax is borne by retail firms. Some states compensate retailers for bearing the administrative costs.[12]

A possible effect of local sales taxation is a loss of retail trade to neighboring jurisdictions where the sales tax is either absent or applied at a lower rate. The migration of retail sales to another taxing jurisdiction can have the effect of reducing employment, business profits in the taxing jurisdiction, or both. This, in turn, could decrease the actual amount of taxes collected. Only partial shifting to consumers of the retail sales tax would occur if the tax caused sales to migrate. This means that retail prices would not rise by the full amount of the tax. The tax would decrease the net incomes of local sellers. If the consumption tax base were elastic with respect to the rate of taxation, then increases in the rate of sales taxation would result in less, not more, revenue collected.

In some cases, a local tax can be levied on items purchased in neighboring jurisdictions but used in the taxing jurisdiction. This is accomplished through *use taxes*. For example, for an automobile purchased outside the taxing jurisdiction, the state or locality levying the tax can require the tax to be paid before the automobile can be registered in that area. Use taxes are difficult to enforce for consumption goods that are not required to be registered. Empirical evidence has indicated that sales tax rate differentials among neighboring taxing jurisdictions (for example, the central city and the suburbs) do have significant effects on per capita retail sales distribution among the taxing jurisdictions.[13] Many state governments have been under pressure to raise more revenue. To do so, several state governments have raised their sales tax rate. In 2012, 34 states, including the District of Columbia, had basic sales tax rates of 5 percent or more, and in many cases local sales taxes were piggybacked on to the state sales tax rate. In 2012, California had the highest state sales tax set at 7.25 percent. New Jersey, Mississippi, Tennessee, Indiana, and Rhode Island had the second highest sales

---

[12]For a complete discussion of sales tax administration, see John F. Due and John L. Mikesell, "State Sales Tax Structures and Operations in the Last Decade—A Sample Study," *National Tax Journal* 32 (March 1980): 21–43.

[13]John L. Mikesell, "Central Cities and Sales-Tax Differentials," *National Tax Journal* 23 (June 1970): 213.

tax rate at 7 percent. In many large cities that have a local sales tax, the total rate paid by consumers is close to 10 percent.

Also, more revenue can be raised from sales taxes by broadening the sales tax base instead of raising tax rates. For example, in states where food is exempt from the tax, additional revenue can be obtained by taxing food. Taxation of services, such as rentals of housing and other products, cable television services, and lawn care, also would generate more revenue and several states tax these services. In 1987, Florida expanded its retail sales tax base to include services to consumers and some services sold to businesses. The new taxes were very unpopular and were repealed shortly after their introduction.

Because the retail sales tax is a state and local tax in the United States, ample opportunity exists to avoid the tax. One way of avoiding the tax is to purchase items in one state for delivery to a residence in another state. This can be accomplished either by visiting the state or through a mail order. Typically, the transaction is viewed as an out-of-state sale if the buyer has a residence in another state and if the seller does not operate in the state in which the buyer resides. No sales tax is levied on the sale by the originating state, and in most cases the buyer can avoid paying the tax to the state in which he resides. Some states have passed laws that make local residents liable for sales tax on out-of-state mail order purchases, but these taxes have proved difficult to collect.

Issues in State and Local Sales Taxation

Retail sales taxes generated 31.5 percent of the total revenue raised by state governments in 2011. However, some states rely even more heavily on the retail sales tax. In Washington, the retail sales tax accounted for 61 percent of total tax collections in 2011. During the same period in Florida, retail sales tax revenue accounted for 58.4 percent of state tax collections. Other states relying on the retail sales tax for 40 percent or more of their tax collections include Arizona, Hawaii, Indiana, Michigan, Mississippi, Nevada, South Dakota, Tennessee, and Texas. Only five states did not tax retail sales in 2012: Alaska, Delaware, Montana, New Hampshire, and Oregon.

Because retail sales taxes tend to exempt services, revenues from the tax have been growing slowly because services have been growing as a share of consumer spending. Since 1960, the share of GDP accounted for by goods has declined while the share attributed to private services has increased. American households allocated 41 cents of each dollar of consumption toward the purchase of services in 1960. By 2009, the share of the consumption dollar allocated to services had grown to 60 cents.

Initially when sales taxes were first introduced on the state level, services were exempt from taxation for administrative reasons. At that time, service establishments were small and were not required to keep detailed financial records, as was the case of goods producers that had to record inventory transactions. It was generally regarded as too costly to enforce taxes on service organizations. And because services were a relatively small share of total consumption at that time, states gave up little revenue by not taxing them. Now with services commanding more and more of consumption, many states in financial crisis are being forced to consider taxing services.

Aging of the population can also adversely affect state sales tax revenue as long as services remain exempt from taxation. Evidence indicates that as the percentage of state populations over the age of 65 increases, state consumption becomes more weighted to services, pharmaceuticals, and medical products currently exempt from sales taxation.[14]

Most state sales taxes do not attempt to tax purchases by government agencies and nonprofit organizations. Taxable sales have fallen from about 45 percent of total sales in 1977 to about 40 percent of total sales in 1997.[15] Electronic commerce poses another challenge for the retail sales tax. Attempts by state governments to apply their retail sales taxes to Internet purchases have met with only limited success. One estimate indicates that the inability to effectively tax Internet sales cost state governments an amount equivalent to 3 percent of total state revenues in 2006.[16] The development of more sophisticated software for taxing Internet sales and agreements or requirements that Internet merchants collect state sales taxes may be necessary to avoid these revenue losses.

Excise Taxes

Excise taxes are selective taxes levied on certain types of consumption activities. As such, they distort choices among goods and services and result in efficiency losses to the economy. These stem from the tax wedge inserted between relative prices, as perceived by consumers and producers and explained in Chapter 11.

Some excise taxes are designed to raise revenue, while others are intended to discourage particular consumption activities. Excise taxes on tires, for example, are primarily designed to raise revenue, while taxes on liquor consumption, although they do raise considerable revenue, also are intended to discourage liquor consumption. A special "gas guzzler excise tax" has been in place for several years to discourage purchase of cars with poor fuel economy. For example, a car that got less than 12.5 miles per gallon in 2011 was subject to a unit excise tax of a whopping $7,700! However, this tax only applies to cars—all trucks, including SUVs, are exempt from the tax. Some types of tariffs are designed to discourage consumption of foreign merchandise. A *tariff* lowers the net price received by foreign suppliers but raises the price paid for goods to consumers. In effect, a tariff redistributes income from the domestic consumers and foreign suppliers of the merchandise to the owners and workers of the protected domestic industries. At the same time, it increases revenues of the federal government.

Both federal and state governments tax liquor and cigarette consumption. Federal excise taxes are also levied on gasoline, telephone service, and tires. In many cases, the consumption activities singled out for taxation are alleged to generate negative externalities or can be considered luxury goods or services.

Prior to 1913, the federal government relied extensively on customs duties as a revenue source. Today, tariffs represent less than 1 percent of revenues collected by the federal government. The rates applied to many items are high and are clearly designed to discourage importation of foreign merchandise rather than to raise revenue. In a sense, tariffs that are successful revenue instruments cannot fulfill their function as protective devices for domestic industries simply because the high

---

[14]Paul L. Menchik, "Demographic Change and Fiscal Stress," *National Tax Association Proceedings*, 2001, pp. 90–98.

[15]See Robert Tannenwald, "Are State and Local Revenue Systems Becoming Obsolete?" *National Tax Journal* 60, 3 (September, 2002): 467–489.

[16]*Ibid.*, 480.

revenue capability implies that they are ineffective in discouraging domestic consumption of foreign merchandise.

The incidence of a tariff depends on the income elasticity of the protected merchandise. When the tariff succeeds in inducing consumers to substitute domestic merchandise for cheaper foreign goods, the effect is to redistribute income from consumers toward the high-cost producers of domestic goods. When the protected commodities are consumed largely by high-income households and produced by low-income workers, the resulting redistribution of income can be progressive. However, a net efficiency loss to the economy results from the indirect subsidization of the relatively inefficient domestic producers.

When the tariff is ineffective in reducing the consumption of foreign goods, it reduces the real income of consumers of these goods and increases government revenue without affecting the domestic production of the protected goods. The overall incidence of the tariff in this case depends on the income class of consumers of the good upon which the duty is levied and on the disposition of the additional federal revenue.

Incidence of Sales and Excise Taxes

A common criticism of retail sales and excise taxes is that they are regressive with respect to income. This is based on the notion that annual consumption expenditures, as a percentage of annual income, are higher for low-income taxpayers relative to high-income taxpayers, and that the tax is shifted forward so that it is borne according to purchases. The alleged regressiveness of these taxes has been challenged by research that suggests that the tax might not be reflected in higher prices in the first place.[17]

However, the common belief that the tax is regressive has led many states to exempt specific consumption items from the tax bases. For example, in the United States in 2012 only six states with a sales tax subjected food to full taxation, and most states fully exempted food or taxed it at lower rates than other purchases. All states exempt prescription drugs with the exception of Illinois, which taxes these drugs at a rate of 1 percent.

Research by Pechman on the incidence of retail sales and excise taxes in the United States concluded that they were regressive with respect to income. The research showed that the rates paid declined steadily from about 9 percent of income for the lowest-income groups to a little more than 3 percent for the highest-income groups.[18] Analysis of the short-lived Florida sales tax on some household and business services concluded that the incidence of the tax on services in Florida was regressive.[19] The national effects of sales taxes are likely to be similar to those of a national consumption tax. The tax would be borne according to labor income. One study concluded that sales taxes are fully reflected in prices and in some cases, because of market imperfections, are shifted in excess of 100 percent, which could add to their regressivity with respect to income.[20] Other empirical research indicates that on average about 60 percent of the sales tax is borne by

---

[17]See Edgar K. Browning, "The Burden of Taxation," *Journal of Political Economy* 86 (August 1978): 649–671.

[18]Joseph A. Pechman, *Who Paid the Taxes: 1966–1985?* (Washington, D.C.: The Brookings Institution, 1985).

[19]See John J. Siegfried and Paul A. Smith, "The Distributional Effects of a Sales Tax on Services," *National Tax Journal* 11, 1 (March 1991): 41–54.

[20]See Timothy J. Besley and Harvey S. Rosen, "Sales Taxes and Prices: An Empirical Study," *National Tax Journal* 50, 2 (June 1999): 157–178.

PUBLIC POLICY PERSPECTIVE

Origins, Destinations, E-Commerce, and Issues in Collecting Sales Taxes

In 1967, the U.S. Supreme Court ruled in the case of *National Bellas Hess v. Illinois Department of Revenue* that on the basis of the interstate commerce clause in the U.S. Constitution, states could not require mail order firms located in other states to collect their state sales taxes if the firm does not maintain business sales facilities in the state where the purchaser resides. Since that decision, the mail order business has grown substantially as a result, in part, of the Internet, and state governments hard-pressed for revenue have continued to pursue taxing out-of-state purchases. A number of states have passed legislation requiring residents to declare their out-of-state purchases and pay state sales tax on them, even though that sales tax is not collected by the seller. For example, the state of North Carolina requires its residents to pay state sales taxes on out-of-state purchases. However, these use taxes on out-of-state purchases have proved to be very difficult to collect.

The possibility of avoiding sales taxes has been a boon to mail order sales in the United States. Here's the way the current system works. As long as a seller that mails catalogs or similar information to residents in a state does not maintain a business presence in that state through offices or retail sales outlets, it is not required to collect sales tax on orders shipped to that state. If you order a jacket from L.L. Bean in Maine and L.L. Bean has no sales outlets in your state, then you do not pay the sales tax for either the state of Maine or your state. On the other hand, if Eddie Bauer has a retail store in your city and you place a mail order for a similar jacket with this firm, Eddie Bauer will then have to collect the sales tax on the shipment. You also can avoid the sales tax in many cases if you make a purchase while visiting another state and then have the purchase shipped to your home state. Under those circumstances, you pay neither the sales tax of the state in which you buy the item nor the sales tax levied by your home state.

Sales taxes in the United States are based on the *destination principle*, which argues that taxes on consumption can be levied only at the point at which the item is consumed. This principle implies that a purchase by a resident of the state of North Carolina either from a New York mail order firm or from a New York seller made while visiting New York and shipped to North Carolina is not taxable by New York State because the destination of the good for consumption would be North Carolina. It is up to North Carolina to levy a use tax on the consumption if it can feasibly track it down. This destination principle provides a loophole in sales tax administration that costs state governments revenue. Naturally, firms that specialize in mail order sales are not eager to collect sales taxes for out-of-state governments. However, some large mail order firms have agreed to start collecting sales taxes for destination states to avoid the threat of litigation.

Some sales taxes are based on the *origin principle*. Under those circumstances, a tax would be levied by states on the production of all items no matter where they are consumed. If retail sales taxes were based on the origin principle, you would pay out-of-state sales taxes on your purchases. This would mean that if you ordered an item from L.L. Bean in Maine, you would pay the sales tax prevailing in Maine.

The value-added tax (VAT), which is a common form of sales tax used by nations of the European Union, is collected from sellers irrespective of the destination of consumption. The World Trade Organization sets rules for international trade and allows rebates of origin-type sales taxes. So a Mercedes produced in Germany and subject to the German value-added tax can have the tax rebated to the manufacturer when the car is exported to the United States. This rebate lowers the price of the Mercedes to U.S. buyers and makes the car more competitive in U.S. markets. The rules also allow imposition of origin taxes on imports; that is, a U.S. aircraft exported to

Germany would be subject to German VATs. This imposition of the tax makes U.S. aircraft more costly and therefore less competitive in German markets. Because European nations use more origin-based sales taxes than we do to tax corporate businesses, this could put us at a competitive disadvantage in European markets. The corporate income tax in the United States puts upward pressure on the price of corporate products, but it is a direct tax that cannot be rebated on exports or imposed on imports according to World Trade rules.

The principles that apply to sales taxation of mail order catalog sales also apply to products sold over the Internet through so-called e-commerce. However, given the growth of e-commerce, taxation of Internet sales has become a hot issue for tax policy. State governors have become concerned that as e-commerce grows, state governments will lose significant amounts of tax revenue from online transactions. If an Internet merchant maintains a business presence in the state to which it ships products, then it is obligated to pay sales taxes on those shipments. Major corporations, such as Apple, shipping computers and other electronic items ordered on the Internet routinely add the state sales tax applicable at the items' destination address.

Although it is a hot issue for tax policy, the concerns about revenue loss for state governments from e-commerce are apparently a bit overblown.[1] Much of e-commerce involves business-to-business sales that are not normally subject to state sales taxes because they are intermediate rather than final transactions. Other transactions on the Internet involve travel services, financial services, and other services that are typically exempt from state sales taxes. One estimate is that as of 1998, 40 percent of e-commerce transactions involved sales that are not normally subject to tax by state government retail sales taxes. Of the remaining 60 percent, computer sales accounted for about half and the major computer online retailers were already collecting sales tax

on the destination principle and paying it to the appropriate state treasuries. In 1998, Goolsbee and Zittrain estimated that revenue losses to state governments amounted to less than one-quarter of 1 percent of total sales tax revenue and concluded that even if the Internet sales were to continue to grow at the current rate, retail sales tax losses will be less than 2 percent of revenue by 2003.[2] Although governments can tax any transaction they choose, it does not appear that new tax laws are necessary to tax Internet commerce. The issues involved in taxing e-commerce are exactly the same as those that apply to mail order sales.

However, some argue that the growth of e-commerce offers an opportunity to make the retail sales tax a more general levy on consumption. Currently, most states exempt services and purely financial transactions from the tax. Some states tax intermediate sales. A general tax on consumption taxes all final sales to consumers at a fixed rate. Applying this principle to Internet transactions would require all retail sales to be taxed.[3] Business-to-business and capital equipment sales would be exempt. It would be a simple matter for software to be installed for Internet orders that would apply the tax according to the destination principle. Internet retailers could then remit taxes monthly to state governments. Of course, this would bring up issues of equity and discrimination against online sales unless other retail services were taxed in the same way.

---

[1]See Austan Goolsbee and Jonathan Zittrain, "Evaluating the Cons and Benefits of Taxing Internet Commerce," *National Tax Journal* 52, 3 (September 1999): 413–428. Also see William F. Fox and Matthew N. Murray, "The Sales Tax and Electronic Commerce: So What's New?" *National Tax Journal* 50, 3 (September 1997): 573–592.

[2]Goolsbee and Zittrain, pp. 415–416.

[3]This approach is proposed by McClure. See Charles E. McLure, Jr., "Electronic Commerces, State Sales Taxation, and Intergovernmental Fiscal Relations," *National Tax Journal* 50, 4 (December 1997): 731–749.

consumers with the remainder borne by the sellers. According to research by Raymond Ring, the distribution of the tax burden between buyers and sellers varies from state to state and ranges from 28 to 89 percent of the burden borne by buyers.[21]

TURNOVER TAXES

Turnover taxes are multistage sales taxes that are levied at some fixed rate on transactions at all levels of production. The effective tax rate on various goods and services is conditioned by the number of stages of production. The turnover tax has been used in Germany and other European countries as a major revenue source. Germany, however, replaced its turnover tax with a VAT in 1968. The turnover tax provides an incentive to vertical integration among firms so as to reduce the number of production stages and interfirm transactions and consequently reduce the tax liability. The tax usually is reflected in higher final consumption prices. However, the rates of taxation vary with the number of stages of production. The distributive effects of the tax depend on consumer preferences for and among goods and services that entail a number of stages in their production.

The turnover tax is an extremely productive levy, producing high, stable yields at very low rates. The relatively low rate employed at any level of transaction is believed to discourage tax evasion. The reason for the high yield is the sheer number of transactions taxed, plus the pyramiding of tax rates on tax rates for multistage production, considerably increasing the final effective rate of taxation. Pyramiding occurs when firms apply percentage markups to purchase prices to include the tax.

The turnover tax, as used in Germany, was criticized by some as being regressive. However, empirical studies have shown that the tax actually was somewhat progressive.[22] This is because the effective rates on many food items were lower than those on clothing and other manufactured goods. Any changes in production techniques that alter the number of processing stages could influence the final effective tax rates. It is administratively difficult to grant specific exemptions under turnover taxation relative to retail sales taxation. The turnover tax is not a truly general tax, because it applies discriminatory rates to alternative goods and services that are dependent on the number of productive stages.

VALUE-ADDED TAXES

The **value-added tax (VAT)** is a general tax on consumption levied on the value added to intermediate products by businesses at each stage of production. Various forms of the VAT are in use in more than 50 nations of the world, including Canada, Japan, several Latin American countries, and all nations of the European Union (EU). The tax was first adopted in 1954 by the French National Government. When a

---

[21]See Raymond J. Ring, Jr., "Consumers' Share and Producers' Share of the General Sales Tax" *National Tax Journal* 52, 1 (March 1999): 79–90.

[22]See John F. Due's classic work, *Sales Taxation* (Urbana: University of Illinois Press, 1957): 59.

nation is admitted to the EU, it is required to introduce the VAT as a condition of membership. The VAT, though not currently used by the U.S. federal government, has been seriously considered in the past. The tax has been considered both as a full or a partial substitute for the existing corporate income tax and also as a new source of revenue.

The Meaning of *Value Added*

The value-added tax is simply a multistage sales tax that exempts the purchase of intermediate goods and services from the tax base. *Value added* is the difference between sales proceeds and purchases of intermediate goods and services over a certain period. For example, the value added for a grocery store in a given month is the difference between the total sales receipts that month and the total invoices for goods and services from its suppliers. Suppose the store had total sales receipts of $150,000 that month. If it purchased $75,000 of groceries from its suppliers and $10,000 of goods and services from other firms, its value added would be $65,000 that month.

Total transactions less intermediate transactions (that is, purchases made from firms by other firms) is equal to the sum of wages, interest, rent, and other input payments in the nation, summing up to the GDP. This may be expressed as the following identity:

$$Value\ Added = Total\ Transactions - Intermediate\ Transactions$$
$$= Final\ Sales = GDP \qquad (16.7)$$
$$= Wages + Interest + Profiles + Rents + Depreciation,$$

where intermediate transactions represent purchases by firms of goods and services to be further processed in production. For example, the purchase of steel by an automobile manufacturer is an intermediate purchase, because the steel is to be further processed and converted into automobile frames and other parts of automobiles that then will be incorporated into the value of the final product when it is sold. In measuring GDP, such intermediate sales are netted out to avoid double-counting the steel both as an input and as part of the automobile. Similarly, seed and fertilizer purchases are intermediate purchases for farmers because both items will be further processed into agricultural produce, which will reflect, in part, the cost of the seed and fertilizer to the farmer.

Netting out the dollar value of intermediate transactions from all transactions leaves the dollar value of final sales. Because final sales must cover the producers' costs, with profit left over as a residual, it follows that such final sales represent the dollar value of all domestic wages, interest, rents, depreciation, and profits. This is the definition of GDP. It becomes clear that the sum of value added by all business firms at each stage of production is merely another way of defining GDP. A general tax on value added would be equivalent to a tax on national product.

Different types of VATs customarily are classified according to the manner in which they apply to a firm's purchase of capital goods. One approach is to allow no deduction from the tax base, either for a firm's initial outlays on capital goods or for amortized deductions on such outlays. This is known as a *product-type* VAT. A second alternative, known as an *income-type* tax, allows no deduction for the costs of capital equipment in the year of purchase but permits a deduction for annual depreciation over the life of the equipment. A third alternative, known as a *consumption-type* tax, allows the full cost of capital to be deducted in the year of purchase. In short, the base for the consumption-type tax is the same as that for a general tax on comprehensive consumption, while that for the income-type tax is the same as for a proportional income tax.

The consumption-type tax is used in most nations. As it is commonly administered, the tax base for the VAT is equivalent to that of any general consumption tax. One study of the U.S. tax system has suggested that if a consumption-type value-added tax were to be substituted for all taxes currently used, considerable reduction in the excess burden could result. Based on the system of taxation prevailing in the late 1970s, the study concluded that the excess burden per dollar of revenue could be reduced from about 24 cents to 13 cents if the consumption-type VAT were substituted for existing taxes.[23] A more recent study estimated that compared with an income tax surcharge raising $150 billion additional revenue in the United States, a VAT raising the same revenue would add about 0.4 of a percentage point to the U.S. annual savings rate in the long run by lowering the cost of capital. In the long run, this would add a 5 percent increment to the nation's capital stock and would allow income to grow by about 0.8 percent more per year over the long run. However, the cost of administering and complying with a new and complex VAT like that used in Europe would run from $5 billion to $8 billion per year, and these administrative costs would offset much of the benefits of improved efficiency in capital markets and would absorb much of the extra income generated by faster growth.[24] The consumption-type VAT would lower costs of production in capital-intensive industries (including agriculture) but raise costs of production in labor-intensive industries.

Administration of the VAT

Administration of a VAT does not require firms to calculate value added. The most common means of administering the tax is the invoice method developed in France and used in EU nations to collect the tax. Under the invoice method, all transactions are taxed at a fixed proportional rate regardless of whether they are final or intermediate transactions. Taxpayers then are allowed to deduct the taxes paid on intermediate purchases from the taxes collected from their sales in determining their tax liability. This is called the *invoice method* because payment of the tax merely requires firms to maintain invoices on sales and purchases for each tax payment period (usually monthly or quarterly). Tax liability is determined simply by applying the fixed rate of taxation to total sales invoices and then deducting the amount of VAT paid previously on intermediate purchases as indicated on purchase invoices, where the tax is usually separately itemized.

---

[23]This is based on an uncompensated elasticity of supply of labor of 0.15 and an uncompensated elasticity of supply of savings of 0.4. See Charles L. Ballard, John B. Shoven, and John Whalley, "The Total Welfare Cost of the United States Tax System: A General Equilibrium Approach," *National Tax Journal* 38 (June 1985): 125–140.

[24]Congress of the United States, Congressional Budget Office, *Effects of Adopting a Value-Added Tax* (Washington, D.C.: U.S. Government Printing Office, February 1992). Also see, James M. Bickely, "A Value-Added Tax Contrasted with a National Sales Tax," Issue Brief for the United States Congress (Washington D.C.: Library of Congress, Congressional Research Service, 2003).

This method results in taxation of value added without the need to actually calculate value added:

$$\text{Tax Liability} = \text{Tax Payable on Sales} - \text{Tax Paid on Intermediate Purchases}$$
$$= [(t)(\text{Sales})] - [(t)(\text{Purchases})]$$
$$= (t)(\text{Total Sales} - \text{Total Intermediate Purchases}) \quad (16.8)$$
$$= (t)(\text{Value Added}),$$

where t is the rate of taxation.

In effect, the tax is charged to purchasers at each stage of production. At the final stage of production, consumers purchase goods with the VAT included in the price; and because consumers have no intermediate transactions to offset the tax liability, they end up paying the entire amount of the tax, with no tax offset. Only producers can offset their tax liability to the extent to which they purchase intermediate goods and services.

Firms that make capital purchases are allowed an additional tax credit for taxes paid on capital goods. So, the tax liability of a firm that makes capital purchases in a given tax period would be

$$\text{Tax Liability} = [(t)(\text{Total Sales} - \text{Total Intermediate Purchases})]$$
$$- [(t)(\text{Capital Purchases})]$$
$$= (t)(\text{Total Sales} - \text{Total Purchases} - \text{Capital Purchases}) \quad (16.9)$$
$$= (t)(\text{Value added} - \text{Investment}).$$

In most nations that use the VAT, it is customary not to itemize the tax on the final transaction. However, it would be simple to itemize the tax to consumers by simply tacking it on to the sale, as is done for the retail sales tax in the United States. Because of this practice of not itemizing the tax at the retail level, in many European nations, the VAT is often accused of being a hidden tax, which is likely to result in fiscal illusion on the part of consumers, who pay the final tax. This need not be the case because the VAT easily can be made visible by collecting it from consumers at the fixed rate t on final sales.

Also, the invoice method embodies a sort of built-in anti-evasion mechanism. If any firm fails to pay its tax liability at some stage of production, it then becomes the tax liability of the producer in the following stage of production. This is not to say that tax evasion is impossible. In some nations that use the tax, it has been evaded by arrangements between firms and consumers to engage in transactions without issuing invoices. Without an invoice, no record of the transaction exists, and the tax becomes difficult to collect. Problems of tax evasion have been most acute for small firms and professional services, such as those of physicians, lawyers, and insurance salespersons, where the costs of enforcement are high. Compliance has been fairly good for larger firms.

The VAT is typically rebated on export sales. This makes goods of nations that use the tax more competitive in international markets when they are exported to nations, such as the United States, where there is no national sales tax. Imported products are subject to the VAT, which increases their prices to domestic consumers. Many nations allow rebate of the tax on tourist purchases of items for export. For example, Canada allows foreign tourists to receive an instant rebate of their VAT taxes on nonfood purchases of goods and services at the Canadian border by presenting their receipts for hotels and nonfood purchases for export.

GLOBAL PERSPECTIVE

Current Use of the VAT

Currently, the value added tax is the most commonly used consumption-based tax in the world. All 30 member nations of the Organization for Economic Cooperation and Development (OECD) except for the United States use the tax. Basic rates for the tax range from a low of 5 percent in Japan to a high of 25 percent in Iceland, Denmark, Hungary, Norway, and Sweden. In general, basic tax rates tend to be higher in European nations than in Asian and Pacific nations.[1] On average, the VAT accounts for about 18 percent of revenue for nations that employ it. However, the VAT actually used by these nations can in no way be considered a general tax on consumption. It is common for the tax to include exemptions, and attempts are made to achieve various income redistribution goals through the VAT by taxing certain goods at rates higher and lower than the basic rate to adjust the tax in accordance with commonly held notions of the ability to pay.

The average basic rate used by European nations in administering the VAT has been about 15–25 percent. Some countries apply lower rates to particular transactions and higher rates to others. In addition, many transactions are exempt from the tax and are taxed effectively at a zero rate. The tax rates of various classes of goods in the nations of the EU are now being harmonized so they will be the same in all member nations.[2] This high rate is usually applied to luxury goods, such as jewelry, furs, cashmere items, and certain hobby equipment (photographic goods and sporting equipment, for example). The lower rates are usually applied to food, clothing, books, and other such items. The tax, as used in European nations, does not share the bias of exempting personal services from taxation that is inherent in the retail sales tax as used by state governments in the United States.

In many nations using the VAT, the tax is applied to entertainment services, transportation services, legal and other professional services, telephone service and other public utility services, some real estate services, and certain financial transactions. It is common to tax food items at a reduced rate. Books and newspapers have been exempt from the tax in the United Kingdom and Ireland but are subject to taxation in most other nations. Except in France, used equipment, including used cars, has been subject to the VAT. Medicines, housing services, hospital services, security transactions, insurance transactions, postal service, and some public utility services also are commonly exempt from the tax.

The net effect of such exemptions, and the application of reduced rates of taxation, is to change the VAT from a general consumption tax to a selective consumption tax, which is likely to distort choices among various consumption alternatives and distort the basic work-leisure choice.[3] The selective tax rates apparently are successful in relieving the regressive effects of the tax on income distribution. Estimates of the distribution of tax burden from the tax in France and Italy indicate that the incidence of the VAT in those countries has been roughly

One criticism of the VAT is that its costs of administration and compliance are relatively high compared with other taxes. If it were introduced as a new tax in the United States, setup costs, such as new tax forms and computer programs, would add to both administrative and compliance costs for the government and businesses. The Congressional Budget Office estimates that administrative and compliance costs for a new VAT could be as much as $8 billion per year. Costs of administering the VAT in Europe range from 0.4 to 1 percent of revenue collected. In general, it is more costly to administer a complex VAT that taxes different types of goods at different rates than it is to administer a general VAT that taxes all goods at the same rate. Other nations that use the tax—such as Canada, Japan, and New Zealand—have chosen to tax all transactions at the same rate as a way of minimizing the costs of collecting the tax. For example, the national General Sales Tax (GST) in Canada taxes all transactions except groceries (all of

proportional with respect to income.[4] Judicious taxation of goods complementary with leisure also could reduce the excess burden in the labor market by discouraging leisure activities. For example, high taxes on sporting equipment, hobby equipment, second homes, and vacation-related activities could offset some of the excess burden that results from the distortion in the work-leisure choice.

Concern about the impact of income taxes on saving and investment makes the consumption-type VAT an attractive alternative to income taxes for many economists.

The following table shows the standard VAT rate used by OECD Nations:

Standard VAT Tax Rates, 2011

NATION	TAX RATE
Australia	10.0
Austria	20.0
Belgium	21.0
Canada	5.0
Chile	19.0
Czech Republic	20.0
Denmark	25.0
Estonia	20.0
Finland	23.0
France	19.6
Germany	19.0
Greece	23.0
Hungary	25.0
Iceland	25.5
Ireland	21.0
Israel	16.0
Italy	20.0
Japan	5.0
Korea	10.0
Luxembourg	15.0
Mexico	16.0
Netherlands	19.0
New Zealand	15.0
Norway	25.0
Poland	23.0
Portugal	23
Slovak Republic	20.0
Slovenia	20.0
Spain	18.0
Sweden	25.0
Switzerland	8.0
Turkey	18
United Kingdom	20.0
Average	18.5

[1]See Jeffrey Owens, "Fundamental Tax Reform: An International Perspective," National Tax Journal 59, 1 (March 2006): 131–164.
[2]For a comprehensive analysis of the VAT in practice see Liam Ebrill, Michael Keen, Jean Paul Bodin, and Victoria Summers, (eds.), The Modern VAT (Washington, D.C.: International Monetary Fund Washington, D.C., 2001).
[3]For a discussion of the use of the tax in European nations, see Henry J. Aaron, (ed.), The Value-Added Tax: Lessons from Europe (Washington, D.C.: The Brookings Institution Washington, D.C., 1981).
[4]Ibid., 8–9.

which are exempt) at 5 percent. It is also more costly for small firms to comply with the tax than it is for large firms, and it is typical to exempt small businesses from the tax.

CHECKPOINT

1. Is the retail sales tax, as used by state and local governments in the United States, a general tax on consumption?
2. What are the issues involved in determining the incidence efficiency loss effects of retail sales taxes?
3. What is a VAT?

SUMMARY

A consumption tax is equivalent to an income tax that excludes saving from the tax base. A consumption tax, in effect, exempts interest income from taxation. Many argue that consumption is a better index of the ability to pay than income. These arguments are based on the notion that well-being in any given year depends on a person's consumption. Those who save sacrifice present satisfaction for increased satisfaction in the future. Income taxes discriminate against those who defer consumption, because interest obtained from saving is taxable. Because interest is simply the payment for deferred consumption, savers pay higher taxes relative to individuals who do not save, even if lifetime labor income is the same for both the saver and the nonsaver. This argument implies that lifetime consumption, including bequests, is a better index of economic capacity than income to ensure equal treatment of savers and nonsavers. The consumption tax does not affect the interest rate because interest is nontaxable. It is equivalent to a tax on labor income.

A general tax on comprehensive consumption is called an expenditure tax. It would be administered like an income tax. Individuals would compute annual consumption by excluding additions to net worth from their income. Progressive rates of taxation could be applied to consumption so as to adjust the burden of taxation with notions of equity.

A general tax on comprehensive consumption does not result in any losses in the efficiency with which choices regarding saving and investment are made, because the tax does not affect the interest rate. Compared with an equal-yield tax on comprehensive income, the consumption tax would reduce excess burden in capital markets to zero. However, because a consumption tax excludes saving, higher rates on labor income would be necessary to raise the same revenue as an income tax. This would result in added efficiency loss in labor markets as the wage is further reduced by a consumption tax rate that exceeds that of an equal-yield income tax. A consumption tax is likely to be borne according to labor income, with little shifting in the form of higher prices or reduced interest.

Retail sales taxes are used extensively by state governments in the United States. Retail sales taxes exempt many consumption items and, in some cases, tax capital outlays. They are not general taxes and are likely to distort the pattern of consumption, as is the case for excise taxes.

Other forms of sales taxes include turnover taxes and VATs. The VAT is used extensively in Western Europe. Most nations use a variant of the tax that exempts investment purchases and saving from taxation.

LOOKING AHEAD

Chapter 17 concludes the analysis of taxes on alternative economic bases with a discussion of taxes on wealth. The advantages and disadvantages of taxes on wealth are highlighted. The economic effects of a general tax on wealth are compared with those of general taxes on income and consumption. This is followed by a discussion of the local property tax in the United States.

KEY CONCEPTS

Comprehensive Consumption

Excise Taxes

Retail Sales Tax

Turnover Taxes

Value-added Tax (VAT)

REVIEW QUESTIONS

1. How could the current personal income tax be modified so that it becomes a consumption tax? What are the advantages of taxing consumption in this way?
2. Explain why many economists argue that an income tax penalizes savers but a consumption tax would not. In what sense can consumption be regarded as a better index of the ability to pay taxes than income?
3. Show how under an income tax the present value of the amount of tax paid over a person's lifetime will vary with the difference in saving for two individuals who begin the life cycle at age 18 and have equal economic capacity. Why is the tax paid

independent of the timing of income under a consumption tax?

4. An income tax that taxes only labor income would be equivalent to a consumption tax. Do you agree?

5. How would loans be treated under a general tax on comprehensive consumption? What are some of the problems encountered in defining the tax base?

6. Why must the tax rate on a general tax on consumption exceed that of a general tax on income if the two are to raise the same revenue?

7. Why will substitution of an equal-yield general consumption tax for a general income tax reduce efficiency losses in capital markets but increase efficiency losses in labor markets? Why is the

consumption tax likely to be regressive with respect to income?

8. How do retail sales taxes, as used in most states, tax a base that is smaller than a comprehensive consumption base? What are the consequences of excluding certain items from the consumption base?

9. What is a VAT? How can it be administered without any need for a firm to calculate value added? Why is a general consumption-type VAT equivalent to a tax on comprehensive consumption?

10. Explain why the invoice method of collecting the VAT does not require firms to compute value added. How does the invoice method act to discourage tax evasion?

PROBLEMS

1. Suppose two workers earn labor incomes of $20,000 per year in each of three tax accounting periods. One worker saves 20 percent of her labor earnings in each of the first two periods and spends all her savings and accumulated interest in the final period. The other worker never saves any of her labor earnings. The market rate of interest is 10 percent.

   Calculate the discounted present value of taxes paid over the three periods for each of the workers under a 15 percent comprehensive income tax. What would be the effect of substituting a comprehensive consumption tax for a comprehensive income tax? Comment on the equity and efficiency aspects of each of the two taxes.

2. Your state has a retail sales tax of 10 percent but it exempts food, prescription drugs, and all services, including housing services, repair services, and consumption of electricity and other public utility services. Use supply-and-demand analysis to explain how the prices of untaxed consumption items can be affected by the retail sales tax even though they are not subject to taxation. How can changes in the prices of nontaxed items affect the incidence of the retail sales tax?

3. Suppose legislation were passed that abolished all state and local sales taxes and replaced them with one uniform sales tax on all consumption, including consumption of services. The federal government would collect the tax and then return the revenue collected to the state governments. Discuss the economic effects of such a national sales tax on work effort and saving as well as the changes in behavior that would result from moving to a national as opposed to state and local sales tax base.

4. A furniture manufacturer sells $500,000 worth of tables, chairs, and other items in a given year. The manufacturer earns a profit of $100,000 that year. His purchase invoices indicate that he bought $200,000 worth of lumber, varnish, nails, and other materials during the year. His labor costs were $150,000, and he purchased $50,000 of new equipment that year. Calculate his tax liability under a 15 percent consumption-type VAT.

5. Suppose the current corporate income tax in the United States is replaced with a general equal-yield consumption-type VAT. What would the impact of such a tax reform be for labor markets and capital markets? What is the likely differential incidence of such a substitution?

ADDITIONAL READINGS

Aaron, Henry J. (ed.). *The Value-Added Tax: Lessons from Europe*. Washington, D.C.: The Brookings Institution, 1981. A collection of articles on the use of the value-added tax in European nations and the prospects for its use in the United States.

Aaron, Henry J., Harvey Galper, and Joseph A. Pechman (eds.). *Uneasy Compromise: Problems of a Hybrid*

Income-Consumption Tax. Washington, D.C.: The Brookings Institution, 1988. A collection of essays on issues involved in tax systems that seek to provide incentives to save and to invest.

Bradford, David F. "Consumption Tax Alternative: Implementation and Transition Issues." In *Frontiers of Tax Reform*, Michael J. Boskin, Palo Alto, (eds.).

Calif.: Hoover Institution Press, 1996. A discussion and analysis of some of the issues involved in setting up a national consumption tax.

Cnossen, Sijbren, "Global Trends and Issues in Value Added Taxation." *International Tax and Public Finance* 5, 3 (July 1998): 399–428. A discussion of use of the VAT worldwide.

Due, John F., and John L. Mikesell. *Sales Taxation: State and Local Structure and Administration*, 2nd edition. Washington, D.C.: Urban Institute Press, 1994. A comprehensive analysis of the economic effect of all types of sales taxes.

Kaldor, Nicholas. *An Expenditure Tax*. London: Allen and Unwin, 1955. A classic analysis of the expenditure tax. Chapter 1 contains Kaldor's arguments in favor of consumption as a superior index of the ability to pay.

Mieszkowski, Peter. "The Choice of the Tax Base: Consumption versus Income Taxation." *In Federal Tax Reform: Myths and Realities*, Michael J. Boskin, (ed.), 27–53. San Francisco: Institute for Contemporary Studies, 1978. A discussion of the difference between income and consumption bases, the advantages of a tax on comprehensive consumption, and some of the problems involved in implementing such a tax.

U.S. Congress of the United States, Congressional Budget Office. *Effects of Adopting a Value-Added Tax*. Washington, D.C.: U.S. Government Printing Office, February 1992. An analysis of the economic effects of introducing a VAT in the United States as a way of raising an additional $150 billion of revenue annually.

U.S. Department of the Treasury. *Blueprints for Basic Tax Reform*. Washington, D.C.: U.S. Government Printing Office, 1977. Contains the outline of a cash-flow tax and discusses some of the implementation problems and economic effects of introducing such a tax into the tax structure in the United States.

Zodrow, George R. *State Sales and Income Taxes: An Economic Analysis*. College Station, Tex.: Texas A&M University Press, 1999. A scholarly analysis of retail sales taxes in the context of state and local finance.

INTERNET RESOURCES

http://www.taxadmin.org

The home page of the Federation of Tax Administrators can be used to access information on state sales taxes.

http://www.oecd.org

Information on use of the VAT by member nations of the Organization for Economic Co-operation and Development can be accessed at this site.

http://www.ecommercetax.com

This Web site contains up-to-date information on issues relating to taxation of Internet transactions.

Chapter 17

TAXES ON WEALTH, PROPERTY, AND ESTATES

LEARNING OBJECTIVES

After reading this chapter, you should be able to:

- Discuss the issues involved in implementing a general tax on a comprehensive wealth tax base, including problems involved in the assessment of property value.

- Show how a comprehensive wealth tax is related to a comprehensive income tax and how the tax can be viewed as falling on accumulated saving.

- Analyze the incidence and effect on resource use of a general tax on comprehensive wealth and the economic effects of property taxation in the United States.

- Discuss estate, inheritance, and gift taxes.

I f you were to own your own home, you would have to pay property taxes on it. In the United States, most real estate is taxed by local governments. Land and structures on the land used for housing, for commercial trade, or for agriculture and manufacturing are taxed at varying rates depending on the city, town, or county in which they are located. Property taxes are used to finance local government services and schooling.

In the United States, nearly 90,000 local government jurisdictions use the local property tax. The tax is levied primarily on one form of wealth—real estate—and the variety of tax rates numbers in the thousands. Naturally, because the property tax is a local tax, it can influence the location of investment. For example, suppose you were to receive a job offer in New York after you graduated from college and wanted to buy a home in the New York metropolitan area. You could choose among thousands of communities in three neighboring states (New York, New Jersey, and Connecticut) where you could live and commute to your job in the city. In each town, you would pay a property tax on your home and get a bundle of government services such as schools, trash collection, and police and fire protection in return for the taxes you pay. Where you locate your home will depend, in part, on the tax rates in the various towns in the metropolitan area and the services you get in return for those taxes.

The impact of the property tax is complex and strongly influences both investment and locational decisions. In this chapter, we examine the economic impact of taxes on wealth and property. First, we look at the economic effects of a general wealth tax on all forms of wealth. We then explore the economic effects of a national tax that is levied primarily on real estate. Once we understand the effects of national taxes on property, we can then trace out the complicated effects of the system of local property taxation as used in the United States. Finally, we examine taxes on transfers of wealth through estate, gift, and inheritance taxes.

A COMPREHENSIVE WEALTH TAX BASE

Wealth is the market value of accumulated assets in a nation. People can acquire wealth through saving or, if they are lucky enough, from gifts or inheritances from their parents or other relatives or friends. A person who never saves any income and receives no gifts and inheritances will never accumulate wealth. To obtain wealth, people must refrain from consuming all their income in a given year. A comprehensive wealth tax base would include all wealth in the economy.

The wealth tax has a long history of utilization by governing authorities.[1] A general property tax was used in England during the medieval period to finance the Crusades. Such taxes were levied on rents and movable property. Evidence also exists that the tax was utilized in ancient Rome. In the colonial period of the United States, wealth taxes were utilized by many of the colonial governments. Although colonies initially relied on poll taxes to finance their modest requirements

---

[1]For a good discussion of the historical development of property taxation, see Arthur D. Lynn, Jr., "Property-Tax Development: Selected Historical Perspectives," in *Property Taxation: U.S.A.*, ed. Richard W. Lindholm (Madison: University of Wisconsin Press, 1967): 7–19. Also see John Joseph Wallis, "A History of the Property Tax in America," in *Property Taxation and Local Government Finance*, ed. Wallace E. Oates (Cambridge Mass.: Lincoln Institute of Land Policy, 2001): 123–147.

for public expenditures, they switched to taxes on real and personal property as differences in wealth developed among the colonists.

Many economists have observed that the utilization of wealth as the base for taxation appears to run a cyclical course. This "property tax cycle" is correlated with the economic development of a society.[2] The tax first appears as a per unit levy on land alone. As income and wealth differentials become more pronounced during economic development, it becomes a proportional tax on the holding of all wealth—land, other real assets, and personal property. Finally, as the society reaches economic maturity and wealth takes on new and heterogeneous forms, the general property tax becomes difficult to administer effectively; essentially, it becomes a tax on real estate. **Real estate or real property** refers to land and structures.

The bulk of the revenue currently raised by property taxes in the United States comes from taxes on real estate. The property tax is used mainly by local governments in the United States.

Many argue that it is necessary to tax wealth, in addition to income and consumption, in order to achieve an equitable tax structure. Quite often, individual households with relatively low incomes have substantial holdings of wealth in the form of real assets. In the case of homes and other consumer durables that yield nonmonetary returns, households might escape taxation completely under an income tax because of problems associated with measuring imputed rent and service flows.

Measuring Wealth

Wealth can be measured by determining the net value of financial assets, capital assets, and land owned by citizens of a nation. The value of these assets represents the value of accumulated savings in a nation. A tax on wealth can be viewed as equivalent to a tax on the return earned in any given year on all savings and investments.

Administering a wealth tax is complicated by the fact that wealth is a stock rather than a flow like income and consumption. A **stock** is a variable with a value defined at a particular point in time. To administer a wealth tax, the value of taxable assets must be determined at a particular point in time. It is often difficult to determine the value of assets that are infrequently traded on markets. Moreover, the value of assets can change quite rapidly. Without frequent reevaluation of the taxable asset values, serious inequities are likely to result.

To determine the base for wealth, all forms of property owned by taxpayers must be listed, and values must be assessed. In listing property, care must be taken to avoid double-counting assets. Assessing the value of wealth that is not often sold on the market is one of the most difficult aspects of property taxation.

Of the two approaches to listing the wealth of taxpayers, the first considers only the net assets of households, while the second considers the net assets of both people and corporations. Both methods yield the same results. The first approach merely takes into account the fact that corporations are ultimately owned by people, and the net assets of such corporations are reflected in the value of outstanding corporate stock.

---

[2]*Ibid.,* 16.

Using the first approach, total wealth is considered to have the following three components:

1. All *real property* (that is, land and improvements thereon) owned by households.
2. All *tangible personal property* owned by households. This includes all movable assets, such as cars, furniture, clothing, and jewelry.
3. All *intangible personal property* owned by households. This includes stocks, bonds, cash, and other "paper" assets that reflect claims on assets owned by corporations and governments.

Furthermore, all debt incurred by households and firms (for example, mortgages and loans) has to be subtracted from the tax base to obtain a measure of net wealth and to avoid double-counting assets. This is because such debt represents paper claims against such assets as homes owned by households and is already included in the tax base. A fourth possible form of wealth that might be included in the tax base is human capital. This includes special skills people are endowed with or acquire through educational investments. However, it is difficult to assess the value of human capital.

The second approach includes the assets of corporations but excludes intangible property that represents claims on the assets of such corporations. Thus, this approach does not tax outstanding corporate stock, for to do so involves double taxation of corporate assets. In addition, this approach deducts from the tax base all debt incurred by the private sector to obtain a measure of net wealth.

Of course, problems are encountered in implementing a general property tax in an economically mature society. This stems, in part, from the complexities of listing all forms of property, particularly tangible personal property and intangible property. Many forms of movable personal property, such as jewelry, are easy to conceal, and this encourages tax evasion. Taxes on personal property often place a disproportionate share of the burden on honest taxpayers, who list all their movable personal assets, even though they realize that the costs of checking the validity of their listings are so prohibitive as to prevent governments from enforcing honest listings. Except for movable personal property that must be registered with local governments, such as automobiles, taxes on this form of wealth prove both easy to evade and difficult to enforce. The same holds true for intangible personal property. For unregistered securities, concealment is relatively easy and, again, enforcement of tax laws can prove costly to governing authorities.

The administrative problems encountered in taxing both tangible and intangible personal property have led to a wealth tax that falls mainly on real estate and exempts other forms of wealth. This is in accordance with the property tax cycle previously discussed. Taxes on real estate are difficult to evade, because it is virtually impossible to conceal such assets. Real estate is registered with local authorities, and the structures on land are open to view by all. The problem now becomes one of determining which real estate is taxable and then assessing the value of such real estate.

In the United States, all localities exclude from the tax base most property owned by religious, educational, and charitable institutions. This is largely real estate owned by churches, schools, and colleges or universities. In addition, constitutional law prohibits local governments from levying taxes on real estate owned by the federal government. However, the federal government often makes payments in lieu of taxes to localities in which it owns property. State government property is usually exempt from local property taxes, but some state governments make payments to local governments in lieu of property taxes.

ASSESSMENT OF PROPERTY VALUE

After all property subject to taxation has been listed, it is necessary to estimate, or assess, the value of the property before the tax can be implemented. **Assessment** is the valuation of taxable wealth by government authorities. Assessment practices are often criticized as being too subjective. In fact, for infrequently traded assets, assessment is often more of an art than a science. Ideally, the assessed value of an asset should reflect its current value.

In a general property tax, assessors estimate the value of both real estate and movable personal property. If assessment is to be reasonably accurate and fair, the asset value of property should closely approximate the market value. Typically, the property tax is levied as a percentage of assessed valuation.

The assessor's task is relatively easy for intangible personal property. Well-organized markets exist for trading stocks, bonds, mortgages, and other paper assets; and prices are available on a daily basis. Similarly, good markets exist for trading automobiles. But, markets for the most prevalent form of taxable wealth, real estate, are not as well organized. The assessor often approximates the value of such assets on a subjective basis.

One method that the economist might suggest to assess the value of real estate is to attempt to determine the capitalized value of such assets. This entails estimating both the net annual rent flowing from the land and structures thereon in monetary terms and the probable life of the structure. Once estimates of these two parameters are made, it is a simple matter to compute the present value of the real estate using a discount rate that reflects the opportunity cost of capital. However, it can be difficult to estimate rentals for nonincome-producing property and vacant lots.

Often, the assessor projects rents into the future based on expected future development in the area. Assessors typically keep records of recent sales of property within an area. They also must be acquainted with growth trends in the area to predict possible changes in property values over time. Property must be reassessed periodically to reflect changing market values. In a particular community with a given supply and demand of real estate, values of structures are likely to vary with such factors as location, age of structure, quality of construction, size of structure, and appearance.

A COMPREHENSIVE WEALTH TAX

A **comprehensive wealth tax** is one that would be levied on all forms of capital and land at a flat rate. Because capital and land represent assets that yield flows of productive services over time, a general wealth tax can be thought of as being levied on the discounted present value of those land and capital services over time. Comprehensive wealth, W, is

$$W = \sum \frac{R_i}{(1+r)^i},$$
(17.1)

where R_i is the annual dollar return to savings and investments and r is the market rate of interest. If the tax rate under the wealth tax is t_W, annual revenue from the tax would be $t_W W$. Exactly the same annual tax revenue could be obtained from an annual tax on the return to savings. Because R_i is the annual dollar return to saving, the annual revenue from a savings tax levied at a rate t_S would be $t_S R_i$. The effective tax on savings under a wealth tax can be computed by setting $t_W W$ equal to $t_S R_i$. Thus, the effective tax on the annual return to accumulated savings associated with a comprehensive wealth tax at rate t_W is

$$t_s = \frac{t_w W}{R_i}.$$ (17.2)

The wealth tax directly reduces the return to savings or to holding land and accumulating capital. It has the effect of reducing interest income from accumulated savings no matter what the form of the savings, such as land, capital equipment, or financial assets. In effect, it is a tax on interest and rental income. If a person earns an annual dollar return of R_G on accumulated savings in any given year, the net return earned after taxes would be $R_N = R_G - t_W W$.

For example, suppose total wealth in a nation amounts to \$100 trillion. A flat-rate wealth tax of 1 percent would yield a total of \$1 trillion annual revenue. If the dollar return to invested capital is \$10 trillion per year, which amounts to 10 percent of assets, the property tax revenue of \$1 trillion is equivalent to a 10 percent annual tax on the return to accumulated savings.

Most of the problems of administering a general wealth tax stem from the fact that capital is a stock rather than a flow. This leads to difficulty in developing fair and accurate mechanisms to assess and reassess the value of the tax base. As previously discussed, one of the most difficult problems encountered would be the treatment of human capital. If a tax on wealth excluded human capital, strong incentives would exist to invest in this form of wealth, as opposed to physical forms of wealth. Despite the constraints imposed by the administrative problems involved, it is worthwhile discussing the hypothetical effects of a general wealth tax as the basis for dealing with the economic effects of specific wealth taxes, such as those levied mainly on real property.

Because substitutes in production exist for capital, it is reasonable to assume that the demand for capital is somewhat elastic. The economic effects of a general wealth tax depend on the elasticity of supply of all forms of saving for the purpose of accumulating assets. First, consider a closed economy (no opportunities exist for exporting capital) in which taxpayers are unwilling to substitute consumption for saving in response to changes in the return to saving. Under such circumstances, the elasticity of supply of savings would be zero.

Impact of a Comprehensive Wealth Tax When the Supply of Savings Is Perfectly Inelastic

The effect of a proportional tax on all forms of wealth on the market for investable funds is shown in Figure 17.1. Assuming a perfectly inelastic supply of savings, the impact of the tax is to reduce the return to savings by the full amount of the tax. The curve labeled D gives the gross percentage return, r_G, earned on investments before payment of the tax. The net return is the annual return minus the annual wealth tax as a percentage of the dollar return to savings, $t_S = t_W W/R_i$. For example, a 1 percent annual comprehensive wealth tax is equivalent to a 10 percent tax

FIGURE 17.1 Impact of a General Wealth Tax When the Supply of Savings Is Perfectly Inelastic

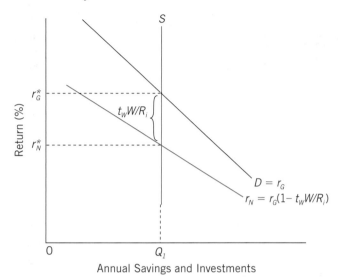

If the supply of savings is perfectly inelastic, a general wealth tax reduces the annual return to savings by the full amount of the tax as a percentage of the dollar annual return to savings, $t_W W/R$. Although the annual savings are unchanged, the tax does result in an excess burden because it causes a substitution effect that is offset by an equal and opposite income effect.

on the return to savings and investments when the equilibrium gross return is 10 percent. The wealth tax reduces the percentage return to savings from r_G to $r_N = r_G(1 - t_W W/R_i)$. A 1 percent wealth tax, which is equivalent to a 10 percent tax on a gross return to savings of 10 percent, will reduce the net return to savings to $r_n = 0.1(1 - 0.1) = 0.09$ or 9 percent.

The impact of the tax is to reduce the annual return to savings and investments from r_G^* to r_N^*. Because the supply of savings is perfectly inelastic in this case, the return falls by the full percentage equivalent of the ratio of annual wealth tax payments to the dollar annual return to savings, $t_W W/R_i$. The incidence of the tax is likely to be progressive because it would be paid in accordance with the ownership of wealth. In most nations, the distribution of capital is heavily concentrated in the hands of middle- and upper-income groups. This implies that these groups would pay higher wealth taxes in relation to their income than would lower-income groups.

The excess burden of the tax is not likely to be zero, even if the supply of savings is perfectly inelastic. This is because a perfectly inelastic supply curve of savings is consistent with behavior for which the income effects of interest changes are offset by equal substitution effects. As shown in Chapter 13, a decrease in the return to saving results in a substitution effect that tends to decrease saving but an income effect that tends to increase saving. When the two effects exactly offset each other, the aggregate supply of saving is perfectly inelastic. However, because the tax does result in a substitution effect that decreases saving, it would result in a reduction in saving compared with that which would prevail under a lump-sum tax. This is because the lump-sum tax could raise the same revenue as the wealth tax but would generate *only* income effects.[3]

Impact of the Tax When the Supply of Savings Is Responsive

When the supply of savings is not perfectly elastic, either because the economy is open so that capital can be exported or because savers are willing to substitute consumption for saving, the tax would result in an increase in the gross return to savings and investments. In addition, further losses in efficiency would occur in investment markets as annual savings and investments decline.

This is illustrated in Figure 17.2. As before, the tax shifts the investment demand curve downward from $D = r_G$ to $r_N = r_G(1 - t_W W/R_i)$. Because the supply of savings is presumed not to be perfectly inelastic, the quantity of funds supplied for investment falls from Q_1 to Q_2. The gross return to investment rises from r_G^* to r_{G1}^*, but the net return to investment falls to r_{N1}. The fall in the return to capital in this case is less than the annual wealth tax, expressed as a percentage of annual savings. The increase in the market rate of interest caused by the tax shifts the burden to those other than savers. Higher interest rates increase costs of production and could result in increases in the price of goods and services, which shifts the tax to consumers. Also, the annual reduction in investment caused by the tax eventually would reduce the capital–labor ratio in production, thereby lowering worker

---

FIGURE 17.2   Impact of a General Wealth Tax When the Supply of Savings Is Responsive to Changes in Annual Return

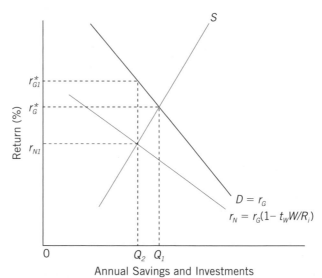

When the supply of savings is responsive to changes in the net return, a general wealth tax reduces the annual amount of saving and investment and increases the annual gross return to investment.

© Cengage Learning

---

[3]The point is illustrated in Chapter 13 for the case of a perfectly inelastic labor supply curve.

productivity in the long run. This would result, in the long run, in the burden of taxation shifting to workers in the form of lower wages.

Finally, the substitution effect of the tax-induced decline in the net return to savings is larger than when the supply of savings is perfectly inelastic. As a result, when the supply of savings is responsive to changes in its return, the excess burden of the tax is correspondingly greater. For a complete analysis of the implications of tax-induced reductions in the return to savings and investments, see Chapter 13.

It follows that when the elasticity of supply of savings exceeds zero, owners of capital succeed in transferring part of the burden of the tax to others as the cost of capital as an input rises. The incidence of the tax in this case is more difficult to determine, because the tax reduces both the return to capital and the income of workers. The tax in this case reduces annual investment. As a result, it adversely affects the rate of economic growth.

If, as many economists contend, the supply of savings is responsive to changes in interest, the wealth tax would be detrimental to the incentive to save. Compared with equal-yield income and consumption taxes, it would result in greater distortion in investment markets, because the tax rate on savings would be higher inasmuch as all revenue would be raised from taxes on capital income. On the other hand, a general wealth tax has no effect on the return to work effort. A person who never saves will never accumulate assets, and the tax is avoided. The tax is independent of labor earnings; the wage is not reduced. The amount of tax that a person pays over a lifetime depends on how that person allocates wage income over time so as to accumulate assets, and on the capital assets acquired through transfers, such as bequests. Thus, when compared with equal-yield taxes on income and consumption, the wealth tax does not distort the work-leisure choice.

In practice, a wealth tax is not likely to be completely general because administrative difficulties encountered in measuring and assessing all forms of wealth. In particular, it is reasonable to assume that human capital escapes taxation, even under a comprehensive wealth tax. If this is the case, then the wealth tax induces a reallocation of investment choices toward human capital and away from other assets, resulting in still further efficiency loss.

If the supply of savings is moderately responsive to its return, the incidence of the general wealth tax would be borne largely according to a person's holdings of capital, with some shifting to labor as wages decline in the long run in response to decreased productivity attributable to lower capital-labor ratios. Given that the bulk of the tax is borne according to ownership of capital, which is heavily concentrated in the hands of upper-income groups, it is likely to be progressive with respect to income.

CHECKPOINT

1. What is wealth?
2. List the major components of wealth, and discuss some of the difficulties involved in assessment of the wealth tax base.
3. Explain why a general wealth tax would be equivalent to a tax on savings, and discuss the possible economic effects of a general wealth tax on resource use and income distribution.

SELECTIVE PROPERTY TAXES

A general tax on wealth is likely to prove administratively infeasible. Most property taxes are selective taxes in the sense that they are levied on only certain forms of wealth. Taxes on real assets (land and improvements thereon) account for nearly 90 percent of all revenue collected from property tax levies in the United States.

As a tax on real estate, the property tax provides an incentive to substitute alternative inputs for real property. In addition, in states where personal property is not taxed, or is taxed at lower rates than real property, the tax, other things being equal, can affect choices between the consumption of real property and that of consumer durables by making the latter relatively more attractive. Therefore, it is possible that the property tax discourages the production and consumption of housing.

The property tax, as it is utilized in the United States, also is likely to induce some locational adjustments because it is a local levy, and rates of taxation differ among communities. The property tax can be a factor in determining the location of an industry. Real property-intensive industries, other things being equal, tend to locate in areas where the property tax is relatively low. However, to include all factors in a firm's location decision, the benefits financed by property taxation in alternative location sites also must be considered. Communities with low property tax rates might lack essential public services or have lower-quality public services to be utilized by industry.

In effect, a selective wealth tax, such as that which mainly affects property held in the form of real estate, can be viewed as a discriminatory tax on the investment income from taxed assets. To abstract from the complications ensuing from local variation in tax rates, assume that all real estate is taxed nationally at the same rate. The long-run impact of such a tax can be analyzed with the aid of a model similar to that developed by Harberger for analyzing the incidence of the corporate income tax (see Chapter 15).[4] Assume first that a national tax on real estate exists, with all real estate subject to the same proportional rate of taxation irrespective of its location. Suppose as well that the aggregate supply of saving is perfectly inelastic and that owners of real estate do not raise rents to cover the tax. It is easy to demonstrate that, in the long run, such a tax would be borne by the owners of all forms of capital.

The tax would disturb the initial capital market equilibrium by reducing the return to real estate investment relative to alternative forms of holding assets. In the long run, investment funds would be reallocated away from real estate and toward investments in alternative assets, where the return is not subject to taxation. This would reduce the quantity of annual savings supplied to real estate investments, thereby raising the net return to holding real estate. Likewise, the tax would increase the supply of savings funds for alternative investments, thereby depressing their return.

Investable funds would continue to flow among the various sectors until the return on real estate, net of taxation, once again is equal to the return available on alternative investments. The end result would be a reduction in the net return to investment in *all* forms of capital. Thus, in the long run, the

---

[4]Arnold C. Harberger, "The Incidence of the Corporation Income Tax," *Journal of Political Economy* 70 (June 1962): 215–240.

incidence of the tax on real estate would be similar to that of a general wealth tax. It would be borne by those who supply funds to create capital. The analysis is exactly the same as that employed in Chapter 15 for the corporate income tax.

If the aggregate supply of savings were not perfectly inelastic, the effect of the national real estate tax would be more complex. In this case, the tax also would induce a flight of savings out of the country so that the burden of taxation could be avoided, or reduce the rate of saving as individuals substitute consumption for saving to avoid the tax. The quantity of investment funds supplied would diminish, and the market rate of interest would rise, resulting in a tendency for prices of consumer goods and services to rise along with the increased cost of capital. Over the long run, the reduction in investment would result in a shifting of part of the burden of taxation to labor, as already described for a general wealth tax.

Local Property Tax on Real Estate

Now, consider the case that reflects most accurately the actual use of the property tax in the United States: a locally administered tax on real estate, with tax rates collectively chosen by citizens of each local governing authority. Given the diversity that exists among local governments, there is considerable variation among the rates of taxation from jurisdiction to jurisdiction. In this case, movements of investment funds caused by the tax would be still more complex. In addition to the investment flows resulting from a national property tax discussed previously, there would be movement of investment among political jurisdictions due to differentials in rates of taxation among jurisdictions. Other things being equal, those local governments where property tax rates are higher than the national average can expect a reduction in local investment; those for which the rates of taxation are below the national average can expect an increase in investment.

The average rate of property taxation reflects the portion of the property tax that is common to all jurisdictions; therefore, it cannot be avoided by changing the jurisdiction in which investments are made. That portion of the tax lowers the return to capital in all uses similar to the way a national property tax would lower the return to capital. **Property tax rate differentials** are differences above or below the national average rate of property taxation. Tax rate differentials above or below the average rate of taxation among jurisdictions can be avoided, however, by reallocation of investment from high- to low-tax jurisdictions. These differentials can be shifted to noncapital input owners.

In states with positive tax differentials where property taxes exceed the national average, a reduction in annual investment would result. Investment would be reallocated to low-tax jurisdictions. As this process of tax-induced reallocation of investment would continue, the stock of capital eventually would decline in high-tax areas but increase in low-tax jurisdictions. This, in turn, would result in shifting the tax burden to owners of other inputs. For example, a reduction in building and construction in the high-tax areas eventually would reduce the ratios of capital to land and capital to labor. This would result in decreases in the productivity of labor and land at those locations. If labor did not migrate out as investment declines, local wages would decline. Land, of course, is an immobile input. Reductions in the capital-land ratio caused by high property taxes would definitely reduce land rents. Conversely, land rents would rise in low-tax jurisdictions that benefit from the reallocation of investment.

Some of the burden of the property tax rate differentials is transferred to workers and local landlords through input price changes caused by capital migration. These changes in local input prices, in turn, can affect the prices of locally produced goods and services. This portion of the tax is similar to an excise tax in its effect on prices. The impact tax differential on price is sometimes referred to as an *excise tax effect*.[5]

Many locally produced services, most notably housing services, are sold in local markets, where they need not directly compete with similar services produced in other parts of the nation. Therefore, other things being equal, communities with positive property tax differentials—their rates of taxation are higher than those of other jurisdictions—can expect to lose resources as developers invest in real estate located in jurisdictions where property taxes are lower. In such areas, this reduction in the supply of capital to real estate investments would make housing and other locally sold services scarcer. The price of those services would be raised, and some of the burden of the positive property tax differential would be transferred to consumers of such services as housing. Renters might suffer reductions in real income as housing costs rise when the tax is shifted. However, housing costs would fall in areas where increased investment takes place as a result of negative property tax differentials.

A Recapitulation

The impact of the local property tax, as used in the United States, is of a twofold nature. First, the average tax that is common to all jurisdictions serves to reduce the return to all capital assets (including land) as a result of the long-run market re-equilibrium process and the investment flows thereby induced. This portion of the tax is borne by owners of capital.

Second, the tax differentials among communities induce regional investment movement. These differentials tend to be positively associated with regional income, implying that the shifting of the tax, in ways that reduce real income of owners of noncapital inputs, is most likely to occur in regions where average income is greater than the national median.[6] In other regions with lower income, the capital inflows induced by the tax increase real income.

From the point of view of particular localities, increases in property tax rates are likely to be shifted in ways that result in either increased prices of locally produced goods or decreased income to owners of land and labor in the community, depending on the extent of reduced investment caused by any increase in tax rates.[7]

---

[5]See Peter M. Mieszkowski, "The Property Tax: An Excise Tax or a Profits Tax?" *Journal of Public Economics* 1 (April 1972): 73–96, and Henry J. Aaron, *Who Pays the Property Tax?* (Washington, D.C.: The Brookings Institution, 1975).

[6]*Ibid.*, 45–49.

[7]See Charles E. McClure, Jr., "The 'New View' of the Property Tax: A Caveat," *National Tax Journal* 30 (March 1977): 69–75. Also see George R. Zodrow, "The Property Tax as a Capital Tax: A Room with Three Views," *National Tax Journal* 54, 1 (March 2001): 139–156.

TAX CAPITALIZATION

Tax capitalization is a decrease in the value of a taxed asset equal to the discounted present value of future tax liability of its owners. Property tax differentials among taxing jurisdictions can be capitalized into lower property values. Tax differentials result from variance in the property tax rates among communities and among various classes of property. Recall that the portion of the property tax rate common to all taxing jurisdictions causes a decrease in the return to capital in all uses. Tax capitalization is a discount in the price of a taxed asset that adjusts the annual market return of the asset to a level that is competitive with other assets not subject to the tax. Capitalization can be full or partial. The extent to which the burden of a tax is capitalized into lower asset values depends on the degree to which owners of the taxed asset can adjust the amounts available in response to the tax.

The process of tax capitalization can be illustrated algebraically. The present value of any capital asset depends on (1) the annual dollar return earned by holding the asset, (2) the life span of the asset, and (3) the rate of discount for the economy. The rate of discount represents the opportunity cost of holding any one particular form of wealth; it roughly can be considered the average market return to investment in the economy. Thus, the value of any capital asset that yields an annual return of Y dollars each year can be expressed as follows:

$$V = \sum_{i=0}^{n} \frac{Y}{(1+r)^i},\tag{17.3}$$

where V is the market value of the asset, n is the number of years that the asset will last, and r is the rate of discount. If it is assumed that the asset has an infinite life, then $n = $ infinity and Equation 17.3 reduces to

$$V = \frac{Y}{r}.\tag{17.4}$$

This is because the value of the ratio $1/(1 + r)^i$ gets smaller and smaller as i, the life of the asset, increases. As i approaches infinity, the sum represented by Equation 17.3 approaches a limit, represented by Equation 17.4.

For example, Equation 17.4 can be used to calculate the value of a parcel of land that will last indefinitely. If the annual rent expected on the parcel is $10,000 per year and the market rate of interest is 10 percent, then the value of the parcel is $10,000/0.10 = $100,000. If an asset that yields $10,000 per year in rent had less than infinite life, its value would be somewhat less.

Suppose a parcel of land is subject to a property tax rate that is t percent greater than the national average. The t percent property tax rate differential is likely to be fully capitalized. The tax at rate t reduces the annual rent earned on the land by the amount tV_t, where V_t is the market value of the parcel after the tax is imposed. The posttax annual dollar return on the asset is $Y - tV_t$. The new market value of the asset can be expressed as follows:

$$V_t = \frac{Y_t}{r} = \frac{Y - tV_t}{r},\tag{17.5}$$

where Y_t is the posttax return. Solving for V_t, Equation 17.5 can be reduced to

$$V_t = \frac{Y}{r+t}.\tag{17.6}$$

Equation 17.6 is the formula for full capitalization of a tax on an asset of infinite life. The expression for the effect of the tax on the market value of an asset of less than infinite life can be easily derived, but it is somewhat more complicated than Equation 17.6. In effect, full tax capitalization puts the entire burden of taxation on current property holders who are selling the assets. For assets that yield the same annual return, the magnitude of reduction in price varies directly with the anticipated life span of the asset.

For example, suppose a wealth tax of 5 percent is levied on one specific asset of infinite life having a pretax return of $10,000 per year. If the rate of discount is 5 percent, the pretax market value of that asset is $10,000/0.05 = $200,000, from Equation 17.4. By substituting in Equation 17.6, the effect of full capitalization of the tax on market value of the asset can easily be determined. The new value of the asset is $10,000/(0.05 + 0.05), or only $100,000. Thus, full capitalization of the tax reduces the value of the asset subject to taxation by a factor of 50 percent! If the asset has a shorter life span, the reduction in market value accordingly is less.

Also, the annual property tax bill in the preceding example would be (0.05) ($100,000) = $5,000. The $100,000 decline in the market value of the asset equals the discounted present value of future tax liability of its owners. This is $5,000/0.05 = $100,000. The seller of the asset must sell it at a capital discount equal to the present value of all future taxes, assuming that other assets are not subject to the tax.

CAPITALIZATION AND THE ELASTICITY OF SUPPLY OF TAXED ASSETS

Full capitalization occurs only if the owners of the taxed asset cannot adjust the quantity supplied in response to the decrease in the annual return to holding it caused by the tax. This is clearly the case for land which, in the aggregate, is in perfectly inelastic supply. Because landholders cannot make land any scarcer in response to the tax, the market rents do not increase, and the landlords bear the full tax burden. However, other taxed assets, such as structures, equipment, and vehicles, are likely to have elastic supply curves in the long run. A reduction in investment in these forms of taxable wealth in the long run is likely to make these assets scarcer and therefore increase their market rents. A tax-induced increase in market rents will prevent full capitalization of property tax differentials.

When market rents of taxed assets rise in response to the tax, part of the annual burden of the tax is shifted to users of these assets by their owners. This is illustrated in Figure 17.3. Suppose the current rent per square foot of housing per year is $100. Assume that all housing structures last indefinitely, so that Equation 17.4 can be used to compute their values. If the market rate of interest is 10 percent, then the pretax value per square foot of housing is $100/0.10 = $1,000. Now, suppose that housing is subject to a differential property tax rate of 10 percent. If the tax were to be fully capitalized, the market value of each square foot of housing would be reduced to $100/0.2 = $500, based on Equation 17.6 for full capitalization.

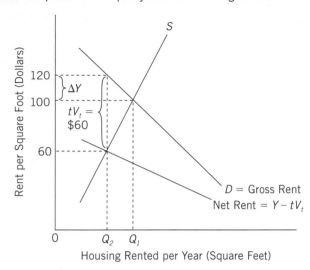

FIGURE 17.3   Impact of a Property Tax on Housing Rents

The decrease in the quantity of housing supplied per year after the property tax is imposed results in an increase in housing rents from $100 to $120 per year. The net rents received by building owners do not fall by the full amount of the annual property tax per square foot.

Suppose, however, in the long run, the decrease in the net return to housing caused by the tax reduces the annual quantity supplied from Q_1 to Q_2, as shown in Figure 17.3. This raises the annual market rent from $100 per square foot to $120 per square foot in the long run. The $20 increase in rent offsets some of the burden of the annual property tax to owners of housing. Call ΔY the increase in market rent caused by the tax-induced decrease in the quantity of housing supplied. The value of each square foot of housing now is

$$V_t = \frac{Y + \Delta Y}{r + t} = \$120/0.2 = \$600. \qquad (17.7)$$

The tax-induced increase in market rents offsets some of the tax capitalization. The market value of each square foot of housing falls by only $400 instead of $500. It follows that whenever the property tax can be shifted to tenants in the form of an increase in rents, only partial shifting takes place. Then, net rent per square foot received by building owners falls to $60. This equals the market rent of $120 less the tax of 10 percent of the new $600 value of each square foot.

Only differentials in the rate of taxation among local governments, or among classes of property within a local jurisdiction, can result in tax capitalization effects. Because the portion of the property tax common to all jurisdictions results in a decline in the return to investment (including investment in land) everywhere in the economy, it has the effect of lowering the rate of discount itself and has no effect on the relative prices of capital assets.

With a few exceptions, empirical research has indicated a marked capitalization of tax differentials among communities. Several studies also have shown that capitalization results from discriminatory taxation among various types of real estate within a given jurisdiction.[8]

CHECKPOINT

1. Why would a national tax on real estate reduce the return to all forms of investment (not only real estate)?
2. Explain how the system of local taxation of property in the United States causes resource flows across regions that can affect both land prices and the price of housing at various locations.
3. What is tax capitalization? Explain why a national property tax on all forms of wealth could not be capitalized. Under what circumstances is a property tax fully capitalized?

PROPERTY TAXATION IN THE UNITED STATES

The administration of the property tax in the United States varies from state to state and from locality to locality. A good part of the dissatisfaction with the tax, often expressed by individual citizens, stems from assessment practices and the method of payment of the tax rather than from any intrinsic deficiency in the tax itself.

The actual tax base varies greatly from state to state. Several states attempt to levy the tax on all forms of physical property, including personal property and intangible financial assets representing claims against corporations located outside of the state. Other states limit the taxable base to real estate. About two-thirds of the taxes collected are from those levied on single-family, nonfarm homes.

Assessment Practices and Effective Tax Rates

A peculiar phenomenon in the administration of the property tax is the practice of fractional assessment of property. Fractional assessment exists when real property is assessed at only a fraction of its market value. Much of the observed fractional assessment results from infrequent assessment of property in periods of rising property values. However, some fractional assessment is the result of state law.

Under fractional assessment, the property tax rate overstates the real rate of taxation. For example, if the property tax rate is nominally 3 percent but the

---

[8]See Wallace E. Oates, "The Effects of Property Taxes and Local Public Spending on Property Values: An Empirical Study of Tax Capitalization and the Tiebout Hypothesis," *Journal of Political Economy* 77 (November–December, 1969): 957–971; Larry L. Orr, "The Incidence of Differential Property Taxes on Urban Housing," *National Tax Journal* 21 (September 1968): 253–262; Albert M. Church, "Capitalization of the Effective Property Tax Rate on Single Family Residences," *National Tax Journal* 27 (March 1974): 113–122; and David N. Hyman and E. C. Pasour, Jr., "Real Property Taxes, Local Public Services, and Residential Property Values," *Southern Economic Journal* 29 (April 1973): 601–611.

PUBLIC POLICY PERSPECTIVE

Capitalization of Property Tax Rate Differentials

A number of studies have provided empirical confirmation and measurement of tax capitalization in the United States. For example, one study analyzed the impact of Proposition 13 on housing prices in northern California. Proposition 13, approved by California voters in 1978, placed a ceiling on effective property rates applied to real property under local property taxation in that state. In effect, the passage of this proposition resulted in a massive reduction in local property tax rates in California. Furthermore, the tax rate ceilings resulted in a substantial reduction in the tax rate differentials among taxing jurisdictions in the state. At the same time, the state government used its own tax revenues to maintain the level of local public services among taxing jurisdictions. The reduction in tax rate differentials resulting from the passage of Proposition 13 was expected to increase property values of homes in jurisdictions that had positive tax differentials prior to 1978.

Research by Kenneth T. Rosen has isolated the impact of the reduction in property tax differentials on housing prices in northern California.[1] His research indicates that the reduction in property tax differentials in the San Francisco Bay area were partially capitalized in the year following passage of Proposition 13. Each $1 reduction in positive property tax differentials in a high-tax jurisdiction increased home values in that jurisdiction by about $7. Nothing changed in the quality or level of government services to these local communities because the state government intervened to finance these services at the pretax reduction levels. Therefore, the observed increase in property values could be attributed entirely to the reduction in relative property tax bills. Other factors influencing property values were adjusted for conducting the statistical analysis of property values.

Another study investigated the impact of interjurisdictional differences in property tax rates applied to commercial property on the value of office buildings in the Boston metropolitan area. Research by William Wheaton supports the hypothesis that the bulk of property taxes on commercial property is borne by owners of buildings and is therefore capitalized into lower property values.[2] Wheaton argues that this is because the demand for office space in a particular area is quite elastic. Decreases in the local annual quantity of office space in response to positive property tax differentials in an area do not result in significant increases in market rents per square foot of office space. Wheaton's research confirms that positive property tax rate differentials are not associated with positive differentials in office leasing rates in the Boston metropolitan area. This provides support for the hypothesis that the incidence of property taxes on commercial property is borne by landlords and investors. Because office leasing rates do not rise substantially, only a small percentage of the tax can be shifted to consumers or workers. This research also suggests that jurisdictions where property tax rates are greater than the average of all jurisdictions in a region can expect to suffer a reduction in growth as the quantity of square feet of commercial property demanded per year declines.

[1]Kenneth T. Rosen, "The Impact of Proposition 13 on House Prices in Northern California: A Test of the Interjurisdictional Capitalization Hypothesis," *Journal of Political Economy* 90 (February 1982): 191–200.
[2]William C. Wheaton, "The Incidence of Interjurisdictional Differences in Commercial Property Taxes," *National Tax Journal* 37 (December 1984): 515–527.

assessment ratio is only 33.3 percent of true market value, then the effective rate of taxation would be merely 1 percent.

To illustrate variability in tax rates, Table 17.1 shows effective property rates in the largest city in each state and the District of Columbia, ranked according to their level of taxation in 2010, along with the nominal tax rates and assessment levels. In cases where the assessment level is less than 100 percent, the nominal tax rate overstates the effective rate of taxation. As you can see, effective tax rates varied considerably from a high of 3.04 percent in Providence, Rhode Island, to a low of 0.34 percent in Honolulu, Hawaii. The median tax rate for the cities in the sample

TABLE 17.1			Residential Property Tax Rates in the Largest City in Each State 2010		
RANK	CITY	ST	NOMINAL RATE PER $100	ASSESSMENT LEVEL	EFFECTIVE RATE PER $100
1.	Providence	RI	3.04	100.0%	3.04
2.	Louisville	KY	2.86	100.0%	2.86
3.	Indianapolis	IN	2.84	100.0%	2.84
4.	Bridgeport	CT	3.96	70.0%	2.77
5.	Philadelphia	PA	8.26	32.0%	2.64
6.	Detroit	MI	6.73	38.7%	2.60
7.	Columbus	OH	7.36	35.0%	2.58
8.	Salt Lake City	UT	2.53	100.0%	2.53
9.	Milwaukee	WI	2.53	100.0%	2.53
10.	Houston	TX	2.52	100.0%	2.52
11.	Baltimore	MD	2.27	100.0%	2.27
12.	Omaha	NE	2.18	96.0%	2.09
13.	Burlington	VT	2.03	100.0%	2.03
14.	Columbia	SC	48.93	4.0%	1.96
15.	Jacksonville	FL	1.83	100.0%	1.83
16.	Portland	ME	1.83	100.0%	1.83
17.	Wilmington	DE	3.83	47.2%	1.81
18.	Billings	MT	6.40	28.2%	1.81
19.	Memphis	TN	7.22	25.0%	1.80
20.	Newark	NJ	3.18	56.2%	1.79
21.	Manchester	NH	1.79	100.0%	1.79
22.	Atlanta	GA	4.42	40.0%	1.77
23.	Boise	ID	1.72	98.9%	1.70
24.	Des Moines	IA	3.45	48.5%	1.67
25.	Jackson	MS	16.71	10.0%	1.67
26.	Fargo	ND	38.51	4.3%	1.67
27.	Kansas City	MO	8.56	19.0%	1.63
28.	Anchorage	AK	1.57	96.0%	1.51
29.	Little Rock	AR	7.05	20.0%	1.41
30.	Wichita	KS	12.20	11.5%	1.40
31.	New Orleans	LA	13.98	10.0%	1.40
32.	Albuquerque	NM	4.11	33.3%	1.37
33.	Sioux Falls	SD	1.58	85.0%	1.34
34.	Oklahoma City	OK	11.43	11.0%	1.26
35.	Minneapolis	MN	1.27	96.8%	1.23
36.	Portland	OR	2.08	57.6%	1.20

TABLE 17.1 Continued					
RANK	CITY	ST	NOMINAL RATE PER $100	ASSESSMENT LEVEL	EFFECTIVE RATE PER $100
37.	Boston	MA	1.19	100.0%	1.19
38.	Charlotte	NC	1.30	88.9%	1.15
39.	Las Vegas	NV	3.29	35.0%	1.15
40.	Los Angeles	CA	1.12	100.0%	1.12
41.	Phoenix	AZ	9.73	10.0%	0.97
42.	Washington	DC	0.85	100.0%	0.85
43.	Seattle	WA	1.01	83.9%	0.85
44.	Charleston	WV	1.40	60.0%	0.84
45.	Virginia Beach	VA	0.89	92.9%	0.83
46.	Birmingham	AL	6.95	10.0%	0.70
47.	Cheyenne	WY	7.10	9.5%	0.67
48.	New York City	NY	17.36	3.7%	0.64
49.	Denver	CO	7.04	8.0%	0.56
50.	Chicago	IL	4.73	10.0%	0.47
51.	Honolulu	HI	0.34	100.0%	0.34
	Unweighted Average		$6.22	58.6%	$1.62
	Median		$3.18	57.6%	$1.67

Note: All rates and percentages in this table are rounded.

Effective tax rate is amount each jurisdiction considers based on assessment level used. Assessment level is ratio of assessed value to assumed market value. Nominal rate is announced rates it levied at taxable value of house.

Source: Government of the District of Columbia, Department of Finance and Revenue, Tax Rates and Tax Burdens in the District of Columbia: A Nationwide Comparison, annual.

was 1.67 percent. Such variability still prevails and is reflected in wide variation in the share of revenue raised by property taxation among states.

Taxation of Business Property

Business property is also subject to taxation under the local property tax. Local governments tax both business real estate and tangible business assets, including inventories. However, because high property taxes can discourage businesses from locating in a local jurisdiction, it is not uncommon for a local government to offer tax abatements to encourage businesses to locate their business activities within the area. Some evidence suggests that this tax competition is intensifying as state and local government jurisdictions must compete not only with each other but also with foreign sites for business location. For example, in 2000, New York City reported that it granted property tax relief to businesses amounting to $586 million or about 7 percent of city property tax revenues in order to encourage economic development!

Another problem with taxation of business property is that intangible business assets, such as trademarks, patents, and other intellectual property, generally are not subject to taxation. As production has shifted from manufacturing and other activities with taxable inventory and capital, property tax revenues can be adversely affected. Service industries also have employees with significant amounts of human capital embedded in their skills that, of course, is not subject to property taxation. The shift to services and intangible business assets as manufacturing declines in the United States could adversely affect local property tax revenue collections.

Incidence of the Property Tax in the United States

Considerable controversy exists concerning the incidence of the property tax in the United States. One point of view is that the tax is regressive with respect to income because a major portion of the tax is equivalent to a tax on the consumption of housing. However, economic theory suggests that the burden of the local property tax is likely to be progressive with respect to income.

Studies indicating that the property tax is regressive are based on a number of assumptions regarding the shifting of the tax, even though these have not been empirically verified. The studies assume that the bulk of the burden of the local property tax falls on housing. Inasmuch as housing expenditures tend to decline as a percentage of income as income rises, the effect of a major portion of the tax would appear to be regressive with respect to income. Netzer, for example, has argued that the local property tax can be viewed as analogous to a sales tax on housing.[9] Given this view of the tax and the belief that much of the tax falling on business property is reflected in higher prices, the conclusion has been that the tax is regressive with respect to income.

This view of the tax conflicts with theoretical analysis of the impact of the local property tax in the United States.[10] As discussed, much of the local property tax is reflected in a lower return to all uses of capital. Because the distribution of ownership of capital is concentrated in the hands of upper-income groups, the incidence of this portion of the tax probably is progressive with respect to income.

The local property tax also causes regional reallocation away from jurisdictions where property taxes exceed the national average and toward low-tax jurisdictions. Jurisdictions with positive property tax rate differentials above the national average suffer a reduction in annual investment. In the long run, these regions lose capital to regions with negative property tax rate differentials below the national average. The ratio of capital to land in the high-tax jurisdictions declines in the long run. This decline in the capital-land ratio lowers land rents and reduces the income of landowners in the high-tax jurisdictions. On the other hand, land rents in the low-tax jurisdictions *increase* because the capital-land ratio increases in those areas. Similarly, if labor is relatively immobile, the decline in capital in high-tax jurisdictions also can contribute to lower wages in those jurisdictions over the long run as the ratio of capital to labor declines. Conversely, wages increase in low-tax jurisdictions in response to increases in capital investment in those areas.

---

[9]See Dick Netzer, *Economics and Urban Problems*, 2nd ed. (New York: Basic Books, 1974): 249.

[10]See Mason Gaffney, "The Property Tax Is a Progressive Tax," *Proceedings of the 64th Annual Conference on Taxation*, 1971 (National Tax Association, 1972).

The evidence seems to indicate that regions with positive property tax rate differentials are those with citizens who have income that is, on average, greater than the national median income. This suggests that regions where land rents and wages are likely to fall are those in which citizens have income greater than the national median. Rent and wage declines in these areas are offset by increases in land rents and wages in areas where the property tax rates are less than the national average (negative property tax rate differentials exist). These jurisdictions are likely to be located in the poorer regions of the nation. The earnings of workers and landlords decline in the upper-income regions of the nation relative to the poorer regions as a result of the tax-induced shifts in investment. This implies that the burden of the property tax rate differentials is likely to be progressively distributed with respect to income.

The question of who bears the burden of the property tax remains controversial. Tax differentials are significant in that they range from less than 20 percent of the median rate to more than five times the average tax rate (ATR). Thus, the effect on prices of inputs other than capital is likely to be significant, because much of the tax is in the form of a differential. As with the case of corporate income tax, the incidence of the local property tax remains unresolved. Considerable disagreement remains concerning who bears the tax; it is probably shared by consumers in general, owners of capital, workers, and landlords.[11]

Tax Preferences

Despite increased reason to believe that the burden of the property tax is progressively distributed with respect to income, many states have granted special property tax relief to certain groups in recent years. Among the most common group to be singled out for such special property tax relief is the elderly.

Many often argue that the elderly find it difficult to pay property taxes because their income is much lower at retirement than it had been in the past. And, insofar as they live in homes with heavy property tax liability, they would be forced to sell those homes to pay the tax. However, in computing the eligibility of the elderly for special property tax relief, no state attempts to include the imputed value of rent accruing to the taxpayers in granting such relief.

In many cases, individuals with low money income are living in homes that are considered to be expensive at current market prices and that are owned without any mortgage debt. The real problem concerning their difficulty in meeting property tax bills is one of cash flow rather than poverty. The problem could be alleviated by allowing the state to borrow money against the value of the property in question to obtain the tax due. Then, at the death of the taxpayers, the property would be sold, with the amount pledged against taxes given to the local governments and the remainder given to the heirs of the taxpayers. In the absence of such an arrangement, any subsidy received by elderly taxpayers eventually ends up as a benefit to their heirs, who might not be in low-income groups.

In the United States, more than 30 states currently grant special property tax exemptions to the elderly or the poor. Still others make use of a *circuit-breaker* approach in the form of state income tax credits to offset some of the burden of local

[11]A recent study on property taxation in Texas concluded that county and school property taxes were proportional to slightly progressive with respect to income but city taxes were mildly regressive with respect to income. See Elizabeth Plummer, "Evidence on the Incidence of Property Taxes Across Households," *National Tax Journal* 56, 4 (December 2003): 739–753.

property taxes. The details of these various tax relief packages vary from state to state. All these packages suffer from the problem of inadequately measuring income.

LAND TAXES

A common criticism against the property tax, as administered in the United States, is that it decreases incentives for land development and redevelopment, particularly in high-tax areas. For this reason, strong support is often voiced to substitute a tax falling on land alone for the existing tax on real estate. Those who support this idea argue that it would have no excess burden and would have progressive redistributive effects. Because, in effect, the supply of land is perfectly inelastic, a tax on land results in no substitution effects. A land tax is equivalent to a lump-sum tax. That is, a national tax on land alone, with no exclusions, does not affect the quantity of land supplied to any particular area, because landowners cannot control the amount of land. Therefore, the tax induces no change in behavior to affect the quantity of land on the market. The rent earned on the land is a pure economic surplus that can be taxed without any effect on quantity supplied. The land tax reduces rents earned on the land by the full amount of the tax, and land prices fall to reflect the future tax burden.[12] As shown in Figure 17.4, a tax on land reduces gross rents received by landlords from R_G^* to R_N^*, where R_N is the gross rent less the annual property tax per acre, tV.

Taxes on land alone have a long history of advocacy in the United States. Perhaps the most important name associated with land taxation is that of Henry George (1839–1897).[13] George's ideas have led to an almost fanatical advocacy of the "single-tax doctrine" under which all taxes except those levied on land would be rescinded.[14] The tax on land then would be such as to appropriate all rents from landlords. George correctly reasoned that rent was a pure economic surplus and that its full taxation would not alter the quantity of land supplied.

George further believed that such high rates of land taxation would encourage investment in the land in the form of structures of various sorts, thereby accelerating economic development. Although the utilization of the land tax as a single tax today would scarcely yield enough revenue to finance state and local public expenditures, to say nothing of federal expenditures, many economists believe it would be an improvement over current taxation of real estate (both land and structures) because it would result in a more efficient land use pattern. To separate the value of land from the value of structures thereon, however, may be administratively difficult.

A land tax would not cause any substitution effects and therefore would have no excess burden. Land developers would be forced to develop parcels to offset the burden of the tax. The incentive would be to use land in the most efficient manner because the development of land would not directly affect the tax bill insofar as the land value can be taken to be independent of the value of structures on the land.

---

[12]Feldstein challenges the conclusion that a tax on land is fully borne by landlords. He argues that the decrease in the price of land, initially caused by the tax, results in a portfolio disequilibrium for investors. The decreased value of land increases demand for land by investors who seek to balance risk associated with holding various assets. The portfolio reallocation raises the price of land and thereby shifts part of the burden of the tax to others. The conclusion of zero excess burden remains the same. See Martin Feldstein, "The Surprising Incidence of a Tax on Pure Rent: A New Answer to an Old Question," *Journal of Political Economy* 85 (April 1977): 349–360.

[13]For a discussion of George's ideas, see Reid R. Hansen, "Henry George: Economics or Theology?" in *Property Taxation*, Richard W. Lindholm ed., 65–76.

[14]George qualified his "single-tax doctrine" to allow for taxes on liquor, gambling, and bequests, as well. See *Ibid.*, 68.

FIGURE 17.4   Impact of a Land Tax

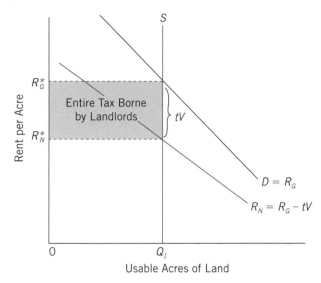

Because the supply of usable acres is fixed at Q_1, a tax on land results in no change in quantity available. The entire tax is borne by landlords as net rents received per acre fall by tV, where V is the market value of an acre and t is the tax rate.

© Cengage Learning

The historical tendency in most nations is for the value of land to decline as a percentage of gross domestic product as the economy grows. A land tax therefore can yield only relatively small amounts of revenue, even at very high tax rates.[15]

Special Treatment of Agricultural Land

Another form of fiscal relief adopted in many states in recent years is the special treatment for land used in agriculture. Such treatment consists of special provisions that commonly permit assessment of agricultural land to be based on the value of that land in agricultural use rather than on its market value. In effect, this provides benefits only for owners of farmland near urban areas, where differentials exist between the value of land in agricultural use and the value of land in urban use. In such areas, urban growth pushes the value of farmland above its value in agriculture. The objective of such special provisions for farmers is to slow down the process of urban development by subsidizing farmers so that they remain in agriculture, despite the temptation to sell their land to urban developers for prices that exceed the discounted present value of that land in current agricultural use. Many often argue that such subsidization also would benefit urban residents by preserving open space near the city and improving urban environmental quality. Further, many assert that such provisions provide benefits to poor farmers, who otherwise might not remain in farming.

In many cases, however, the farmer finds that the best alternative, in terms of maximizing income, is still to sell the land to urban developers, despite the subsidy that would be received by remaining in agriculture. Even though many states

---

[15]For an estimate of the revenue that might be obtained by taxing all rents, see *Ibid.*, 70.

require that farmers who sell their land to developers pay back taxes equal to the subsidies that they received when holding their land in agricultural use, many farmers still decide to sell.

CHECKPOINT

1. What is fractional assessment?
2. What issues must be resolved to uncover the actual incidence of the system of local property taxes used in the United States?
3. Why will a tax on land be fully capitalized and result in zero excess burden?

PROPERTY TRANSFER TAXES

Property transfer taxes include estate, inheritance, and gift taxes. These taxes are levied on transfers of wealth among citizens. Property transfer taxes represent a feasible method of taxing accumulations of wealth that normally escape other forms of taxation. When wealth is transferred at time of death, the government supervises the administration of the bequest. Because reasonably accurate data exist on the accumulation of wealth, it is relatively easy for the government to levy taxes on wealth accumulations transferred from one generation to another.

Estate, Inheritance, and Gift Taxes

Estate and inheritance taxes are sometimes referred to as *death duties*. They are levied essentially as excise taxes on the rights to transfer property at time of death. The federal government levies taxes on property transfers before death as well in the form of gift taxation. Federal death taxes are levied on taxable estates.

Federal estate taxes in 2009 accounted for about 1 percent of total federal revenue. Although levied according to a fairly progressive rate scale, the tax allows many exemptions. It allows, for example, a generous basic exemption, plus other specific deductions and exemptions, and taxes the remainder according to a progressive rate structure. Included among the specific deductions from the tax base are legal and funeral expenses, debts, and charitable contributions. In addition, estates may be left to the surviving spouse, exempt of all taxes. When the surviving spouse dies, the remainder of the estate presumably is bequeathed to the remaining heirs.

In the absence of a federal gift tax, all estate taxes could be avoided by transferring property prior to death. The federal gift tax prevents such avoidance to some degree. Gift taxes are levied on the individual who makes the gift. Since 1977, the rates and lifetime exemptions that apply to gifts have been the same as those existing under the estate tax for a combined base of gifts and estates.

Most states levy taxes on inheritances. These taxes are the liabilities of the beneficiaries of the estate. Many often argue that this is a more equitable property transfer tax because the effective tax rates can be correlated with the ability of the heirs to pay. Furthermore, higher exemptions and lower effective tax rates are generally allowed to closer relatives of the deceased.

TABLE 17.2	Federal Estate Tax Maximum Rates and Exemptions, 2005–2012	
YEAR	HIGHEST ESTATE AND GIFT TAX RATE (%)	AMOUNT EXEMPT FROM ESTATE TAX ($)
2005	47	1.5 million
2006	46	2 million
2007	45	2 million
2008	45	2 million
2009	45	3.5 million
2010	Top Individual Income Tax Rate for Gift Tax Only, Estate Tax Repealed.	
2011	35	5 million
2012	35	5.12 million

© Cengage Learning

Legislation enacted in 2001 phased out the federal estate tax in the United States. The amount of funds transferred at death exempt from taxation was increased in steps. Estate tax rates were also reduced in phases. The tax was fully repealed by 2010. The estate tax was reinstated by Congress in 2011 but there remain political pressures to repeal it permanently.

Table 17.2 shows the federal estate tax rates for 2005 through 2012 based on the law in effect in 2012. The top tax rate in 2012 fell from the 50 percent rate that was in effect in 2002 to 35 percent. The amount exempt from the estate and gift tax rose from the $1 million that was in effect in 2002 to $5.12 million in 2012.

The *American Taxpayer Relief Act of 2012* increased the maximum federal tax rate on estates to 40 percent and introduced an annual inflation-adjusted $5 million (based on 2011 dollars) exclusion for the estates of decedents effective in 2013.

Critics of repealing the tax argue that its repeal will largely benefit a few rich families and contribute to increased regressiveness of the tax system with respect to income. The U.S. Department of Treasury estimated that in 1998 of a total of $20.3 billion of tax revenue collected from the estate tax in that year, $4.4 billion, about 22 percent, came from 374 estates valued at more than $20 million each. In 1998, more than half of the estate tax was from 3,000 estates valued at $5 million or more. However, the proportion of estates paying the tax has increased sharply from about one-half of 1 percent in the mid-1980s to more than 2 percent in the late 1990s.[16] Property transfer taxes can be avoided by establishing trusts that are not subject to estate taxation until dissolved. Wealthy individuals make extensive use of this provision. In addition, bequests to charitable foundations are deductible, without limit, from the tax base.

Economic Effects

Estate and gift taxes represent levies on accumulated wealth. They can be viewed as taxes on accumulated savings that reduce the return to savings when that wealth is

---

[16]For a discussion of issues in repeal of the estate tax see William B. Gale and Joel Slemrod, "Rhetoric and Economics in the Estate Tax Debate," *National Tax Journal* 54 (September 2001): 613–617. Gale and Slemrod point out that the estate tax in the United States is a highly progressive tax paid mainly by the richest 2 percent of the population.

transferred. Some people argue that it is a good idea to tax gifts and estates as transfers to the heirs because they are not taxed as income to the recipients. Remember, the U.S. tax code flatly declares that gifts and other transfers are *not* income despite the fact that they would be included in income under the Haig–Simons definition. You also can argue that a gift or inheritance will have an income effect that is unfavorable to the work effort of its recipient. An estate (or inheritance) tax along with a gift tax could have the desirable social effect of reducing the undesirable income effect to the recipient of the transfer by reducing the amount of the net transfer.

However, high estate and inheritance taxes could adversely affect the work incentives of prospective donors. For example, if you wanted to leave a large fortune to your children, you might think twice about it if you knew that half of everything you worked hard for would be taxed away at your death rather than transferred to your chosen heirs. The tax has a substitution effect that is unfavorable to the work effort of prospective donors. However, the estate tax also has an income effect on the work incentive of prospective donors. If you stubbornly wanted to leave $1 million to your children, you might work *harder* because of the estate tax so that you could accumulate that amount *after taxes* to bequeath to your heirs! Because estate taxes have both income and substitution effects on the incentives of donors, we really can't predict the effect that the tax would have on their incentives to work and save.

However, estate taxes also can have an effect on the way that a donor transfers wealth to heirs. The estate, gift, and inheritance taxes are levied only on transfers of financial wealth and physical capital such as real estate. A prospective donor could avoid the tax by investing heavily in his or her children's education rather than by accumulating savings in taxable form that would be subject to the tax when transferred. Thus, very high property transfer taxes could encourage overinvestment in human capital.

Wealth transfer taxes are levied on the wealth itself rather than as income of the recipient of the transfer. Separate taxation of wealth transfers would be less desirable if a comprehensive income tax were used. Under a comprehensive income tax, any transfer received would be treated as income to the recipient, and it would be taxed accordingly. Under progressive taxation, treatment of the transfer as income could have the effect of taxing large transfers heavily—to the extent that they would push the recipient into high tax brackets. The effective tax rates on accumulated capital probably would be much higher than is currently the case with estate and gift taxes, which tax the transfer as wealth, rather than as income to the recipients. Thus, the tax on the transfer is lower than would be the case if it were treated as capital income to the recipient.

Although many argue that generally an estate tax is necessary to reduce inequality of income, it can actually increase income inequality if saving is responsive to the tax rates for the estate tax. This is because the tax, insofar as it reduces capital accumulation, reduces capital-labor ratios in the long run, thereby reducing labor productivity and income. This has the effect of increasing the share of income going to capital in the long run.

It is also possible that the estate tax in the United States provides incentives for charitable donations. These donations are deductible from the estate tax liability. A significant portion of charitable giving in the United States is at death, as a portion of a decedent's estate is willed to organizations that qualify for charitable tax status. Reduction in rates or elimination of an estate tax could reduce charitable giving.[17]

[17]See Jon M. Bakija, William G. Gale, and Joel B. Slemrod, "Charitable Bequests and Taxes on Inheritance and Estates: Aggregate Evidence from across States and Time," *American Economic Review* 93 (May 2003): 366–370.

SUMMARY

General wealth taxes are levied on all forms of wealth, while selective property taxes are levied only on certain forms of wealth. Most of the revenue collected through property taxation in the United States comes from the real estate tax.

Determining the value of wealth that is infrequently traded is one of the most difficult aspects of property taxation. A comprehensive wealth tax is difficult to administer because of problems involved in measuring all forms of wealth, especially human wealth. The estimation of the value of an asset is called assessment. Accurate assessment closely approximates the market value of an asset. Property must be reassessed periodically to reflect changing market values.

Compared with equal-yield general taxes levied on the alternative economic bases of income and consumption, a general wealth tax is more detrimental to saving incentive but less detrimental to work incentive. If the supply of savings is perfectly inelastic, a general wealth tax is borne by owners of capital. The tax can be shifted only when the quantity of savings supplied is responsive to changes in its return.

The process through which the prices of taxed assets fall in value relative to untaxed assets is called tax capitalization. In tax capitalization, the full burden of future tax payments is concentrated on owners of taxed wealth at the time the tax is initially levied. If the property tax results in decreases in real estate investment so that rent is raised, the depressing effect that the tax has on asset prices may be offset.

The property tax in the United States tends to reduce the return to capital in all uses. The positive property tax differentials among communities are reflected in lower land rents and lower wages in areas where investment declines. Tax-induced reduction in investment in new housing and in local goods and services also can contribute to higher prices for housing and other goods and services. Although considerable controversy concerns the incidence of the property tax, many economists now believe that its effects on the distribution of income are progressive.

LOOKING AHEAD

The property tax is the main source of tax financing for local governments. Part 5 considers questions of public finance and government expenditures within the context of a federal system. The advantages and disadvantages of decentralized government compared with those of centralized government are extensively examined in Chapter 18. Intergovernmental fiscal relations and local fiscal problems also are discussed in Chapter 18.

KEY CONCEPTS

Assessment

Comprehensive Wealth Tax

Property Tax Rate Differentials

Real Estate or Real Property

Stock

Tax Capitalization

Wealth

REVIEW QUESTIONS

1. Explain why a comprehensive wealth tax is equivalent to a tax on the annual return to savings. If the annual return to holding wealth is 10 percent, calculate the tax rate on annual savings and investments associated with a 1 percent wealth tax.

2. How is the tax base defined for a comprehensive wealth tax? What are some of the problems associated with measuring wealth? Why would inclusion of the assets of corporations and outstanding corporate stock double-count the wealth of corporations?

3. Who bears the incidence of a general wealth tax when the interest elasticity of supply of savings is zero? Why is the incidence most likely to be progressive?

4. How can a general wealth tax be shifted to workers and consumers when the aggregate supply of saving is not perfectly inelastic? What effect does the tax have on the work-leisure choice? What are the consequences of excluding human capital from the tax base?

5. Why is a national tax on real estate likely to be at least partially borne by owners of all forms of capital regardless of the use to which that capital is put?

6. How can property tax differentials be shifted to others who do not own capital? Why is the average property tax rate likely to be borne by owners of all forms of capital?

7. Suppose the discount rate is 10 percent. Calculate the tax capitalization resulting from a property tax rate differential of 5 percent above the national average for an asset with a $5,000 annual income before taxation, assuming that the tax is fully capitalized and that the asset has an infinite life.

8. Under what circumstances will a property tax be only partially capitalized?

9. Suppose property in state X is assessed at 60 percent of its market value and the nominal property tax rate is 4 percent. Calculate the effective tax rate.

10. Why is the property tax often asserted to be regressive with respect to income in the United States? Do you agree with this view?

PROBLEMS

1. The annual return to savings is currently $100 billion per year in a certain nation. The estimated value of wealth in the nation is $1 trillion. Calculate the percentage gross return to savings. Assuming that the supply of saving is perfectly inelastic, calculate the impact of a 1 percent tax on wealth on the gross and net percentage return to savings. How would your answer differ if the interest elasticity of supply of savings were positive rather than zero?

2. Suppose you were appointed economic advisor to a less-developed nation in Africa. The nation seeks to encourage capital formation and wants to increase the rate of saving of its own residents and encourage foreigners to invest in their nation. What role would you assign to property taxes in this nation to achieve its objectives?

3. A parcel of land is expected to yield annual rents equal to $10,000 per year forever. If the market rate of interest is 10 percent, calculate the market price of the parcel. Suppose you purchase the parcel of land. After your purchase, a 5 percent property tax on the land is imposed. Calculate the impact of the tax on the market value of the land parcel. Can you avoid the tax by selling the land?

4. Suppose, as a result of the imposition of a 5 percent local property tax, the rent on a parcel of property increases from $12,000 to $12,500 per year. Assuming that the current rate of discount is 8 percent and that the property will last forever, calculate the value of the property before and after the imposition of the tax. How much of the tax is capitalized and how much of it is shifted to others rather than absorbed by the owner of the property at the time the tax is imposed?

5. Go to Table 17.1 and find the property tax rate for the largest city in your state. Is that rate above or below the national average? If it is above the national average, what effect on property values is likely? If it is below the average, what effect is likely to result? Why is the national average property tax rate likely to affect the return to capital in investments other than real estate?

ADDITIONAL READING

Aaron, Henry J. *Who Pays the Property Tax?* Washington, D.C.: The Brookings Institution, 1975. An analysis of the incidence of the property tax.

Lindholm, Richard W., ed. *Property Taxation: U.S.A.* Madison: University of Wisconsin Press, 1967. A collection of papers on the history and administration of and problems in using property taxes.

Mieszkowski, Peter M. "The Property Tax: An Excise Tax or a Profits Tax?" *Journal of Public Economics* 1 (April 1972): 73–96. A provocative and influential analysis of the impact of the property tax as used in the United States.

Wallace E. Oates, ed. *Property Taxation and Local Government Finance*, Cambridge Mass.: Lincoln Institute of Land Policy, 2001. A collection of essays on the property tax as used in the United States.

Zodrow, George W. "The Property Tax as a Capital Tax: A Room with Three Views." *National Tax Journal* 54, 1 (March 2001): 139–156. A comparison and analysis of theories about the incidence of the property tax in the United States.

INTERNET RESOURCE

http://www.census.gov
The home page of the Census Bureau of the U.S. Department of Commerce can be used to access information on taxable property values by state and to obtain Census Bureau reports on property taxes and local finance.

Most cities and counties in the United States now have information on the World Wide Web. Look up the Internet home page for your city or county government to find information on property tax rates in your region. For example, to find information on Raleigh, North Carolina, go to http://www.raleighnc.gov

PartFive

STATE AND LOCAL GOVERNMENT FINANCE

CHAPTER 18 Fiscal Federalism and State and Local Government Finance

Chapter 18

FISCAL FEDERALISM AND STATE AND LOCAL GOVERNMENT FINANCE

LEARNING OBJECTIVES

After reading this chapter, you should be able to:

- Define the concept of fiscal federalism, and discuss issues relating to the supply of public goods in a multilevel system of government.

- Use the Tiebout model of supply for local public goods in a system of decentralized governments to analyze the relationship between local government finance and location decisions.

- Explain the consequences of interjurisdictional externalities.

- Describe how the elasticity of local tax bases acts as a constraint on state and local government tax policy.

- Discuss variation in fiscal capacity among state and local governments, intergovernmental grants, the impact of grants on resource allocation, and current fiscal problems of state and local governments in the United States.

Most of you rely on state and local governments to provide road maintenance, criminal justice, police and fire protection, and primary and secondary education. State and local governments also are active in the provision of health care to the needy and the subsidization of higher education. The federal government assists state and local governments in performing their functions. Federal grants to state and local governments finance nearly a quarter of the outlays of those governments in the aggregate. These grants account for more than 16 percent of the federal government's total budget. However, many of these grants go to individuals in the form of mandated programs, such as Medicaid and Temporary Assistance to Needy Families (TANF), that provide support to the poor. In fact, nearly two-thirds of federal grants to state and local governments finance income support in cash or in-kind to eligible citizens.

Since the 1980s, our intergovernmental system has come under increased fiscal discipline. On the state and local government level in the 1990s, taxpayer resistance to higher tax rates and political demands for reduced taxes have also put a cap on the growth of government spending. Open-ended programs, such as income support to the poor, are now capped through a system of block grants to the states that limits annual federal spending. State governments now have considerable leeway in policies to deal with poor families to help them become self-sufficient in a new environment that limits eligibility for income support to a maximum of five years for each aid recipient.

On the state and local government levels, there is a push to privatize many government services or achieve greater self-finance of such government enterprises as roads, recreational facilities, and university education through user charges. As a result, many of you are now paying higher tuitions to attend state universities and higher tolls to use bridges and roads around major cities. Increasingly, governments contract with private firms to provide such services as trash pickup, security, toll collection, and even administrative tasks. If we exclude payroll taxes, state and local governments, in the aggregate, now collect about the same amount of revenue as the federal government to finance their activities. The balance of power and responsibility between state and local governments and the federal government will certainly be more equal in the 21st century than it has been at any other time in the nation's history.

In 2009, most state governments were experiencing sharp declines in revenues as a result of a major recession that increased unemployment rates and reduced both incomes and consumption. Shortfalls of revenue relative to spending forced many state governments to cut spending and search for new sources of revenue. As state and local governments bear more of the responsibility for public services, they are being forced to look for ways to balance their budgets as is required in most cases by state laws. In fiscal year 2009, 42 states used across-the-board spending cuts to ease revenue shortfalls. Fiscal year 2010 was proving to be very difficult for state governments with over three-quarters of the states forced to cut their budgets because of revenue shortfalls. Many states were laying off or furloughing workers, and some states were cutting basic programs such as education and public safety. Given the slow recovery from the recession of 2007–2009, most state budgets were impacted as a result of revenue shortfalls in fiscal years 2011 and 2012, and many have already taken measures to raise taxes to avoid draconian cuts in state government services.

Most states have refrained so far from cutting such basic services as education, Medicaid, and public safety. However, as citizen resistance to tax increases remains strong, some states are even beginning to cut funding for these basic services.

In 2009, the *American Reconstruction and Reinvestment Act* had provisions that provided funds to state and local governments to ease the effects of the recession on their budgets. A total of $8.8 billion in block grants was allocated to state governments to offset the effects of recession-induced budget cuts on state services. Another $4 billion was allocated to assist state law enforcement agencies. In addition, provisions of the Act to fund infrastructure and education directly or indirectly assisted state governments in dealing with the fiscal crisis brought on by the recession. Most of this special assistance from the federal government expired in 2012. As of 2012, Medicaid expenditures were still straining most state budgets and many state and local governments remained under extreme fiscal pressure to cut expenditures.

In this final chapter, we examine some of the issues involved in state and local government finance in a federal system. We discuss theoretical issues relating to the division of responsibility for supplying public goods among various levels of government. We also examine such practical issues as the problems of local government in raising revenues and the implications of reduced federal aid to state and local governments.

FISCAL FEDERALISM

The United States has a **federal system of government** characterized by numerous levels of government, each with its own powers to provide services and raise revenue. The levels of government can be divided into three broad categories: federal or central, state, and local. The various local governments range from large counties and cities with populations in the millions to small towns and special districts with fewer than 1,000 citizens.

A multilevel governing system raises some interesting and important questions. What is the most efficient allocation of responsibilities among alternative levels of government? In general, the more decentralized the government, the greater is the opportunity for expressing the desire for various kinds of government services and for obtaining the means to finance those services. However, diversity can be accompanied by fragmented or noncoordinated collective decision making among jurisdictions. In addition, government provision of services on a small scale often results in higher average costs because all economies of scale cannot be realized.

Fiscal federalism is the division of taxing and expenditure functions among levels of government. Economic theory offers some insights into the consequences of alternative arrangements for supplying public goods and services and for financing them among the various levels of government. In general, collective choices by citizens will probably result in the central government's undertaking of those functions most likely to have benefits that are collectively consumed on the national level. Accordingly, in most nations, the supply and finance of armed forces is observed as a central government function. All citizens, regardless of their location, collectively benefit from national defense and other public services that have the characteristics of pure public goods. They can reasonably be expected to agree to a national public choice arrangement for determining the level of such services and a system of finance in which all citizens pay a share for such services, independent of the region or locality in which they reside.

Many government-supplied services require central coordination and can be costly or impossible to provide in a decentralized way by local governments. It is almost inconceivable to expect a local or state government to undertake its own economic stabilization program. Such programs would be doomed to failure by virtue of the simple fact that the economic base for state and local governments is heavily dependent on those in other regions of the nation. Any attempt by state and local governments to alleviate inflation and unemployment within their own borders, either by adjusting aggregate demand through fiscal policy or monetary demand through restrictions on credit, will do little to solve these problems because much of the spending by local citizens will be for goods and services produced in other states. Increased demand that results from a tax reduction in one state is likely to provide increased income in all states, because citizens spend only a fraction of their income on locally produced goods.

No one state can control its own inflation and unemployment rates because these are tied to events in national markets that cannot in any way be controlled by the economic policies of the state or the locality. Monetary and fiscal policies can be more effectively implemented by a national government.

Similarly, attempts by local or state governments to engage in social programs that significantly redistribute income among their citizens are likely to result in resource flows that limit the effectiveness of such programs. Although state and local governments do redistribute income among citizens with some degree of success, these programs are likely to entail efficiency losses higher than those that would be encountered if the central government undertook the same level of redistribution. This is because it is easier to avoid state and local taxes than federal taxes and because the availability of transfers at one location as opposed to others is likely to induce in-migration of eligible recipients. As a result, the costs to finance a given amount of redistribution per recipient probably will be higher than anticipated, as the tax base declines due to out-migration of local resources and as the number of eligible recipients rises due to in-migration.

A national income redistribution program would be less wasteful because it would not encourage migration of eligible recipients in response to differential transfer payments among jurisdictions. The taxes necessary to finance collectively agreed-upon transfers would be impossible to avoid by changing the location of personal residence within the nation. Opportunities for a centralized governing authority to redistribute income are less limited than those for local governments, principally because the mobility of resources between nations is much less than mobility among areas within a nation.[1]

The Supply of Local Public Goods in a Federal System

Local public goods are public goods with benefits that are nonrival only for that portion of the national population who live within a certain geographical area. Such goods and services are likely to be most effectively produced by local governing units. Local governments are likely to be formed almost exclusively for producing such goods and services and financing them by taxes that are paid entirely by local residents. Among the services that are likely to result in locally consumed collective benefits are police and fire protection, public sanitation and refuse collection,

---

[1]A strong case for centralized supply of stabilization and redistributive programs is made by Oates. See Wallace E. Oates, *Fiscal Federalism* (New York: Harcourt Brace Jovanovich, 1972), Chapter 1. However, some basis does exist for a limited role by noncentral governments in supplying these two services. For an analysis of the desirability of local government participation in stabilization and redistribution programs, see Albert Breton and Anthony Scott, *The Economic Constitution of Federal States* (Toronto: University of Toronto Press, 1978).

GLOBAL PERSPECTIVE

Fiscal Federalism in the European Union

The European Union (EU) is an economic and political partnership between 27 European countries of which 17 (called the euro zone countries) share the same currency. Although there is a European Parliament located in Brussels, Belgium, as well as a European Commission and European Council, there is really no central government for the member nations. The EU does not have a framework for fiscal federalism as it exists in the United States of America.

The European Union cannot be viewed as a "United States of Europe" as it is currently set up. It is, instead, a loose confederation of sovereign nations whose citizens speak different languages and have their own separate legal systems. There is no real central authority with powers to enforce laws, make foreign policy, or supply public services. Even the European Central Bank does not have the same regulatory authority that the Federal Reserve System has in the United States. And although the euro zone countries share the same currency, the risk of default on sovereign debt in several of these nations is causing doubt that the single currency will survive.

A comparison of fiscal federalism as it exists in the United States of America and other nations with that existing in the European Union shows that federalism is lacking in the confederation of European nations. The administrative bodies of the European Union do wield significant regulatory power in such areas as environmental protection and antitrust enforcement. Most of the regulation of productive activity and industrial standardization rules emanate from laws enacted by the European Parliament and are administered by the European Commission based on priorities established by the European Council, which meets four times each year. However, regulation is basically the only power the EU central authority possesses.

The EU has no power to tax. It does not provide national defense services, social insurance, and police protection, nor does it have its own foreign policy. Instead each member state in the EU has its own military, social security system, foreign policy, health insurance system, and safety net of income support for its citizens. The basic central government functions that exist in the United States are instead functions of the sovereign nations that compose the EU. The function of the EU central government is only regulation of intercountry externalities and direct regulation of productive activities across borders. The EU bureaucracy plays no role in education policy and provision of infrastructure. It lacks the powers to impact the legal systems of sovereign nation members in any significant way. EU activities are financed primarily by contributions (more like dues) from member nations, and these are capped at only a little more than 1 percent of GDP of each member nation. The bureaucracy that runs the European Commission in Brussels, Belgium, amounts to a small force no bigger than a typical European city government.

Finally, political decisions regarding regulation and any other political actions undertaken by the EU typically require the unanimous consent of member nations or at least a supermajority of 70 percent or more of representatives in the European Parliament. The collective choice rule of unanimity or close to unanimity makes it very difficult for the EU to enact legislation. Even the representatives of the smallest EU nations can effectively veto legislation that adversely affects citizens of their nations.

In short, as it is currently set up, the European Union cannot really be regarded as a central government with the power possessed by federal governments such as that of the United States of America. It is also unlikely that the member nations of the EU will ever give up their sovereign powers to control such central government functions as national defense, social security, income support, health and foreign policy to the EU Parliament and Commission in Brussels.

traffic control and roads, water and sewer services, and educational services. Similarly, services that are typically financed by state governments result in collectively consumed benefits on a somewhat larger scale, such as state road networks, bridges, a share of educational programs, highway patrols, and certain social services.

The main advantage of local and regional supply and finance of government-provided services is that it allows the system of governments to accommodate a wide array of tastes and demands for their services in accordance with local variations in demand patterns and cost conditions. Each local governing unit with its own political institutions can articulate the demands for government-supplied services within its own collective choice process. This adds great flexibility to the political process and allows citizens the option of locating their residences with at least some consideration of the types of government-provided services offered at alternative locations. In fact, citizens with similar tastes in certain public services tend to congregate together and form local governments.

Thus, communities whose citizens have strong preferences for recreation can choose to tax themselves to pay for parks and other public recreational facilities. Other communities, whose citizens are relatively more interested in the arts, can choose collectively to have few public parks and instead use significant amounts of their resources for public concerts, art exhibits, and libraries. In a sense, the political process is most efficient when individuals of relatively similar preferences congregate in local communities, where they can best satisfy their preferences for public services. Under these conditions, both transactions costs and external costs of political action are likely to be low.

CENTRALIZED VERSUS DECENTRALIZED GOVERNMENT

National versus Local Political Equilibria

Under centralized government, collective choices on government-provided services are made nationally. Central provision of these services tends to result in uniformity of the quality and quantity of public goods across all regions of a nation. The resulting collective choices represent national political equilibria. Under centralized provision of government-supplied services, all citizens vote on the quantity and kinds of services to be supplied at all locations. If such choices are made under majority rule, the resulting equilibrium is likely to reflect the preferences of the median national voter (see Chapter 5).

A national consensus on the amount of public goods with truly national collective benefits is necessary because those goods, when provided, are consumed by all residents, independent of the location of their residence. With local public goods (those with geographically constrained collective benefits), a national consensus on the amount to provide makes less sense, because when these goods are produced, they are consumed by only a subset of the population. For such goods, decentralized decision making provides the advantage of taking into account variations in preferences for those goods among residents of specific communities. Allowing local public choice of the amount of these goods provides more flexibility and improves efficiency because government output then can respond to variations in tastes.

Under decentralized collective choices made by majority rule, the political equilibrium reflects the median most-preferred outcome of local voters. The quantity and kinds of government-provided services preferred by these voters can vary considerably across regions and might be very different from the median most-preferred outcome of all national voters on similar issues.

The means of financing government-provided services can vary with local desires when government is decentralized. Communities with strong interests in encouraging certain types of development, such as housing or new industry, can adapt their tax structures to provide incentives to achieve those goals. Similarly, insofar as notions of fairness in taxation vary across jurisdictions, a decentralized system of government can adjust its tax structure to attain those objectives.

However, as will be made clear presently, the tax and expenditure decisions in one governing jurisdiction are not independent of those in other jurisdictions. Within a system of decentralized government, citizens can be viewed as "shopping" for places to reside. Their locational decisions are influenced, in part, by the menu of services and the associated taxes at alternative local government jurisdictions. By the same token, local governments can find their goals upset by reactions to their local political decisions. For example, a local jurisdiction that tries to tax the rich heavily while excusing the poor from taxes might find that its population mix changes over time as the rich leave, or choose not to reside there, while the poor flock in.

An Example

At the extreme, imagine a group of individuals who have similar tastes and who live together in a local community, each one of whom places a zero benefit on tennis courts. In such a community, under decentralized, local collective decision making, an election to consider government provision of such a good would receive no votes. In fact, it would be unlikely that any resident would even propose that such an issue be put up for vote, because a locally provided tennis court would benefit no one in town. If, however, the number of tennis courts per town were decided in a national election, with given tax shares under majority rule, the outcome would be the national median most-preferred number of tennis courts per town.

If the preferred number of tennis courts per town in other communities is greater than zero, the resultant equilibrium is likely to be some positive number of tennis courts. This means that residents in the town where no one wants tennis courts, even at zero price, would be forced to submit to construction of tennis courts in their town and to pay taxes to finance those tennis courts. Such an outcome is not efficient, and welfare can be improved by allowing each town to decide locally whether collectively to provide and finance such services. This assumes that tennis courts are local public goods and that no one living in other communities would be harmed or benefited in any way by the choice of a particular community to forgo tennis courts.

For certain government-provided services that have the characteristics of pure national public goods, uniformity across all regions is inevitable, and centralized provision of uniform amounts of such services in all locations is efficient relative to local government attempts to supply diverse services. The opportunities for local diversity in national defense, economic stabilization, and income redistribution programs are nil, or at best limited, as discussed previously.

Advantages of a Federal System of Government

The central problem of fiscal federalism is to understand the process by which various government functions are paired with various levels of government. This, in turn, requires an investigation of the linkage between the geographical portion of the population that makes collective choices on various public goods, the legal boundaries of political jurisdictions, and the range of external benefits for various government-supplied services. Likewise, given the size of government and the variation in tastes among citizens and regions, the variation in costs of producing government services also must be studied. In a normative sense, the problem of fiscal federalism is to find the efficient pairing of responsibility for deciding how much of and what kinds of government-provided goods and services to produce with geographically defined subsets of the population.[2]

CHECKPOINT

1. What resource allocation issues are relevant to fiscal federalism?
2. What are local public goods?
3. What are the advantages of a federal system of government?

CITIZEN MOBILITY AND DECENTRALIZED GOVERNMENT

A **political jurisdiction** is a defined geographical area within which individuals make collective choices on government functions and government-provided services. Each political jurisdiction has a governing authority and its own political institutions. In a federal system of government, political jurisdictions are both centralized and decentralized. This provides both a national, or central, government as well as lower levels of government. Each citizen is within the jurisdiction of the central government. Lower levels of government represent subsets of the population, defined in terms of geographic boundaries. Only citizens of local political jurisdictions can participate in public choices that affect the provision of government-supplied services in that jurisdiction. Also, taxes to finance locally provided government services are paid mainly by residents of the political jurisdiction.

The Tiebout Model

Some useful insights into government expenditures within such a decentralized system of local jurisdictions are obtained from a classic model developed by Charles M. Tiebout.[3] Tiebout points out that the level and mix of local expenditures and taxes are likely to exhibit wide variations among local political jurisdictions. Therefore, many citizens will choose to live in communities where the government budget best satisfies their own preferences for public services, provided they are not restricted in their mobility among communities. Thus, government expenditure and revenue

---

[2]See David E. Wildasin, "The Institutions of Federalism: Toward an Analytical Framework," *National Tax Journal* 57, 2 (June 2004): 247–272.

[3]Charles M. Tiebout, "A Pure Theory of Local Expenditures," *Journal of Political Economy* 64 (October 1956): 416–424.

patterns tend to be set on the local level, and the mobile citizen maximizes personal well-being by choosing to live in some particular political jurisdiction.

The Tiebout model assumes that all citizens are fully mobile among communities and possess full knowledge of the government budgets in alternative political jurisdictions. Many communities offer similar employment opportunities to citizens. An optimal community size is defined as that which corresponds to minimum unit costs of government services. Communities larger than the optimal size try to discourage new residents, while communities smaller than the optimal size attempt to attract new residents.

Under this set of restrictive assumptions, a quasi-market equilibrium is attained when all residents are located in the community that best satisfies their political preferences, subject to the constraint that all communities are providing government services at minimum unit costs. The constraint implies that some citizens might have to be content with a second-choice community. If all communities can supply government services at constant costs, implying no economies or diseconomies of scale, then equilibrium will be completely analogous to a market equilibrium. This is because, in the extreme case, an iconoclast can establish a one-person community that provides all the government services he or she requires, and an infinite number of communities is available to satisfy every citizen's preferences. In this situation, competition among communities would result in an efficient solution similar to that produced by a perfectly competitive market economy.

Applicability of the Tiebout Model

Although the Tiebout model's basic assumptions are extremely restrictive, it does offer insights into some of the unique problems of government expenditure analysis within a decentralized context. Citizens are not completely mobile among communities and often they possess only imperfect knowledge of local government budgets. Although there are a large number of communities within the federal system, they differ in their employment opportunities and in geographical and climatic conditions. That is, many factors other than political preferences for government expenditure are likely to affect the locational choices of citizens. The Tiebout model is relevant, though, because, at least at the margin, some households do respond to differences among government budgets in alternative communities.

In particular, the model appears to be useful in partially explaining the exodus of households from the central city to surrounding suburban communities that has occurred in the United States since the end of World War II. Clearly, mobility of households is not perfect. But, within a constrained geographic area, a citizen can change his or her place of residence to one in a neighboring political jurisdiction while maintaining his or her employment in his or her old political jurisdiction. The proliferation of private automobiles in the post-war era and generally improved roads made such moves relatively easy.

In part, citizens are motivated to move to smaller political jurisdictions in the suburbs of central cities because of lower tax rates and better-quality, government-provided services, such as schools, relative to those prevailing in the central cities. This is in accord with the basic tenets of the Tiebout hypothesis. Thus, the model is useful in explaining movements within a constrained geographic area constituting one relatively large labor market. It is not very useful in explaining moves across larger geographic areas, such as interstate, because of the impediments to mobility and the variety of other factors that influence locational choices.

Interjurisdictional Externalities and Locational Choices

Interjurisdictional externalities are costs or benefits of local government goods and services to residents who live in other political jurisdictions. These interjurisdictional externalities create problems for efficient operation of a federal system of governments because they result in benefits or costs that spill across the geographic boundaries of political jurisdictions. Interjurisdictional externalities also complicate the Tiebout model, because they cause residents of local communities to make decisions based on inadequate data. The Tiebout approach implies that local taxes are analogous to prices for local government services. Citizens who desire high quality and quantity of government services gravitate to those communities with relatively higher tax rates. The model suggests that citizens shop for a set of local government services in much the same manner as they shop for automobiles. Their choices of communities as residence sites depend on tax rates, local government services financed by revenues, and relative preferences for government and private expenditures. If, however, all government services are not financed through taxes on local bases, the alternative community tax rates do not accurately reflect the costs of those services and cannot be considered the full prices for such services. Furthermore, when local jurisdictions receive state or federal aid, the prices paid by residents are subsidized by higher levels of government.

The deduction of state and local taxes from the federal income tax base is an example of a cost spillover that enables local communities to finance their government services through a reduction in federal income tax collections. Thus, where there are spillover costs and benefits of local government activities, the competition among local governments is less likely to achieve efficiency.

A Recapitulation

In summary, the ability of households to express their preferences for alternative local government budgets by "voting on their feet" provides a partial explanation of residential choices in a constrained metropolitan area that comprises a relatively large labor market. The Tiebout model suggests that citizens choose their residence among communities solely on the basis of their demand for local public goods. The Tiebout equilibrium is efficient because, given personal demands for public services, no single voter can be made better off by moving to another political jurisdiction. The model implies that citizens of similar tastes congregate together in communities based on their preferences for local public goods.

Impediments to mobility on the regional and national levels, chiefly due to restrictions in employment opportunities, make the conclusions of the Tiebout model questionable if applied to regional residential choices.

Local taxes are not likely to be an accurate measure of the prices for local government services because of the existence of spillover costs and benefits. All these factors result in an equilibrium residential choice pattern that is not efficient. At any point in time, some persons are dissatisfied with their current political jurisdiction but for one reason or another are not able to move. Other residents can move either into or out of a community in response to tax rates that do not represent the true marginal costs of local government services.

THE THEORY OF TAXATION WITHIN A DECENTRALIZED SYSTEM

Local Tax Base

The ability of tax bases to migrate partially from one taxing jurisdiction to another creates problems that constrain the revenue-raising capabilities of local governing units. The possibility of induced locational effects of local taxation is well recognized by local governing authorities.[4] Such recognition might account, in part, for local reliance on property taxation in the United States. Real property is relatively immobile compared with the other tax bases. It is impossible to relocate land from one community to another, and shifts in the supply of structures on the land generally occur only in the long run. However, this does not suggest that local property tax policy can have no effect on the value of the property tax base. Unrestrained property taxation can result in reduced economic development of a locality and consequently reduced value of its real property tax base.

However, the local government-supplied goods and services financed with local taxes also can have an effect on property values in a community. If a community uses its property taxes to finance high-quality schools, the demand for property in that jurisdiction could be increased. The increase in the demand for real property increases its price in the jurisdiction. This increase in price could more than offset the reduction in price due to positive differentials in property tax rates.

Elasticity of the Local Tax Base

The **elasticity of the tax base**, E_T, is the ratio of the percentage change in the tax base attributable to any given percentage change in the tax rate applied to that base:

$$E_r = \frac{\Delta B/B}{\Delta t/t} = \frac{t\Delta B}{B\Delta t},$$ (18.1)

where B is the tax base in dollars and t is the percentage rate of taxation. Tax revenue is equal to tB. For example, if the tax base is $10 million of labor income per year and the tax rate is 20 percent, tax revenue is (0.2)($10 million), which is $2 million per year.

The elasticity of the tax base is usually negative. Two opposing influences are exerted on the revenues collected when tax rates are changed. An increase in tax rates causes a favorable effect on revenues, stemming from the increase in the rates themselves. On the other hand, an offsetting effect decreases revenues, resulting from the decrease in the size of the tax base induced by the rate increases. Which effect dominates depends on the magnitude of the elasticity of the tax base with respect to the tax rate.

The three possibilities are that the tax base may be elastic ($E_T < -1$), of unitary elasticity ($E_T = -1$), or inelastic ($E_T > -1$). If it is elastic, any given percentage increase in the tax rate is offset by a larger percentage decrease in the size of the tax base. Under such circumstances, an increase in tax rates will reduce tax revenues collected because the change in revenues collected is the combined effect of the

---

[4]See Advisory Commission on Intergovernmental Relations (ACIR), *Interstate Tax Competition* (Washington, D.C.: U.S. Government Printing Office, March 1981).

percentage increase in tax rates and the percentage decrease in the size of the tax base. When the tax base is elastic, the percentage decrease in the size of the base exceeds the percentage increase in tax rates, causing a fall in revenues.

By similar reasoning, if the elasticity of the tax base with respect to the tax rate is unitary, any given percentage change in tax rates will be exactly offset by an equal and opposite percentage change in the tax base, causing total revenues collected to remain constant. Only in those circumstances for which the elasticity of the tax base with respect to the tax rate is greater than -1 (that is, closer to zero) can an increase in the rate of taxation increase revenues collected. The relation among elasticity of the tax base, tax rates, and revenues collected is summarized in Table 18.1.

Tax bases are very elastic when individuals can engage in the taxed activity in alternative political jurisdictions, where the tax is not present or exists at lower rates. This is of particular concern to state and local governments. If, for example, one state increases its income tax rates significantly above the rates in neighboring states, some workers and employers will relocate to neighboring states where the income tax rates are lower. At the extreme, if the tax rate differential becomes very high, the high-tax state might find tax revenues actually decreasing in response to high tax rates. Local taxing authorities are concerned with the elasticity of the local tax base with respect to the rate of taxation. So long as resources are mobile among political jurisdictions, the knowledge of elasticities is crucial to the implementation of effective local tax and expenditure policies. If the local tax base is elastic with respect to the rate of taxation, then increases in the rates of taxation result in a reduction, rather than an increase, in tax revenue collected. An increase in the rate of taxation applied to any base results in an increase in revenue collections from that base if and only if the tax base is inelastic with respect to the rate of taxation.

Among the factors that determine the elasticity of the tax base are the degree of mobility of taxed resources, the rates of taxation applied to similar tax bases in surrounding communities, the public services supplied by surrounding communities, and the initial amount of revenues collected from that base compared with, for example, local income. In addition, services financed through the increase in tax rates affect locational choices by households and business firms, which, in turn, affect the value of the local tax base. If individual economic units feel that extra taxation exceeds the benefits that they obtain from increased public expenditure, they will consider relocation, other things being equal.

Because of mobility of resources and the presence of alternative tax jurisdictions that provide similar public services, taxes that might be neutral when imposed on the

TABLE 18.1 Tax Base Elasticity, Tax Rates, and Revenues (Assuming a Negative Relationship between the Tax Base and Tax Rates)

VALUES OF E_T	CHANGES IN t (TAX RATES)	CHANGES IN REVENUES (t_B)
$E_T > -1$ (Inelastic)	An increase in t A decrease in t	Revenues increase Revenues decrease
$E_T = -1$ (Unit Elastic)	Either an increase or decrease in t	No change in revenues
$E_T < -1$ (Elastic)	An increase in t A decrease in t	Revenues decrease Revenues increase

© Cengage Learning

national level can have distorting effects when imposed on the local level. For example, a lump-sum tax has zero excess burden on the national level but is likely to induce locational effects when imposed on the local level if households are mobile and alternative communities exist. Individuals who wish to avoid the local lump-sum tax can simply move to another community where the tax is not used. If the adult population (the tax base under the lump-sum tax) of the locality is elastic with respect to the rate of taxation, any increase in the tax results in a decrease in revenue.

Taxes that account for only very small percentages of taxpayers' income are likely to have tax bases that are inelastic with respect to the rate of taxation. For example, an increase of 10 percent in the rate of taxation applied to a tax base that currently yields revenue equal to less than 1 percent of local income results in fewer resource transfers among communities than does an equivalent increase applied to a tax base that currently yields 15 percent of local income. In general, the greater the degree of uniformity among local tax and expenditure policies, the less elastic is the local tax base. Within local taxing jurisdictions in the federal system, no tax base is completely inelastic. Injudicious taxation of any given base eventually erodes that base, as resources are reallocated among jurisdictions to avoid the burden of local taxation.[5] Because tax rates are often changed in discrete rather than in continuous variations, threshold levels of taxation come into play beyond which any sharp increases induce economic decision-making units to relocate their economic activities. The tax base also is likely to become more elastic over time, as it often takes time for citizens to make the adjustments required to avoid taxes.

Tax Competition and Tax Exporting

The elasticity of tax bases often results in competition among communities for residents and business firms whose economic activities increase the value of local tax bases. Such competition often acts as a constraint on the sizes of local public budgets. Local tax jurisdictions hesitate to increase tax rates for fear of putting themselves at competitive disadvantages relative to other jurisdictions as sites for the conduct of various kinds of economic activities. The expenditure sides of local budgets also are considered factors in the location decisions of economic units. Jurisdictions that are reluctant to raise taxes might lack public services that attract citizens as residents.

The willingness of local residents to support higher taxes also can depend on the extent to which local jurisdictions succeed in exporting their taxes to residents of other political jurisdictions. Thus, a $1 increase in taxes might be valued at less than $1 by local taxpayers if they know that part of the increase in taxes will be paid by residents of other political jurisdictions.

Tax exporting is common in many resort communities, where environmental attributes make them unique and popular with tourists. Taxes on hotel accommodations are likely to be paid exclusively by tourists and other nonresidents, but they might be used to finance locally produced public services. To the extent to which cities also must provide public services to these nonresidents, it can be argued that those taxes finance police departments and sanitation services that are necessarily

---

[5]Elasticities of supplies of inputs to particular areas are much higher than their national levels. Research estimates indicate that those elasticities vary from 20 to 100. See Timothy W. McGuire and Leonard A. Rapping, "The Role of Market Variables and Key Bargains in the Manufacturing Wage Determination Process," *Journal of Political Economy* 76 (September–October 1968): 1015–1036, and "The Supply of Labor and Manufacturing Wage Determination in the United States: An Empirical Estimation," *International Economic Review* 11 (June 1970): 258–268.

bigger to meet the demands for services by these nonresidents, particularly during peak-season periods.

In a sense, the deductibility of state and local income taxes from federal income taxes is a form of tax exporting. It allows state and local governments to shift a portion of their taxes to the national level in the form of reduced federal income tax collections.

1. What are the assumptions and major conclusions of the Tiebout model of decentralized government?
2. What are interjurisdictional externalities?
3. Why are local tax bases more elastic than national tax bases?

VARIATION IN FISCAL CAPACITY

Fiscal capacity is a measure of the ability of a jurisdiction to finance government-provided services. The fiscal capacities of local governing units are likely to vary with the values of local tax bases and with the ability to "export" taxes. Taxing jurisdictions with relatively low tax bases in dollar terms find it more difficult to raise tax revenues than do wealthier high-income jurisdictions. Insofar as the demands for local public services do not increase with fiscal capacities, low-tax-base communities are likely to encounter difficulties in supplying acceptable minimum levels and qualities of public services. Given the tax revenue required, the lower the average income in a community, the higher the tax rates.

For example, consider the fiscal consequences of different per capita income levels among states. If each state supplies the same per capita amount of public services at the same cost to its citizens and finances all these expenditures by income taxes that fall solely on residents in the state, then it follows that the proportionate per capita tax burdens as a percentage of income are greater in those states with lower incomes. Alternatively, if tax rates are the same in all states, and all public expenditures are financed by state taxes, then those states with lower per capita income supply fewer and lower-quality public services.

Measures of Fiscal Capacity

Among the commonly used measures of fiscal capacity for state and local governments are per capita income; per capita retail sales; and assessed valuation per capita, or per pupil, for school districts. All these measure the value of the tax base per person in the political jurisdiction. Because local governments rely heavily on property taxes, the measure most relevant for this level of government would be *assessed valuation per capita*. When the property tax base is used mainly to finance schooling services, *assessed valuation per pupil* might be a better measure of the capacity to finance government-supplied services. These measures are imperfect in that they do not consider the extent to which a jurisdiction exports tax burdens to residents of other jurisdictions, and vice versa.

In addition to measuring fiscal capacity, it is useful on occasion to measure the extent to which subnational governments provide services to their residents. A common measure of this is *per capita expenditure*. However, per capita expenditure is only imperfectly correlated with actual per capita services because of unit cost variations.

It is also useful to measure the extent to which the fiscal capacity of a state compares with that of other states. Usually, this is done by dividing measures of the fiscal capacity, such as per capita income, of that state or locality by the national average of that measure. Similarly, per capita expenditure could be divided by the national average for other nonfederal governments. States and localities with fiscal capacity less than the national average, and per capita expenditure less than the national average, would be candidates for fiscal equalization grants by the central government.

Revenue Effort

Revenue effort is the ratio of tax collections from all sources in a taxing jurisdiction, as a percentage of personal income in that jurisdiction, to the national average of that ratio for all jurisdictions. As a measure of the extent to which a local government is tapping its tax base, revenue effort has a number of serious shortcomings. It does not consider the fact that jurisdictions with low levels of personal income require high revenue effort to maintain the same level of per capita public expenditure financed in jurisdictions that have high levels of personal income. Differences in revenue effort also can be explained by different costs and demands among the taxing jurisdictions. In general, areas with higher population densities and greater percentages of their populations living in cities require greater levels of local government expenditure. Differences in revenue effort also reflect differences in collective choices among communities for the allocation of resources between public and private uses.

A value for revenue effort that is greater than 100 percent for a given type of taxing jurisdiction implies that the jurisdiction is raising a greater amount of revenue than the national average per dollar of personal income. This, in turn, can imply a number of things. First, citizens in this taxing jurisdiction might have strong demands for local government-supplied services compared with other communities. Second, it might be that the community has a lower level of per capita income relative to other communities and requires greater revenue effort to maintain the national average of per capita government expenditure. Finally, it could be that this community, because of either geographic or demographic characteristics, requires more per capita expenditure than the national average to meet the basic demands for government-provided services by its populace.

The chief shortcoming of the revenue effort measure is the fact that it ignores the expenditure side of the budget. The extent to which citizens in a community wish to tax themselves depends on the collective choices made concerning the allocation of resources between government and private uses. Revenue effort statistics must be used in conjunction with data on per capita expenditure and per capita tax base values to provide useful information on the need for fiscal equalization of the capacity to finance goods and services.

INTERGOVERNMENTAL FISCAL RELATIONS

Variation in fiscal capacity among states and local governments provides a basis in intergovernmental aid to ensure minimum levels of certain public services in all regions of a nation. Intergovernmental aid is also a way to help achieve a more efficient allocation of resources in the government sector by internalizing interjurisdictional externalities. In fiscal year 2011, federal aid was a major source of revenue to state and local government, accounting for 23.3 percent of revenue. Local governments also rely heavily on grants from state governments to finance their expenditures. Grants are intergovernmental transfers of purchasing power that can be used to help achieve a wide variety of social objectives.

Grants differ mainly in terms of the restrictions that are placed on the use of funds by recipient governments. Some grants are transfers with literally no strings attached. Other grants merely require that the recipient government spend the funds in a broad general area, such as education or transportation. The most restrictive types of grants are those that the recipient government must spend on a particular service or project. A review of the various types of grants currently in use is an appropriate way to start the analysis of intergovernmental fiscal relations.

State and local governments have become dependent on fiscal assistance from a higher level of government for significant amounts of funds. Some of this assistance is for entitlement programs that the lower level of government is required to provide within certain guidelines by the higher level. Many government officials regard the dependence on grants as risky because grant programs can be reduced, eliminated, or fail to keep up with rising costs. In recent years, more than two-thirds of grants from the federal government to the states have financed payments to individuals through such programs as Medicaid. Funds for these programs finance programs mandated by the federal government and are not used to finance capital projects.

Local governments are very dependent on state governments for fiscal assistance and, on average, grants from state to local governments finance 35 percent of local expenditures. State aid is very important for school districts and education finance. In some school districts, state aid accounts for more than half of revenues.

Types of Grants

A **categorical grant-in-aid** is a transfer of funds from a higher level of government to a lower level, with specified conditions attached to the expenditure of the funds. Many categorical grants from the federal to state and local governments are for payments to individuals for income support or health care. The Medicaid program is a categorical grant to states to provide health services to low-income persons and is the largest federal grant-in-aid program. Federal highway grants are categorical grants to states to help fund roads and bridges. Some federal grants contain the requirement that recipient jurisdictions match each dollar of federal aid with a certain amount of locally raised revenue. These are known as **matching grants**. General **unconditional grants** differ from categorical grants in that revenues are shared among governments, with no strings attached to the use of the funds.

Federal aid to encourage expenditure on particular projects is used as an inducement to state and local governments to pursue activities in general accord with national goals. Perhaps the most famous example of an early categorical grant-in-aid program is the 19th-century *Morrill Act*, which established the so-called land-grant colleges in the states. Essentially, this program granted both land and funds to states that agreed to establish colleges of various kinds. In effect, this served to internalize some of the interjurisdictional benefits associated with higher education by subsidizing state expenditure for public colleges.

Federal Grants

Federal categorical grants that provide transfers to individuals have increased enormously since 1970. The bulk of these grants has been to state and local governments to fund federally mandated entitlements to individuals under such programs as Medicaid and cash transfer programs that provide public assistance to the poor. Nearly two-thirds of total federal grants to state and local governments as of 2011 was for programs that are essentially grants to individuals rather than grants to governments.

Table 18.2 shows that federal grants-in-aid to state and local governments grew rapidly in the 1970s and then slowed down considerably in the 1980s. Federal grants grew more quickly in the early 1990s, both as a share of federal revenue and as a share of gross domestic product (GDP), than they did in the 1980s mainly because of the growth in grants to individuals through entitlement programs. In 2011, 63.9 percent of all federal grants to state and local governments was accounted for by Medicaid and public welfare payments to individuals. Table 18.3 shows trends in federal grants by category from 1960 to 2011.

The major functions for which federal transfers are made directly to local governments include education, housing and community redevelopment, waste-treatment facilities, and airport construction. Again, these are areas of expenditure likely to have spillover effects. If categorical grants are to be efficient tools for internalizing externalities, they must be allocated according to a system that accurately evaluates spillovers and their ranges. To internalize externalities, a grant must reduce the net cost to local citizens of the activity that generates the externality to citizens of other local governments. In addition, if opportunities exist for communities to engage in bargaining to internalize externalities, then categorical grants are unnecessary and their use could result in inefficiencies.

States also make grants to their own local governmental subdivisions. As in federal aid, the bulk of such funds appears to be designed to internalize externalities caused by inappropriate sizes of the collective decision-making units. The major local functions subsidized by state-aid programs are education, public welfare, and highways.

When spillovers exist, the tendency is for either overspending or underspending, depending on whether costs or benefits are spilling over and on the extent of spillovers among communities. When the spillovers lead to an undersupply of public services, matching categorical grants-in-aid are reasonable tools to use to subsidize government activities that generate external benefits. The existence of a categorical grant program for a particular function induces an increase in local expenditure. However, in most functions that generate external benefits, all the benefits are not appropriable by the communities that are responsible for supply decisions. Educational expenditure, for example, tends to spill out because some of the recipients of education relocate to other areas after they finish their schooling. On

| TABLE 18.2 | Federal Grants-in-Aid Summary: Selected Fiscal Years 1970 to 2011 |

| | CURRENT DOLLARS | | | | | |
| | | | GRANTS TO INDIVIDUALS | | GRANTS AS PERCENTAGE OF INDIVIDUALS | | |
YEAR	TOTAL GRANTS (MILLIONS OF DOLLARS)	ANNUAL PERCENTAGE CHANGE AVERAGE[a]	TOTAL (MILLIONS OF DOLLARS)	PERCENTAGE OF TOTAL GRANTS	STATE-LOCAL GOVERNMENT OUTLAYS[b]	FEDERAL OUTLAYS	GROSS DOMESTIC PRODUCT
1970	24,065	19.3	8,727	36.3	19.0	12.3	2.4
1975	49,791	14.8	16,762	33.7	23.5	15.0	3.3
1980	91,451	9.7	32,652	35.7	26.3	15.5	3.5
1985	105,852	8.5	49,352	46.6	21.3	11.2	2.7
1988	115,342	6.4	62,434	54.1	18.6	10.8	2.4
1989	121,928	5.7	67,353	55.2	18.6	10.7	2.4
1990	135,325	11.0	77,132	57.0	18.7	10.8	2.5
1991	154,519	14.2	92,497	59.9	19.5	11.7	2.7
1992	178,065	15.2	112,185	63.0	20.8	12.9	3.0
1993	193,612	8.7	124,289	64.2	21.2	13.7	3.1
1994	210,596	8.8	135,232	64.2	21.8	14.4	3.2
1995	224,992	6.8	145,793	64.8	22.2	14.8	3.2
2000	284,700	6.4	182,600	64.1	24.2	15.9	2.9
2002	351,550	11.0	227,373	65.0	26.3	17.5	3.4
2005	426,243	4.9	273,464	64.2	25.2	17.2	3.5
2007	443,800	3.7	284,400	64.1	22.6	16.3	3.2
2011	606,766	−0.3	387,806	63.9	23.3	16.8	4.1

[a]Annual percentage change from prior year shown.
[b]Outlays as defined in the national income and product accounts.
Source: Office of Management and Budget, Historical Tables, Budget of the United States Government, FY2013.

the other hand, many recipients of educational services do remain in the community in which they are educated. Thus, efficiency considerations imply that some matching of funds is desirable.

Ideally, the federal share of costs for a program is equal to the percentage of net benefits spilling out from a particular local area. The local share is based on an estimate of the benefits retained by the community. Although this is desirable in principle, accurate computations of spillouts virtually are impossible because of problems in quantifying and evaluating collectively consumed goods. However, some reasoned estimates of appropriate matching formulas are useful and are likely to improve resource allocations.

Unrestricted Grants and Fungibility

For the purpose of studying intergovernmental relations, it is useful to discuss unrestricted and restricted intergovernmental grants separately. Unrestricted grants

| TABLE 18.3 | Trends in Federal Grants to State and Local Governments, 1960–2011 (Outlays; Dollar Amounts in Billions) |

	1960	1965	1970	1975	1980	1985	1990	1995	2000	2002	2005	2007	2011
Distribution of Grants by Function:													
Natural Resources and Environment	0.1	0.2	0.4	2.4	5.4	4.1	3.7	4.1	4.6	5.1	5.9	6.1	8.3
Agriculture	0.2	0.5	0.6	0.4	0.6	2.4	1.3	0.8	0.7	0.9	0.9	0.8	0.9
Transportation	3.0	4.1	4.6	5.9	13.0	17.0	19.2	25.8	32.3	41.0	43.4	47.9	60.1
Community and Regional Development	0.1	0.6	1.8	2.8	6.5	5.2	5.0	7.2	8.7	10.5	20.2	20.7	19.9
Education, Training, Employment, and Social Services	0.5	1.1	6.4	12.1	21.9	17.8	23.4	34.1	36.7	44.8	57.2	58.1	89.1
Health	0.2	0.6	3.8	8.8	15.8	24.5	43.9	93.6	124.8	158.7	197.8	206.3	292.9
Income Security	2.6	3.5	5.8	9.4	18.5	27.2	35.2	55.1	68.7	81.5	90.9	91.0	113.6
Justice	—	—	a	0.7	0.5	0.1	0.6	1.2	5.3	5.7	4.8	4.6	4.9
General Government	0.2	0.2	0.5	7.1	8.6	6.8	2.3	2.2	2.1	2.5	4.4	3.6	7.6
Other	0.2	0.3	0.6	7.2	9.3	7.6	3.1	3.0	0.9	1.0	2.6	2.8	9.5
Total	7.0	10.9	24.1	49.8	91.4	105.9	135.3	225.0	284.7	351.6	428.0	443.8	606.8
Composition:													
Current Dollars:													
Payments for Individuals	2.5	3.7	8.7	16.8	32.6	49.3	75.7	141.2	182.6	227.4	273.9	284.4	387.9
Physical Capital	3.3	5.0	7.1	10.9	22.6	24.9	27.2	39.6	48.7	58.7	60.8	70.8	92.0
Other Grants	1.2	2.2	8.3	22.2	36.2	31.6	32.5	44.2	53.4	65.5	93.3	88.7	126.9
Total	7.0	10.9	24.1	49.8	91.4	105.9	135.3	225.0	284.7	351.6	428.0	443.8	606.8
Percentage of Total Grants:													
Payments for Individuals	35	34	36	34	36	47	56	63	64.2	64.7	64.2	64.1	63.9
Physical Capital	47	46	29	22	25	24	20	18	17.6	16.7	14.3	15.9	15.2
Other Grants	17	20	34	45	40	30	24	20	18.2	18.8	21.5	20.8	20.9
Total	100	100	100	100	100	100	100	100	100	100	100	100	100

a$50 million or less.

Source: U.S. Office of Management and Budget, Historical Tables, Budget of the United States Government, FY2013.

include what often are referred to as **general revenue sharing**. The United States had a general revenue sharing program that was terminated in 1986. Restricted grants are those available only for a specific purpose, and they must be spent on that purpose. Restricted grants have auditing requirements that limit the way the funds, once granted, can be spent. **Block grants**, a principal type of unrestricted grant, have only minimal restrictions on the uses to which the funds can be put and rarely require matching funds raised locally. TANF is the major block grant to states used to provide income support to the poor.

The distinction between restricted and unrestricted grants is somewhat artificial because of the **fungibility** of money, which means that money can be used for more than one purpose. A grant, with or without restrictions on the use of funds, frees local tax monies that otherwise would be spent on government-provided services. The receipt of the grant could allow tax reductions that benefit citizens of recipient communities. If taxes are reduced as a result of the grant, citizens can increase their consumption of private goods and services beyond the amounts that would be possible if they had to finance all government-supplied goods and services through locally raised tax revenue. In other words, the funds might end up being used for any purpose, even though they were intended for a specific use. However, matching grants tend to stimulate government spending to a greater degree than nonmatching grants. A grant increases net resources flowing to a local or state government only to the extent to which the grant increases the net funds available for both government and private spending in that community over and above the federal, or central, government taxes paid by the local citizens in that community to finance the grant program expenditures in all localities.

CHECKPOINT

1. What is fiscal capacity?
2. How well does revenue effort measure fiscal capacity?
3. How do matching grants differ from unconditional grants?

THE THEORY OF GRANTS

Grants and other forms of intergovernmental fiscal assistance are essentially gifts, or subsidies, from one level of government to another level. Usually, the recipient government is on a level lower than that of the donor government. These subsidies can be expected to affect the political equilibrium, with consequent changes in the observed expenditure and tax policies collectively agreed upon by citizens who live in the recipient political jurisdiction. The process by which such grants change behavior patterns in recipient jurisdictions must be understood in order to predict whether the grant will accomplish the result for which it is intended.

Matching grants, under various categorical grant programs, are more likely to stimulate citizens of recipient governments to agree collectively to expanded production of public goods than are equal-dollar-amount general-purpose grants. The latter grants neither require matching funds raised from local taxes nor restrict the purpose for which the grant funds must be spent. The basic reason for the more stimulative effect attributed to matching grants is the fact that such grants reduce the marginal and average cost of the public good to citizens of the recipient government. This sets up both income and substitution effects that influence citizens' collective choices. A nonmatching grant, such as that used for revenue sharing or general fiscal assistance, results only in income effects and is less effective in increasing the willingness of citizens to support increased local public spending.

Suppose the distribution of taxes among citizens per unit of a public good, such as a road, is given. For example, say each citizen pays $1 per mile of new road surfaces supplied per year. A matching grant for public goods will be available only if citizens allocate local tax revenue to the project. For example, if the grant requires a 50 percent matching of revenue, matching funds will be made available if local authorities allocate from their own revenue 50 cents per citizen per mile of new roads. In effect, *in terms of local taxes*, the matching grant reduces the marginal cost of each mile of road from $1 to 50 cents per citizen. This 50 percent reduction in the tax per mile of road per citizen results in a substitution effect, leading individual citizens to support more government spending on roads.

The income effect of the grant depends on the income elasticity of the demand for public goods. Depending on the individual tastes of citizens, the income elasticity can be positive or negative. The impact of the income effect of any grant on the political equilibrium therefore is difficult to predict. The income effect is likely to have the effect of increasing consumption of both private goods and public goods, as its effect on the political equilibrium might be to induce citizens to support local tax reductions.

General-purpose or categorical grants without matching requirements result *only* in income effects. No substitution effect is caused because such grants do not reduce the tax per unit of government-provided goods to individual citizens. Therefore, it is conceivable that under certain circumstances general-purpose grants can decrease the amount of government-supplied goods and services produced by the recipient community if enough citizens in the community view these goods and services as inferior (negative income elasticity of demand). This is less likely to be the result with matching grants because substitution effects always will occur to counter any income effects acting to decrease the consumption of the public good.

MATCHING VERSUS GENERAL-PURPOSE GRANTS: AN APPLICATION OF THE THEORY OF COLLECTIVE CHOICE UNDER MAJORITY RULE

Consider the case of two equal grants that finance a single public good. Assume that the grants are equal in amount but that one grant has a matching requirement while the other is simply a direct transfer to the recipient government. Assuming that collective choices are made by simple majority rule in the recipient jurisdiction, Bradford and Oates have shown that the matching grant will result in a political equilibrium at a higher level of production for the public good.[6]

---

[6]David F. Bradford and Wallace E. Oates, "Towards a Predictive Theory of Intergovernmental Grants," *American Economic Review* 61 (May 1971): 440–449. The analysis presented here follows Bradford and Oates.

The Initial Political Equilibrium

Suppose that collective choices in the recipient government are made under simple majority rule and that taxes per unit of the public good are given for each voter. If, as illustrated in Figure 18.1, the marginal tax per unit of the public good of each voter is t_i, then the initial budget line for each voter would have slope $-t_i$. This slope gives the expenditure on private goods per year that must be given up by each citizen to finance each extra unit of the public good, such as miles of new roads, per year. In actuality, the marginal tax per unit of the public good, t_i, varies from voter to voter.

In Figure 18.1, the indifference curves of the voter whose budget line is illustrated are omitted to avoid cluttering the diagram. Assume, however, that the indifference curves have the standard shapes and that, given the voter's tax per unit of the public good and his preferences, the voter has his most-preferred mix of expenditure on private goods per year and units of public goods per year, represented by point E.

At that point, he consumes Q_{P1} units of the public good, gives up AM of his income in taxes, and retains $0M$ of his income for expenditure on private goods. Assume that the voter whose equilibrium is illustrated in Figure 18.1 is the median voter. It follows that his individual optimum will correspond to the political equilibrium, provided that all voters have single-peaked preferences (see Chapter 5).

Other voters whose most-preferred mixes of expenditure on private goods and public goods do not correspond to the median will end up consuming either more or less than their most-preferred amount of the public good after the political equilibrium is reached.

FIGURE 18.1 Political Equilibrium: A Matching Grant versus a Nonmatching Grant of Equal Value

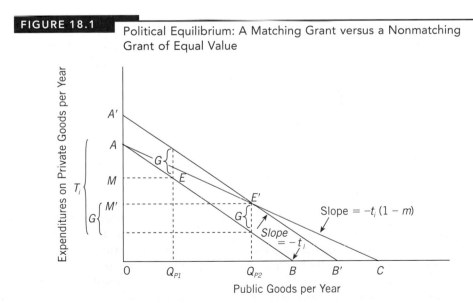

A matching grant lowers the tax per unit of local public goods. Matching grants are more effective in increasing local government expenditures than nonmatching lump-sum grants, with an equivalent reduction in taxes to the median voter of G per year.

Impact of a Matching Grant on the Political Equilibrium

Suppose now that a matching grant is made available to citizens in the local jurisdiction. The effect of the grant is to reduce the tax rate per unit of the public good for each voter. If the donor government's proportionate share of increased costs associated with more public goods is m, then each voter's tax share would fall by m times his original tax share. The tax share of each voter now is $t_i(1 - m)$. For example, if $m = 0.5$, the tax per unit of the public good would fall by 50 percent for each citizen. This would rotate the voter budget line from AB to AC as the introduction of the matching grants reduces tax rates per unit of the public good for all voters by the same fraction, m. Suppose again that the voter whose budget lines are illustrated in Figure 18.1 is the median voter. This voter's most-preferred outcome would move from E to, say, E'. This implies an increase in the output of the public good to Q_{P2} and an increase in taxes to the voter from AM to AM'. The full cost of producing the public good, however, is $AM' + G$, where G is the voter's imputed dollar share of government grant to the community. Because the voter illustrated is the median voter, his most-preferred outcome is the political equilibrium. As long as the demand curve for the public good is downward sloping for each voter, all voters would prefer more annual amounts of the public good per year under the matching arrangement. It is therefore certain that the new median peak, or most-preferred outcome, would correspond to increased production of the public good and correspond to a point such as E'.

Bradford and Oates point out that the impact of the grant is equivalent to a tax reduction equal to the fraction of the tax per unit of the public good to individual voters.[7] This result indicates that the effect of the grant could be duplicated, in terms of the political equilibrium it generates, by a tax credit to all voters equal to the fraction, m, of each voter's share of the total budget spent on the public good. For example, if the median voter is told that he will receive a cash payment in terms of a tax rebate each year equal to a fraction, m, of the amount actually paid in taxes, his most-preferred amount of the public good would be Q_{P2}. He would pay $T_i = (AM' + G)$ in taxes but would receive G as a rebate equal to mT_i. His net taxes would be AM'.

This is a very interesting and useful result. It suggests that nothing is uniquely special about matching grants to governments. Insofar as these grants upset the political equilibrium in recipient governments, they do so by altering the tax shares to citizens. Provided that the grant itself does not change the basic political institutions of the recipient government, its effects are equivalent to a reduction in taxes to individual taxpayers, and the impact of the grant can be duplicated by simply giving local taxpayers tax credits against their local tax bills.

This model of grants assumes that the bureaucrats and politicians respond to the desires of the median voter. Some models suggest that the mechanism involved in government grants is such that the normal political process can be bypassed by bureaucrats who spend the funds. These models presume that the bureaucrats who receive the grant funds will spend the money according to their own goals without voters ever being given the opportunity to express their desires. The bypassing of the normal political process by local bureaucrats is called the **flypaper effect**. The

---

[7]See Bradford and Oates, "Towards a Predictive Theory."

funds seem to stick to the hands of the local politicians and get spent before voters can be polled. In fact, some evidence shows that the tendency to spend grant money on government programs is higher than the tendency to spend private income on such programs.

Impact of a Nonmatching General-Purpose Grant on the Political Equilibrium

Now, consider the effect of a nonmatching lump-sum or general-purpose grant, with no strings attached, made available to a local government. Essentially, this is a gift to citizens in that political jurisdiction and can be thought of again as a reduction in local taxes to individual citizens. To compare the effect of the general-purpose grant with the matching grant, suppose that the individual's imputed share of the general-purpose grant is G, equal to the matching grant at the political equilibrium of Q_{P2} units of the public good, as illustrated in Figure 18.1 and discussed previously. Such a grant can be illustrated as a parallel shift upward of the budget line by G to $A'B'$. For each voter, the aggregate grant to the government is equivalent to a subsidy, G, equal to the imputed share of what the voter would receive under the matching grant. The grant, because it has no strings attached, could allow voters to continue consuming Q_{P1} units of the public good and pocket the grant as a net increase in income to each taxpayer equivalent to AA'. However, this extreme result would occur only in the unlikely case that the income elasticity of the demand for public goods was zero for all voters. More likely, the grant will have the effect of increasing the production of public goods and allowing some reduction in tax rates to local citizens so as to enable them to consume more private goods and public goods.

The new political equilibrium will be that corresponding to the most-preferred outcome of the median voter. As long as the income elasticity of demand for public goods is positive for at least some voters, an increased output of public goods is implied. This same political equilibrium could be generated by a federal income tax reduction for all citizens in the recipient government proportionate to local citizens' local tax share in the total cost of the public good. In other words, the political outcome that results from a gift to the local government could have been achieved by a set of gifts to individual voters in that community. General-purpose grants can be thought of as implicit subsidies that increase the income of residents of local jurisdictions and induce them to spend such increases in income on both public and private goods.

The impact of the general-purpose grant on the output of the public good will be less than is the case under the equivalent matching grant. The basic reason for this, as discussed, is that the matching grant will result in both income and substitution effects that influence the behavior of others, while the general-purpose grant always will result in a political equilibrium to the left of point E' in Figure 18.1. The median voter is likely to be in equilibrium under the lump-sum grant at a point to the left of E', implying that he or she consumes relatively less of the public good and retains more of the grant for other purposes through reduced local tax payments.[8]

---

[8]See Bradford and Oates, "Towards a Predictive Theory," for a more complete proof.

Matching Grants and Efficiency

Categorical grants with matching requirements can be used to internalize interjurisdictional externalities and thereby promote efficiency. To see this, suppose that pollution control by local governments provides benefits not only to the citizens of the local jurisdiction but also to *all* citizens. Suppose that the local political equilibrium results in the level of pollution control that corresponds to the point at which the sum of the marginal benefits of local residents equals the marginal social cost of abatement. If a positive interjurisdictional externality exists, less than the efficient amount of annual pollution abatement will be supplied by this local government, even though $\Sigma MB = MSC$ for local residents.

In Figure 18.2, a local government must spend $10 to remove each pound of a certain pollutant from waste water. The current political equilibrium at point E corresponds to the point at which the sum of benefits to local citizens of the jurisdiction, ΣMB_L, equals the marginal social cost of pollution abatement, MSC, where MSC is assumed to be constant. At that point, 100,000 pounds of the pollutant are removed each year at a cost to local taxpayers of $1 million per year. However, at point E, the marginal social benefit of pollution abatement exceeds its marginal social cost. This is because local pollution abatement results in positive interjurisdictional externalities to residents of other areas.

The efficient level of pollution abatement for this jurisdiction corresponds to point E^*, at which the sum of the *national* marginal benefits equals the marginal social cost of abatement. The sum of the national marginal benefits, ΣMB_N, is the marginal social benefit of pollution control, MSB. The efficient level of local abatement corresponds to 150,000 pounds per year.

A matching grant for pollution control can get the local residents to choose the efficient level of abatement. Local residents will demand 150,000 pounds of

FIGURE 18.2   Matching Grant

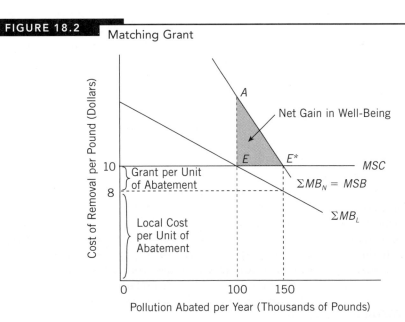

A matching grant can internalize interjurisdictional externalities. The grant allows a net gain in well-being.

abatement per year if the price per pound is reduced from $10 to $8. This can be accomplished through a 20 percent matching grant. The federal government would agree to pay 20 percent, or $2 per pound, of pollution abatement. The local government would pay the remaining 80 percent of the costs. At a net price of $8 per pound, local citizens agree to provide 150,000 pounds of local pollution abatement. The total cost of this annual abatement is $1.5 million. Local taxpayers, however, pay only $1.2 million. The remaining $300,000 per year is paid and financed by the federal government.

The net increase in well-being to all citizens made possible by the matching grant is represented by the triangular area *EAE**. If the matching grant is provided to *all* localities, the increment in well-being would be equal to the gain in net benefits made possible by the improvement in efficiency in the pollution abatement decisions of *all* local jurisdictions.

CHECKPOINT

1. How does a matching grant affect the price per unit of the local public goods it helps finance?
2. What is the "flypaper effect" of intergovernmental grants?
3. How can a matching grant improve resource allocation when used to finance local public goods for which interjurisdictional externalities prevail?

EDUCATION FINANCE

In the United States, public elementary and secondary education is primarily the responsibility of state and local governments. The federal government finances only about 10 percent of the total cost of primary and secondary education, and the bulk of federal spending on education is on programs designed to improve equality of educational opportunity. The federal government also finances research and development programs to stimulate educational reform.

Spending for public schools amounts to one-third of the combined budgets of state and local governments. It is the largest single category of expenditure for these governments. In many states, the primary responsibility for financing education falls on local governments: cities, counties, and school districts set up for the sole purpose of financing elementary and secondary education for local residents. The provision of basic schooling has significant effects on the well-being of citizens and their children. Deprivation of quality schooling or inequality of educational opportunity can have devastating impacts on the lives of students and all of us through its effect on future taxpayers' productivity. For this reason, many citizens demand that government play a strong role in the supply of schooling to ensure that each child in the nation receives a satisfactory amount of schooling of a certain standard of quality.

The Decentralized Supply of Schooling

The supply of schooling in the United States has traditionally been decentralized. Early in the history of the nation, it was primarily the responsibility of families and religious institutions. Surprisingly, public schools did not exist on any major scale in the nation until the late 1800s. Tax-financed schooling was not common when most of the original states of the union adopted their constitutions; government supply and tax finance of education was not widely accepted until around 1850.[9] When public schooling did become a widespread government function, states gave local governments the responsibility of supplying it to children and financing it with their own revenue sources. The states' role in financing education through grants to local government and other means increased in the mid-20th century. The federal role in education has always been minimal.

In New England towns where public education began, separate school districts within each town were set up as taxing authorities to finance education. Thus, the school district began as a submunicipal unit within a town. There was always some inequality of capacity to finance education among towns, but citizens demanded local control. The tradition of local supply and control of primary and secondary schooling remains strong in the United States. Today, the desire for local control is tempered by desires for equality of educational opportunity and desires for even more parental control in school choice and curricula.

A decentralized system of public schooling and finance has the advantage of allowing a community to tailor its mix of schooling and other services to the demands of its citizens. A retirement community with few young children will naturally spend less on schooling than a community composed primarily of young couples. If the demand for schooling is income elastic, we can also expect high-income communities to spend more per pupil than low-income communities. According to the principles of the Tiebout model, people will decide in which community to locate by considering the quality of schooling services. In fact, in modern metropolitan areas, there are several school districts from which to choose, and parents often make their residence choice on the basis of school quality.

Equalization of Expenditures per Pupil: The Role of the States

While decentralization has advantages in terms of matching demand for education with supply, it also has some unfortunate side effects. Those who are least mobile, namely, the poor, are often stuck in areas where resources to finance schooling are low and where the quality of schooling is poor. The classic manifestation of this problem is a large central city with a core of impoverished residents who attend poorly funded schools that are surrounded by many suburban jurisdictions with few poor residents and with high-value property tax bases to finance education. In many cases, zoning laws that require minimum lot sizes keep low-income residents out of the area. Much of the disparity in expenditure per pupil arises from differences in taxable property values per pupil among jurisdictions. Remember, the main source of local tax revenues is the property tax.

To compensate for disparity in educational quality among local taxing jurisdictions, most state governments have formulas for state aid to local jurisdictions that are inversely related to property values and incomes in each jurisdiction. In the United States today, more than 50 percent of revenues to finance local education

---

[9]See the classic work in the history of public education in the United States, Ellwood P. Cubberly, *Public Education in the United States: A Study and Interpretation of American Educational History* (Boston: Houghton Mifflin, 1919).

is provided by state government. The amount of state aid per student varies from state to state, and some states, such as Hawaii, fully fund schooling and assure equal expenditure per pupil in all local jurisdictions. There are those who argue, however, that equal expenditure per student is not enough to ensure equality of opportunity. Given the obstacles that low-income students in impoverished areas face to learning, such as crime-ridden neighborhoods and home environments that do not foster study, some believe that equal educational output among districts requires that expenditure per pupil be higher than the average in impoverished school districts.

In the 1970s, there were a number of court challenges to decentralized school finance in the United States, the most notable one being *Serrano v. Priest*, 1971 and 1976, in California. These challenges resulted in changes in school finance in California and other states. Basically, the challenges argued that local finance allows variation in expenditure per pupil based on differences in property tax base per student. Property-rich districts could therefore tax themselves at a lower rate than property-poor districts and yet still get high expenditure per pupil. Although it is not always the case that districts with low-value property are inhabited by low-income people (for example, there could be a lot of high-value industrial and commercial real estate in a city dominated by low-income residents), these court cases have revolutionized school finance in many states. In effect, the educational reform in California increased state aid to local education and more or less equalized expenditure per pupil across jurisdictions.[10] In states in which locally based decentralized school systems were declared unconstitutional, spending variations among communities per pupil have been sharply reduced, and the state share of the cost of schooling has risen sharply.

In most states, district power equalization plans subsidize education with grants that are inversely related to the districts' fiscal capacity. Usually, districts for which the property tax base per pupil is below the state average receive such aid while those with above-average property tax receive none. Other plans try to establish equality with grants that set a foundation level of expenditure per student and aid districts in which very high local property tax rates would be needed to meet that standard.

However, there is scant evidence that these reforms have actually improved educational quality. In fact, in California there is some evidence that the shift to state finance of education actually resulted in a decline in expenditure per pupil relative to other states as demands on state funds for other uses reduced overall funding for education. Nor is there any evidence that standardized test score differences between rich and poor districts have narrowed as a result of the reform.[11]

Voucher Systems and School Productivity

Dissatisfaction with public school quality has led to demands that there be more competition among schools to encourage innovations and improve student performance. One program intended to improve schools' productivity is the voucher system, which designates state funds to be used to finance tuition at private schools. The idea of a government-issued voucher to pay for education was introduced in

---

[10]See Joseph T. Henke, "Financing Public Schools in California: The Aftermath of *Serrano v. Priest* and Proposition 13," *University of San Francisco Law Review* 21 (Fall 1986): 1–39.

[11]Thomas Downes, "Evaluating the Impact of School Finance Reform on the Provision of Public Education: The California Case," *National Tax Journal* 45 (December 1992): 405–420.

the 1970s by the famous economist Milton Friedman. With this plan, each family receives a voucher to pay for educational service for each child that can be redeemed for cash by either public or private schools supplying educational services. Naturally, officials of public school systems have opposed voucher systems. Many believe that the vouchers, if used at parochial schools, violate separation of church and state doctrine. By allowing parents to choose schools for their children, presumably those schools that do a good job will prosper while those that cannot effectively educate students will fail. Although there were a few early experiments with vouchers, they are still not widely used in the United States. However, increased pushes now to "privatize" public services could increase the demand for this form of finance.

There is some evidence that productivity in public schools has, in fact, declined in recent years. After adjustment for inflation between 1982 and 1991, productivity has fallen by between 2.5 and 3 percent per year. Public schools have hired more teachers per pupil and more teachers with master's degrees since 1965. However, over the same period, student performance has not improved. Public schools apparently lack incentives to improve student performance while economizing on cost. One reason for the decline in productivity could be the increased proportions of students who have received special-education services in recent years, but this does not entirely explain the decline.[12] However, if public schools are, in fact, doing a poor job in producing output of qualified students, then a voucher plan that gives parents more choice among schools and encourages schools to innovate could help improve the situation.

Federal support for education has increased somewhat in recent years, and increased involvement by the federal government in establishing national educational standards has been proposed. State governments have also become involved in setting minimal standards for schools and have been using statewide tests to evaluate the output of schools. Some states have increased the number of days of schooling during the year and have tried to improve the quality of teachers by increasing qualification requirements and using merit pay systems to award teachers whose performance in the classroom is good. However, there remains wide diversity in the quality of education within states and localities and wide variations in expenditures per pupil despite state equalization programs and federal aid to schools with high proportions of disadvantaged students. However, the perceived decline in the quality of schools in the United States is going to provoke continued demands for more governmental innovation to improve educational output of elementary and secondary schools. The issue of more choice, perhaps through the use of vouchers and schemes to provide incentives for educational innovation, is undoubtedly going to be important in the future.

Vouchers are perhaps the most controversial method of providing more choice. Public teachers' unions and officials of public schools are firmly opposed to vouchers. If vouchers were used, public schools would have to compete with private schools. Instead of having their revenue come from guaranteed tax appropriations, funding of public schools would depend on the demand for their services. If they failed to perform in the marketplace where spending depended on vouchers, they would have to shut their doors. Many argue that if private schools emerged as winners under a voucher plan, the quality of education and equality of educational opportunity could actually improve. This is because many public schools have a

---

[12]See United States Department of Education, *Developments in School Finance*, 1996.

geographic base of students in low-income disadvantaged neighborhoods. Under a voucher plan, geographic segregation of students need not be the norm and, at least in theory, low-income families could choose to send their children to any school. This could promote educational equality and more diversity in schooling.

Those who support vouchers argue that there is already an element of choice in schooling that favors upper-income groups. These groups often choose their residence location, in part, based on the quality of schooling. Low-income groups who lack mobility and often cannot afford housing in school districts where the quality of schooling is best are thereby deprived of choice in education. A voucher plan could give low-income families more choice in the education of their children.

However, critics of voucher financing of education argue that competitive markets cannot prevail for schooling. Information on quality of schools is not freely available. Poorly educated parents could lack the ability to evaluate alternative schools, and their choices could be based on criteria other than quality of education. It is also disruptive to transfer students among schools, and transportation resources may not be available to low-income households to get their children to the best-performing schools. The critics argue that public schooling with minimum standards guaranteed to students is a better option than vouchers in assuring equality of educational opportunity. They further argue that right now private schools perform better than some public schools because they attract better students and children of families where there is more support for education in the home.

There have been some experiments with vouchers. Milwaukee engaged in an experimental voucher program in the 1990s in which a limited number of students (about 1.5 percent of the school enrollment) were given vouchers and allowed to choose their schools. Few parents used the vouchers and a large number of students who used the vouchers to attend private schools transferred back to public schools after a year. However, some students who remained in private schools did seem to perform better. It is difficult to say whether this experiment provided any useful information about how a widespread voucher program would perform.[13]

Vouchers are not the only schemes that have been considered to improve performance of schools in the United States. Some have advocated turning over control of public schools to private managers instead of having them run by bureaucrats or civil servants. School districts would hire specialized firms to run the schools with the goal of improving educational output. In the few cases where this has been tried, management teams have concentrated on providing more training for teachers and on developing suitable teaching materials. This is an alternative to actually privatizing public schools. Other alternatives to vouchers include charter schools, which are directly managed by parents or other groups closer to the schooling process instead of by a centralized school district.

The charter school represents part of a broader movement to decentralize education. Decentralization of public education shifts control of schools to principals, teachers, and parents from larger bureaucracies in school districts. Many argue that this allows schools to better cater to the needs of students enrolled and provides parents with more incentive to participate in the process because they would have greater influence in curriculum and teaching methods.

---

[13]For evaluation of the Milwaukee experiment, see Cecilia Elena Rouse, "Private School Vouchers and Student Achievement: An Evaluation of the Milwaukee Parental Choice Program," *Quarterly Journal of Economics* 113, 2 (May 1998): 553–602.

CHECKPOINT

1. Which level of government has primary responsibility for supplying public elementary and secondary education in the United States?
2. What role do state governments play in helping supply education?
3. How would the use of voucher systems affect public education?

SUMMARY

A federal system of government allows both centralized and decentralized collective choices. The more decentralized the government, the greater the opportunity to supply diverse levels and kinds of government-provided services. Fiscal federalism is the division of taxing and spending functions among levels of government. Central government most efficiently supplies those services most closely resembling pure public goods that benefit all citizens regardless of their location. However, many public goods have only regional or local benefits, and these are possible to supply in a decentralized fashion through local government and local political institutions.

Stabilization and income redistribution are two functions that have national collective benefits and are most effectively supplied by central government. The advantage of decentralized supply of government-supplied services, when feasible, is that it allows accommodation of a diversity of demands for such services within a nation. When individuals of similar tastes for government-provided services live together within a political jurisdiction, political externalities are minimized.

Pairing government-supplied services with political jurisdictions is a central problem of fiscal federalism. As the size of a political jurisdiction increases, so does the number of taxpayers; this decreases the per capita cost per unit of government output. This advantage is balanced against increased congestion costs when the size of the jurisdiction is expanded.

Citizen mobility allows individuals of similar tastes to congregate for the purpose of supplying government-provided services and sharing the costs of such services. This decreases political externalities within such jurisdictions. The Tiebout model examines the consequences of mobility in a decentralized system of government and concludes that mobility improves efficiency. In the Tiebout model, citizens are assumed to "shop" for local jurisdictions in which to reside in much the same way that they shop for any consumer good.

Interjurisdictional externalities are caused by improper size of political jurisdictions. Such benefits or cost spillovers provide bases for government consolidation or federal subsidies to internalize the external effects. Local tax bases generally are more elastic than national tax bases simply because individuals can easily avoid local taxes by changing the location of their economic activities.

Fiscal capacity is used as a basis of support for federal grants to equalize the capacity to finance basic public services among communities. Per capita expenditures are often used as an index of variations in government-supplied services among jurisdictions. Revenue effort is a crude index of the extent to which a jurisdiction is taxing its residents relative to a national average.

Grants and other forms of intergovernmental fiscal assistance represent gifts, or subsidies, to recipient governments. As such, they disturb the political equilibrium in those governments and can influence the mix between public and private spending in the recipient jurisdiction. In general, matching grants are more likely to induce local governing authorities to increase public spending than are general-purpose grants.

KEY CONCEPTS

Block Grants

Categorical Grant-in-Aid

Elasticity of the Tax Base

Federal System of Government

Fiscal Capacity

Fiscal Federalism

Flypaper Effect

Fungibility

General Revenue Sharing

Interjurisdictional Externalities

Local Public Goods

Matching Grants

Political Jurisdiction

Revenue Effort

Unconditional Grants

REVIEW QUESTIONS

1. What are the advantages and disadvantages of decentralized government? Why can a federal system of government take advantage of both centralized and decentralized collective decision making?

2. Which public services are most likely to be efficiently provided by central government? What are the basic characteristics of such services?

3. Why are local governments likely to be limited to a greater degree than the central government in the extent to which they can engage in redistribution and stabilization programs?

4. Explain why the equilibrium quantities of government services supplied by a central government under majority rule, with all citizens voting, will differ from local political equilibria for the amount of such goods when local elections are also decided by majority rule.

5. How many political jurisdictions do you reside in? List the government-provided services that you obtain from each of your jurisdictions. What kinds of taxes are levied in each jurisdiction to pay for those services?

6. Why does citizen mobility increase the desirability of decentralized decision making in relation to efficiency? What does Tiebout mean by "voting on your feet?" How does the Tiebout model explain residential location patterns?

7. What are interjurisdictional externalities? What problems does their existence create for a federal system?

8. How does the fungibility of money limit the value of the distinction between restricted and unrestricted grants?

9. Explain how a matching grant results in both income and substitution effects that affect the willingness of citizens to support increased local government spending. Why do nonmatching grants result only in income effects?

10. Why are matching grants likely to be more effective in increasing local government spending than are equal-dollar nonmatching grants? Explain how matching grants can help achieve efficiency by internalizing interjurisdictional externalities.

PROBLEMS

1. The average cost of employing each police officer per year is $30,000 for a small town. The current population of the town is 1,000. Calculate the per capita cost per police officer. Explain why increased congestion costs associated with increased population can result in increased per capita taxes, even though the per-capita cost per police officer declines with population.

2. Municipal zoning laws often are used as a means of controlling the population and income levels of citizens in a political jurisdiction. How can zoning laws that require homes to be built on a minimum lot size of one acre per residence affect the size and income level of a community? Why would a high-income community pass laws outlawing mobile homes and requiring minimum construction standards for homes?

3. The elasticity of the property tax base for the town of Elderberry is estimated to be 22. Assuming that this estimate is correct, what effect would a 10 percent increase in the property tax have on property value and tax revenue for Elderberry?

Explain what economic factors could cause the results that you calculated.

4. All voters in a city pay an equal marginal tax rate of $10 per mile of roads paved per year. The federal government has a matching grant program of road paving, whereby 75 percent of the cost of road paving is paid. Show how the matching grant affects the budget constraint for a typical voter. In equilibrium, the community receives $1 million per year for road paving under the matching grant program. Prove that the matching grant will be more effective in increasing road paving than a $1 million annual lump-sum grant.

5. Explain why using the local property tax to finance a given quantity and quality of public schooling can result in low tax rates in rich jurisdictions but high tax rates in poor jurisdictions. How do state governments supplement local finance of education to insure equality of opportunity in education? Go to your state government's Web site and find out how elementary and secondary education is financed in your state.

ADDITIONAL READINGS

Brunori, Brunori. *Local Tax Policy*, 3rd edition. Washington, D.C.: The Urban Institute Press, 2011. A discussion of local government revenue systems in the United States within the context of the problems faced by these governments and the federal system.

Brunori, David. *State Tax Policy*. Washington, D.C.: The Urban Institute Press, 2001. An analysis of state tax systems within the context of a federal system where the central government is shifting more responsibility to the states.

Fisher, Ronald C. *State and Local Public Finance*. Glenview, Ill.: Scott Foresman and Company, 1988. A textbook emphasizing issues in state and local government finance.

Hanushek, Eric, Dale Jorgenson, eds. *Improving America's Schools, The Role of Incentives*. Washington, D.C.: National Research Council, 1996. Analyzes the role of incentive-based approaches, such as teacher merit pay, in improving the quality of schools in the United States.

Inman, Robert P., and Daniel L. Rubinfeld. "Rethinking Federalism." *Journal of Economic Perspectives* 11, 4 (Fall 1997): 43–64. An overview of theories of fiscal federalism with new insights. Includes a discussion of welfare reform and its impact on federalism. The same issue of this journal has other articles on fiscal federalism as part of a symposium on the subject.

Oates, Wallace E. *Fiscal Federalism*. New York: Harcourt Brace Jovanovich, 1972. A classic analysis of public finance in a federal system. Discusses the question of optimal jurisdiction size and optimal division of responsibility among levels of government. Includes empirical analysis.

Oates, Wallace E. "Federalism and Government Finance," in *Modern Public Finance*. John M. Quigley and Eugene Smolensky, eds. Cambridge, Mass.: Harvard University Press, 1994, 126–164. An analysis of issues in local government finance, including discussion of how tax exporting can lead to inefficient levels of spending by state and local governments and how such distortions justify federal grants.

Oates, Wallace E. "An Essay on Fiscal Federalism." *Journal of Economic Literature* 37, 3 (September 1999): 1120–1149. A review of the literature and of issues in fiscal decentralization. Discusses both theory and practice as of the late 1990s.

Steuerle, C. Eugene, Van Doorn Ooms, George Peterson, and Robert D. Reischauer. *Vouchers and the Provision of Public Services*. Washington, D.C.: The Urban Institute Press, 2000. An analysis of how vouchers are used to finance public services, including education and housing, in the United States and other nations.

INTERNET RESOURCES

http://www.nasbo.org

This is the home page of the National Association of State Budget Officers. You can find information about current state government finance issues and the impact of changes in federalism on state governments.

http://www.ntanet.org

The home page of the National Tax Association has many useful links to other sites to obtain information about state and local government spending and finance.

http://nces.ed.gov

From the U.S. Department of Education's National Center for Education Statistics, you can access information on federal programs for primary, secondary, and higher education. Click on Annual Reports to access the Digest of Education Statistics, which gives information on public financing of federal education programs.

A

Ability-to-pay Principle   Maintains that taxes should be distributed according to the capacity of taxpayers to pay them.

Accelerated Depreciation   Deduction of more than the actual economic depreciation from a firm's income each year.

Ad Valorem Taxes   Taxes levied as a percentage of the price of a good or service.

Adjusted Gross Income (AGI)   Gross income minus any allowable adjustments.

Arrow's Impossibility Theorem   A theorem by Kenneth Arrow which states that it is impossible to devise a voting rule that meets a set of conditions that can guarantee a unique political equilibrium for a public choice.

Assessment   The valuation of taxable wealth by government authorities.

Asset-Substitution Effect   The reduction of the incentive to save that results from the promise of a Social Security pension.

Average Effective Tax Rate   Actual taxes as a percentage of a measure of gross (rather than taxable) income for each group.

Average Indexed Monthly Earnings (AIME)   A worker's average monthly earnings on which payroll taxes are paid.

Average Tax Rate (ATR)   Total dollar amount of taxes collected divided by the dollar value of the taxable base.

B

Backward Shifting   A transfer of a tax's burden from buyers who are liable for its payment to sellers through a decrease in the market price of the taxed good.

Benefit Principle   Argues that the means of financing government-supplied goods and services should be linked to the benefits that citizens receive from government.

Bequest Effect   Strong incentives for parents to leave bequests to their children.

Block Grants   A principal type of unrestricted grant, having only minimal restrictions on the uses to which the funds can be put and rarely require matching funds raised locally.

Bracket Creep   An increase in the effective rates of taxation of real taxable income when the tax rate schedules are based on nominal values of income rather than real values.

Budget Deficit   The excess of government outlays over receipts taken in from taxes, fees, and charges levied by government authorities.

Budget Incidence   The evaluation of the effects of both government expenditure and tax policies on the distribution of income in the private sector.

Budget Surplus   The excess of government receipts over government outlays.

Burden of the Debt   The redistributive effect of debt financing.

Bureaucracy   A government body in charge of implementing public choices made through political institutions.

C

Capital Gains   Increases in the value of assets over the accounting period.

Capitation Payments   Fixed amounts per patient per year received by health care providers in managed care facilities.

Categorical Grant-in-Aid   A transfer of funds from a higher level of government to a lower level, with specified conditions attached to the expenditure of the funds.

Coase Theorem   States that governments, by merely establishing the rights to use resources, can internalize externalities when transactions costs of bargaining are zero.

Coinsurance   The amount paid as an out-of-pocket cost by the individual, which varies from (insurance) plan to plan, but is typically 20 percent of the cost. The insurance plan pays the remaining 80 percent of covered expenses (after a patient incurs the deductible expense of the plan).

Command and Control Regulation   A system of rules established by government authorities that requires all emitters to meet strict emissions standards for sources of pollution and requires the use of specific pollution control devices.

Compensated Demand Curve Demand curve of a good that shows the relationship between the price and the quantity demanded of a good due only to substitution effects of price changes.

Compensated Labor Supply Curve A curve that shows how hours worked per day (or per year) vary with wages when the income effect of wage changes is removed. It reflects only the substitution effects of wage changes.

Compensated Supply Curve Supply curve of an input that reflects only the substitution effects of input price changes.

Compensation Criteria Criteria, which attempt to measure the value of the gains to gainers in dollar terms and compare these with the dollar value of the losses to losers.

Comprehensive Consumption Annual comprehensive income minus annual savings.

Comprehensive Income The sum of a person's annual consumption expenditures and the increment in that person's net worth in a given year.

Comprehensive Wealth Tax Tax that would be levied on all forms of capital and land at a flat rate.

Congestible Public Goods Those goods for which crowding or congestion reduces the benefits to existing consumers when more consumers are accommodated.

Constitutions The generally accepted set of rules by which decisions are made in a society.

Corporation A business that is legally established under state laws that grant it an identity separate from that of its owners.

Corrective Subsidy A payment made by government to either buyers or sellers of a good so that the price paid by consumers is reduced.

Corrective Tax Tax designed to adjust the marginal private cost of a good or service in such a way as to internalize the externality. It is designed to internalize a negative externality by making sellers of the product pay a fee equal to the marginal external costs per unit of output sold.

Cost-Benefit Analysis A statement of pros and cons of a particular activity over a period of time.

Cost-Effectiveness Analysis A technique for determining the minimum-cost combination of government programs to achieve a given objective.

D

Deadweight Loss The extra benefit a recipient can enjoy from the dollar amount of a price-distorting subsidy if instead the grant was received in a lump sum.

Debt Finance Use of borrowed funds to finance government expenditures.

Deductible A certain amount of health care expenditure to be incurred first by the patients, as required by a typical insurance plan, before the plan starts paying benefits.

Deferral of Taxable Income Income that is ordinarily taxable can be excluded or deducted from gross income in the current year but will be taxed eventually along with the accrued interest and capital gains.

Differential Tax Incidence The resulting change in the distribution of income when one type of tax is substituted for some alternative tax, or set of taxes, yielding an equivalent amount of revenue in real terms, while both the mix and level of government expenditures are held constant.

Dividends The portion of a corporation's profits paid out to its stockholders.

Donations Voluntary contributions to governments from individuals or organizations.

E

Earmarked Taxes Special taxes designed to finance specific government-supplied services.

Earned Income Tax Credit (EITC) A payment from the IRS to workers with dependent children and some single workers equal to a certain percentage of wage and salary income to those eligible.

Earnings Test Reduces Social Security benefits by $1 for each $2 of earnings over a certain maximum amount of earnings that is adjusted each year when they retire before the year they reach their full retirement age.

Economic Depreciation Measures the decrease in the market value of the durable physical capital used by firms in the productive process as that capital is "used up."

Efficiency Criterion Criterion that is satisfied when resources are used over any given period of time in such a way as to make it impossible to increase the well-being of any one person without reducing the well-being of any other person.

Efficiency-loss Ratio The ratio of the excess burden of a tax to the tax revenue collected each year by that tax.

Elasticity of the Tax Base   The ratio of the percentage change in the tax base attributable to any given percentage change in the tax rate applied to that base.

Entitlement Programs   Transfer programs that require payments to all those people meeting eligibility requirements established by law.

Equity   The difference between the value of a corporation's assets (including the cash that could be obtained if its equipment and real estate were sold) and the value of its outstanding debt.

Excess Burden of the Subsidy   The difference between the cost of the program to taxpayers and the gain in net benefits to the tenants.

Excise Taxes   Selective taxes levied on certain types of consumption activities.

Expenditure Incidence   The evaluation of the effects of alternative government expenditure projects on the distribution of income.

Expensing a Capital Asset   Deduction of the full purchase price of an asset in the year of its acquisition.

External Debt   Funds borrowed from abroad.

Externalities   Costs or benefits of market transactions not reflected in prices.

F

Federal System of Government   Numerous levels of government, each with its own powers to provide services and raise revenue.

Fiscal Capacity   A measure of the ability of a jurisdiction to finance government-provided services.

Fiscal Federalism   The division of taxing and expenditure functions among levels of government.

Fixed Allotment Subsidies   Subsidies that give eligible recipients the right to consume a certain amount of a good or service each month either through direct allotment of the item or through the issuance of vouchers that can be used only to buy a specific item.

Flat-rate Tax   Tax with a proportional rate structure.

Flypaper Effect   The bypassing of the normal political process by local bureaucrats.

Forward Shifting   A transfer of a tax's burden from sellers who are liable for its payment to buyers as a result of an increase in the price of the taxed good.

Free-rider   A person who seeks to enjoy the benefits of a public good without contributing anything to the cost of financing the amount made available.

Fully Funded Pension System   A pension system in which benefits are paid out of a fund built up from contributions by, or on behalf of, members in a retirement system.

Fungibility   A characteristic that exists in money; which means that money can be used for more than one purpose.

G

General Obligation Bonds   A type of security backed by the taxing power of the government that issues the securities.

General Revenue Sharing   A revenue sharing program of unrestricted intergovernmental grants, which was terminated by the United States in 1986.

General Tax   One that taxes all of the components of the economic base, with no exclusions, exemptions, or deductions from the tax base.

General Theory of Second Best   States that when two opposing factors contribute to efficiency losses, they can offset one another's distortions.

Gini Coefficient   A summary index of the information contained in a Lorenz curve, which measures the degree of inequality for any income distribution by calculating the ratio of the area between the Lorenz curve corresponding to that distribution and the 45-degree line to the total area under the 45-degree line.

Government Goods and Services   Goods and services, such as roads, schooling, and fire protection, that are not usually sold in markets.

Government Purchases   Those that require productive resources (land, labor, and capital) to be diverted from private use by individuals and corporations so that such resources can be used by the government.

Government Transfer Payments   Government expenditures that redistribute purchasing power among citizens.

Government-induced Inflation   Sustained annual increase in prices caused by expansion of the money supply to pay for government-supplied goods and services.

Governments   Organizations formed to exercise authority over the actions of people who live together in a society and to provide and finance essential services.

Gross Income   All income received during the year from taxable sources, which includes wages and salaries, interest income from taxable sources, dividends, rental income, and profits from business activity. Also included in gross income, under rules prevailing in 2012, are realized capital gains from sale or exchange of securities and other property.

Gross Replacement Rate (GRR)   A worker's monthly retirement benefit divided by monthly earnings in the year prior to retirement.

H

Head Tax   An example of a lump-sum tax that would require all adults to pay an equal amount each year to governing authorities.

High-Employment Deficit or Surplus   A calculation that estimates the budget deficit or surplus that would prevail at a certain designated level of unemployment in the economy.

Historic Cost   The acquisition price of the asset.

Horizontal Equity   Achieved when individuals of the same economic capacity (measured, for example, by income) pay the same amount of taxes per year (or over their lifetimes).

I

Implicit Logrolling   A practice that occurs when political interests succeed in pairing two (or more) issues of strong interest to divergent groups on the same ballot or the same bill.

Incidence of a Tax   The distribution of the burden of paying tax.

Income-in-Kind   Income in the form of goods and services rather than cash payments.

Individual Excess Burden of a Tax   The loss in well-being of the taxpayer on paying T in taxes under the price-distorting tax instead of under the lump-sum tax.

Induced-Retirement Effect   Results from the fact that Social Security benefits and the earnings test for such benefits tend to provide incentives for early retirement and less work during retirement years.

In-kind Benefits   Noncash benefits that increase the quantities of certain goods and services that will be consumed by the recipients.

Interjurisdictional Externalities   Costs or benefits of local government goods and services to residents who live in other political jurisdictions.

Internal Debt   The portion of a government's indebtedness owed to its own citizens.

Internalization of an Externality   Occurs when the marginal private benefit or cost of goods and services is

adjusted so that the users consider the actual marginal social benefit or cost of their decisions.

Itemized Deductions   Expenses that can be legally deducted as an alternative to the standard deduction from adjusted gross income in figuring taxable income.

L

Lindahl Equilibrium   Exists when the voluntary contribution per unit of the public good of each member of the community equals his or her marginal benefit of the public good at the efficient level of output.

Lindahl Prices   The equilibrium contributions per unit of the public good.

Local Public Goods   Public goods with benefits that are nonrival only for that portion of the national population who live within a certain geographical area.

Logrolling   A vote-trading process that occurs when intensities of preference differ on issues and there are incentives for groups to trade votes for those issues of great interest to them.

Long-term Care Services   Medical, support, and rehabilitative services for patients who have functional limitations or chronic health problems and need daily assistance with the normal activities of living.

Lorenz Curve   A graph that gives information on the distribution of income by size brackets.

Lump-sum Tax.   A fixed sum that a person would pay per year, independent of that person's income, consumption of goods and services, or wealth.

M

Marginal Conditions for Efficient Resource Allocation   Conditions that require resources to be allocated to the production of each good over each period so that MSB (marginal social benefit) $= MSC$ (marginal social cost).

Marginal External Benefit (MEB)   The benefit of additional output accruing to parties other than buyers or sellers of the good.

Marginal External Cost (MEC)   The extra cost to third parties resulting from production of another unit of a good or service.

Marginal Net Benefit   Difference between a good's marginal social benefit and its marginal social cost.

Marginal Private Benefit (MPB)   The marginal benefit that consumers base their decisions on.

Marginal Private Cost (MPC)   The marginal cost that producers base their decisions on.

Marginal Rate of Time Preference   The slope of an indifference curve for present and future consumption multiplied by -1.It is a measure of the willingness of savers to forgo current consumption in exchange for future consumption.

Marginal Social Benefit   Extra benefit of a good obtained by making one more unit of that good available per month (or over any other period).

Marginal Social Cost   Minimum sum of money required to compensate the owners of inputs used in producing a good for making an extra unit of the good available.

Marginal Tax Benefit   Relates to the extra tax benefit of an activity; the extra tax reduction that results when an individual engages in the activity.

Marginal Tax Rate (MTR)   Additional tax collected on additional dollar value of the tax base as the tax base increases.

Matching Grants   Federal grants that contain the requirement that recipient jurisdictions match each dollar of federal aid with a certain amount of locally raised revenue.

Means Test   Establishes that those passing the status test also have incomes or asset levels that are below the minimally required amounts to be eligible for aid.

Median Voter Rule   Also called the median most-preferred outcome of all voters, this rule states that one and only one outcome of the three emerges as victorious: the one corresponding to the median peak.

Median Voter   One whose most-preferred outcome is the median of the most-preferred outcomes of all those voting.

Medicaid   A program that provides benefits for most of those eligible for TANF and SSI cash subsidies and others who pass a means test.

Medicare   A health insurance plan, under which the elderly are covered by hospitalization insurance, which is financed by a special payroll tax amounting to a combined rate of 2.9 percent for employees in 2012 on all labor income.

Mission (of a government agency)   Is comparable to a business firm's product.

Mixed Economy   An economy in which government supplies a considerable amount of goods and services and regulates private economic activity.

Moral Hazard of Health Insurance   The increase in the incentive to consume and supply health care services that results from the reduction in price to consumers when third parties pay the bulk of medical expenses.

Most-Preferred Political Outcome   The quantity of the government-supplied good corresponding to the point at which a rational person's tax share is exactly equal to the marginal benefit of the good.

Multiple-Peaked Preferences   An implication that people who move away from their most-preferred alternative become worse off at first but eventually become better off as the movement continues in the same direction.

N

Negative Externalities   Also called external costs, these are costs to third parties other than the buyers or the sellers of an item not reflected in the market price.

Negative Income Tax (NIT)   A cash assistance program that would provide a minimum income guarantee for Americans. All those with income below the floor would receive cash subsidies from the government, whereas those above the floor would pay taxes.

Net Federal Debt   A portion of the debt of the federal government held by the general public, excluding the holdings of U.S. government agencies, trust funds, and the Federal Reserve banks.

Net Replacement Rate (NRR)   A better measure of the generosity of the pension benefits that is calculated as monthly social security pension benefits divided by monthly labor earnings after payment of taxes in the year prior to retirement.

Net Worth   The value of a person's assets held at any point in time less the value of a person's liabilities, or debts.

Nominal Interest Rate   The sum of the real interest rate and the rate of inflation.

Nonexclusion   Implies that it is too costly to develop a means of excluding those who refuse to pay from enjoying the benefits of a given quantity of public good.

Nonmarket Rationing   Distribution where government goods and services are not made available to persons according to their willingness to pay and their use is not rationed by prices.

Nonrival in Consumption   Implies that a given quantity of a public good can be enjoyed by more than one consumer without decreasing the amounts enjoyed by rival consumers.

Normative Economics   Designed to formulate recommendations as to what *should* be accomplished. This approach evaluates alternative policies and actions on the basis of underlying value judgments.

O

Old-Age, Survivors, and Disability Insurance (OASDI)
A tax-financed pension system under which retirement benefits are financed through taxes levied on the working population.

P

Pay-as-You-Go Pension System   A pension system that finances pensions for retired workers in a given year entirely by contributions or taxes paid by currently employed workers.

Personal Exemption   A certain sum of money that a taxpayer is allowed to deduct from AGI that varies with the number of dependents claimed on the return.

Physical Infrastructure   A nation's transportation and environmental capital, including its schools, power and communication networks, and health care systems.

Political Equilibrium   An agreement on the level of production of one or more public goods, given the specified rule for making the collective choice and the distribution of tax shares among individuals.

Political Externalities   The losses in well-being that occur when voters do not obtain their most-preferred outcomes, given their tax shares.

Political Institutions   Institutions that constitute the rules and generally accepted procedures that evolve in a community for determining what government does and how government outlays are financed.

Political Jurisdiction   A defined geographical area within which individuals make collective choices on government functions and government-provided services.

Political Parties   A group of individuals with similar ideas on the role of government and other issues.

Political Transactions Costs   The additional costs of the political process that measure the value of time, effort, and other resources expended to reach and enforce a collective agreement.

Pollution Abatement   The reduction in pollution that results from reduced emissions.

Pollution Rights   Transferable permits to emit a certain amount of particular wastes into the atmosphere or water per year.

Positive Economics   Scientific approach to analysis that establishes cause-and-effect relationships among economic variables.

Positive Externalities   Benefits to third parties other than the buyers or the sellers of a good or service not reflected in prices.

Poverty Threshold   The level of income below which a household is classified as poor in the United States.

Price-Distorting Subsidies   Subsidies that reduce prices to consumers below the market price.

Price-distorting Tax   A tax that causes the net price received by sellers of a good or service to diverge from the gross price paid by buyers.

Price-Excludable Public Goods   Public goods with benefits that can be priced.

Private Goods and Services   Items, such as food and clothing, usually made available for sale in markets.

Private Goods   Goods that are rival in consumption.

Program Budgeting   A system of managing government expenditures by attempting to compare the program proposals of all government agencies authorized to achieve similar objectives.

Program   A combination of government activities producing a distinguishable output.

Progressive Tax Rate Structure   One for which the average tax rate increases with the size of the tax base.

Property Tax Rate Differentials   Differences above or below the national average rate of property taxation.

Proportional Tax Rate Structure   One for which the average tax rate, expressed as a percentage of the value of the tax base, does not vary with the value of the tax base.

Prospective Payment System   The system used by Medicare, which gives hospitals a fixed payment per patient for the expected costs of treating patients with specific illnesses.

Public Choice   A choice made through political interaction of many people according to established rules.

Public Finance   The field of economics that studies government activities and the alternative means of financing government expenditures.

Public Goods   Goods with benefits that cannot be withheld from those who do not pay and are shared by large groups of consumers.

Pure Market Economy   An economy in which virtually all goods and services would be supplied by private firms for profit and all exchanges of goods and services would take place through markets, with prices determined by free interplay of supply and demand.

Pure Private Good   A good that, after producers receive compensation for the full opportunity costs of production, provides benefits only to the person who acquires the good, and not to anyone else.

Pure Public Good   A public good that is nonrival in consumption for an entire population of consumers, and its benefits have the characteristic of nonexclusion.

R

Rational Ignorance   The lack of information about public issues that results because the marginal cost of obtaining the information exceeds the apparent marginal benefits of doing so.

Real Budget Balance   A measure of the change in the federal debt after adjustment for the effects of inflation and changing interest rates on the real market value of the outstanding net debt.

Real Estate or Real Property   Refers to land and structures.

Regressive Tax Rate Structure   One for which the average tax rate declines as the size of the tax base increases.

Retail Sales Tax   An ad valorem levy of a fixed percentage on the dollar value of retail purchases made by consumers.

Retained Earnings   The portion of corporate profits kept by the corporation.

Revenue Bonds   A type of security backed by the promise of revenue to be earned on the facility being financed by the bonds.

Revenue Effort   The ratio of tax collections from all sources in a taxing jurisdiction, as a percentage of personal income in that jurisdiction, to the national average of that ratio for all jurisdictions.

Ricardian Equivalence   An idea that both tax finance and deficit finance have the same impact on current aggregate spending and future economic growth.

Risk Averse   The preference to incur a certain modest cost for insurance rather than risk high costs as a result of an unforeseen prospect.

S

Selective Tax   One that taxes only certain portions of the tax base, or might allow exemptions and deductions from the general tax base.

Shifting of a Tax   The transfer of the burden of paying a tax from those who are legally liable for it to others.

Simple Majority Rule   A rule under which a proposal is approved if it receives more than half the votes cast in an election.

Single-Peaked Preferences   An implication that individuals behave as if a unique optimal outcome exists for them.

Small-Number Externalities   The kinds of externalities for which the Coase theorem is relevant.

Social Opportunity Cost of Funds   The cost that depends on the rate at which savers and investors are willing to give up either consumption or investment to finance a government project.

Social Rate of Discount   The return that can be earned on resources employed in alternative private use.

Social Security and Insurance Programs   Programs benefiting diverse groups of citizens including government-provided pensions, disability payments, unemployment compensation, and health benefits.

Special-Interest Groups   Organizations that seek to increase government expenditures that benefit their constituents.

Standard Deduction   A fixed dollar amount that is adjusted for inflation each year and varies with the filing status of the taxpayer.

Status Test   Ensures that those falling under into demographic categories belong to one of the particular groups that is eligible for poverty relief.

Stock   A variable with a value defined at a particular point in time.

Straight-Line Depreciation   Deduction of the same fraction of the cost of an asset each year over its useful economic life.

Supplemental Nutrition Assistance Program   A federally financed subsidy program that began in 1971. Under this program administered by state governments, recipients receive electronic benefits transfer (EBT) cards that can be redeemed for food and related items at stores.

Supplemental Security Income (SSI)   A federally funded and operated program that provides cash transfers to the aged, the blind, and the disabled who pass a means test.

T

Tax Avoidance   Change in behavior of taxpayers to reduce tax liability.

Tax Base   Item or economic activity on which a tax is levied.

Tax Bracket   Gives the increment of annual income associated with each marginal tax rate.

Tax Capitalization   A decrease in the value of a taxed asset equal to the discounted present value of future tax liability of its owners.

Tax Evasion   Noncompliance with the tax laws by failing to pay taxes that are due.

Tax Expenditures   Losses in tax revenues attributable to tax preferences.

Tax Preferences   Exclusions, exemptions, and deductions from the tax base.

Tax Rate Structure   Describes the relationship between the tax collected during a given accounting period and the tax base.

Tax Shares   Also called tax prices, these preannounced levies assigned to citizens and are equal to a portion of the unit cost of a good proposed to be provided by government.

Taxable Income   The portion of income received by individuals that is subject to the personal income tax.

Taxes   Compulsory payments associated with certain activities.

Tax-Financed Pension System   Social security retirement program in which retirement benefits are financed through taxes levied on the working population.

Temporary Assistance to Needy Families (TANF)   A welfare assistance program that provides family support payments on a temporary and limited basis through grants to state governments, which in turn determine eligibility by income and conditions for receiving welfare payments.

Third-Party Payments   Payments by third party that finance the system of health care provision in the United States, where the third party is neither the purchaser nor the seller of the service.

Total Excess Burden of a Tax   An additional cost to society over and above the amount of dollars that citizens pay in a tax.

Total Social Benefit   A certain amount of satisfaction that is obtained by consuming any given quantity of an economic good available per month (or any other period).

Total Social Cost   Value of all resources necessary to make a given amount of a good available per month.

Transactions costs   The time, effort, and cash outlays involved in locating someone to trade with, negotiating terms of trade, drawing contracts, and assuming risks associated with the contracts.

Turnover Taxes   Multistage sales taxes that are levied at some fixed rate on transactions at all levels of production.

U

Unconditional Grants   Revenues shared among governments, with no strings attached to the use of the funds.

Unemployment Insurance   A program which provides income support for those temporarily out of work because they have been laid off or have lose their jobs for reasons other than misconduct or a labor dispute.

Unit Tax   A levy of a fixed amount per unit of a good exchanged in a market.

User Charges   Prices determined through political rather than market interaction.

Utility-possibility Curve   Curve that presents the maximum attainable level of well-being (or utility) for any one individual, given the utility level of other individuals in the economy, their tastes, resource availability, and technology.

V

Value-added Tax (VAT)   A general tax on consumption levied on the value added to intermediate products by businesses at each stage of production.

Vertical Equity   Accomplished when individuals of differing economic ability pay annual tax bills that differ according to some collectively chosen notion of fairness.

W

Wage Rate Subsidies (WRS)   A government wage supplement program where minimum-wage legislation would be repealed and workers would be induced to search for jobs at the market-determined wage. Those working at the lowest wages would receive subsidies from the government to raise their incomes to some minimum level.

Wealth   The market value of accumulated assets in a nation.

Subject Index